Politics in the Developing World

More from Oxford University Press

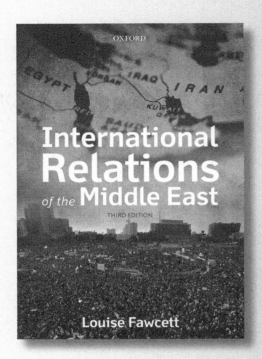

International Relations of the Middle East
THIRD EDITION
Louise Fawcett

'*International Relations of the Middle East* has established itself as the standard text in the study and teaching of the region... A must read!'
Fawaz A. Gerges, LSE

'This text sets the standard for excellence in human rights teaching.'
Shareen Hertel, University of Connecticut

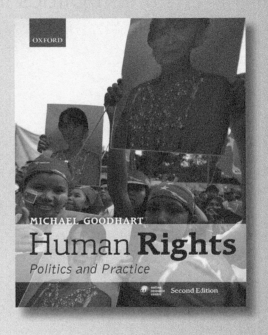

MICHAEL GOODHART
Human Rights
Politics and Practice
Second Edition

See our full range of Politics and International Relations textbooks at:

http://ukcatalogue.oup.com/category/academic/highereducation/politics.do

Make your voice heard: join the OUP politics student panel

To help us make sure we develop the best books for you, the student, we've set up a student panel.

To find out more visit www.oxfordtextbooks.co.uk/politics/studentpanel/

Politics in the Developing World

FOURTH EDITION

Edited by

Peter Burnell

Lise Rakner

Vicky Randall

OXFORD

UNIVERSITY PRESS

OXFORD

UNIVERSITY PRESS

Great Clarendon Street, Oxford, OX2 6DP,
United Kingdom

Oxford University Press is a department of the University of Oxford.
It furthers the University's objective of excellence in research, scholarship,
and education by publishing worldwide. Oxford is a registered trade mark of
Oxford University Press in the UK and in certain other countries

© Oxford University Press 2014

The moral rights of the authors have been asserted

First edition 2005
Second edition 2008
Third edition 2011

Impression: 2

Published in the United States of America by Oxford University Press
198 Madison Avenue, New York, NY 10016, United States of America

British Library Cataloguing in Publication Data

Data available

Library of Congress Control Number: 2013949103

ISBN 978–0–19–966600–3

Printed in Great Britain by
Clays Ltd, St Ives plc

Preface

This fourth edition of *Politics in the Developing World*, just like the previous editions, has benefited substantially from feedback by referees and readers. The editors wish to thank all those who offered comments and also Oxford University Press for its decision to commission a fourth edition. We would also like to thank Vegard Vibe, University of Bergen, for excellent research assistance throughout this fourth edition of *Politics in the Developing World*, as well as for help with the online resources. Thanks are also due to Ane Thea Djuve Galaasen for research assistance on Chapter 11. On a sadder note, we must relate that Adrian Leftwich died while we were assembling this edition; he has been an outstanding scholar in the field, as well as a key contributor to this volume, and will be greatly missed.

In terms of content, the fourth edition includes newly commissioned material, including chapters on social movements and governance. Other new additions include the presentation of the ten case studies grouped around four key challenges currently facing the developing countries: regime change (Part 5); strong versus fragile states (Part 6); human rights and development (Part 7); and South–South cooperation (Part 8). We hope that, by structuring case studies around common themes, the conditions for comparing across cases and countries have been enhanced.

All of the chapters retained from the third edition have been revised and updated to include recent global events and developments. In the case of Chapter 12, on theorizing the state, it is Lise Rakner and Vicky Randall, as editors, who are responsible for this revision. The edited chapters contain, among other things, fresh illustrative material and pedagogic content, which extend to new sample questions and guidance on further reading. Throughout, a conscious attempt has been made to emphasize gender issues more adequately, although doubtless there is scope to do even more in this regard. The overall composition of authors is both more international and closer to gender parity.

Finally, the Online Resource Centre contains new extra material, including case studies of politics in high-profile countries such as Syria. Readers of the book are urged to consult this invaluable resource.

New to this Edition

- Two new chapters have been written, focusing on 'Social Movements and Alternative Politics', and 'Governance'.
- Four restructured parts appear, containing ten case studies illustrating the following overall themes of politics in the developing world: regime change; strong versus fragile states; development and human rights; and South–South cooperation.
- A new case study on Brazil is added to this edition.
- All chapters have been updated to reflect the ongoing evolution of political regimes and development policies in the wake of recent events such as the global financial crisis, the role of new social movements, and social revolts in the Middle East.
- The Online Resource Centre has also been updated with new case studies, including Syria and Zambia.

Acknowledgements

The authors and publisher would like to thank: the United Nations Conference on Trade and Development (UNCTAD) for data presented in Tables 4.1, 4.2, and 4.3 (the United Nations is the author of the original material); the Inter-Parliamentary Union (IPU) for data presented in Table 9.1; the United Nations Development Programme (UNDP) for data presented in Boxes 26.2 and 26.3; and the World Bank for data presented in Table 16.2.

The data presented in Table 3.1 is taken from Gretchen Helmke and Steven Levitsky (eds) *Informal Institutions and Democracy: Lessons from Latin America* (Baltimore, MD: Johns Hopkins University Press), 14, Fig. 1.1. © 2006 Johns Hopkins University Press. Reprinted with permission of Johns Hopkins University Press.

The publishers would be pleased to clear permission with any copyright holders that we have inadvertently failed, or been unable, to contact.

Guided Tour of Textbook Features

We have developed a number of learning tools to help you develop the essential knowledge and skills you need to study politics in the developing world. This guided tour shows you how to get the most out of your textbook.

2
Colonialism and Post-Colonial Development

James Chiriyankandath

Chapter contents
- Introduction: The Post-Colonial World 29
- Pre-Colonial States and Societies 31
- Colonial Patterns 33
- Post-Colonial Development 36
- Conclusion: The Colonial Legacy 40

Overview

The variety of states and societies found in the developing two-thirds of the political diversity. The contemporary polities of the global South bear the colonialism, but are also marked both by their pre-colonial heritage and their experiences. This chapter argues that while the historically proximate exper had a significant impact on post-colonial political development, attention to political agency after independence yield a more nuanced perspective on across the developing world. The different ways in which post-independ adapted to—and were constrained by—the past legacies and present sit helped to determine the shape of the new polities.

Introduction: The Post-Colonial World

Sixty years ago, the world was still dominated by mainly European empires. By 1921, 84 per cent of the earth had been colonized and there were as many

as 168 colonies, most became independent, tres of colonial history of politance of the

Overview

The variety of states and societies found in the developing two-thirds of the world is reflected in their political diversity. The contemporary polities of the global South bear the imprint of the legacy of colonialism, but are also marked both by their pre-colonial heritage and their different post-colonial experiences. This chapter argues that while the historically proximate experience of colonialism has had a significant impact on post-colonial political development, attention to the *longue durée* and to political agency after independence yield a more nuanced perspective on the varied politics found across the developing world. The different ways in which post-independence politicians reacted and adapted to—and were constrained by—the past legacies and present situations of their countries helped to determine the shape of the new polities.

Overviews

Each chapter opens with an overview outlining what you can expect to cover in the chapter.

Boxes

BOX 3.4 TRUTH COMMISSIONS

The 'first' truth commission was set up in Uganda in 1974, whilst Idi Amin was still firmly in power, to inquire into the 'disappearances of people'. Although hearings were public, the report was never published and the **regime**'s infamous brutality persisted. As of 2012, truth commissions had been deployed in thirty-five different countries, including Argentina's 1983 National Commission on the Disappeared, Chile's post-Pinochet 1991 National Commission of Truth and Reconciliation, Guatemala's 1994 Historical Clarification Commission, perhaps the most celebrated of all, South Africa's post-**apartheid** 1998 National Commission of Truth and Reconciliation, and South Korea's 2005 Truth and Reconciliation Commission.

Truth commissions have been defined as 'temporary bodies,

2001: 2). W
prosecution
collective v
innate diffi
vast amoun
search for '
difficult to
clear in the
Philippines,
(Brahm 200
commission
as: how res
been, limita
instance, co

Throughout the book boxes give you extra information on particular topics, define and explain key ideas, and challenge you to think about what you've learned.

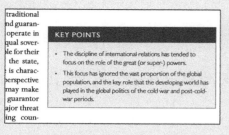

Key points

Each main chapter section ends with key points that reinforce your understanding and act as a useful revision tool.

KEY POINTS

- The discipline of international relations has tended to focus on the role of the great (or super-) powers.
- This focus has ignored the vast proportion of the global population, and the key role that the developing world has played in the global politics of the cold war and post-cold-war periods.

Questions

End-of-chapter questions probe your understanding of each chapter and encourage you to think critically about the material you've just covered.

? QUESTIONS

1. Does the state 'matter' in sustaining female subordination or moving so
2. Discuss key turning points in history, political institutional development, 'Arab Spring', which potentially open political space for women's government.
3. Under what conditions do 'private' or 'personal' issues become politi associated with violence against women.

Further reading

Annotated recommendations for further reading at the end of each chapter identify the key literature in the field, helping you to develop your interest in particular topics.

FURTHER READING

Escalante, F. (2012) *El Crimen como Realidad y Representación* (Mexico City: the treatment of violence in the Mexican public sphere.

Greene, K. F. (2007) *Why Dominant Parties Lose: Mexico's Democratizati* Cambridge University Press) A theoretical and empirical analysis of hegemo

Grillo, I. (2011) *El Narco: Inside Mexico's Criminal Insurgency* (New York: Bloor cal drug trafficking and contemporary drug violence in Mexico.

Guerrero, E. (2012) 'La Estrategia Fallida', *Nexos*, 1 December, available onlir

Web links

Carefully selected lists of websites direct you to the sites of institutions and organizations that will help develop your knowledge and understanding.

WEB LINKS

http://blds.ids.ac.uk The British Library for Development Studies claims to social and economic change in developing countries.

http://www.eldis.org Thousands of online documents, organizations, and development policy, practice, and research.

http://www.gdnet.org The site of the Global Development Network, a w institutes aiming to generate research at the local level in developing countri to those originating in the more developed world.

Glossary terms

Key terms appear in bold in the text and are defined in a glossary at the end of the book, identifying and defining key terms and ideas as you learn, and acting as a useful prompt when it comes to revision.

Gini coefficient A commonly used measure of inequality (household income or consumption): the higher the figure, the more unequal the distribution.

global justice movement A loose, increasingly transnational network of non-governmental and social movement organizations opposed to neoliberal economic globalization, violence, and North–South inequalities; they support participatory democracy, equality, and sustainable development.

global stewardship Referring to resources that are said to be part of the common heritage of humankind

HIV/AIDS
retrovirus
tem; it is w
AIDS (acq
characteriz

human ca
capabilitie

human de
tions Deve
being, and
Human D

Guided Tour of the Online Resource Centre

www.oxfordtextbooks.co.uk/orc/burnell4e/

The Online Resource Centre that accompanies this book provides you with ready-to-use learning materials. These resources are free of charge and have been created to take your learning further.

> **Case Study: Political Parties, Their Social Ties a[...]**
> **Change**
> **Vicky Randall**
>
> **Overview**
> This is a case study of a form of political institution, political part[...] state. There is a great variety and number of political parties in [...] has also been a tendency to study them in terms of western exp[...]

Case studies

Additional case studies have been included to encourage you to consider the political situations in different developing countries, including Syria and Zambia.

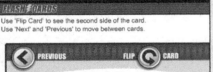

> **FLASH CARDS**
> Use 'Flip Card' to see the second side of the card.
> Use 'Next' and 'Previous' to move between cards.
>
> PREVIOUS   FLIP   CARD
>
> A state that is failing in respect o[...] of its functions without yet having [...] stage of 'collapse'.

Flashcard glossary

A series of interactive flashcards containing key terms allows you to test your knowledge of important concepts and ideas.

> **Chapter 2**
>
> 1. If the idea of postcoloniality is fundamental to ex[...] developing world today, then why do the politics[...] country to another?
>
> 2. What are the most notable features of the colon[...] politics of developing countries today?

Study questions

Additional questions are designed to support your understanding of each chapter and encourage you to think critically about the material in the textbook.

> **Chapter 12: Theorizing the State**
>
> www.transparency.org/
> Website of Transparency International, offering impor[...] corruption plus the annual Corruption Perception Inde[...] to navigate to the annual Global Corruption Report.
>
> www.gsdrc.org/
> Website of the Governance and SocialDevelopment[...]

Web links

Carefully selected lists of websites direct you to the sites of institutions and organizations that will help develop your knowledge and understanding of politics in the developing world.

Brief Contents

Detailed Contents

List of Figures

List of Boxes

List of Tables

List of Abbreviations

9/11	11 September 2001 terrorist attacks on the United States
ACP	Africa-Caribbean-Pacific states
AIDS	acquired immune deficiency syndrome
AKP	Justice and Development Party (Turkey)
ALBA	Bolivarian Alliance of Latin America
ANC	African National Congress (South Africa)
AOSIS	Alliance of Small Island States
APRM	African Peer Review Mechanism
ARPCT	Alliance for the Restoration of Peace and Counter-Terrorism (Somalia)
ASEAN	Association of South-East Asian Nations
Attac	Association pour une Taxation des Transactions financieres pour l'Aide aux Citoyens (Association for the Taxation of Financial Transactions and Aid to Citizens)
AU	African Union
AZAPO	Azanian People's Organization (South Africa)
BASIC	Brazil, South Africa, India, and China
BIS	Bank for International Settlements
BJP	Bharatiya Janata Party (India)
BRICs	rapidly developing emerging economies comprising Brazil, Russia, India, and China
BRICS	BRICs plus South Africa
BRICSAM	BRICs plus South Africa and Mexico
BSPP	Burma Socialist Programme Party
CACIF	Comité de Asociaciones Agrícolas, Comerciales, Industriales y Financieras (Guatemala)
CACM	Central American Common Market
CAN	Andean Community
CAP	Common Agricultural Policy (of the EU)
CARICOM	Caribbean Community and Common Market
CBO	community-based organization
CCI	Contemporary Capabilities Index
CCP	Chinese Communist Party; Comparative Constitutions Project
CCTV	China Central Television
CDB	China Development Bank
CDSA	South American Defense Council
CEDAW	UN Convention on the Elimination of All Forms of Discrimination against Women
CFCs	chlorofluorocarbons
CIA	Central Intelligence Agency (US)
CIDA	Canadian International Development Agency
CIS	Commonwealth of Independent States
CIVETS	Colombia, Indonesia, Vietnam, Egypt, Turkey and South Africa
CNG	compressed natural gas
CODESA	Convention for a Democratic South Africa
COMESA	Common Market for Eastern and Southern Africa
COPE	Congress of the People (South Africa)
COSATU	Congress of Trade Unions (South Africa)
CPA	Coalition Provisional Authority (Iraq)
CPI	Corruption Perceptions Index
CPRC	Chronic Poverty Research Centre
CSGR	Centre for the Study of Globalisation and Regionalisation
CSR	corporate social responsibility
CTAs	clandestine transnational activities
DAC	Development Assistance Committee (of the Organisation for Economic Co-operation and Development)
DLP	Democratic Liberal Party (South Korea)
DPKO	Department of Peacekeeping Operations (UN)
DPRK	Democratic People's Republic of Korea
DRC	Democratic Republic of the Congo (formerly Zaire)
DS	development studies
DSB	Dispute Settlement Body (WTO)
ECOSOC	Economic and Social Council (United Nations)
ECOWAS	Economic Community of West African States
EFFORT	Endowment Fund for the Rehabilitation of Tigray (Ethiopia)
ELN	National Liberation Army (Colombia)
EPB	Economic Planning Board (South Korea)
EPRDF	Ethiopian People's Revolutionary Democratic Front
EPZ	export-processing zone
EU	European Union
EZLN	Zapatista Army of National Liberation (Mexico)
FAO	Food and Agriculture Organization
FARC	Revolutionary Armed Forces of Colombia

FDI	foreign direct investment	IFE	Federal Electoral Institute (Mexico)
FH	Freedom House	IFI	international finance institution
FIS	Front Islamique du Salut	IFP	Inkatha Freedom Party (South Africa)
FOCAC	Forum on China–Africa Cooperation	IGC	Iraqi Governing Council
FOMWAN	Federation of Muslim Women's Associations in Nigeria	IMF	International Monetary Fund
		IOC	international organized crime
FRELIMO	Mozambican Liberation Front	IPU	Inter-Parliamentary Union
FRETILIN	Revolutionary Front for the Independence of East Timor	IR	international relations
		ISAF	International Security Assistance Force
FRG	Frente Republicano Guatemalteco (Guatemala)	ISI	import-substituting industrialization; Directorate of Inter-Services Intelligence (Pakistan)
FSB	Financial Stability Board (BIS)		
FSC	Forestry Stewardship Council		
FTA	free trade agreement	ISO	International Organization for Standardization
FTAA	Free Trade Area of the Americas	IT	information technology
FPTP	first past the post	ITEC	Indian Technical and Economic Cooperation
G8	Forum of eight established industrial countries comprising Canada, France, Germany, Italy, Japan, Russia, UK, US, plus EU representation	KDP	Kurdish Democratic Party (Iraq)
		LACDD	Latin American Commission on Drugs and Democracy
G20	Forum of finance ministers and central bank governors of leading industrialized and developing economies	LFO	Legal Framework Order (Pakistan)
		LTTE	Liberation Tigers of Tamil Eelam (Sri Lanka)
		MAD	mutually assured destruction
G77	Group of 77 least developed countries	MAR	Minorities at Risk
GAM	Aceh Freedom Movement (Indonesia)	MAVINS	Mexico, Australia, Vietnam, Indonesia, Nigeria, and South Africa
GATT	General Agreement on Tariffs and Trade		
GDP	gross domestic product	MCA	Millennium Challenge Account (US government)
GEF	Global Environment Facility		
GHG	greenhouse gas	MDGs	Millennium Development Goals (of the United Nations)
GM	genetically modified		
GMOs	genetically modified organisms	MDP	Millennium Development Party (South Korea)
GNI	gross national income	MENA	Middle East and North Africa
GNP	gross national product	MEND	Movement for the Emancipation of the Delta (Nigeria)
GNU	Government of National Unity (South Africa)		
H1N1	swine flu	MERCOSUR	Southern Common Market (Latin America)
H5N1	avian influenza virus	MINUGUA	Misión de las Naciones Unidas en Guatemala
HCI	heavy and chemical industries	MKSS	Mazdoor Kisan Shakti Sangathan (India)
HDI	Human Development Index	MNCs	multinational corporations
HIPCs	heavily indebted poor countries	MST	Movimento dos Trabalhadores Rurais Sem Terra (Landless Rural Workers, Movement) (Brazil)
HIP(I)C	Heavily Indebted Poor Countries (Initiative)		
HIV	human immunodeficiency virus		
IAU	Inter-Agency Information and Analysis Unit (on Iraq)	NAFTA	North American Free Trade Agreement
		NAM	Non-Aligned Movement
IBRD	International Bank for Reconstruction and Development (of the World Bank)	NATO	North Atlantic Treaty Organization
		NDA	National Democratic Alliance (India)
IBSA	India, Brazil, South Africa	NDD	non-DAC donor
ICG	International Crisis Group	NEPAD	New Economic Partnership for Africa's Development (AU)
IDA	International Development Association		
IDB	Inter-American Development Bank	NGO	non-governmental organization
IDEA	International Institute for Democracy and Electoral Assistance	NIC	National Intelligence Council
		NICs	newly industrialized countries (mainly East Asia)
IFAI	Federal Institute for Access to Public Information (Mexico)		
		NIE	new institutional economics

NLD	National League for Democracy (Myanmar)
NORAD	Norwegian Agency for Development Cooperation
NPT	Non-Proliferation Treaty
NRS	National Revenue Service (Ghana)
NSSD	National Strategy for Sustainable Development
OAS	Organization of American States
OAU	Organization of African Unity
OBCs	Other Backward Classes (India)
ODA	official development assistance
OECD	Organisation for Economic Co-operation and Development
OPEC	Organization of the Petroleum Exporting Countries
ORHA	Office for Reconstruction and Humanitarian Assistance (in Iraq)
PAC	Pan Africanist Congress (South Africa)
PAN	National Action Party (Mexico)
PARLASUR	Parliament of the Common Market of the South (MERCOSUR)
PD	Democratic Party (Indonesia)
PDI-P	Indonesia Democratic Party–Struggle
PDP	People's Democratic Party (Nigeria)
PDPA	People's Democratic Party of Afghanistan
PES	payments for ecosystem services
PFN	Pentecostal Fellowship of Nigeria
PKB	National Awakening Party (Indonesia)
PKI	Communist Party of Indonesia
PKS	Justice and Welfare Party
PML(Q)	Pakistan Muslim League (Quaid)
PNUD	Programa de las Naciones Unidas para el Desarollo
POPs	persistent organic compounds
PPC	People's Plan Campaign (India)
PPP	Pakistan People's Party; purchasing power parity
PRC	People's Republic of China
PRD	Party of the Democratic Revolution (Mexico)
PRI	Institutional Revolutionary Party (Mexico)
PRN	National Revolutionary Party (Mexico)
PRSP	Poverty Reduction Strategy Process
PUK	Patriotic Union of Kurdistan (Iraq)
R2P	responsibility to protect
RCT	randomized control trial
REDD	reducing emissions from deforestation and forest degradation
RENAMO	Mozambican National Resistance
ROC	Republic of China
ROK	Republic of Korea (South Korea)
RPF	Rwandan Patriotic Front
RSS	Rashtriya Swayamsevak Sangh (India)
RUF	Revolutionary United Front (Sierra Leone)
SA	South Africa
SACP	South African Communist Party
SALs	structural adjustment loans
SAPs	structural adjustment programmes
SARS	severe acute respiratory syndrome; South African Revenue Services
SAVAK	Organization for Intelligence and National Security (Iran)
SCO	Shanghai Cooperation Organization
SLORC	State Law and Order Restoration Committee (Myanmar)
SME	small and medium-sized enterprises
TAC	Treatment Action Campaign (South Africa)
TEAM-9	Techno-Economic Approach for Africa-India Movement
TEPJF	Electoral Tribunal of the Judicial Power of the Federation (Mexico)
TERI	The Energy and Resources Institute (India)
TFG	Transitional Federal Government (Somalia)
TI	Transparency International
TNA	Transitional National Assembly (Iraq)
TNCs	transnational corporations
TRC	Truth and Reconciliation Commission (South Africa)
TRIPS	Agreement on Trade-Related Aspects of Intellectual Property Rights
UAE	United Arab Emirates
UDF	United Democratic Front (South Africa)
UIC	Union of Islamic Courts (Somalia)
UK	United Kingdom
UN	United Nations
UNAIDS	Joint United Nations Programme on HIV/AIDS
UNAM	National Autonomous University (Mexico)
UNAMI	United Nations Assistance Mission for Iraq
UNASUR	Union of South American Nations
UNCAC	United Nation Convention against Corruption
UNCED	United Nations Conference on Environment and Development
UNCTAD	United Nations Conference on Trade and Development
UNDP	United Nations Development Programme
UNEP	United Nations Environment Programme
UNFCCC	United Nations Framework Convention on Climate Change
UNHCR	United Nations High Commissioner for Refugees
UNICEF	United Nations Children's Fund
UNIDO	United National Democratic Opposition (Philippines)
UNIFEM	United Nations Development Fund for Women
UNITA	National Union for Total Independence of Angola

UNMIT	United Nations Integrated Mission in Timor-Leste
UNMOGIP	United Nations Military Observer Group in India and Pakistan
UNOCHA	UN Office for the Coordination of Humanitarian Affairs
UNODC	United Nations Office on Drugs and Crime
UNRISD	United Nations Research Institute for Social Development
UNSC	United Nations Security Council
UNSCN	United Nations Standing Committee on Nutrition
UNTAET	United Nations Transitional Authority in East Timor
UNU-WIDER	United Nations University's World Institute for Development Economics Research
UP	Uttar Pradesh (India)
URA	Uganda Revenue Authority
URNG	Unidad Revolucionaria Nacional Guatemalteca (Guatemala)
US	United States
USAID	United States Agency for International Development
USSR	Union of Soviet Socialist Republics
VAT	value added tax
WB	World Bank
WFP	World Food Programme
WGA	World Governance Assessment
WGI	World Governance Indicators
WHO	World Health Organization
WMDs	weapons of mass destruction
WSF	World Social Forum
WSSD	World Summit on Sustainable Development
WTO	World Trade Organization
WWF	World Wide Fund for Nature

About the Contributors

Tony Addison is Chief Economist and Deputy Director of the United Nations University's World Institute for Development Economics Research (UNU-WIDER) in Helsinki, Finland.

Nadje Al-Ali is a professor of gender studies and Director of the Gender Studies Centre, School of Oriental and African Studies, University of London, UK.

Leslie Elliott Armijo is Visiting Scholar, Mark O. Hatfield School of Government, Portland State University, US.

Edward Aspinall is a professor in the Department of Political and Social Change, School of International, Political, and Strategic Studies, Australian National University, Canberra, Australia.

Deborah Bräutigam is a professor of international development and comparative politics, and Director of the International Development Program, Johns Hopkins University School of Advanced International Studies, Washington DC, US.

Peter Burnell is a professor in the Department of Politics and International Studies, University of Warwick, UK.

James Chiriyankandath is Senior Research Fellow with the Institute of Commonwealth Studies, School of Advanced Study, University of London, UK.

Peter Ferdinand is a reader in the Department of Politics and International Studies, University of Warwick, UK.

Michael Freeman is a research professor in the Department of Government and was formerly Deputy Director of the Human Rights Centre, University of Essex, UK.

Siri Gloppen is a professor in the Department of Comparative Politics, University of Bergen and Senior Researcher at the Chr. Michelsen Institute, Bergen, Norway.

Jeff Haynes is a professor in the Department of Law, Governance, and International Relations, London Metropolitan University, UK.

Stephen Hobden is a senior lecturer in international politics in the School of Humanities and Social Sciences, University of East London, UK.

Nicole Jackson is an associate professor in the School for International Studies, Simon Fraser University, Vancouver, BC, Canada.

Adrian Leftwich was a senior lecturer in the Department of Politics, University of York, UK.

Emma Mawdsley is a Fellow of Newnham College and a senior lecturer in the Department of Geography, University of Cambridge, UK.

Peter Newell is a professor of international relations at the University of Sussex.

Marina Ottaway is Senior Scholar at the Woodrow Wilson International Center for Scholars, Washington DC, US.

Jenny Pearce is a professor of Latin American politics in the Department of Peace Studies, University of Bradford, UK.

Nicola Pratt is an associate professor of international politics of the Middle East in the Department of Politics and International Studies, University of Warwick, UK.

Lise Rakner is a professor in the Department of Comparative Politics, University of Bergen, and Senior Researcher at the Chr. Michelsen Institute, Bergen, Norway.

Vicky Randall is Emeritus Professor in the Department of Government, University of Essex, UK, and President of the Political Studies Association, UK.

James R. Scarritt is Emeritus Professor in the Department of Political Science and formerly Faculty Research Associate in the Institute of Behavioral Science at the University of Colorado at Boulder, CO, US.

Andreas Schedler is a professor of political science in the Department of Political Studies, Centro de Investigación y Docencia Económicas (CIDE), Mexico City, Mexico.

Rachel Sieder is Senior Researcher, Centro de Investigación y Educación Superior en Antropología School of Advanced Study (CIESAS), Mexico City, and a senior lecturer in Latin American politics at the Institute for the Study of the Americas, School of Advanced Study, University of London, UK.

Kathleen Staudt is a professor of political science at the University of Texas at El Paso, TX, US.

Astri Suhrke is Senior Researcher, Chr. Michelsen Institute, Bergen, Norway, and Fellow, Asia-Pacific College of Diplomacy, The Australian National University, Canberra.

David Taylor is Director of the Aga Khan University Institute for the Study of Muslim Civilisations and a Senior Research Fellow at the Institute of Commonwealth Studies, University of London, UK.

Torunn Wimpelmann is a researcher at the Chr. Michelsen Institute, Bergen, Norway.

Stephen Wright is a professor of political science at Northern Arizona University, Flagstaff, AZ, US.

Introduction

Peter Burnell, Lise Rakner, and Vicky Randall

The aim of this book is to explore the changing nature of **politics** in the **developing world** in the twenty-first century. It analyses central developments and debates, illustrated by current examples drawn from the global South, covering such issues as **institutions** and **governance**, but also the growing importance of alternative politics and **social movements**, security, and post-conflict state-crafting. The present edition builds on earlier editions, but brings the discussion up to date. It looks at the 'Arab uprisings' considered as social movements or from the perspectives of religion, **gender**, and democracy, offering a new online case study of Syria. And it highlights the growing importance of South–South relations with case studies of China, India, and (new to the book) Brazil.

Both 'politics' and the 'developing world' are concepts that require further elaboration, and which are discussed more fully next. By 'politics', we mean broadly activities associated with the process and institutions of government, or the state, but in the context of wider power relations and struggles. By the 'developing world', we are primarily referring to those regions that were formerly colonized by Western powers, which have been late to industrialize, and which sustain relatively high levels of poverty—that is, Africa, Asia, the Middle East, and Latin America, including the Caribbean.

In our analysis of politics in the developing world, the complex and changing nexus between state and society has centre stage. This is because it is the reciprocal interaction of state and society, and the influence that each one exerts on the other, that most accounts for the distinctive character of developing countries' politics. Needless to say, that influence varies in both degree and kind, over time, as between individual states and inside states. The book does not set out to present a case for saying that the state is now marginal for the political analysis of developing countries; nor does it argue that we must 'bring the state back in'. On the contrary, it recognizes that issues concerning the state have been, are, and will remain central to the political analysis, notwithstanding important developments—political, financial, economic, technological, and even social at the sub-state, regional, and especially global levels—that are reshaping the nature, size, role, and performance of individual states.

A book about politics in the developing world is not the same thing as a book about development per se, or about development studies. Indeed, the book does not have as its main objective an emphasis on the politics *of* development by which is meant the elucidation of different development theories. There are other books that have been designed for this purpose. Certainly, there has been a trend in the study of development to comprehend development in an increasingly holistic sense—one that emphasizes its multifaceted nature and the interconnectedness of the various parts, of which politics provides one very important element. And while the chapters of the book do explore key relationships between politics and society, and between politics and the economy, they do so without any mission to demonstrate that politics is in some sense the 'master science' that unlocks all other subjects. Instead, the consequences that development can have for politics in the developing countries are as much a part of the analysis in this book as the implications that the politics have for development. So, although the book's primary focus is politics rather than development, we hope that its contents will still be of interest to anyone who is involved in development studies more generally.

A word is also needed explaining the geographical coverage of the book. As will be related shortly, the boundaries of the developing world are neither uncontentious nor unchanging. We have already suggested which regions have tended historically to be associated with it. However, this book's coverage—and more especially its case studies—do not include all of the possible candidates, primarily for pragmatic reasons. Thus Cuba, Vietnam, and some other countries that at one time claimed to be socialist, even Marxist–Leninist, are just as much part of the developing world as are the many countries that now defer to capitalism and adopt political pluralism. But notwithstanding the financial and economic traumas that hit the global system in 2008, such countries remain a small band. A few, such as Bolivia and Ecuador, are currently pioneering redistributive social and economic policies, but the forces

of **globalization** in the post-Soviet, post-cold-war world do seem to militate against a more widespread radical socialist transformation. Indeed, China, whose credentials to be considered part of the developing world are open to debate, shows no intention of reverting to communism as an organizing principle for political economy even though it remains a one-party communist state. However, because contemporary China's relations with developing countries are increasingly significant and the distinctive combination of China's own politics with its rapid economic development appears to some to be a model for others to follow, a chapter on China's relations with the developing world is included in this book.

There are other parts of the world, beyond the regions traditionally included, that might now be considered to fall into this 'developing world' category. Although no express reference is made in the book to those elements of the post-communist world, a handful of the new European and Central Asian states that formerly belonged to the 'Second World' have certain characteristics long associated with the developing world. Some of them have come to acquire developing country status, in as much as the Organisation for Economic Co-operation and Development's (OECD) Development Assistance Committee (DAC) has made countries such as Albania and Armenia eligible for **official development assistance (ODA)**. By comparison, the post-communist world's more advanced members were styled 'countries in transition' and judged ineligible for such aid. Readers are free to apply the concepts and propositions in this book to an examination of all of these other countries if they wish, just as area specialists seeking insights into those countries will find here material that resonates for their own subject. After all, the growing interdependence of states, and the rise of trans-territorial and supranational issues, such as those embraced by what might be called the 'new security agenda', certainly do not respect all of the distinctions between categories of countries, let alone national borders. The geopolitical unit of analysis that is most relevant to understanding the issues can easily straddle different states only some of which possess all of the main traits conventionally associated with developing countries. Similarly, there are regions and localities inside the wealthiest countries ('the South in the North') that share certain 'Southern' or 'Third World' characteristics, relative economic and social deprivation being one such characteristic, which the global economic recession since 2009 brought into sharper relief.

From Third World to Developing World

The developing world has been variously referred to as the 'Third World', the 'South', and the 'less developed countries (LDCs)', among other titles. Some of the members are rightly deemed 'emerging economies', and there is a distinctive group—the so-called BRICs (Brazil, Russia, India, China—supplemented by South Africa since 2010 and now referred to as BRICS)—that current debate singles out as rising powers, the harbingers of a new emerging multipolarity or more fragmented world. For example, four of these countries—Brazil, South Africa, India, and China—played a key role alongside the United States in negotiating the Copenhagen Accord of the United Nations Climate Change Conference (December 2009), and the same countries, plus Argentina, Indonesia, Mexico, Saudi Arabia, South Korea, and Turkey, also formally belong to the G20 group of the world's leading economies, taking part in, for example, the succession of summit talks on tackling global economic crisis and promoting economic development, most recently held in Mexico in 2012 and St Petersburg in 2013.

In fact, the question of the meaningfulness of the Third World as an organizing concept has long been the subject of as much dispute as the term's precise definition or true origins. Successive rationales for marking out a distinct Third World associated this world with a stance of non-alignment towards the capitalist and communist superpowers, with post-colonial status, with dependence on Western capitalism, and with poverty and economic 'backwardness'. Together, this comprised a confusing melange of external, as well as internal, economic and political descriptors. Following the collapse of Soviet power, the disappearance of the 'Second World' served to hasten the decline of the 'Third World' as a category name. Here is not the place to revisit the history of the debates about a term that, by and large, have now been brought to a conclusion. An abundant literature exists (Wolf-Phillips 1979; Berger 1994; Randall 2004). In keeping with the general trend, then, we have preferred to use the term 'developing world' for this book. In so doing, we do not mean to imply that this term is entirely uncontroversial or unproblematic. Assuming a conventional understanding of 'development', there are many parts of the developing world in which such a process is little in evidence and some in which it might even seem to be in retreat. There are also those who question the validity of such conventional understandings of 'development'—who indeed see development itself as an ideological construct subservient to the interests of Western donors, the international aid 'industry', and suchlike. We recognize the force of many of these arguments. At any rate, whatever term is favoured, there has also been a growing appreciation of the very considerable diversity to be found among and within those countries traditionally seen to come under its umbrella, and the widening of differences in their role and stance towards major issues in world politics.

Notwithstanding what, in many instances, has been a shared colonial past, some of the differences have always been there, such as the enormous range in demographic and territorial size. At only the lower end of the scale, the distinction between 'small' and 'micro' states that in total make up around 40 per cent of all developing countries and territories is a topic for debate. In contrast, in a regional context, some of the larger developing countries now appear to be approaching almost superpower-like status, even while remaining vulnerable to major external shocks. Thus a country such as India, a nuclear power with a population that exceeds 1 billion people, has very strong claims to be admitted to the permanent membership of the United Nations Security Council (UNSC). Some people champion similar claims for Brazil and Nigeria, although the latter is less stable politically and its fortunes continue to rest heavily on a very narrow base of energy exports.

Similarly, the developing world has always been noted for considerable variety in terms of economic dynamism and technological progress, and recent decades have served only to make these contrasts more pronounced. Just as average incomes were in decline in many parts of Africa in the latter years of the twentieth century (although in the second decade of the twenty-first century there are real signs that this may be changing), so some of the so-called 'tiger economies' in East Asia have become developed countries in all but name. South Korea is a member of the OECD and now a member of the DAC. Its inclusion as a case study in this book illustrates how far and how quickly countries can develop, if political and other conditions are favourable. Yet in many parts of the developing world, including India, China, and large parts of Latin America, great inequalities persist alongside the growing prosperity of an emerging middle class and political elite. It may be significant that, when the World Economic Forum met in Davos in January 2013, hundreds of economic experts from around the globe agreed that the biggest challenge facing the world is the increasing income gap between rich and poor. It was noted that not only is there an income gap between individual countries, but also many developing countries are currently experiencing dramatic income disparities between various groups.

Until the 1980s, despite the differences in size and economic performance, it was possible to argue that most countries in the developing world had in common certain domestic political traits. These included a tendency towards authoritarian rule, whether based on the military, a single ruling party or personal dictatorship, or severe instability and internal conflict, and endemic **corruption**. But, more recently, political differences that were already there have become much more pronounced—and nowhere more so than in the recognition that some states are failing or are even close to collapse. We are increasingly aware of the wide disparities in state strength and of the significance (not least for development) of variations in the quality of governance. The role played by ethnic and religious identity in politics has also come more to the fore, with the misfortunes of Iraq since the fall of Saddam Hussein providing a vivid example. In contrast, in Latin America, ethno-nationalism and religious conflict have been relatively minor themes—which is not to say that they are absent: indigenous peoples have started to come out of the shadows. Examples of 'alternative politics' and **non-violent action** by social movements are demanding increasing attention in this and some other parts of the developing world, whilst the complex chain of events originating in the 'Arab Spring' continues to defy confident categorization and prediction.

In sum, we are increasingly conscious of change, complexity, and diversity in the developing world and of significant disagreements that follow from differences such as those related to national power. Some common features among developing countries, such as the colonial experience, are now receding into history, which makes old manifestations of 'Third World solidarity', such as the Non-Aligned Movement (NAM), harder to keep alive in their original form. This means that the many differences within the developing world now appear in sharper relief even as new ways of constructing shared interests vis-à-vis the rich world and forging new South–South links among governments and non-governmental actors also proceed apace.

Politics as Independent or Dependent Variable?

Most people—still more so politics students—will have some idea of what is intended by the term 'politics'. Generally, political scientists understand it to refer to activities surrounding the process and institutions of government or the state, and that is a focus that we share in this book. However, there is another tradition, which some describe as 'sociological', that tends to identify politics with power relationships and structures, including, but by no means confined to, the state. They include, for instance, relationships between socio-economic classes or other kinds of social group, and between genders. When studying politics in the developing world, we believe it to be particularly important to locate analysis of political processes in their narrower sense within the wider context of social relationships and conflicts. Here, one of the themes and puzzles is the relationship between the more formal aspects of political processes and institutions, which may, to some degree, have been imposed or modelled on Western prototypes, and their 'informal' aspects. The latter can be very resilient, and may even be regarded as more authentic. The informal hierarchies of power between patrons and clients are a specific example that applies especially, although not exclusively, to the developing world.

Despite our insistence on the need to understand politics in the wider power context, this does not rule out what is sometimes referred to as the 'autonomy of the political'—that is, the ability of politics to have independent and significant effects of its own. Thus any account of politics in the developing world that goes beyond the merely descriptive can have one or both of two objectives: to make sense of the politics; and to disclose what else the politics itself helps us to understand better. Succinctly, politics can be treated as *explanandum* or *explanans*, and possibly as both.

For some decades, there was a large movement in political science to view politics as the dependent variable. Analysts sought to advance our understanding of politics and to gain some predictive potential in regard to future political developments by rooting it in some 'more fundamental' aspects of the human condition, sometimes called structural 'conditions'. This was nowhere more evident than in the tendency to argue that the kind of political **regime**—namely, the relationship between rulers and ruled, usually depicted somewhere along the continuum from a highly authoritarian to a more liberal democratic polity—is a product largely of economic circumstance. The level of economic achievement, the nature and pace of economic change, and the social consequences were all considered highly important. It was not only Marxists who subscribed to broadly this kind of view; there were also others who sought to explain politics, especially in some parts of the developing world, more as an outcome of certain cultural conditions. This invoked a matrix of social divisions much richer and potentially more confusing than a simple class-based analysis would allow. These and other inclinations that view politics as contingent are still very much in evidence in contemporary theorizing about politics in the developing world, as several of the chapters in Parts I and II of the book will show.

However, over recent decades in political science, the larger study of comparative politics and area studies too have increased the weight given to the idea of politics as an independent variable, claiming in principle that politics matters: not only is it affected, but it too can have effects. Mair (1996) characterized this as a shift from an emphasis on asking what causes political systems to emerge, to take shape, and possibly to persist towards questions about what outputs and outcomes result from the political processes, and how well various political institutions perform. Making sense of the politics now goes beyond only explaining it; it extends also to investigating the impact of politics and its consequences. That includes the way in which contemporary politics are affected by the political history of a country—a proposition that is sometimes given the label of 'path dependence', which in its more narrow and most meaningful application suggests that institutional choices tend to become self-reinforcing (see Pierson 2000).

This move to view the more autonomous side of politics coincides with the rise of new institutionalism in political studies. New institutionalism has been described in a seminal article by March and Olsen (1984: 747) as neither a theory nor a coherent critique of one, but instead 'simply an argument that the organisation of political life makes a difference'. The new institutionalism (explored more fully in Chapter 3) directs us to the study of political process and political design, but not simply as outcomes or in terms of their contextual 'conditions'. This is not a completely new mood. As March and Olsen (1984) rightly say, historically, political science has emphasized the ways in which political behaviour is embedded in an institutional structure of norms, rules, expectations, and traditions that constrain the free play of individual will. The implications of this approach, and of tracing what political forms and political choices mean for a large set of issues of public concern—environmental issues, for instance—are explored in Parts 3 and 4 of the book especially. In doing so, the chapters provide a bridge to studying the larger phenomenon of **human development**. Here, we take our cue from the United Nations Development Programme (UNDP), which said that its 2002 Human Development Report was 'first and foremost about the idea that politics is as important to successful development as economics' (UNDP 2002: v). The UNDP's understanding is that human development, an idea that has grown in acceptance across a broad spectrum of development studies, aims to promote not simply higher material consumption, but also the freedom, well-being, and dignity of people everywhere. Development, then, has a political goal, just as politics is integral to how we understand the meaning of development.

Global Trends

Notwithstanding the increasing differentiation within the developing world, it is a fact that, over the last few decades, there has also been a growing convergence. This is the result of the presence of a number of major interconnected trends, political and economic, domestic and international. But these trends, far from reconfirming the more old-fashioned notions of the Third World, are instead ensuring that some of the most striking similarities emerging in the developing world today have a very different character from the Third World of old. This point is well worth illustrating before moving on.

One such trend, entrenched towards the end of the last century, comprised pressures from within and without the societies to adopt the so-called **'Washington consensus'** of the Bretton Woods institutions—the International Monetary Fund (IMF) and World Bank—on economic policy and national economic management. These developments have been held responsible in part for a near-universal movement in the direction of **neoliberalism** and marketization. There has been a shift from public ownership and the direct control of economic life by the state towards acceptance and encouragement of for-profit enterprise and growing opportunities for non-governmental development organizations. Although proceeding at different paces in different places and experiencing widely varying degrees of success, the implications of such changes for politics generally and for the state specifically can be quite profound. Ultimately, the same might be true of the 'post-Washington consensus', which is now commonly said to have succeeded the earlier development and which appears to give a bit more priority to tackling poverty, as well as to highlighting the developmental importance of attaining '**good governance**'. How this trend may be further modified by the growing importance of the new non-DAC donors, especially China (see Part VIII), it is too early to say.

If *economic* liberalization has been one prong of a growing convergence among developing countries, then pressures towards *political* liberalization and democratization have been a second and, according to some accounts, symbiotically related development. The amount of substantive change that has actually taken place and its permanence are both open to discussion. Indeed, after a time in the early 1990s when the third wave of democratization seemed to have unstoppable momentum and some observers talked about the 'end of history', far more cautious claims are now much in evidence. By 2013, the reality has become more confused: authoritarian or semi-authoritarian persistence in some places sits alongside evidence of democratic reversal in yet others. While a number of the 'new democracies' are of questionable quality, the progress made by others has confounded the cynics. Yet, irrespective of how truly liberal (in the political sense) or even democratic most developing countries really are and of how many possess market economies that are truly vibrant, recognition of the importance of governance in whatever way we define it (the definitions are many, some of them so vague or all-encompassing as to be almost useless— see Chapter 15) is ubiquitous. All of these agendas have been driven strongly by developed world institutions and, notwithstanding the varied responses and reactions, the developing world now looks a rather different place from the way in which the Third World was formerly understood.

Underpinning these and many other contemporary developments—such as the campaigns for gender equity, the salience of 'new security' issues, and international monitoring of **human rights**—there is the growing significance ascribed to globalization. Here, globalization is understood at a minimum as 'the

process of increasing interconnectedness between societies such that events in one part of the world more and more have effects on peoples and societies far away' (Baylis and Smith 2001: 7). The influence may be direct, and positive or negative, or both. It can also work indirectly. And, of course, the developing countries are touched unevenly and in different ways, as is made clear in this book. In purely economic terms, some are largely bystanders. They may share few of the claimed benefits even while incurring accidental and unintended costs. Their continuing vulnerability to fluctuations in the world market for their commodities is illustrative. Globalization theorists tell us that the sites of power are becoming more dispersed, and some say that power is leaking away from the state—more so in the case of many developing countries that are small or very poor, or have weak governance structures, than for big countries such as the United States, Japan, Russia, China, or even the other BRICS. This unevenness is an unwritten assumption in much of the international political economy literature on globalization, which, by its own admission, biases attention towards the economically more developed parts of the world (see, for example, Phillips 2005). It provides one more reason for arguing that treating the developing world as a distinct, but not separate, entity continues to make sense.

Thus while the old order summed up by 'First', 'Second', and 'Third' Worlds has disappeared and the international system appears to be edging to a very uncertain future characterized by a greater dispersion of power compared to the cold war and its immediate aftermath, differences still exist between the developing world and its counterpart in the more affluent North. And if US foreign initiatives after the **terrorist** attacks of 11 September 2001 ('9/11'), especially in the Middle East, caused widespread resentment in developing regions triggered by perceptions of a new imperialism reminiscent of older struggles for liberation from colonial rule, then claims to developing world solidarity might be credited with some purchase even now. A shared sensitivity to incursions or infringements of their sovereignty still supplies a common cause, one that China quite expressly promotes, although, of course, unlike European Union (EU) member states, countries such as the United States are hardly keen to surrender **political autonomy** either. Perhaps the dividing lines are nowhere more evident than in the North–South alignment over how to respond to global climate change. Most of the developed world sees a reduction in global greenhouse gas emissions as the priority, but many developing countries—including India and, at least until recently, China—have seemed less convinced and rather draw attention to the urgency of climate adaptation in developing countries, and to the rich world's obligation both to cut emissions and to offer help. Interests and issues like these share with identities a responsibility for how the different worlds are constructed, or construct themselves—sometimes expressly in opposition to one another.

Even so, we should be continually challenging ourselves to distinguish between, on the one side, what, how, and how far changes really are taking place in developing world politics, and on the other side the changes in our understanding that owe most to the lens through which we study the subject. Here, history tells us that, for the most part, the lens tends to originate, or comes to be ground more finely, outside and not inside the developing world. This is an important point: registering major developing world contributions to the way in which developing world politics is understood by observers in the developed world is crucial, but, while far from impossible, is not an easy or straightforward task.

Organization of the Book

The book comprises eight parts, the last four of which (Parts 5–8) contain case studies that illustrate some of the key concepts and themes presented in the first parts of the book (Parts 1–4). Each part is introduced by its own brief survey of contents; these short introductions can be read alongside this opening chapter. Part 1 on analytical approaches and the global context should be read first. The aim of this part is to provide an introduction to general theoretical approaches that offer different ways of making sense of the politics in the developing world. These simplifying devices enable us to bring some order to a great mass of facts. They are useful both for directing our inquiries and because they provide a lens or lenses through which to interpret the empirical information. They suggest explanations for what we find there. Ultimately, the point of theorizing is not simply to explain, but also to provide a gateway to prediction. And however tenuous social science's claims to be able to predict with any confidence may be, the book aims both to assess the present of developing countries in the light of the past and to identify the major political uncertainties facing them in the foreseeable future.

So it is entirely appropriate that, immediately following the analytical overview, there is a chapter on colonialism and post-coloniality—themes that still resonate in so many different ways. Special attention is then given to institutional perspectives, followed by the changing international context. The glib conviction that now, more than ever, all of humanity resides in 'one world' betokens a very real fact of growing interconnectedness and interdependence, albeit highly asymmetric. There is increasing global economic integration at its core, but important political and other expressions of globalization, including new patterns in relationships among developing countries and China, should not be ignored either. The different analytical approaches that these chapters offer should not be viewed as entirely mutually exclusive. Each can quite plausibly have something valuable to offer, even though the emphases may shift when applied to different country situations and historical epochs. Readers must form their own judgements about which particular theoretical propositions offer most insight into specific issues and problems, or the more general condition of politics in developing countries. It is not the book's aim to be prescriptive in this regard, other than to restate that, where possible, notable perspectives from the developing world should be reflected.

Parts 2 and 3 set out to illuminate the changing nature, role, and situation of the state in relation to key social variables within developing countries. The two parts are a mirror image of one another. Together, they explore both how the politics reflects or is affected by social context, and how states specifically have responded to the challenges posed by society, and the social effects. Particular attention is given to what this means in terms of the changing use and distribution of political power among state institutions and other actors. Thus Part 2 introduces the themes of inequality, ethnopolitics and nationalism, religion, gender, **civil society**, and alternative politics and social movements, in that order. Part 3 proceeds to theorize the state, before going on to examine the distinctive features of states that are trying to escape violent conflict at home. This is followed by an examination of the conditions of democratization and of the relations between democratization and development, and by a discussion of governance, in which emphasis is placed on how power is exercised and checked once a government is in office.

Part 4 identifies major policy issues that confront all developing countries to a greater or lesser degree. In general terms, the issues are not peculiar to the developing world, but they do have a special resonance and their own character there. And although the issues also belong to the larger discourse on development per se, Part 4 aims to uncover why and how they become expressly political. It compares different political responses, and their consequences both for politics and development. The issues range from economic development and the environment, to human rights and security. Some of these could just as well have been introduced in earlier chapters of the book. This is because the presentations in Part 4 do not concentrate purely on the *details* of policy, but rather, out of necessity, seek to locate the policies within the context of the policy *issues* as such. However, all of these more policy-oriented chapters are grouped together because they are representative of major challenges for society and for government. Of course, where readers prefer to relate material from a chapter in Part 4 more closely to the material that comes earlier in the book, then there is no need for them to follow the chapters in strict numerical order.

Parts 5–8 aim to illustrate in some depth, or by what is sometimes called 'thick description', principal themes raised in the earlier parts, so complementing the use there of examples drawn more widely from around the developing world. While space limitations mean that the case studies are not designed to cover all aspects of a country's politics, the cases have been selected both with an eye to their intrinsic interest and for the contrasts that they provide in relation to one or more of the larger themes introduced earlier. Also, attention has been given not simply to illustrating developing country problems and weaknesses, but also to highlighting cases that offer a more positive experience. A deliberate aim of the book is to show the developing world as a place of diversity and rapid transformations. All of the main geographical regions are represented in Parts 5–8, together with the supplements offered by the book's Online Resource Centre. Part 5 includes two case studies, of Pakistan and Indonesia, focusing on **regime change**. In Part 6, focus shifts to the debates over state power, and over fragile and strong states, illustrated by the cases of Iraq, Mexico, and South Korea. Part 7 draws on the debates about development and human rights discussed in more detail in Part 4, illustrated by two case studies: of Nigeria and Guatemala, respectively. In the final

section (Part 8), emphasis is put on the increasingly strong South–South relations. The new role of developing countries in international politics is illustrated through country case studies of Brazil, China, and India.

In total, the country studies once again highlight the great range of experience in the developing world. They also demonstrate the benefit to be gained from a detailed historical knowledge of the individual cases. But although the cases differ not least in respect of their relative success or failure regarding development in the widest sense and politics specifically, none of them offers a simple or straightforward picture. The case studies should be read in conjunction with the appropriate chapter(s) from the earlier parts and are not intended to be read in isolation.

The editors' view is that a final chapter headed 'Conclusions' is not needed. The chapters each contain their own summaries; such a large collected body of material is not easily reduced without making some arbitrary decisions—and, most importantly, readers should be encouraged to form their own conclusions. It is almost inevitable that readers will differ in terms of the themes, issues, and even the countries or regions about which they will most want to form conclusions. And it is in the nature of the subject that there is no single set of 'right' answers that the editors can distil. On the contrary, studying politics in the developing world is so fascinating precisely because it is such a rich field of inquiry and constantly gives rise to new rounds of challenging questions.

So we finish here by posing some overarching questions that readers might want to keep in mind as they read the chapters. These questions might be used to help to structure the sort of general debate that often takes place towards the end of courses or study programmes that this book aims to serve. In principle, the individual subject of each of the chapters and of each of the case studies merits further investigation. But for courses occupying a very limited number of weeks, lectures or tutor presentations might concentrate only on material drawn from Parts 1–4, and the allotted preparatory student reading each week might include the relevant case study material.

- Is politics in the developing world so very different from politics elsewhere that understanding it requires a distinct theoretical framework?

- Is there a single theoretical framework adequate for the purpose of comprehending politics in all countries of the developing world, or should we call on some combination of different frameworks?

- Are the main political trends experienced by the developing world in recent decades summed up best by 'increasing diversity' or by 'growing convergence', and are these trends likely to continue in the future?

- What are the advantages of applying a gendered framework of analysis to the study of politics in developing countries, and does one particular gendered framework offer equivalent insights in all countries?

- In what political respects is the developing world truly developing and in what respects are significant parts of it *not* developing—or even travelling in the opposite direction?

- What grounds are there for being optimistic, or pessimistic, about the ability of states to resolve conflict and to manage change peacefully in the developing world?

- Are the role of the state and the nature of the public policy process fundamentally changing in the developing world, and if so, in what respects?

- What principal forces, domestic or global, are creating incentives and pressures for fundamental political change and what forces are resisting or obstructing such change?

- How should developing countries' policies concerning the major public issues of our time differ from the typical policies that we see widely adopted in developed countries?

- What lessons most relevant to other societies can be learned by studying politics in the developing world and to which countries, or groups of countries, are these lessons most relevant?

- Drawing on what you understand about politics in the developing world, should China be included among the countries that are studied as part of the developing world?

WEB LINKS

http://blds.ids.ac.uk   The British Library for Development Studies claims to be Europe's largest research collection on social and economic change in developing countries.

http://www.eldis.org   Thousands of online documents, organizations, and messages convey information on development policy, practice, and research.

http://www.gdnet.org   The site of the Global Development Network, a worldwide network of research and policy institutes aiming to generate research at the local level in developing countries and to provide alternative perspectives to those originating in the more developed world.

PART I
Approaches and Global Context

Politics in the developing world offers an enormously rich and fascinating canvas of material for investigation. If we are to make sense of what we find, we must approach the subject in a structured and orderly way, with a clear sense of purpose. That means having an adequate framework, or frameworks, of analysis comprising appropriate concepts lucidly defined, together with a set of coherent organizing propositions. Propositions are advanced to explain the political phenomena in terms of their relationships both with one another and with other variables—including the influencing factors and the factors that are themselves influenced by, and demonstrate the importance of, politics. This part of the book introduces analytical approaches to the study of politics in the developing world. It reviews the contribution that can be made by a particular focus on institutions and the analytical purchase that adopting such a focus entails. It also sets out to situate politics within both an historical and an international and increasingly globalizing environment, as befits the increase of interdependence ('one world') and supraterritoriality that appear so distinctive of modern times.

This part has two aims. *First*, it aims to identify the most enlightening analytical approaches for an understanding of politics in the 'developing world'. Is this a sufficiently distinct entity to warrant its own theory, or can we usefully apply approaches that are current in 'mainstream' political science? It compares the main broad-gauge theoretical frameworks that, at different times, have been offered for just this very purpose. Have the theoretical approaches that were pioneered in the early years of decolonization and post-colonial rule now been overtaken and made redundant by the other and more recent critical perspectives such as those offered by post-modern and post-structuralist thinking, orientalism, and the like? Do some theories or perspectives work better for some cases than for others? It also considers the application of a specific approach, the 'new institutionalism', which is currently widely deployed in the discipline as a whole. How helpful is this approach and what adaptations need to be made?

The *second* aim is to show why and in what ways it is becoming increasingly difficult to understand, or even just to describe, politics within developing countries without taking account firstly of the influence of pre-colonial and colonial legacies. How, and to what extent, have these shaped trajectories of the state and development in the developing world? The second and essential contextual consideration is the role of factors in the contemporary international system. These latter inter-state and supra-state influences originate in economic, financial, diplomatic, cultural, and other forums. Many of these influences can penetrate state borders without having either express consent or tacit approval from government. They collaborate and collide with a variety of intra- and non-state actors, reaching far down to the sub-state and subnational levels. At the same time, developing countries also participate in and seek to influence regional networks and wider international organizations. The so-called BRICS (referring to Brazil, Russia, India, China, and South Africa) are a good example: even if the potential of this group of states to act as one in international affairs is not fully realized, recent changes on the international stage plus the emergence of China and India as new development donors suggest a paradigm shift in North–South, as well as South–South, relations. The nature of 'South–South' relations should be compared with 'North–South' relations before and since the end of the cold war. This part helps us to consider the developing world's place within the global system as a whole: such questions as how far are developing country politics conditioned by powerful constraints and pressures originating outside? Are those pressures and constraints, and their impact, in any sense comparable to 'neo-colonialism' or, indeed, the imperialism of old? Is power in the developing world now being ceded not so much to governments in the rich world as to a more diffuse and less controllable multilayered set of global commercial, financial, and economic forces and institutions? Or does their possession of valuable resources and growing presence enable at least some countries to be increasingly assertive in respect of their **political autonomy** and influence on world affairs?

Readers are encouraged to consult relevant case studies, and in particular Chapters 27, 28, 29 in Part 8 on 'South–South Relations' and the changing landscape of international development cooperation, alongside the chapters in Part 1.

1

Changing Analytical Approaches to the Study of Politics in the Developing World

Vicky Randall

Chapter contents

Overview

Two contrasting broad approaches long dominated political analysis of developing countries. One was a politics of modernization that gave rise to political development theory, then to revised versions of that approach that stressed the continuing, if changing, role of tradition and the need for strong government, respectively. Second was a Marxist-inspired approach that gave rise to dependency theory and subsequently to neo-Marxist analysis that focused on the relative autonomy of the state. By the 1980s, both approaches were running out of steam, but were partially subsumed in globalization theory, which emphasized the ongoing process, accelerated by developments in communications and the end of the cold war, of global economic integration, and its cultural and political ramifications. In the absence of a systematic critique, an alternative to this mainstream perspective was provided in the literatures on orientalism and post-coloniality, and on post-development, and more generally from a post-structural perspective. Nowadays, the very concept of a developing world is increasingly hard to sustain and, with it, the possibility of identifying one distinct analytic approach, as opposed to middle-range theories and a particular focus on the role of institutions more widely evident in contemporary political studies. However, certain key themes and agendas provide some degree of coherence. Similarly, there is no distinctive set of methodological approaches, but rather the application of approaches more generally available in the social sciences.

Introduction

This chapter provides an introduction to the main broad analytical approaches or frameworks of interpretation that have been employed in studying **politics** in the **developing world**. The 'developing world' contains numerous highly diverse political systems. To varying degrees, its analysts have looked to theories or frameworks of analysis to provide appropriate concepts or containers of information, and to allow comparison and generalization across countries or regions. Some frameworks have been relatively modest or 'middle-range', but others have been much more ambitious. Moreover, despite aspirations to scientific objectivity and rigour, they have inevitably reflected the circumstances under which they were formulated—for instance political scientists' underlying values, domestic political pressures, and funding inducements, as well as perceived changes in the developing countries themselves. We all need to be aware of these approaches, and the surrounding debates, if we are to read the literature critically and form our own views.

We begin with 'the politics of **modernization**', emerging in the United States in the 1950s. This approach, including political development theory and its various 'revisions', operated from a mainstream, liberal, or (to its left critics) pro-capitalist perspective. The second and opposed approach, stemming from a critical, Marxist-inspired perspective, has taken the form, first, of **dependency theory**, and then of a more state-focused Marxist approach. More recently, the dominant, although by no means unchallenged, paradigm has been **globalization theory**, to some degree incorporating elements of both developmentalist and dependency perspectives. Globalization theory, however, has also served to problematize politics in the developing world as a coherent field, partly because it tends to undermine the premise of a distinct developing world. For this and other reasons, some have suggested that the field is currently in crisis. The latter part of this chapter considers how far a distinctive and coherent approach to politics in the developing world is still discernible in the present day, and also asks whether such an approach would be desirable.

'Politics' and the 'Developing World'

Before considering the three main approaches themselves, we need briefly to revisit the central notions of 'developing world' and 'politics'. As noted in the introduction to this part, the term 'developing world' has conventionally referred to the predominantly postcolonial regions of Africa, Asia, Latin America and the Caribbean, and the Middle East, perceived to be poorer, less economically advanced, and less 'modern' than the developed world. 'Developing world' is preferred to 'Third World', because that latter term carries some particular historical connotations that make it especially problematic.

But even when we use the less problematic 'developing world', there have always been questions about what exactly are the defining features that these countries have in common and which distinguish them from the 'developed world'. These questions have become yet more pressing as the differences within the 'developing world' have widened: does it make sense to discuss the World Bank's 'lower-income countries' or the United Nation's 'least developed countries' (LDCs) alongside 'upper middle' income countries or the BRICs (Brazil, Russia, India, and China)? Still more basically, some seek to question the assumptions underlying the notion of 'development'. From what to what are such countries supposed to be developing, and from whose perspective?

Similarly, 'politics' is a highly contested notion. On one understanding, it is a kind of activity associated with the process of government and linked with the 'public' sphere; on another, it is about 'power' relations and struggles not necessarily confined to the process of government or restricted to the public domain. This volume takes the view that neither perspective on its own is sufficient—in general, but particularly in a developing world context. A further important question concerns the **autonomy of politics**: how far is politics, as a level or sphere of social life, determined by economic and/or social/cultural dimensions of

---

KEY POINTS

- The expression 'developing world' is preferable to 'Third World', but the increasing diversity of the countries included still makes generalization problematic.

- Studying politics in developing countries means investigating both central government processes and power relations in society.

- A further important question concerns the relative autonomy of politics.

society, and how far does it independently impact on those dimensions? Is the autonomy of politics itself variable? The different approaches to be considered all address this question, more or less explicitly, but arrive at very different conclusions.

Dominant Theoretical Approaches

Most studies of politics in developing countries have been informed to some degree by one or other of three main dominant approaches: modernization theory; Marxism-inspired theory; and globalization theory. These approaches, or theoretical frameworks, themselves have not necessarily been directly or centrally concerned with politics; however, both modernization theory and dependency theory have helped at least to generate more specifically political approaches.

The politics of modernization

The emergence of the 'politics of modernization' approach reflected both changing international political circumstances and developments within social science, and specifically within political science. Out of the Second World War a new world was born, in which, first, two superpowers—the United States and the Soviet Union—confronted one another, and second, a process of decolonization was set in train, leaving a succession of constitutionally independent states. Soon, the two powers were vying for influence in these states. Within the United States, social scientists—and increasingly political scientists—were encouraged to study them.

For this, the field of comparative politics at that time was ill-equipped; it concentrated on a narrow range of Western countries, was typically historical and legalistic in orientation, and was not systematically comparative at all. Responding to this new challenge, comparative politics drew on two developments in the social sciences: first, the 'behavioural revolution' encouraged a more 'scientific' approach that sought to build general social theories and test them empirically; second, especially in sociology, but also in economics, interest was growing in tracing and modelling processes of 'modernization'. Whilst modernization theory took different forms, its underlying assumption was that the process of modernization experienced in the West provided a valuable guide to what to expect in the developing world.

Political development theory

In this context, interest grew in elaborating a specific concept and theory of political development. The framework of analysis developed by Gabriel Almond was particularly influential. He developed a structural-functional approach to comparing politics in different countries, and as a basis for his concept of political development, which distinguished a series of political functions and then examined their relationship with particular structures or **institutions** (see Box 1.1). There were four 'input' functions: political socialization (instilling attitudes towards the political system); political recruitment; and the 'articulation' and 'aggregation' of interests (demands). On the 'output' side, three functions were identified: rule-making; rule implementation; rule adjudication; and a more pervasive function of political communication.

Almond originally suggested that political development could be understood as the process through which these functions were increasingly associated with specialized structures—parties for interest aggregation, legislatures for rule-making, and so on—and with the emergence of modern styles of politics (achievement-based versus ascriptive, and so forth). Later, he identified five political system 'capabilities' (extractive, regulative, distributive, symbolic, and responsive), which were expected to grow as structures became more specialized and political styles more modern. These capabilities in turn would help the system to deal with four main problems (some writers later referred to these as 'crises')—of state-building (with the focus on state structures), **nation-building** (focusing on cultural integration), participation, and distribution.

Almond's approach has been extensively and justly criticized, although it must be said that political scientists continue to use many of the concepts he developed, such as state-building (see Chapter 12) and nation-building. Similar criticisms were made of other attempts to conceptualize political development, with the added observation that they were excessively diverse, demonstrating a lack of consensus on what political development actually was (Pye 1966).

Political development theory, in this form, was in decline by the late 1960s, not least because supporting funding was drying up. But it has not entirely disappeared; indeed many of its characteristic themes resurfaced in the literature emerging from the 1980s concerning democratization and governance (see

---

BOX 1.1 ALMOND'S FRAMEWORK FOR COMPARATIVE ANALYSIS

Political systems

Input functions (*and typical associated structures*)

Political socialization (*family, schools, religious bodies, parties etc.*)

Political recruitment (*parties*)

Interest articulation (*interest groups*)

Interest aggregation (*parties*)

↓ Political communication ↑

Political systems develop *five capabilities*:

- extractive (drawing material and human resources from environment);

Output functions (*and typical associated structures*)

Rule-making (*legislatures*)

Rule implementation (*bureaucracies*)

Rule adjudication (*judicial system*)

- regulative (exercising control over individual and group behaviour);
- distributive (allocation of different kinds of 'good' to social groups);
- symbolic (flow of effective symbols, for example flags, statues, ceremony); and
- responsive (responsiveness of inputs to outputs).

These help them to face *four kinds of problem*:

- state-building (need to build structures to penetrate society);
- nation-building (need to build culture of loyalty and commitment);
- participation (pressure from groups to participate in decision-making); and
- distribution (pressure for redistribution or welfare).

Source: Almond and Powell (1966)

Chapters 14 and 15). Before leaving political development theory, though, two further developments should be noted.

Modernization revisionism

One strand of criticism of political development theory—modernization **revisionism**—centred on its oversimplified notions of tradition, modernity, and their interrelationship. Taking up arguments voiced by social anthropologists against modernization theory, some political scientists questioned what they perceived as an assumption that political modernization would eliminate 'traditional' elements of politics such as **caste** and ethnicity (the topic of religion was largely ignored until the 1980s—see Chapter 8). Instead, they suggested that aspects of political modernization could positively invigorate these traditional elements, albeit in a changed form, and also that these elements would invariably influence in some measure the form and pace of political change.

This perspective also drew attention to the ubiquity and role of **patron–client relationships**. In their 'traditional' form, local notables, typically landowners, acted as patrons to their dependent clients, typically peasants, in relationships that were personalized, clearly unequal, but framed in terms of reciprocity and affection. With greater 'modernization', and extension of state and market into the 'periphery', a modified

kind of relationship emerged between peasant/clients and local 'brokers' who could mediate their dealings with the centre. But at the centre, emerging, seemingly modern, political institutions—political parties and bureaucracies—also often operated on the basis of informal, but powerful patron–client relationships, which moreover often linked into those at the periphery. Where such relationships pervaded government, scholars drew on sociologist Max Weber's typology of forms of rule (Weber 1970), to talk about '**patrimonialism**', or '**neo-patrimonialism**'. This insight into the realities of **patronage** and **clientelism** was extremely valuable, and has continuing relevance (see Box 1.2; see also Chapters 6 and 10). Indeed, with the more recent emphasis on the role of political institutions, discussed further later in this chapter and in Chapter 3, there has been renewed interest in these relationships, as part of the wider question of the relationship between formal and informal processes within institutions. Despite further criticisms that have been made of modernization revisionism in its turn, this perspective has greatly enhanced our understanding of political processes in the developing world.

Politics of order

Samuel Huntington (1971) launched a scathing attack on political development theory for its unrealistic optimism, suggesting that, rather than political

BOX 1.2 PATRON–CLIENT RELATIONS (TWO ILLUSTRATIVE QUOTATIONS)

An anthropological account of a traditional patron–client relationship between landlord and sharecropper:

A peasant might approach the landlord to ask a favour, perhaps a loan of money or help in some trouble with the law, or the landlord might offer his aid knowing of a problem. If the favour were granted or accepted, further favours were likely to be asked or offered at some later time. The peasant would reciprocate—at a time and in a context different from that of the acceptance of the favour in order to de-emphasize the material self-interest of the reciprocative action—by bringing the landlord especially choice offerings from the farm produce or by sending some members of the peasant family to perform services in the landlord's home, or refraining from cheating the landlord, or merely by speaking well of him in public and professing devotion to him.

(Silverman 1977: 296)

Patron–client relationships in Mexican party politics:

Given PRI monopolization of public office, for much of the post-revolutionary period the most important actors in the competition for elected and appointed positions have been political *camarillas* within the ruling elite. *Camarillas* are vertical groupings of patron–client relationships, linked at the top of the pyramid to the incumbent president. These networks are assembled by individual politicians and bureaucrats over a long period of time and reflect the alliance-building skill and family connections of the patron at the apex.

(Craig and Cornelius 1995: 259–60)

development, it might be more relevant to talk about political decay. He criticized an assumption in political development theory that, in developing societies, **economic growth** would lead to social change conducive to liberal democracy. Instead, he argued that rapid economic growth from low initial levels could be profoundly destabilizing, generating excessive pressures on fragile political institutions. In this context, what mattered was not what form of government existed (whether democratic or communist), but the degree of government.

Critics accused this 'strong government', or '**politics of order**', perspective of inherent conservatism and authoritarianism. But it also injected a welcome dose of realism into the discussion, as well as drew attention to the ability of political institutions not only to reflect economic and social development, but also themselves to make an active difference—that is, to the 'relative autonomy of the political'. Significantly, this theme re-emerged in the 1990s with the emphasis on institutions such as the World Bank on 'governance' (see Chapter 15).

Marxist-inspired approaches

The second main category of approaches to be examined stems from a broadly Marxist perspective. As such, it opposed the 'politics of modernization' school as reflecting bourgeois or capitalist interests, and stressed the determining role of processes of economic production and/or exchange and the social class relationships embedded in them. In fact, dependency theory, which emerged in the late 1960s, was primarily concerned to refute orthodox models of economic development and also modernization theory; its implications for politics, at least in the narrower governmental sense, were almost incidental, although its impact was considerable.

One main reason was that it drew attention to a serious shortcoming of all forms of political development theory: their near-total neglect of the international context and implied assumption that politics in developing countries were shaped by purely domestic forces. Dependency theory originated in South America and reflected that continent's experience, but was quickly applied to other parts of the developing world. It has taken numerous forms, but will be briefly illustrated here through the arguments of a leading exponent, Gunder Frank (see also Chapter 5).

Frank (1969) maintained that the developing world had been increasingly incorporated into the capitalist world economy from the sixteenth century onwards. In fact, development of the developed world (known as the 'metropolis', or 'core') was premised upon '**underdevelopment**' of the developing world (known as 'satellite economies', or the 'periphery'); development and underdevelopment were two sides of the same coin. Despite formal political independence, former colonies remained essentially dependent because the metropolis was able to extract most of their economic surplus through various forms of monopoly. Even when such economies appeared to be developing, this was only dependent and distorted development. Frank argued that the only way in which a satellite economy could end this dependence was to drastically reduce ties with the metropolis; later he recognized that even this was not really an option.

Whilst, for a time, dependency theory was extremely influential, it was also increasingly and justly criticized for the crude generalization and determinism of its economic analysis. Not all versions were quite as deterministic as Frank's. Wallerstein (1979), for instance, recognized a 'semi-periphery' of countries such as the East Asian 'tigers' that, over time, had been able to improve their position within the overall 'world system', and by their example offered others on the periphery the hope of doing so too. By the 1980s, dependency theory was losing currency, although ironically the emerging 'debt crisis' of that same decade and imposition of structural adjustment requirements has seemed one of its best illustrations.

What did dependency theory have to say about politics in developing countries? Frank tended to minimize the independent effects of politics. He argued that both the state and the national political elite in such countries were identified with the 'comprador' economic class, which served as the local agent of metropolitan capital and consequently had a vested interest in the status quo. The only real possibility of change would be a revolution of those at the end of the chain of **exploitation**—the peasantry and urban poor—who had nothing to lose. Short of that, the different forms of politics, contests between political parties and so forth, had little significance. Again, there were some variations in this position. Wallerstein had more to say about politics and a less reductionist view of the state, but still ultimately saw strong states as a feature of the developed world and reinforcing capitalist interests. In general, dependency theory shed little direct light on the political process as such within developing countries. Its real contributions were to insist on the intimate link between politics and economics, which had been largely neglected in the politics of modernization literature, and to demonstrate that the domestic politics of developing countries was incomprehensible without reference to their position within the world capitalist system.

Neo-Marxism rediscovers politics

Despite its Marxist associations, dependency theory had many neo-Marxist critics. They rejected its economic analysis, which, they argued, was based on falsely equating capitalism with the market, rather than seeing it as a system of production. They also cherished hopes that the socialist revolution that had failed to materialize in the West would begin in the developing world. Such hopes were raised by a 'third wave' of revolutionary developments from the late 1960s (following a first wave centred on China, and a second wave from the late 1950s including Cuba and Algeria), which included communist victories in Vietnam, Cambodia, and Laos, revolution in Ethiopia, the overthrow of Portuguese **regimes** in Africa, and revolution in Nicaragua (Cammack 1997). For these reasons, neo-Marxists engaged in a much more detailed and rigorous analysis of social structure that was, in some sense, aimed at assessing the eligibility of different social categories—peasants, the lumpenproletariat (the urban poor who were not regular wage-earners), and so on—to inherit the role of revolutionary vanguard originally attributed to the industrial working class.

At the same time, there was a new interest in what Marxists typically referred to as the **'post-colonial state'**. Marx himself generally depicted the state as a simple instrument of class domination—in the famous words of the *Communist Manifesto* (1872): 'The executive of the modern state is but a committee for managing the common affairs of the whole bourgeoisie.' But his writings sometimes alluded to a second possibility, as in France during the second empire under Louis Napoléon, when the weakness or divisions of the bourgeoisie allowed an authoritarian state to emerge that was 'relatively autonomous' from any particular social class. This notion, as developed by neo-Marxists such as Antonio Gramsci (1891–1937) and later Nicos Poulantzas (1936–79) analysing capitalist states in the West, was later seized on to explore the relationship between the state and social classes in post-colonial societies. Hamza Alavi (1979), for instance, argued, with particular reference to Pakistan, that the post-colonial state enjoyed a high degree of autonomy. This was, first, because it had to mediate between no fewer than three ruling classes, but second, because it had inherited a colonial state apparatus that was 'overdeveloped' in relation to society because its original role was holding down a subject people (although others later questioned whether the post-colonial state in Africa could be described as overdeveloped).

Globalization theory

By the early 1980s, and despite their diametrically opposed starting points, the lines of thought evolving out of early political development theory, on the one hand, and dependency theory, on the other, were converging around a re-appreciation of the independent importance of 'the political' and an interest in strong government and/or the state. But both of these lines of thought were also tending to run out of steam. Modernization-based approaches were particularly vulnerable to the charge of insufficient attention to the economic and international context. In the meantime, dependency theory was increasingly challenged by apparently successful cases such as the oil-producing Gulf states and the **newly industrializing countries (NICs)**, whilst the neo-Marxist focus on socialist revolution appeared increasingly anachronistic.

Reflecting these changes in the global environment, by the 1990s a new 'macro' approach was emerging, globalization theory, which tended both to absorb and displace the previous two (for a valuable early overview, see McGrew 1992). Globalization theory (see also Chapters 4 and 12) should more properly be referred to as 'globalization theories', since it has taken many different forms. As with the previous two approaches, it can also often seem closer to an ideology or policy strategy than a theoretical framework. Globalization theory focuses on a process of accelerated communication and economic integration that transcends national boundaries, and increasingly incorporates all parts of the world into a single social system. Although this process is often seen as originating in the distant past, there is general agreement that it accelerated in particular from the 1970s, spurred by developments in transport and communications, and subsequently by the collapse of the Soviet bloc and end of the cold war.

Probably the most important dimension of this process is economic, with particular attention paid to developments in global trade, foreign direct investment (FDI), and finance (see Chapter 4). Associated with these economic trends, however, has been a significant cultural dimension of **globalization** that is increasing cultural awareness and interaction across national boundaries. Central to this process has been the remarkable development and expansion of information technology and the new electronic mass media, enormously extending the scope and immediacy of communication. The consequences of this process are undoubtedly complex and contentious. For globalization pessimists like Sklair (1991: 41), the predominance of US-based media conglomerates has meant the diffusion of images and lifestyles that promote the 'culture-ideology of consumerism'. Powerful media industries have emerged in a number of developing countries such as India, Brazil, and Mexico. Pieterse (2011) writes about the popularity of Thai soap operas in China and of Turkish soap operas in Saudi Arabia. Yet it is questionable just how truly 'global', in the sense of multidirectional, cultural communications have become. By the same token, however, the perceived threat of cultural globalization has prompted complex counter-trends, including reassertion of local and national cultural identities (on religious identity, see Chapter 8).

Different forms of globalization theory have emphasized different aspects—economic, cultural, and so on. They differ in what they understand to be the prime moving mechanism of the globalization process: some see it as driven by the underlying logic of unfolding capitalism associated in particular with an aggressive **neoliberalism**; others, as primarily a consequence of developments in communications; others, as a combination of factors. Some accounts, echoing modernization theory, are essentially optimistic: they stress, for instance, the extent to which a globalizing economy, in which capital is increasingly mobile, hugely extends opportunities for investment and employment for those who are enterprising and adaptable. Others, echoing the mistrust and many of the arguments of dependency theory, have been more pessimistic; they have depicted an increasingly unfettered global capitalism, ruthlessly exploiting people and resources. Globalization theory has taken stronger forms—sometimes referred to as 'hyperglobalization'—and more cautious, moderate forms. The debate too has changed over time: Jones (2010: 12), in his overview of key globalization thinkers, traces an evolving dialogue involving emphatic statements, sceptical reactions, more cautious reformulations, and so forth, although he suggests that there is a growing consensus that 'globalization does amount to something "new"'.

Although the voluminous literature on globalization has had relatively little directly to say about politics in the developing world, its implications are far-reaching. First, it suggests changes in the character of politics as a whole. While it would be premature to talk about a process of political globalization comparable with what has been claimed in the economic and cultural spheres, one can point to a series of developments that incline that way. There is the increasing perceived urgency of a range of issues—such as global warming, refugee flows, **terrorism**—the origins of and solutions to which transcend national borders. Correspondingly, we have seen a proliferation of international regulatory organizations and governance regimes, such as the **international human rights** regime, discussed in Chapter 18, of **non-governmental organizations (NGOs)** and of transnational **social movements**, including the so-called 'anti-globalization' movement itself. (see Chapter 11)

At the same time, globalization theory has emphasized ways in which the nation-state is losing autonomy. It is increasingly difficult for the individual state to control the flow of information across its borders or to protect its people from global security threats. Likewise, globalizing trends have greatly reduced its economic options, for instance its ability to fend off the consequences of economic upheaval elsewhere, such as the 1997 East Asia financial crisis, or to successfully promote 'Keynesian' economic policies, to enhance welfare and protect employment, when these run counter to the logic of the global economy. With reduced autonomy, it is argued, comes reduction in the state's perceived competence and accordingly in its **legitimacy**. It comes under increasing pressure from within, as well as without, contributing to a process of 'hollowing out' the state. This increased vulnerability of the nation-state has particular relevance for poorer countries of the developing world. Clapham (2002: 785) suggests that, in such countries, 'the logic of incorporation into the modern global system . . . has undermined the state's coercive capabilities, weakened its legitimacy and subverted its capacity to manage the inevitable engagement with the global economy'.

Globalization theory also creates difficulties for the notion of a distinct developing world. Even if we talk about a 'developing world' rather than a 'Third World' and are careful about which countries we include or exclude, this still implies a distinct geographic entity. However, globalization theorists like Berger have argued that if we want to retain the idea of a Third or developing world, this should be conceived of in sociological rather than geographic terms. The ongoing process of economic globalization means that economically based social classes are increasingly transnational or global in span. Thus dominant classes in the developing world are more oriented to Western capitalist centres, where 'they have their bank accounts, maintain business links, own homes and send their children to school', than to their own countries (Berger 1994: 268). Meanwhile countries in the developed world, not least the United States, each have their own underclass (or 'Third' or developing world), even if there are few signs that such underclasses are coming together at a global level.

An overall assessment of globalization theory as a framework for understanding politics in the developing world is made difficult by the fact that it has taken such a variety of forms and reflects such a range of ideological positions. Perhaps the theory's most valuable contribution in this regard is that, like dependency theory, it emphasizes the impact of global processes. But in other ways it has posed problems for this field of study, first by calling into question the concept of the 'developing world', and second by depicting economic or technological change as driving cultural and political change, thereby downplaying the independent importance of politics and the state.

Having said that, in recent years, there have been increasingly audible revisionist voices where the state's importance is concerned. Observers have firstly debated the significance of the 'new 'regionalism' evident from the 1980s, and which Gamble and Payne (1996: 2) defined as 'a state-led or states-led project designed to recognize a particular regional space along defined economic and political lines'. By 2007, there were 380 regional trade associations notified to the World Trade Organization (WTO), including such South–South associations as the Southern Common Market (MERCOSUR) in South America, the Association of South-East Asian Nations (ASEAN), and the Common Market for Eastern and Southern Africa (COMESA). The question was whether these were to be seen as stepping stones en route to global economic integration or as stumbling blocks and a form of resistance.

Second, critics of the globalization hypothesis have long argued that it greatly overstates the threat posed to the nation-state, pointing out, for example, that many states, including the East Asian NICs, have actively promoted and benefited from the process of economic globalization, and suggesting that states may be able to invoke or harness nationalist reaction to globalizing pressures as an alternative source of legitimacy, as in

India. More recently, such debates have paid more systematic attention to the experience of developing countries. Mosley (2005) found that, in a number of the more developed countries in South America and where there was the political will, the state was better placed to resist these global pressures. Following the 1997 financial crisis and during the most recent global financial crisis (2008–09), it has been noted that a number of emerging economies—notably China and India, but also others such as Malaysia and Indonesia—had retained sufficient protective regulation in place to withstand the worst economic consequences.

With renewed acknowledgement of the independent agency of the nation-state, has come re-appreciation of the role of the state itself, for instance in development and security. If neoliberalism, with which globalization theory has been closely associated, tended to advocate a reduced role for the state in favour of the market, already by the end of the 1990s there were signs of reappraisal. The World Bank's 1997 report, *The State in a Changing World*, and the emerging so-called 'post-**Washington consensus**' recognized the importance of an effective state to complement and support the activities of markets (Stiglitz 1998). In South America, many commentators have pointed to a 'return of the state' over the last decade, associated with a succession of left-leaning governments, as in Bolivia and Ecuador

(Grugel and Riggirozzi 2012). So, as with modernization and dependency perspectives, over time globalization approaches have been modified by increased awareness of the role and efficacy of the (nation) state.

Critical Perspectives

As the field of developing country politics has become more fragmented and complex, with no clearly dominant narrative in the way in which the 'modernization' narrative dominated before, so it has become more difficult to identify a main line of critique. Within the broad compass of globalization theory, the debates between the liberal-modernizers and radical-socialists certainly persist, as we can see for instance in disagreements over the criteria for democratic consolidation or deepening (see Chapter 14), or for **good governance** (Chapter 15). **Feminist** critiques and agendas of inquiry have also grown in number, scope, and sophistication, as discussed in Chapter 9. At the same time, alternative critical perspectives have emerged, although these are directed less at politics, as commonly understood, and more at social science understandings of development and non-'Western' societies.

First is the critique associated with the notion of **orientalism**. In his influential book, first published in 1978, Edward Said wrote about the lens of 'orientalism' through which many Western scholars have interpreted Asian and Middle Eastern societies, in imperial times. This discourse, which tended to 'essentialize' such societies, rendering them as exotic and 'Other', could also be seen as instrumental to the political aims of the imperialist powers (although it was not confined to them, as demonstrated in Marx's account of the 'Asiatic' mode of production). Although Said was primarily writing from a historical and cultural viewpoint, subsequently he argued that orientalist discourse was being revived in the post-cold-war context, and especially after 9/11, to help to justify US policy in the Middle East. Huntington's (1996a) **clash of civilizations** hypothesis (see Chapter 8) could seem to bear out this perception.

Said's work is said to have inspired a broader movement of 'post-colonial studies'. Specifically, in India, it stimulated the emergence of 'subaltern studies', the original rationale of which was to rewrite India's colonial history from the standpoint of the oppressed, subaltern classes (for a fuller discussion of these developments, see Chapter 2). At the same time, it

---

KEY POINTS

- The politics of modernization approach emerged in the 1950s, initially taking the form of political development theory.

- Political development theory was criticized by 'revisionists' for simplifying and underestimating the role of tradition, and by advocates of political order for excessive optimism.

- From the left, dependency theory criticized the modernization approach for ignoring former colonies' continuing economic and thus political dependence.

- Neo-Marxists criticized dependency theory's determinism, and explored the relative autonomy of politics and the state.

- Globalization theory, drawing on both modernization and dependency theory, emphasizes increasing global economic integration.

- Globalization theory calls into question both the importance of the state (although revisionist arguments are emerging) and the existence of a distinct developing world.

generated much criticism. Halliday (1993), for instance, claims first that Said insufficiently acknowledged earlier formulators of this critique, and second, that the notion of orientalism has itself been too static and overgeneralized.

Second is the critique that has emerged in different forms of the assumptions of development theory and the development 'industry', referred to as 'post-development theory'. This entails a criticism of development as discourse. One influential exponent, who explicitly situates himself within the parameters of discourse theory, is Arturo Escobar (1995). Escobar, who incidentally acknowledges a debt to Said, suggests that whatever kind of development is advocated, whether capitalist or 'alternative', there is still the assumption that developing countries have to be made to change, which helps to rationalize continuing intervention of outside interests, experts, perspectives, and so forth. Ferguson (1997) has also written about external intervention in Lesotho, drawing a contrast between the repeated 'failure' of development projects and the significance of their apparently unintentional political side-effects (see Box 1.3). Again, such arguments have generated much counter-criticism, not least that 'development' is not only an elite preoccupation, but also an almost universal aspiration.

Both of these kinds of critique—of orientalist thinking and of developmentalism—have implications for the way in which we think about politics in developing countries. It is probably fair to say that they are stronger on pointing out problematic assumptions in mainstream literature than in offering satisfactory alternative approaches. Nonetheless, considering that these potential critiques have been around for well over ten years, their impact in this field has so far been quite limited.

KEY POINTS

- In addition to continuing arguments between liberal and socialist-inspired camps, and critical feminist perspectives, new critiques of conventional forms of social science emerged, drawing on discourse theory.

- In particular, the critique of orientalism and post-development arguments has been relevant for studying politics in developing countries, although its impact has been limited.

Current Approaches

A state of 'disarray'?

Both modernization-based approaches and Marxist-inspired approaches were found increasingly wanting by the 1980s. Although globalization theory incorporates significant elements of both, it too tends to undermine the rationale for studying politics in the developing world as a distinct field. Moreover, globalization theory reflects changes in the real world, including increasing differentiation amongst countries of the 'developing world', which pose further problems for meaningful generalization.

These developments within the field have coincided with a wider disillusionment with attempts at grand theory-building in the social sciences. One general school of thinking, originating in linguistics and philosophy, which contributed to and helped to articulate such misgivings, has been **post-structuralism**. The approach adopted by post-structuralists, discussed further later in this chapter, questioned the epistemological basis and claims of all of the great theoretical

---

BOX 1.3 THE DEVELOPMENT INDUSTRY IN LESOTHO

Lesotho is a small landlocked country in southern Africa, with a population of around 1.3 million. Ferguson (1997) lists seventy-two international agencies and non- and quasi-governmental organizations operating in Lesotho, and notes that, in 1979, it received some US$64 million in **official development assistance (ODA)**.

What is this massive internationalist intervention, aimed at a country that surely does not appear to be of especially great economic or strategic importance? . . . Again and again development projects in Lesotho are launched, and again and again

they fail: but no matter how many times this happens there always seems to be someone ready to try again with yet another project. In the pages that follow, I will try to show . . . how outcomes that at first appear as mere 'side-effects' of an unsuccessful attempt to engineer an economic transformation become legible in another perspective as unintended yet instrumental elements in a resultant constellation that has the effect of expanding the exercise of a particular sort of state power while simultaneously exerting a powerful depoliticizing effect.

(Ferguson 1997: 7–21 *passim*)

approaches or 'meta-narratives' such as **liberalism**, Marxism, or indeed 'modernization'.

There has also been a steady growth of information about politics in different developing countries since the first attempts at generalization in the 1950s. Western governments—above all the US government—have funded research and teaching, some of it under the rubric of 'area studies'. Professional associations of area specialists, conferences, and journals have proliferated. At the same time, political science expertise—concerning both the country in question and politics in developing countries more broadly—is expanding in a growing number of developing countries: not only in India, where authors such as Rajni Kothari have been challenging received thinking over many decades, but also, for instance, in Mexico, Chile, Argentina, Brazil, Thailand, South Korea, Taiwan, and South Africa. Admittedly, such indigenous authors often gravitate to the relative comfort and security of American universities; Africa, for instance, has its own 'academic diaspora'. The ranks of these indigenous authors are swelling all the time, but include, for example: Guillermo O'Donnell, from Argentina, who devised the influential concept of '**delegative democracy**' (see Chapter 14); Arturo Escobar from Colombia, associated as we have seen with the notion of 'post-development'; Doh Chull Shin from South Korea, who has written on democracy, with special reference to that country's experience (see Chapter 24); and Claude Ake, from Nigeria (who died in 1996).

All of this has heightened awareness of the complexity and diversity of politics across this great tranche of the world's countries. Surveying all of these developments, one might well conclude that politics in the developing world no longer even has pretensions to being a coherent field of study; rather, as Manor (1991: 1) had already suggested more than twenty years ago, it is 'in disarray'.

Themes and agendas

If this remains to some extent true, the globalization background provides one element of commonality, whilst in the foreground one can also discern three, partly overlapping, themes or research issues that have tended to predominate and shape lines of more recent comparative inquiry, supplemented or even challenged in the last few years by a fourth.

The first is democratization (see Chapter 14). When the **third wave of democracy** broke in the mid-1970s,

spreading through South America in the 1980s and much of tropical Africa in the 1990s, it served to confound the expectations of a generation of political scientists who had come to see political authoritarianism or decay as an intrinsic political feature of the developing world. The global reach of democratization extended not only as a consequence of pressures within developing countries, or of the collapse of the Soviet bloc and end of the cold war, but also through more deliberate interventions of Western governments and intergovernmental organizations. As Chapter 14 describes, these included attaching political conditions to forms of economic assistance, but also more direct international **democracy promotion** through financial and other forms of support to democracy projects. Linked to this drive, Western government and research foundation funding helped to generate a huge literature apparently covering every aspect of democratic transition, including analysis of the effectiveness of international **democracy assistance**.

Already in the 1990s, Diamond (1996) was asking whether democracy's third wave was over; increasingly, in the new millennium, the literature has come to focus on the limitations and failures of the democratizing process, and the survival or revival of authoritarianism in democratic guise. However, the arrival of the so-called 'Arab Spring' in 2011 (see Chapters 11 and 14) encouraged a new surge of 'demo-optimism', with speculation that this could even herald a 'fourth wave'. Two years on at time of writing, such expectations are considerably tempered, but it would be wrong to write off these dramatic recent developments in the Middle East and North Africa.

The second theme is the relationship between politics and economic development or growth. An influential strand of thinking now sees good governance, and even democracy, as a prerequisite of economic growth. This represents an inversion of the early political development literature in which economic growth was generally assumed to be a condition of democracy (Leftwich 1993). We have already noted a reassessment of the importance of the state by bodies such as the World Bank, which opened its 1997 report, *The State in a Changing World*, by declaring that the state is central to economic and social development, not so much as a direct provider of growth, but rather as a partner, catalyst, and facilitator. The 2008–09 global financial crisis has reinforced this interest as observers debate which kinds of political arrangement have been associated with the most resilient economies. It has also led to an interest in the economic role played by **civil society** organizations and **social capital**. This theme, again, lacks a fully elaborated theoretical context, but owes something to the strong government variant of the politics of modernization. But again, like the democratization theme, it is clearly partly driven by concerns of Western governments and intergovernmental organizations.

A third prominent theme concerns peace, stability, and security versus conflict and risk. Again, this overlaps with the two previous themes: domestic conflict inhibits the emergence of political conditions conducive to economic growth, for instance, whilst many champions of democratization believe that democratic values and institutions provide the best guarantee both of domestic and of international security and order. The growing focus on causes and consequences of conflict and instability within developing countries is also, however, a result of the perception that such conflict has been on the increase since the end of the cold war. An additional impetus has been the perceived need to combat international terrorism, heightened in the wake of 9/11. In this context, there has been particular interest, on the one hand, in the pathology of 'failing' and 'failed', or collapsed, states, and on the other, in the 'politics of identity', especially ethnic and religious identity, in developing countries (see Chapters 7 and 8). Building on this theme, the most recent trend has been in analysis of the record and challenges of state-building in post-conflict societies (see Chapter 13).

These three themes do not amount to, or derive from, one coherent analytic framework, although they echo and incorporate elements of the earlier dominant paradigms, as well as globalization ideas. But they do overlap in the sense that democratization, economic performance, and the presence or absence of internal conflict either do or are seen to significantly affect one another. These themes also clearly relate to observable trends in the developing world, but also reflect the concerns, interests, and research-funding priorities of international agencies, Western governments, and to a lesser extent NGOs (see Chapter 10).

A fourth emerging theme, however, also requires mention: the implications of China's growing ascendancy. India is sometimes coupled with China in this context, but its rise is seen in more provisional and future terms. This China theme does not dovetail so neatly with the other three, although it is regularly discussed in relation to them. Increasingly, in the new

century and especially since the global financial crisis, China has come to be seen as a key global player, at the least one of the four designated BRIC countries, with the possibility of being part of a G2 or even global hegemon. Its rise has compounded the conceptual difficulties of defining and demarcating a developing world. China likes to present itself as a Third World or developing country (see Chapter 28), but some see in its relationship with other developing countries an element of North–South imperialism rather than South–South solidarity. The complexity of its internal relations also tend to undermine the North–South distinction; rather, China contains its own 'north' and 'south' (Eckl and Weber 2007).

Perhaps the most debated aspect of China's rise concerns the economic implications. By 2010, with a population of more than 1.3 billion, it had become the world's second largest economy, the largest exporter, and the second largest importer of goods in the world (see the discussion in Chapter 4). We have seen that this has raised big questions about China's impact on the (modified) neoliberal agenda associated with globalization and how far China offers an alternative development model, sometimes referred to as the 'Beijing Consensus' (Ramo 2004). But along with this growing economic influence, observers have anticipated more directly political effects. Questions have been asked about not only the prospects for democracy within China, but also the implications of China's rise for relatively fragile new democracies in East Asia (Kraft 2006; Diamond 2012). There have been concerns about the apparent lack of **conditionality** attached to Chinese foreign aid in Africa, which could

---

KEY POINTS

- The decline of modernization- and Marxist-based approaches and the ascendancy of globalization theory have coincided with questioning of the need for grand theory in political studies.

- Expanding scholarship has increased awareness of the empirical complexity of the field.

- However, some coherence is provided by key themes of democratization, politics and economic development, conflict/post-conflict, and increasingly the role of China.

- Recent scholarship is marked by a preference for middle-range theory, with an emphasis on the role of political institutions.

undermine the Development Assistance Committee (DAC) donors' good governance agenda (Tan-Mullins et al. 2010).

Strategies and Methods of Analysis

We need to consider, finally, the strategies, categories, and more specific methods of analysis that have been typically deployed to analyse the politics of developing countries. As already noted, the tendency has been to apply those developed initially within 'mainstream' and Western political science. This is even more noticeable now that the notion of a distinct 'developing world' is increasingly problematized. An important contemporary illustration is the focus of much recent analysis of politics in developing countries on political institutions, which is part of a broader trend in political science from the 1980s (see Chapter 3).

The politics of individual developing countries is studied in the context of area or regional studies (for instance centred on Latin America, the Caribbean, or South Asia), or as part of cross-national and regional thematic inquiries (for instance into executive–legislative relations or **corruption**). There has also latterly been some tendency to emphasize the international or global dimension of politics, for example the increasing salience of the religious dimension of politics (see Chapter 8) in individual developing countries, especially those in sub-Saharan Africa. The implicit argument is that, in such countries, external determinants are so powerful that apparently domestic political processes are best understood through the prism of international political economy and international relations approaches.

Most commonly, studies of developing country politics fall into the broad category of comparative politics. Accordingly, we find a range of comparative 'strategies' deployed. First is the case study approach, in which the politics of a single country is explored in some depth. In theory, at least, such exploration should be informed by a research agenda reflecting a wider body of comparative research, and should aim to test or generate propositions relating to that research. Case studies that simply celebrate the 'exceptionalism' of the country in question would not be considered proper social science, although of course even the idea of an 'exception' implies a broader pattern that is being deviated from. More middle-range comparative studies focus on particular questions.

They may use a subset of cases (such as countries, local governments, parties) selected to illuminate the matter in question. In a methodological distinction going back to J. S. Mill (1888), cases in a 'most similar' design will be similar in a number of key respects, whilst differing in regard to the variable being explored. In a 'most different' design, they will differ in many key respects, but not as regards that variable. In-depth qualitative analysis, often involving a historical perspective, will aim to identify particular factors associated with the variable under review. A good example of such an approach is Bratton and Van de Walle's study of *Democratic Experiments in Africa* (1997). Alternatively, studies take a 'large N' of cases and use statistical methods to analyse comparative data. The availability of such data is steadily growing. They include, for instance, election results and survey data collected through instruments such as Latinobarometer and Afrobarometer, and the databases collected by Freedom House, Transparency International, and the Governance Matters project (see Chapter 15). Such an approach, increasingly favoured within mainstream political science and international relations, can yield valuable and counterintuitive findings, but is of course heavily dependent on the availability of data that are reliable, valid, and appropriate. (For an excellent account of these issues, see Landman 2003.)

In arriving at propositions to be explored, or even tested statistically, studies draw on existing studies and middle-range theorizing. Some, however, establish their own central propositions more systematically and deductively, building on the precepts of rational choice theory. This is an approach that takes as its primary unit of analysis the individual actor, who is presumed to make rational choices on the basis of self-interest. Within the framework of the 'new institutionalism', the focus is on the way in which institutional incentives and opportunities influence the individual's strategic calculations. As discussed further in Chapter 3, this approach has recently been very evident in work on constitutional and electoral systems design in new democracies.

The dominant assumption in the 'mainstream' comparative strategies and methods of analysis explored so far is that it is appropriate to apply them in contexts differing from those in which they first evolved. This is, in many ways, an attractive argument that emphasizes what is common and continuous in human experience—in contrast to those that point to possibly unbridgeable cultural differences, as is said to be the case in forms of 'orientalism' discussed earlier. Nonetheless, there is a danger, unless these approaches are used sensitively, that aspects of politics in developing countries will be wrongly assumed or misinterpreted. For a long time, comparative political analysts have been urged to ensure that the concepts they use actually do 'travel'. For instance, doubts have been raised about the relevance of rational choice theory in contexts in which cultural values weigh heavily; indeed, the notion of rational choice itself could be seen as the product of a specific US social science culture.

The approaches discussed so far are also, to a large extent, empirical and positivist. But there is an alternative type of approach that focuses more centrally on issues of meaning (sometimes referred to as 'interpretavism') and thus incidentally potentially suffers less from problems of cultural imposition or misinterpretation. This comes in what might be called stronger and weaker forms, ranging from post-structuralism and discourse theory to types of social constructivism. It also tends, although not inevitably, to be associated with more radical, or critical, accounts of politics.

Post-structural or 'discourse' approaches question the very epistemological foundations of knowledge, including political science. Within the study of politics, the ideas of Michel Foucault (1926–84) have been especially influential. He understood political processes, institutions, and indeed 'subjects' (actors) to be constructed through dominant 'discourses', understood not simply as language and ideas, but also as the practices embodying them. A central concern of discourse theorists, then, has been to trace the originating historical practices (genealogy) of such discourses. We have seen how Said's critique of 'orientalism' and radical critiques of the discourse of development have drawn on post-structural methods of analysis.

Constructivism does not go so far, but still argues that central concepts such as 'power' or 'ethnicity' through which we organize our understanding are themselves 'socially constructed'. It makes use of notions such as 'framing', or the way in which political issues are constructed to reflect and favour different interests and agendas. It has been especially influential within the study of international relations. Feminists have, for instance, drawn upon it to critically deconstruct use of the notion of the 'empowerment' of women by development agencies (della Faille 2011). Within comparative politics, including the study of developing polities, it has been used to analyse the construction of political identities, for instance ethnopolitical identity (see Chapter 7). It has been especially prominent in analysis both concerning and stemming from the new social movements and their 'alternative' political projects (see Chapter 11).

Conclusion

The dominant paradigms in the past, associated with modernization theory and dependency theory, were valuable to the extent that, by suggesting the importance of particular factors or relationships, they helped to generate debate; also, they encouraged political analysis and generalization beyond the particularities of individual country case studies. But at the same time they were overgeneralized, excessively influenced by Western ideological assumptions and agendas—whether 'bourgeois' or 'radical'—and Western historical experience, and based on inadequate knowledge and understanding of the developing world itself. They created, as Cammack et al. (1993: 3) phrased it, 'a problem of premature and excessive theorization'.

Over time, our knowledge of the developing world has grown, and with it, inevitably, our awareness of its diversity and complexity. Moreover, that developing world itself has become increasingly differentiated. Especially in the context of globalization theory, this greater recognition of diversity has called into question the coherence of the developing world as a geographic—and political—category. These developments have coincided with a tendency for political science to rein in its theoretical aspirations, focusing on 'middle-range' rather than grand theory. Post-structural thinking has also diminished the appeal of grand interpretative narratives.

Presently, then, whilst globalization theory continues to provide an implicit backdrop to much political analysis, the field of politics in the developing world has become less obviously coherent. However, it is possible to perceive an implicit agenda of inquiry, focusing around democracy or governance, development, conflict, and, increasingly, the implications of China's rise, which remains strongly influenced by Western interests and perspectives. At the same time, radical, critical perspectives persist. In addition to a continuing Marxist-inspired materialist critique can be found alternative critiques, some of them emanating from 'indigenous' sources, which seek to problematize the whole enterprise of 'Western' attempts to understand and influence politics in developing countries. For many of us, this may be a step too far, but we should by now recognize the need to proceed with all caution and humility.

QUESTIONS

1. What are the implications of globalization theory both for the character of politics in the developing world and the way in which it should be studied?

2. In what sense and for what reasons is the study of politics in the developing world currently in 'disarray'?

3. Do we need a distinct theoretical framework for analysing politics in the developing world?

4. In what ways is Said's critique of 'orientalism' relevant to the understanding of politics in developing countries?

5. Is it either possible or desirable to arrive at an 'objective' analysis of politics in developing countries?

6. Discuss, with examples, the extent to which the concepts and assumptions of political development theory still influence the way in which we understand politics in the developing world.

FURTHER READING

Berger, M. (ed.) (2004) 'After the Third World?', Special issue of *Third World Quarterly*, 25(1) Collection of articles that reflect upon the historical significance and contemporary relevance of the notion of a 'third world'.

Cammack, P. (1997) *Capitalism and Democracy in the Third World: The Doctrine for Political Development* (Leicester: Leicester University Press) Well-argued, critical reflection, from a left-wing perspective, upon 'mainstream' accounts of the political development literature.

Hagopian, F. (2000) 'Political Development Revisited', *Comparative Political Studies*, 33(6/7): 880–911 Retrospective overview of political development thinking.

Higgott, R. A. (1983) *Political Development Theory* (London/Canberra: Croom-Helm) Account of the development and persistence of political development thinking.

Jones, A. (2010) *Globalization: Key Thinkers* (Cambridge: Polity) Accessible and up-to-date overview of the strands and development of globalization thinking.

Landman, T. (2003) *Issues and Methods in Comparative Politics*, 2nd edn (London: Routledge) Clear and engaging introduction to comparative analysis.

Manor, J. (ed.) (1991) *Rethinking Third World Politics* (London: Longman) Collection of essays, some using post-structuralist concepts or approaches, seeking to go beyond old theoretical perspectives.

Randall, V. and Theobald, R. (1998) *Political Change and Underdevelopment: A Critical Introduction to Third World Politics*, 2nd edn (London: Macmillan) Provides an account of theories and debates concerning politics in the developing world, from political development to globalization.

Said, E. (1995; 1978) *Orientalism* (Harmondsworth: Penguin) Influential critique of 'orientalist' approaches to history and culture.

Smith, B. C. (2008) *Understanding Third World Politics*, 3rd edn (Basingstoke: Palgrave) Useful, recently updated, overview of themes in the study of the politics of the developing world.

WEB LINK

http://faculty.hope.edu/toppen/pol242/   Hope College course website providing materials on the scope and methods of political science.

For additional material and resources, please visit the Online Resource Centre at:
http://www.oxfordtextbooks.co.uk/orc/burnell4e/

2

Colonialism and Post-Colonial Development

James Chiriyankandath

Chapter contents

Overview

The variety of states and societies found in the developing two-thirds of the world is reflected in their political diversity. The contemporary polities of the global South bear the imprint of the legacy of colonialism, but are also marked both by their pre-colonial heritage and their different post-colonial experiences. This chapter argues that while the historically proximate experience of colonialism has had a significant impact on post-colonial political development, attention to the *longue durée* and to political agency after independence yield a more nuanced perspective on the varied politics found across the developing world. The different ways in which post-independence politicians reacted and adapted to—and were constrained by—the past legacies and present situations of their countries helped to determine the shape of the new polities.

Introduction: The Post-Colonial World

Sixty years ago, the world was still dominated by mainly European empires. By 1921, 84 per cent of the earth had been colonized and there were as many as 168 colonies (Go 2003: 17). Although, by the mid-1960s, most were at least nominally independent, subsequent decades showed how much the spectre of colonization still loomed. While the varied history of **post-colonial states** illustrates the importance of their pre-colonial past, as well as of factors such as geography, geopolitics, and political agency, Hall (1996: 246, 253) points out that the fact that countries are not 'post-colonial' in the same way does not mean that they are not 'post-colonial': colonization 'refigured the terrain' everywhere. The concept of the post-colonial offers a point of entry for studying the differences between formerly colonial societies (Hoogvelt 1997: xv).

Whatever the varied reality of their present condition, their colonial background is still used to identify the contemporary states of the **developing world** with a pre-modern, traditional, backward past—the antithesis of the 'modern' post-imperial West (Slater 2004: 61–2). In this way, a colonial cast of mind persists, one that geopolitical power relations (North–South, West–non-West) make it very hard to shake off. One important result is the remarkable resilience of racialized discourse in the West when it comes to discussing issues such as migration and development, albeit one that shifted from being expressed in biological terms during the heyday of colonialism to being voiced in a socio-cultural idiom in the wake of decolonization (Duffield 2006; see also Wallerstein 2003: 124–48).

It is to this reality that the rise of post-colonial theory, especially in the field of cultural studies, sought to draw attention. Influenced by post-modernist and **post-structuralist** perceptions, it was born of disillusionment with the failure of the Third World to, in the words of Frantz Fanon (1967: 255), start a new history and 'set afoot a new man'. Going beyond a temporal understanding of post-colonialism, post-colonial theory sought to analyse its cultural aftermath: the 'cultures, discourses and critiques that lie *beyond*, but remain clearly influenced by colonialism' (McEwan 2009: 17).

Colonialism was the obvious place to start explaining why political independence had not resulted in the **emancipation** for which people like Fanon, a black psychiatrist from the French Caribbean who devoted himself to the Algerian struggle for independence, yearned. The problem appeared to be that the emancipatory project, belying the hope expressed by Fanon, had been fatally undermined by its 'imperial genealogy' (Cooper 2005: 25). While a number of political scientists, historians, and anthropologists (Crawford Young, Mahmood Mamdani, Bernard Cohn, and Nicholas Dirks among them) sought to analyse the lasting impact of colonialism on the colonized, much post-colonial theory has followed Edward Said's (1993; 1995) seminal work on '**orientalism**' in focusing attention more on imperial intent than colonial consequence (for example Viswanathan 1990). That the colonial past might be of great significance in determining the future of post-colonial states was recognized even as decolonization proceeded, although then it was adherents of what they saw as the imperial mission who were more inclined to do so. Margery Perham (1963: 18), colonial historian of British Africa, remarked: 'Our vanishing empire has left behind it a large heritage of history which is loaded with bequests good, bad and indifferent. This neither they [the critics of colonialism] nor we can easily discard.'

Thirty years later, the interest aroused by post-colonial theorists served to refocus attention on the nature of the colonial legacy. Birmingham (1995: 6–8), writing of post-colonial Africa, highlights lasting geographical, financial, and cultural legacies: the remarkable persistence of colonial borders, trade and currency links (especially in the ex-French colonies), and the way in which 'the minds of many Africans continued to work on colonial assumptions'. Mayall and Payne (1991: 3–5), dealing with the 'Commonwealth Third World', suggested that the more durable legacies of the British Empire may have been its military and statist characteristics rather than ideologies such as **liberalism** and nationalism. It is also argued that direct British rule led to more successful development (Lange 2009), and that the reason why former British colonies may have fared better was the role of Christian Protestant missions and the autonomy that they enjoyed in relation to the colonial state (Woodberry 2004).

That the impact of colonialism has been transformative rather than transitory is now widely accepted. Half a century or more after their independence, developing countries still live with colonialism (Sharkey 2003: 141; Dirks 2004: 1; see Box 2.1). While some such as the Kenyan academic and **human rights** campaigner Makau Mutua (2008: 34) maintain that 'colonialism has been the single most important variable in determining the future of Africa', others see colonialism's impact as more indirect—a conditioning agency rather than a determinant factor (Hyden 2006: 26). Still, in concluding his comparative study of Spanish America, Mahoney (2010: 269) says: 'Colonialism usually brought countries to relative levels of development that have been remarkably enduring . . . the international hierarchy created from colonialism will not be easily rearranged.'

Despite the differences in formation and practice between the European colonial powers, it is argued that the phenomenon of colonialism is united to a large extent by its legacies (Dirks 2004: 2). Yet differences in the trajectories of post-colonial development matter and require explanation. One way of attempting to do so that has been gaining currency is **path**

BOX 2.1 COLONIZING THE MIND

How to come to terms with the survival of not only institutional forms (administrative, legal, educational, military, religious) and languages (English, French, Portuguese, Spanish, Dutch), but also the mentality bequeathed in part by the colonial heritage has been a preoccupation of Third World intellectuals. Some, like the Kenyan writer Ngũgĩ wa Thiong'o (1986), sought a resolution to the dilemma by abandoning the colonial language (English) to write in their native tongue—in Ngũgĩ's case, Gĩkũyũ. However, mentality is shaped by much more than just the language used, and Partha Chatterjee (1986) and Ramachandra Guha (1989) have noted nationalism's role in embedding colonialist historiography into Indian understandings of India, European history serving as a kind of *metahistory*

(Chakrabarty 2003) that relegated the people of the developing world to being 'perpetual consumers of modernity' (Chatterjee 1993: 5). When it came to defining state forms and political structures, Indian nationalist and post-independence leaders, 'coloured by the ideas and **institutions** of Western colonialism' (Jalal 1995: 11), preferred the familiar structures of the British Raj. Although no African or Asian state went to the extent of the founders of the Brazilian republic who, in 1889, adapted the motto of Auguste Comte, the nineteenth-century French Positivist philosopher, in adding the words 'order and progress' to their flag, the post-Christian myth of modernity (Gray 2003: 103) certainly found many devotees across the developing world.

---

dependence, an idea borrowed from economics. This emphasizes the importance of choices made and the difficulties of changing a course once set. Yet, as we shall see, other factors also matter—geopolitical and strategic considerations, and political agency.

KEY POINTS

- **Politics** in developing countries are influenced by their pre-colonial heritage, and colonial and post-colonial experiences.

- Virtually all developing countries are in some sense post-colonial, although not necessarily in the same ways. Post-colonial theory seeks to examine the continuing impact that colonialism has on post-colonial development.

- The impact of colonialism was transformative, rather than transitory. As well as reshaping economic and political forms, it also changed the way in which people, especially the educated, came to see the world.

- 'Path dependence' emphasizes the importance of history in shaping choices for states and societies.

Pre-Colonial States and Societies

It is plausibly argued that among the best predictors of the resilience of post-colonial states is whether the societies they contain possess a significant pre-colonial experience of statehood (Clapham 2000: 9). From this perspective, it is instructive to consider the political map of the pre-colonial world. Eighteenth-century Asia was dominated by states that included some of the world's largest empires (Ottoman Turkey, Safavid Iran, Mughal

India, and Manchu China), with only sparsely populated Central Asia and the interior of the Arabian Peninsula occupied by nomadic pastoral societies. In contrast, prior to the sixteenth-century Spanish and Portuguese conquest, the Americas were largely inhabited by dispersed hunter-gatherer, fishing, and farming communities. The important exceptions were the Inca Empire on the western seaboard of South America and, in Central America, the Aztec empire, a number of smaller kingdoms, and Mayan city-states. Before being overwhelmed in the nineteenth-century European **scramble for Africa**, more than two-thirds of the African continent was also occupied by non-state societies, with kingdoms and other state formations found only along its Arabized Mediterranean coast and scattered across more densely populated pockets south of the Sahara.

In the Americas, colonization by European settlers resulted in the creation of some twenty independent settler states in the century following the US Declaration of Independence in 1776, making America 'post-colonial' before some European colonial powers such as Germany, Italy, and Belgium had even become states, let alone acquired colonies (McEwan 2009: 51). In the 1900s, Australia and New Zealand also became self-governing British dominions. The post-colonial experience of the United States, Canada, Australia, and New Zealand is thus quite distinct from that of Asian and African states, while Latin American states are distinguished by the varying admixture of European and indigenous American elements in their social make-up. In recent years, Latin American political leaders, especially those of, at least partly, non-European descent, such as Hugo Chávez in Venezuela (president from 1999 to 2013) and Evo Morales in Bolivia (president from

2006), have sought to emphasize the latter, still visible in syncretic political, religious, and social practice. In Africa and Asia, European settlement was not a significant feature of colonization except for isolated instances such as French Algeria, the 'white' highlands of Kenya, and, most importantly, South Africa, where the white supremacist **apartheid** state was only displaced in 1994.

Pre-colonial Africa featured a variety of polities, among which were the city-states (for example Kano) and empire-states (such as Songhai, Ghana, Mali, Asante) of the west (Mazrui 1986: 272–3), as well as conquest states, such as that of the Zulus in the south, emerging in the period preceding European colonial rule. African scholars (for example Mazrui 1986: 273; Mamdani 1996: 40) have stressed the discontinuity between the pre- and post-colonial state, Mahmood Mamdani blaming, in particular, the deliberate colonial generalization of the conquest state and the administrative chieftainship as the basic modes of African rulership that were to serve as the template for their practice of **indirect rule** (see later in the chapter). The colonial rulers disregarded differences between societies and the restraints sometimes placed by tradition upon rulers. For instance, among the Akan of southern Ghana, the king (Asantehene) was chosen by a group of 'kingmakers' from among a number of candidates from a royal matrilineage and could be removed if deemed to have breached his oaths of office (Crook 2005: 1). In contrast, societies in northern Ghana had kings who ruled in a much more authoritarian manner, or had chiefs imposed by the British of a kind that did not previously exist. Basil Davidson (1992), in contrasting the achievements of Meiji Japan with the Asante state, argued that colonialism prevented the potential for the natural maturing of pre-colonial African institutions, but this is unconvincing given the continent's relative economic backwardness and the deeply rooted historical factors that gave rise to the logic of **extraversion** (see Box 2.2). Reinforced by its relative isolation, nineteenth-century Japan was a nation-state in being— 'Meiji political nationalism [creating] the modern Japanese nation on the basis of aristocratic (*samurai*) culture and its ethnic state' (Smith 1991: 105). There were hardly any pre-colonial nation-states in sub-Saharan Africa— although there might be a case for suggesting that Buganda in East Africa, what is now southern Uganda, was one (Green 2010)—an important reason why most African countries remain preoccupied with state formation rather than state consolidation (Hyden 2006: 70).

Pre-colonial Asia represented a considerable contrast to sub-Saharan Africa in being dominated by

---

BOX 2.2 AFRICA'S GEOGRAPHY AND THE CONCEPT OF EXTRAVERSION

The history of Africa has been profoundly influenced by its geography. Clapham (2000: 5) described the bases for states in pre-colonial sub-Saharan Africa as 'peculiarly feeble', with the few relatively densely populated pockets creating a very discontinuous pattern of state formation across the vast continent. It is this historical geography that the French political scientist Jean-François Bayart (1993: 21–2) had in mind when elaborating the concept of extraversion to explain the politics of post-colonial Africa. He argued that the relatively weak development of its productive forces and its internal social struggles had combined to make political actors in Africa disposed to mobilize resources from their relationship with the external environment. The collaboration of African rulers in the transatlantic slave trade that resulted in the transportation of an estimated 11 million Africans to the Americas between the sixteenth and nineteenth centuries was the most notorious aspect. Colonialism and its legacy served to emphasize the operation of the logic of extraversion, reinforcing a strong indigenous tendency to favour trade and commerce over manufacture (Chabal 2009: 117).

---

states, albeit diverse in size, depth, and durability. Indeed, the Mughal Empire that flourished in India between the sixteenth and eighteenth centuries dwarfed its European counterparts in extent, population, and wealth, as did the Ming and, subsequently, Manchu empires in China and the Ottoman, and Safavid empires to the west. Only in the Philippines did the establishment of Spanish dominion in the sixteenth century largely succeed in erasing the pre-colonial past from history (the country has the dubious distinction of being the only post-colonial state that bears the name of a colonial ruler, Philip II of Spain). In terms of prior state tradition, there is no gainsaying the antiquity of those in the rest of Asia. Yet, at first glance, the lineage of the post-colonial states of Asia too seems to owe far more to their immediate colonial predecessors than to their historic traditions.

There are a number of reasons for this. Perhaps most important are the obvious institutional, and more subtly influential ideological, legacies of colonialism, both of which appear more tangible despite the efforts to trace a pre-colonial ideological lineage, not least by nationalist leaders such as India's Jawaharlal Nehru (1961). Typically, descriptions of post-colonial institutions *begin* with the colonial past. Four decades after the Indian parliament came into being, an account of its historical origins by its secretary-general devoted barely two unconvincing pages to the pre-colonial period, almost wholly focused on ancient India—the two millennia prior to the advent of British rule merited less than a sentence (Kashyap 1989: 1–3). While between one and two centuries of British dominion over the subcontinent may have left only a slight imprint on aspects of the everyday lives of many people, it was long enough, and the nature of the contrast stark enough, to have altered the context of government and politics fundamentally.

Anthropologists have been better at capturing this alteration than political historians or political scientists (Cohn 1996; Dirks 2001). Bernard Cohn (1996: 18) noted that while 'Europeans of the seventeenth century lived in a world of signs and correspondences . . . Indians lived in a world of substances'. His phrase captured a profound shift in how people first constituted, and then transmitted, perceived, and interpreted authority and social relations. In the mentality of government, the malleability and pliability afforded by 'substance' gave way to the unyielding notional rigour of scientific classification—the intention being to set rigid boundaries so as to control variety and difference. As Cohn (1996: 16) put it, the 'command of language' was paired with the 'language of command'. While this did not erase the legacy of the pre-colonial, it transformed it. How it did so is what we shall now consider in examining patterns of colonial rule.

KEY POINTS

- Varying patterns of state formation in pre-colonial Africa, Asia, the Americas, and Australasia influenced both the kind of colonization they experienced and post-colonial development.

- The post-colonial experience of areas that were the focus of European settlement is quite distinct from that of Asia and Africa. However, in Latin America, indigenous American influences are still perceptible.

- It has been argued that the geography and demography of Africa has had a significant influence in the persistent weakness of states, as reflected in Bayart's theory of extraversion.

- Even in Asia, where the pre-colonial era was dominated by state societies, the colonial state profoundly affected the development of politics and government.

Colonial Patterns

The era of European colonialism overseas was proclaimed in 1493, a year after Christopher Columbus's 'discovery' of America when Pope Alexander VI apportioned newly discovered non-Christian lands between the two main Catholic maritime powers of the day, Spain and Portugal. The greatest impact was felt in Central and South America, where the Spanish swiftly conquered the Aztec and Inca empires in the 1520s and 1530s, while the Portuguese focused on the coastline of much more sparsely populated Brazil. In under a century, the populations of the two great pre-colonial American empires declined by as much as 90 per cent to fewer than 2 million, decimated not so much by Spanish arms as by European-borne diseases such as smallpox, measles, yellow fever, and influenza (Mahoney 2010: 60, 68). The new Iberian empires were mercantilist until the eighteenth century, when they belatedly followed the British in undertaking liberal economic reforms, at the same time professionalizing and modernizing the absolutist state.

Over the next four-and-a-half centuries, the scope of European settlement and dominion expanded to cover the whole of the Americas, and much of South and South East Asia, Oceania (including Australia and New Zealand), Africa, and the Arab Middle East. Typically beginning with small coastal, generally commercial enclaves, they subsequently expanded to cover the hinterland as conquest followed trade. The different periods in which regions were colonized by a number of European states (Spain and Portugal being followed by Holland, England, and France in the course of the sixteenth and seventeenth centuries, and by Belgium, Germany, and Italy in the nineteenth century) gave rise to a varied pattern of colonialism. The emergence of the United States (Hawaii, Cuba, Puerto Rico, Guam, and the Philippines) and Japan (Taiwan, Korea, and Manchuria) as overseas colonial powers by the end of the nineteenth century added to the variety, as did the peculiar situation of China.

After being defeated by Britain in the First Opium War of 1839–42, China suffered further military humiliation in the following decades (including at the hands of Japan in 1894–95) and had to acquiesce to leasing coastal territories to Britain, France, Germany, Russia, and Japan, and conceding territorial rights and consular jurisdiction to as many as nineteen, mainly European, countries (Feuerwerker 1983: 128–53). This 'treaty-port form of colonialism' (Maddison 2007: 167) survived until 1943. When the Communists established the new People's Republic in 1949, after more than a decade of war against, first, the invading Japanese, and then the Guomindang (Nationalist) government, Mao Zedong declared that the Chinese people had stood up, ending a period in which they had fallen behind 'due entirely to oppression and **exploitation** by foreign imperialism and domestic reactionary governments' (Mao Zedong 1977: 16–17).

Although their respective colonialisms expressed distinctive experiences of statehood, colonial powers also borrowed and learned from each other, by the early twentieth century perceiving themselves as being engaged in a common progressive endeavour of developing 'scientific colonialism' (Young 1998: 105). While the pattern varied, it is possible to discern certain common features across the colonial world. Referring to Michel Foucault's characterization of power as 'capillary', the African historian Frederick Cooper (2005: 49) argues that power in most colonial contexts was actually 'arterial'—'strong near the nodal points of colonial authority, less able to impose its discursive grid elsewhere'. This was in part because, as a number of writers put it, the colonial intent was to 'rule on the cheap' (Sharkey 2003: 122; Cooper 2005: 157). On the eve of its transfer from the brutally exploitative personal rule of King Leopold II to the Belgian state in 1908, the Congo Free State had only 1,238 European military and civilian officers covering more than 900,000 square miles (Young 1994: 107). In British India, the centrepiece of Britain's colonial empire, the entire European population in 1921 amounted to just 156,500 (or 0.06 per cent) out of a total of over 250 million (Brown 1985: 95). The colonial state was coercive and extractive, yet thin, with local collaborators, especially those recognized as 'traditional' rulers, forming an indispensable element. Such a state also made the exercise of symbolic, as well as punitive, power very important. The routine British use of aircraft to both awe and bomb into submission rebellious Arab tribes in Iraq in the 1920s was an innovative case.

Until relatively late in their history, colonial states had a poor record of investment, with barely a tenth of total British overseas investment in the Victorian era going to the non-white colonies (Chibber 2005). Davis (2001: 311) damningly notes that India recorded no increase in its per capita income in 190 years of British rule, with the colonial **regime** operating a policy of deliberate neglect when it came to development (Tomlinson 1993: 217). Lord Lugard (1965: 617), the Indian-born first governor-general of Nigeria credited with introducing the policy of indirect rule to British Africa, admitted that 'European brains, capital, and energy have not been, and never will be, expended in developing the resources of Africa from motives of pure philanthropy'. The fact was that the philanthropic element was not readily evident. The widespread consequence of cheap colonialism was uneven development and wide disparities between small, more-or-less Westernized elites and the rest (Dirks 2004: 15). In addition, the movement of labour between colonies to work in the plantation sector in particular introduced new social and economic divisions. In the course of the nineteenth and early twentieth centuries, hundreds of thousands of Indians, mainly indentured labourers, were transported to British colonies in the Caribbean, as well as to Burma, Ceylon, Malaya, Fiji, South Africa, Kenya, and Mauritius—a factor that contributed to ethnic political tensions in all of these territories after they became independent.

Leftwich (see Chapter 12) reviews the chief characteristics of the colonial state; the focus in this chapter is more upon its cultural and ideological impact. For colonial powers such as Britain and France, the paradox of their rule was that its survival depended on *failing* to fulfil the universal promise of their liberal state ideology. The **rule of law** in British India was necessarily despotic in that the rulers could not be held to account by those whom they governed, but only by their imperial masters in London. In the French colonies, the concept of assimilation (that is, to ultimately make colonial subjects French) was never officially jettisoned, although by the 1920s it was obvious that the language of assimilation was merely the 'rhetoric of colonial benevolence' (Dirks 2004: 14). It could scarcely be otherwise since 'if the colonized. .. is found to be exactly the same. .. the colonizer is left with no argument for his supremacy' (McEwan 2009: 67). Under such circumstances, it was logical that the post-eighteenth-century European Enlightenment discourse of rights should become translated into the language of liberation for the Western-educated colonized elite (Young 1994: 228).

A feature of colonial rule that was to have far-reaching consequences for the post-colonial world was what Nicholas Dirks ('Foreword' to Cohn 1996: ix–xv; also Dirks 2004: 1) described as a 'cultural project of control', one that 'objectified' the colonized, and reconstructed and transformed their cultural forms through the development of a colonial system of knowledge that outlived decolonization. It was an approach that reified social, cultural, and linguistic differences, causing the colonial state to be described as an 'ethnographic state'

(Dirks 2001). Yet while imperial anthropologists such as Herbert Risley, census commissioner and later Home Secretary in British India in the 1900s, helped to furnish 'a library of ethnicity, its shelves lined with tribal monographs' (Young 1994: 233), what colonial regimes generally did was adapt and develop pre-colonial differences and processes of identification rather than create them where none previously existed.

In India, the British rulers learned from the practices of their Mughal, Hindu, and Sikh predecessors in categorizing their Indian subjects, the novelty lying in their systematic method, modern 'scientific' techniques, and the scale on which they sought to enumerate and classify **castes**, tribes, and religions (Bayly 1999). The effect, as in Africa (Chabal 2009: 33), was to make the consciousness and instrumentalization of such group identities far more pervasive and politically potent. The creation of separate representation and electorates in the representative and elected bodies that were introduced from the 1900s on (Chiriyankandath 1992) also served to institutionalize these identities, making them less fluid than they had been. While such categorization may have initially had as its primary purpose making intelligible, and encompassing, an alien public sphere (Gilmartin 2003), it also proved useful in deploying divide-and-rule tactics against emergent anti-colonial nationalism. In the Indian case, the eventual outcome was the partition of the subcontinent in 1947, with the creation of Muslim Pakistan, and a post-independence politics in which such group identities remain of central significance (see Chapter 20).

The colonial investment in emphasizing the traditional character of the colonized 'others' produced another of the peculiar paradoxes of colonialism—the civilizing colonizer's nostalgia for, in the words of the British imperial writer Rudyard Kipling (1987: 183), 'the real native—not the hybrid, University-trained mule—[who] is as timid as a colt'. Yet deprecating the 'inauthentic' hybrid did not prevent colonial regimes from often favouring politically useful pre-colonial elites in imparting Western education, thereby creating a monocultural elite that created a nationalism in their own image; in more extreme cases such as Pakistan and Sudan, this proved impossible to sustain in the multicultural context of the post-colonial state (Alavi 1988; Sharkey 2003). However, internalizing the colonial representation of them as the 'other' caused Asians and Africans to stress their 'dedicated' non-Western identities (Sen 2006: 102), ironically making the identities shaped under colonialism the force for decolonization (Dirks 2004: 30). Anti-colonial nationalists sought to distinguish between a material 'outer' masculine domain of economy, statecraft, science, and technology in which they acknowledged the superiority of Western modernity, and a spiritual and cultural 'inner' feminine domain of language, religion, and family—the 'private essences of identity' (Young 1994: 275)—the distinctness of which had to be preserved (Chatterjee 1993: 6–9).

Despite overarching commonalities, there were important differences between colonies (see Box 2.3). While the British colonial state left behind an

---

BOX 2.3 COLONIAL MUTATIONS OF THE MODERN STATE

Colonialism in Africa created mutations of the modern state. Among the ways in which this has been theorized is in terms of a 'gatekeeper' (Cooper 2002) or, from a different perspective, 'bifurcated' (Mamdani 1996) state. Unlike the night-watchman state favoured by libertarians (Nozick 1974), the role of the colonial **gatekeeper state** was not to serve its inhabitants, but to control the intersection of the colony and the outside world, collecting and distributing the resources that control brought. However, while such a state was conceived as weak in terms of its social and cultural penetration, the same could not be said of the bifurcated colonial state. Seen as the prototype for the apartheid regime in South Africa, Mamdani (1996: 29) describes it as the outcome of the simultaneous operation of two different modes of dominion: a racially discriminatory direct rule, based on the exclusion of most, if not all, natives

from civil rights, in urban centres; and a method of indirect rule resting upon the institution of customary tribal authority that produced a system of **decentralized despotism** in the rural hinterland. The latter generally involved the conflation of a variety of forms of pre-colonial authority into one essentially monarchical, patriarchal, and authoritarian model (Mamdani 1996: 39) that was also territorially demarcated. Such an approach had the effect of disassociating power from authority in a way that subsequently came to pose a formidable challenge to post-colonial African rulers seeking to establish their **legitimacy** (Chabal 2009: 41). Elements of this model could be discerned in colonial practices outside Africa, most notably in the colonial search for—or creation of—a more authentically native aristocracy to enlist as subordinate collaborators.

entrenched legacy of autocratic government in both India and Africa, in India this was tempered by nearly three decades of a widening measure of partly representative quasi-constitutional self-government at the provincial level, as well as a superior administration (the Indian Civil Service) that was nearly half Indian when independence came (Chandra et al. 1999: 18) and which maintained a tradition of political neutrality that ensured administrative continuity (Burra 2010). Although anti-democratic tendencies persisted in post-independence India (and, much more obviously, in Pakistan) (Jalal 1995), the contrast with the rapid breakdown of post-colonial constitutional government in Britain's erstwhile African colonies was striking.

From the outset of the establishment of colonial rule, the weak demographics that underpinned what Bayart calls the politics of extraversion meant that the primary focus of colonial extraction in Africa was labour rather than land revenue, as in the much more densely populated Indian subcontinent (Young 1994: 273). From their relatively late inception, mainly in the late nineteenth century, the European colonial states in Africa relied heavily on the institution of various forms of forced and tributary labour. Although its most brutal manifestations, as in King Leopold II's Congo Free State, largely disappeared after the First World War, the practice survived well into the first half of the twentieth century. The colonial economics of sub-Saharan Africa resulted in either the absence of—or a much weaker—indigenous capitalist class, with Africans effectively excluded from all but petty trade in most regions (Tordoff 1997: 42; Hyden 2006: 46–7). European companies and immigrant Asian merchants dominated larger-scale economic activity, with African integration in the global economy mainly taking the form of cash crop farming, especially in French and British West Africa, and labouring in diamond, gold, copper, bauxite, and other mines, particularly in central and southern Africa. These features, together with the relatively brief span (between sixty and eighty years) of colonial rule across much of the continent, had the consequence that both the colonial state in Africa and indigenous political and economic forces were more weakly developed than in India, the colonial powers having not modernized society enough (Hyden 2006: 232).

Colonies have been described as 'underfunded and overextended laboratories of modernity' (Prakash 1999: 13). They were laboratories within which the subjects of the experiments proved unwilling to live.

Through specific ideologies such as Gandhian nationalism in India, Negritude, Pan-Africanism and African socialism in sub-Saharan Africa, Arabism in the Arab Middle East, and varieties of nationalism influenced by pre-colonial Muslim identity across the Islamic world and Buddhism in South East Asia, the anti-colonial nationalism of the Western-educated elite succeeded in mobilizing a mass following. Yet while this evocation of what Chatterjee termed the 'inner domain' proved effective as an anti-colonial tool, colonialism left a material legacy in the institutions of state (bureaucratic, judicial, and educational systems, police and military) and entrenched patterns of trade and exchange (for example the French franc zone and the British sterling area in Africa). It also bequeathed ideologies exported from the West—nationalism itself, liberalism, and socialism—as well as global languages of power (English, French, Spanish, and Portuguese). The rest of this chapter describes how this polyglot legacy has served post-colonial states and societies.

KEY POINTS

- The era of European colonialism stretched over five centuries, during which different colonial powers emerged and patterns of colonialism changed.

- The colonial state was typically extractive in intent, and autocratic and coercive in form. A thin, cheap state, it relied on local collaborators to maintain its authority.

- Colonialism developed a system of knowledge that 'objectified' the colonized, one consequence being to harden and highlight ethnic and religious distinctions.

- Variations in colonial rule had repercussions for post-colonial development, as in the contrasting experience of decolonization in much of Africa and in India.

- Colonialism created mutations of the modern state. In Africa, this has been described variously in terms of a 'gatekeeper' or 'bifurcated' state.

Post-Colonial Development

In contrast to the drawn-out history of colonization, the tide of decolonization came in fast across Asia, the Middle East, Africa, the Caribbean, and the Pacific. Beginning in Asia, the Middle East, and North Africa in the decade after the Second World War, it covered most of sub-Saharan Africa within a few years of Ghana (formerly the British Gold Coast) becoming the first independent black African state in 1957, and by 1980 had taken in much of the rest of the erstwhile European colonial empire in the Caribbean, the Persian Gulf and South Arabia, and the Pacific. This rapid transformation was in part the outcome of geopolitical factors: the perceptible weakening of European power following the two world wars; and the emergence of the United States and the Soviet Union, each competing to win over anti-colonial nationalists to their respective camps, as the pivots of the post-war bipolar cold war world. However, it was increasing pressure from anti-colonial nationalism, inspired in part by Indian independence in 1947, that forced the pace of change.

But how much change did decolonization bring? The passionate desire of anti-colonial idealists such as Fanon (1967: 252) not to imitate Europe starkly contrasted with the imperial paternalism of colonial officials such as Phillip Mitchell, the British Governor of Kenya, who could say as late as 1945 that, faced with 'the choice of remaining a savage or of adapting our civilisation, culture, religion and language, [the African] is doing the latter as fast as he can' (quoted in Cooper 2002: 73). The post-colonial reality belied both Mitchell's belief and Fanon's hope. Colonialism, by globalizing the European template of an international system constituted of sovereign nation-states, determined that the primary object of anti-colonial nationalism would be the transformation of colonies into independent nation-states within a system that bore the deep impress of the erstwhile colonizers. Despite seeking to assert their political and cultural autonomy, anti-colonialists demanding independence had little choice but to operate within this system, since it was the only one that was also imaginable to their rulers (Cooper 2003: 67). This was the dynamic that helped to ensure that while, for instance, pan-African and pan-Arab dreams remained unrealized, Muslim insecurities in British India resulted in partition and the creation of Pakistan as a separate 'Muslim' nation-state.

The new states faced the unprecedented challenge of fashioning 'a peculiarly *modern* form of statehood', modelled not on earlier, more basic, forms of the state, but on the elaborate modern Western state that had been developed over centuries (Clapham 2000: 6–7). They were also inhibited by the fact that the conditions in which power was generally transferred were far from optimal. Even though, in the majority of cases, independence was not accompanied or preceded by war or violence, it was marred by the

hurried transfer of administrative responsibilities, belated and unsustainable political compromises, economic dependence, and largely untested legislatures and governments. In noting how colonialism fatefully structured political choices along regional and ethnic lines in Britain's most populous African territory, Nigeria, Nolutshungu (1991: 100) observed that the political systems of post-colonial societies 'carried. . . in their genes—the heritage of the colonialism that designed them, authoritarian in its day, but also, invariably, in its retreat, a champion of elitist and paternalist notions of democracy'. In Nigeria, the system quickly, and tragically, gave way—successive military coups in 1966, six years after independence, being followed by a three-year civil war that claimed between 1 million and 3 million lives.

Whether states achieved independence via a negotiated constitutional transition or a war of liberation did not appear to make much difference to the lasting influence of the colonial legacy. Certainly, in Africa, the trajectory of development of the minority of post-colonial states that were the outcome of armed struggle (Algeria, the ex-Portuguese colonies of Guinea-Bissau, Angola, and Mozambique, as well as Zimbabwe, Namibia, and Eritrea) showed much in common with that of their neighbours (Young 1998: 107). Although peaceful transfers of power may have assisted what Crawford Young (2004: 29) calls the inertial forces favouring the retention of colonial legal and bureaucratic legacies, the troubled post-independence histories of the liberated colonies demonstrates that it was not possible to remove the long shadow cast by the colonial past through struggle. In fact, the bitterness of the struggle itself seems, in some cases (Algeria, Angola, Mozambique), to have contributed to subsequent civil war. Being accepted as legitimate by its population was a major preoccupation for post-colonial states. Their colonial predecessors had demanded obedience, not consent, and been content with commanding fear rather than affection. This presented a formidable challenge, given the generally multi-ethnic and multi-religious character of most post-colonial states, and often, especially in Africa and the Middle East, the absence of a pre-colonial state tradition. While the legacy of anti-colonial nationalism was helpful, especially where, as in India, it encompassed decades of struggle and mass engagement, this plural context meant that the concept of development was particularly attractive to nationalist leaders pursuing popular acclaim and concerned with getting their publics to shake off habits of disobedi- ence to the colonial state institutions that they had inherited. Even in India, one of the main nationalist criticisms of British rule was that, having brought the gift of science, they were stunting India's growth and arresting her progress (Nehru 1942: 433–49; 1961: 508). A developmental ideology thus became central to the self-definition of the post-colonial state (Chatterjee 1993: 203)—in 1945, Jawaharlal Nehru (1961: 504), soon to become independent India's first prime minister, felt that 'planned development under a free national government would completely change the face of India within a few years'.

In Africa, the predilection on the part of post-colonial leaders to embrace the cause of development was strongly influenced by the late British and French colonial interest in ushering in a **developmental state**. A belated attempt to justify colonialism as it found itself under challenge—the shift from a primarily exploitative and preservationist colonialism to one that claimed to actively champion and invest in progress and development—did not save the colonial state (see Box 2.4). Indeed, Cooper (2002: 66) suggests that, in Africa, it was the lead that the British and French took in this shift that ensured that it was their empires that first started giving way as the changes introduced stimulated growing demands for self-government. The developmentalist authoritarianism subsequently pursued by their post-colonial successors also failed to secure their regimes. The successful military coup in Ghana in 1966 against President Kwame Nkrumah epitomized this failure (inheriting the economically interventionist and centralizing late colonial state in the Gold Coast, Nkrumah had assumed dictatorial powers and pursued a succession of wasteful and ill-planned projects aimed at transforming Ghana into an industrialized state).

In most of Africa, the patterns of post-colonial government that developed in the 1960s and 1970s traced their lineage to colonial forms: 'Africanised but . . . still impervious, greedy and coercive' (Chabal 2009: 90). However, there were important differences that caused the post-colonial state to be seen as 'an albatross, a yoke . . . round the neck of Africa' (Mutua 2008: 2). Mamdani's 'bifurcated' colonial state mutated into two types. In the majority of cases, conservative post-colonial decentralized despotisms were not really transformed by the reintroduction of multi-party systems in many countries in the 1990s (for example Kenya under President Daniel arap Moi in the 1990s). A minority turned into radical centralized despotisms in which local authority was dismantled without central government being democratized (for example Uganda in the first decade after Yoweri Museveni's National Resistance Movement took control in 1985).

Alternatively, Cooper's gatekeeper state in its post-colonial form, lacking its predecessors' external coercive capacity or financial resources, was left dependent on either the former colonial power or one of the main protagonists in the cold war—the United States, the Soviet Union, or, in a few cases, Communist China. This was perhaps most obvious

BOX 2.4 INGREDIENTS FOR POST-COLONIAL SUCCESS: EAST ASIA AND BOTSWANA

Despite lingering until the 1990s, developmentalist authoritarianism in Africa proved a dead end. Whereas, in East Asian states such as South Korea and Taiwan, both Japanese colonies in the first half of the twentieth century, it was credited with producing an economic miracle, post-colonial Africa was very different. It lacked the societal cohesion, state tradition, and cold war geopolitical significance of the East Asian states, as well as the peculiar legacy of state-led capitalist development left by a colonial power that was close both geographically and culturally. In this connection, it is noteworthy that Botswana, despite inheriting a 'colonial state not worth the name' and long serving as a labour reserve for the South African mining industry (Samatar 1999: 95), represented a rare African success story, recording average annual growth of over 6 per cent even in 1985–95, a decade during which most other African states recorded negative growth

(World Bank 1997: 214–15). While very different in other respects, Botswana benefited, like Korea and Taiwan, from an ethnically homogenous society with a cohesive dominant class and a purposeful leadership under the country's first president, Seretse Khama, also the hereditary chief of the Ngwato, the biggest *morafe* (nation) in the country. The colonial mediation of indigenous socio-political institutions and practices, and the post-colonial incorporation of indigenous authorities in the bureaucratic structures of the modern state through rational-legal means, were crucial elements in producing a strong state with a sustainable government (Gulbrandsen 2012), capable of building successful public development institutions (the Botswana Meat Commission and the Botswana Development Corporation), and of avoiding the rampant **corruption** and autocratic tendencies that disfigured post-colonial Africa.

in the Francophone states in West and Central Africa, most of which belonged to the *Communauté française d'Afrique* (French Community of Africa) and had their currencies pegged to the French franc (and, after 1999, the euro). Into the early twenty-first century, France continued to be an important source of economic aid. Often maintaining a long-standing military presence, she intervened militarily to prop up post-colonial rulers in several former French colonies. To a lesser extent, Britain played a similar role in countries such as Sierra Leone, intervening to end the civil war there in 2000–02. Political independence, by placing the resources of the 'gate' in local hands rather than changing the nature of the state, simply intensified the struggle for the gate, making the beleaguered new gatekeepers, usually ethnically defined, dependent on external agencies for international recognition and aid (Cooper 2002: 200).

These trajectories of dependent political development can be interpreted in different ways. Some see it as basically an adaptation of the inherited Western colonial template of **modernization** as Eurocentric development and progress, albeit inflected locally through a continuing process of hybridization (Ahluwalia 2001: 67–71). Others reject the extraneous nature of the post-colonial state. Bayart (1993: 265), for instance, suggests that what is negatively described in terms of 'tribalism' or 'instability' in Africa reflects the local appropriation of alien institutions. He evokes the image of a rhizome—a continuously growing underground stem constantly generating both shoots and roots—to explain the dynamic linkage of African societies to institutions of the post-colonial state (Bayart 1993: 220–1). However, these links can be viewed more critically as reflecting the emergence of a form of **clientelism** that, while drawing upon pre-colonial customary patrimonial relations between rulers and ruled, is more instrumentalist and unaccountable (Chabal 2009: 95).

Bayart's notion has the value of conceiving of the post-colonial as part of a historical continuum (the *longue durée*), but in doing so it risks underplaying the impact of colonialism. Bayart's rhizome concept avoids the link between political regimes in post-colonial states and the **globalization** of capitalism that European colonialism did so much to bring about. From a Marxist perspective, there was no gainsaying that 'two-thirds of the world's people do not have liberal states because of the structure of the capitalist world-economy, which makes it impossible for them to have such regimes' (Wallerstein 2003: 164).

The European export of the idea of the monocultural nation-state left most post-colonial states with the dilemma of how to reconcile this with ethnically and religiously plural societies. Chatterjee (1993: 11) identifies this 'surrender to the old forms of the modern state' as the source of 'postcolonial misery'. In some countries, such as Iraq, created under a British League of Nations mandate in 1921 and formally independent by 1932, the shallow foundations of colonial rule necessitated recourse to particularly high levels of violence, setting a pattern for post-colonial government that has persisted (Dodge 2003: 157–71).

As in Africa, colonialism in South Asia left in its wake visions of society and polity that were distorted. Some outside observers have suggested that India owes its comparatively stable post-independence political and economic development to its 'relative immunity from western ideologies' (Gray 2003: 18), but this argument is hard to sustain. More to the point perhaps are three kinds of ingredient that were more evident in the post-colonial Indian mix than, say, in Africa. First, in the realm of cultural politics there ran a deep vein of the non- (if not pre-) modern. Gandhi tapped into this in developing the 'saintly' idiom of Indian politics (Morris-Jones 1987: 60), and the metaphor of the sanctified and patriarchal extended family has been described as one of the most important elements in the culture of Indian nationalism (Chakrabarty 2003: 71).

Second, the phenomenon of caste associated with Hinduism, while rendered less fluid, more regulated, and institutionalized under colonialism, gave to India a particularly encompassing, yet supple, resource in adapting colonial institutions (Rudolph and Rudolph 1967).

Third, there was the important role played by political agency—in this case, the Congress Party that had spearheaded the campaign for independence. Already more than sixty years old at independence, Congress, under the leadership of Nehru, reinforced India's liberal democratic institutional framework by accommodating not only the dominant classes, but also a variety of caste, religious, linguistic, and regional identities, both through the party and in the structures of government (Adeney and Wyatt 2004: 9–11).

In contrast, lacking in these ingredients, India's subcontinental neighbours, Pakistan and Sri Lanka, proved far less successful, both in sustaining stable constitutional government and in preventing civil war. While India experienced localized civil wars, these outbreaks were insulated and ultimately defused (in this respect, Kashmir, a bone of contention between India and Pakistan since independence, remains the exception). However, as the 'formal' democracy of the British Dominion of Ceylon (as it was until 1972) was displaced by the more brash and intolerant 'social' democracy of the Republic of Sri Lanka (Wickramasinghe 2006: 160), the island state witnessed a descent into decades of civil war between the Sinhala Buddhist majority and the minority Tamils. In contrast, although the 'democratization' of Indian democracy through the politicization of previously oppressed and marginalized lower castes and other peripheral groups (Yadav 1996) confronted the state in India with formidable challenges, its post-colonial institutions coped. The partition of the subcontinent, by removing roughly two-thirds of the Muslim population, might have made the issue of state and **national identity** in India less problematic. Even so, it is because the post-colonial state in India transcended, in some measure, the colonial logic of divide and rule that it has been better at digesting ethnic and religious plurality. Despite the recent political salience of Hindu chauvinism, it is still possible to conceive of Indian culture as 'constructed around the proliferation of differences' (Ghosh 2002: 250).

KEY POINTS

- In contrast to colonization, decolonization occurred apace and, twenty-five years after the Second World War, was largely achieved.

- Colonies became nation-states despite the form being ill-suited to most post-colonial societies.

- Development was prominent as a legitimizing motif for late colonialism and became central to the self-definition of its post-colonial successors, albeit often degenerating into unsuccessful developmentalist authoritarianism.

- While the development record of many post-colonial states was disillusioning, a few registered conspicuous success owing to history, geopolitical situation, and political agency.

Conclusion: The Colonial Legacy

As the tide of decolonization was reaching its peak, both the departing colonizers and the anti-colonial nationalists anticipating freedom were disposed to strike a positive note. The colonial historian Margery

Perham (1963: 99) held, in 1961, that 'Britain on the whole was the most humane and considerate of modern colonial nations and did most to prepare her subjects for self-government'. As power was handed over by the last British Governor of the Gold Coast, Kwame Nkrumah, Ghana's first leader, declared confidently: 'We have won independence and founded a modern state' (James 1977: 153). Yet, less than a decade later, on the eve of losing power, Nkrumah summed up his misgivings about the reality of independence in a book entitled *Neo-Colonialism*:

> The essence of neo-colonialism is that the State which is subject to it is, in theory, independent and has all the outward trappings of international sovereignty. In reality its economic system and thus its political policy is directed from outside.

(Nkrumah 1965: ix)

A quarter of a century later, one international relations theorist coined the phrase 'quasi-states' to describe the majority of post-colonial states (Jackson 1990).

In the early twenty-first century, there was a resurgence of interest in the West in the idea of a **liberal imperialism**, if not the actual restoration of formal empire, as a solution to the continuing political and economic crisis that many post-colonial states, especially in Africa and the Middle East, faced (Cooper 2004; Ferguson 2004; Lal 2004). Echoing earlier justifications for colonial rule, adherents of a revival of paternalist imperialism shared a sense of civilizational superiority, and disregard of the logic of domination and exploitation that underpinned European colonialism. This logic had also been apparent in the behaviour of the United States, the first post-colonial imperial power, towards native, African, and Hispanic Americans in extending its domain across North America in the course of the nineteenth century, and then in the Philippines, Latin America, and the Caribbean in the years following the Spanish–American War of 1898 (Slater 2006: 15, 44–53). Attributable to a 'geopolitical amnesia' engendered by imperial—and post-imperial—culture in the West (Slater 2006: 148), the renewed fascination with liberal imperialism can be seen as both a reflection of post-cold-war Anglo-American hubris and a legacy of colonialism's 'civilizing mission' (Watt 2011: 1–12). Liberal imperialism may be perceived in the Western-led occupations of Afghanistan (2001) and Iraq (2003), and other military interventions in post-colonial states. However, more

BOX 2.5 ASSESSING THE COLONIAL LEGACY

In an ambitious effort to examine the legacy of colonialism comparatively, James Mahoney (2010: 3) studied the experience of fifteen mainland Latin American countries colonized by Spain, seeking to develop hypotheses that might explain variations in levels of colonialism (that is, the extent of settlement and institutional implantation), and post-colonial economic and social development. The study found that, under mercantilist colonialism, there was an inverse relationship between the levels of colonialism and post-colonial development. Peripheral or marginal colonial territories (Argentina, southern Brazil, Chile, Costa Rica, Uruguay) achieved higher levels of development, while erstwhile important colonial centres (Bolivia, northeast Brazil, Mexico,

Peru), in which powerful coalitions of merchants and landowners blocked successful adaptation to an advancing capitalist world economy, fared less well. Significant in terms of social development was the fact that the people of the former were more European by descent, and their societies were thus not built around excluding a subordinated indigenous and African majority from social goods. The study also argued that, under a liberal colonizing power such as Britain, the intensity of colonialism was positively related to post-colonial development—the four British settler colonies (the United States, Canada, Australia, and New Zealand) and the city-states of Hong Kong and Singapore serving as prime examples (Mahoney 2010: 256).

subtle and widespread has been the post-cold-war effort to globalize a hegemonic discourse of democratization and **governance** that, it is argued, interprets self-determination for post-colonial societies in terms of 'the "freedom" to embrace the rules, norms and principles of the emerging [informal imperial] (neo) liberal global order' (Ayers 2009: 21).

While virtually the entire developing world experienced colonialism, the experience differed from place to place, and this is reflected in the varied legacy (see Box 2.5). To begin with, the settler and slave societies of post-colonial Latin America and the Caribbean present a contrast to Africa and Asia. For example, in the Caribbean, the private hierarchies of exploitation that underpinned slavery, and the subsequent drawn-out history of slave emancipation and struggle for political rights, helped the state structures, closely modelled on the British parliamentary system, to gain acceptance as autochthonous (Sutton 1991: 110).

In the African case, the patchiness of pre-colonial state traditions, and the relative brevity and 'thinness' of colonial rule, generally resulted in post-colonial states incapable of achieving the ambitions of nationalist leaders and the expectations of their peoples. By the end of the twentieth century, a large part of the colonial state legacy in many African countries had been effaced by institutional decay (Young 1998: 116), eroding 'the explanatory power of the post-colonial label' (Young 2004: 49). What also needs to be reckoned is the legacy of the anti- and post-colonial movements in Africa. The characteristics of these responses to colonialism militated against a transition to multiparty

democratic politics, instead leading to a personalization of politics (Hyden 2006: 48, 232).

This is not to negate the continuing historical significance of the colonial, and indeed pre-colonial, past. For instance, contrasting the former Belgian Congo with regions that possessed effective states before colonialism, such as the south of Uganda (Buganda) and Ghana (Asante), and northern Ethiopia, the latter have proved better able to survive phases of bad government (Clapham 2000: 9). Although the model of the nation-state has proven a burdensome legacy for contemporary Africa, the consequences of **state collapse** in Somalia, Liberia, Sierra Leone, and Congo in the 1990s and 2000s showed the high human cost exacted by its absence. The lesson seemed to be that, in a world of states, vulnerable regions and their inhabitants are left dangerously exposed by state collapse. Although some (Clapham 2000) argue that societies might conceivably be able to function without states, it is difficult to foresee them being tolerated for long in the globalized world of states, and the unresolved question for many African countries remains how to fashion a sustainable state (Cooper 2002: 186).

Historical differences reflected in institutional weakness may have compounded the crisis faced by the post-colonial state in Africa, but in Asia too the colonial legacy presented post-colonial states with their greatest challenges, especially in grappling with issues of political identity. The problem in countries such as Sri Lanka was that the concept of multiculturalism introduced by the British colonial rulers stressed the fragmentary nature of society (Wickramasinghe 2006: 13). By doing so, it left the post-colonial state with its composite identity particularly vulnerable to being torn apart by incompatible visions of the nation.

The condition of the post-colonial state today is determined by a combination of factors marked by its colonial past: history and geopolitical situation; internal political agency; location in the world economy; and the influence of Western powers, and international governmental and non-governmental institutions, latterly expressed through a globalized discourse and practice of democratization and governance.

? QUESTIONS

1. Is the 'post-colonial' label still useful in discussing the politics of developing countries?

2. How far did colonialism efface pre-colonial patterns of development?

3. How much does the colonial legacy inform contemporary views of the global 'South' and 'North'?

4. How far can differences in post-colonial development be explained with reference to differing colonial pasts?

5. How useful are the concepts of the 'gatekeeper' and 'bifurcated' colonial state in understanding post-colonial political development?

6. To what extent is the idea of development undermined by its past association with colonialism?

7. How far do the international institutions and practices of the contemporary world bear the imprint of colonialism?

FURTHER READING

Chatterjee, P. (1993) *The Nation and Its Fragments: Colonial and Postcolonial Histories* (Princeton, NJ: Princeton University Press) An insightful examination of the impact of colonialism on the nationalist imagination in Asia and Africa by a leading Indian political theorist.

Chiriyankandath, J. (1992) '"Democracy" under the Raj: Elections and Separate Representation in British India', *Journal of Commonwealth and Comparative Politics*, 30(1): 39–63 Shows how the British introduction of communal forms of political representation helped to shape the post-colonial politics of the Indian subcontinent.

Cooper, F. (2002) *Africa since 1940: The Past of the Present* (Cambridge: Cambridge University Press) Considers the post-colonial development of Africa from a historical perspective, with particular reference to the concept of the 'gatekeeper' state.

Hall, S. (1996) 'When Was "The Post-Colonial"? Thinking at the Limit', in I. Chambers and L. Carti (eds) *The Post-Colonial Question: Common Skies, Divided Horizons* (London: Routledge), 242–60 A thoughtful exploration of the term 'post-colonial'.

Hyden, G. (2006) *African Politics in Comparative Perspective* (Cambridge: Cambridge University Press) A review of the development of post-colonial Africa.

Mahoney, J. (2010) *Colonialism and Postcolonial Development: Spanish America in Comparative Perspective* (Cambridge: Cambridge University Press) A wide-ranging empirical inquiry into the developmental legacies of colonialism in Latin America and beyond.

Slater, D. (2006) *Geopolitics and the Post-Colonial: Rethinking North–South Relations* (Oxford: Blackwell) A political geographer's perspective on the post-colonial world, which devotes special attention to Latin America.

Young, C. (1994) *The African Colonial State in Comparative Perspective* (New Haven, CT: Yale University Press) Wide-ranging comparative study of the colonial state by a political scientist.

— (2004) 'The End of the Post-Colonial State in Africa? Reflections on Changing African Political Dynamics', *African Affairs*, 103: 23–49 Young's reconsideration of the condition of the post-colonial African state.

WEB LINKS

http://bostonreview.net/chibber-good-empire   Link to the article by Indian political sociologist Vivek Chibber (2005) 'The Good Empire: Should We Pick Up Where the British Left Off?', *Boston Review*, 30(1), a damning critique of Niall Ferguson's (2004) *Colossus: The Rise and Fall of the American Empire* (London: Allen Lane) and of the poor scholarship that lies behind the early twenty-first-century idea of a new liberal imperialism.

http://hdr.undp.org/en/reports/global/hdr2004/papers/HDR2004_Nicholas_Dirks.pdf   Link to the background paper for the United Nations Development Programme in which a historical anthropologist specializing in South Asia, Nicholas Dirks (2004) *Colonial and Postcolonial Histories: Comparative Reflections on the Legacies of Empire*, considers the colonial legacy.

For additional material and resources, please visit the Online Resource Centre at:
http://www.oxfordtextbooks.co.uk/orc/burnell4e/

3

Institutional Perspectives

Lise Rakner and Vicky Randall

Chapter contents

Overview

This chapter focuses on the role of institutions and how institutionalism is increasingly applied in the analysis of politics in the developing world. It presents central theoretical concepts and approaches helping us to understand institutional origins and change, and further explores the interrelationship between formal and informal institutions through two case studies. By way of conclusion, the chapter discusses the merits of the new institutionalism as a tool of analysis for developing countries.

Introduction

As noted in Chapter 1, a marked feature of the literature relating to **politics** in the **developing world** since the 1980s has been the centrality assigned to **institutions**. This 'new institutionalism', which actually includes many different scholarly traditions, holds that institutions explain political outcomes, and may provide a solution to political and economic problems across nations. In considering institutionalism as an approach, this chapter will also touch on the character of political institutions in developing countries, thereby anticipating chapters in Part 3 of this book that focus on political processes and the state. We begin by reflecting on the increasing popularity of institutionalism within analyses of politics in developing countries. We then discuss the theoretical underpinnings of 'new institutionalism', before looking more directly at instances of its application to institutions in developing countries, both formal and informal. In a final section, we assess the appropriateness of institutionalist analyses in developing countries.

New institutionalism and the study of the developing world

Institutionalism has always been a prominent approach in mainstream political science. In the early years, there was an emphasis on historical and legal aspects of political institutions and on constitutions. The 'behavioural' revolution from the 1950s, and subsequently the development of rational choice analysis, entailed a reaction against this kind of institutionalism in favour of approaches that focused on the individual, conceived as a broadly autonomous actor. Obviously, this did not mean that the study of institutions ceased, but it was not until the 1980s that the beginnings of a counter-revolution in political science was discernible, famously launched by March and Olsen (1984) as the 'new institutionalism'.

'Old' and 'new' institutionalism

This new institutionalism had much in common with the 'old'. It also took a number of different forms, as we shall see. Nonetheless, these shared some important and novel features (Peters 2005; Lowndes 2010). In particular, comparing old and new forms of institutionalism, one can trace the following shifts. First, institutions were no longer implicitly identified with organizational structures; instead, the focus of analysis moved towards rules and even norms. Second, where the focus had originally been on formal institutions, there was now at least as great an interest in **informal institutions**. In addition, the new institutionalism was more explicitly theoretical than the old institutionalism had been and more interested in processes of institutional change.

The new institutionalism then emerged within 'mainstream' political science from the 1980s and, in its different guises, has become increasingly prevalent, leading to the claim 'we are all institutionalists now' (Pierson and Skocpol, cited by March and Olsen 2006: 5). As part of this trend, it has also been increasingly applied in the analysis of politics in developing countries.

political science, together with the declining sense that developing countries need their own specialized analytic frameworks. The new emphasis in the scholarly literature also coincided with a shift in the policies of the international financial institutions toward the developing world from the late 1980s. During the 1970s and 1980s, major international organizations such as the World Bank de-emphasized the role of state institutions in terms of forging development in the South. Inspired by neoclassical economic analyses, the international financial institutions argued that a particular feature of the least developed nations was corrupt and inefficient state institutions, and that they encouraged a reduced role for the state. However, recognizing that the '**Washington consensus**' had neglected the need for appropriate institutional design for achieving development, the World Bank in the 1990s began actively to promote the role of institutions to protect property rights and contract, and to encourage **civil society** and **good governance** (World Bank 1994; see also Chapter 15). Key in the new development scholarship and the policies of the multilateral institutions was the interest in institutions, and how institutional practices could be built and nurtured to secure accountability in new and fragile democracies in the developing world. This focus on institutions has not waned over time; most recently, it has been applied to issues of conflict and security by the World Bank (2011), which notes that '[w]eak institutions are particularly important in explaining why violence repeats in different forms in the same countries or subnational regions'.

This (new) institutionalism is everywhere apparent in the study of politics in developing countries. It arises in numerous thematic contexts and across regions, for instance in studies of democratization in Latin America (Helmke and Levitsky 2006), in accounts of parliaments in Asia, and in relation to African politics (Posner 2005; Lindberg 2006). To assess its implications for studying politics in developing countries, we need now to consider more systematically the theoretical foundations and complications of the new institutionalism.

New Institutionalism Applied to the Developing World

The growing application of the new institutionalism in analysis of the politics of developing countries is partly explicable in terms of more general developments in

---

KEY POINTS

- In mainstream political science, 'new institutionalism' has emerged since the 1980s.
- Compared with old institutionalism, new institutionalism focuses less on organizational structures and more on

rules and norms; it is more explicitly theoretical and interested in processes of change.

- The application of the new institutionalism to developing countries is partly a consequence of the recognition that the 'Washington consensus' neglected the role of appropriately designed institutions for achieving developmental goals.

The Theoretical Underpinnings of Institutionalism

The premise of the new institutionalism is that 'institutions matter' and that, to quote Peters (2005: 155), 'scholars can achieve greater analytic leverage by beginning with institutions rather than individuals'.

Three kinds of institutionalism

However, the new institutionalism actually embraces several different approaches. In an influential article, Hall and Taylor (1996) identified three main forms—sociological, rational choice, and historical. Although many other candidates have emerged and Peters (2005) claimed to have found seven types, for present purposes it is helpful to review the main differences between these original three.

Sociological institutionalism

Sociological institutionalism is also referred to as 'cultural', or 'normative', institutionalism. As its name implies, this perspective has been heavily influenced by a tradition in sociology concerned with how collective institutions establish forms of social control over individual action. But it also draws on the sociological study of organizations (Selznick 1948). March and Olsen (1984; 1989), in some ways the founding fathers of the new institutionalism, broadly fall into this category. Like other new institutionalists, they do not equate institutions with formal organizations; rather, they define an institution as 'a relatively enduring collection of rules and organized practices' (March and Olsen 2006: 5). Sociological institutionalists tend to stress the role of norms and values in constituting institutions, and in socializing individuals into conforming behaviour through what March and Olsen (2006: 7) term a 'logic of appropriateness'. By the same token, they tend to see individual preferences as shaped by the institutions within which they become embedded rather than arising exogenously.

Rational choice institutionalism

Although the 'new institutionalism' can be understood as a reaction against what was seen as the extreme methodological individualism of behavioural and rational choice approaches, this form of institutionalism comes from within the rational choice perspective itself. It has been strongly influenced by developments in economics within which the dominant neoclassical paradigm has involved idealized free agents interacting in an idealized free market. Institutional analysis within economics has reacted against this by showing how collective action can be institutionally embodied, and can thereby shape and constrain individual choice. New institutionalism within economics is represented most prominently by the Nobel laureate Douglass North (1990), whose ideas have been extensively taken up in political science.

A key premise of rational choice institutionalist approaches in political science is that individual behaviour can be regarded as rational, in the sense of rationally linking means to desired ends. Institutions are seen to represent rules and incentives that constrain and enable individual action. Significantly, within this perspective, the fundamental principles of political behaviour are the same across different political systems despite seemingly different configurations of institutions and political phenomena. Rational actors respond to institutional contexts in identical ways regardless of strategic position, and institutions emerge and persist because of the value and benefits of their functions for the actors who cooperate voluntarily. Contrary to 'the logic of appropriateness' of sociological institutionalism, rational choice institutionalism considers actors to behave according to a 'logic of consequentiality': rules reflect the explicit intent and powers of individual actors. One of the first analysts to apply the rational choice perspective to the study of institutions in developing countries is Robert Bates, whose work has generated huge interest amongst both scholars and policymakers (see Box 3.1).

Historical institutionalism

The third strand to be introduced, although possibly the first to emerge, is historical institutionalism. An early statement of its approach can be found in Thelen and Steinmo (1992). Historical institutionalism is not a unified intellectual enterprise: some scholars within this tradition, relying on quantitative approaches, treat history as the outcome of rational and purposeful behaviour; other, more qualitatively oriented, scholars emphasize the role of randomness and accidents. Historical institutionalism views institutions as the formal and informal procedures, routines, norms, and conventions embedded in the organizational structure of the polity or political economy. Institutions range from the rules of a constitutional order or the standard operating procedures of a bureaucracy to the conventions governing trade union behaviour or bank–firm relations (Hall and Taylor 1996: 6–7). What differentiates historical institutionalism from the two other strands is the emphasis on historical context. At its simplest, the historical institutionalist argument is that the choices made as an institution (or policy) is being formed, and the commitments that the institution comes to embody as a consequence, will continue to shape its subsequent development through a process of 'path dependence' (Pierson 2000). Path dependence analysis also includes the notion of critical junctures—or a critical moment in history with lasting consequences (Thelen 2004). Dramatic historical moments, such as independence from a colonial power, may create new institutions and substantially change power resources of various groups in society.

What is an institution and how does it affect individual behaviour?

Given the central role of institutions in the new institutionalism, a crucial question to be asked is what we should understand an institution to be. Within 'classical' institutionalism, institutions were frequently identified with organizations or formal structures. Within all three strands of the new institutionalism—and although in practice there is still much interest in organizations—an institution is more

typically understood as a 'stable, recurring pattern of behaviour' (Goodin 1996: 22), or as defined by North (1990: 3), 'the rules of the game in society, or, more formally, the humanly devised constraints that shape human interaction'. Thus, in an institutionalized setting, behaviour is more stable and predictable.

How do institutions emerge and change?

Institutions, although stable, are not eternal, but answers to the question of how institutions arise have been various, and often vague and unsatisfactory. Goodin (1996) suggests that there are three main ways in which institutions could have come about—by accident, through a process of evolution, or intentionally—and that, in practice, any actual instance of institutional change will almost certainly involve a combination of these three elements. However, in practice, sociological institutionalists have tended to depict institutions as emerging out of their social context and often as embodying dominant social values. Deriving from this perspective, the important notion of 'political institutionalization' as a process has been widely taken up, either in reference to the regularization of political processes as a whole, or especially in reference to political parties. On the other hand, rational choice institutionalists have been criticized for having an implicitly functional approach in which institutions are consciously designed by individuals to reduce **transaction costs** and increase efficiency.

More thought has been addressed to the connected question of how institutions change. Generally, the assumption is that changes are exogenous—that is, driven by outside pressures—but more recent research points to a more complicated process in which external pressures or opportunities combine with the effects of internal dynamics and opportunism of 'institutional entrepreneurs' (Lowndes 2010).

Political Institutions in Developing Countries

Influenced by and drawing on these theoretical developments, political scientists have focused with renewed interest on a range of political institutions in developing countries. Examining institutions at the centre of government, they have considered executive and legislative institutions and their interrelationship. Long-standing arguments about the respective merits of presidential and parliamentary executive arrangements are now being rehearsed in a developing world context (see Box 3.2). Related to this, generally, until recently, the assumption was that executive power

in such countries, through both formal and informal means, dominated the legislature—where it existed—to such an extent that the latter institutions barely warranted independent study. Increasingly, scholars are taking legislatures seriously not only in established democracies such as India, or some Latin American countries, where it has been argued that 'legislatures play a vital role' (Huneeus et al. 2006: 422), but also in Africa (Nijzink et al. 2006).

Two further and overlapping subjects for extensive political analysis have been political parties and party systems, and electoral systems. Randall and Svåsand (2002) consider the 'institutionalization' of political parties, distinguishing between 'internal' and 'external' aspects of the process. They conclude that, with notable exceptions, political parties in developing countries tend to be weakly institutionalized, but also warn against imposing expectations derived from an uncritical account of parties in the developed world. Mainwaring and Scully (1995) analyse the institutionalization of party systems, which they relate closely to the democratization process, in Latin America. These concepts have been further 'operationalized' and applied in later studies (for a fuller account see the 'Political Parties' case study available on the Online Resource Centre).

It is widely accepted that political parties, and especially party systems, are significantly affected by electoral systems. Beyond the familiar distinction between majority or 'first past the post' (FPTP) electoral systems, those embodying some form of proportional representation, and 'mixed systems', there are all

BOX 3.2 PARLIAMENTARY VERSUS PRESIDENTIAL SYSTEMS

In presidential systems, the president is head of government and state, popularly elected for a fixed term; in parliamentary systems, the prime minister or head of government is selected by the legislature and depends upon its support to continue in office. In between are various kinds of 'semi-presidential' system, such as when a directly elected president coexists with a prime minister dependent on parliamentary support. Whilst instances of all three types of governmental system can be found in the developing world, parliamentary systems cluster in South Asia (India, Bangladesh, and currently Pakistan) and the Caribbean, whilst presidential systems predominate in Africa (exceptions include Botswana, Mauritius, and South Africa, the 'president' of which is actually elected by the legislature) and especially Latin America.

In the context of democratic transition, a lively debate has arisen about the respective merits of presidential and parliamentary systems. Some political scientists have agreed with Linz (1990), who famously warned against the 'perils of presidentialism', suggesting that parliamentary systems were preferable because they offered greater democratic stability. Others, such as Shugart and Carey (1992), have questioned whether presidential systems are in fact less stable, and argued that they provide greater democratic transparency and accountability. It is, however, increasingly clear that the way in which these systems operate in practice is strongly shaped by contextual institutional factors, such as the degree of fragmentation of the party system and the prevalence or otherwise of informal neo-patrimonial relationships.

manner of possible variations, with claimed consequences for the quality of representation, including women's presence in legislative bodies, on the one hand, and government stability and conflict resolution, on the other. In practice, partly as a legacy of colonial rule, FPTP systems predominate in Africa and Asia, though proportional representation largely prevails in Latin America. However, it is important, when estimating the consequences of electoral systems, especially in a developing world context, to recognize that they do not exist in a vacuum, but interact with other institutional features, such as whether the government is unitary or federal, and the pattern of social divisions.

Designing political institutions

Given this focus on political institutions and belief in their independent consequences, there has been particular interest, both theoretical and practical, in **intentional institutional design**, or how institutions can be designed *ab initio* or modified in order to

achieve particular desired ends. A major area for this kind of work is the design and critique of electoral systems, but its scope is far wider, including the design of systems of party regulation and of constitutions (see Box 3.3).

Interest is growing in the possibilities of engineering or modifying party systems, which are increasingly seen as playing a key role in successful democratic consolidation. One approach that has been adopted in a succession of developing countries is to devise a national system of party regulation. This is often aimed at encouraging the formation of national parties and involves specifying, for instance, that parties must field candidates in a certain minimum proportion of constituencies. There is also interest in using the electoral system to modify the party system. Thus, in Turkey, parties must win at least 10 per cent of the national vote before they can be represented in the national legislature. Or, in fragmented or polarized party systems, electoral systems can be used to try to encourage greater cooperation between the parties (Reilly and Nordlund 2008).

BOX 3.3 DESIGNING CONSTITUTIONS

The process of making a new constitution can involve assemblies, executives, ordinary legislatures, or the public, and most utilize several actors in the constitution-making process. There is a trend towards including the population in the ratification process and earlier in the process. Based on data from the Comparative Constitutions Project (CCP), Ginsburg et al. (2009) find that processes that are either very long or very short tend to occur in non-democracies and can sometimes be unstable. Also the size of the deliberative body may matter: too many may be problematic.

Elster (1997) claims that constitutions produced in more democratic processes will be more democratic. The CCP shows that constitutions in which public participation had been used as part of the process on average yielded more rights and provided more opportunities for participation of citizens later on.

In general, however, it is very hard to establish what makes a constitution 'good' or 'bad'. A central idea is that constitutions should provide stability. Enduring constitutions are considered good because they may provide for a more stable environment for both investment and democratic stability (Ginsburg et al. 2009). Most constitutions do not last very long and 50 per cent of constitutions are dead by the age of 18 years. However, there

are large regional disparities. Constitutions in Western Europe last, on average, three times longer than African or Latin American constitutions. Internal factors that are considered to ensure constitutional longevity are linked to the inclusiveness of the constitution's origins and the constitution's ability to adapt to changing conditions (Ginsburg et al. 2009). More specific constitutions will be able to anticipate potential problems in the future. This includes both attention to detail and scope of events covered. An inclusive constitution will tend to be more democratic and, since more people will know of the constitutional provisions, it will provide a clear focal point for citizens and thus be more self-enforcing. This counts for both the drafting stage and the approval stage. Adaptable constitutions will be more able to resist shocks through either formal amendments or informal amendments that come from interpretative changes.

An example of a constitutional process that did not succeed in providing stability and democracy is Iraq's constitution. This is mainly owing to issues relating to a lack of **legitimacy** and latent religious, ethnic, and economic tensions (Elkins et al. 2008: 34–5). The case of Iraq highlights some of the importance of extra-constitutional variables in explaining constitutional outcomes.

Whilst many political scientists, as well as multilateral agencies and national governments, have taken up such schemes enthusiastically, however, others remain more sceptical. Acknowledging that sometimes there is no option but to create or engineer new institutions, Bastian and Luckham (2003) nonetheless caution against the risks of unintended consequences. It is also important to consider the political context in which such engineering is attempted—who is supporting it, whose vested interests may it in fact promote, and whose may suffer? In other words, what is the hidden political agenda?

Transplanting political institutions

Closely related to designing new political institutions is the option of transferring or transplanting institutions, or institutional models, from other countries. This could be said to have a long history in much of the developing world, with governing institutions modelled on those of departing colonial powers, as in the 'Westminster' model of government. But, post-independence, such experimental borrowing has persisted whether freely chosen by the sovereign government, or under pressure from donor countries or multilateral agencies. Recent examples include anti-**corruption** commissions or agencies, truth

commissions (see Box 3.4), and women's national policy machinery (see Chapter 9). Generally, the direction of borrowing has been from developed to developing countries, but South–South exchanges are also increasingly in evidence. The wisdom of such transplanting exercises is disputed. We have seen that the rational choice assumption is that the principles governing political behaviour are broadly similar whatever the regional or cultural context. Others are more wary about the consequences of applying 'lessons' from one political context to another very different one. In practice, institutional transplanting may be, to some degree, an unavoidable aspect of policy innovation, On the other hand, it could be part of a strategy of cosmetic change and policy avoidance. Any assessment of 'success' needs to take such contextual factors into consideration.

KEY POINTS

- Political scientists are increasingly interested in the role of formal political institutions in developing countries.
- In this context, there is specific interest in intentionally designing, or transplanting, institutions.

BOX 3.4 TRUTH COMMISSIONS

The 'first' truth commission was set up in Uganda in 1974, whilst Idi Amin was still firmly in power, to inquire into the 'disappearances of people'. Although hearings were public, the report was never published and the **regime**'s infamous brutality persisted. As of 2012, truth commissions had been deployed in thirty-five different countries, including Argentina's 1983 National Commission on the Disappeared, Chile's post-Pinochet 1991 National Commission of Truth and Reconciliation, Guatemala's 1994 Historical Clarification Commission, and perhaps the most celebrated of all, South Africa's post-**apartheid** 1998 National Commission of Truth and Reconciliation, and South Korea's 2005 Truth and Reconciliation Commission.

Truth commissions have been defined as 'temporary bodies, usually with an official status, set up to investigate a past history of human rights violations that took place within a country during a specified period of time' (Chapman and Ball

2001: 2). Whilst potentially providing a 'third way' between prosecution, which would hardly be feasible given the scale of collective violence, and blanket amnesty, they have all faced innate difficulties, not least in gathering and processing the vast amount of potentially relevant data, and in squaring the search for 'truth' with reconciliation. 'Success' is, in any case, difficult to define and measure, although failure is relatively clear in the cases of commissions in Bolivia and in the Philippines, which broke up before their task was completed (Brahm 2007). But, in practice, the impact of truth commissions has varied enormously, affected by such factors as: how restrictive the terms of their original mandate have been, limitations of time, and resource limitations (for instance, contrast Haiti, with around US$1 million funding and seventy-five staff, with South Africa, with roughly US$28 million funding and, at its peak, more than 400 staff (Chapman and Ball 2001: 16–17)).

Formal and Informal Institutions

As the previous discussion has made clear, a growing focus on the role of formal political institutions, including those that have been intentionally designed or transplanted, has been accompanied by a recognition, especially in relation to developing countries, that their performance can be highly variable, unpredictable, and often disappointing. Amongst the numerous explanations, a key contributory factor must be the impact of informal institutions. A distinguishing feature of the new institutionalism is, in any case, its emphasis on the role of informal institutions. But it is with its application to developing countries that this dimension has really come to the fore.

Chapter 1 of this book discusses the '**modernization revisionism**' that emerged in reaction to some of the cruder depictions in **modernization** theory of the relationship between tradition and modernity. Rather than expecting modernization to eliminate tradition, it was more realistic to recognize the persistence and reworking of tradition in new symbiotic forms with modernity. The present interest in informal institutions to some extent echoes that argument and examines some of the same kind of phenomena, especially forms of **patron–client relationship** that work in and through formal political institutions. However, informal institutions cannot simply be equated with tradition or culture; they are both less and more than this. Helmke and Levitsky (2006: 5) suggest the following definition of informal institutions: '… socially shared rules, usually unwritten, that are created, communicated and enforced outside officially sanctioned channels.'

Formal institutions involve defined organizational patterns, rules, and procedures that govern the behaviour of groups and individuals. Informal institutions interact with formal political institutions in highly significant ways. In many cases, informal political institutions–such as political **clientelism**, corruption, the 'big man' syndrome, customary law–undermine the formally specified political rules, but in a few cases the working of formal political institutions can actually be facilitated by a set of informal rules and conventions. Specifically in the context of democratization, Helmke and Levitsky (2006) build on the initial analysis of Lauth (2000) to suggest four different possible kinds of interaction (see Table 3.1).

- As the name suggests, *competing* informal institutions compete with and subvert weak formal institutions, a very common occurrence in new democracies.
- *Substitutive* informal institutions share goals with, and take the place of, weak formal institutions.
- *Accommodative* informal institutions have divergent goals and values from formal institutions, but do not ultimately undermine them.
- In a *complementary* relationship, informal institutions are compatible with, and may actually reinforce, formal institutions.

Indeed an important new insight emerging from the works of authors such as Helmke and Levitsky (2006: 11) is that, in emerging democracies, informal institutions can actually have a positive effect on **governance**.

Two specific examples, set in different continents, Africa and Latin America, illustrate further the complex interaction between formal and informal institutions. In the first case, sub-Saharan Africa from the 1980s, the emphasis is on the way in which informal institutions have tended to undermine formal political institutions, although we note some recent signs of a changing relationship. In the second case, we see how a set of informal institutions has contributed to lessen the problems posed by Chile's formal electoral institutions of strong presidential powers and majoritarian parliamentary elections.

Table 3.1 A typology of relationships between informal and formal institutions

Outcomes/effectiveness	Effective formal institutions	Ineffective formal institutions
Convergent	Complementary	Substitutive
Divergent	Accommodating	Competitive

Source: Gretchen Helmke and Steven Levitsky (eds) Informal Institutions and Democracy: Lessons from Latin America (Baltimore, MD: Johns Hopkins University Press), 14, Fig. 1.1. © 2006 Johns Hopkins University Press. Reprinted with permission of Johns Hopkins University Press.

Formal and informal institutions in sub-Saharan Africa

The role of informality has been particularly marked in analyses of politics in sub-Saharan African countries and new institutionalist perspectives have illuminated our understanding of African politics. They have demonstrated the continuing salience and impact of informal institutions, especially those associated with **neo-patrimonialism**. Most recently, however, they have also been associated with a new and cautious optimism that perhaps formal institutions, or rules of the game, really are beginning to matter as well.

Neo-patrimonialism in African politics

One classic neo-patrimonial account is Bratton and van de Walle's (1997) analysis of democratic transitions in Africa from the early 1990s (see Box 3.5). Situating themselves firmly in the 'new institutionalist' school, they pose the question of how far these apparent transitions really constitute a turning point in African political development. They note areas of change, but also strong elements of continuity, such as the de facto persistence, despite ostensibly competitive elections, of traditional leaders and the old political elite. And they suggest that transition has not in general strengthened political institutions—by which they mean political parties, legislatures, and electoral institutions. Instead, they show how the operation of such formal democratic political institutions has been affected by the persistence of largely informal institutions associated with the preceding neo-patrimonial regimes.

Chabal and Daloz, authors of another influential study, *Africa Works* (1999), similarly affirm the importance of informal institutions and processes. They suggest that the ongoing economic crisis in Africa is contributing to a growing trend towards the informalization of politics. They find only a superficial resemblance between African political institutions and those in the West (Chabal and Daloz 1999: xx): 'In reality it is the patrimonial and infra-institutional ways in which power is legitimated which continue to be most politically significant.'

Formal rules and presidential politics

This perception of African politics in which informal, neo-patrimonial institutions pervade and largely undermine formal institutions remains widespread, and indeed largely appropriate. But in this case study we want also to bring attention to the emergence of a new theme in the literature, which suggests that formal political institutions in Africa are beginning to affect the behaviour of political and economic elites. Posner and Young (2007: 126), reflecting on some recent trends in African presidential politics, conclude that '[t]he formal rules of the game are beginning to matter'. They note the increasing importance of elections—by 2000–08, 98 per cent of presidential elections were contested (although, even then, incumbent presidents were re-elected more than 85 per cent of the time). They also note that, since 1990, more than thirty-six African countries have adopted new constitutions, most of which do not permit a third presidential term. It is encouraging that no incumbent president has tried to get rid of the constitution altogether and that nine out of eighteen agreed to step down after two terms. The remaining nine sought to change the constitution: three failed—Chiluba in Zambia, Muluzi in Malawi, and Obasanjo in Nigeria—although six, including Nujoma of Namibia and Museveni of Uganda, succeeded. Posner and Young (2007) accept that the role of external pressures in modifying presidential behaviour should not be underestimated. Nonetheless, they find grounds for 'cautious optimism' in what appears to be the unwillingness of presidents to openly defy growing public support for contested presidential elections and presidential term limits. In this context, it is worth mentioning the military coup in Niger (February 2010), which was blamed on the president's successful referendum extending his term of office. This could be seen as a further encouraging

---

BOX 3.5 NEO-PATRIMONIALISM DEFINED

In neo-patrimonial regimes, the chief executive maintains authority through personal patronage rather than through ideology or law. . . . Relationships of loyalty and dependence pervade a formal political and administrative system and leaders occupy bureaucratic office less to perform public service than to acquire personal wealth and status. The distinction between private and public interests is deliberately blurred. The essence of neo-patrimonialism is the award by public officials of personal favours, both within the state (notably public sector jobs) and in society (for instance, licences, contracts, and projects). In return for material rewards, clients mobilize political supporters and refer all decisions upwards as a mark of deference to patrons.

(Bratton and van de Walle 1994: 458)

sign, although the fact of military intervention in itself is less reassuring. In 2012, in Senegal, President Wade was permitted, despite mass protests, to stand for an unconstitutional third term, but then conceded defeat when he lost the election.

Other formal institutions: courts and anti-corruption commissions

This kind of argument has been echoed in other institutional contexts. Suberu (2008) looks at the role of Nigeria's Supreme Court. He notes the widely held view that Western-style institutions such as courts are simply facades for neo-patrimonial rule, but he argues that 'the neo-patrimonial framework of such analysis often trivializes the significant recent advances towards democratization, liberalization and institutionalization of power in Africa' (Suberu 2008: 458). This neo-patrimonial interpretation might have been appropriate for the Supreme Court before 1999, but since the transition in that year from military to civilian rule, the Court has emerged as 'a prominent and independent adjudicator of intergovernmental disputes'. He demonstrates this by means of an analysis of all fifteen major intergovernmental disputes, concerning central government and Nigeria's thirty-six state governments, from 1999 to 2007. Beyond establishing the Supreme Court's increasing independence and integrity, he also points to the contributory role of two other institutions, the National Judicial Council and the Federal Judicial Service Commission, which, under the 1999 Constitution, helped to ensure that members of the Supreme Court have been recruited on the combined basis of seniority and merit (see also Chapter 25).

Lawson (2009) focuses on the issue of anti-corruption reform, comparing the achievements in this respect of Kenya's Anti-Corruption Commission with Nigeria's Economic and Financial Crimes Commission (for further discussions of corruption, see Chapter 15). She points to the way in which earlier studies tended to emphasize how incumbent elites used anti-corruption campaigns to target their political enemies. Lawson does not deny this aspect of anti-corruption initiatives, but argues that a subtler analysis is needed. In Kenya's case, she found that the Anti-Corruption Commission was indeed sidelined, but in the Nigerian case the Commission had a degree of success. More generally, she suggests that factors such as timing and 'unintended consequences' of reform can make a difference. If an anti-corruption

clean-up following an election were too obviously targeted at the previous incumbents, this could alienate public support. In addition, those heading up the new organizations could, as appeared to happen in Nigeria, seek to assert their independence from the new political leaders by adhering to and implementing their formal organizational mandate.

Accommodating formal rules: the case of Chile's electoral institutions

Chile returned to democracy in 1990 with a weak congress and strong presidential powers, as embodied in the 1980 Constitution under Pinochet. At the centre of the preceding military government's project of social transformation was an attempt to reduce the number of political parties through electoral engineering and the adoption of a majoritarian two-member district parliamentary electoral system (known as a 'binominal' system). This institutional 'heritage' of a presidential system, weak legislature, and a majoritarian electoral system in principle creates major challenges and disincentives for cooperation and coalition formation (Mainwaring and Scully 1995). But, since the democratic transition, Chile has followed a stable pattern of two-coalition competition with an alliance on the left (the *Concertación*) and an alliance on the right (*Alianza por Chile*). Rather than reducing the number of political parties, the electoral system has encouraged relatively stable coalition formation. Instead of deadlock and instability, as scholars would predict, Chile has experienced stable coalition governments marked by extensive consensus-building among political elites. One of the most striking elements of Chilean politics since the return to democracy in 1990 (and up until the most recent general election in 2009) is the stability of the coalition government *Concertación*, representing a broad alliance of four major parties. This stability contrasts with the coalition fluidity characterizing Chile's pre-Pinochet democratic experience. According to Siavelis (2006: 34), a complex set of informal institutions has contributed to lessen the problems posed by Chile's inflexible formal electoral institutions and helped to moderate the actions of presidents with formal powers to act in an authoritarian manner.

The role of the *cuoteo* (quota)

Under the first post-authoritarian government in Chile, elites made an informal pact to counteract the negative characteristics of the constitutional powers vested in the presidency and the exclusionary characteristics of the electoral system. This pact has been referred to as the *cuoteo*, which translates as 'quota'. The informal quota system refers to the distribution of executive-appointed positions based on party affiliation and the quota of parliamentary candidates allotted to each party within the government alliance. These informal institutions have been crucial to the maintenance of the government coalition and the legislative success of presidents, and by implication to the stability of democracy in Chile since 1990 (Siavelis 2006: 40).

Managing coalition governments: the role of the *partido transversal*

The model of Chilean coalition governments in the past, and in particular during the years of Salvador Allende's Popular Unity Government (1970–73), was a situation of different parties negotiating to maximize their own gains at the expense of attention to collective problems. Another informal institution that has been critical to governing and the success of the *Concertación* coalition post-1990 is the informal group of leaders that held crucial roles in the first democratic government, who refer to themselves as the leaders of the coalition government. Known as the *partido transversal*, an informal, yet well-organized cadre of party elites, whose loyalty lies equally with the coalition as with their individual parties, form a network between themselves, the parties, and the coalition government. Their object is to control the potentially damaging consequences of co-party government, in which each party might otherwise seek to maximize its own utility or advantage (Siavelis 2006: 47). The members, centred on the presidency and holding key ministerial positions, facilitate cross-party communication among actors in different branches of government, which helps to build consensus among the parties in the government coalition.

Democracia de los acuerdos: securing agreements

Multiparty presidentialism creates many negative incentives for coalition formation and the building of legislative majorities. In the case of post-authoritarian Chile, this was made more complicated by strong political elites fearing the electoral powers of the *Concertación*. To overcome this threat to legislative success, presidents post-1990 have consistently engaged in a pattern of informal negotiations that has become known as *democracia de los acuerdos*, or 'democracy through consensus'. These negotiations have been carried out with congressional opposition and powerful social groups outside parliament. Since the 1990s, presidents have routinely consulted with legislators of the government and opposition to reinforce coalition unity, and to ensure that the budget and other important bills are acceptable to the coalition partners.

Two member district elections and coalition strategies

Chile's binomial legislative electoral system ensures that all districts elect two representatives to Congress. Each list on the ballot may therefore include up to two candidates. The lists are open and voters indicate a preference for one of the candidates within their preferred list. Seats are allocated by the D'Hondt method, which means that the first placed list in a district can win both seats only if it more than doubles the total vote of the second-placed list; if not, each of the top two lists wins one seat each. Combined with the multiparty system, Chile's electoral system, known as the 'M = 2' system, brings complexity for candidates, parties, and coalition leaders. Because of the high threshold for two-seat victories, most lists may expect one defeat in each district. Carey and Siavelis (2006) argue that the *Concertación* coalition has responded to the challenges imposed by the M = 2 formula by creating and sustaining an informal institution for ensuring strong candidates who incur risk on behalf of the coalition against the vagaries of the electoral marketplace. This is done through rewarding good losing candidates with appointed government positions. This 'insurance system' may be considered as a complementary institution in Helmke and Levitsky's model, because it serves to compensate for dilemmas posed by formal institutions that run the risk of undermining cooperation.

The Chilean example shows that, when formal institutions are strong and the costs of changing institutions are high, accommodating informal institutions may emerge when political actors face difficulties in terms of operating within formal institutions. The case of Chile's electoral institutions shows how informal institutions may contribute to political stability and governability and the endurance of democratic electoral institutions.

Formal–informal institutional interrelations in the developing world

The case studies have illustrated the variety of national and thematic contexts in which the interrelationship of formal and informal institutions has increasingly been explored. Whilst the traditional assumption might be that informal institutions would tend to vitiate and compete with formal institutions of democracy and governance, the cases have shown a more varied and complex picture. In sub-Saharan Africa, where regimes have long been seen as quintessentially neo-patrimonial, with informal power relations subverting weak formal representative and administrative institutions, there may be signs that formal institutions are beginning to matter. In Chile, with strong formal democratic institutions, informal practices have helped to sustain viable democracy.

KEY POINTS

- Interest is growing in the interaction of formal with informal political institutions in developing countries.

- The case of sub-Saharan Africa illustrates the salience of neo-patrimonial politics and *competing* informal and formal institutions, but also offers examples of formal institutions beginning to shape the behaviour of political and economic elites.

- The case of Chile illustrates how informal power-sharing institutions may allow elites to achieve their goals within an inflexible formal institutional context.

Conclusion: Institutionalism and the Developing World

The new institutionalism that now pervades mainstream political analysis represents a welcome reaction to the reductionism of earlier individual actor-based approaches. Whilst it takes different guises, all institutionalist approaches include in their analyses a focus upon both formal and informal rules, organizations, and procedures. Moreover, these different strands can be regarded as complementary (Goodin 1996). Although the new institutionalism has been criticized for internal ambiguities, and for inadequately engaging with questions of the origins of institutions and how institutions change, this is part of an ongoing dialogue in which such shortcomings are being addressed.

The new institutionalism is increasingly applied in analysis of politics in the developing world. We have seen that this partly reflects the new institutional emphasis of development economics, as purveyed by

international bodies such as the World Bank. Sound, effective governance institutions are seen as a prerequisite of development. This raises the question of the extent to which the new institutionalism is an appropriate tool of analysis for developing countries. Actors and institutions engaged in promotion of good governance and sound institutions for development have turned to institutional analyses in search of tools for designing institutions that may achieve desired goals. But the question of intentional institutional design raises a number of critical questions. Can institutional designs 'travel' from different political settings? What are the potential unintended consequences of creating new formal institutions in political contexts in which the informal institutions may not be accommodating the stated aims of the formal institutions designed?

Arguably, institutional analyses have tended to ignore the uneasy relationship between formal institutions designed with external assistance and deeply embedded local informal institutions. Remmer (1997: 50), emphasizing the fragility and constrained character of institutions in developing countries, argues that the new institutionalism, with its emphasis on domestic issues, has ignored the overwhelming importance of international actors and institutions for the developing world, as well as domestic economic constraints. She finds it ironic that new institutionalism places politicians and bureaucrats at the centre of analysis at a time when the activities, resources, and relative weight of the state are being reduced through processes of **privatization**, **globalization**, and the emphasis on civil society.

Some writers go further in questioning whether an institutional emphasis is really illuminating. Sangmpan (2007: 201) maintains that 'empirical evidence reveals that outcomes in developing countries consistently defy institutions as explanation and prescription'. He wants to distinguish three aspects of political systems—politics, institutions, and the state—and argues that, in developing countries, it is what he calls 'society-rooted politics' that imprints and even determines the other two aspects. Sangmpan's conception of politics is avowedly 'sociological', referring to interests within society that compete for property, goods, services, values, and political power. His argument is that an institutional approach marginalizes such factors. Although Sangmpan directs his criticism against the new institutionalism and its application to developing countries, he maintains that this new institutionalism, like the old institutionalism, tends to focus on formal institutions. We have argued, however, that one of the great virtues of the new institutionalism has been its interest in informal institutions and their interaction with the formal sphere, which Sangmpam deliberately chooses to ignore. Even so, his notion of society-rooted politics is broader than anything typically connoted by informal institutions and to that extent he may be right to argue that the new institutionalism runs the risk of exaggerating the significance of institutions, as opposed to fundamental political interests and conflict.

In conclusion, the new institutionalism offers an exciting tool of analysis if used with sensitivity to context and without hegemonic claims to be the only proper approach to politics in developing countries.

An important feature of the application of the new institutionalism to developing countries has been a special emphasis on the role of informal institutions and their interaction with formal institutions. This emphasis on the interactions between formal institutional structures and informal practices offers important insights into why some formal institutional arrangements 'stick' and guide political actors behaviour, why in some instances formal institutions change because they do not serve the interest of the elites, and under what circumstances informal norms and practices simply render formal written constitutions irrelevant. Our case studies demonstrated some of the productive ways in which this kind of analysis has been used.

? QUESTIONS

1. What explains the new emphasis on institutional analyses applied to the developing world?

2. Compare the sociological, historical, and rational choice institutionalist approaches to understanding institutional change.

3. How do institutions emerge and how do institutions change?

4. Discuss how a cultural and a rational choice approach may interpret traditional agrarian economies differently.

5. With particular reference to developing countries, how would you evaluate the 'success' of a (written) constitution?

6. What are the potential pitfalls and unintended consequences of designing institutions with external assistance in a developing country setting?

7. With reference to Table 3.1, provide empirical examples of formal–informal institutional relations that are complementary, accommodating, substitutive, and competitive.

8. How persuasive do you find the argument of Posner and Young (2007) that, in Africa, 'formal rules of the game are beginning to matter'?

≋ FURTHER READING

Goodin, R. (1996) *The Theory of Institutional Design* (Cambridge: Cambridge University Press) A comprehensive review of major theoretical approaches to institutional design and change.

Hall, P. A. and Taylor, R. C. R. (1996) 'Political Science and the Three New Institutionalisms', *Political Studies*, 44 (5): 936–57 A useful overview of the central debates between institutionalist approaches.

Helmke, G. and Levitsky, S. (eds) (2006) *Informal Institutions and Democracy: Lessons from Latin America* (Baltimore, MD: The Johns Hopkins University Press) A valuable framework for analysing formal and informal institutional relations, with detailed case studies from Latin America.

Lowndes, V. (2010) 'The Institutionalist Approach', in D. S Marsh and G. S Stoker (eds) *Theory and Methods in Political Science*, 3rd edn (Basingstoke: Palgrave), 60–79 An excellent overview.

March, J. and Olsen, J. P. (1989) *Rediscovering Institutions: The Organizational Basis of Politics* (New York: Free Press) A central text within new institutionalism.

Peters, G.D (2005) *Institutional Theory in Political Science: The New Institutionalism*, 2nd edn (London: Continuum) A thoughtful and thorough overview.

Powell, B. J. (2000) *Elections as Instruments of Democracy: Majoritarian and Proportional Visions* (New Haven, : Yale University Press) A central text discussing key aspects of democratic institutional design.

Thelen, K. and Steinmo, S. (1992) *Structuring Politics: Historical Institutionalism in Comparative Analysis* (New York: Cambridge University Press) A key introduction to historical institutionalism.

WEB LINKS

http://genderindex.org/   Social Institutions and Gender Index

http://globalresearch.ca/   Centre for Research on Globalization (CRG)

http://plato.stanford.edu/entries/social-institutions/   Social Institutions

http://www.cgdev.org/section/topics/ifi   Center for Global Development

http://www.isnie.org/   International Society for New Institutional Economics

For additional material and resources, please visit the Online Resource Centre at:
http://www.oxfordtextbooks.co.uk/orc/burnell4e/

4

The Developing World in the Global Economy

Stephen Hobden

Chapter contents

Overview

This chapter and the following interlinked one provide an overview of the international context in which politics in the developing world operates. In this chapter, the focus is on the global economy. Over the past fifty years, there has been a marked increase in global economic integration, often described as globalization. The chapter focuses on three key features of the global economy—trade, foreign direct investment, and financial flows—discussing their significance for the developing world. As the twenty-first century progresses, two distinguishing features are apparent: the most profound economic dislocation for eighty years; and the gradual erosion of the economic dominance of the 'North' (specifically Europe and North America).

Introduction: Trends in the Global Economy

For the purposes of this chapter, the term 'global economy' is understood as all international economic transactions that occur across national borders: trade;

financial flows; and foreign direct investment (FDI). Many observers claim to see evidence of increasing global economic integration, a feature usually associated with **globalization**. However, the meaning of the concept of globalization is a subject of much debate and, in particular, there is considerable disagreement

BOX 4.1 GLOBALIZATION

Globalization is a term much used in contemporary social sciences. Some suggest that it 'might justifiably be claimed to be the defining feature of human society at the start of the twenty-first century' (Beynon and Dunkerley 2000: 3). However, it is a deeply problematic term, because there is no accepted definition and little agreement about how to measure the process or even whether the term provides a useful way of assessing contemporary global developments (Hirst et al. 2009). O'Brien and Williams (2010: 425) regard globalization as characterized by the process of deterritorialization, which 'involves the shrinking of time and space, as well as the creation of new sets of social relations and new centres of authority'. When we turn to the developing world, the key argument is about whether globalization increases or decreases levels of poverty. As with the discussion over definition and measurement, there is little agreement over the impact.

The following are two rather divergent views:

Globalization has been a force for higher growth and prosperity for most, especially for those in the bottom half of the world's population.
(Bhalla 2002: 11)

Globalization speeds up the economy magnifying the chasm between [rich and poor]. Both at home and abroad, the extremes of wealth and deprivation have become so great that the stability of the global system is threatened.
(Isaak 2005: xxi)

How are such divergent views possible? One reason is that that there is no agreement as to what constitutes poverty. Should poverty be measured in absolute or relative terms? The most widely used absolute measure of poverty is the World Bank's figure for the number of people living on little more than US$1 a day. Measures of relative poverty compare the proportion of global wealth enjoyed by the richest people in the world with that of the poorest. Although the figures are disputed, most absolute measures suggest that poverty is declining (there are fewer people living on less than a dollar a day), whilst relative measures suggest that poverty is increasing (the gap between the richest and poorest is getting wider). Attitudes towards globalization may depend on the way in which poverty is measured. The picture is complicated when the situation within countries is also considered: the population of China living on the country's eastern edge has benefited much more from the country's recent rapid growth compared to the large rural population living on the western side.

Globalization is best understood as a multifaceted process that affects different countries and different social groups within countries differently. Most observers would agree that levels of inequality have increased, both nationally and internationally, while levels of absolute poverty, when examined globally, have decreased.

---

over the precise implications for economic well-being in the **developing world** of increased economic integration (see Box 4.1).

A major component of the emergence of a global economy has been the growth in the value of trade. For many writers, the **economic growth** of the West is largely explained by its involvement in an international trading system, leading to the view that 'free trade' is inherently beneficial. Yet despite the developing world's increasing inclusion in the global economy, few of the benefits from trade appear to have reached the large proportion (1.4 billion people, or one in four of the human population) of the globe's population who live in absolute poverty (on less than US$1.25 a day). Indeed, although the developing world increased its share of world manufacturing output from a mere 5 per cent in the early 1950s to close to 25 per cent by the end of the twentieth century, much of this was accounted for by only a handful of countries, which include China, Brazil, South Korea, and Taiwan (Dicken 2003: 37). The same is true of the increase in merchandise exports, where again China and Hong Kong dwarf other exporting countries such as Mexico, Singapore, and Taiwan. The arguments that lead many to suggest that the enormous benefits to be gained from joining the world economy need to be balanced against a consideration of the reasons why developing countries are not always able to exploit the potential gains from trade. There is evidence of trade between different social groups for as long as written records have existed and it has provided much of the motivation for global exploration. By the end of the nineteenth century, much of Asia and Africa had been included in the European empires, and trade between the colonial powers and their subject states provided the bulk of trade between what came to be called 'First' and 'Third' Worlds. The colonies provided guaranteed sources of essential raw materials and also markets for manufactured goods from the metropolitan centres. One historian of empire notes that 'Britain prospered...by manufacturing articles for sale abroad, which her customers paid for in raw materials and food' (Porter 1996: 4). An international division of labour developed in which European powers exported manufactured goods to the colonies and imported the materials needed to make these goods (McMichael 2008: 31–42). One way of imagining this process is to think of the international trading system as a number of segments, each segment comprising the colonial power and its colonies. A considerable amount of trade took place within the segment, and to have an empire was seen as essential for the economic well-being of the core.

Standing outside this segmented economic system was the United States, which, in the early twentieth century, was becoming a significant source of global production. Successive US administrations sought a larger role in the international economy, which would require the breaking up of the European imperial systems of trade. At the outbreak of the Second World War, planners in the United States started to think about what the post-war economic and political order might look like. The fruits of this planning emerged in a document known as the 'Atlantic Charter', signed by President Roosevelt and Britain's Prime Minister Churchill in 1941. At the core of the Charter was a commitment to the end of empire and the creation of an open world economy.

Despite the resistance of the European powers, decolonization gradually occurred following the end of the Second World War. However, as a result of the cold war, a world economy segmented by the European colonies was replaced by a world economy divided between, on the one hand, the United States, its allies, and client states, and, on the other, the Soviet Union, its allies, and client states. These systems resembled in many ways the imperial systems that had preceded them, in the sense that the cores provided manufactured goods, whilst developing countries were major sources of raw materials.

One major attempt to overcome this reliance on the export of raw materials was the development of a policy of import-substituting industrialization (ISI). Such a policy was attempted, for example, by the countries of Latin America in the period immediately after the Second World War. The promotion of local manufacturing was seen to have several advantages. It would employ local labour and thereby reduce unemployment, and allow production of manufactured goods at prices lower than available on international markets. Producing locally would reduce imports, potentially allow some of the production to be exported, and promote the introduction of new technology. To allow local industries to develop without competition, tariffs were imposed on imports.

Import-substituting industrialization is regarded as having been a failure for the developing world. In general, ISI did not promote the stated objectives, but resulted in rather inefficient government-owned industries that were unable to compete internationally. The reason for this is generally cited as being a reluctance to move towards reducing the tariff walls so that the industries are forced to compete internationally. Particularly in Latin America, pressure was put on governments to maintain subsidies and high levels of protection underpinning the industries. A further problem was that, in many developing countries, the market was not large enough to reap economies of large-scale production. Finally, ISI did not even break the reliance on imports: instead of relying on imported manufactured goods, the countries became reliant on the import of machine tools, spare parts, and specialized knowledge. Although ISI is normally now depicted in negative terms, it should be remembered that much of European and US industrialization occurred behind tariff walls, and that the success of the **newly industrializing countries (NICs)** of East Asia depended to varying degrees on this approach (see Box 4.2).

Despite an increasing level of contact between the capitalist and communist systems, it was not until the collapse of Communist Party rule in the Soviet Union that it became possible to start talking of a global economy—a single, exclusively capitalist, system.

While trade has been a feature of human societies dating back thousands of years, there are two other features of economic activity, also associated with the term 'globalization', but which have gained greater significance over recent decades. The first of these is FDI. This refers to the practice of firms, usually described as transnational corporations (TNCs), locating production and marketing facilities in other countries. The level of this FDI has increased massively over recent years and concerns have been raised about whether the activities of TNCs have assisted or undermined economic development. A further recent development has been the enormous financial flows occurring in the global economy. While FDI can be seen as a relatively long-term form of investment, financial flows are primarily

BOX 4.2 THE NICS OF SOUTH-EAST ASIA AND EXPORT-LED INDUSTRIALIZATION

The so-called newly industrializing countries (NICs) include Taiwan, South Korea, Hong Kong, and Singapore, with perhaps a second wave including Malaysia, Indonesia, and the whole of the People's Republic of China (PRC). The NICs have seen a remarkable turnaround in their economic fortunes, developing from being very poor, largely agricultural economies in the wake of the Second World War to become industrialized countries, some with average incomes comparable to those of the developed world. Free trade advocates have cited the NICs with varying justification as models for how to develop an economy.

The economic success of the NICs has many possible explanations, for example their exceptionally favourable geopolitical location during the cold-war period and even the cultural attributes of the people. But to most economists a major reason is their adoption of policies of export-led industrialization. This can be contrasted with the policies of import-substituting industrialization (ISI). The policy of the NICs has been to direct industrialization to fulfil the demands of world markets and gradually to expose their industries to world competition through lowering tariff barriers. They have been prepared to switch production in order to maintain their position of **comparative advantage**—starting with textiles, then moving into mass-production items such as toys, and then into

more high-tech goods. The NICs in particular have been successful in specializing in areas of production that have become unprofitable in the more developed world.

Economists who wish to promote free trade have seen the NICs as a good model because of their willingness to trade in the global economy and their readiness to reduce tariff barriers over time. Furthermore, the NICs have succeeded in exploiting their comparative advantage. However, the position is more complicated. It is true that the NICs have reduced tariffs over time so that their industries are now more exposed to international competition. But they have been prepared to use tariffs to protect their industries in the early stages while they were becoming established. This is known as 'infant industry protection', and was used as an argument for the protection of industry in Europe during the nineteenth and early twentieth centuries. A further point that is often overlooked is the important role that the state played in developing industry in the NICs (see Chapter 24 for more on the South Korean example). The state-maintained subsidies and investment as a way of developing parts of the economy were perceived to have the greatest potential, or were strategic in some sense. As with infant industry protection, this suggests that the history of the NICs is more complicated—and perhaps more difficult to replicate—than free market proponents suggest.

short-term. They refer to the buying and selling of currencies, and stocks and shares, in local economies. While FDI refers to investments such as buildings and machinery, and therefore takes some time to create, vast amounts of money in the financial system can be moved by the pressing of a computer button. Concerns have therefore been raised as to whether rapid financial movements can be destabilizing to developing world economies—although it should also be noted that economies in the developed world are not immune to the turbulence caused by rapid and speculative financial flows.

By the second decade of the twentieth-first century, two important features of the global economic system have become apparent: first, there has been a major dislocation in the economic system, with implications for both developed and developing countries; and second, some commentators are pointing to a shift in economic power from Europe and North America to Asia. At the forefront of this shift have been the economies of China and India, both of which have been enjoying substantial growth rates. These growth rates were negatively affected by the

global economic slowdown in 2008–09, yet still remain substantial. This shift of economic power may signal profound changes in the character of international relations, an issue that will be developed in the next chapter.

KEY POINTS

- The global economy comprises three main activities across national borders: trade; investment; and financial movements. There is a long history of trade between different societies, although large-scale FDI and financial flows are relatively more recent.

- Under European colonialism, the major pattern of trade was for the colonies to export raw materials, while metropolitan cores exported manufactured goods. These structures of trade have persisted into the post-colonial period.

- Post cold war, a single global, capitalist economy has emerged. Two contemporary features are a significant slowdown in economic activity and a shift in economic power to Asia.

Trade

Patterns of global trade

During the second half of the twentieth century, the rate of growth of trade far outstripped that of production. Between 1950 and the close of the twentieth century, world trade increased almost twenty times, while production increased only sixfold (Dicken 2011: 18). Yet this growth has not been at a constant rate and has been subject to considerable fluctuation. During the 1950s, levels of trade grew extremely rapidly as the world, and in particular Western Europe, recovered from the Second World War. In contrast, the rate of growth was much slower during the 1970s as the international economy contracted in the wake of large oil price rises.

World trade is relatively concentrated. Table 4.1 shows the breakdown among different regions of the world of their contributions to merchandise and trade in services. The developed world is responsible for the majority of exports in merchandise and services, although the rapidly increasing contribution of China to merchandise exports suggests that the character of the global economy is undergoing a profound transformation. Manufactured goods make up approximately 75 per cent of merchandise trade and one of the striking developments is the increasing amount of manufactured goods flowing from the developing world. Despite the large increases in the proportion of manufactured goods coming from some countries in the developing world, many maintain their traditional role of providing raw materials and agricultural products. Many countries in sub-Saharan African rely on just one primary product for over 50 per cent of their exports (Harrison 2004: 219).

The promotion of free trade

The relative prosperity of the developed world during the latter half of the twentieth century is linked by many economists to the rapid rise of global trade. The idea that unimpeded trade will lead to a material benefit to developing countries is a core idea of the neoliberal agenda, and is expressed in what became known as the Washington Consensus. The neoliberal agenda derives from classical liberal economics. The 'consensus' denotes the primacy of related ideas taken up by the key international finance institutions (IFIs)—the World Bank and the

Table 4.1 Relative shares in global exports by region and for selected countries, 2011

	Merchandise (%)	Services (%)
Developed world	53	67
Germany	8	6
US	8	14
Japan	4.5	3
CIS & SE Europe	4	3
Developing world	43	30
Africa	3	2
S. Africa	0.6	0.3
Asia (excluding Japan)	33	24
China	10	4
Latin America (incl. Caribbean)	6	3.5
Brazil	1	0.4
Mexico	1	0.3

Note: CIS = Commonwealth of Independent States

Source: UNCTAD (2012a: Tables 1.1.1 and 5.1.1). The United Nations is the author of the original material.

BOX 4.3 THE 'BRETTON WOODS' ORGANIZATIONS

Three organizations dominate international trade and finance: the World Bank; the International Monetary Fund (IMF); and the World Trade Organization (WTO). Collectively, these are known as the 'Bretton Woods organizations', because their origins can be traced to a conference held at the holiday resort of that name in the United States in July 1944. The aim of the conference was to create international **institutions** that would prevent the recurrence of the Great Depression of the late 1920s and 1930s, seen as a contributory factor in the outbreak of the Second World War. All three organizations have been highly significant in their impacts on developing countries.

- The IMF has existed primarily to help countries undergoing balance-of-payments crises (that is, those that arise when the value of imports has exceeded exports). Member countries experiencing a financial crisis are able to borrow money in tranches—but the more that is borrowed, the stricter the terms of **'conditionality'** (that is, economic policies set by the IMF that the borrowing country is obliged to implement).

- The World Bank is a more complex network of institutions, and it therefore makes more sense to talk of a 'World Bank group' rather than a specific organization. At the core is the International Bank for Reconstruction and Development

(IBRD), which started off with the purpose of making loans to aid the reconstruction of Europe following the Second World War, but which now specializes in making loans to countries in the developing world.

A controversial feature of both the IMF and the World Bank is that decisions are not made on a 'one member, one vote' basis. Instead voting is based on the size of the quota that each country pays the organizations. This, in turn, is related to the size of the country's economy. As a result, the developed world always has a majority in terms of the decisions that these organizations make.

- The WTO, by comparison, has a 'one member, one vote' decision-making process. The WTO did not emerge directly from the Bretton Woods conference, although its possibility was discussed; what emerged initially was the General Agreement on Tariffs and Trade (GATT). Whilst the name sounds like a one-off agreement, there were a number of GATT rounds, the prime aim of which was to promote international trade by reducing tariff levels. During the Uruguay Round (so-called because the first meeting was held in Uruguay in 1986), the decision was made to create the WTO as a more formal organization to oversee global trade and to adjudicate on trade disputes.

International Monetary Fund (IMF), both based in Washington (see Box 4.3 on the 'Bretton Woods' institutions). These ideas have proven to be very powerful. Policies based on the theory of comparative advantage, implemented by international organizations, have dramatically affected the lives of millions of people around the globe. (For a clear discussion of the theory of comparative advantage, see Dunn and Mutti 2004: ch. 2.)

The package of measures associated with the neoliberal economic agenda comprises both national and international elements. At the national level, free trade policies fall into two main areas: the promotion of a more efficient use of labour; and the reduction of the state's role in the economy. At the international level, policies aim to remove hindrances to trade and to promote the inflow of FDI. Tariffs are a form of taxation levied on the value of goods that are entering or leaving a country. They can be both a form of revenue and a way of protecting domestic industries. For free trade advocates, tariffs are seen as acting to undermine the potential gains to be derived from comparative advantage. Free traders have also argued in favour of allowing currencies to float freely rather than

being managed by governments. As part of free trade **regimes**, countries have been persuaded to allow their currencies to float freely. This often means devaluation of the currency, making domestic production more competitive internationally, while increasing the cost of imports. Many developing countries also placed considerable restrictions on the permitted levels and forms of international investment in their economy. Restrictions on the parts of the economy in which foreign investment is allowed, higher levels of taxation for international firms, and limits on the expropriation of capital have all been typical in the past, especially before the 1980s. However, free market policies argue that there should be no discrimination against foreign capital wishing to invest in the country and that any barriers to investment should be removed. The NICs of South-East Asia are often seen as examples of the successful implementation of free trade policies (see Box 4.2).

Since the 1990s, the Washington Consensus has been criticized. This has been partially as a result of prolonged growth in a number of countries where the policy has been rejected and also as a result of criticism of the handling by the IMF of the Asian financial crisis (Stiglitz 2002). Following on from this criticism—and led in particular by the World Bank—a revised set of policies has emerged. These have been described as the 'post-Washington Consensus'. While there is still a focus on market mechanisms, and 'getting the prices right', the state is seen as playing an important role in terms of overseeing the financial system, and providing education and instituting infrastructural projects.

Limits on comparative advantage for developing countries

The examples of the Asian NICs suggest that, in certain circumstances, free market policies can contribute to rapid economic growth. Why have other developing countries not been able to replicate this success? Why has the enormous growth in international trade not resulted in a wider distribution of the fruits of that trade, as the theory of comparative advantage would suggest? And why have some parts of the developing world barely participated at all in the growth of world merchandise trade? Africa's share of such trade is now less than its contribution of over 5 per cent in 1980, for example, and the developing countries of the Americas have remained static at just under 6 per cent (UNCTAD 2008a). Critics of the neoliberal agenda suggest that, in some ways, much of the developing world is disadvantaged in the global economy compared to more developed countries.

Following decolonization, the same basic pattern whereby the developing areas under colonialism were primarily providers of raw materials and markets for manufactured goods has largely persisted, with some notable exceptions (see Weiss 2002). For many non-Asian developing countries, over 70 per cent of exports still comprise primary products. In Africa, the contribution of manufacturing to gross domestic product (GDP) is falling (UNCTAD 2012b). This can be a problem for developing countries because of the failure of the prices of primary commodities to keep pace with manufactured goods (known as the 'declining terms of trade'). Also primary commodities have historically been liable to confront very large fluctuations in prices, coffee being a particular example.

Between 1997 and 2001, the United Nations Conference on Trade and Development (UNCTAD) combined price index of all commodities in US dollars fell by 53 per cent in real terms—that is, primary commodities lost more than half their purchasing power relative to manufactures (UNCTAD 2003: 19).

While commodity prices rose during the first decade of the twenty-first century, fluctuations make it harder to predict what revenues will be derived from exports in any particular year. Agricultural products are particularly prone to large price fluctuations. Years during which there is a glut in production can lead to price falls, while crop failures can lead to massive price increases. Agricultural production can also be hit by changes in fashion in the developed world. One exception to this pattern for primary commodities has been oil (see Box 4.4).

Many developing countries have also been hampered in their attempts to participate more fully in the global economy by a continuing and chronic shortage of capital. Investment is significant for trade, particularly in the modern world economy, because it is possible to compete in the most profitable areas only with the most up-to-date equipment. When equipment is outmoded or the technology outdated, it becomes harder to manufacture goods, or even to extract raw materials or grow crops that can compete on the global market. Patterns of FDI are discussed in the next section.

A further problem that developing countries confront is that of protectionism. Perhaps the simplest form is the implementation of a trade tariff, the application of a tax on imports. A large element of the Common Agricultural Policy (CAP) of the European Union involves the use of tariffs to protect farmers from certain agricultural products from outside Europe. One effect of these tariffs is that countries within the European Union produce more than 40 per cent of the world's agricultural exports (WTO 2012: Table II.13). Another form of protectionism is the use of subsidies: for example, US cotton farmers receive large subsidies on their production, to the disadvantage of African producers such as Egypt. Furthermore, there are non-tariff barriers, such as quotas, whereby only specified quantities of a product can be imported, and other restrictions such as safety requirements, and environmental or labour standards that must be adhered to, and which might be judged unreasonable (see Chapter 17). This whole area has been described as the **'new protectionism'** because governments have sought to defend domestic industries, while at the same time honouring commitments to lower trade tariffs as part of international agreements.

It has been estimated that developing countries are losing US$1,000 billion each year from protectionist measures in industrialized countries (O'Brien and Williams 2010: 153). Tariff barriers are far higher in

BOX 4.4 THE ORGANIZATION OF THE PETROLEUM EXPORTING COUNTRIES (OPEC)

In terms of commodity exports, oil represents a special case. Nevertheless, it highlights further the difficulties that commodity exporters face. The Organization of the Petroleum Exporting Countries (OPEC) was founded in 1960 by a number of oil-producing countries in the developing world in an attempt to increase export revenues. In the 1950s, world oil consumption was growing rapidly. But oil prices fell throughout the decade. However, between 1970 and 1973, OPEC succeeded in doubling oil prices, through negotiation with Northern governments. Then, between October 1973 and January 1974, OPEC was able to further quadruple oil prices, by reaching an agreement between the members to restrict supply. In the 1970s, OPEC's success in increasing oil prices seemed to be a signal to developing countries that others too could get a better price for their commodity exports. But was oil a special case?

OPEC is an example of an export quota commodity agreement. Its members have been able to manipulate the price by regulating the supply. But this is not easy, especially because not all major producers are members. On the supply side, export quota commodity agreements tend to be fragile because there is always a temptation for producers to defect. When prices rise through joint action to limit supply, there is always a risk that some member(s) will exploit the situation by increasing their supply to take advantage of the higher price. At times, this has been a problem for OPEC and would be a much bigger issue were the number of producers to be larger, for example millions of coffee growers. Moreover, oil is not

perishable and to leave it in the ground does not affect its quality, unlike agricultural goods, which cannot be stored indefinitely. On the demand side, there are ways of reducing its use (seeking other non-OPEC-controlled sources; using increased insulation; using coal, nuclear power, or synthetic substitutes; reducing energy use generally), but these take time to introduce. Oil is still an essential item even if the requirements of climate mitigation recommend using less. And although oil as a proportion of total energy use has declined since the 1970s (in 1973, oil supplied 46.1 per cent of the world's energy requirements, compared to 34.4 per cent in 2006), this decline has to be seen in the light of an overall increase in demand for oil, particularly from rapidly growing economies such as China and India.

Since 2003, oil prices have been rising rapidly, reaching a peak in the summer of 2008. This has been the result partially of events in Afghanistan and Iraq, and partially of an increased demand for oil. For many oil-importing countries in the developing world, this has resulted in a worsening in their economic position. Compared to developed countries, developing countries use more than twice as much oil to produce one unit of economic output. However, for oil-producing countries, the increased oil price has provided increased export earnings and government revenue. Some argue that this allows authoritarian governments in oil-producing countries to entrench their positions, contrary to a global shift towards democracy (Friedman 2006), whereas Youngs (2009) takes a more sceptical view

Sources: International Energy Agency (2008); BP (2009)

---

developed countries than in the rest of the world. At the same time, the richest countries in the world have increased their subsidies to their agricultural industries, making it harder for developing countries to compete.

KEY POINTS

- Since 1945, there have been significant increases in the levels of international trade.

- Although there are some exceptions, many countries in the developing world do not appear to have benefited greatly.

- Although the theory of comparative advantage suggests that all countries would benefit from participation in trading, the 'gains from trade' are not shared equally, for various reasons.

Foreign Direct Investment

The theory of comparative advantage suggests that a country should specialize in those goods that it can produce relatively more cheaply. One area in which the developing world has a distinct economic advantage is in labour costs. Throughout the developing world, it is cheaper to employ workers than in developed economies. It would therefore seem logical for companies from the developed world to relocate production from those economies in which labour costs are high to those in which such costs are lower. For some companies, the employment of female workers has been particularly attractive (see Box 4.5).

With improvements in transportation and communications associated with globalization, it has become easier for companies to set up production facilities in different parts of the world. O'Brien and Williams

BOX 4.5 WOMEN IN THE GLOBAL ECONOMY

In 2008, of the 3 billion people in paid employment worldwide, 1.2 billion were women. Of these 1.2 billion, only 18 per cent were employed in industry (compared to 26.6 per cent of men). Women are consistently overrepresented in the agricultural sector, especially in Asia and Africa, and a larger proportion of women are employed in the service sector. Women tend to be subject to more insecure employment, and have less choice in terms of sector of employment and working conditions. Wage inequality between men and women is a worldwide phenomenon. In most countries, women can expect to earn 70–90 per cent of their male counterparts' pay, and in some parts of Asia and Latin America, even lower proportions (ILO 2009).

One issue that has been particularly relevant to the role of women in the global economy has been the employment of women in export-processing zones (EPZs) in developing countries. Export-processing zones have been set up by governments to encourage inward investment by foreign companies, manufacturing products such as electronics, toys, and clothes. The factories are often described as 'sweat shops' because of the poor conditions for workers. Women are disproportionately represented (although in some countries this trend may be slowing) (Braunstein 2006), because they are deemed more suitable—that is to say, passive and prepared to accept low wages and no job security, as well as being nimble-fingered and amenable to training (Elson and Pearson 1981).

(2010: 186) define FDI as 'investment made outside the home country of the investing company in which control over the resources transferred remains with the investor'. In other words, a key feature of FDI is that production will be directed by (and presumably organized to benefit) a corporation from outside the territory in which the investment is made. One of the aims

of much recent policy promoted by the World Bank and IMF has been to encourage governments in the developing world to promote inwards investment—for example by reducing taxation levels and removing controls on capital flows. However, there has been much debate about the extent to which investment by TNCs benefits the host economies, with accusations

BOX 4.6 ADVANTAGES AND DISADVANTAGES OF FOREIGN DIRECT INVESTMENT

Advocates of FDI argue that TNCs offer the following benefits.

- *They introduce additional resources.* In particular, they bring capital—a resource of which many developing countries are particularly short. Furthermore, they bring technology, financial resources, managerial expertise, and access to foreign markets.

- *They increase tax revenues.* In general, TNCs will contribute to government revenues by paying local taxes.

- *They increase efficiency.* By providing links to the global economy, TNCs introduce competition into the local economy, thus encouraging more efficient local production.

- *They improve the balance of payments.* It is suggested that TNCs achieve this by producing local goods that previously had been imported and by producing goods for export.

Critics suggest that TNCs bring with them the following disadvantages.

- *They bring little in the way of new technology.* Most of the activities carried out by TNCs primarily involve assembly of

parts produced elsewhere and involve very little in the way of high technology.

- *They contribute little to the local economy.* Through a process known as 'transfer pricing', TNCs are able to ensure that they pay their taxes on profits in countries with low tax regimes (usually in the developed world). Furthermore, critics argue, TNCs drive local firms out of business by using unfair competitive practices.

- *They worsen the balance of payments.* It is argued that TNCs can have a negative impact on the balance of payments as a result of the need to import machinery and spare parts, and to make payments to the parent company.

- *They adversely affect the local culture.* By introducing global brands, TNCs can undermine the market for locally produced goods and tastes.

- *They have a negative effect on the political system.* Because TNCs are so large and powerful, and have a large impact on a small economy, they are able to extract concessions from governments by threatening to withdraw their facilities, or as a result of bribery and **corruption**.

Table 4.2 Foreign direct investment inflows by region (US$bn)

Region	1980		1990		2000		2011	
	Total	% of total	Total	% of total	Total	% of total	Total	% of total
World	54.1		207.5		1,400.5		1,524.4	
Developed world	46.6	86	172.5	83	1,138.0	81.3	747.9	49
Developing world	7.5	14	34.9	17	255.5	18.2	684.4	44.9
Central and Eastern Europe	0.02	0.03	0.07	0.03	7.0	0.5	92.2	6.1
Africa	0.4	0.7	2.9	1.4	9.7	0.7	42.7	2.8
Latin America and the Caribbean	6.4	11	8.9	4.3	97.8	7	217.0	14.2
Asia	0.5	0.9	22.6	10.9	147.8	10.6	423.2	27.8

Source: UNCTAD (2012a: 7.2.1). The United Nations is the author of the original material.

that they use their size to extract inordinate benefits (see Box 4.6). This is an area of much controversy, and it is better to look at the actions of individual TNCs in different countries rather than necessarily to draw general conclusions.

There are considerable data on levels of FDI, and one feature of this activity is that it fluctuates year on year. Levels of FDI dropped off quite considerably following the **terrorist** attacks on the World Trade Center in New York in 2001, although they now appear to be increasing again. Tables 4.2 and 4.3 present data taken from statistics compiled by UNCTAD. From these tables, a few general observations can be derived, as follows.

Table 4.3 Top ten recipients of foreign direct investment in the developing world, 2011

Country	US$bn	% of developing world total
China	124.0	18
Hong Kong, China	83.1	12
Brazil	66.7	10
Singapore	64.0	9
British Virgin Islands	53.7	8
India	31.6	5
Mexico	19.6	3
Indonesia	18.9	3
Chile	17.3	3
Saudi Arabia	16.4	2

Source: UNCTAD (2012a: Table 7.2.1). The United Nations is the author of the original material.

- Levels of FDI have risen considerably since the early 1980s. In 2011, levels of FDI were nearly thirty times higher than they had been in 1980. The bulk of this expansion occurred between 1980 and 2000. Although levels of FDI decreased from their peak in 2008, they have now started to show some recovery.

- Developing economies are now receiving increased levels of FDI. In 1980, developing economies accounted for only 14 per cent of FDI. By 2011, this had risen to almost 45 per cent. In 2010, the proportion of FDI flowing into developed economies dropped below 50 per cent for the first time—signalling the significance in this shift. It is also worth noting that TNCs from the developing world are now some of the largest companies in the world, for example PetroChina, the largest Chinese oil company.

- Although the proportion of FDI flowing to the developing world is increasing, it is very concentrated. Just ten countries absorb more than 50 per cent of FDI directed to the developing world. In 2011, China was the largest recipient, and the combined figures for China and Hong Kong account for 30 per cent of developing world FDI, although this figure has been higher in previous years. The relative proportion of FDI flowing into Africa remains very low.

KEY POINTS

- Foreign direct investment is a major component of global financial flows.
- Although much investment occurs in developed countries, a small number of developing countries receive a significant, and increasing, proportion of the global total.
- There is considerable debate over the costs and benefits of FDI for developing countries.

Financial Flows

Trade and FDI are the more visible aspects of the global economy, yet in numerical terms they are dwarfed by the movements of money through the world's foreign exchanges. World merchandise trade amounts to approximately US$18 trillion per year (UNCTAD 2012a: Table 1.1.1). This is the equivalent of just over

BOX 4.7   SUSAN STRANGE ON THE IRRATIONALITY OF FINANCIAL MARKETS

Mad. . . is exactly how financial markets have behaved in recent years. They have been erratically manic at one moment, unreasonably depressive at others. The crises that have hit them have been unpredicted and, to most observers surprising. Their behaviour has very seriously damaged others. Their condition calls urgently for treatment of some kind.

(Strange 1998: 2)

four days' trading on the world's money markets (BIS 2010: 6). The sheer size of these financial flows compared to the volume of global production suggests that a large component of these transactions is speculative (see Scholte 2005: 166). The operation of financial markets and the rapid flows of what is described as 'hot' money are often perceived as having an adverse effect on local economies, especially those in the developing world, and have been the subject of considerable criticism (see Box 4.7).

These financial flows comprise two main elements. First, quite simply, is the buying and selling of money. Some of these transactions are related to trade and investment. For example, if a company in Britain were to want to purchase goods from Ghana, it would first need to purchase Ghanaian cedi in order to pay the supplier. However, much of the activity on the global currency markets could be more closely equated to gambling. Since the 1980s, many of world's major currencies have been free-floating. In other words, governments have allowed the value of the currency to be largely dictated by the sentiments of the market. Some investors have made, and continue to make, large fortunes simply based on the buying of currencies that they anticipate will go up in value and selling those that they expect will become worth less. These financial movements can have implications for even the largest of economies: in 1992, Britain was forced out of the European Exchange Rate Mechanism following large-scale selling of sterling.

A second feature of global financial flows is investment in the stock markets of other countries, usually described as 'portfolio investment', or indirect foreign investment. Foreign direct investment usually involves the construction of factories and offices, and the purchase of machinery. If the owner wishes to move production to another country, these need to be disposed of or transferred, which may be a time-consuming activity. Holders of portfolio investments, however, do not have a direct link to the bricks and mortar of the company concerned; they can sell their holdings of shares in overseas territories at the press of a computer button. This buying and selling of shares can take the pattern of a herd instinct. Certain countries or regions become very popular, meaning that large numbers of shares are bought, leading to stock market booms. At other times, the same regions suddenly become unpopular, meaning that large numbers of shares are sold, leading to stock market crashes. These sudden changes of sentiment often have very little to do with the underlying economic stability or potential of the countries concerned. However, as with the buying and selling of currencies, for the insightful (or lucky) investor there are fortunes to be made by 'buying cheap and selling dear'. Furthermore, rapid movements of money into and out of economies can be extremely destabilizing to the domestic economy.

During the late 1980s and early 1990s, many countries in the developing world were encouraged to open their economies to these kinds of financial flow. Financial liberalization involved removing restrictions on the buying and selling of the country's currency, and on the movements of capital in and out of the country. Such policies were adopted by many countries in Latin America, East Asia, and the former Soviet Union. For many analysts, it is not a coincidence that these regions were afflicted by severe financial disruption during the 1990s. Examples are the Mexican peso crisis of 1994–95, the Brazilian crisis of 1998-99, Russia's rouble crisis of 1998, and a crisis in Argentina dating from 2000.

Perhaps the most famous of the financial crises of the 1990s was the one that swept through East Asia in 1997. There is much debate about the causes, and no simple explanation. However, one factor might be that these countries were simply the victims of their own success. As discussed in Box 4.2, East Asian countries were very successful at following export-led models of development. They also were enjoying very high levels of domestic saving and low inflation—a perfect conjunction for continued growth. However, following financial liberalization, the perceived profitability of the region led to a vast inflow of speculative investment that the countries' domestic financial institutions were not able to manage. A speculative boom was followed by a crash. Bankruptcies in South Korea and Thailand led to a rapid withdrawal of funds from the entire region. The outcome was reductions in the rate of growth and in GDP per head, the second taking

several years to recover. Analyses by the World Bank and IMF now suggest that the pace of financial liberalization was the problem. It is also worth pointing out that India and China, two of the fastest-growing economies in the world, have not implemented equivalent levels of financial liberalization and were only indirectly affected by the crisis that swept through the region.

The Global Economy in Crisis: Implications for the Developing World

Many commentators claim that the global economic crisis that has persisted since 2007 is the most serious since the Great Depression of the 1920s and 1930s. In 2009, global gross national product (GNP)—that is, the aggregated GNP of all the world's economies—dropped for the first time since the Second World War. While there was something of a rebound in 2010, rates of growth in developing countries have been decreasing since, prompting fears of a prolonged economic downturn (see ILO 2013: 1). In particular, concerns focus on the economic instability and debt problems in the eurozone, which have the potential to spill over into the rest of the world, so that any recovery might be short-lived, with further disruption on the way. Although the crisis originated in the developed world, particularly the United States, it became a global crisis with particular implications for developing areas. Whilst the origins of the crisis may look complicated, in essence it was an old-fashioned credit crisis, sparked by ill-advised mortgage lending in the United States (the so-called 'sub-prime' market). This crisis spread to the banking sector more generally, resulting in an unwillingness by banks to make loans. As a result, economic activity slumped in the world's most advanced economies. This had a ripple effect on the global economy, creating some specific problems for developing regions.

First, there have been substantial impacts on world trade. According to the WTO, the rate of growth in 2007 was 5.5 per cent, down from 8.5 per cent in 2006. The level of trade declined by 11 per cent in 2009 (Deshpande and Nurse 2012: 3). As more developing countries become integrated into the world economy, and often rely on exports to contribute substantially to GDP, this is significant. Commodity prices have been affected. In the initial phases of the crisis, commodity prices declined, although there has been a recovery since 2009. Many developing countries are heavily reliant on the export of raw materials and are vulnerable to fluctuations in commodity prices. According to the World Bank, non-oil commodity prices declined by 38 per cent in the second half of 2008. There are some benefits from a drop in commodity prices. For oil-importing countries in the developing world, the drop in the price of oil from its July 2008 peak provided some relief on the import side, but the price began climbing again in late 2009.

The loss of income from exporting has been compounded by a reduction in financial flows into developing countries. The level of FDI increased dramatically since the 1980s with an increasing proportion of investment taking place in developing countries. Growth of FDI has slowed considerably over the past decade, with the levels in 2011 not far above those of 2000. However, an increasing proportion of this is directed towards developing economies.

Two further sources of income for developing countries, remittances and international development aid, will be affected. Remittances are money transfers from workers in one country back to their families in their country of origin. For some countries, remittances (especially from the Gulf states to South Asian countries) can contribute significantly to GDP, and for many families in the developing world remittances from a family member working abroad can make a sizeable addition to the household income. In previous economic crises, rich country governments have cut their aid budgets (UNCTAD 2009b) and this seems likely to happen again, as they spend heavily on bolstering domestic economic activity.

Countries in the developing world are therefore affected by multiple reductions to their economic well-being—including loss of income from exporting

possibilities, fluctuating commodity prices, and cuts in FDI, remittances, and aid. Many developing countries (in Africa especially) are more likely to be affected by the economic downturn: most do not have the financial resources to substitute increased public spending for reduced capital and income streams from abroad. However, this goes beyond the purely economic realm. The global economic crisis is likely to result in increased numbers living in absolute poverty, throwing into reverse recent modest reductions in the numbers. According to the United Nations Standing Committee on Nutrition (UNSCN), the numbers living in extreme poverty have increased by 130–155 million in 2005–08, with a further increase of 53 million expected in 2009 (UNSCN 2009). The global position is increasingly gloomy, with unemployment levels estimated to be 29 million higher in 2011 than would have been expected based on pre-crisis trends (ILO 2012: 34). The most recent edition of the Food and Agriculture Organization (FAO) report *The State of Food Security in the World* indicates that while considerable advances have been made in reducing hunger and malnutrition in the developing world, the global economic crisis has brought hunger reduction to a standstill (FAO 2012: 11).

KEY POINTS

- Since 2007, the global economy has entered a period of considerable instability. A credit crisis in the world's most developed economies has expanded outwards towards all sectors and regions of the global economy.

- Developing countries have been particularly susceptible to the downturn as a result of the slowdown in the rate of global trade and reductions in investment, remittances, and aid.

Conclusion

Since 1945, the global economy has seen not only massive increases in the levels of world trade, but also an enormous growth in the prosperity of the developed world. With the emergence of a single global economy since 1990, these processes have accelerated. For most analysts, these two features are closely linked. Yet the benefits of greater engagement in the global economy do not appear to have been obtained by the poorest countries. Why, in an era of a global economy and neoliberal policies, does the gap between the richest and the poorest appear to be widening?

A free market analysis would suggest that there are still too many blockages to the free movement of investment and goods. Poorer countries have undermined their own prospects of development by working against the market. A second position maintains that greater engagement is potentially beneficial, but that, because developing countries are behind the developed world in terms of industrialization, reforms to the global economy are required. A more radical position would argue that the global economic system entrenches inequality between the richest parts of the world and the poorest. For the past twenty years, the free market philosophy has dominated development policy (see Chapter 16). But although many developing countries have followed neoliberal prescriptions, they still face protectionist measures imposed in the developed world. This makes it more difficult to persuade them to proceed more quickly or in a more comprehensive fashion. Protectionist measures in the developed world have caused WTO talks on further trade liberalization to stall.

The reasons for the disparity of wealth in the global economy will be disputed indefinitely. For the foreseeable future, developing countries will have to make their way within a global capitalist environment. The operation of global markets has the potential to generate enormous wealth, as well as the capacity to exploit the most vulnerable. The governments of developing countries have the awesome task of trying to minimize the negative impacts of global capitalism, while attracting the potential benefits for their populations. Economic crisis makes this task even more difficult. China's rise (see Chapter 28) displays the possibilities for developing countries in a global economy. Indeed, China's rapid economic expansion is a contributory factor in decreases in global absolute poverty. Yet China has not played, so far, by the globalization 'handbook'; its participation in the global economy is by its own rules. Thus far, this seems to have been to its benefit, although consequences flowing from its accession to the WTO in December 2001 are now causing some resentment. Meanwhile, governments of the developed world also confront a challenge: how to resolve the contradiction of promoting free trade as a solution for the developing world while maintaining protectionism at home. Until they resolve this, it would appear that the global economy operates largely in the interests of the rich and powerful, and against some of the poorest and least influential parts of the world.

? QUESTIONS

1. Has globalization been a positive or negative force for developing countries?

2. Who benefits most from the global trading system?

3. Should developing countries be wary of foreign direct investment?

4. What was the Asian financial crisis? What are its lessons for developing countries?

5. What is protectionism? What are its implications for developing countries?

6. Explain how the recent financial crisis, in particular in the eurozone, affects the global economy and how this creates specific problems for developing regions?

≋ FURTHER READING

Dicken, P. (2011) *Global Shift: Mapping the Changing Contours of the World Economy*, 6th edn (London: Sage) Clear overview of the emergence of a global economy, with good sections on the NICs

Mandle, J. R. (2003) *Globalization and the Poor* (Cambridge: Cambridge University Press) A good overview of arguments for and against economic globalization

O'Brien, R. and Williams, M. (2010) *Global Political Economy: Evolution and Dynamics*, 3rd edn (Basingstoke: Palgrave Macmillan) Clear discussion of the development of the global economy and key contemporary issues in international political economy

Scholte, J. A. (2005) *Globalization: A Critical Introduction*, 2nd edn (Basingstoke: Palgrave) A superb discussion of the subject and associated literature

Todaro, M. and Smith, S. (2009) *Economic Development*, 10th edn (Harlow: Pearson) Regularly revised and updated, contains excellent chapters on the role of developing countries in the global economy and on theories of trade

Valdez, S. (2007) *An Introduction to Global Financial Markets*, 5th edn (Basingstoke: Palgrave) Effective introduction to the murky world of global finance

Van Marrewijk, C. (2002) *International Trade and the World Economy* (Oxford: Oxford University Press) Excellent introduction to theories of trade and investment in the global economy

WEB LINKS

http://www.cato.org/research/international-economics-development The site of the Cato Institute ('individual liberty, free markets, and peace'), a Washington DC-based, non-profit, public policy research foundation committed to the principles of limited government and free markets, including free trade

http://www.oxfam.org The site of the non-governmental organization Oxfam (UK), containing many of its reports on trade and protectionism

http://www.twnside.org.sg/trade.htm Third World Network page on trade issues; provides research critical of current global economic policies

http://www.unctad.org The site of the United Nations Conference on Trade and Development, containing voluminous data on trade and investment, and reports on the latest developments in the global economy

http://www.undp.org The site of the United Nations Development Programme—the UN body that focuses on development issues and produces an annual Human Development Report

For additional material and resources, please visit the Online Resource Centre at:
http://www.oxfordtextbooks.co.uk/orc/burnell4e/

5

The Developing World in International Politics

Stephen Hobden

Chapter contents

Overview

The previous chapter examined the role of the developing world in the global economy. In this chapter, the emphasis changes to the role of the developing world in international politics. International relations, as a discipline, has traditionally overlooked the significance of the developing world in global politics. The chapter opens by discussing the reasons for this and why such an oversight is lamentable. It then looks at the position of the developing world throughout the large structural changes that have occurred in the international system since 1945: the cold war; the post-cold-war world; and the emerging multipolar world, in which China is anticipated to return to the centre of international politics.

Introduction: International Relations and the Developing World

The **developing world** has been 'on the periphery' of the study or discipline of international relations (IR) (Thomas and Wilkin 2004). The discipline has primarily been concerned with relations between the great (or super-) powers. Although perhaps understandable, this focus is deeply problematic. First, it has meant that at least four-fifths of the global population were excluded as a subject of study; second, it overlooks the central role played by developing countries as actors in international **politics**, and as sites of confrontation and competition. This has reflected a North American and European perspective on the world. It fails to acknowledge that while, during the cold war, there was a 'long peace' in Europe, many parts of the developing world were deeply mired in violent conflict, in which the superpowers were frequently involved. Superpower rivalry was played out in a way that was far from 'cold', fuelling **proxy wars**, for instance in southern Africa and Central America. Third, it overlooks and underestimates fundamental changes to the international system: the dissolution of the European empires; and the increasing power of a number of countries, but in particular China.

The focus on the superpowers may reflect a deeper problem with the discipline. That is quite simply that traditional IR theory lacks the tools with which to understand the developing world. In the traditional world view of IR, the state is the key actor and guarantor of the 'good life' for its citizens. States operate in a situation of 'anarchy' in which all have equal sovereignty and must, in the final instance, be liable for their own self-defence. Within the confines of the state, there is order and hierarchy, while outside is characterized by unregulated disorder. From the perspective of the developing world, this world view may make little sense. The state, rather than being the guarantor of the 'good life', has frequently been a major threat to individual well-being. Many developing countries have been governed at some time or another by military **regimes**, which have targeted sections of the society for repression. The states of Latin America have, by and large, lived at peace with each other since the 1930s, but regimes in virtually every country in the region have committed major **human rights** violations. The anarchy has been on the inside rather than the outside. Furthermore, the state, rather than being the key actor, has had to compete with numerous other powerful actors, such as **warlords**, guerrilla groups, and drug cartels, which in some places appear to threaten its very existence. International financial institutions (IFIs), such as the International Monetary Fund (IMF) have played significant roles in overseeing the running the economies of states that have signed up to **structural adjustment programmes (SAPs**—see Chapter 16). At the same time as domestic politics in the developing world perspective can be viewed as disordered, the external world appears to be more hierarchical, with the most powerful states determining the fates of the less powerful. Sovereignty, the right of states to govern within their own territory without external interference, a fundamental tenet of the Charter of the United Nations, has been breached many times since 1945 (see Dickson 1997: ch. 1; Neuman 1998: 2–12).

While traditional approaches have tended to focus on those states with the most power, there have always been perspectives that attempted to incorporate an analysis of the developing world. Marxist approaches, in particular dependency and world-systems schools, have stressed the importance of a global economic system in which the developing world has played a key role as the supplier of cheap labour and raw materials, and as a market for surplus production. More recently, post-colonial theorists (heavily influenced by **post-structuralist** approaches) have focused on questions of identity during and after the colonial period (see Chapter 2).

KEY POINTS

- The discipline of international relations has tended to focus on the role of the great (or super-) powers.

- This focus has ignored the vast proportion of the global population, and the key role that the developing world has played in the global politics of the cold war and post-cold-war periods.

North–South Relations during the Cold War

The cold war

The term 'cold war' refers to the period of confrontation between the United States and the former Soviet Union between 1945 and 1990. The international system during this time is often described as 'bipolar', meaning that there were two superpowers, although the now obsolete notion of a 'Third World' is also closely linked to this period. This term is derived from a perceived tripartite division of the world:

- a 'First World', comprising the United States and its allies;

- a 'Second World' comprising the Soviet Union and Eastern Europe; and

- a 'Third World' comprising the rest—that is, the newly decolonized countries of Asia and Africa, and the countries of Latin America, most of which had gained their independence at the start of the nineteenth century.

This was a ridiculous oversimplification, although the ideological and strategic conflict played out between the superpowers certainly had a major impact on most Third World countries. This conflict took a variety of forms. There were cases of direct military intervention by the superpowers, such as the United States in Vietnam and the Soviet Union in Afghanistan. There were many examples of indirect intervention using either the 'carrot' of aid, or the 'stick' of sanctions, or the threat of the withdrawal of aid. There was also the use of proxy fighting forces to avoid direct intervention. Examples here include US funding of the Mujahidin to challenge the Soviet Union in Afghanistan and the use of the Cuban army to support leftist governments in southern Africa.

Once both superpowers had access to nuclear weapons, any direct confrontation would have been, in the terminology of the time, MAD—that is, 'mutually assured destruction'. However, a history of the cold war is incomplete without a consideration of how superpower competition was conducted in the developing world. A range of interests underpinned the superpowers' policies towards the developing world. For both, there were security issues, both had trading concerns, and for both there were ideological issues that related to their views of themselves as nations. These different interests played out differently at different times.

In the beginning of the cold war (1945–55), the US government's main interest in developing areas was in supporting calls for decolonization, in line with its world view that a decolonized world would be more in its own interests. This was coupled, however, with concern that newly independent countries should not fall under Soviet influence. Therefore there was a tension between the United States' support for decolonization and its wish to maintain international stability. Additionally, with the triumph of Mao's revolutionary army in China and North Korea's invasion of the South of the country, there was fear that communist influence was spreading in East Asia. The Soviet Union was barely engaged at this time. Stalin, now in physical decline, did not try to exploit Lenin's theory that the developing world was a weak link for

the capitalist system and had done little to support the Communist Party in China.

From the late 1950s and through the 1960s, both superpowers increased their activities in the developing world. The United States was particularly active in its own 'backyard', supporting the overthrow of democratically elected President Arbenz in Guatemala (1954) and attempting to overthrow the revolutionary regime in Cuba (1961 onwards). Throughout this period, it also became increasingly involved in the war between North and South Vietnam. Following the death of Stalin, the Soviet Union gave more attention to the newly independent countries, seeking to draw them under its influence. However, it lacked the power projection to protect potential satellite states. For example, in 1960, Prime Minister Lumumba of the Congo sought military aid to counter secessionists in his newly independent country, but the Soviet Union was not able to respond and the country soon came under the rule of Joseph Mobutu, who looked to the West. Likewise, in the autumn of 1962, the Soviet Union withdrew the missiles that it had placed on Cuba rather than risk a direct military confrontation with the United States.

As, through the 1960s, the United States became increasingly drawn into the Vietnam quagmire, confidence about its role in the world declined, and anti-US sentiment grew. The Soviet Union was now getting closer to strategic parity with the United States and was able to project its power with greater confidence. It gave direct support to revolutionary movements in Vietnam, Ethiopia, and Angola, and as a result gained strategic bases in Africa and Asia. It also supported revolutionary movements in Central America, giving it influence very close to the United States. This growing confidence led it to launch a major military intervention in Afghanistan in late 1979 to support a friendly regime on its southern border.

The global situation changed dramatically in the following decade. It was now the Soviet Union that was mired in a foreign war, and the United States, under President Reagan, exploited the situation. The United States sought 'rollback'—reversing Soviet gains of the 1970s—and under the 'Reagan doctrine' support was given to anti-communist guerrillas. In Afghanistan, the United States supported the Mujahidin, in Nicaragua, the 'Contras', and in Angola, the National Union for Total Independence of Angola (UNITA). As the decade drew on, the cold war moved to a close. Mikhail Gorbachev's 'new thinking' as leader of the

Soviet Union sought a new relationship with the West and a Soviet withdrawal from Afghanistan. The impact of the Afghan war on the Soviet Union was at least comparable to that of the Vietnam War on the United States. Although not the sole cause of the Soviet Union's collapse, within two years of the withdrawal from Afghanistan, Communist Party rule had ended. At the same time, material support for former satellite states, even Cuba, also ended.

The cold war was a time of great upheaval for the developing world. In the period immediately after the Second World War, most of it was still under colonial control. By the end of the cold war, it was mostly independent. This wave of decolonization was accompanied by an international conflict between the two superpowers, fought over and in developing countries. For their governments, it meant choosing to align with one superpower or the other. This pressure provoked the creation of the Non-Aligned Movement (NAM) in 1961—a collection of states that claimed to reject both superpowers, although in reality most states (Cuba, for example) were aligned with one or other. The NAM has survived the end of the cold war and its 120 members continue to meet on a tri-annual basis.

The existence of two competing superpowers meant that a choice existed for developing countries. Many countries were courted by both sides, with rival offers of financial and economic aid. For some, the possibility existed of switching allegiances (or at least of threatening to switch). Egypt in the early 1970s

changed its alignment from the Soviet Union to the United States, becoming one of the largest recipients of aid. The cold war provided these countries with at least an option between two superpowers with two ideologies concerning the operation of social and economic systems, and the goals and modalities of development (see Halliday 1989; Allison and Williams 1990; Merrill 1994; Westad 2005).

The United Nations

The United Nations (UN) was created during the latter part of the Second World War as an organization the key role of which was the maintenance of international peace and security. Although most would argue that the UN has been singularly unsuccessful in this respect, it has played a significant role in a number of others. In addition to its security remit, the Charter of the organization also commits its members to cooperation on economic and development issues, and these have had a number of implications for developing countries. In this development sphere (or the 'other UN'), the organization can perhaps claim the largest area of success (see Box 5.1). Furthermore, the organization had an inbuilt predisposition towards decolonization. Charter signatories with responsibilities for non-self-governing territories (in other words, colonies) committed 'to develop self-government, to take due account of the political aspirations of the peoples, and to assist them in the progressive development of their

---

BOX 5.1 THE UNITED NATIONS' ACHIEVEMENTS IN DEVELOPMENT

The UN has been involved in development issues in a number of ways, including:

- as an information source, with experts in economics, agriculture, and industrial development;

- offering direct assistance in emergency situations;

- the creation of regional organizations to address the particular problems of specific areas, for example the Economic Commission for Asia and the Far East;

- specific development responsibilities of UN agencies, for example the UN Development Programme (UNDP) and the UN High Commissioner for Refugees (UNHCR);

- numerous resolutions in the General Assembly related to development issues; and

- a series of 'development decades', intended to keep issues such as global inequality on the agenda.

The UN can point to a number of areas of success, including:

- life expectancy globally has increased;

- child mortality rates for under-5s have decreased;

- immunization levels have improved, as have access to primary health facilities, the availability of clean water, and literacy levels; and

- an achievement that can be directly attributed to a UN agency is the eradication of smallpox, coordinated by the World Health Organization (WHO).

That the organization retains such goals is demonstrated by the Millennium Declaration adopted in September 2000. This pledged that member states would work towards ambitious goals, including halving the proportion of the world's population living on less than US$1 a day and ensuring that all of the world's children receive a primary education (see Chapter 16).

BOX 5.2 THE UNITED NATIONS AND DECOLONIZATION

The end of the European empires is one of the most significant developments of the last century. The oversight of this process is perhaps one of the UN's greatest achievements. The notion of self-determination is at the core of the Charter, articulated in Article 1(2) and repeated in Article 55. Furthermore, a pledge to develop self-government in non-self-governing territories (a euphemism for colonies) is made in Article 73.

In the immediate aftermath of the Second World War, a small number of countries became independent, for example India gained independence from Britain in 1947. The first move of newly independent countries was to take up a seat in the UN General Assembly as a mark of sovereignty and independence. The newly independent states were critical of the continuation of empire and the General Assembly became the main forum in which calls for decolonization were voiced. By 1960, there were sufficient members to allow the passing of Resolution 1514, which condemned the continuation of colonialism. In the 1960s, several African states became independent and further resolutions were passed calling for colonialism to be eradicated.

The UN also acted in a very practical way to smooth the process of decolonization. The withdrawal of colonial powers from territories was seldom straightforward, frequently leaving civil strife and disastrous levels of **underdevelopment**. The UN was frequently drawn into such situations, as peacekeeper and provider of essential services. With the withdrawal of the British from India, massive unrest broke out between the Hindu and Muslim populations of India, and the newly created state of Pakistan. There was massive loss of life and displacement of population. The UN Security Council voted to send an observer group to monitor the situation in the hope that an outside group might calm the situation. The United Nations Military Observer Group in India and Pakistan (UNMOGIP) was created in 1949 to patrol the border area in Kashmir. It remains in place today.

Decolonization also transformed the organization itself. There were fifty-one original members in 1945, and the United States and the West in general had a built-in majority in the General Assembly. By 1960 (when Resolution 1514 was passed), the situation had changed dramatically—to 100 members, of whom sixty-six were from the developing world, including forty-six from Africa and Asia. By this point, the General Assembly was supporting the position adopted by the United States in around half of all votes taken. By 1980, more than half of the UN consisted of non-founder members, which had not been sovereign states in 1945. Their loyalty to a US-dominated world order was low, and the vast majority of the votes in the Assembly were against the US position and in support of the Soviet Union. As a result, the General Assembly became the forum for issues that were a priority for the developing world.

free political institutions' (UN Charter, Article 73.B). As discussed in Box 5.2, the UN played a key role in the process of decolonization, and in turn the character of the organization was transformed.

KEY POINTS

- During the cold war, the superpowers intervened in the developing world in a variety of different ways.

- The superpowers were motivated by a variety of interests, including military security, trade, and ideology, the significance of which differed over time and location.

- The cold war brought instability for many developing countries. However, in a world in which neutrality from the global struggle was difficult, there was a choice of ideology and model of development.

- A key feature of the cold war period was the dissolution of virtually all of the European colonies. The United Nations was a key actor in, and was itself transformed by, this process.

North–South Relations after the Cold War

A new world order?

The end of the cold war in the late 1980s was greeted with optimism. The United States emerged as the 'winner' of the contest, and appeared to enjoy an unassailable position in terms of economic, military, and political power. Some argued however, that this dominant position (or unipolarity) might be short-lived (see Krauthammer 1991). How would the remaining superpower employ that considerable power and what would be the implications for the developing world? The father and son presidencies of George H. W. Bush (1989–93) and George W. Bush (2001–09) appeared to demonstrate very different visions of what came to be called the 'new world order'.

In a 1991 speech, US President George H. W. Bush spoke of a new world order that would be 'an historic period of cooperation … an era in which the nations of the world, East and West, North and South, can prosper and live in harmony' (quoted in Acharya 1999: 84). In the early 1990s, there was a sense that a new form of global cooperation could solve many of the world's problems. For many in the developed world, this sense of peace and well-being was enhanced by a prolonged economic boom through much of the 1990s.

For developing countries too, there were reasons to be optimistic. The cold war had been a cause of instability, and its end promised greater peace and stability. Accompanying the end of the forty-year superpower conflict, a number of regional conflicts were also resolved—particularly in southern Africa (Mozambique, Namibia, and temporarily in Angola) and Central America (Nicaragua and El Salvador). A new spirit of cooperation in the UN Security Council enabled that organization to become more active in conflict resolution. The UN achieved notable successes in Namibia, El Salvador, and Cambodia. It authorized an international military response to Iraq's invasion of Kuwait in 1990. Furthermore, a number of corrupt regimes that had been supported by one side or the other were replaced by democratic governments. There was much talk of a 'peace dividend' and considerable reductions in arms spending, which could be funnelled towards development projects. At the Millennial UN General Assembly, ambitious commitments were made by the member states to reverse global poverty. Also, the prospect of a truly global economy appeared to promise more extensive trading links, with the hope of generating greater wealth.

Such developments did indeed suggest that the world had reached the 'end of history', as claimed by Francis Fukuyama in 1992. There were indications, however, that this view might be optimistic. A UN-sponsored intervention in Somalia resulted in humiliating withdrawal following the killing of eighteen US soldiers. In 1994, the global community looked the other way while **genocide** occurred in Rwanda. A more sombre account of post-cold-war international relations was provided by Samuel Huntington's view that the cold war would be replaced by a **clash of civilizations** (see Box 5.3). The **terrorist** attacks on the United States in 2001 ('9/11') appeared to confirm this gloomy prognosis and the euphoria of the immediate post-cold-war period was replaced by a 'global melancholy' (Halliday 2002: 214). The prospects for developing countries started to look less promising. While the end of the cold war did provide greater stability in some areas, there has been greater instability in other regions. Afghanistan, for example, has been in a constant state of upheaval, and the Democratic Republic of Congo descended into chaos, with its neighbouring countries intervening on opposing sides.

With the election of George W. Bush, concerns started to surface about how the United States would use its position as the only superpower. The unipolar era of cooperation appeared to transform into one in which 'cooperation' would be very much on the terms and in the interests of the dominant power. In the aftermath of 9/11, the US government declared its willingness to act unilaterally and pre-emptively to further its national security interests, and the invasion of Iraq in 2003 occurred without the clear support of the UN Security Council (see Box 5.4).

BOX 5.3 THE 'END OF HISTORY' OR A 'CLASH OF CIVILIZATIONS'?

With the end of the cold war and the emergence of the United States as the dominant world power, two accounts of international politics made a crossover from the academic arena into the wider policy and media arenas. Both had implications for North–South relations. In 1989, Francis Fukuyama published a much-discussed article in which he speculated whether, with the demise of the Soviet Union as an ideological and military threat to the United States, the human race had reached the end of history:

The triumph of the West, of the Western *idea* is evident first of all in the total exhaustion of viable systematic alternatives to Western liberalism. What we might be witnessing is not just the end of the Cold War, or the passing of a particular period of post-war history, but the end of history as such: that is the end

of mankind's ideological evolution and the universalisation of Western liberal democracy as the final form of human government. The vast bulk of the Third World remains very much mired in history and will be a terrain of conflict for many years to come, but large scale conflict must involve large states still caught in the grip of history, and they are what appear to be passing from the scene.

(Fukuyama 1989: 4, emphasis original)

Fukuyama's was essentially an optimistic liberal account. The global future was liberal democracy. Crucially, because conflict between democratic states was unlikely (the so-called **'democratic peace theory'**), the future prospect was for a more peaceful world.

A different view was offered by Samuel Huntington in an equally famous article, published in 1993. Rather than having reached the end of history, when conflict over the best form of social organization was over, Huntington argued that there were real differences at a civilizational level that would, in the future, lead to conflict:

The fundamental source of conflict in this new world will not be primarily ideological or primarily economic. The great divisions among humankind and the dominating source of conflict will be cultural. Nation states will remain the most powerful actors in world affairs, but the principal conflicts of global politics will occur between nations and groups of different civilizations. The clash of civilizations will dominate global politics. The fault lines between civilizations will be the battle lines of the future.

(Huntington 1993: 22)

This more pessimistic, **realist**-influenced view of global politics suggests that the future will be dominated by conflict between the developed and the developing world, although primarily divided by civilization.

This gloomier sentiment has been echoed by Andrew Bacevitch (2011), perhaps marking an end to the vision that Fukuyama popularized at the end of the cold war. Writing in the *Washington Post*, Bacevitch argues that:

[T]he beliefs to which the end of the Cold War gave rise— liberal democracy triumphant, globalization as the next big thing and American dominion affirmed by a new way of war— have all come to rest in that unmarked grave reserved for failed ideas.

(Bacevitch 2011)

BOX 5.4 US PRESIDENT GEORGE W. BUSH, 9/11, AND THE 'WAR ON TERROR'

There has been much discussion about whether the administration of George W. Bush, the attacks of 11 September 2001, and the subsequent **'war on terror'** marked a distinct turning point in US foreign policy. Two aspects of the Bush administration policy looked particularly important. First, the United States appeared more prepared to act unilaterally, and to be openly hostile to global organizations and commitments. Before 9/11, the Bush administration had signalled that it would withdraw from the Kyoto Agreement, which the previous Clinton administration had been involved in negotiating. Following 9/11, the invasions of both Afghanistan and Iraq occurred without a UN Security Council mandate. The invasion of Iraq occurred after an attempt to get UN authorization had been blocked in the Security Council. This leads to a second perceived area of major change: the so-called 'Bush doctrine'. Under this doctrine, the United States claimed a right to intervene in other countries not only to *prevent* an imminent threat of attack on the United States, but also to *pre-empt* such a threat from emerging. According to the September 2002 US National Security Strategy:

For centuries, international law has recognized that nations need not suffer an attack before they can lawfully take action to defend themselves against forces that present an imminent danger of attack. . . We must adapt the concept of imminent threat to the capabilities of today's adversaries. . . The United States has long maintained the option of preemptive actions to counter a sufficient threat to our national security. . . To *forestall* or prevent such hostile attacks by our adversaries, the United States will, if necessary, act preemptively.

(White House 2002, emphasis added)

The presidential letter accompanying the Strategy document (White House 2002) puts the point more directly: 'As a matter of common sense and self-defense, America will act against such emerging threats before they are fully formed.'

These two developments appear of particular concern to countries of the developing world. International organizations and international law provide some measure of protection for the weak against the strong. By distancing itself from such arrangements, the US government indicated that it was not prepared to be constrained by international commitments. Likewise, the claimed right to intervene in countries solely on the basis that a threat to US security *may emerge* is open to abuse.

However, did foreign policy under the Bush administration change dramatically? Although it played a central role in the creation of much of the current international architecture, the United States has always had vacillating relations with international organizations. Relations with the UN have been uneasy since the General Assembly became dominated by countries from the developing world following decolonization. They were particularly difficult during the Reagan era, when the United States fell into serious financial arrears. Furthermore, the United States has displayed a consistent pattern of intervention in countries of the developing world, during and after the cold war. In the immediate aftermath of the cold war, the United States invaded Panama (during the presidency of George W. H. Bush)—a country that could hardly be considered a threat to US security. The most distinctive feature of US foreign policy during the George W. Bush presidency was perhaps the readiness of policymakers to be explicit about the rationale of foreign policy (Slater 2004: 190).

President Obama: change and continuity in US foreign policy

With the inauguration of a new US president in January 2009, there were signs of a change of tone in relations between the United States and the rest of the world. In the early phase of the Obama presidency, there appeared to be significant attempts to re-forge the relationship with the Muslim world. Indications included the 'Cairo' speech in June 2009 and hints that pressure would be put on Israel to negotiate with the Palestinians. On the basis of this change in approach, Obama was awarded the Nobel Peace prize in 2009—an award that many commentators thought was, to say the least, premature.

Hopes for a radical change in the direction of US foreign policy were disappointed during Obama's first term. While relations between the US administration and the Israeli government have been tense, there has been no progress on an Israeli–Palestinian peace process, and no indication that the US government would be prepared to use its considerable financial leverage to pressurize Israel to negotiate. The US military completed a withdrawal from Iraq in 2011, ending a conflict that Obama had consistently criticized. However, the US military remained in Afghanistan, making this a conflict comparable in length to that in Vietnam. There has also been considerable criticism of the continuation of drone attacks against targets in Pakistan. Generally seen as a stain on the reputation of the United States internationally, the detention camp at Guantanamo Bay, Cuba, remains active despite Obama's promise to close it within the first year of his presidency.

A more sympathetic assessment of the first Obama presidency would point to the spectrum of problems that the new president faced, particularly with regard to the US economy. These have limited the time and resources that the US president has been able to devote to an international agenda. To an extent, these problems reflect the declining international position of the United States and the transition to a period beyond the post cold war. The United States remains militarily dominant, but in relative terms its economic power is weakening, along with its political and ideological capabilities.

The global picture for developing countries during the period of US dominance was mixed. Some states benefited from a greater stability, while for many global citizens the end of the cold war has

meant greater instability. The post-cold-war boom of the 1990s also offered increased possibilities for more countries to participate in the global economy. However, the demise of the Soviet Union removed an option of choice: there was now one global economy and one system—capitalism—and the costs of defaulting from this system became higher. The option of playing one superpower off against the other no longer existed and hence the room for manoeuvre was reduced (see Mesbahi 1994; Swatuck and Shaw 1994; Fawcett and Sayigh 1999; Halliday 2002).

KEY POINTS

- At the end of the cold war, the United States appeared to be in an unchallengeable position. This had implications for the developing world.

- A post-cold-war peace dividend has failed to appear for the developing world. Although some areas experienced greater stability, many have not. Fears increased regarding the deployment of US power, especially under George W. Bush.

- The period of US predominance in international affairs now appears to be drawing to an end.

All Change? The Developing World in the 'Chinese Century'

The changing structure of the international system

Since 1945, the international system has experienced three major structural changes. Thus far, we have discussed decolonization and the end of the cold war, which resulted in a (short) period of US pre-eminence. This section assesses the third transformation, currently under way and perhaps the most significant of all. Its most prominent feature is the rapid economic development of China. (See Box 5.5 for a discussion of some views on the implications of China's rise and see also Chapter 28.)

While China's economic development is breathtaking, it should not blind us to developments in other parts of the world (particularly India and Brazil), and the appearance of a new grouping of economically dynamic countries. These have been described by Parag Khanna (2009) as the 'second world' (not to be confused with the communist Second World of the

BOX 5.5 THE END OF THE WESTERN WORLD?

Traditional accounts of the modern world have tended to depict the European example both as somehow exceptional and a model for the rest of the world. Europe and North America have been the dominant powers for the last 200 years. However, developments in the writing of world history (see Frank 1998; Hobson 2004) suggest that this was something of an exception and that, for most of recorded history, the East has been the leading power in economic, scientific, military, and political terms. Furthermore, the rapid growth of China's economy leads some to argue that the brief period of Western/North American domination is drawing to a close. But what does the rise of China mean for international relations?

Is it the end of the Western world?

In his provocatively entitled *When China Rules the World*, Martin Jacques (2012: ch. 11) argues not only that China is likely to become the dominant power internationally, but also that it will provide a very different model of society and development from that which the West has promoted.

Does it mean that conflict is inevitable?

For realist writers, power transitions (that is, when one hegemonic power is challenged by another) rarely occur without conflict. China's rise and the United States' apparent decline indicate that such a power transition is occurring, and is unlikely to happen peaceably. Thus Mearsheimer (2010: 382) warns:

China's rise. . . is likely to lead to an intense security competition between China and the United States, with considerable potential for war. Moreover, most of China's neighbors, to include India, Japan, Singapore, South Korea, Russia, Vietnam—and Australia—will join with the United States to contain China's power. To put it bluntly: China cannot rise peacefully.

Yet Chinese President Hu Jintao (2003–13) stated in his report to the Eighteenth Congress of the Chinese Communist Party that 'China will unswervingly follow the path of peaceful development and firmly pursue an independent foreign policy of peace'.

cold war). He argues that the countries of this second world are crucial to understanding developments in international politics; he notes that 'the second world shapes the global order as much as the superpowers do' (Khanna 2009: x). While, for Khanna, China is both part of the 'second' world, and one of three competing empires (together with the United States and European Union), another formulation has been to group it with Brazil, Russia, and India as the BRICs (or sometimes BRICS, which includes South Africa).

The BRICs are seen by some analysts as a rival grouping to Western-based organizations such as the G8, and a challenge to Western domination in organizations such as the World Trade Organization (WTO), IMF, and World Bank. The basis for much discussion of the BRICs was a report produced by the accounting firm Goldman Sachs, entitled *Dreaming with BRICS: The Path to 2050* (Wilson and Purushothaman 2003). Its startling conclusion was that, by 2050, the BRICs' combined gross domestic product (GDP) would exceed that of the current six largest economies (the United States, Japan, Germany, Britain, France, and Italy). While some of the report's underlying assumption may be questionable (pessimism about growth rates in the current largest economies; over-optimism regarding growth prospects of the newly emerging economies), it does indicate that even if the comparative growth rates for the BRICS are less than expected,

major changes can be expected in the global architecture that could have enormous implications for all global actors, and especially developing countries (see Box 5.6). The economic crisis that has engulfed much of developed economies since 2008 (as discussed in Chapter 4) has hastened these trends. By 2011, China had become the second largest economy, with Brazil passing Spain in 2009, Italy in 2010, and the UK in 2011 to become the sixth-largest economy in the world. Similarly, the economies of Russia and India are moving up the ranks of the world's ten largest economies.

Implications for the developing world

Significant changes are occurring to the structure of the international system. A particular feature is the coming to prominence of large countries that would previously have been considered as developing (especially Brazil, China, and India)—potentially a truly revolutionary change. This section examines some of the possible implications for the developing world (see also Chapter 28 on China).

China's reach

China, according to one Chinese government official, is 'all over Africa' (cited in Large 2008). A striking impact of China's economic rise is the extent to which its influence is being exerted over regions formerly

BOX 5.6 THE BRICS ARE COMING!

The term 'BRICs' to designate Brazil, Russia, India, and China was coined by Goldman Sachs economist Jim O'Neill in 2001. Since 2008, this label has gone from being an economic label to a political reality, with the BRICs members holding regular summit meetings to discuss a range of economic and political issues. In 2010, South Africa was invited to join the grouping, after which the acronym became 'BRICS'. South Africa hosted the fifth summit meeting of the group in March 2013. These countries are seen not only as economic challengers to the current core economies, but also as representing a distinct set of interests, possibly at odds with the present dominant powers.

Without disputing the current exceptional growth rates of these countries, the view that the BRICS constitute a coherent bloc is questionable. First, their economies are radically different: Brazil and Russia's prime connection to the global economy is dependent on the export of raw materials; China,

on assembled manufactured goods; India, largely on services. Second, they have radically different political systems: India and Brazil are fully functioning and lively democracies; South Africa is a functioning democracy, although dominated by one party; Russia is a quasi-democratic authoritarian state; while China is a one-party state. Furthermore, China has not always had the most peaceable relations with Russia and India.

The formulation of the term BRICs/BRICS has led financial analysts to dream up a number of alternatives, such as CIVETS (Colombia, Indonesia, Vietnam, Egypt, Turkey and South Africa) and MAVINS (Mexico, Australia, Vietnam, Indonesia, Nigeria, and South Africa). These groupings, however, reflect the concerns of analysts looking to make investments in rapidly growing economies. At the current time, none of these subsequent groupings reproduce the potential political challenge of the BRICs.

within the European and North American spheres of influence. This may offer benefits to many developing countries, but also comes with potential risks. This has been particularly marked over areas of Africa. Rising commodity prices during the early years of the twenty-first century are often connected to China's enormous demand for raw materials (Johnson and Blas 2009). China has become a major trading partner with a number of African countries and also a major aid donor. The significance of this growing relationship between China and the continent of Africa was demonstrated when China held a November 2006 summit in Beijing that was attended by representatives from more than fifty African countries. A range of trade investment and aid proposals were announced. A major feature of this growing influence has been a 'no strings attached' basis for trading and aid relations. China has been prepared to enter into friendly relations with countries considered to be pariah states by European and North American countries. For example, China has received considerable criticism for its relations with Sudan, a significant source of oil for the Chinese economy. While China has provided a ready market for many of Africa's exports, it has done little to alter the composition of those exports. This has led to fears that the neo-colonial relations with the West might be being reproduced, albeit with a different power. Former South African President Thabo Mbeki warned about the possible unequal relationship between African countries and China: 'China cannot just come here and dig for

raw materials and then go away and sell us manufactured goods' (cited in Alden 2007: 120). Despite these potential fears, China has been able to expand its contacts with African countries, prompting fears in North America and Europe that it may become the dominant power on the continent. There are also indications of the growing influence of China in Latin America, a traditional site of US hegemony (Roett and Paz 2008).

Increased North–South conflict

The emergence of competing centres of power in the international system, and in particular the alternative development and political model offered by China, has reintroduced the possibility of choice of alliances for developing countries. There is some evidence that this increased range of possibilities has prompted developing countries to be more prepared to challenge the dominance of Europe and the United States in international financial institutions. A key example of this is the breakdown by 2008 of the Doha Round of WTO trade agreements. Developing countries in a variety of coalitions blocked discussions of a range of issues of interest to the United States and Europe, pending progress helpful to their agricultural exports. Hurrell and Narlikar (2006) provide a detailed account of the possible contours of future North–South confrontation.

The return of bipolarity

The discussion of the cold war earlier in this chapter indicated that, while there was peace in Europe, the conflict between the superpowers was very far from 'cold' in the developing world, with a range of interventions through Asia, Africa, and Latin America. One possibility of the end of the unipolar moment and the appearance of China as a possible second polar power is the return of great power confrontation and action along the lines that were evident during the cold war. Some US writers have already indicated their concerns about increased Chinese influence in Africa (see Campbell 2008) and growing links with Latin America. A direct military confrontation between China and the United States would be, as in the cold war, 'MAD', but this does not exclude the possibility of their rivalry again being played out in military form in the developing world.

Regional integration

The overlap between the international economy and international politics is also found in the attempts of developing countries to pursue policies of regional integration. Regionalism emerged as a separate strategy with a first wave in the 1960s, but that had run its course by the early 1970s and a second wave of, or 'new', regionalism in the 1990s. The prime aim of the first wave of regionalism was to increase the size of the market for locally produced manufactures. Regional blocks were also thought potentially to increase negotiating power in international organizations. One of the features of the first wave of regional organizations, such as the Caribbean Community and Common Market (CARICOM, established in 1973), was the attempt to implement a high level of political control over production, so that decisions about the siting of industrial production were supposed to be made at a regional level. The idea was that, by sharing out industrial production, the benefits from economies of scale could be maximized. This proved to be both politically and economically unviable. The first wave of regionalism foundered when the required degree of political cooperation and coordination failed to materialize. The maintenance of high tariffs once again resulted in inefficient industries, unable to compete internationally. Weak transport and other infrastructural links also played a part.

By the mid-1970s, many of the first wave of regional organizations were moribund in all but name. However, in the 1990s, a 'new' regionalism emerged, inspired by the European Union. These organizations adopted a much larger free market agenda, without the political baggage associated with the first wave. Some formerly dormant organizations, such as the Central American Common Market (CACM), have been revitalized, and other new groups have emerged, such as MERCOSUR—the Common Market of the Southern cone, in South America (see Box 5.7). The aim of these organizations has been to promote interregional trade through the lowering of internal tariffs, without ambitious attempts at controlling the economic diversification of the countries involved.

In some ways, this can be seen as a reaction to the impacts of **globalization**. As a way of protecting their economies from the pressures of the global economic market, countries in different parts of the world have joined together to form regional blocs. However, in some ways, the 'new regionalism' can be viewed as a way of accelerating the speed of globalization. The aim of the old regionalism was to erect *external* barriers to protect domestic production; the aim of the new regionalism is to *reduce* internal barriers to trade as a means of promoting trade within the region (Payne 2004: 16–17).

Nuclear proliferation

A further area of change in relations between North and South is with regard to nuclear weapons, and their proliferation. In 2009, there were eight known nuclear weapons states: the United States; Britain; France; China; Israel; India; Pakistan; and North Korea. At the start of the twenty-first century, there are fears that the non-proliferation regime is breaking down and that more states will be drawn into developing nuclear weapons, as a form of defence both against their neighbours and against a perceived threat from a unilateralist superpower.

Central to limiting the spread of nuclear weapons has been the Non-Proliferation Treaty (NPT), which came into force in 1970. In essence, the NPT sought to limit the spread of nuclear weapons technology and to push for disarmament (or at least a reduction in the numbers of nuclear weapons), while allowing non-nuclear states to develop nuclear energy under international supervision. Implicit in the Treaty was an agreement between nuclear and non-nuclear states: the nuclear states would move towards disarmament; and the non-nuclear states would not attempt to develop, or obtain, the technology. With the exception of North Korea, it could be argued that the Treaty has 'worked' in the sense that, as far as

BOX 5.7 A PROFILE OF MERCOSUR, THE COMMON MARKET OF THE SOUTH

The origins of MERCOSUR date back to 1985, when Presidents Raúl Alfonsín of Argentina and José Sarney of Brazil agreed an 'Argentina–Brazil Integration and Economics Cooperation Program'. MERCOSUR itself came into existence in 1991, comprising Argentina, Brazil, Uruguay, and Paraguay. Venezuela became a full member in July 2012 and Bolivia is moving towards full membership at the time of writing. Chile (since 1996), Colombia (since 2004), Ecuador (since 2004), and Peru (since 2003) are associate members, which means that they can enter trade agreements with member states, but remain outside the institutional mechanisms of the organization.

The stated aims of the organization are to increase the free movement of goods, capital, services, and peoples amongst member states, with the possible introduction of a common currency being considered. As an intergovernmental organization, it is often compared to the European Union, and is one of the most developed regional trade agreements in the developing world in institutional terms. In terms of area, it is four times the size of the EU, with a population of 250 million people. The economic activity of MERCOSUR comprises more than three-quarters of that on the South American continent.

While, in relation to previous attempts at regional integration, MERCOSUR could be counted a success, it has not been without problems. Deepening of integration, in particular a move towards a full customs union, has been delayed by the economic storms that have swept the continent, in particular Argentina's financial and economic collapse in 2001. There have also been trade disputes between Brazil and Argentina over car production, and between Uruguay and Argentina over the construction of pulp mills on the Uruguay–Argentine border. Furthermore, the two smaller members, Paraguay and Uruguay, have complained that they enjoy only restricted market access to the economies of the two larger members.

On the international stage, MERCOSUR has clashed with the United States over the possibility of creating a Free Trade Area of the Americas (FTAA). While in principle all countries in Latin America seek to be part of the FTAA, disputes have concerned both the nature of the agreement and the process of its creation. MERCOSUR members, in particular Brazil, have sought to counter what is regarded as a neoliberal agenda implicit in the agreement. Furthermore, they have encouraged the countries to negotiate as a bloc, rather than as individual states, which has increased the continent's bargaining power related to the United States. The failure to agree an FTAA in many ways parallels the collapse of the Doha Round of the WTO: the issues, in particular rich country farm subsidies, were similar; Brazil played a key role in both.

Sources: Carranza (2004); BBC News (2008).

---

we know, no other signatory has obtained nuclear weapons. India, Pakistan, and Israel have never been signatories. North Korea was a signatory, but announced its withdrawal from the Treaty in 2003. The Islamic Republic of Iran is now considered to provide the most serious challenge to the non-proliferation regime. Yet it is very unclear whether Iran is seeking nuclear weapons or merely developing a nuclear energy capacity (for an excellent discussion, see Lodgaard 2007).

Since the attacks on the United States on 11 September 2001, the issue of non-proliferation has become entwined with the 'war on terror'. The concern has been that (given that the attacks indicated the organizational ability and murderous intent of non-state actors) nuclear materials might be obtained by groups planning such attacks. This became part of the motivation for the 2003 attack on Iraq and the enormous international pressure currently being placed on Iran.

KEY POINTS

- The structure of international politics is again in flux with a (relatively) declining United States confronting a resurgent China, plus a group of 'second world' countries enjoying rapid **economic growth** and enhanced international influence. This affects the developing world in several ways.

- In particular, China has emerged as a major alternate source of influence, trade, aid, and investment. This may result in a return to confrontation in the developing world between the United States and China.

- Regionalism has increased significantly, with regional blocs perceived as a possible source of confrontation between North and South.

- The nuclear non-proliferation regime appears to be under strain, with Iran a current focus of concern. (See the Online Resource Centre for a case study.)

Conclusion

The notion of a 'Third World' was primarily a construction of the cold war. As the conflict drew to an end, increasing diversity between regions, based on divergent rates of economic growth and competition between countries for the supposed fruits of globalization, has eroded the perception of shared interests that underlay earlier groupings, such as the Non-Aligned Movement (NAM). Regional groupings are now tending to replace specific Third World organizations. The increasing economic power and confidence to act on a global stage displayed by countries such as India, and especially China, indicate the major changes that are occurring in the international system. The implications for all actors in the international system are enormous. While it may not be the end of the 'Western world', the 200-year period in which Europe and North America have been dominant appears to be drawing to a close, with a multipolar and culturally plural world replacing Western dominance.

The central argument of this chapter has been that countries in the developing world have had, and continue to have, a major impact on international relations. Through the various permutations (bipolar, unipolar, multipolar) that have constituted the international system, the countries of the developing world have consistently played a significant role in international relations—as sources and sites of conflict, and as challengers to the existing political and economic order. Part of this contribution has come through the form of international organizations, such as the NAM. The diversity of patterns of development now means that organizations claiming to represent all less-developed countries are unlikely to be effective. The new drive to regionalism offers an alternative forum and possibilities of exerting greater influence in negotiations with the developed world. The emergence of a global economy also offers immediate advantages to some. Where capital is more mobile, developing countries can exploit their advantage as sites of low wage production. Countries in which there are high educational standards are particularly likely to be able to gain from this. For example, India has been particularly successful in attracting jobs in the information technology and call centre sectors. India, Brazil, and China are all regional superpowers, able to exert their influence internationally. In due course, the first two might gain more formal institutional recognition in the UN Security Council if that body is reshaped. The emergence of what has been described as a 'global **civil society**' offers additional possibilities. **Neoliberalism** is under attack from some quarters in the developed world, as the anti-globalization movement has demonstrated. There are increasing avenues for the development of transborder and supraterritorial alliances between the peoples of the North and South.

The character of the global system remains unsettled following the end of the cold war. But the situation of the majority of the world's population who reside in the developing world should become a more central area of study for those who seek to comprehend international processes.

?   QUESTIONS

1.   Account for the failure of international relations theorists to include North–South relations in their analyses.

2.   How significant was the developing world in the cold war conflict between the Soviet Union and the United States?

3.   Assess the significance of decolonization on the international system.

4.   Have events since 11 September 2001 proved that Fukuyama's claim that we have reached the 'end of history' was incorrect?

5.   What are the implications for the Western liberal order of the rapid economic growth of China?

6.   Does the changing structure of the international system imply more friction in the relations between developed and less-developed countries?

7.   Does the increased significance of regional trading organizations mean that globalization has stalled?

FURTHER READING

Duffield, M. (2001) *Global Governance and the New Wars: The Merging of Development and Security* (London: Zed) Analyses the position of the developing world in the emerging world (dis?)order.

Jacques, M. (2012) *When China Rules the World: The End of the Western World and the Birth of a New Global Order* (London: Allen Lane) Excellent study of China's rise and its implications for the international system.

Jawara, F. and Kwa, A. (2004) *Behind the Scenes at the WTO: The Real World of International Trade Negotiations* (London: Verso) Accessible account of the WTO, detailing negotiating practices of the member states.

Payne, A. (2005) *The Global Politics of Unequal Development* (Basingstoke: Palgrave) Superb discussion of issues of development and underdevelopment from a new political economy (NPE) perspective.

Slater, D. (2004) *Geopolitics and the Postcolonial: Rethinking North–South Relations* (Oxford: Blackwell) Outstanding overview of approaches to thinking about North–South relations, influenced by post-colonial and post-structuralist approaches.

Westad, O. A. (2005) *The Global Cold War: Third World Interventions and the Making of Our Times* (Cambridge: Cambridge University Press) Recent account of the cold war, focusing on the key role played by the developing world and the implications for contemporary international relations.

WEB LINKS

http://www.brics.utoronto.ca   The BRICS Information Centre, run by the University of Toronto, containing a wealth of information on developments within the BRICS.

http://www.economist.com/topics/mercosur   News on the MERCOSUR region from *The Economist*.

http://www.iaea.org/newscenter/focus/iaeairan/index.shtml   International Atomic Energy Agency page detailing negotiations with Iran relating to the Non-Proliferation Treaty.

http://www.imf.org   Official site provides details of role of the International Monetary Fund.

http://www.twnside.org.sg/econ_1.htm   Third World Network reports on international organizations.

http://www.un.org   Official site provides overview of the organization and workings of the United Nations.

http://www.worldbank.org   Official site provides complete overview of the operation of the World Bank Group.

http://www.wto.org   Overview of history, purpose, and working of the World Trade Organization.

For additional material and resources, please visit the Online Resource Centre at:
http://www.oxfordtextbooks.co.uk/orc/burnell4e/

PART 2
Society and State

In Part 2, we introduce the social and cultural aspects of developing countries within which their **politics** are embedded, and which are so central to understanding political behaviour.

The part has two main aims. The *first* is to indicate the great diversity of social structure found in the **developing world** and in countries individually; the variety in terms of religious, ethnic, and other identities; and the divisions to which these features, together with **gender**- and economically based inequalities, give rise. In contemporary social science, **civil society** also ranks very high as both a constituent feature and determining influence upon politics; that too can vary widely in practice. The role played by **social movements** and 'alternative politics' is also gaining in recognition.

The *second* aim is to show the political significance of these complex social contexts and diverse forms of social and political organization, and how problematic they can be for political management. They pose challenges, as well as opportunities, for the institutional arrangements centred on the state—in some cases expressly demanding political solutions outside of, and alternative to, the conventional mechanisms and processes of the state. The contents of this part thus set the scene for the investigation in Part 3 of how developing world states have responded to the many internal and external demands on them, and to their transformation in recent decades. So, for instance, societal features introduced in Part 2 can help to explain tendencies towards **state collapse** and the pressures to engage in political liberalization and democratization, as well as the forces resisting those agendas.

The illustrative material included in Part 2 is drawn widely from around the developing world. By comparison, case studies of individual countries selected to illustrate specific themes can be found in Parts 5–8. For example, tendencies towards social fragmentation and political disintegration in developing countries are revisited in Chapters 22 and 23 on Iraq and Mexico, respectively. The political ramifications of extreme inequality are illustrated in Chapter 26, with the case of Guatemala. This choice of countries illustrates the multiplicity of social, as well as economic and political, challenges that can be present during attempts at post-conflict reconstruction. It also shows how easy it is to oversimplify the consequences of diversity for political unity, especially when set against a background of rapid change from more authoritarian and less inclusive forms of political rule to governing arrangements that resemble more closely Western-style liberal democracy (as in Indonesia—see Chapter 21).

Readers are encouraged to study the introductions to Parts 5, 6, and 7, and to consult the relevant case studies in that section when reading the chapters in Part 2.

6

Inequality

Jenny Pearce

Chapter contents

Overview

Inequality is at the heart of discussions on the political economy of development, whether amongst development economists, sociologists, political geographers, or political scientists. The debate on the meaning, significance, and measurement of inequality, however, has taken many twists and turns. The two questions that have dominated development debates are: does growth inevitably lead to inequality? And if so, does it matter, as long as poverty declines? The debate around these questions began in the 1950s, with Simon Kuznets' 'inverted U-hypothesis', which posited that relative inequality increases, but only temporarily, in the early stages of economic development, improving once countries reach middle-income levels. Ultimately, initial inequality precipitated by economic growth does not prevent poverty reduction, although it might delay it. However, by the 2000s, while global poverty *and* inequalities between nations had declined overall (although the gap between the very richest and very poorest nations has continued to grow), inequality within many countries has increased and has prompted some to announce the 'end of the "Inverted-U"' (Palma 2011: 87). According to *The Economist* (Beddoes 2012: 13), 'more than two-thirds of the world's people live in countries where income disparities have risen since 1980 often to a startling degree'. The pattern that is of particular concern is the way in which the income share of the richest 1 per cent has risen not only in the United States, but also in the rising economic powers, such as China and India: the former had ninety-five billionaires and the latter, forty-eight, by 2013 (Beddoes 2012: 3). The combination of this extreme concentration of wealth, and the character and impact of the 2008 global crisis, gave rise to a new question: does inequality in fact hinder growth?

Introduction

This chapter first reviews the key conceptual debates on inequality until the end of the Second World War and the birth of the field of 'development'. It will then explore how inequality thinking impacted on the **developing world** during and after the cold war. An implicit post-war consensus emerged in the industrialized world in the 1950s that government had a responsibility to address inequalities. The cold war played its role in the debate. Western financial institutions sought to demonstrate that capitalist economics could address poverty and growth more effectively than socialist egalitarianism. By the mid-1970s, however, the distribution of income was deteriorating in many 'Third World' countries, as they were then known, and the debate on poverty and inequality intensified. A new paradigm of market **liberalism** and state retreat arose in the 1980s, underpinned by the rising interest in monetarist and neoclassical economics. These posed a serious theoretical and practical challenge to redistributive theories of justice. Concern with income inequality as a goal of development policy declined. Pro-poor growth became the core theme of development rather than the impact of growth on income distribution. This was reinforced by the post-cold-war so-called 'Washington Consensus' around **neoliberalism**; the **Millennium Development Goals (MDGs)** reflected the ascendency of this perspective.

However, the debate on inequality remained lively, nourished by new theoretical contributions outside of economics. The collapse of universalizing social theory, for instance, resulted in an unprecedented uncovering of differential life experiences throughout societies all around the world, which has favoured new thinking on social stratification dynamics. The cultural dimensions of inequality were exposed, while recognition of human differences suggested that the 'equality of man' is not necessarily the best foundation for egalitarian theory. In its 2001 *World Development Report*, the World Bank acknowledged that 'high initial inequality' did reduce the poverty impact of a given rate of growth (similar to Kuznets' arguments), and that there may even be circumstances in which addressing asset inequality can enhance economic efficiency and benefit growth. It also recognized that **gender** inequalities have a particularly negative impact on **economic growth**, as well as poverty reduction. Interventions

in the market can, it argued in a challenge to prevailing orthodoxies, aid poverty eradication amongst such socially disadvantaged groups as indigenous peoples, and certain **castes** and tribes. In 2005–06, both the World Bank and the United Nations Development Programme (UNDP) produced annual development reports dedicated to the themes of equity and inequality.

As some developing countries began to overtake the developed world in rates of economic growth, but manifested high rates of within-country inequality, the debate around inequality took on new intensity. This time, the debate is as much about the rich as the poor. While there are ongoing discussions about whether or how inequality matters to development, a growing number of voices even in the mainstream have begun to agree that inequality does indeed matter not only to growth, but also to political community and to **governance**. At the grass roots, inequality has become a source of **social movement** activity in the global North, particularly in the wake of the 2008 global financial crisis. Occupy Wall Street, for instance, juxtaposed the 99 per cent against the super-rich 1 per cent of the United States, one of the countries of the global North in which inequality had risen greatly since the 1970s (see Chapter 14). In the global

---

KEY POINTS

- Post-war acceptance that economic development can enhance inequality and that governments have some responsibility to redress this was questioned in the 1970s and 1980s, and overturned post cold war by the rise of neoliberalism.

- Major development institutions began to acknowledge in the new millennium that high existing inequality can retard poverty reduction.

- Recognition of human differences challenges the idea of 'equality of man'.

- Inequality within emergent economies added a new dimension to the debate in the 2000s and, by the second decade of the millennium, inequality within nations was rising, just as inequality between nations seemed to be reducing.

- Inequality has political, not only economic, impacts on the exercise of citizenship, and ultimately influences who determines development goals within and between nations.

South, middle-income countries of Latin America and mineral-rich Southern Africa are by far the most unequal regions of the world (Palma 2011). By the second decade of the second millennium, new approaches to conceptualizing and measuring inequality over time, as well as space, generated a raft of new questions about **globalization**, inequality, and their effects on life chances and choices of an imagined global citizenry (cf. Milanovic 2012a).

Key Conceptual Debates

The importance that we attach to the issue of inequality is rooted in some fundamental questions of political philosophy, and shifting values and norms. There is much disagreement about the meaning of 'inequality' and whether it matters, and conversely whether equality is a legitimate aspiration, and if so, how it is to be achieved.

Over the past two centuries or more, these questions have been discussed repeatedly. During this period, there was a 'steady erosion in the legitimacy accorded to social inequality . . . for students of social stratification, this . . . is perhaps the most important feature of the nineteenth and twentieth centuries' (Béteille 1969: 366). However, by the end of the twentieth century, the pursuit of greater social and economic equality had become increasingly discredited; such concepts as 'social exclusion' and 'pro-poor growth' gained ground. The poor became 'targets' of anti-poverty programmes. Traditional leftist concerns about distribution and '**exploitation**' were abandoned. At the same time, interest grew in human diversity. Identity and culture, and their relationship with equality, led to what Fraser (1997) calls a shift from the '**politics** of redistribution' to the 'politics of recognition'. Such a shift appeared to imply abandonment, or at least weakening, of the idea of economic equality in favour of more robust mechanisms for ensuring political equality. But does equality of civil and political rights compensate for, or even work in the context of, social and economic inequalities? The twist in the second decade of the millennium has been the return of income inequality to mainstream debate. The trigger has been the process of concentration of income amongst the very rich, highlighted by the 2008 global economic crisis. This section traces the ebbs and flows of these conceptual debates.

Ontological equality and equality of outcome

The idea that men are born equal emerged in the eighteenth century as a philosophical challenge to the prevailing assumption that social stratification was a result of natural differences of rank between individuals. The ancient Greeks had built the *polis* on that assumption and equality existed only in the political realm. However, their belief in political equality irrespective of social or economic **status** remains an abiding reference point for many (despite the notorious exclusion of women, slaves, and foreigners). Rousseau, in his *Discourse on Inequality* (1755), began his investigation into inequality by assuming instead the equality of man in a pre-social original state of nature—an assumption of **ontological equality**. In the course of the eighteenth century, the idea that men are equal, rather than unequal, by nature took hold, with powerful political and intellectual consequences. But it inevitably led to the question: what are the origins therefore of inequality? Rousseau's answer is usually summed up as 'private property'. Those who came to see private property as a social evil emphasized the need for society to promote **equality of outcome** despite individual human differences. Karl Marx made equality of outcome the central tenet of his vision of the good society.

For Marx, writing in 1845–46, inequality had its origins in the division of labour, as well as private property. It is the former that 'implies the possibility, nay the fact that intellectual and material activity—enjoyment and labour, production and consumption—devolve on different individuals'; with the division of labour comes the question of distribution and 'indeed the *unequal* distribution, both quantitative and qualitative, of labour and its products, hence property, the nucleus, the first form of which lies in the family, where wife and children are the slaves of the husband' (Marx 1970: 52). Capitalism is the most advanced system of labour division yet, in which the capitalist class owes its wealth to its exploitation of another class with only its labour to sell. Marx not only places this unequal relationship to the means of production at the heart of his class analysis of history, but also his emphasis on exploitation indicates that such inequality between classes is unjust, which became a very influential argument for socialist, and often nationalist, movements of the nineteenth and twentieth centuries.

Marxist thinking tapped into deeply felt injustices at the popular level. For some, largely pre-industrial, developing societies, Marxist ideas appealed to the desire to retain some of the primitive communal forms of equality that persisted in agrarian societies and to restrain the differentiating process that comes with socio-economic change. Much Third World sociology in the post-war years was an effort to clarify its distinct forms of class composition and social inequality, and the relationship between class formation and development. A particularly vibrant debate concerned the analytical categories for exploring relationships between the developed and underdeveloped worlds. Could one nation exploit another? Gunder Frank (1971) powerfully argued that it could and traced the history of **underdevelopment** from 'core' to 'periphery'. He was criticized by others who claimed that he saw feudalism and capitalism only in terms of market exchange, not in Marx's true sense of relations to production and class exploitation. The ideas of **unequal exchange** and dependency would nevertheless provide one of the most important frameworks for understanding inequalities between countries in the North and the South in the early post-war decades.

Differentiating inequalities: class, status, and power

Max Weber, writing early in the twentieth century, provided a more differentiated categorization than Marx. He argued that social divisions and the distribution of power that they convey encompass a range of non-economic, as well as economic, determinants. In addition to class stratifications that emerge out of a person's relationship to the market, there is status—a quality of social honour or a lack of it, which is mainly conditioned as well as expressed through a specific style of life. A status group can be closed ('status by descent') or it can be open.

Weber's understanding of the distinctiveness of status groups was particularly helpful for those wishing to understand social differentiations in situations in which market transactions were fairly simple and class formation limited. He also observed, however, that technological advances and economic transformation threaten stratification by status, and will push the class situation further into the foreground.

In terms of the developing world, Weber was able to draw into the picture the forms of social stratification that Marxists have often found particularly

difficult to explain, such as caste and tribe, and the distinctions between them. Caste, Weber argued for example, belonged to the 'closed status group', in which status distinctions are guaranteed not only by conventions and laws, but also by rituals, such as stigmatizing any contact between lower and higher castes through religious acts of purification. He explored the complexity of the **Hindu caste system** in India in some detail, seeking to explain its relationship to economic change, and its 'elasticity' and hence survival in the face of the logic of labour demands in the modern economy.

The nature of these traditional relationships and the impact of processes of economic change are particularly significant for an understanding of social divisions in the developing world. Systems of 'inherited inequality', such as those based on descent, lineage, and kinship, have persisted in many parts of the developing world. Anthropologists have long studied the lineage and kinship stratifications of indigenous populations. For example, Sahlins (cited in Béteille 1969: 239), who studied kinship in Polynesia in the 1950s, referred to 'a graduated series of different degrees of stratification'. He distinguished between stratified and egalitarian societies, and implied that ranking processes emerge in all human societies, but noted that they vary a great deal in terms of ranking criteria and how far they formally sanction social inequality (see Box 6.1). This is why writers such as Béteille (1969) have emphasized the values and norms that underpin social inequality or its qualitative dimensions. It has often been assumed that ranking on the basis of the hereditary principle will disappear with the process of economic development, and that industrialization will overcome the differentials associated with

BOX 6.1 BÉTEILLE ON INEQUALITY

Béteille (1969: 365) points out that the sanctioning of social inequality has taken place on very distinct grounds often legitimized by religious systems that paradoxically and simultaneously contain messages of equality. In the United States, commitment to the equality of man was a strong feature of cultural values and political ideals—even though, for many years, black people were denied the vote and were evidently not treated as equals by the dominant white population. Most societies have denied, and many still deny, women formal, as well as informal, social, economic, and political equality.

traditional and agrarian societies. The persistence of caste in India, where status is determined by birth and legitimized by religio-cultural belief, questions that assumption. In modern India, caste and class intersect in particularly complex ways, creating a potent and enduring source of social, economic, and political inequality.

But across the developing world even where 'closed status group' systems such as caste do not exist, kinship and ethnic group identity have been the basis of stratified, as well as segmented, forms of social differentiation. Ethnic coexistences have become the source of ethnically based stratifications at various points in history. Pre-colonial conquests, colonialism, and post-colonial political mobilization have all played a critical role in privileging some ethnic groups over others, and usually for some political, as well as economic, gain. As market economies expanded, so some ethnic groups were in a more privileged position than others to take advantage of opportunities. In this context, the debate about whether emerging stratifications are derived from market positioning, or from the logic of capital and its search for exploitable labour, or from **ethnic identity** per se has been particularly protracted. Thus relationship to production is a source of inequality, but not the only source of social differentiation. When class and status, and economic and social power all coincide, however, one of the most potent sources of inequality is created with the capacity to perpetuate itself through the generations.

The politics of inequality

One means by which inequality perpetuates itself is through the political system that develops around it. Unequal societies, no matter what the source of inequality, generate differential means of influencing political processes. This is true at all levels, from micro to macro, and in traditional as well as more 'modern' development contexts. That means that power and powerlessness emerge out of inequality, and create the source for recycling it. As societies undergo transitions from more traditional to 'modern' economies, traditional power structures and ways of exercising power have often adapted to changing social conditions, so that they survived more or less intact, or persisted in new, but recognizable, forms. As the idea of political contestation (if not modern democracy) began to take root in the developing world, it frequently did so in contexts in which political and economic power were

already tightly meshed. The 'delivery' of the political support of a dependent rural population to particular leaders and interests quickly became the norm. Such practices were then adapted to urban contexts, where the rapid growth of cities without adequate services or employment gave brokerage power to individuals with access to elites and decision-makers. **Clientelism** and **patronage** networks emerged throughout the developing world, creating vertical links to tie the poor to political power structures through favours granted in return for support. Such networks reflect differentials in power and income, and act as obstacles to independent political action and democratization, further entrenching the pre-existing structures of inequality. More than this, the relationships between dominated and dominant create internalized feelings of humiliation that have a lasting impact on generations of poor people (Scheper-Hughes 1992).

In Latin America, where inequalities across class, gender, and ethnic lines are so deeply entrenched, it is not surprising that centuries of humiliation can be overcome only when the denigrated group members gain dignity through building a positive identity around themselves. At the same time, this can serve to mobilize the previously dispossessed politically. This is clear, for instance, in the case of those indigenous people of Guatemala who, towards the end of the twentieth century, began to see themselves as 'Mayans' as a way of revaluing themselves and their differences from the non-indigenous elites who have dominated and oppressed them historically (see Box 6.2; see also Chapter 26).

BOX 6.2 HOW HISTORICALLY OPPRESSED GUATEMALAN INDIANS FIND DIGNITY IN THE WORD 'MAYA'

The term 'Maya' began to be used to unify identities beyond the local and linguistic groups, and for that reason also, they have called themselves 'pan Maya' (all the Mayans). To call themselves 'Maya' includes an entire shift towards a positive self-recognition. The terms 'Indian' and 'indigenous' were imposed by the invaders and their descendants, and have a negative weight, of stigma, that leads to subordination. In the face of those, 'Maya' is a term chosen voluntarily by the actors themselves, who consciously refer to belonging to a distinct group with historic roots and connected to a grand and ancient civilisation.

(Bastos and Camus 2003: 102)

KEY POINTS

- The ancient Greeks believed in the equal right to participate politically irrespective of social and economic inequalities.

- Both Rousseau and the French Revolution challenged assumptions that inequality was natural or divinely sanctioned; a good society should be dedicated to overcoming inequality.

- Marx believed that inequality derived from the division of labour, as well as private property, and advocated equality of outcome.

- Weber's notions of status and honour, derived from non-economic as well as economic determinants, assisted understanding of social stratification in the developing world.

- Social stratifications have exclusionary political consequences; clientelism and patronage are ways in which political brokers have used inequality to build a power base amongst the poorest.

The Politics and Economics of Inequality in Developing Countries: The Cold War and its Aftermath

In the twentieth century, the discussion around the relative weight to be accorded to equality as a goal in **human development** was intense and conflictive. In the mid-twentieth century, Tawney (1952: 106) made a case against the assumption that inequalities in industrial societies were simply the outcome of individual effort or failures. He argued that *opportunities* to rise were only one side of the picture and appealed for measures (for example progressive taxation and trade union rights) that would ensure that society actively aimed at 'eliminating such inequalities as have their source, not in individual differences, but in its own organization' (Tawney 1952: 57).

It was agreed that governments had some responsibility to pursue strategies of greater equality, although there was less agreement on what they were. Yet, by the 1960s, social scientists on both sides of the Atlantic questioned whether their societies were becoming more equal despite the welfare state, estate duties, and higher taxation (in the United Kingdom),

and equal opportunity measures (the United States). This raised important questions about the relationship between equality strategies and social justice theories. John Rawls (1971: 62), in his influential *Theory of Justice*, proposed that '[a]ll social values—liberty and opportunity, income and wealth and the bases of self-respect—are to be distributed equally unless an unequal distribution of any, or all, of these values is to everyone's advantage'. In other words, inequalities (benefits to those with greater talents, training, etc.) can be justified only if they are to the benefit of the least advantaged, and attached to offices and positions open to all under conditions of equality of opportunity.

During the cold war, these debates in the industrialized world impacted on policies towards the developing world, while in the developing world itself political movements emerged with equality as their stated goal and occasionally became governments. Huge controversies surrounded the efforts to put that goal into practice. This section discusses the controversies and the eventual demise of these efforts as neoliberal economics challenged the very foundations of the argument for equality. It also introduces the complex question of measuring inequality.

Equality as a political and moral goal

Moral and political arguments for an equitable model of economic development found concrete expression in a number of experiments that spanned the post-war decades, such as the model of socialism that followed the 1959 revolution in Cuba, the 1967 Arusha declaration and *Ujamaa* (Swahili for 'community-hood') socialism of Nyerere's government in Tanzania, and the Chilean road to socialism of Salvador Allende between 1970 and 1973. These experiments went further than economic egalitarianism. They were also about new forms of political participation and how to address the impact of economic inequality on political decision-making. They encountered hostility from Western governments opposed to non-capitalist paths to development. Cuba and Allende's Chile faced attempts at destabilization from the United States in their pursuit of more egalitarian development. Tanzania, one of the most heavily aided countries, found its strategy of self-reliance and equality extremely difficult to combine with growth and development.

Measuring inequality

The inequality question in development was partly about moral and political arguments at this time, but it was also partly about the facts and how to measure them. Development economists in the Bretton Woods institutions (the World Bank and the International Monetary Fund, or IMF) and universities were concerned with measuring the potential trade-off between economic growth and inequality that Kuznets had highlighted. Their objective was to understand the contribution that factors of production such as land, labour, and capital make to output, and not who gets what and why. Inequality mattered if it impacted negatively on growth and development. Quantitative surveys during these decades broadly tended to confirm Kuznets' findings, but they did not show a fixed relationship in all cases. However, the argument that inequality was impeding development appeared to have been partially accepted when, in the mid-1970s, the World Bank embarked on a new strategy of 'redistribution with growth'. At the same time, arguments that a 'new international economic order' should address the inequalities between nations were also topical.

Income distribution measurement is by no means straightforward. Unreliable data, choices over the best unit of measurement (individuals or households), the timescale of measurement, and the definition of income itself, which, given the high level of informal and unregistered earnings, is particularly problematic in developing countries, all represent significant problems.

The most frequently used approaches to measurement are the Lorenz curve and the **Gini coefficient**.

- The Lorenz curve, named after the American statistician Lorenz who developed it in 1905, uses a vertical axis (percentage of income earned) and horizontal axis (percentage of the population earning that income); the greater the bow of the curve, the larger the degree of inequality.

- The Gini coefficient, named after the Italian statistician who created it in 1912, uses areas of the Lorenz curve, and is the ratio of the area between the line of equality and the Lorenz curve, and the total area under the line of equality. It offers an aggregate measure of inequality between 0 (perfect equality) and 1 (perfect inequality). The Gini coefficient for countries with highly unequal income distribution tends to lie between 0.50 and 0.70.

Following Kuznets' challenge, many studies in the 1960s and 1970s examined the impact of economic growth on income distribution, and vice versa. Large-scale, cross-country surveys were undertaken. Some confirmed the trend towards rising inequality in the less-developed countries, although they varied in terms of whether the trend was weak or strong. Evidence was clearly not uniform across countries. Chenery et al. (1974) argued that ultimately the evidence and judgements cannot be separated from 'social and ethical postulates'. In other words, the patterns of growth and distribution reflected political priorities and values in particular countries. He discussed three models: growth-oriented patterns, illustrated by Brazil and Mexico, including an equity-oriented, low-growth variant, illustrated by Sri Lanka; rapid growth with equity, illustrated by Taiwan, Republic of Korea, and Singapore; and an average pattern illustrated by India, the Philippines, Turkey, and Colombia, where patterns of growth and distribution follow the average relations of the Kuznets curve.

Structuralist and non-structuralist approaches to inequality

A great many qualitative, but empirically based, studies tried to identify the causes of income inequality, and some examined its consequences. A division arose between structuralists and non-structuralists. The former emphasized the impact on income inequality of such factors as historically unequal landownership patterns and social structures that excluded people on such bases as caste, race, sex, or religion. The concentration of physical and financial capital, as well as land, in the hands of small elites enabled them to buy access to educational opportunity and to control an ever greater proportion of national product. The consequences of this unequal distribution included malnutrition, poor housing, and little or no education for the majority, resulting in low levels of productivity. In contrast, the argument was made that a redistribution of income would increase production by boosting the consumption, and hence the health and productivity, of the poor.

Non-structuralists countered that inequality was the logical (some would say inevitable) outcome of economic growth. The apparent increase in inequality during the early stages of development is because development does not start at the same time in all parts of the economy. Growth in a poor, underdeveloped country will always raise some people's income before others—notably those where the growth is first located, for instance in urban rather than rural areas. Shifts in a country's structure of production will inevitably create inequalities between those engaged in agriculture compared to those in new, more highly remunerated industries. The non-structuralists argued that these inequalities would not necessarily result in absolute impoverishment, but only a relative decline in income of the poorest. The argument that the poor would see their living standards rise through economic growth, even though their relative share of income might not, gained ground in the 1980s.

However, in the 1970s, even the president of the World Bank, Robert MacNamara, was forced to admit that, despite a decade of unprecedented increase in the gross national product (GNP) of the developing countries, the poorest segments of their population had received relatively little benefit. Policies aimed primarily at accelerating economic growth in most developing countries had benefited, at most, the upper 40 per cent of the population.

Equality questioned

By the 1980s, support for the idea that reducing inequality is a task of government eroded in the Anglo-American world especially and in the international **institutions** that it influenced. The global economic recession that followed the 1973 oil shocks had resulted in a shift from Keynesian policies of demand management and welfare-oriented state interventions to monetarism, which cuts public expenditure on welfare and prioritizes investment and profitability. Monetarists, as they were called, denounced the coercive and bureaucratic state needed, they argued, to pursue egalitarian goals.

Many developing world egalitarian states had indeed shown that these dangers were real. Even where such states had consciously sought to avoid such tendencies, for example Nyerere's Tanzania (1962–85) and the Sandinistas' Nicaragua (1979–90), they could not entirely avoid state-heavy political structures that concentrated power in new elites, such as the 'bureaucratic bourgeoisie' of the former and the party *caudillos* of the latter. Bauer (1981) also maintained that promotion of economic equality and the alleviation of poverty are distinct and often conflicting goals, and that to make the rich poorer does not make the poor richer.

The broad trend in thinking away from government regulation and intervention in markets for any purpose, including social justice, gathered pace in the 1980s. The argument against Kuznets that inequality had no inevitable consequences for poverty was boosted by the publication of several time-series studies showing that income inequality does not, in any case, change much over time, so economic growth must reduce poverty to some extent. The pattern of overall distribution of goods in society now seemed less important than individual well-being and freedom to pursue private interests in the marketplace. These arguments paved the way for market liberalization, which was expected to reduce poverty through growth. It was followed by emphasis on political liberalization and governance reform, aimed at enhancing the institutional framework for growth and poverty reduction. Inequality was no longer considered a major issue for development, and would creep back only in the course of the 1990s and the new millennium as neoliberal globalization began to generate evidence of rising inequalities within nations, and thinking went beyond income to recognize the multiple domains of inequalities and their persistence.

KEY POINTS

- From the 1960s, egalitarian thinking influenced several policy experiments in developing countries, but most ran into difficulties.

- Measurement of inequality became an important field of study, whilst structuralists and non-structuralists debated the relationship between inequality and the economy.

- From the 1970s, as agreement grew that economic **modernization** was not benefiting the poor, international development policies focused on raising their living standards, but without radical redistribution.

- In the 1980s, priority shifted to market-driven growth and new arguments claimed that economic growth benefited the poor.

Inequalities in the Age of Globalization

❝ There are at the beginning of the second decade of the 21st century hardly two more politically charged economic terms than 'globalization' and 'inequality'. ❞

(Milanovic 2012b: xvi)

The arguments around the inequality effects of market liberalization and the globalization of the economy over the three decades or more since the end of the cold war began to gather pace amongst economists at the turn of the new millennium, and particularly in the wake of the 2008 global economic crisis. A new global landscape developed over these decades, in which a range of developing countries began to outstrip the developed world in economic growth, at the same time as levels of inequality within them grew apace.

However, the first range of critiques came not from economists, but from sociologists, political theorists, and philosopher economists (Amartya Sen and Martha Nussbaum, for example). They began to question income as the main measure of inequality. The World Bank began to listen, and its 2001 development report was much more nuanced than its 1990 report. Meanwhile, economists began to sharpen their own measurement tools and definitions of inequality. By the second decade of the new millennium, a rich new set of insights was emerging on the nature of inequalities in the age of globalization.

Inequality and human diversity

Interest waned in ideas of equality in the post-cold-war world and even in efforts such as those of Rawls to reach a shared 'theory of justice'. However, explorations into the relationship between human diversity and inequality generated new post-Rawlsian thinking on how substantial freedoms for all could be realized and thresholds of real opportunities established below which no human being should be allowed to fall. This was a period during which violent conflict in the world seemed to reflect what has been called 'horizontal inequalities' between cultural and religious groups, and between geographical regions of the same country (Stewart 2008). The impact of armed conflict on poverty became a central concern of the **international community** and, amongst other factors, drove institutions to embrace some of the new thinking.

Amartya Sen, in *Inequality Re-examined* (1992), offered one of the most sophisticated efforts to address the relationship between human diversity and equality. It has been particularly influential in development studies, refocusing attention away from income to human capabilities—a shift that can be followed in

the evolution of the UNDP's annual Human Development Reports (see Box 6.3). Sen is less interested in equality, as such, than in the question: 'Equality of what?' His thinking is heavily influenced by Rawls, but he has gone beyond Rawls' emphasis on the *means* of freedom, to the **extents of freedom**, meaning the capabilities or freedom to achieve whatever functionings an individual happens to value.

The logic of Sen's argument is based on the assumption of human diversity. Equality claims must come to terms with this fundamental empirical fact, because there are times when equal consideration for all may demand unequal treatment in favour of the disadvantaged. Indeed, because we are diverse in our personal qualities, such as age, gender, talents, proneness to illnesses, and physical abilities, as well as in our external circumstances such as material assets, social backgrounds, and environmental circumstances, insistence on egalitarianism in one field may imply rejecting it in another. Disadvantage is itself diverse. Moreover, disadvantage is not just about consumption of resources. Our capabilities to achieve whatever we

BOX 6.3 THE HUMAN DEVELOPMENT INDEX

The UNDP's annual Human Development Reports contain a range of indices that try to take into account non-income measures of development, and enable us to view the performance of a country in terms of both growth and freedoms. The best known is the Human Development Index (HDI), which incorporates data for human longevity and educational attainment, as well as material living standards. Comparing countries by their place in the HDI produces a very different picture from a rank that is based on the Gini coefficient alone. For example, Chile and Guatemala have a comparable level of inequality measured by the Gini coefficient that is very high. But in human development terms, Chile easily qualifies among the top fifty countries (high human development), whereas Guatemala is in the middle of the medium human development range, placed many countries below Chile. The contrast between, for instance, South Korea and Rwanda is even greater. Similar in terms of the Gini coefficient (in which case both appear significantly more equal than, say, the United States or the United Kingdom) in human development, Rwanda features among the least developed countries anywhere, while South Korea features in the top thirty countries of the world.

value do not ultimately depend on income, but on all of the physical and social characteristics that make us what we are. Substantial inequalities in well-being and freedom can, given our variable needs and disparate personal and social circumstances, result directly from an equal distribution of incomes. As Sen noted, some countries with higher per capita incomes enjoy lower life expectancies. The Indian state of Kerala has one of the lower real per capita incomes in India, but the highest life expectancy, lower infant mortality, and higher general literacy—particularly female literacy. This is true even if the average GNP is adjusted for distributional inequality: Kerala remains, even with this statistical adjustment, one of the poorer Indian states. The explanation lies in the history of public policy, most notably education, health services, and food distribution, which reaches the rural as well as urban population (Sen 1992: 128). Thus these conceptual debates show their importance also to policy.

Inequalities, power, and politics

The emphasis on the diversity of inequalities led to a focus on the way in which politics and power impact on inequalities, and vice versa. Anne Phillips (1999) argued that political inequality cannot be addressed without addressing economic inequality. Disparities between rich and poor impede recognition of equal human worth. Political equality assumes equal worth, as well as equal access to political influence:

66 The problem for democracy is not just how to equalize people's political resources but how to establish their equal human worth; the problem with economic inequality is not just that it constrains the exercise of political rights but that it shapes (and damages) perceptions of fellow citizens. 99

(Phillips 1999: 83)

When, in its 2001 *World Development Report*, the World Bank acknowledged that social discrimination can have economic effects that will undermine efforts at pro-poor growth, it advocated making 'public spending pro-poor', recognizing that this would encounter political resistance:

66 Governments face important political issues in redistributing public spending to support asset accumulation by poor people. With finer targeting, public funds may in principle reach more poor people. But such targeting may lack political support from powerful groups that may lose out. Hence the importance of building pro-poor coalitions. 99

(World Bank 2001: 82)

(For more on the policy issues, see Chapter 16.) While political liberalization in the post-cold-war decade opened up some new political spaces for participation, these were often filled by self-appointed allies of the poor, such as **non-governmental organizations (NGOs)**. These organizations could at least advocate policies that might equalize the playing field politically and/or economically. Collective action remained another means by which the disadvantaged might make their voice heard, and social movements proliferated in the developing world in this period (see Chapter 11). Such movements saw struggles in terms of rights and **entitlements**, and challenged the mainstream thinking that the poor are a 'target group' for policies, which ultimately maintains the division between 'rich' and 'poor'. Political leaders often emerged to mobilize the poor on grounds of class and ethnic exclusion, such as Hugo Chávez in Venezuela and Evo Morales in Bolivia. However, whereas in India the space for such movements remained relatively open, in China it did not. And these countries were both contributing to growth and poverty reduction in the new millennium, but also to rising inequalities.

Gradually, the policy debate on inequality moved beyond income inequality, to explore the relationship between social and political inequalities, and economic inequalities, and between all of these and poverty and development. This renewed mainstream interest in inequality and its relationship to development is reflected in the 2005 and 2006 reports of the UNDP and World Bank, respectively, which were devoted to inequality (UNDP) and equity (World Bank). (On the World Bank report, see Box 6.4.) These reports explore the deep effects of income inequality on wider life chances of people in developing countries, including staying alive. The reports go well beyond income inequality in their understanding of the relationship between inequality and development, a trend that has been led by the discussion on gender inequality. The impact of inequalities in race and ethnicity, as well as gender, began to be analysed. Brazil, for instance, revealed

BOX 6.4 THE WORLD BANK ON INEQUALITIES OF POWER AND THE QUALITY OF INSTITUTIONS

How do societies develop equitable non-market institutions? First, there must be sufficient political equality—equality in access to the political system and in the distribution of political power, political rights, and influence. Poor institutions will emerge and persist in societies when power is concentrated in the hands of a narrow group or an elite…Because the distribution of power, through its impact on institutions, helps to determine the distribution of income, the possibility of vicious and virtuous circles is clear. A society with greater equality of control over assets and incomes will tend to have a more equal distribution of political power. It will therefore tend to have institutions that generate equality of opportunity for the broad mass of citizens.

(World Bank 2006: 108)

a large discrepancy in income inequality between population groups based on skin colour. Brazil has the second largest population of African descent in the world after Nigeria (almost half of all Brazilians are of African descent). Yet in 2005 about 33 per cent of Afro-Brazilians lived in poor households whose incomes were below 50 per cent of the median income of the country, compared to 14 per cent of whites falling into this group (Gradin 2009). Similarly, in South Africa, where income inequality had risen in the post-**apartheid** years, measured by a Gini coefficient that went from 0.64 in 1995 to 0.69 in 2005, it is the inequality between black African and white people that continues to drive overall inequality, although there is evidence of growing inequality also amongst black Africans.

Economic and political inequalities have been created around human differences, and embedded over time in structured social relationships. The mainstream financial and development institutions came to acknowledge that this impacts on democracy, governance, and the quality of institutions. This recognition took place at the same time as neoliberal economics was still unchallenged. The global financial crisis of 2008 led to new questions about the relationship between neoliberal globalization and inequality, and the debate returned to income inequality.

The economists return to inequality

The construction of a World Income Inequality Database in the late 1990s by the United Nations University's World Institute for Development Economics Research (UNU–WIDER) produced more reliable time-series data on income inequality, and led to a research project into the relationship between income inequality and poverty reduction. On the basis of these data, Cornia and Court (2001) concluded that worsening inequality resulted less from the traditional causes, such as landownership patterns and **urban bias**, or the impact of new technologies on skilled and unskilled wages, although all these remain significant, than from new causes including, most notably, macroeconomic stabilization, labour market and financial deregulation, and excessively liberal economic policies. The debate on the relationship between market liberalism, globalization, and inequality intensified.

Statistical evidence portrayed a stark picture of the extent of income inequality in the first decade of the new millennium, particularly in Latin America and sub-Saharan Africa. The Gini coefficient for sub-Saharan Africa is 0.72 and for Latin America it is 0.57, compared to 0.52 for East Asia, 0.43 for Central and Eastern Europe and the Commonwealth of Independent States (CIS), 0.37 for the high-income Organisation for Economic Co-operation and Development (OECD) countries, and 0.33 for South Asia (UNDP 2005: 55). Countries with high income inequality, it was argued, require much higher rates of growth for poverty reduction than those with lower inequality (Ravallion 2001). Ravallion (2005) went on to question other assumptions of the previous decade, for instance that absolute poverty in terms of income is the overriding issue in poor countries and that only economic growth can reduce it. He emphasized the significance of initial inequality and how it might affect the poverty reduction effects of growth. 'Making growth more pro-poor', he argued, 'requires a combination of more growth, a more pro-poor pattern of growth and success in reducing the antecedent inequalities that limit the prospects for poor people to share in the opportunities unleashed in a growing economy' (Ravallion 2005: 15).

His 'convergence' hypothesis of 2012 highlighted the point that economic growth did not reduce inequality in countries where it was historically high.

In this debate, the experiences of emerging economies—those making the main contribution to global gross domestic product (GDP) from the developing world—provided new evidence. China, India, Brazil, Mexico, Russia, and South Africa are such emerging economic powers, in which rapid growth took place in the 1990s and 2000s. The shifting patterns in the global economy and the impact of the 2008 global economic crisis led economists to take a fresh look at inequality.

An important contribution from World Bank economist Branco Milanovic (2012a) has been to clarify terminology. He has pointed out that there are three potential measures of inequality. The first is in terms of mean incomes across all nations, without taking population size into account. A second conceptualization does take population into account. In both cases, the calculation is based on country averages: the first income measure shows a rise in inequality between nations during the years of neoliberal globalization; while the second, which brings in the per capita averages, shows a decline, or greater convergence. China and India contribute a great deal to the latter finding, given their large populations. For much of the 1990s, China alone accounted for greater convergence, with its rapid rise in per capita incomes, until Indian economic growth added its statistical weight (Milanovic 2012a). In other words, as poorer and larger countries have caught up with richer countries, they have pushed global income inequality down, albeit only slightly.

However, a third conceptualization of inequality takes as its unit of measurement individuals, rather than countries, and their actual income. The data is based on household surveys of incomes or consumption, which are not available everywhere and are not always reliable. The first available such surveys in China were in 1982, for example. Some of the countries that do not have reliable surveys (Afghanistan, Sudan, Congo, Somalia, Eritrea) are amongst the poorest in the world (Milanovic 2012a: 10). The calculation also has to be adjusted using the purchasing power parity (PPP) dollar measure, which takes account of 'cheaper' living costs in some countries. Milanovic shows that global inequality is higher when measured in a way in which every citizen counts, and increased between the late 1980s and 2005. This third approach highlights what is happening to income disparities within countries rather than between countries. A divergence emerges between countries rather than the greater convergence on the average per capita GDP measure. The most consistent increase in inequality took place in China, the Gini coefficient of which climbed from about 0.30 in the early 1980s to about 0.45 in 2005 (Olinto and Saavendra 2012: 2). In Latin America, inequality declined in Brazil, but rose in Costa Rica, Guatemala, and Honduras. While inequality in Brazil remained high, its decline, as measured by the Gini coefficient from 0.607 in 1990 to 0.537 in 2009 (Lopez-Calva 2012: 5), attracted considerable interest, particularly for the role of innovative social policies, such as its conditional cash transfer (*Bolsa Familiar*) programme to poor families in exchange for ensuring educational and health investments in their children. In terms of global patterns of within-nation inequality, there were now far more OECD countries in which inequality had increased rather than decreased, notably Finland, Germany, New Zealand, Sweden, the UK, and the United States (Olinto and Saavendra 2012: 3)

One of the emerging social trends in Brazil and other rising economies has been the emergence of a middle class. And with this emergence have come some interesting patterns analysed by the economist Gabriel Palma (2011). One of these is that some 80 per cent of the world's population now live in regions or countries with a median Gini coefficient of around 0.40; Latin America and Southern Africa, however, remain outliers to this pattern, with very high levels of inequality still despite the decline in Brazil. He concludes that over half the world's population (in the categories of middle and upper middle classes) have gained strong 'property rights' over half of their respective national incomes. However, the other half of national income is distributed between the very rich and the poor. The figures of Milanovic (2012a) also show that while the bottom third of the global income distribution have made gains over the last decades, the exception is the poorest 5 per cent of these. At the top of the pyramid, on the other hand, the highest 1 per cent, and to a lesser degree the top 5 per cent, have gained significantly. It is now also acknowledged that the very rich tend not to fill in household surveys, so that their share of income is often underestimated. The financial crisis of 2008 highlighted the extraordinary rewards that could accrue to the super-rich, including the financial class of the developed world widely felt to be responsible for the crisis. But now, parts of the developing world also boasted their own class of global billionaires.

What has changed the terms of the debate, however, is the acknowledgement by economists that inequality matters. *The Economist*, an influential and mainstream source of analysis on the global economy, published a special report on inequality in 2012, which reflected the emerging consensus amongst the international financial institutions that inequality harms growth and society:

❝ The economics establishment has become concerned about who gets what. Research by economists at the IMF suggests that income inequality slows growth, causes financial crises and weakens demand. In a recent report the Asian Development Bank argued that if emerging Asia's income distribution had not worsened over the past 20 years, the region's rapid growth would have lifted an extra 240m people of out extreme poverty. More controversial studies purport to link widening income gaps with all manner of ills, from obesity to suicide. The widening gaps within many countries are beginning to worry even the plutocrats. A survey for the World Economic Forum meeting at Davos pointed to inequality as the most pressing problem of the coming decade (alongside fiscal imbalances). In all sections of society, there is growing agreement that the world is becoming more unequal, and that today's disparities and their likely trajectory are dangerous. **❞**

(Beddoes 2012: 6)

KEY POINTS

- New awareness of social and cultural diversity increased the complexities of the inequality issue, and encouraged a focus on 'recognition' of difference, as well as 'redistribution' of income.

- Sen argued that policies need to recognize that people are diverse in their disadvantages and advantages, and the UNDP introduced new measures to estimate non-income aspects of inequality.

- Inequality is a source of contentious politics in the developing world, which can be positive in the case of self-empowering social movements, but can also be negative, polarizing, and potentially violent.

- By the new millennium, economists returned to the inequality debate, with new measurement tools for income inequality.

- Neoliberal globalization generated growth that decreased poverty overall and led to a rising middle class in a range

of countries mostly from the global South, which became motors of global economic change.

- As these poorer and larger countries caught up with richer ones in terms of GDP, the global income gap between nations reduced.

- However, inequalities within countries grew significantly, particularly in some of the emerging economic powers, but also in the global North. Latin America and Southern Africa continued to be the most unequal regions of the world.

- Mainstream economists came to accept that inequality matters to growth and financial stability.

Conclusion: Inequality Matters

The conceptual waters of the inequality debate have ebbed and flowed since the eighteenth century, with ontological equality challenged by the end of the twentieth century by the idea of equality based on human diversity. Sen has advanced on Tawney's vision of the 'largest possible measure of equality of environment', to the multiple environments that must be tailored to the capability enhancements of a diverse humanity. However, humankind is a long way from constructing the new social, political, and economic arrangements that would enable inequalities to be addressed in the multiple 'spaces' in which they appear. Equality practice has foundered on the power at the global, national, community, and family levels that protects embedded inequalities, and which allows some people to exploit, marginalize, and deprive others of a full life. In turn, inequality impacts on the political system, limiting participation of poor and discriminated people, and hence the possibilities of prioritizing the search for new solutions that might truly enhance the life chances of all.

By the second decade of the second millennium, the negative impacts of inequality had come to concern the international community once again. The assumption that market liberalism would reduce inequality was not borne out, although numbers in absolute poverty declined as new economic powers emerged amongst highly populated and poor countries of the developing world. A new middle class had come into being across the globe, but a significant proportion of people remained with a negligible share of their nation's income, while a very few had become a super-rich class of global billionaires, many from the emerging economies of the global South. The description of the *Human Development Report 2002* (UNDP 2002) of the level of worldwide inequality as 'grotesque' still hangs in the air as policymakers and politicians grapple with the aftermath of the economic crisis of 2008 and the subsequent global recession.

? QUESTIONS

1. Is inequality unjust?

2. Discuss the persistence of caste inequalities in India since India has become an emerging economic power.

3. To what extent should the state address the question of inequality as well as poverty in its development strategies?

4. How does gender inequality impact on economic growth?

5. How has the World Bank's understanding of inequality shifted since 1990?

6. Compare the inequality impact of the approaches to development and growth of either Brazil and India, or India and China.

7. Discuss Gabriel Palma's claim that Kuznets' 'inverted-U' hypothesis was buried by the early twenty-first century.

8. Why do Latin America and Southern Africa remain the most unequal regions of the world?

FURTHER READING

Beddoes, Z. M. (2012) 'For Richer, for Poorer', *The Economist*, 13 October, available online at http://www.economist.com/node/21564414 A useful short piece highlighting evidence of wealth concentration.

Béteille, A. (ed.) (1969) *Social Inequality* (Harmondsworth: Penguin) A good set of conceptual and anthropological essays on social inequalities that still merits reading.

Fraser, N. (1997) *Justice Interruptus: Critical Reflections on the 'Postsocialist' Condition* (London: Routledge) A very useful discussion on the relationship between the redistributionist and recognitionist emphases within inequality thinking.

Gradín, C. (2009) 'Why is Poverty so High among Afro-Brazilians? A Decomposition Analysis of the Racial Poverty Gap', *Journal of Development Studies*, 45(19): 1426–52 A useful attempt to understand the differential poverty levels between whites and blacks in Brazil.

Kuznets, S. (1955) 'Economic Growth and Income Inequality', *American Economic Review*, 45: 1–28 An important benchmark study on the relationship between inequality and development.

Lopez-Calva, L. (2012) 'Declining Income Inequality in Brazil: The Proud Outlier', *Inequality in Focus*, 1(1): 5–8 A short piece on the impact of Brazil's income support programme on inequality.

Milanovic, B. (2012a) *Global Income Inequality by the Numbers: In History and Now—An Overview*, World Bank Policy Research Working Paper No. 6259, available online at http://elibrary.worldbank.org/content/workingpaper/10.1596/1813-9450-6259 A significant paper on measuring inequality.

—— (2012b) 'Introduction', in B. Milanovic (ed.) *Globalization and Inequality* (Cheltenham: Edward Elgar), ix–xxiii A helpful introduction to what is one of the best collection of contemporary debates on inequality.

Olinto, P. and Saavedra, J. (2012) 'An Overview of Global Inequality Trends', *Inequality in Focus*, 1(1): 1–4 Useful short discussion of global inequality in the second decade of the second millennium.

Palma, J. G. (2011) 'Homogenous Middles vs. Heterogenous Tails, and the End of the "Inverted-U": It's All about the Share of the Rich', *Development and Change Forum*, 42(1): 87–153 A provocative and insightful analysis of contemporary patterns of global inequality.

Phillips, A. (1999) *Which Equalities Matter?* (Cambridge: Polity Press) A very lucid discussion of the relationship between political and economic equality.

Ravallion, M. (2001) 'Growth, Inequality and Poverty: Looking beyond Averages', *World Development*, 29(11): 1803–15 A good discussion of the relationship between growth, distribution, and poverty.

—— (2005) *Inequality is Bad for the Poor*, World Bank Policy Research Working Paper No. 3677, available online at https://openknowledge.worldbank.org/handle/10986/8625 This background paper to the 2006 World Development Report on Equity and Development puts forward the arguments for bringing the issue of inequality back into development debates, with useful sections on China and India.

Rawls, J. (1971) A *Theory of Justice* (Oxford: Oxford University Press) A very influential contribution to the political philosophy of inequality.

Sen, A. (1992) *Inequality Re-Examined* (Oxford: Oxford University Press) Includes good discussions of both the state of welfare economics measurement, and the relations between aggregative and distributional considerations and economic efficiency.

Stewart, F. (ed.) (2008) *Horizontal Inequalities and Conflict: Understanding Group Violence in Multiethnic Societies* (Basingstoke: Palgrave Macmillan) An important exploration of how inequalities around ethnic, religious, and subnational identities relate to armed conflict.

Tawney, R. H. (1952) *Inequality* (London: Allen and Unwin) A classic essay on inequality that challenges the notion that equality of opportunity is a sufficient approach to the question.

WEB LINKS

http://ucatlas.ucsc.edu   The University of California, Santa Cruz Atlas of Global Inequality, includes downloadable maps and graphics.

http://www.undp.org   Site of the United Nations Human Development Programme contains links to its annual Human Development Report.

http://www.wider.unu.edu/   Includes access to the United Nations University–World Institute for Development Economics Research Database on world income inequality.

http://www.worldbank.org/poverty/inequal   The World Bank Group site on the concept of inequality and its links to poverty and to socio-economic performance, and pro-poor growth specifically. The briefing paper *Inequality in Focus*, which the World Bank began to produce in April 2012, can be downloaded from this site.

For additional material and resources, please visit the Online Resource Centre at:
http://www.oxfordtextbooks.co.uk/orc/burnell4e/

7

Ethnopolitics and Nationalism

James R. Scarritt

Overview

This chapter stresses the significance of both: (1) differences among ethnic, ethnopolitical, and national identities; and (2) different types of relationship among groups having these identities in countries of the developing world. Ethnic identities are constructed and reconstructed over time, and some, but not all, are politicized. Specific processes for construction and politicization, and their variations across countries, are discussed. National identities in the developing world, which are inherently political, vary in strength as well as the degree to which they are civic, multi-ethnic or multicultural, or ethnic, and the chapter explains these variations. Both types of identity have been strongly influenced by European colonialism. Both types interact variously with group morphology, group advantages and disadvantages, organizations, institutions, mobilization and state response histories, and international influence. Based on such interactions, ethnopolitical groups engage in conflict, competition, and cooperation with one another and the state in different countries and at different points in time. Different interaction patterns are explored. Since national identities are relatively weak in many developing countries while subnational ethnopolitical identities and groups are often stronger, developing states more or less successfully engage in a variety of nation-building activities; the chapter describes these activities, and explains their degree of success in the current era of electoral democracy, globalization, and the 'war on terror'.

Introduction

Defining ethnicity and nationalism in ways that are uncontroversial is probably an impossible task. Yet these are vitally important topics in the **politics** of the **developing world**, affecting and affected by the other social and economic cleavages and characteristics discussed in this volume, the nature of the state and its degree of democratization, and policies for economic development and **human rights** protection. Boldly stated, a reasonably strong sense of civic or multi-ethnic nationalism and interactions among politicized ethnic groups based primarily on cooperation and institutionalized competition, rather than on conflict, tend to moderate economic and religious cleavages, strengthen **civil society**, and enhance state-building, democratization, economic development, and the provision of human rights. Although these generalizations are only tendencies rather than universal relationships, and reverse causal effects of other cleavages, civil society, state-building, democratization, economic development, and human rights on ethnopolitics and nationalism are also important, these relationships leave no doubt about the vital importance of ethnicity and nationalism.

Rather than dwell on controversies about the definition of ethnicity and nationalism, this chapter assumes that:

- they are different and only sometimes closely related;
- both are socially constructed identities (as discussed in Abdelal et al. 2009; Chandra 2012) that are subject to change in interaction with group morphology, group advantage or disadvantage, political organizations and **institutional** rules, mobilization histories, and international influences; and
- ethnicity is only politicized in some cases, but nationalism has an inherent political component.

The discussion thus begins with the construction and politicization of **ethnic identities**—in other words, the construction of ethnic and **ethnopolitical identities**—and then turns to the construction of a variety of nationalist identities. The next section deals with the conflictual, competitive, and cooperative interactions of groups based on these identities with one another and with states, while the final section before the conclusion deals with states' efforts to mould these interactions in ways that enhance the **legitimacy** of state-based nations and their support from various groups.

The Construction and Politicization of Ethnic Identities

Ethnic identities are constructed when some people self-consciously distinguish themselves from others based on perceived common descent, frequently combined with shared cultural attributes, such as values, norms, goals, beliefs, and language (Chandra 2012). There is thus a wide variety in the specific contents of these identities even within a single country, to say nothing of across the countries of the developing world. Actual commonalities of language, a broader culture, or a common line of descent are often, but not always, included in ethnic identities. In spite of this wide variety in specific content, the common characteristics of these identities are sufficient to separate them clearly from other identities and to justify generalizing broadly about them (Horowitz 1985: 51–64; Eriksen 1993: 10–12; Gurr 2000: 3–5; Chandra 2012). Religious identities can be attributes of ethnic identities, but, as discussed in Chapter 8, it is sometimes useful to separate them.

Many, but not all, ethnic identities are politicized or, as Chandra and Wilkinson (2008: 523–6; see also Chandra 2012) put it, 'activated in politics'. This distinction is obviously very important for the analysis of the role of ethnicity in politics in the developing world and elsewhere. Ethnopolitical identities are those ethnic identities that have been politicized. This term deliberately emphasizes the interactive causal significance of the ethnic and political components of these identities in their formation, continuing mobilization, and interaction with concrete organizations, institutional rules, and international influences (Gurr 2000: 5–8; Mozaffar et al. 2003: 382–3). There is much debate about the relative strength of each component of ethnopolitical identities, with a majority of recent analysts giving predominance to the political. But their relative strength, as well as the specific form of their interaction, may vary across ethnicities or countries and over time, so what is crucial is to emphasize their interaction and examine it empirically in different cases. Young (2001: 176) suggests that the political component is more important in Africa than in Eurasia. The fact that ethnopolitical identities are constructed through the processes discussed and thus change over time does not, however, mean that they are not often held with deep emotional intensity. They are constructed through a variety of interactions between leaders and masses in which everyone's rational calculations are structured by their existing values, norms, and identities.

With very few exceptions, the countries of the developing world experienced European colonialism, which played a crucial role in the construction of ethnic identities, and an even more crucial role in their politicization and organization into ethnopolitical groups. But the timing of colonial rule, the European powers involved, and the specific policies that affected ethnic identities varied sharply between Latin America and the Caribbean, on the one hand, and Asia, the Middle East, North Africa, and sub-Saharan Africa, on the other, and to a lesser extent among and within the latter areas. The Spanish and Portuguese colonized virtually all of Latin America and much of the Caribbean from the sixteenth century until the first quarter of the nineteenth century. They brought in large numbers of settlers from their own countries and other European countries, and it was the Creoles—the American-born descendents of these settlers (Young 1976: 84; Anderson 1991: 47)—who seized power from the decaying colonial empires at the time of independence. In many of these countries, they were outnumbered by indigenous Indians alone, or (as in Brazil) in combination with imported African slaves, although extensive intermarriage created intermediate groups of people, many of whom adopted Creole identities. European or Creole, mixed race or Mestizo, Indian and African ethnopolitical identities developed over the following decades, roughly in that order. The increasing strength of Indian identities as disadvantaged minorities—more focused on individual 'tribes' than on multitribal Indian populations in specific countries—has been the primary change in the landscape of ethnopolitical identities in recent decades. Ethnopolitical mobilization and the **globalization** of information have played crucial roles in strengthening these identities, as discussed later in the chapter. British and French colonialism in the Caribbean began slightly later, and the British held on to their colonies until the end of the Second World War. Descendants of former slaves from Africa are the overwhelming majority of the population in most of these countries. However, those countries with substantial East

Indian populations are deeply divided in terms of ethnopolitical identities.

English, French, Dutch, and Spanish/American colonialism in South and South-East Asia occurred somewhat later, beginning as early as the sixteenth century in the Philippines and as late as the late nineteenth century in Indochina, and lasting until after the Second World War. Very few permanent European settlers were brought in, although Chinese and Indian settlers were brought into some South-East Asian countries. A core pre-colonial ethnic identity existed in many, but not all, Asian colonies, and was usually reinforced and given increased political significance by colonial rule. Burma is a clear example of this pattern. But minority ethnic identities within or outside the core were recognized and also politicized, especially by the British. Minority identities were strengthened in the process of resistance to the colonial reinforcement of the core identity. The two largest Asian colonies—British India and Dutch Indonesia—and a few others were amalgamations of a vast array of ethnic identities without a single dominant core. The British politicized these multiple identities more intensively and intentionally (through granting limited **political autonomy** to indigenous princely states) than the Dutch did, but the latter's classification of customary law zones constructed and politicized the ethnicity of their residents (Young 1994: 270), and amalgamation of groups into a common state inevitably had a politicizing effect. Post-independence politics have intensified group politicization in both countries, reinforced by international support for some disadvantaged minorities.

English, French, Belgian, and Portuguese colonialism in sub-Saharan Africa occurred much later, not really penetrating the subcontinent beyond a few coastal areas, the Portuguese-influenced Kongo Kingdom (most of which is now in Angola), and areas of European settlement in South Africa until the 1880s. Colonial rulers' reliance on local agents to cope with the dilemma of maintaining control at low cost encouraged these agents to differentiate their groups from those not so privileged by colonial authority, either by recombining and redefining existing objective markers of ethnicity, or by accentuating previously minor group differences. Colonial rulers' creation of administrative units to secure additional economies in the cost of **governance** incorporated culturally disparate groups within single administrative units or separated culturally similar groups into separate units.

At independence, therefore, sub-Saharan African countries inherited a distinctive **ethnic morphology** (the form and structure of groups) with three defining features:

- very few ethnopolitical groups comprise an outright majority in a country, although some comprise a large plurality;
- limited cultural differences among groups in most countries; and
- the territorial concentration of many ethnic groups that facilitates their construction as cohesive units for collective political action.

These three features have combined with the accommodation by post-colonial **regimes** of instrumental ('pork-barrel') ethnopolitical demands to foster *communal contention* as the typical pattern of political interactions in which ethnopolitical groups serve as cost-effective resources for organizing political competition. Communal contention discourages political entrepreneurs from exaggerating cultural differences among groups, and encourages them instead to maintain strong group and coexisting subgroup identities that are sustained by their ability to access the state, and to secure valued goods and services for their followers (Mozaffar et al. 2003: 382–3).

In sub-Saharan Africa, construction of *ethnopolitical* groups occurred through organized group mobilization, articulation of grievances by leaders claiming to speak for a group, participation in collective action or conflict with other groups or the state, being subjected to state violence, encapsulation within or domination of an officially designated administrative unit, occupying a disproportionate number of high positions in the bureaucracy or the military, controlling disproportionate socio-economic resources, or forming or joining an ethnic or multi-ethnic political party (Mozaffar et al. 2003: 383).

French and British colonialism came to North Africa with the French occupation of Algeria in 1830—fifty years before neighbouring Morocco and Tunisia—and the British occupation of Aden in 1839. The presence of numerous French settlers in Algeria, who campaigned to incorporate the colony permanently into France, was eventually a major force in politicizing Algerian and regional (Maghreb) Arab identity. Colonial rule by the same European powers came to the Asian Middle East the latest of all regions (the end of First World War, in which the Ottoman Empire—the

former colonial power in most of this region—was defeated), and lasted less than thirty years. Ottoman rule was assimilative rather than alien, but it was more interventionist and integrative than previous localized rulers, and thus stimulated Arab nationalism within its territories, especially in its waning years. Post-independence interventionist states continued this process, as did the conflict surrounding the arrival of large numbers of European Jews in Palestine before and after the founding of Israel in 1948. Other Arab countries have had few European settlers. Thus the construction and politicization of Arab as the dominant ethnopolitical identity in the entire bi-continental region was a long process in which European colonialism played a more limited role than in other regions (Young 1976: 373–427). Apart from the Kurds of Iran, Iraq, and Turkey, whose identity was politicized primarily in the twentieth century, and Berber speakers in western North Africa, the main lines of division are religious. The Western powers have been seen as opposed to the emergence of a transnational Arab identity, and not only with respect to Palestine. This opposition has been a powerful politicizing force.

KEY POINTS

- Ethnic identities are constructed and then are often politicized to become ethnopolitical.

- The ethnic and political components of ethnopolitical identities are both important, but their relative importance varies among groups, countries, and regions.

- Most ethnopolitical (politically relevant ethnic) identities in the developing world were constructed during the colonial period, but some have been modified by post-independence politics.

- Differences among regions of the developing world in the timing of colonialism, the policies of the major colonial powers, and the presence of European settlers significantly affected the construction of ethnopolitical identities.

Varieties of Nationalism in the Developing World

National identities are inherently political, emphasizing the autonomy and unity of the nation as an actual or potential political unit (Hutchinson and Smith 1994: 4–5). They can be broadly characterized as civic, multi-ethnic and multicultural, ethno-national, or a combination of these types (Eriksen 1993: 118–20; Croucher 2003: 3–5; Scarritt and Mozaffar 2003). Civic national identities involve unity among citizens of an autonomous state. Whatever social cleavages may divide these citizens are irrelevant; their common citizenship unites them. The only cultural uniformity that is demanded is commitment to the existence of the nation and its political institutional norms and values. **Ethno-national identities** define the nation in ethnic terms, attaining unity through the merger of ethnic and national identities, and demand autonomy for ethnic nations. **Multi-ethnic/multicultural national identities** define the nation in terms of several ethnic identities that are united by, or nested within, citizenship and political interaction in an autonomous state, while often excluding other ethnic identities. They differ from **civic nationalism** in accepting the legitimacy and political utility of ethnopolitical identities, as long as they do not undermine national unity. This difference is not sufficiently recognized in the literature on nationalism. Very few national identities in the developing world are purely civic, but a substantial majority of them contain civic or multi-ethnic aspects, so that they do not identify the nation with a single ethnic group. Consequently, there is an ongoing tension between the ethnic, multi-ethnic, and civic aspects of these identities in their interaction with group advantages and disadvantages, concrete organizations, institutional rules, and international influences.

Since nationalism is a constructed identity, the significant variations in the specific nature of nations in the developing world are not surprising. Colonialism played an even greater role in the construction of national identities than it did in the construction of ethnopolitical identities. The boundaries of the vast majority of developing states were determined by colonial rulers, and the varieties of nationalism are products of the interaction between the states that rule within these boundaries and the morphology of ethnopolitical identities, the tactics of ethnopolitical groups, and the presence of alternative identities within the same boundaries, as discussed in the next section of this chapter: 'The normative model of the contemporary polity calls for the coincidence of nation and state' (Young 1976: 70). States attempt to create national identities that are coextensive with their boundaries, and the constituent ethnopolitical groups support or oppose these identities. Disadvantaged minority groups are especially likely to oppose

ethno-national identities, and groups that are politically dominant demographic majorities are likely to oppose civic or multi-ethnic national identities, but other patterns of support and opposition also occur. National identities are still being constructed, and this process is more advanced in some regions of the developing world than in others. But only in a very few developing countries have national identities become banal—that is, accepted as a matter of course and constantly reinforced by popular culture—as these identities are in most developed countries (Billig 1995). Thus nationalism in every country—one nation in a world of nations—develops in relation to nationalism in all other countries, but especially in relation to nationalism in neighbouring countries and to the strong nationalism of the former colonial powers, including the United States, which is all the more galling to the developing world because it is banal. It is impossible to specify exactly the number of nations or potential nations in the developing world, but if one includes every state and every ethnopolitical identity that engenders an ethno-nationalist movement, there are probably several hundred.

Latin American states are former colonial administrative units: 'The first century of independent life saw the gradual transformation of what began primarily as the territorial heirs to colonial administrative divisions into nation-states' (Young 1976: 85). These countries officially pursue civic nationalism, but until the late twentieth century this was actually a cover for Creole assimilationist ethno-nationalism. Since the awakening of indigenous and/or African ethnopolitical identities in most countries, there has been a struggle by these groups to redefine national identity in more multi-ethnic/multicultural terms. Because of Creole elite resistance, the outcome of this struggle is very much in doubt. Civic and ethnic nationalism tend to merge in racially homogeneous Caribbean countries, but civic national identities are much weaker and ethno-national ones much stronger in countries such as Trinidad and Guyana with significant East Indian populations.

Nationalism in Asian countries containing politicized ethnic cores has tended to be ethno-nationalism focused on these cores, and thus is often rejected by members of non-core cultural groups who advocate civic or multi-ethnic nationalism or desire secession. As discussed in the next section, this can lead to violent conflict over the definition of the nation. In substantially different ways, multi-ethnic India and

Indonesia constructed relatively strong multi-ethnic/multicultural national identities during the struggle for independence and the first decades of post-colonial rule. In India, the multiplicity of types of ethnic identity and the integrating force of the multi-ethnic and nationalist Congress Party facilitated the emergence of a multi-ethnic national identity, while the adoption of a lingua franca developed through trade as the national language did the same for Indonesia. These multi-ethnic national identities have weakened substantially in recent decades, as discussed in the following section and in Chapter 21 on Indonesia. The role of religion in weakening these identities is discussed in Chapter 8.

Sub-Saharan Africa is the region in which multi-ethnic nationalism is most commonly found, although ethno-nationalism is by no means absent there. The predominance of ethnopolitical cleavages, their complex multilevel morphology already described, the absence of large cultural differences in most African countries (in contrast to the multi-ethnic/multicultural societies of Asia, Latin America, and the Caribbean) except those divided by religion, and the aforementioned politics of communal contention combine to produce multi-ethnic national identities that most effectively integrate national and ethnopolitical identities in this context. The presence of substantial numbers of foreign Africans in the presently or formerly wealthier African countries helps to solidify the multi-ethnic national identities that exclude them, but include all ethnic groups comprising primarily citizens. It should be noted that these identities are emerging, rather than fully formed, and that they mitigate, rather than eliminate, ethnopolitical conflict. A minority of African societies are deeply divided and thus torn by conflicts about national identity. That small cultural differences do not always eliminate such conflict is amply illustrated by Rwanda and Burundi, which can be called culturally homogeneous because the pre-colonial Tutsi conquerors adopted the culture of the conquered Hutu, but in which colonial policies and post-independence political competition have created violent, deeply divided societies.

In the Middle East and North Africa, the national identities of states with colonially (Ottoman or European) created boundaries compete with: the transnational Arab nationalism, the primary competitor in the middle decades of the twentieth century; transnational Islamist identities (see Chapter 8), a primary competitor today; transnational non-Arab identities (Berber in Algeria and Morocco, and Kurdish in Iran, Iraq, and Turkey); and Sunni–Shi'a ethno-religious identities. Consequently, these national state identities are probably among the weakest in the developing world. The high level of violence among ethnopolitical groups in Iraq that has followed the American military intervention (see Chapter 22) demonstrates the weakness of efforts to construct civic or multi-ethnic national identities in that country.

KEY POINTS

- National identities are inherently political.
- National identities can be ethno-national, multi-ethnic/multicultural, and civic in varying degrees.
- Most national identities in the developing world were constructed during the colonial period, but some have been modified by post-independence politics.
- Differences among regions and countries of the developing world in the morphology of ethnopolitical identities, the tactics of ethnopolitical groups, the policies of the major colonial powers and post-independence states, and the presence of alternative identities significantly affected the construction of national identities.

Ethnopolitics in Multi-Ethnic and Deeply Divided Societies

Ethnopolitical morphology

The discussion of the construction of ethnopolitical and national identities in various regions of the developing world has revealed that the morphology of ethnopolitical groups varies greatly among the developing countries. Borrowing from Young (1976: 95–7), it is possible to specify five patterns of ethnopolitical morphology:

(1) homogeneous societies, such as Korea, Lesotho, and Haiti;

(2) societies with a single clearly dominant group, numerically and socially, and minorities, such as Algeria, Burma, and Nicaragua;

(3) bipolar, or deeply divided, societies, such as Burundi, Guyana, Rwanda, and Sri Lanka;

Table 7.1 Numbers of ethnopolitical groups in the developing world (minimum 1% of the population)

Region	Fearon (2003)	Scarritt and Mozaffar (1999)	Gurr (1993, 2000); MAR (2009)	Cederman et al. (2010)
Latin America–Caribbean	84		33	54
Asia	108		49	119
Sub-Saharan Africa	351	382	75	215
Middle East–N. Africa	70		40	83
Total	613	382	197	471

(4) multi-polar societies, divided primarily on a single dimension, with no dominant groups, such as many sub-Saharan African countries; and

(5) societies with a multiplicity of cultures, with more than one dimension of differentiation, such as India and Indonesia.

Countries with patterns (4) and (5), and those with pattern (2) in which the minorities do not cohere (a substantial majority of societies in that pattern at most points in time), can be called multi-ethnic societies.

Another approach to comparing ethnopolitical morphologies is to develop an index of fractionalization or fragmentation for each country. To do this, one must first specify all of the ethnic or ethnopolitical groups that exist in each country of the developing world because of past construction processes. Fearon (2003) and Cederman et al. (2010) have attempted to do this; Scarritt and Mozaffar (1999) have attempted to do it for Africa; Gurr and his associates in the Minorities at Risk (MAR) project (Gurr 1993, 2000; MAR 2009) have attempted to specify a narrower list of

groups 'at risk'. These authors have different definitions of politically relevant ethnic groups; it may be the case that different groups have been politicized for different purposes, including economic policymaking (Fearon), civil war (Cederman et al.), electoral politics (Scarritt and Mozaffar), and political protest and rebellion (Gurr), and that construction and politicization are ongoing processes. But it is nevertheless useful to examine these efforts to specify groups, as in Table 7.1, in order to get an idea of the very large number of them and to show that two regions are ranked in the same order in the three global data sets in terms of the number of groups specified: sub-Saharan Africa first; Asia second.

Only Fearon's data present a comparison of countries and regions in terms of fractionalization, which varies in his scale between 0 (homogeneous) and 1 (totally fragmented). These data (Fearon 2003: 204, 209, 215–19), summarized in Table 7.2, show that, within the developing world, the average level of ethnic fractionalization is lowest in Latin America–Caribbean, slightly higher in Asia and the Middle East–North Africa, and much higher in sub-Saharan Africa. The

Table 7.2 Ethnic fractionalization in the developing world

Region	Average	Range	% of countries with majority group
Latin America–Caribbean	0.41	0.743–0.095	78
Asia	0.44	1.00–0.002	78
Sub-Saharan Africa	0.71	0.953–0.180	28
Middle East–N. Africa	0.45	0.780–0.039	84

range of countries in terms of fragmentation is greatest in Asia, almost as great in sub-Saharan Africa, and less in the other two regions. Finally, the percentage of countries in which the largest group comprises the majority of the population is only 28 per cent in sub-Saharan Africa, and between 78 per cent and 84 per cent in the other three regions. Thirty African countries (70 per cent of the total) have fragmentation scores above 0.7, while only four Asian countries (including the two largest ones, India and Indonesia), three Middle Eastern countries, and one Latin American country have scores this high. Fearon's data thus support the conclusion that most African countries are far more fragmented than most countries in other regions.

Other relevant aspects of ethnopolitical morphology are geographic concentration, the extent of cultural differences among groups, and the presence of ethnic groups that have not been explicitly politicized, as described earlier. Available data indicate that ethnopolitical groups in sub-Saharan Africa tend to be the most geographically concentrated and tend to have the smallest cultural differences, and that there are more ethnic groups that have not been politicized there than in other regions of the developing world (Gurr 1993: 344–51; Fearon 2003: 211–14; Scarritt and Mozaffar 2003: 9–10).

Collective action and interaction

These different ethnopolitical morphologies interact with group advantage or disadvantage, political organizations and institutional rules, mobilization and state response histories, and international influences in causing different types of collective action by ethnopolitical groups and different types of interaction among them or with the state. Human agents who are rational within their belief and normative frameworks carry out these processes enabled and constrained by social structures (Mozaffar 1995; Gurr 2000: 65–95; Mozaffar et al. 2003: 380–2, 385–7). Ethnopolitical interactions cannot be fully explained without taking all of these factors and their interactions into account; the following presentation is organized factor by factor, but incorporates interactions among factors into the discussion of each one. Group advantage or disadvantage can be economic, political, or cultural, or any combination of these forms. Crucial political organizations include various civilian state agencies, the military and police,

political parties, and interest associations that are not ethnically based. Some are more institutionalized than others. Institutional rules can be broadly categorized as democratic, transitional, or autocratic (Gurr 2000: 154). Rules about the formation and control of ethnopolitical associations and the conduct of elections are of special importance. Group collective action and state responses have historical patterns that have varied in violence and intensity in different countries of the developing world, although these patterns are more firmly established in some countries than in others. These patterns are, of course, subject to change, but they have self-perpetuating qualities that resist change unless the forces supporting it are sufficient to overcome them. Finally, although ethnopolitics is primarily internal to states, it is significantly influenced by several aspects of globalization, diffusion, and contagion among identical or similar groups across state boundaries, and external political and material support.

Interaction among groups and between them and the state can be categorized as cooperative, competitive, or conflictual. The boundaries among these three types of collective interaction are by no means perfectly clear, and a given action by a group or the state may involve any two or all three types vis-à-vis various targets. The relative importance of these interaction patterns nevertheless provides a very useful way of comparing ethnopolitics in the countries of the developing world. As illustrated in Box 7.1, the literature on ethnopolitics there (Young 1976; Horowitz 1985; Gurr 1993, 2000) emphasizes the complex causation of conflict involving some degree of violence and, to a lesser extent, competition, but a greater emphasis on the latter and the inclusion of cooperation are necessary for a more balanced treatment. To highlight this point, it is useful to separate—within the discussion of each factor and its interactions with others—the explanation of cooperation, institutionalized competition, and peaceful protest from the explanation of conflict and non-institutionalized competition.

Cooperation and institutionalized competition among ethnopolitical groups and states in the developing world do not get much attention in the global media, yet they occur with great frequency and have significant consequences. They are substantially greater in frequency and consequences than conflict is in many countries, although they often coexist with conflict (involving the same or other groups). Peaceful protest attracts more media attention. It is not

BOX 7.1   TWO CONCEPTIONS OF THE CAUSES OF ETHNOPOLITICAL CONFLICT

An adequate theory of ethnic conflict should be able to explain both elite and mass behavior. Such a theory should also provide an explanation for the passionate, symbolic, and apprehensive aspects of ethnic conflict. Group entitlement, conceived as a joint function of comparative worth and legitimacy, does this—it explains why the followers follow, accounts for the intensity of group reactions, even to modest stimuli, and clarifies the otherwise mysterious quest for public signs of group status.

(Horowitz 1985: 226)

The motivations at the heart of ethnopolitics are assumed to be a mix of grievance, sentiment, solidarity, ambition, and calculation. It is simplistic to argue that one kind of motivation is primary and others subsidiary. Ethnopolitical protest and rebellion are consequences of complex interactions among collective experience, normative commitments, contention for power, and strategic assessments about how best to promote individual and collective interests.

(Gurr 2000: 66)

institutionalized, but is more properly seen as competition rather than conflict, although it is easy for such protest to turn violent and thus become conflictual through the actions of the protesters or the authorities (usually the police). This is one reason why the boundaries between cooperation and competition, and between competition and conflict, are often difficult to draw. On the other hand, conflict in the forms of violent protest, rebellion, and repression, as well as its almost indistinguishable cousin, non-institutionalized violent competition, get a great deal of attention from global media (and scholars); they are 'newsworthy'. The consequences of such conflict can indeed be horrific, but this is not always the case, and the media's view of ethnopolitical conflict as prevalent in most developing countries is distorted.

Ethnopolitical morphology and types of ethnopolitical interaction

Cooperation, institutionalized competition, and peaceful protest, aspects of the politics of communal contention, are much more frequent and consequential in multi-ethnic than in deeply divided societies, although they are not limited to the former type. The impossibility of majority support for the regime (which is important even for autocratic regimes) in the absence of such cooperation in the former type of society, and the tendency towards the mutual fears and hopes of ethno-nationalist 'winner takes all' politics among both groups in the latter type of society, account for this difference. Small cultural differences and the presence of non-politicized groups (impossible in deeply divided societies) facilitate cooperation, while geographic concentration (less likely in deeply divided societies) has more ambivalent effects. Conflict and non-institutionalized violent competition are

more likely to occur in deeply divided, than in multi-ethnic, societies, although they are not limited to the former type. The reasons for this are the inverse of those for the greater significance of cooperation in the latter type of society. Organizations such as political parties and the military tend strongly to be arenas of conflict in deeply divided societies (Horowitz 1985: 291–525). But within each type of society, other factors account for substantial differences in cooperation, competition, and conflict.

Group advantages and disadvantages, and types of ethnopolitical interaction

Cooperation is easier the smaller the advantages or disadvantages of different groups. Advantages or disadvantages can be economic, political, or cultural, and can be the result of discrimination in either state policies or well-established social structures, or of more accidental factors such as regional differences in resource endowments. Disadvantages that are seen as caused by discrimination in state policies make cooperation especially difficult (Gurr 1993: 34–60; Gurr 2000: 105–32), but disadvantages caused by social structural discrimination and not counteracted by state policies also hinder it. Since many groups in most countries of the developing world have advantages or disadvantages caused by discrimination (as described later in the chapter), ethnopolitical cooperation and the reduction of discrimination through state policies tend to go together.

Conflict is more likely to occur the greater the advantages or disadvantages of different groups, especially if these advantages or disadvantages are seen to result from discrimination in state policies. Horowitz (1985: 32) indicates that 'virtually all ranked systems of ethnic relations [in which class and ethnicity coincide] are in a state of rapid transition or of increasing coercion by the superordinate group to avert change'. Almost 90 per cent of the 186 groups in the developing world that were included in the MAR survey in the mid-1990s because they were judged to be at risk of being involved in violent conflict experienced one or more forms of discrimination, and most of the rest were at risk because of advantages gained from such discrimination. More than two-thirds of these groups experienced economic discrimination and 40 per cent experienced high levels of such discrimination. Within the developing world, economic discrimination is greatest in Latin America and the Caribbean (where indigenous peoples are subject to severe discrimination of all types), followed by the Middle East and North Africa, Asia, and sub-Saharan Africa, in that order. Political discrimination is even more prevalent in the developing world. Over 80 per cent of the 186 groups experienced political discrimination in the 1990s and over half experienced high levels of such discrimination. This form of discrimination is also greatest in Latin America and the Caribbean, and least in sub-Saharan Africa, but Asia ranks a close second in this case. Finally, cultural discrimination is less frequent, with small majorities of groups experiencing it in Latin America and the Middle East, a large minority of groups in Asia (mainly 'hill tribes'), and only a few groups in sub-Saharan Africa. Unlike the other forms of discrimination, a majority of groups that experience cultural discrimination experience it at low or medium levels. These forms of discrimination were highly correlated with group disadvantages (Gurr 2000: 105–27).

Organizations, institutional rules, and types of ethnopolitical interaction

Cooperation among ethnopolitical groups occurs primarily within the previously listed political organizations, operating with more or less firmly institutionalized rules. Institutional differences are probably the most important factor in explaining cooperation in such organizations. Cooperation requires a relatively high degree of institutionalization of the organizations within which it occurs, although it is impossible to specify the required level exactly. Democratic institutions, particularly if they are strong (highly institutionalized), promote cooperation, are the primary basis of institutionalized competition, and allow—and

in some ways encourage—relatively peaceful protest. Institutional rules providing relatively unrestricted freedom for group activities are crucial for both institutionalized competition and peaceful protest. Not surprisingly, the MAR data demonstrate the greater use of peaceful protest and less ethnopolitical conflict in democratic countries, and, perhaps more surprisingly, in transitional countries in the developing world as well.

In multi-ethnic societies, political parties contesting democratic elections need multi-ethnic support to win, unless one group constitutes a majority of the population or is close enough that a non-proportional electoral system can give that group control of a majority of seats in the legislature. But even in the latter cases, democratic institutions value inter-ethnic cooperation (and thus multi-ethnic parties) more than autocratic institutions do. Multi-ethnic parties predominate in sub-Saharan Africa and are found in a number of countries in other regions of the developing world. There is considerable debate about whether proportional representation or 'first past the post' (FPTP) electoral institutions are more likely to promote cooperation in multi-ethnic parties. The influence of such electoral institutions is probably outweighed by other factors. Horowitz (1985: 291–440) has analysed the ways in which ethnic parties, the support for which comes overwhelmingly from a single ethnopolitical group, enhance conflict in deeply divided societies by unreservedly pursuing the interests of that group and failing to form stable majority coalitions.

Conflict and non-institutionalized violent competition occur within and among the organizations in which cooperation occurs (Horowitz 1985: 291–525), but more frequently occur outside formal organizations in the forms of violent protest, armed rebellion, and state repression varying from restrictions on civil and political liberties, through conventional policing, to **genocide**. Conflict has been most violent in deeply divided societies, when groups are severely disadvantaged by multiple forms of discrimination, and under weak autocratic institutions. In the MAR data, violent rebellion between 1985 and 1998 had a mean annual magnitude in autocracies that was two-and-a-half times that in new democracies. Rebellion in transitional regimes was much closer to the level in new democracies. Partial or failed transitions in the developing world tend to increase protest, but decrease rebellion (Gurr 2000: 151–63). The data show that, in part, democratization decreases conflict by decreasing discrimination (Gurr 2000: 163–77). Thus, while the institutional instability engendered by democratization can increase ethnopolitical conflict, as Snyder (2000) suggests, this is not its most common effect, at least beyond the transition period.

Mobilization, state response, and types of ethnopolitical interaction

Ethnopolitical identity construction and ethnopolitical group mobilization are closely related processes that tend to occur together over time. As discussed previously, mobilization of ethnic associations is part of the politicization of ethnic identities, which then leads to ethnopolitical mobilization through political parties. Thus ethnopolitical mobilization has a history going back to the colonial period in most countries of the developing world. Since independence, such mobilization has been most intense and most violent in deeply divided societies, when groups are severely disadvantaged by multiple forms of discrimination, under weak autocratic institutions, and in the presence of international political and material support for or against mobilization. It has been least intense and most peaceful in highly multi-ethnic societies, when few or no groups are severely disadvantaged by any form of discrimination, under strong democratic institutions, and in the absence of international political and material support. The longer a specific pattern of mobilization occurs, the more likely it is to be self-perpetuating unless changed deliberately by powerful actors. It is very difficult to change a primarily conflictual pattern of collective interaction into a primarily cooperative pattern, or vice versa, and somewhat difficult to institutionalize un-institutionalized competition or to change violent protest into peaceful protest.

The tendency for patterns of mobilization to be self-perpetuating is reinforced by state repression of a pattern of mobilization or the absence of such repression. Not surprisingly, the more intense and violent the mobilization, the more severe the repression. In the MAR data, repression varies from conventional policing to genocide (the extermination of an ethnic group) and **politicide** (the extermination of political enemies). Between 1955 and 1995, extensive ethnopolitical repression occurred in all areas of the developing world. It involved the largest number of groups in Asia and sub-Saharan Africa, but was least intense in Latin America and the Caribbean during the last decade of that period. Repression was far more likely to intensify violent mobilization than to stop it. Harff (2003: 66) found that genocide or politicide is most likely to occur or to be repeated after political upheaval in autocracies based on the support of advantaged minorities with exclusionary ideologies. State response to peaceful protest, most common in democratic states, has often been to grant only a small proportion of the protesters' demands, but not to engage in repression. This response has typically led to the continuation of peaceful protest.

International influences and types of ethnopolitical interaction

International influences have fostered both ethnopolitical cooperation and ethnopolitical conflict. Scholars have given some attention to the direct diffusion or indirect contagion of ethnopolitical conflicts across national borders through the presence of the same or closely related groups on both sides of the border. Much less attention has been paid to the diffusion of ethnopolitical cooperation, which is more difficult to study. But as democracy has been diffused to much of the developing world since the end of the cold war, it is possible to argue that ethnopolitical cooperation and institutionalized electoral competition have often been diffused with it.

During the cold war, the superpowers and former colonial powers frequently gave material, political, and/or military support to parties in ethnopolitical conflict in the developing world. This was done to further the objectives of the powers giving aid, but it undoubtedly substantially exacerbated such conflict in a number of countries, including Afghanistan, Angola, Ethiopia, Guatemala, and Nicaragua. It is argued in the next section that international intervention in ethnopolitical conflicts has been less self-interested since the end of the cold war, but the combination of the persistence of some degree of self-interest and lack of adequate information about the consequences of specific forms of intervention mean that political and/or material support can still have conflict-enhancing effects. French intervention in Rwanda in favour of the existing government (and thus of its followers who were bent on genocide) before and during the genocide of 1994, and increased Sunni–Shi'a–Kurd conflict in Iraq after the Anglo-American invasion are cases in point. Regional powers within the developing world have also supported parties to ethnopolitical conflict in their regions out of self-interest, which formerly included rewards from their cold war patrons. Finally, regional and international organizations—governmental and especially non-governmental—have struggled to resolve a number of ethnopolitical conflicts, with consequences that have varied from success to exacerbating the conflict, but it appears that some of these organizations are becoming more successful.

Globalization has stimulated ethnopolitical mobilization and probably **terrorism** as tools in ethnopolitical conflict, but it has also strengthened international norms of democratization, human rights, and non-discrimination. International norms now favour ethnopolitical cooperation, institutionalized competition, and the peaceful resolution of ethnopolitical conflicts to a greater extent than ever before. However, this may be changing with terrorism and Anglo-American reactions to it, as discussed next. Economic globalization has strengthened national identities in the developing world, while also weakening the capacity of most developing states to carry out nationalist policies that challenge multinational corporations or international financial institutions. Globalization of communications has provided new tools for constructing ethnopolitical groups as well as nations. But, as Billig (1995: 128–43) argues, global culture cannot serve as the primary basis of resistance to economic globalization, because it is less banal than the cultures of the developed nations, which support such globalization.

KEY POINTS

- Ethnopolitical morphology takes a variety of forms in the countries of the developing world, ranging from highly multi-ethnic to deeply divided and homogeneous.

- Interaction among ethnopolitical groups, and between them and states, involves a mixture of cooperation, competition, and conflict.

- Cooperative interactions are most easily achieved in multi-ethnic societies that have small group advantages and disadvantages, democracy based on relatively institutionalized multi-ethnic parties, a historical pattern of non-violent ethnopolitical mobilization and minimal repression of it, and international influences that support 'managed heterogeneity' rather than one side of ethnopolitical conflicts.

- Cooperation is possible when some of these conditions are absent.

The State and Nation-Building in the Developing World

Nationalism was relatively weak in most developing states at independence, and was essentially absent in those that lacked meaningful nationalist movements, and which won their independence through a combination of the spillover effect of nationalist movements in neighbouring countries and the colonial powers' desire to extricate themselves from their colonies: 'The initial "nation-building" ethos [in Africa] proposed to resolve the ethnic question by confining it to the private realm' (Young 2001: 174). Civic nationalism was asserted ideologically in spite of its empirical weakness. But authoritarian 'banishment of ethnicity from political assertion merely drove it underground' (Young 2001: 176), while rulers continued to make ethnopolitical calculations in appointments to high political positions and the placement of development projects. Many essentially similar histories of failed efforts to extinguish ethnopolitical identities and movements, and either to create civic nationalism by fiat or to assimilate minorities into the core ethno-national identity by force, are found in other regions of the developing world. Forced assimilation to ethno-nationalism has had the more severe consequences; in deeply divided societies with long histories of ethno-political mobilization, especially those characterized by great group differences, and external material and political support for one side or the other, it has usually led to extremely violent conflict.

Owing in part to the desire to reduce the negative effects of economic globalization and the support received from international norms and the globalization of communications, there has been a shift in some developing states from these unsuccessful policies of trying to impose civic nationalism by fiat or majority ethno-national identities by force towards accepting multi-ethnic/multicultural national identities as a viable compromise. As Sen points out (see Box 7.2), there is a substantial difference between state policies promoting rational multiculturalism and policies promoting plural monoculturalism. In the former, national identity is based on a freely chosen blend of diversity and commonality among interacting ethnic groups; in the latter, full diversity is enforced by isolated groups and national identity is based on a 'federation' of group identities. The shift to rational multiculturalism/multi-ethnicity has been easier in multi-ethnic societies than in societies with a single dominant group or deeply divided societies, but such national identities are potentially viable in all of these societies (Snyder 2000: 33). They tend to make state and nation mutually reinforcing; 'the persistence of states, however challenged or changed by globalization they may be, offers a partial explanation for the continuation of nationhood as a salient form of belonging' (Croucher 2003: 14). Immigration compels states to clarify and reinforce national boundaries; responses to terrorism have the same effect; 'Nationhood, then, continues to be a functional, familiar, and legitimate mechanism for belonging' (Croucher 2003: 16). The aspirations of stateless peoples to national states prove its value.

Gurr (2000: 195–211, 275–7) presents data to show that the number and severity of ethnopolitical conflicts have declined since the end of the cold war, reversing the upward trend of the preceding three decades. He attributes this change to the emergence of a 'regime of managed ethnic heterogeneity, shorthand for a bundle of conflict-mitigating doctrines and practices' (Gurr 2000: 277–8). This regime has both domestic components—essentially those previously described as promoting ethnopolitical cooperation—and international components—that is, international norms and changes in the behaviour of outside states and transnational organizations, reflecting decreased self-interest and increased competence. It fosters multi-ethnic/multicultural nationalism. But Gurr (2000: 223–60) also acknowledges that some ethnopolitical groups are still at risk of being involved in future violent conflicts, because they maintain the interaction patterns with other groups and states that have led to violent conflict in the past.

The United States, an important player in this international regime, moved back to self-interest and interventionism under the Bush administration,

although the Obama administration has reversed this trend slightly. The consequences of this change for national identities are uncertain. As mentioned already, Iraqi national identity was weakened, rather than strengthened, by the Anglo-American invasion (see Chapter 22), and the same can be said even more emphatically for national identity in Afghanistan. Terrorists tend to promote transnational identities. On the other hand, national identities have probably been strengthened in countries such as Venezuela and Bolivia, in which elected leaders have both reached out to indigenous groups and defied US pressures. It is far too soon to declare the demise of ethnopolitical conflict, exclusionary ethno-nationalism, or their exacerbation through foreign intervention and terrorism.

KEY POINTS

- Many states of the developing world have attempted to suppress ethnopolitical identities and conflicts by declaring civic nationalism by fiat or assimilating minorities into their core ethno-national identity by force, but more are now accepting multi-ethnic national identities as a viable compromise.

- National identities in the developing world, usually based on existing states, continue to be viable in the era of globalization and offer a basis for resisting the negative effects of economic globalization.

- The number and severity of ethnopolitical conflicts have declined since the end of the cold war because of the emergence of a 'regime of managed ethnic heterogeneity', but some violent conflicts persist.

Conclusion

In conclusion, we can briefly summarize the major themes of this chapter. Ethnopolitical and national identities are different, although both are socially constructed, and thus change over time. The pattern of ethnopolitical identities (the ethnopolitical morphology) within countries involves the number and relative size of groups, their geographic concentration and degree of cultural differences, and varies from deeply divided to highly multi-ethnic. National identities are civic, multi-ethnic, or ethno-national. Collective action by ethnopolitical groups, and cooperative, competitive, and conflictual interactions among them and with states, are influenced by the interaction of ethnopolitical morphology, group advantages and disadvantages, political organizations and institutional rules, mobilization and state response histories, and international influences. Cooperative interactions are most easily achieved in multi-ethnic societies that have small group advantages and disadvantages, democracy based on relatively institutionalized multi-ethnic parties, a historical pattern of non-violent ethnopolitical mobilization and minimal repression of it,

and international influences that support 'managed heterogeneity' rather than one side of ethnopolitical conflicts. These interactions, in turn, tend to promote **nation-building** through multi-ethnic/multicultural nationalism. There is evidence of a shift in this direction in some countries of the developing world, but conflictual interactions and failures of nation-building still occur all too frequently.

QUESTIONS

1. If ethnopolitical and national identities are constructed, and thus can change, why do they not change more frequently and rapidly?

2. What are the major types of national identity and how different are they?

3. Why do you think scholars disagree on how many ethnopolitical groups there are in the developing world and its various regions?

4. Does the nature of ethnopolitical and/or national identities determine whether democracy can be effective in the developing world?

5. If the amount of violent ethnopolitical conflict has declined in the developing world as a whole, why is such conflict still so strong in some countries?

6. What are the effects of globalization and foreign intervention on national identities in the developing world?

7. What are the effects of policies of plural monoculturalism and reason-based multiculturalism (as defined by Sen) on different types of national identity?

8. What are the major differences in ethnopolitics and nationalism among the four regions of the developing world?

FURTHER READING

Chandra, K. (ed.) (2012) *Constructivist Theories of Ethnic Politics* (Oxford: Oxford University Press) Presents a new definition of ethnic identities that relates attributes to categories, and a new model for analysing how these identities are politically activated and changed. Relations of ethnicity to electoral politics, patronage, riots, and state disintegration and reconstruction are discussed.

Eriksen, T. H. (1993) *Ethnicity and Nationalism: Anthropological Perspectives* (London: Pluto Press) Presents an anthropological perspective on ethnicity, identity, ethnic relations, nationalism, and relations between states and ethnic minorities.

Fearon, J. D. (2003) 'Ethnic Structure and Cultural Diversity around the World: A Cross-National Data Set on Ethnic Groups', *Journal of Economic Growth*, 8: 191–218 Describes a global data set under construction on ethnic and linguistic/cultural groups, and compares it to other data sets; highlights the difficulties encountered in specifying ethnic groups cross-nationally.

Gurr, T. R. (2000) *Peoples versus States: Minorities at Risk in the New Century* (Washington DC: United States Institute of Peace Press) The second book from the Minorities at Risk project identifies communal groups at risk, and analyses forms of risk, group grievances, group mobilization, group protest and rebellion, and the resolution of group conflicts, along with the role of democracy and the risk of future ethnic violence. It includes a number of illustrative sketches from the developing world.

Horowitz, D. L. (1985) *Ethnic Groups in Conflict* (Berkeley, CA: University of California Press) Presents a definition of ethnicity and a theory of ethnic conflict among unranked groups derived primarily from social psychology. Also discusses the roles of political parties and the military in ethnic conflict and strategies for its resolution, and emphasizes deeply divided societies in South-East and South Asia, Africa, and the Caribbean.

Hutchinson, J. and Smith, A. D. (eds) (1994) *Nationalism* (Oxford: Oxford University Press) A very comprehensive reader that includes selections from classic works on the definition of nationalism, theories of nationalism, nationalism in the developing world, and the effects of trends in the international system on nationalism.

Sen, A. (2006) *Identity and Violence: The Illusion of Destiny* (New York: W. W. Norton) Argues that all people have multiple identities and that movements that restrict relevant identities to ethnic or national ones only promote violence.

Young, C. (1976) *The Politics of Cultural Pluralism* (Madison, WI: University of Wisconsin Press) Discusses cultural pluralism, identities, the state, nationalism, and cultural mobilization in Africa, the Arab world, Asia, and Latin America, illustrated with comparative case studies from these regions.

WEB LINKS

http://www.cidcm.umd.edu/mar/   The website of the Minorities at Risk project, covering almost 300 politically active ethnic groups coded on approximately 1,000 variables. Qualitative assessments of every group's risk are included.

http://www.icr.ethz.ch/data/growup/epr-eth   The website of Cederman et al., *Ethnic Power Relations*, cited in Table 7.1.

http://www.stanford.edu/~jfearon   Go to egreousrepdata.zip for Fearon's data, which is summarized in this chapter in Tables 7.1 and 7.2.

For additional material and resources, please visit the Online Resource Centre at:
http://www.oxfordtextbooks.co.uk/orc/burnell4e/

8
Religion

Jeff Haynes

Chapter contents

Overview

Recent decades have seen widespread involvement of religion in politics, especially, but not exclusively, in parts of the developing world. This chapter, examining the relationship between religion and politics, is structured as follows. First, the concept of religion is defined, and its contemporary political and social salience in many developing countries is emphasized. Second, the chapter examines how religion interacts with politics in the developing world, not least because it is often associated with religious competition and conflict. Third, we look at how 'religion'—especially identifiable religious institutions and organizations—interacts with the state in the developing world, because of the importance of these relationships for the wider issue of religion and politics. Fourth, we examine how religion is involved in democratization in the developing world, with special focus on the phenomenon known as the 'Arab Spring'. Fifth, the chapter considers the extent to which, after 11 September 2001—that is, the epochal day on which the United States was attacked by al-Qaeda terrorists, resulting in the loss of around 3,000 lives—the world changed in terms of the political salience of religion. We examine the importance of both domestic and external factors in conflicts characterized by religious concerns in the developing world.

Introduction

'Religion and **politics**' is everywhere. Newspapers, television news broadcasts, blogs, and other sources of information incessantly feature stories and commentary about how and why religion and politics interact. Often, the focus is on the competition and conflict that derive from this relationship, especially in the **developing world**. For example, a recent recurring theme is the issue of the role of religion in the widespread political changes in the Middle East and North Africa (MENA), known as the 'Arab Spring'. There is also the long-running issue of the mainly Muslim Palestinians and the Israeli Jews, whose decades-long political dispute today centres on the **status** of holy sites—especially Jerusalem—claimed by the two sides, as well as political and economic concerns of the Palestinians. In addition, in the early months of 2013, international attention was drawn to the adjoining countries of Algeria and Mali, beset by Islamist militants seeking to change the political configurations of those countries.

These events remind us that Islamic militancy has a long track record in both domestic and international politics. For example, from the early 1990s, Algeria endured a decade of civil war between Islamist militant rebels and the state. The roots of this conflict go back to a contested election, and, more generally, highlight the often problematic political relationship between religious and secular actors in the MENA region. In December 1991, Algeria held legislative elections that most independent observers characterized as amongst the freest ever held in the MENA region. The following January, however, Algeria's armed forces seized power to prevent what was likely to be a decisive victory in the elections by an Islamist party, the Front Islamique du Salut (FIS). The assumption was that if the FIS were to achieve power, it would then erode Algeria's newly refreshed democratic **institutions**. In London, *The Economist* posed the question, 'What is the point of an experiment in democracy if the first people it delivers to power are intent on dismantling it?' (2 January 1992). The answer might well be: 'This is the popular will, it must be respected—whatever the outcome.' Instead, Algeria's military leaders imposed their preference. The FIS was summarily banned, thousands of its supporters were incarcerated, and between 150,000 and 200,000 Algerians died in the subsequent civil war. Even now, nearly twenty years after the initial outburst of violence, Algeria still endures intermittent attacks from Islamist rebels, unhappy about the nature of the political system in the country.

It is worth noting at this point that there is no obvious reason why **political Islam** cannot compete for power democratically. Events in the Arab Spring since 2011—which include at least initial electoral victories for Islamists in Egypt and Tunisia—provide evidence of this contention. Generally, 'political Islam' refers to diverse political movements that are, however, all animated by an ideological belief in the desirability of what is known as the 'Islamic state', an ideal polity with often diverse characteristics that, at various times, has included elements of many other political movements, while simultaneously adapting the religious views of Islamism. In various Muslim-majority countries in recent years, including the Palestinian authority, Iraq, Turkey, Pakistan, and the aforementioned Egypt and Tunisia, Islamists have gained power either alone (Hamas in the Palestinian authority, and the Justice and Development Party, or AKP, in Turkey) or as part of a ruling coalition (Iraq, Egypt, and Tunisia). In these cases, we see Islamists to an extent being willing to play by the democratic rules of the game.

Elsewhere in the developing world, Islamists are also politically active. For example, in Africa, Nigeria is increasingly polarized politically between Muslim and Christian forces, with the phenomenon of Boko Haram the most recent manifestation of an apparently intransigent Islamist militancy, and fragmented Somalia has continuing conflict centrally involving various Islamists, while Sudan lurches from crisis to crisis in the aftermath of the country's long-running civil war between Muslims and non-Muslims. In these cases, Islamists have not sought to use the ballot box to achieve influence and power—but, then again, that particular option has not been available as a result of constitutional restrictions or constraints, or wider political factors.

Not only Islamists pursue political goals related to religion. In officially secular India, a growth in militant Hinduism was highlighted by, but not confined to, the Babri Masjid mosque incident at Ayodhya in 1992, which was instrumental in transforming the country's political landscape. This mosque, according to militant Hindus, was built on the birthplace of the Hindu god of war, Rama. As long ago as 1950, the mosque was closed down by the Indian government, because militant Hindus wanted to build a Hindu temple there. Since then, Hindu militants, whose primary political organization is the Bharatiya Janata Party

(BJP), have grown to political prominence. From 1996 to mid-2004, the BJP was the dominant party in three ruling coalitions. Since then, the BJP has competed electorally and is, at the time of writing (mid-2013), the leading opposition party in the country, expected to do well in India's next general elections, due in 2014.

On the other hand, religion can significantly contribute to political and social stability, for example in the way in which the Roman Catholic Church was a leading player in the turn to democracy in Latin America in the 1980s and 1990s. In that region, however, the rise of a strand of Protestantism known as Pentecostalism has served to challenge the Catholic Church's historical hegemony.

KEY POINTS

- The last three decades have seen widespread involvement of religion in politics, especially in many countries in the developing world.

- Several religious traditions have experienced increased political involvement.

- Religion and democracy do not always seem compatible, although religious actors have contributed to democratization.

Religion and Politics

Before proceeding, it is necessary to define 'religion'. In this chapter, religion has two analytically distinct, yet related, meanings.

In a *spiritual* sense, religion pertains in three ways to models of social and individual behaviour that help believers to organize their everyday lives.

(1) It is to do with the idea of *transcendence*—that is, it relates to supernatural realities.

(2) It is concerned with *sacredness*—that is, a system of language and practice that organizes the world in terms of what is deemed holy.

(3) It refers to *ultimacy*—it relates people to the ultimate conditions of existence.

In another, *material*, sense, religious beliefs can motivate individuals and groups to act in pursuit of social or political goals. Very few—if any—religious groups have an *absolute* lack of concern for at least *some* social and political issues. Consequently, religion can be 'a

mobiliser of masses, a controller of mass action . . . an excuse for repression [or] an ideological basis for dissent' (Calvert and Calvert 2001: 140). In many countries, religion remains an important source of basic value orientations; this may have social and/or political connotations.

One final point concerns the relationship between religion and ethnicity. As Chapter 7 demonstrates, religion is one of the bases for **ethnic identity**. For instance, in India, Sikh ethnic identity has been defined largely in terms of adherence to a common religion. It could seem, then, that ethnicity is the overarching concept and religious identification is one subtype. However, there are situations in which people sharing a single religion are divided by ethnicity, such as in Pakistan, where people share a common Islamic faith, but are ethnically divided on the basis of region and language. Moreover, appeals to religion often seek to transcend particular local or ethnic identities in the name of a supposedly universal ideal. It is wisest, therefore, to see ethnicity and religion as terms the potential meaning and content of which overlap, but remain distinct.

An American commentator, George Weigel, claims that there is an '**unsecularization** of the world'—that is, a global religious revitalization (quoted in Huntington 1993: 26). This is manifested in a global resurgence of religious ideas and **social movements** not confined to one faith or only to poor, developing countries. This unexpected development can be explained in various ways. No simple, clear-cut reason or single theoretical explanation covers all of the cases. Yet the widespread emergence of religious actors with overtly social or political goals is often linked to **modernization**—that is, the prolonged period of historically unprecedented, diverse, massive change, characterized by urbanization, industrialization, and abrupt technological developments that people around the world have experienced in recent times. Modernization is said not only to have undermined traditional value systems, but also to have allocated opportunities—both within and between countries—in highly unequal ways. This has led many people to feel both disorientated and troubled, and as a result some, at least, (re)turn to religion for solace and comfort. In doing so, they seek a new or renewed sense of identity, something to give their lives greater meaning and purpose.

A second, although linked, explanation for apparent religious resurgence moves away from the specific impact of modernization to point to a more generalized 'atmosphere of crisis'. A key factor is said to be widespread popular disillusion with the abilities of secular state leaders to direct their socio-economic polities so that people generally benefit. Such disappointment can then feed into perceptions that these leaders hold power illegitimately—a sense bolstered when leaders resort to political oppression. Adding to the sense of crisis is widespread popular belief that society's traditional morals and values are being seriously undermined, not least by the corrosive effects of **globalization**, Westernization, and **secularization**—that is, the reduction in influence or even withdrawal of religion from the public realm. These circumstances are said to provide a fertile milieu for many people's 'return' to religion.

This suggests that the influence of religion will not be seen 'only' in relation to personal and social issues. Commentators have additionally pointed to *political* effects of the 'return of religion' where, in many developing countries, highly politicized religious groups, institutions, and movements have emerged—or adopted a higher profile—in recent years. Such actors are found in many different faiths and sects, and what they have in common is a desire to change domestic, and in some cases international, arrangements, so as to (re)instate religion as a central societal and political influence. They adopt a variety of tactics to achieve their goals. Some actors confine themselves to the realm of legitimate political protest, seeking reform or change via the ballot box; others resort to violence and terror to pursue their objectives.

Other explanations are offered for what is widely seen as a global religious revival and revitalization, but some commentators suggest that, in the developing world, there is not a religious resurgence per se; rather, political religion is simply more visible—largely as a consequence of the global communications revolution. In other words, religion is not a novel political actor, so much as a stubbornly persistent one. For Smith (1990: 34), 'what has changed in the present situation … is mainly the growing awareness of [global manifestations of political religion] by the Western world, and the perception that they might be related to our interests'. This makes the recent trends only the latest manifestation of *cyclical* religious activity, made more highly visible (and, to many, alarming) by advances in communications technology and availability. In short, globalization is a multifaceted process of change, universally affecting states, local communities, and individuals. Religions are not exempted from its influence; as a result, like other social agents, they participate in and are affected by globalization. Academic

discussions of religion and globalization often highlight trends towards cultural pluralism as a result of globalization, examining how various religions respond (Haynes 2007). Some believers react 'positively', accepting or even endorsing pluralism, including some Christian ecumenical movements. Others emphasize more inter-religious differences, sometimes confronting non-believers in attempts to preserve their particular values from being eroded by globalization.

But they are not necessarily *sui generis*. In the developing world, various religious traditions—for example Hinduism, Buddhism, and Islam—all experienced periods of pronounced political activity in the first half of the twentieth century in what were then mostly colonized countries. In the 1920s and the 1930s, religion was frequently used in the service of anti-colonial nationalism, and was a major facet of emerging **national identity** in opposition to alien rule (see Haynes 1996: 55–6). For example, in various Muslim countries, such as Algeria, Egypt, and Indonesia, Islamic consciousness was the defining ideology of nationalist movements. In 1947, immediately after the Second World War, Pakistan was founded as a Muslim state, religiously and culturally distinct from India, which was 80 per cent Hindu. A decade later, Buddhism was politically important, inter alia, in Burma, Sri Lanka, and Vietnam. Later, in the 1960s in Latin America, both **Christian democracy**—the application of Christian precepts to politics—and **liberation theology**—a radical ideology using Christianity as the basis of a demand for greater socio-economic justice for the poor—were politically consequential. More recently and in diverse countries including Iran, the United States, and Nicaragua, religion (re)appeared as an important political actor. Religious actors became skilled at using the media to spread their political messages (Tarrow 1998: 115). In sum, political religion is nearly always in opposition to the status quo; in the developing world, this has been the case since at least the early years of the twentieth century, a time of widespread external colonial control. Current manifestations of political religion can be located in this historical continuum and context to stress *continuity* rather than *change*.

A key example in this regard is Boko Haram, an Islamist religious sect active in northern Nigeria (Walker 2012). Since 2009, Boko Haram has violently targeted Nigeria's police, rival Muslim clerics, politicians, and **public institutions**. It is said to be leading an armed revolt against several targets, including governmental **corruption**, abusive security forces, strife between the disaffected Muslim north and Christian south, and widening regional economic disparity in an oil-rich, yet impoverished, country. It may be that Boko Haram's actions go beyond narrowly religious issues to include socio-economic concerns that Nigeria's government has shown little capacity to resolve in the country's disaffected Muslim north, a region of deep poverty and limited opportunities for improvement. In August 2011, Boko Haram's bombing of a United Nations building in the capital, Abuja, and claims that it has ties with al-Qaeda led to new Western fears about its growth and influence.

Boko Haram colloquially translates into 'Western education is a sin', which may be a name assigned by the government. The group calls itself *Jama'atul Alhul Sunnah Lidda'wati wal jihad*, which translates as 'people committed to the propagation of the prophet's teachings and jihad'. In July 2009, Boko Haram members refused to follow a motorcycle helmet law, leading to heavy-handed police tactics that set off an armed uprising in the northern state of Bauchi and spread into the states of Borno, Yobe, and Kano. The incident was suppressed by the army and left more than 800 dead. It also led to the execution of Yusuf, the sect's founder and 'spiritual leader', as well as the deaths of his father-in-law and other sect members, which **human rights** advocates consider to be extrajudicial killings. In the aftermath of the 2009 unrest, an Islamist insurrection under a splintered leadership emerged. From that time, Boko Haram began to carry out a number of suicide bombings and assassinations from Maiduguri to Abuja, staged an ambitious prison break-in in Bauchi, freeing more than 700 inmates in 2010, and during 2011–13 regularly attacked Christian churches in northern Nigeria (Walker 2012).

KEY POINTS

- Religion has spiritual, material, and in some cases political aspects.

- Religion played an important political role in many developing countries during the last years of colonialism.

- Patchy modernization and/or a more generalized 'atmosphere of crisis' are said to underpin religious resurgence.

- It is often claimed that there is a near-global religious revival, but globalization may simply be rendering religion in politics more visible.

Religion and the State

The relationship of religion to politics in the developing world centrally informs the importance of **state–church relations**—that is, the interactions in a country between the state and the leading religious organization(s). A major difficulty in trying to survey existing church–state relations in the developing world is that the very concept of *church* reflects a somewhat parochial Anglo-American standpoint with most relevance to Western Christian traditions.

Extending the question of church–state relations to non-Christian and developing world contexts necessitates some preliminary conceptual clarifications—not least because the very idea of a prevailing state–church dichotomy is culture-bound (see Box 8.1). *Church* is a Christian institution, while the modern understanding of *state* is deeply rooted in the post-Reformation European political experience. Overloaded with Western cultural history, these two concepts cannot easily be translated into non-Christian terminologies. Some religions—for example Hinduism—have no ecclesiastical structure at all. Consequently, there *cannot* be a clerical challenge to India's secular state comparable to that of Buddhist monks in parts of South-East Asia

BOX 8.1 RELIGION, NATIONALISM, AND IDENTITY

What is the relationship between religion and nationalism? The first point is that nationalism is a source of identity for many people in the developing world. Many identities are based on shared values, beliefs, or concerns that not only include religion, but which can also extend to ethnicity, nationality, culture, and political ideologies (Gopin 2000, 2005). This does not imply that such expressions of identity are necessarily monolithic entities—because in fact *everyone's* self-conception is a unique combination of various identities that can include, but are not limited to, community, religion, ethnicity, nationalism, **gender**, class, and family. Their relative importance and compatibility will differ at various times and circumstances. For example, race and religion are important sources of identity in some societies, while in others political ideologies and nationalism are judged to be of more significance. In short, both individual and collective senses of identity are socially constructed from a number of available traits and experiences, all of which are subject to interpretation. People *choose* their history and ancestry, and as a result can *create*, as much as *discover*, differences from others (Gopin 2000; Malek 2004).

or of *mullahs* in Iran. However, political parties and movements energized by religious notions—such as Hinduism and Sikhism—have great political importance in contemporary India. Within the developing world, only in Latin America is it pertinent to speak of church–state relations along the lines of the European model. This is because of the historical dominance in the region of the Roman Catholic Church and the creation of European-style states in the early nineteenth century.

The differences between Christian conceptions of state and church, and those of other world religions, are well illustrated by reference to Islam. In the Muslim tradition, mosque is not church. The closest Islamic approximation to 'state', *dawla*, means, conceptually, either a ruler's dynasty or his administration (only with the specific proviso of *church* as generic concept for 'moral community', *priest* for 'custodians of the sacred law', and *state* for 'political community' is it appropriate to use these concepts in Islamic and other non-Christian contexts). On the theological level, the command–obedience nexus that constitutes the Islamic definition of authority is not demarcated by conceptual categories of religion and politics. Life as a physical reality is an expression of divine will and authority (*qudrah*). There is no validity in separating the matters of piety from those of the polity; both are divinely ordained. Yet although both religious and political authorities are legitimated Islamically, they invariably constitute two independent social institutions. They do, however, regularly interact with each other. In sum, there is a variety of church–state relations in the contemporary world (see Box 8.2). Note, however, that this typology is not exhaustive, but instead identifies common arrangements.

In the *confessional* church–state relationship, ecclesiastical authority is pre-eminent over secular power. A dominant religion—Islam in the countries in Box 8.2—seeks to shape the world according to its leadership's interpretations of God's plan for humankind. However, confessional states are rare in the early twenty-first century. One of the most consistent effects of secularization is to separate religious and secular power almost—but not quite—regardless of the religion or type of political system. However, as events in Saudi Arabia after the country's creation in 1932, in Iran since the 1978–79 Islamic revolution, and in Sudan and Afghanistan from the 1980s indicate, several Muslim countries have sought to build confessional polities.

Because of Islam's pivotal role, the overthrow of the Shah of Iran in 1979 was one of the most spectacular political upheavals of recent times. Because of space limitations, however, this chapter contains relatively little on the important topic of religion and politics in that country. (Interested readers will find on the Online Resource Centre a commentary on the issue of religion and politics in Iran.) The Shah's **regime** was not a shaky monarchy, but a powerful centralized autocratic state, possessing a strong and feared security service (SAVAK), and an apparently loyal and cohesive officer corps. Unlike earlier revolutions in other Muslim countries, such as Egypt, Iraq, Syria, and Libya, Iran's was not a revolution from above, but one with massive popular support and participation. The forces that overthrew the Shah came from all of the urban social classes, Iran's different nationalities, and ideologically varying political parties and movements. Nevertheless, when an Islamic Republic was eventually declared, the outcome of the revolutionary process was a clerical, authoritarian regime. In these events, the *ulama* (or Muslim clerics), who adhere like the bulk of Iran's Muslims to the Shi'a tradition, played a central role. Organized in and by the Islamic Republican Party, they came to power, established an Islamic constitution, and dominated the post-revolutionary institutions.

Alongside the confessional states such as Iran there are the 'generally religious' states, such as the United

BOX 8.2 A TYPOLOGY OF CHURCH–STATE RELATIONS

Confessional	'Generally religious'	Established faith	Liberal secular	Marxist secular
Iran, Saudi Arabia, Sudan, Afghanistan (under the Taliban, 1996–2001)	Indonesia, US	England, Norway	Netherlands, Turkey, India, Ghana	China, Albania (until 1991), Russia (until 1991), North Korea

States and Indonesia. They are guided by religious beliefs in general, but are not tied to any specific religious tradition. Both the United States and Indonesia have a belief in God as one of the bases on which the nation should be built. In Indonesia, under General Suharto (1965–98), such a belief formed one of the five pillars of the state ideology, **Pancasila**. This position is very similar to the notion of 'civil religion' in the United States. However, whereas the generally religious policy of religion in Indonesia is an official policy, civil religion in the United States is not formally recognized.

Then there are countries that have an officially established faith, but which are also socially highly secular, of which Norway and England are examples. Over time, the voices of the established churches in public policy issues have generally become increasingly marginal.

Next, and frequently encountered in the modern era, the *liberal secular* model encapsulates the notion of secular power holding sway over religion, with detachment and separation between church and state. Here, the state may try to use religion for its own ends, to 'legitimate political rule and to sanctify economic oppression and the given system' of social stratification (Casanova 1994: 49). Secularization policies are widely pursued as a means of national integration in post-colonial multi-religious states, such as India. It is worth noting, however, that the concept of secularism is not necessarily straightforward. For example, Hindu critics of India's religiously 'neutral' Constitution contend that it is not neutral, but rather privileges India's religious minorities, including Muslims, Sikhs, and Christians.

In the liberal secular model, no religion is given official predominance. In fact, in vigorously modernizing countries such as India and post-Ottoman Turkey, state policies of modernization were expected to lead—inevitably—to a high degree of secularization; hence their constitutions are neutral towards religion. But things turned out differently: in recent years, democratization and secularization have worked at cross-purposes. Increasing participation in the political arena has drawn in new social forces in India—religious Hindus, Sikhs, and Muslims, who, in demanding greater formal recognition of their religions by the state, have been responsible for making religion a central issue in contemporary politics. In Turkey, the accession to power of the AKP in 2002—claiming to be the party of the poor and the

alienated—suggests that even when secularization is pursued with great determination over a long period (in Turkey's case, for eighty years), there is still no certainty that, for important constituencies, the socio-political appeal of religion will wither. Indeed, the AKP, which does not call itself an 'Islamic' party, yet has some Muslim characteristics and credentials, achieved a landslide victory in both the 2007 and 2011 elections, which underlined its wide appeal in Turkey.

Finally, there is the category of *Marxist secular* states. Before the overthrow of communism in 1989–90, Eastern Europe contained anti-religious polities in which religion was stifled by the state. Most Marxist regimes were less hard-line than Enver Hoxha's Albania—where religion was 'abolished'—but religion was typically permitted to exist only as the private concern of the individual. This constituted a kind of promise that the authorities would respect the people's religious faith and practice—as long as it remained behind closed doors. Skeletal religious organizations were, however, allowed to exist—but only so that the state could use them for purposes of social control. They were reduced to liturgical institutions, with no other task than the holding of divine services. Numbers of permitted places of worship were greatly reduced.

Paradoxically, however, even the most strident and prolonged Marxist anti-religion campaigns failed to secularize societies. The pivotal role of the Christian churches in the democratic openings in Eastern Europe and non-Marxist Latin America in the 1980s and 1990s, and the contemporary revival of Islam in some of the formerly communist Central Asian countries, indicate that popular religiosity has retained immense social importance. But we should not take it for granted that Marxist, 'anti-religion' states are only of historical interest. For example, the government of China—home to more than a billion people—launched a fierce, continuing, campaign in the mid-1990s to 'teach atheism to Tibetan Buddhists'. This was necessary, the Chinese government argued, to enable Tibetans to 'break free of the bewitchment' of religion.

In sum, none of the various models of church–state relations has been permanently able to resolve the tension between religion and the secular world. The chief manifestation of this tension in recent times is the desire of many religious organizations not to allow the state to sideline them as—almost everywhere—increasingly secularized states seek to intervene ever deeper into social life.

Religion and Democratization in the Developing World

Until quite recently, there were few democratically elected governments outside Western Europe and North America. Most countries, especially in the developing world, had various kinds of non-democratic government, including military, one-party, no-party, and dictatorships led by individually strong leaders. During the 1970s, 1980s, 1990s, and early 2000s, however, there was a pronounced shift from unelected to elected governments in many developing regions, including Latin America, sub-Saharan Africa, East Asia, and South Asia.

The question of how religious actors might affect democratization has been a controversial issue for decades. Some scholars have stressed the importance of what they call '**political culture**' in explaining success or failure of democratization after the Second World War in West Germany, Italy, and Japan (Huntington 1991; Linz and Stepan 1996; Stepan 2000). In addition, religious traditions—for example Roman Catholicism in Italy and Christian Democracy in West Germany—are said to have been important in the (re)making of those countries' political cultures after their lengthy experience of totalitarian, Nazi, and fascist regimes, from the 1930s until the mid-1940s (Casanova 1994). During the '**third wave of democracy**' (mid-1970s to late 1990s), a lot of attention was paid to the role of religion in democratization (Huntington 1991). For example, in Poland, the Roman Catholic Church played a key role in undermining the communist regime and helping to establish a post-communist, democratically accountable regime (Weigel 2005, 2007). This had a wider political effect beyond Poland, extending from Central and Eastern Europe to Latin America,

Sub-Saharan Africa, and parts of Asia. There was also the rise of the religious right in the United States from the 1980s, and its subsequent impact on the electoral fortunes of both the Republican Party and the Democratic Party. Add to this widespread growth of Islamist movements across the fifty or more countries that comprise the Muslim world, with significant ramifications for electoral outcomes in various countries, including Algeria, Egypt, Morocco, and Tunisia, electoral successes for the BJP in India, and substantial political influence over time for various 'Jewish fundamentalist' political parties in Israel and an Islamist party (Hamas) in the Palestinian authority, and we can see clear and sustained evidence of religion's recent democratic importance in many parts of the developing world.

US-based academics, Juan Linz and Alfred Stepan (1996), argue that religion is *not* generally a key explanatory factor explaining democratization outcomes in the developing world and elsewhere. In relation to Muslim countries, the late Fred Halliday (2005) argues that apparent barriers to democracy are primarily linked to certain shared social and political features. These include, in many cases, long histories of authoritarian rule and weak civil societies, and although some of those features tend to be legitimized in terms of 'Islamic doctrine', there is in fact nothing specifically 'Islamic' about them. On the other hand, for Huntington (1993, 1996), religions have a crucial impact on democratization. He claims that Christianity has a strong propensity to be supportive of democracy, while other religions, such as Islam, Buddhism, and Confucianism, do not.

But, in fact, religious traditions are not necessarily connected to specific political preferences. For example, we have noted that some assert that Christianity has close connections to democracy. However, the fastest growing strand of Christianity in parts of the developing world, notably Latin America, is Pentecostalism. The doctrine behind Pentecostalism fits neatly into a neoliberal market globalism, which is known as the 'prosperity gospel'. This draws on various Christian scriptures that proclaim God's wish generally to bless humanity. In the world view of the prosperity doctrine, this centres on the idea that God's blessings take the form of material wealth and that, in order to achieve this goal, Pentecostalists and others believing in the prosperity gospel must 'bless' others—that is, literally give their money away, typically to a church—so that God can them bless them. In other words,

Christians who give generously will get generous rewards in return. The point is that this fast-growing strand of Christianity tends implicitly to downplay the redemptive power of politics to change people's lives by focusing on the give-and-take relationship inherent in the prosperity gospel.

In terms of the relationship of religion and political change in the developing world, three key points can be made, as follows.

- Religious traditions have core elements that are *more* or *less* conducive to democratization and democracy.

- Religious traditions may be *multi-vocal*—but at any moment there may be dominant voices more or less receptive to, and encouraging of, democratization.

- Religious actors rarely, if ever, *determine* democratization outcomes. However, they may, in various ways and with a range of outcomes, be of significance for democratization. This may especially be the case in countries that have a long tradition of secularization.

The issue of religion's relationship to political change and democratization is central to the phenomenon of the 'Arab Spring', perhaps the most significant and complex political development currently affecting the Arab countries of the MENA region. Like nearly everywhere else in the world, the twenty or more Arab countries of the MENA region are today affected by the observable impact of religion: mainly Islam, although Christianity and Judaism are also important components of the overall political scene in the region. Islam and other regional religions have left their previously assigned place in the private sphere, to become a significant component of various current political issues, competitions, and conflicts between groups, including democratization and civil liberties.

Religion and democratization in the 'Arab Spring'

What is the effect of the 'return of religion' on current democratization in Arab countries? Three questions are important in this context. First, *why* should religious actors in the Arab countries pursue political goals? We shall see that, in the context of the 'Arab Spring', this occurs when religious entities feel that political and/social changes are necessary, and that the state is not well equipped to oversee and lead such changes, not least because the solutions it seeks are secular ones and they do not chime well with religious interpretations.

Second, how *widespread* is the phenomenon among the Arab countries? Judging by media reports, it seems clear that the phenomenon of the 'Arab Spring' is affecting all of the twenty or more countries of the Arab world.

Third, what are the *political consequences* of religion's involvement in the 'Arab Spring'? The short, although not very analytically helpful, answer is that they are variable, as we shall see.

One assessment of the chances of generally successful political changes in the Arab countries, leading to polities with improved political conditions and better civil liberties, is that such an outcome is unlikely to be achieved. Alternatively, the pessimistic, but probably realistic, assessment is that there will be a gradual slide into entrenched and long-term political instability, culminating in some cases in **state failure**, with serious ramifications for regional and international instability.

The overall role of political Islam—including 'traditionalists' (or 'fundamentalists') and 'modernists' (or 'moderates')—in these developments is not clear. On the one hand, some modernist/moderate Islamists have shown themselves willing to play by the democratic rules of the game where elections have been held (Tunisia and at least initially in Egypt), although this has not necessarily helped to dispel fears, especially among secularists, that the ruse of the Islamists is to get into power and then use the circumstances to make sure that they stay there by denying democratic freedoms. The same kind of argument was used in relation to Algeria in the early 1990s to justify a military coup that ushered in a two-decade long civil war, which did nothing for the country's long-term political or economic development.

Much of the suspicion projected by secularists and Western governments results from the fact that many Islamists are understood to have a rather ambivalent attitude towards democracy. But the only empirically verifiable way in which to assess what various kinds of Islamists do with democracy is to see what they do when elected into positions of authority and power. If they try to truncate or diminish democracy, or to undermine its veracity, then the option is always to take to the streets in order to pressurize incumbent rulers to change policies in a pro-democracy direction.

Both Tunisia and Egypt have been significantly politically affected by the events of the Arab Spring. Both have seen Islamist parties take a leading role in the post-uprising political arrangements. At the same time, neither country has managed to find either a quick or easy political *modus vivendi* covering the political way forward or has set out a plausible democratization trajectory. The situation in Egypt since the military take-over in the summer of 2013 is particularly volatile. On the one hand, for both Islamists and secularists, this involves confronting questions of how practically to accommodate demands of faith, and at the same time accept and develop democratic pluralism—a *sine qua non* for successful democratization. On the other hand, in Tunisia and Egypt, new and inexperienced governments have come to power, having to face immediate and very difficult to resolve economic questions. These include the highly significant issue of mass—including, youth—unemployment, the proximate cause of the uprising in the first place.

Both Egypt and Tunisia are in a changed political place, yet the contours of the new political regime are not yet firm or certain. In particular, neither country appears to have a clear or sustainable programme of democratization in place. The US-based commentator, Michael Wahid Hanna (2012) argues that, in Egypt, the electoral triumph of the Islamist Muslim Brotherhood has led to what he calls an 'ambush' style of decision-making. This is characterized by a fundamental lack of consensus and consultation, the antithesis of democratic politics and an unlikely starting point for further or fundamental democratization.

Hanna's assessment vis-à-vis Egypt is similar to what observers have noted in relation to Tunisia. There, an Islamist party, *Ennahda*, is also said to govern via a 'no consensus, no consultation' approach. As in Egypt, this is a politically dangerous strategy that makes development of democratic norms and values very difficult—or impossible—to achieve. Critics also contend that this suggests a real danger of a new post-Arab-uprising period of authoritarianism, this time led by Tunisia's political Islamists.

To explain the apparent approach to governing in both Egypt and Tunisia, it is relevant to note that many among the current Islamist power holders were, for decades, jailed or forced underground or into exile by *ancien régimes*. Certainly, the Islamists' rise to power was both swift and unexpected, while jail, harassment, or exile are not necessarily conducive environments in which to develop a democratic approach to politics.

Yet the swiftness of their ascent to power has also been their Achilles' heel. According to a former senior *Ennahda* adviser, Abou Yaareb Marzouki, *Ennahda* leaders 'thought that governing would be easy… And they imagined that through **governance**, they will reject forced modernism … a policy of westernization under colonial rulers and authoritarian governments' (Marzouki, quoted in Fahim 2013). Now, he claims, *Ennahda* has swung too far in the opposite direction, imposing 'forced easternization'.

The position in both countries is, to some degree, complicated by the fact that both Tunisia and Egypt have active Salafi parties and movements. Salafism is a political ideology the name of which draws on the notion of the Arab word *Salaf* (meaning 'predecessors' or 'ancestors'). *Salaf* provide modern Salafists with inspiration and ideas, because historic *Salaf* are thought to be worthy of emulation as representative of best Islamic practice. Today's Salafists believe that they are the essential keepers of historic—yet timeless—Islamic traditions, with two central beliefs: that politics and Islam are inseparable; and that **Sharia law** should be applied to all Muslims. Salafists believe that, for something to be authentically 'Islamic', it must be acceptable both to Sharia law and the *ulama* (Muslim clerics). Salafists regard 'Western-style' 'liberal' democracy as anti- or un-Islamic. Many Salafists also believe that Muslims collectively are the focal point of a conspiracy involving Zionists and Western imperialists aiming to take over Muslim-owned lands and their oil resources. Such a concern is underlined, on the one hand, by US-owned transnational corporations' 'control' over 'Arab' oil and, on the other, by what the Salafists see as Israel's denial of full political and civil rights to its (mainly Muslim) Palestinians. In Egypt, a main Salafist party was strongly represented in parliament following elections in 2011: the *Al-Nour* party has 121 seats in the legislature (24 per cent). In Tunisia, Salafists decided not to compete for parliamentary seats in the 2011 election, yet their influence appears to be growing: many

---

KEY POINTS

- Christianity is said to be conducive to democratization in the developing world.

- Religious actors in the developing world—including Islamists in the 'Arab Spring'—seek to change political arrangements by a variety of methods.

Salafists are members of a group called *Ansar al-Sharia* founded in 2011 by Abu Ayadh al-Tunisi.

Religion in International Politics after 9/11

So far, we have been concerned primarily with the domestic interaction of religion and politics within developing countries. However, no survey of the issue can legitimately ignore the impact of the **terrorist** events of 11 September 2001 ('9/11') on issues of religion and politics in general, and those of the Muslim world and the West, in particular.

Prior to the eighteenth century, and the formation and development of the international state system, religion was the key ideology that stimulated conflict between social groups. However, following the Peace of Westphalia in 1648 and the consequent development of centralized states, religion took a back seat as an organizing ideology at the international level. As already noted, it was not until the Iranian revolution of 1978–79 that religion resumed a significant political role. Ten years later in 1989, the cold war came to an end. Since then, international politics has been characterized by four significant changes:

- change from a bipolar (US, Soviet Union) to an arguably unipolar (US) structure of power;

- culture replacing ideology as a chief source of identity, leading to changes in extant affiliations and antagonisms in world affairs;

- according to some commentators, a worldwide religious resurgence, excepting Western Europe; and

- change in the nature of international conflict, with fewer inter-state wars.

In relation to the last point, of the 110 major conflicts during the 1990s—that is, those involving more than 1,000 fatalities each—only seven were inter-state wars, while 103 were civil wars. Of the latter, over 70 per cent are classified as communal wars—that is, wars among ethnic and other national groups, with religion very often playing an important part.

Western Europe, including Britain, is characterized by both religious **privatization** and secularization. In contrast, over half of all US citizens claim to attend regular religious, mostly Christian, services.

Moreover, eight words are juxtaposed—'In God We Trust' and the 'United States of America'—on all US currency, both coins and notes.

The issue of what role religion should play there was sharpened by the arguments of the US academic, Samuel Huntington (1993; revised and expanded version 1996a), in his **clash of civilizations** hypothesis. Huntington's key argument is that, following the end of the cold war, future international conflicts are increasingly likely to be along cultural fault lines. Now, he suggests, new rivalries are most important, notably between the (Christian) 'West' and the (mostly Muslim, mostly Arab) 'East'. In short, the core of Huntington's argument is that, in the post-cold-war era, the 'Christian', democratic West finds itself in conflict with radical Islam ('Islamic fundamentalism'), a global anti-Western political movement said to be aiming for fundamental changes to the political order. Another influential US commentator, Francis Fukuyama (1992: 236), argued that what he called 'Islamic fundamentalism' was the antithesis of Western **liberalism**, with 'more than superficial resemblance to European fascism'.

Critics of such arguments maintain that although many radical Islamist movements and political parties would not classify themselves as liberal democratic, we cannot assume that this necessarily implies that such actors are willing to engage in violent conduct, including terrorism, to pursue their aims. The 9/11 atrocities in the United States—as well as the Bali and Kenya terrorist incidents that followed—appear to have been carried out by a shadowy transnational terrorist group, al-Qaeda. However, it is by no means clear that most 'ordinary' Muslim men and women support either its goals or its violent methods.

It is also important to see the struggle in the Islamic world of groups such as al-Qaeda as directed against their own rulers, as well as the West. Since the beginning of Islam in the seventh century, Muslim critics of the status quo have periodically emerged to oppose what they perceive as unjust rule. Important contemporary Islamists, including, arguably, Osama bin Laden, the late leader of al-Qaeda assassinated by US covert action in May 2011, seek to portray themselves as the 'just' involved in struggle against 'unjust', 'anti-religious' rulers and their allies. Bin Laden's key goal was said to be the creation of a pan-Islamic state to revive the glories of the Ottoman caliphate that collapsed after the First World War. Al-Qaeda certainly opposes Western interpretations of democracy, in which sovereignty resides with the people, because it is seen as a system that negates God's own sovereignty. Finally, it is suggested that Western support for so-called 'un-Islamic' rulers in, for example, French support for the military junta in Algeria and US support for Saudi Arabia's allegedly unpopular rulers, led some radical Islamist groups to target the West.

But it would be wrong to attribute the rise of Islamist groups to bin Laden. Instead, we might look to the failure of state-sponsored modernization as a key explanation. Contemporary Islamist resurgence is argued to be a vehicle for popular disillusion with many governments in the Muslim world, which have failed to achieve what they promised—both developmentally and politically—since independence from colonial rule. In addition, existing communitarian structures have been confronted by state power that apparently seeks to destroy and replace them with the idea of a national (increasingly secularized) citizenry. Thus the widespread Islamic awakening can be seen in relation to its *domestic* capacity to oppose what are perceived as oppressive states: 'It is primarily in civil society that one sees Islam at work' (Coulon 1983: 49). The point is that this domestic response does not necessarily translate into a wider Muslim threat to *global* order.

The issue of Islam in international relations was given additional focus at the April 2009 Durban Review Conference, the official name of the 2009 United Nations World Conference against Racism. The aim of the Conference was to review implementation of the Declaration and Programme of Action from the 2001 World Conference against Racism, Racial Discrimination, Xenophobia and Related Intolerance. Many Western countries boycotted the Conference, fearing that it would be used by some Muslim countries, such as Iran and Saudi Arabia, to promote anti-Semitism, laws against blasphemy (seen as contrary to key principles of free speech), and attacks against Western countries for alleged racism and intolerance, but without mentioning such problems in the developing world. Such fears were given credence by a speech from Iranian President Mahmoud Ahmadinejad, who used the opportunity to attack Israel and to accuse the West of using the European Holocaust as a 'pretext' for aggression against Palestinians. His speech polarized opinion among his audience, with delegates from the European Union leaving the conference room, while a number of the remaining delegates applauded him.

KEY POINTS

- Religion now plays a central role in international politics.
- Most Islamic critics of the status quo see their own governments as the main cause of political and developmental failures.
- The terrorist attack of 9/11 is sometimes said to provide evidence of an emerging 'civilizational' clash between Christianity and Islam, but most Muslims were probably appalled by these and related terrorist acts.

Conclusion

The last thirty years have seen much involvement of religion in politics. A serious new threat to world order, some claim, now emanates from Islamist militancy, with 9/11 as the key example. However, such fears do not appear to have very strong foundations. In the case of political Islam, various domestically orientated groups threaten the incumbency of their own rulers rather than the security of the global order. In short, there is very little—if anything—in the spectre of an 'Islamic' threat per se to global order.

Globally, the recent political impact of religion falls into two, not necessarily mutually exclusive, categories. First, if the mass of the people are not especially religious—as is the case in many Western countries—then religious actors tend to be politically marginal. However, in many developing countries, most people are already religious believers. Unsuccessful attempts by many political leaders to modernize their countries have often led to responses from various religious actors. Often, religion serves to focus and coordinate opposition, especially—but not exclusively—that of the poor and ethnic minorities. Religion is often well placed to benefit from a societal backlash against the perceived malign effects of modernization. In particular, various religious actors have sought support from ordinary people by addressing certain crucial issues. These include the perceived decline in public and private morality, and the insecurities of life, the result of an undependable market in which, it is argued, greed and luck appear as effective as work and rational choice. Sometimes, such concerns feed into a direct involvement of religion in democratization, although outcomes in this regard are variable, as the example of the 'Arab Spring' indicates.

And what of the future? If the issues and concerns that have helped to stimulate what some see as 'a return to religion'—including socio-political and economic upheavals, patchy modernization, increasing encroachment of the state upon religion's terrain—continue (and there is no reason to suppose that they will not), then it seems highly likely that religion's political role will continue to be significant in many parts of the developing world. This will partly reflect the onward march of secularization in many countries and regions, linked to the spread of globalization—which no doubt will be resisted by religious leaders and their followers, with varying degrees of success. For this reason, it would be very unwise to neglect religion in analyses of contemporary politics in the developing world.

? QUESTIONS

1. What are the characteristics of religious resurgence in the developing world and how are they important politically?

2. What is the relationship of religion and democratization in the developing world?

3. Why does India, a constitutionally secular country, have an important religious party, in the form of the BJP?

4. Now, a dozen years after 11 September 2001 ('9/11'), is it fair to say that religious issues dominate the international relations of the developing world?

5. Are modernization and secularization the same thing?

6. Does underdevelopment in the developing world increase the significance of religio-political actors or undermine them?

7. To what extent is the Arab Spring a religious uprising?

≋ FURTHER READING

Flanagan, S. (2009) *For the Love of God: NGOs and Religious Identity in a Violent World* (West Hartford, CT: Kumarian Press) The book examines the ways in which history and religious identity influence faith-based organizations in Lebanon, Sri Lanka, and Bosnia Herzegovina, and finds that they often reinforce, rather than transcend, schisms found in the larger society.

Freeman, D. (2012) *Pentecostalism and Development: Churches, NGOs and Social Change in Africa* (Basingstoke: Palgrave Macmillan) This book explains why, and shows how, Pentecostalism informs local-level development processes in Sub-Saharan Africa.

Haynes, J. (2013) *Introduction to Religion and International Relations*, 2nd edn (Harlow: Pearson Education) A survey of how international relations is affected by religious global resurgence.

Huntington, S. P. (1996) *The Clash of Civilizations* (New York: Simon and Schuster) Articulates the hypothesis that the world is poised to enter an era of 'civilizational clashes'.

Mainuddin, R. (ed.) (2002) *Religion and Politics in the Developing World: Explosive Interactions* (Aldershot: Ashgate) Examines a number of key religio-political interactions in the developing world.

Roy, O. (2010) *Holy Ignorance: When Religion and Culture Part Ways* (London: Hurst) The secularization of society was supposed to free people from religion, yet individuals are converting en masse to radical expressions of faith, including Protestant evangelicalism, Islamic Salafism, and Haredi Judaism.

Woodhead, L., Partridge, C., and Kawanami, H. (eds) (2013) *Religions in the Modern World*, 3rd edn (London: Routledge) A very useful survey of the contemporary position of religion.

WEB LINKS

http://www.archive.org/details/iraq_911   A collection of archive video footage and films relating to the 11 September 2001 terrorist attacks against the World Trade Center and Pentagon.

http://www.assr.nl/   Details of a research programme on 'Religion, Politics and Identity' at the Amsterdam School of Social Research.

http://www.calvin.edu/henry/   The Paul B. Henry Institute for the Study of Christianity and Politics at Calvin College, US.

http://www.csmonitor.com/   *The Christian Science Monitor* is a useful source of material on many aspects of religious politics, including in the developing world. It does not have a Christian bias in its coverage.

http://www.uga.edu/islam/   Islam and Islamic Studies resources.

http://www.vanderbilt.edu/csrc/politics.html   Center for the Study of Religion and Culture at Vanderbilt University, US.

For additional material and resources, please visit the Online Resource Centre at:
http://www.oxfordtextbooks.co.uk/orc/burnell4e/

9
Women and Gender

Kathleen Staudt

Chapter contents

Overview

Nearly all nations in the world could be considered still 'developing', or not yet developed, if judged against full democratic standards both of women's representation in decision-making positions and of responsiveness to women's policy interests. Only a few exceptions exist, most notably Scandinavia—but even there countries became more inclusive and responsive to women only in recent decades, a result of women's organized strength (including in unions), progressive public policies since the 1930s, and especially open and democratic political structures. This chapter draws attention to the widespread reality that women have little voice in established politics, and that their 'interests' are muted, given the existence of overwhelming male privilege and preference in the policymaking and policy implementation processes. Here and there, women's activism has produced some change in policies, altering power relations between men and women.

The chapter first examines key ways in which men's privileges became institutionalized in the colonial and post-colonial state, political institutions, and governments during history. In so doing, it will not only incorporate the language of gender that leads to an examination of social structures that 'construct' male and female differently in different nations, regions, and historical eras, but also the political institutions (see Chapter 3) that shape women's and men's lives. While the term 'gender' is contested and does not translate well into all languages, it facilitates emphasis on the larger social structure, including relations between men and women, and away from biology as the essential determinant of behaviour. The chapter then considers women's paid and unpaid work, along with women's reproductive capabilities, in order to outline typical obstacles that women face in different places and why gendered 'stakes' have been maintained or changed in the policy status quo. It moves on to examine women as voters, activists, and decision-makers in different nations, and the effects of their actions on policy responsiveness. Finally, more global and local perspectives are introduced as being essential to moving towards gender-fair politics and policies.

Introduction: Historical Perspectives

In geographic spaces around which national boundaries are drawn, relatively stable **institutional** structures and decision-making patterns have emerged that reflect values and ideologies, including beliefs about men and women. This structure is known as the state (see Chapter 12), and it is different from the regional units of government also known as states, provinces, or districts, such as the State of Coahuila in Mexico, China's Shanxi Province, or the State of Texas in the United States. From the outset of the modern state in Europe, elite men, not people generally, crafted the skeletal structure of the state during an era when men spoke for most women and children in both societies and families, as fathers, husbands, and brothers, and when institutions absorbed **gender** assumptions and practices like these. While wealth, position, and authority concentrated power among the few, virtually all men exercised formal power and authority in 'their' households. Power is relational: the relatively more and less powerful can shift the balance through force, knowledge, and resistance, among other things, opening opportunities for women to exercise power. Men were often the first to benefit from rights to hold office and to vote. These rights and opportunities themselves augmented the social construction of gender in ways that associated men with the public sphere of **politics** and paid labour, and women with the private sphere of family and household.

Patriarchy—the ideology and institutions of male rule, male privilege, and female subordination—exists in most societies to different degrees. Prior to the establishment of states, women exercised some power and authority in societies—such as the queen mothers of particular peoples in Ghana, Benin, and Nigeria—based on age, kinship relationships, religious roles, economic activity and resources, and reproductive capabilities. However, patriarchy is embedded in virtually all indigenous societies and states, made 'normal' and routine in laws and public policies that often change only incrementally over time. By the twentieth century, state policies and laws institutionalized male privilege and, through colonialism, transplanted the tools, ideology, and machinery of privilege from one nation to another. This gender baggage constructed men as family breadwinners, legally and financially responsible for land and households, and attendant policies benefited men through education, training, and employment. For Latin America and the Caribbean, colonial masters included Spain, Portugal, the Netherlands, Britain, and France. For Africa, the masters included Britain, Belgium, France, Germany, Italy, Portugal, and Spain. For Asia, from west to east and south, the masters included France, the United States, Britain, Japan, Portugal, and the Netherlands. Nations such as China and Japan, despite alternative and historically deeper indigenous patriarchal sources in those states, also exhibited male dominance in, and benefit from, the public sphere.

Consider an example from South Africa. High-level political leader (and, at the time of writing, president) Jacob Zuma was charged with the rape of a young woman, used Zulu masculine culture as the justification, and was judged 'not guilty' at the trial in 2006. The case roused people to reflect on misogyny, and organized women pushed parliament (and its large critical mass of female parliamentarians) to pass stronger laws against sexual assault.

Male privilege and gender social constructions have enduring legacies for women's quality of life and opportunity. Life itself may be in question (see Box 9.1).

Forty years ago, scholars and activists focused on 'women', making them visible in research and action. By the 1980s, the term 'gender' offered the opportunity to conceptualize the social construction and

BOX 9.1 'MISSING' WOMEN AND 'SURPLUS MEN' IN INDIA AND CHINA

Economist Amartya Sen (1990) found that 100 million women were 'missing' in India, based on imbalanced demographic sex ratios. Usually, such ratios display relative balance (slightly over or under) of 100:100, but he found skewed ratios as extreme as 88 females to 100 males. In northern India and elsewhere, girl infants and children are ignored so badly that some die needlessly for lack of food, amounting to the waste of enormous numbers of female lives. Moreover, although sex-selective abortion is outlawed, female foetuses are disproportionately aborted. Practices like these have consequences decades later.

In China, surplus young men are referred to as 'bare branches', with nothing attached: generally of lower socio-economic **status**, they rarely marry and have little bargaining power in the marriage market (Hudson and den Boer 2005: 188). In the December 2012 high-visibility media coverage and outrage over the six-man gang rape with a steel rod of an unnamed physiotherapy university student in New Delhi, India, resulting in her death, reference was made to the 15 million excess men, expected to double by 2020 (Timmons and Gottipoti 2012).

consciousness that shape the lives and relationships of women and men from global to national and local levels. A focus on gender also permits one to problematize men and masculinities, whether hegemonic or hyper-masculinity in institutions and behaviour, including war, peace, and security studies (Staudt et al. 2009: 4). In this and other chapters, readers should use a 'gender lens' to understand public policies and power relations, attending also to the intersection of gender with class/income, ethnicity/race, nationality, and sexuality.

KEY POINTS

- Laws, public policies, and decisions about how to implement public policies are deeply and historically embedded in states, with their concentrated political authority in government that affects the whole of society.

- Men captured and controlled these political institutions in ways that disempowered women and muted their policy interests.

- In the **developing world**, this patriarchal state model both emerged from indigenous practices and/or spread through colonialism and persisted in the post-colonial era.

- One may focus on both (or either) 'women' and 'gender', along with other social categories, to gain insightful lenses for research and action.

Women's Policy Interests

Women and men have stakes in any and all public policies, from education to health, safety, and employment. Policies articulate official decisions on issues

that have been perceived as public, rather than private matters; and governments raise money—through taxes, tariffs, and fees—and spend that money (documented in budgets) in ways that may or may not resemble official policies. One must examine policy implementation, for much policy is merely rhetoric, lacking budgetary resources, staff, and commitments to put policy decisions into practice.

From private problems to public policies

The social construction of gender has given men and women different stakes in policies, for the ways in which policies are formulated, finalized, implemented, and evaluated have usually meant that women's and men's 'interests' were benefited and burdened in distinctive ways. **Women's (or gender) policy interests**, then, refer to stakes in issues over which governments exercise decision-making, spending, or authority in policy implementation. The identification of shared stakes is complex, given the intersectional differences of ethnicity, class, age, geography, and other factors. People contest whether policies should be gender-neutral or gender-specific, taking into account realities such as who cares for infants after birth. In other words, questions can be raised about whether public policies should be neutral to gender (for example parental leave from paid employment obligations after birth, rather than only maternal leave) or should recognize gender difference, whether constructed through social norms or reduced to biological factors, such as reproductive organs. The question raises a dilemma: if difference is recognized, will that reinforce and sustain gender difference?

Often, extraordinary efforts are required to bring issues and problems deemed part of a 'private' sphere onto the public policy agenda (Box 9.2). A key example

BOX 9.2 A 'PRIVATE PROBLEM' IS MADE PUBLIC

Only in the last three decades have most governments treated violence against women as a public, rather than a private, problem. Historically, in many cultures worldwide, women moved from the patriarchal control of the father to the husband, reinforced in legal systems. Control often authorized physical punishment, usually short of death. Assault from strangers merited more accountability than assault from intimate partners. In many countries, **feminists** spread awareness in the late 1960s to put violence against women on the public agenda, and to change laws and law enforcement. The study of changing

masculinities explores abusive behaviour, even in police departments, and the conditions under which such behaviour changes. Recall the late 2012 unnamed woman in India whose rape-induced murder roused many—despite women's economic and educational gains over the years—to protest about ineffective law enforcement, rare convictions of rapists, and persistent sexual harassment of women on streets. In a gang rape case that took place in Punjab State, a teenager committed suicide when police humiliated her after her report and suggested that she marry her attackers (Timmons and Gottipati 2012).

is found in sexual assault and domestic violence, which primarily burdens women.

In a methodical cross-national study, Weldon (2002) compared thirty-six countries for their responses on seven violence-against-women policies. She examined cultures, measurements of which are notoriously difficult, women politicians, women's machinery in government, and **social movements** and **non-governmental organizations (NGOs)**, finding that the last two are most strongly correlated with policy adoptions. Governments with better records than most on the issues include Costa Rica in the developing world and Canada.

Police agencies in many countries are dominated by men who work in a militaristic organizational culture that has historically been unresponsive to women. In some countries, special women's police stations have been established, such as Brazil and India. The stations produce mixed results: more crimes are reported, but serial battering and raping persist.

Women and wage inequalities

Until the latter part of the twentieth century, it was legal to pay women lower wages and salaries than men for the same or similar work. International organizations, sparked by scholarship and transnational NGOs, established equality norms and standards that sometimes shaped national policy if and when activists used this leverage. While the United Nations-affiliated International Labour Organization (ILO) produced conventions that established equal pay principles—agreed to in tripartite negotiations among government, business, and labour—national governments enforced these principles to the extent that internal political forces and laws pushed or permitted them. For women who laboured for income in the **informal economy**, laws and regulations had no impact on earnings (see Box 9.3). Economic recessions, such as that following the global financial crisis in 2008, have gendered impacts that vary based on the labour sectors (manufacturing, service) in which women and men predominate.

BOX 9.3 LATIN AMERICAN WAGE STRUGGLES

Labour unions have been slow to organize women workers. Historically, men organized men, viewed as the family breadwinners, to obtain 'family wages' that could support women and children. In many countries, the percentage of economically active people organized into unions diminished by the close of the twentieth century. Informal workers are rarely organized despite their labour burdens: they work outside regulations on minimum wage, social security benefits, and maximum hours.

In most Latin American countries, the commonest paid job for women has been domestic labour: working as servants in other people's households. Live-in maids are notoriously exploited,

with employers calling upon them for more than 40- or 50-hour working weeks. And their pay supplements may consist of discarded clothing and leftover food. Employer–employee relationships take on feudal overtones, and women may be labelled *muchachas* ('girls') well beyond the age of adulthood. Chaney and Castro (1989) document the struggles of domestic workers to organize themselves in cities such as Bogotá, Colombia, and Mexico City. They show that although organized *trabajadoras domésticas* agree on wage rates and hourly commitments, organizing domestic workers is very challenging, given the competition for work and desperation that characterizes many who seek earnings.

Women work in many kinds of occupations, from paid to unpaid. But virtually everywhere, women earn less than men in paid employment. The United Nations Development Programme (UNDP) annual Human Development Report shows no countries without gender wage gaps, even the Scandinavian countries. Where rights-based approaches prevail, individuals may require access to expensive and time-consuming legal services to challenge inequalities, state impunity, and the failure to recognize that women's rights are **human rights** (part of the United Nations Universal Declaration of Human Rights, reiterated at the Vienna Conference in 1993).

Because women generally form at least a third, if not a half, of the labour force, the unequal pay adds up to considerable value or profit that is extracted from, but does not benefit, women or their families who depend on them. Worldwide, labour unions are the collective means by which workers use the power of numbers to threaten work stoppage, to strike, and/or to negotiate with generally more powerful employers, whether nationals or foreigners. A minority of workers belongs to such organizations; genuinely independent unions, able to negotiate on national and transnational bases, are rare. Moreover, lower wages, discriminatory job entry, and/or high unemployment levels leave many women in poverty.

With the rise of the global economy, much attention has focused on the recruitment of young women into export-processing factories such as garment and electronics manufacturing. Compared with work as maids or street vendors, the factory jobs have fixed hours and pay the legal minimum, although artificially low, wages. However, the jobs are often unsafe and insecure, involving minuscule wages compared with profits earned or executives' salaries. In Mexico, workers' minimum wages are less than US$4 daily, compared with US$60 daily across the border in the United States, but only US$1 daily or less in large parts of the world according to the UNDP Human Development Reports.

Unpaid labour in households

Women provide extensive unpaid labour in households, from food cultivation and preparation, to caring for family members, especially children. In **subsistence economies**, which characterize many parts of the developing world in Asia and Africa, women invest considerable time to grow and process food, cook and feed family members, haul water, and gather firewood.

Managing households is a time-consuming activity in most societies, considering the child-rearing and emotional care that is generally thought necessary to hold families together. Women are primary caregivers in families. In societies lacking running water and basic technology, tasks that seem manageable in the developed world become onerous physical and time constraints. For example, carrying water from rivers or collecting firewood from forests surrounding villages can consume an inordinate number of hours each day, as can pounding dried grains to make flour for cooking.

Reproductive choices

State policies and local customs pose challenges to women's ability to make decisions about their bodies and voluntary motherhood. Although, historically, women relied on indigenous knowledge and practices related to birth, most states until the last few decades have been **pro-natalist** (that is, encouraging multiple births, and restricting contraception and abortion). As primary care-givers, multiple births consumed much female time and energy. As **overpopulation** became a global issue, with United Nations conferences beginning in 1972 (Stockholm) and cheap contraception technology widespread, more governments began to legitimate, and to disseminate advice and the means of, contraceptive use. Total fertility rates (average numbers of births per woman) have dropped, with impoverished countries such as Niger, Uganda, and Afghanistan reporting rates of six or seven births per woman, in contrast to countries such as Korea, Indonesia, and China, and in the developed world, with figures of between one and three births per woman (UNDP 2011). Among countries focused on in this volume, Nigeria has the highest total fertility rate (5.4) and the highest maternal mortality rate (840 women die annually per 100,000 live births), compared to single and double digit figures in Korea (11) and the developed world (UNDP 2011). However, the population policy agenda has often appeared to prioritize government planners' desires to slow population growth, rather than to enhance women's choices over healthy and voluntary motherhood, wherein women themselves decide on the timing and spacing of pregnancy, or even the choice to become mothers. In the United Nations International Conference on Population and

Development in Cairo in 1994, delegates and NGO representatives explored the connections between user-friendly women's health and development. Approximately a third of a million women die annually giving birth, yet restrictions are still in place for contraception, emergency contraception, and abortion. A backlash to women's voluntary motherhood is occurring worldwide.

KEY POINTS

- Women may have different policy interests from men, requiring policies that recognize gender rather than those that are gender-neutral.

- Many issues affecting women are defined as 'private', and it is a struggle to get them onto the public agenda.

- International organizations and NGOs establish rights-based, equality, and other norms that activists sometimes use as leverage within their own countries and communities.

- Women workers are regularly paid less than men, and the value of women's unpaid domestic and agricultural labour is insufficiently recognized.

- Women often lack autonomy over reproductive choices about their own bodies.

Policy Injustices

How and why could these unequal gender patterns prevail for so long? The answers involve a confluence of education, discrimination, state inaction, economic inequalities, embedded male privilege, and women's muted political voices. The most privileged people rarely organize to dismantle privilege, so organized constituencies and political parties rarely advocated gender equality until women acquired voices, rights, economic strength, networks, and organizations to promote change. This section looks first at educational inequalities, then voting rights, and finally the growing women's movements.

Mass education arrived only in the twentieth century in most countries, but usually boys had preferential access and wider opportunities for education that prepared the privileged among them for technical, management, legal, business, health, and other professional occupations. Even in the twenty-first century, girls are the majority of illiterates in South Asian and some African countries, although equal access to primary and secondary education now exists in many Latin American countries. Adult literacy rates continue to display huge gender gaps, concentrated in the band of deep patriarchy (West Asia and North Africa), and in the impoverished countries of Africa and South-East Asia (UNDP 2011). Many of those countries contain desperately impoverished majorities, as does Guatemala, with its low percentages of both women and men aged 25 and older with secondary education (15 and 21 per cent, respectively) (UNDP 2011). Usually, though, poverty and opportunity are structured to produce different outcomes for men and women, the essence of a gendered approach: in Pakistan, India, and Nigeria, about half of men aged 25 and older achieve secondary education; this is true for only a quarter of women.

Who is responsible for the massive historical disinvestment in girls' education: parents or governments? In nations without social security and state-provided welfare or poverty-alleviation programmes, parents have typically relied on grown children to support them in old age. Marital and customary settlement patterns tended to result in girl children joining their future husbands' families upon marital age, but with boy children remaining near home, and therefore expected to support their parents. Yet, historically, governments did little to alter inequalities. In recent decades, states such as Bangladesh, Pakistan, and Nepal offered incentives, such as free uniforms, subsidized fees, and books, to parents with girl children in school attendance. These incentives, sometimes funded through international assistance, reduce the costs of female education to parents. However, even under such conditions of equal access, girls' and boys' experiences may be quite different, for subtle, but accumulating, gender cues are communicated to both boys and girls about leadership and paid employment. State interventions to provide credit for women's micro-business, however minuscule, have precedents in India, Mexico, and elsewhere (see Box 9.4).

Even when girls and boys complete primary and secondary school in relatively equal proportions, gender patterns diverge in higher education, especially in coursework that results in marketable employment and political careers. In most societies, leaders emerge from professional, business, and economic careers, providing money to fund political careers and organizations. Men are channelled into these occupations, thereby accumulating wealth and contacts that translate into political recruitment opportunities.

BOX 9.4 ACCESS TO CREDIT VIA WOMEN-FRIENDLY APPROACHES

Women often resort to self-employment, usually as part of the informal economy, in income-generating strategies outside the state regulatory apparatus. Outside the state, women's group members save money and rotate total amounts to individuals, common in Mexico, Indonesia, Kenya, and Nigeria. Many NGOs model themselves on the Grameen Bank in Bangladesh, started by Mohammad Yunus. The Bank channels credit to micro-entrepreneurs, either as individuals or in groups, and peer responsibility provides the guarantee for loans. The approach has flaws, but many view the model as an advance from the male-to-male credit approach that still dominates banking throughout the world.

Although democratic and semi-democratic countries usually provide equal voting rights, it takes advocacy, leadership, and sustained activism around gender and equality issues to make substantial change. Although women participated in movements for independence, they often did so primarily as nationalists, not advocates of women's interests. Yet the voting franchise was often granted to all adults—women and men—once independence came, in countries that instituted elections.

Finally, women's movements have begun to grow in the late twentieth century, challenging policy injustices. Worldwide networking occurred with the global organizing around the United Nations-sponsored International Women's Year of 1975, which turned into an International Women's Decade, followed up with global conferences in 1980 (Copenhagen), 1985 (Nairobi), and 1995 (Beijing). These conferences fostered the development of more global to regional and local gender visibility at other UN meetings. Naturally, women's movements experienced resistance to change from those with stakes in perpetuating the status quo and the privileges that they enjoyed. In 2013, global media covered the story of Pakistani teen Malala Yousafzai, aged 15 and an advocate of girls' education, who survived an assassination attempt by reactionaries.

Women's movements rose hand in hand with the emergence of diverse feminist philosophies, which, at a generic level, focus on inequalities and injustices between men and women, especially in the areas of income, political voice, and violence (Staudt 1998: 18–31). Ironically, many women's movements do not use feminist labels, so as to avoid the appearance of replicating or accepting philosophies developed elsewhere rather than customizing issues within their own communities and nations. Feminist approaches are wide-ranging, preceded with adjectives that provide distinctive ways in which to problematize and address injustices—'liberal', 'socialist', 'radical', 'black', 'maternal', 'conservative', and others. But by the late twentieth century, feminists converged in their efforts to deal with typical widespread injustices such as wage inequalities, domestic abuse, and sexual violence.

Not everyone agrees that political power is the key to generating greater equality. Some focus on strengthening women's ability to earn and control income and other assets. If women had greater economic resources, or resources comparable to those of men, then they could either make individual choices to benefit themselves and their families, or organize collectively to press governments to change. After all, public policy often changes in response to monied constituencies. But it is only changes in public policies and their implementation that systemic change is possible for large numbers of people.

KEY POINTS

- In women's everyday lives, from unpaid and paid work to reproductive activities, the political framework has devalued women's experiences and increased their poverty.

- Gradually, once private issues within the household have entered the public policy agenda, women have made gains that increase their value and autonomy.

- The explanations for past policy disadvantage are numerous, herein focused on (still lingering) educational inequalities, economic inequalities, and delays in women's exercise of their political voices. Those causes for policy disadvantage invite specific solutions: women's increasing economic and political power will enhance their ability to gain responsive and accountable government that serves their interests and needs.

Women's Political Activism: Movements, Non-Governmental Organizations, and Decision-Makers

Women's political activism has gradually increased at the local, regional, national, and transnational levels, both in government organizations and NGOs. Still, however, the power that women exercise collectively is far less than that of men, and few countries exhibit gender-balanced decision-making. Men continue to monopolize politics and much of that monopolization contributes to sustaining male privileges in the status quo. During transitions to democracy, women's civil rights usually increase, but not necessarily their economic and social rights, according to a ten-country study, unless women's interests resonate with the political climate, government, and party in power (Waylen 2007). Thus it is important to consider the political context, as Waylen (2007), Krook (2009), and other comparative political scientists do in their studies. Cynical observers recognize that some political parties hostile to feminism and/or gender equality select women as 'decorations' to mobilize voting support. Moreover, some among the by now more than fifty women presidents and prime ministers gain legitimacy through family and marital connections, as daughters, sisters, and/or wives of prominent men.

In preparation for the United Nations-sponsored Women's Conference in Beijing in 1995, the UNDP Human Development Report produced a special publication on gender (UNDP 1995). One of its chapters focused specifically on women in political decision-making positions and politics. That represents a baseline from which to examine change in women's participation, almost twenty years later.

Political structure matters

In the 1995 UNDP report, the concept of a 'participation pyramid' was introduced and graphed. It illustrated how men's monopolization was stronger at the pinnacle of the pyramid, for chief executives, and how this steep pyramid broadened only slightly in descent from the top, to cabinet members, elected representatives of the legislature, and finally to eligible voters, the bottom of the pyramid, which exhibited greater gender balance. In some parts of the world—namely, western Asia—few or no women serve in cabinets. Often, there is only a token female presence in cabinet, serving in posts with limited resources, staff, and authority. Yet there are differences among countries, based on their political institutions and structures. Even democracies come in different forms and questions have often been raised about which form is the more gender-friendly (see Box 9.5).

Chief executives in government consist primarily of presidents and prime ministers, illustrating two variations in democracy: presidential and parliamentary (although hybrid systems also exist). Presidential forms of government, most common in the Western hemisphere, have three separate branches (executive, legislative, judicial), which ideally are equal and check one another's power. The president is elected separately from legislators in what is often a bicameral congress of a lower and an upper house. The president appoints cabinet members from various walks of life: interest groups; campaign supporters; loyal friends; experts; and/or academics. These appointees are not elected, but are indirectly accountable to the people. Presidential systems, as is evident, are fragmented, consuming a great deal of time for decision-making. Their officials are elected for fixed terms, lending stability to the system, but also less responsiveness. Yet presidential systems also offer many decision points at which to advocate or resist policy change, including policy that concerns women especially.

Parliamentary forms of government, most common in European and former European colonies in Asia and Africa, fuse the executive and legislature in the form of a chief executive called the prime minister. The prime minister is elected to parliament, and rises to executive leadership as a result of leadership in the majority political party or party coalition. Cabinet ministers come from the majority party or a coalition of parties, and are thus elected officials. As is evident, parliamentary systems concentrate power, thus making the decision-making process potentially more efficient and more responsive to the people, because new elections can be called if, on important measures before parliament, a majority vote does not prevail (that is, a 'vote of no confidence').

Women in decision-making positions

Few women have risen to become a chief executive in democratic governments. In the 1995 Human Development Report, only twenty had ever achieved the position, about equal numbers of presidents and prime ministers. In the early twenty-first century, more have been added; the Philippines, Sri Lanka, and Bangladesh are the only countries to have elected two different women as chief executives. In recent years, women have ascended to head of state in several key countries: first ever on the African continent, President Ellen Johnson Sirleaf in post-war Liberia; socialist-feminist President Michele Bachelet in Chile (until her term ended in 2010); President Pratibha Patil in India; President Dilma Roussef in Brazil; President Park Geun-hye of the Republic of Korea; and President Cristina Fernandez de Kirchner in Argentina. The German Chancellor, Angela Merkel, was re-elected to a third term in 2013 and may be the most powerful woman in the world.

Women are beginning to be selected or appointed for cabinet positions in larger numbers than two decades past. For the 1995 report, women held 7 per cent of cabinet posts, and in two out of every five governments, men monopolized all of the cabinet posts. Often, however, women's portfolios involved 'women's affairs', 'family affairs', or peripheral bureaucracies not central to core government missions and budgets. Now the annual UNDP Human Development Reports routinely report on the percentage of women among cabinet members.

Moving to legislatures, the 1995 Human Development Report calculated an average of 10 per cent women's participation, illustrating men's near-monopolization of legislative politics. Women's representation varied by world region a decade ago. Asian, European, and Latin American figures surpassed world averages, while African, Pacific, and Arab countries were well below world averages. But the differences were not dramatic. Since 1995, women's participation in legislatures has risen slightly, to 20 per cent in 2012. The Inter-Parliamentary Union (IPU) compiles data on parliaments for many countries (see Table 9.1). Scandinavian countries and the Netherlands are always near the top, exhibiting critical masses of women, at a third or more of the representatives, with the UK ranked #61 (22 per cent) and the United States, #82 (17 per cent, although up slightly in January 2013). Of course, a third never constitutes a majority—the proportion usually required for voting bills into laws. Updated lists are easily available for readers who wish to consult each and every country (see the IPU web link in the sources to Table 9.1).

The regional patterns outlined nearly two decades ago still persist. That is, among developing countries, the Latin American region retains the highest level of female participation, with African, Asian Pacific, and Arab countries following in that order. As the Table 9.1 source shows, the highest levels in Latin American are found in Cuba (45.2 per cent) and Costa Rica (38.6 per cent). Post-war Rwanda sets the world record, with 56.3 per cent in its lower house, and second on the African continent is South Africa, at 42.3 per cent. In Asia, the

Table 9.1 Women in national parliaments: IPU regional figures

	Single or lower house (%)	Upper house (%)	Both (%)
Nordic countries	42		
Americas	23.8	24.6	24
Europe (excluding Nordic)	21.9	21.1	21.7
Sub-Saharan Africa	20.8	17.4	20.4
Asia	18.5	14.2	18
Pacific	12.7	34.4	15.2
Arab States	14.9	6.4	13.2

Source: Inter-Parliamentary Union: http://www.ipu.org/wmn-e/classif.htm © Inter-Parliamentary Union (IPU)

highest levels are in new nation-state Timor-Leste at 38.5 per cent. In several Pacific, Arab, and/or Middle Eastern countries, there are no women elected to the legislature. Post-war Iraq's Parliament has a quarter women, but the US military occupation was a setback and sex ratios are extremely skewed (Al-Ali and Pratt 2009). Alas, no quantitative data exist on the percentage of feminists—women and men—in legislative bodies.

Why the variation? The answers lie in constitutions and political party rules about the structure of electoral systems and quotas for underrepresented people such as women. Proportional representation electoral systems produce higher percentages of women in politics than do single-member systems.

Female quotas: a solution for inequality and injustice?

In more than 100 countries, governments and political parties have adopted three special measures—reserved seats, party, and legislative quotas—to increase women's representation, but not necessarily to improve gendered outcomes (Krook 2009: 4, 6). In 1992, India passed a law that required women to hold a third of all local council (*panchayats*) seats, although a similar law was not passed at the national level. This introduced nearly a million women into public decision-making positions, theoretically a stepping stone into other political offices (Rai 2003). Yet, in 2013, India fell well below the international median in national representation rates for women: 11 per cent in the lower and upper houses. Feminist scholarly critics point to the problem of 'essentialism' in the implicit promise of female quota systems. Just because a woman is biologically female does not necessary mean that her ideological beliefs will produce political behaviour with policy outcomes that offer more equality and justice. Commitment to gender and social justice is related to more than the female or male bodies of politicians, bureaucrats, and leaders.

The perennial question in women and politics research asks whether women in the legislature expand the policy agenda and/or address gender inequalities. Women often follow different pathways into the political process, such as through NGOs with possible commitments to women's policy interests. As a result, they may also bring a new way of interacting with colleagues and constituents. Once in office, women's party loyalties, ideologies, and constituencies influence their legislative behaviour. Elected and appointed women may come from markedly different and privileged income backgrounds than those of the majority of (poor) people. And women may belong to political parties that operate under ideologies that ignore 'private' injustices. Conservative politicians cut public spending programmes from which poor women may benefit. Yet women have sometimes coalesced across party lines to vote for women's policy interests. This happens periodically in Mexico around anti-violence laws. Yet consider the South Africa rape case cited earlier, which occurred despite the near gender balance in that country's parliament. Neither women nor men share single-minded approaches to ideologies and policies.

Non-governmental organizations

The crucial ingredient for bringing about more gender-just policies and better accountability lies with the political engagement of NGOs and social movements with women (and men) representatives. NGOs come in many different forms, active at the local, regional, national, transnational, and international levels. Some NGOs are registered with the United Nations or with government (the latter seeking to qualify for tax-exempt status), known as non-profit organizations, or *asociaciones civiles* in parts of the Spanish-speaking world. Others are looser informal networks or coalitions, including movements that may avoid registration (particularly with authoritarian governments). Social movements offer opportunities to put new issues on political agendas, to use social media, and to mobilize large numbers of people with the potential for **regime change**. Such was the case in various countries in what was termed the 'Arab Spring'. However, it is too soon to tell whether more doors will open for women or gender equality, or whether setbacks will occur as in Egypt under the Muslim Brotherhood government (2012–13).

In many countries, NGOs work with political parties, legislatures, political executives, and bureaucracies to press for more responsive policies and resources. They push for goals such as equal employment opportunities, non-sexist education, better health care, loans for micro-businesses, and laws to prevent violence against women, among many other areas. In some countries, consultants create organizations, but tend to operate more like a business. Just as governments need to be accountable to their citizens and residents, so also must NGOs become more accountable than many actually are. Generally, NGOs have the potential to give life and energy to democracies, and to the women and men elected and appointed to office.

Tools for policy change

Women are gradually increasing their share of power in public affairs, in NGOs and governments. Women's participation expands public policy agendas to include women's policy interests. What tools exist to ensure that policies are implemented?

Once public officials adopt new policies, some resistance can be expected in the policy implementation process of government bureaucracies. The last quarter-century has pioneered the use of several tools to overcome that resistance, including more academic research and the innovative policy tools associated with gender **mainstreaming**, such as establishing what the United Nations has called women's 'machinery' in government and introducing gendered budget-making (BRIDGE 2003). The popularity of the term 'gender' among international agencies has prompted some feminist scholarly critics to challenge the co-optation potential in this technical approach. They see the possibility of 'disappearing' women and gender altogether once status quo leaders declare that mainstreaming has been accomplished.

Although policymaking is an inherently political process, in which power is brought to bear on policy adoption, the idealized policymaking process involves the application of research findings to policy deliberation and adoption. There is now a considerable body of findings concerning various developmental, education, and health policies relevant to women and gender. This research has been spurred on by the rise of policy, programme, and project evaluation (see Box 9.6).

Other innovations have moved beyond just policy rhetoric that promises greater equality and more responsive **governance** towards initiating real action in government bureaucracies as they interact with people. The first such innovation involved the creation of **women's policy machinery**, or units within government such as women's bureaux, commissions of women, ministries of women, and women's desks. Within ten years, virtually all governments hosted some women's machinery, but many had minimal staff and low budgets. Optimally, they allow government 'insiders' to work with 'outsider' feminist organizations. But many are separate sideline units, unable to 'mainstream' gender in all government efforts—even those without obvious women's policy interests or those based on women's special needs (Goetz 1997; Staudt 1997; Rai 2003; Waylen 2007). The effectiveness of mainstreaming strategies depends on good leadership, adequate resources,

institutional incentives for change, outside constituency strength, and strategic locations within governments that resonate with feminist change.

Budgetary decision-making is at the very heart of the political process, and some countries have pioneered methods to dissect budgets by gender and make the process more transparent in this way, and to involve more women and their organizations. The phrase 'gender audits' has also been used to analyse spending, and it resonates well with the technical accountability tools deemed necessary to exercise oversight on government.

BOX 9.6 EVALUATION RESEARCH AS AN ACCOUNTABILITY TOOL

Evaluation research typically asks the following questions.

- What outcomes occurred as a result of the programme intervention or policy changes?
- Who benefited and who was burdened?
- How well were programme and policy goals accomplished?
- What lessons can be learned for future change?

Evaluation research of this type has lent itself well to addressing inequalities, whether by gender, ethnicity, class, and/or geographic regions.

KEY POINTS

- Women are gaining power both in official positions and in relation to government through social movements and NGOs.

- Political structure and government resonance with feminist agendas matter: democratic systems that are parliamentary, with political parties with female quotas that gain seats through proportional representation that implement goals for more critical masses of women, have higher rates of women representatives than presidential systems, although fewer decisional access points.

- However, once in office, bureaucratic or elected, women decision-makers will respond to women's interests and needs only if committed to justice in a political party that does the same, and where accountable to relevant NGOs.

- Tools are available to nudge the more resistant bureaucracies include mainstreaming strategies, budgets, and audits, but **civil society** 'outsiders' must exercise constant oversight and vigilance to avoid co-optation.

More Global Dimensions

This chapter has focused primarily on nations, but it cannot close without noting the growing global inequalities in which nations are fixed. Even as developed countries exhibit average annual per capita incomes of many thousands of dollars, there are numerous countries in which per capita income is equivalent to only a few hundred dollars (US$1–2 per day). As the annual UNDP Human Development Report documents in grim continuity, the world's richest 10 per cent of people receive as much income as the poorest 50 per cent. Women in developing countries are burdened by this grave inequality and poverty.

International conferences, many of them held under the auspices of the United Nations, have provided space for women to articulate their interests. These meetings range from those that focus specifically on women, such as the women's conferences of 1975, 1980, 1985, and 1995 (mentioned earlier), and those that focus on public policies in which women have stakes, such as the environment, population, and others. Typically, official delegations meet and, at the same time, parallel meetings of international or national NGOs also take place. Transnational networks and bonds are formed, and resolutions are passed. While the United Nations exerts little authority over sovereign countries (save for peacekeeping missions), the passage of resolutions provides leverage for local and national organizations to press their governments for accountability and change. Legal instruments, such as the UN Convention on the Elimination of All Forms of Discrimination against Women (CEDAW), also provide leverage for change. War and civil conflicts take their tolls on all people, but women often bear disproportionate burdens on themselves and their children in refugee and humanitarian crises. The UN Security Council Resolution 1325 stresses women's participation in post-conflict peace operations, but its implementation could be strengthened. Despite the rhetoric, women are rarely liberated during and after military occupation and intervention. During war and conflict, women face special forms of terror, such as sexual assault and torture.

KEY POINTS

- Analysts must think outside the box of nation-states to understand the global politics of over-prosperous women (and men) versus desperate women (and men) struggling for basic amenities. Gender balance within the nation-state obscures those politics.

- Global inequalities and local forces structure women's everyday lives and gender relations.

Conclusion

Women and their policy interests have been marginalized as a result of historic state structures and political institutions that privilege men and their voices in the decision-making process. Over the last century, women have gradually increased their participation in politics as voters, decision-makers, and members of non-government organizations. Public policy agendas have widened, taking into account discrimination and gendered inequalities. Progressive policies have yet to be fully implemented, but various bureaucratic tools and NGO oversight increase the prospects for implementation and accountability. Women are gaining ground in most nation-states, thus altering power relations between men and women. The meagre pace of change in most countries, however, may mean that it is our great-grandchildren who will be among the first to experience a gender-balanced polity in most of the developing (and developed) nation-states.

QUESTIONS

1. Does the state 'matter' in sustaining female subordination or moving society toward gender equality?

2. Discuss key turning points in history, political institutional development, and transitions to democracy, including the 'Arab Spring', which potentially open political space for women's voices and for advocating their issues in government.

3. Under what conditions do 'private' or 'personal' issues become politicized as public policy issues? Use examples associated with violence against women.

4. Do women share identical policy interests? Discuss ways in which one might analyse women's interests by ethnicity/race, class, nationality and other factors.

5. What role does reproductive choice have in gender equality?

6. Will poverty-alleviation policies automatically address gender inequalities? Make reference to education and literacy in your response.

7. Do women in the legislature expand the policy agenda and address gender inequalities?

8. Design a debate around the merits of female quotas in a particular country.

9. Consider the analysis of women versus gender. Provide some examples of how a 'gender lens' might stimulate new questions and avenues of research or action.

FURTHER READING

Basu, A. (ed.) (1995) *The Challenge of Local Feminisms: Women's Movements in Global Perspective* (Boulder, CO: Westview Press) A collection of chapters on grass-roots women's movements in Asia, Africa, and Latin America, most authored by women from those areas.

—— (ed.) (2010) *Women's Movements in the Global Era: The Power of Local Feminisms* (Boulder, CO: Westview Press) An updated (from 1995) collection containing new country chapters and theoretically expanded chapters connecting the global to the local.

BRIDGE Development–Gender (2003) *Gender and Budgets* (Brighton: Institute of Development Studies, University of Sussex) Offers valuable concepts for application to real problems in government and organizations.

Goetz, A. M. (ed.) (1997) *Getting Institutions Right for Women in Development* (London: Zed) About transforming and tinkering with institutional machinery to make it more accountable to women and gender equality.

Jahan, R. (1995) *The Elusive Agenda: Mainstreaming Women in Development* (London: Zed) A comparison of two multi-lateral organizations (the World Bank and UNDP) and two relatively progressive bilateral technical assistance institutions (the Norwegian Agency for Development Cooperation, or NORAD, and the Canadian International Development Agency, or CIDA).

Jaquette, J. S. and Summerfield, G. (eds) (2006) *Women and Gender Equity in Development Theory and Practice: Institutions, Resources, and Mobilization* (Durham/London: Duke University Press) Compares recent analyses on the women in development and gender and development approaches.

Krook, M. L. (2009) *Quotas for Women in Politics: Gender and Candidate Selection Reform Worldwide* (New York: Oxford University Press) This is the latest, perhaps definitive, quota study revealing the variety of techniques and outcomes.

Seager, J. (2009) *Penguin Atlas of Women in the World*, 4th edn (New York: Penguin Press) This is the latest version of eye-catching maps and graphics about women and gender inequality.

Staudt, K., Payan, T., and Kruszewski, Z. A. (eds) (2009) *Human Rights along the US–Mexico Border: Gendered Violence and Insecurity* (Tucson, AZ: University of Arizona Press) Scholars from Mexico and the United States broaden the national security versus human security debates in a focus on everyday violence, migration, and activism.

Waylen, G. (2007) *Engendering Transitions: Women's Mobilization, Institutions, and Gender Outcomes.* (Oxford: Oxford University Press) This ten-country study examines the conditions under which women's civil rights expand during transitions to democracy.

⊕ WEB LINKS

http://libarts.wsu.edu/polisci/rngs   Research Network on Gender Politics and the State.

http://www.amnesty.org   Amnesty International, with a global campaign to stop violence against women.

http://www.awid.org   Association for Women's Rights in Development (English, Spanish, French).

http://www.bridge.ids.ac.uk/   Development–Gender, Brighton Institute of Development Studies, University of Sussex, offers 'cutting-edge' packs on trade, migration, citizenship, participation, and many more issues.

http://www.globalfundforwomen.org   Global Fund for Women (English, Spanish, French, Portuguese, Arabic).

http://www.ipu.org   Inter-Parliamentary Union.

http://www.sewa.org   Self-Employed Women's Association, India.

http://www.un.org/womenwatch   United Nations gateway on women's advancement and empowerment.

http://www.un.org/womenwatch/daw   United Nations Division for the Advancement of Women.

http://www.undp.org/women/   UNDP Women's Empowerment home page.

http://www.unifem.org   United Nations Development Fund for Women (UNIFEM).

http://www.vday.org   Provides organizing ideas, including drama performances of *Vagina Monologues*, a play by Eve Ensler, performed in thousands of cities worldwide (in mid-February, 'V-Day') to raise funds to stop violence against women.

http://www.wedo.org   Women's Environment and Development Organization.

http://www.who.int/gender/en/   World Health Organization's Department of Gender, Women, and Health.

http://www.wluml.org   Women Living under Muslim Laws.

http://www.womenlobby.org   European Women's Lobby, comprising more than 4,000 NGOs.

http://www.womensenews.org   A website and source of daily news about women.

http://www.worldbank.org/gender   World Bank Gender Home Page.

For additional material and resources, please visit the Online Resource Centre at:
http://www.oxfordtextbooks.co.uk/orc/burnell4e/

10

Civil Society

Marina Ottaway

Chapter contents

Overview

The expression 'civil society' has metamorphosed during the 1990s from a relatively obscure concept familiar mostly to scholars of Marxism into a mainstream term freely used by social science analysts in general, and by practitioners in the international assistance field specifically. Several factors contributed to these developments. First, there was growing interest by the United States and many European countries in promoting democracy abroad at that time. The demise of the Soviet Union and the Eastern European communist regimes triggered a wave of more or less successful democratic transitions further afield, where regimes formerly influenced by the Soviet model, and often by the Soviet government, struggled to transform themselves into something both more acceptable to their populations and less anachronistic internationally. This wave of political transformations provided an opportunity for the industrialized democracies to actively promote the spread of political systems similar to their own. As international actors devised democracy promotion strategies, they focused much effort on promoting citizen participation and activism—what quickly came to be known as a vibrant civil society.

Another factor was the changes taking place in the established democracies themselves. Many organizations of what used to be called broadly 'the left', inspired by socialist or social democratic ideals of socio-economic equity and justice, were replaced by newer groups whose concept of justice extended beyond the traditional concerns of socialist parties and labour movements. They embraced a broad array of causes such as environmental protection and sustainability, opposition to globalization, and protection of gay rights (see Chapter 11). The old left was rooted above all in political parties and labour unions. The new activists were organized in smaller non-governmental organizations (NGOs), often loosely tied in broad networks that saw themselves as the embodiment of a mobilized civil society.

Disenchantment with the performance of state institutions was an additional factor, as political leaders made concerted efforts to narrow the functions of government, and to enlarge the spheres of the private and non-profit sectors. At the same time, the corruption and inefficiency of many developing countries' governments prompted international development agencies to rethink the assumption that development required state intervention. As a result, they sought ways in which to bypass governments and implement some development projects and programmes through NGOs.

Needless to say, the popularization of the concept of civil society has led to a blurring of its meaning. It has also led to a blurring of its political connotations: a greater role for civil society is now extolled by conservatives, liberals, and radicals alike as a crucial component of political, and even economic, reform. Analysts of different persuasions do not agree about which organizations should be considered part of civil society and which should not, but they all agree that civil society is a good thing.

Introduction: Defining Civil Society

Defining 'civil society' is difficult because the term is laden with theoretical assumptions, unsolved problems, and value judgements. According to Hegel's oft-cited, but ultimately unsatisfactory, definition (in his *Philosophy of Right*, 1821), civil society comprises the realm of organizations that lie between the family, at one extreme, and the state, at the other. While superficially clear and logical, this definition generates a lot of conceptual confusion and some political booby traps. The result is that very few scholars, and virtually no practitioners of **democracy promotion**, now accept such a broad definition in practice, even if they cite it.

Intellectual conundrums

The definition is clear on one point: civil society is not the whole society, the entire web of social **institutions** and relations, but only one part of it. The problem is how to define that part with any degree of precision. Citing the realm of voluntary associations between the family and the state does not provide sufficient clarification. Three problems deserve special attention in terms of:

- distinguishing organizations that are truly voluntary from those that are not;
- determining whether all voluntary organizations between the family and the state deserve to be considered civil; and

- determining whether there is a conceptual difference between civil society and political society, as some argue, or whether this is a distinction with little analytical value, which has gained currency for reasons of political expediency.

The concept of 'voluntary association' contains ambiguities, particularly when applied to the less formal organizations that constituted civil society in the past and are still important in the **developing world**. According to definitions that stress civil societies' voluntary character, a civil society group is a formally constituted association of which individuals become members as part of a completely free choice—a club, for example, is undoubtedly a voluntary association. The family is not, because membership in it is not chosen. But there is a grey area of groups in which membership is not formally compulsory, but neither is it completely a matter of free choice. Religious associations offer one example. Very often, people are born into a church or another type of religious association by virtue of having been born in a family, and inertia explains continued membership; in other cases, membership in a religious group is a truly voluntary choice. Similarly, people are born members of a clan, tribe, or ethnic group, but membership in an organization that claims to represent that group is a political choice made voluntarily and deliberately by some, but by no means all, members of that particular group. South

Africa provides a telling example of how membership in an ethnic group can be an accident of birth or a voluntary decision to join a group. In the early 1990s, at a time of intense fighting between the supporters of Inkatha, a political party with a Zulu nationalist agenda, and other black South Africans, ethnic Zulus who did not support the party and its agenda referred to Inkatha supporters, but not to themselves, as Zulus.

The ambiguities even extend to organizations that appear at first sight to be clearly voluntary, such as political parties. In the early twentieth century, many Europeans were born as members of social democratic parties, figuratively, because of their families' allegiances, or even literally, being delivered by 'midwives' paid by the party as a service to their members. Membership was voluntary in that anybody could stop paying dues and quit the party, but, for many, membership became part of an identity acquired at birth. A contemporary example of this phenomenon is offered by the Sudan, where major religious brotherhoods, into which people are born when families belong, have formed political parties to which adherence is equally automatic, although not compulsory.

Another common problem in determining whether an association is voluntary arises in relation to ruling political parties and the mass organizations that they control. Membership in the party or mass organization is rarely compulsory, but the absence of membership has negative consequences and many are forced to join. One of the difficult tasks faced by the United States as the occupying power in Iraq in 2003 was to distinguish between committed members of the Ba'th Party, who were part of the defunct **regime** of Saddam Hussein, and those who had joined in order to keep their jobs.

A second thorny problem in determining the boundaries of civil society is ideological in nature, hinging on the interpretation of the word 'civil', which can mean both 'relating to citizens or the general public' and 'civilized'. The expansive definition of civil society as comprising all voluntary associations between family and state is based on the first meaning. For many, this is an unacceptable approach because it combines in one category, for example, **human rights** groups and terrorist organizations. In practice, the term 'civil society' is almost invariably used to denote organizations that share certain positive, 'civil' values. But there is no consensus on that point. During the 1980s, Scandinavian countries considered the organizations fighting **apartheid** in South Africa as 'civil' and

provided support. The United States defined them as terrorist organizations and refused to help; Nelson Mandela, the much acclaimed first president of post-apartheid South Africa, was once considered a terrorist by the United States. Many liberals or radicals have no problem accepting labour unions as organizations of civil society, but are often reluctant to see a federation of employers in the same light.

Another controversial issue influenced by political and policy consideration is whether it is valid to draw a distinction between civil and political society. Those who defend the distinction, first made by Gramsci (1929–35, in his *Prison Notebooks*), admit that both civil society and political society play a political role and seek to influence policy decisions. But the political role of civil society is indirect: civil society groups do not aspire to control the government and exercise power, but see their role as that of influencing policies in the public interest; political society organizations—essentially, political parties—want to control the government. A corollary of this view is that the civil society is virtuously dedicated to giving citizens a voice, while political society is power-hungry, self-interested, and considerably less virtuous. A second corollary is that international agencies seeking to promote democracy can and should provide assistance to civil society organizations; supporting political society, which aspires to power and thus is partisan by definition, would be morally questionable and could also represent unjustifiable interference in the domestic **politics** of another country.

The distinction between civil and political society has theoretical justification. Its usefulness, however, is scant, because most civil society organizations are, overtly or covertly, more partisan and political than they claim to be. True, there are organizations of civil society that act purely as pressure or advocacy groups and have no intention of contesting public office. But civil society activists are often close to specific political parties, and many move freely between civil society organizations and parties. Furthermore, many political parties, including some in power, set up organizations of civil society in an attempt to capture some of the assistance that is available only to civil society organizations.

Examples of the blurring of the lines between political and civil organizations exist in most countries, although more pronounced in some than in others. Civil society organizations may be pushed into close alliance with political parties by government repression. Many **non-governmental organizations (NGOs)** in Zimbabwe, for example, developed during the 1990s as bona fide, non-partisan civil society organizations lobbying for improved human rights, constitutional reform, better legal services for the poor, and a variety of similar causes. As the government turned increasingly repressive, violating laws and human rights principles in order to stay in power, civil society organizations increasingly became part of the political opposition. Formally organized NGOs operating at the national level are particularly likely to become politicized when confronted by a repressive regime. Less formal, local groups, sometimes referred to as 'community-based organizations' (CBOs), rarely become openly political. These CBOs are usually concerned about local-level development and welfare issues, focusing on service delivery or simply self-help.

Politics and expediency

The abstract problems of how to define civil society remain a source of debate among academics, but in the meantime civil society is being defined in practice by the policies of bilateral and multilateral aid agencies, by the governments of countries receiving **democracy assistance**, and by civil society organizations themselves.

Bilateral and multilateral international aid organizations define the boundaries of civil society when they decide which organizations are eligible for assistance under democracy promotion programmes, or which should be consulted in the preparation of an assistance strategy. This definition is based on a mixture of political considerations and administrative requirements. The major political requirement is that such organizations focus their activities either on civic education or advocacy for human rights and democratic reform. Civic education programmes, particularly common in countries in the early stages of political transition, seek to convey the basic meaning of democracy, as well as to teach about the political and institutional mechanisms of democratic systems. In its more sophisticated, advanced form, civic education is also training for political activism: citizens are encouraged to scrutinize the action of politicians, to lobby them to enact reforms, and to hold them accountable by voting them out of office. Advocacy organizations that attract international support focus on human rights, women's rights, legal reform, judicial reform, and, occasionally, environmental sustainability. To be

part of civil society thus means to belong to one of these types of organization.

The aid agencies' definition of civil society is further narrowed by their administrative requirements. The groups must be organized in a formal way because donors cannot provide support for an organization that is not registered in some way, which does not have a name and address, or which cannot be audited. Informal networks or vaguely organized civic movements may play an important part in a society or a democratic transition, but they do not meet donors' needs and few foreign funders will provide support for them on an exceptional basis. For example, during the apartheid era in South Africa, some Scandinavian countries agreed to provide assistance to informal organizations affiliated to the African National Congress (ANC). Such willingness to deal with informal organizations is exceptional, however. For practical reasons, donors also prefer to deal with organizations that speak, literally and figuratively, the same language.

As a result, the donors' civil society is an entity very different either from the society at large or from civil society as the realm of voluntary organizations between the family and the state. The term 'civil society' as used, and financed, by the international aid agencies refers to 'a very narrow set of organizations: professionalized NGOs dedicated to advocacy or civic education work on public interest issues directly relating to democratization, such as election monitoring, voter education, governmental transparency and political and civil rights in general' (Ottaway and Carothers 2000: 11).

Direct funding of civil society is not the only way in which international assistance agencies support that society. The influence of NGOs is strengthened by the requirement, under which many agencies now operate, that they consult with local civil society in implementing a wide variety of development and democracy aid programmes. The World Bank has such civil society requirements and many bilateral agencies also hold wide consultations. In practice, many of the groups so contacted are the same organizations that the assistance agencies helped set up or fund in the first place—the ones that they know and which are capable of sending representatives to meetings.

The governments of countries that are recipients of democracy assistance also try to shape the definition of civil society by imposing registration requirements, which are sometimes very strict and used to prevent the formation of antagonistic organizations. Many also try to limit access to donor funding to only some categories of organization or to prevent it outright. Some international agencies are willing to circumvent such regulations and provide funding covertly; others are more anxious not to antagonize the government.

Civil society activists have also played a very important part in determining which organizations are recognized as part of civil society. Transnational networks of NGOs, usually led by the better-funded groups of the industrialized countries, have been particularly influential here. For example, some networks successfully pressed the United Nations to accept their presence at international meetings; the World Bank agreed to undertake re-evaluations of some of its practices, particularly lending for the construction of dams, and to consult with the NGO sector before reaching decisions on certain issues. And, in the early 2000s, oil companies in Chad were required to pay royalties into specially controlled funds in which they were administered under strict controls with the participation of civil society organizations (the requirement was rescinded by parliament in December 2005). These examples are counterbalanced by more numerous examples in which the militancy of transnational civil society networks has failed to earn them recognition as rightful participants.

KEY POINTS

- The widespread agreement about the importance of civil society is accompanied by a great deal of controversy about what civil society is, not only among theorists, but also among practitioners.

- The term has been given a concrete meaning by the policies of international assistance agencies and, to a lesser extent, by the efforts of civil society organizations.

Traditional and Modern Civil Society

It is common for donors to bemoan the weakness, or even the absence, of civil society in countries in which they try to promote democracy. This concern has spurred governments of industrialized countries, as well as international NGOs and private foundations, to launch an array of civil society assistance programmes to strengthen what is invariably referred to as a 'fledgling' civil society. In many instances, even after years of effort, donors express concern about the

BOX 10.1 POPPY GROWERS AND THE AFGHAN STATE

Poppy cultivation for heroin production has become the most important economic activity in Afghanistan since the overthrow of the Taliban in 2001. In 2006, an estimated 2.9 million farmers, or 12.6 per cent of the population, grew poppies. During this time, poppy growers could obtain production loans from illegal organizations controlling the illicit trade, but farmers growing legal crops could not obtain loans through government banks or extension services. Poppy cultivation generated more than US$3 billion in revenue in 2006, while the government could generate only about US$300 million in custom and tax revenue, and foreign assistance brought the country's total budget to only US$600 million.

slow progress of civil society development and its continuing need for support (see Box 10.1). Paradoxically, in the countries in which civil society is deemed at its weakest, for example in war-torn African countries, the population relies for survival on civil society networks that go well beyond the family, and which reveal a high degree of sophistication and organization. One of the problems faced by countries undergoing political upheaval is that some civil society networks quickly establish themselves in major fields of economic activity and even within parts of the government. The criminalization of the state that has been witnessed in **failing states** in West and Central Africa is the result of the disparity between the power of civil society organizations and that of a duly constituted government and administrative structure.

These considerations point to the need to put the discussion of civil society in a broader perspective. Following the current use of the term, the discussion so far has dwelt on 'modern' civil society—that is, the part of civil society organized into formal, professionalized NGOs typical of the late twentieth century. But in all countries, including the industrialized ones, there is another civil society: 'traditional society'. This society is organized more informally, often through networks rather than formally structured organizations, and often following patterns that existed in earlier times.

Traditional forms of civil society exist in most countries today, particularly when the state is weak. Organizations that are traditional in form do not necessarily perform only traditional roles; on the contrary, they grow in new directions in response to contemporary needs and requirements. West African Sufi brotherhoods such as the Mourides are ancient, but when they establish control over the wholesale rice trade in Senegal, or set up mechanisms to help members to emigrate to the United States and find jobs there, they are performing definitely non-traditional functions in response to new challenges.

Modern and traditional civil society stand in inverse relation to each other. In countries in which the state is strong, **traditional civil society** is weak and **modern civil society** is strong. If the state is weak, so is modern civil society, but traditional civil society is strong (Migdal 1988). This explains the paradox outlined above: in countries in the throes of a difficult, state-weakening transition, citizens rely on civil society networks in many aspects of their lives even as donors bemoan the weakness of civil society.

Traditional civil society

Organizations of civil society have taken a great variety of forms traditionally, from the very informal to the highly structured. Loosely structured, but culturally sanctioned, mechanisms for swapping labour and joining efforts in the performance of large collective tasks exist in all societies, as do more structured mechanisms—for example the rotating credit associations that exist, under different names, almost everywhere (see Box 10.2). Compared to modern ones, traditional civil society organizations were less specialized and formal.

They were extremely unlikely to have full-time organizers and certainly not offices. Even in industrial countries, the professionalization of civil society—hence its separation from the society at large—is a recent phenomenon. When Alexis de Tocqueville visited the United States in the first half of the nineteenth century and wrote *Democracy in America* (published in two volumes, in 1835 and 1840), he was struck by the American propensity to form intermediate associations in the pursuit of a wide range of interests and projects; he was looking at loosely structured, ad hoc groups, not at formal organizations with professional staffs.

Modern civil society, defined as a set of NGOs, has clear boundaries that separate it from the family and indeed from the rest of society, as well as from the state. The expression 'members of civil society' refers to a rather small number of people who belong to, and very often work for, such NGOs, not to all citizens.

BOX 10.2 FROM ROTATING CREDIT ASSOCIATIONS TO MICRO-CREDIT

Rotating credit associations exist in all countries and provide loans, usually small, to people who do not have access to, or who do not trust, banks. Members of such associations pay a small fee to the association every week, and every week one of the members, in turn, receives the entire amount. Women use such credit associations to capitalize small businesses, to pay school fees, or to finance a celebration. Shoeshine boys in Addis Ababa use the system to cover the costs of a can of polish or a new brush.

The modern, formal variant of the rotating credit association is **micro-credit**. The Grameen Bank in Bangladesh pioneered the idea. The bank grants small loans to clients—predominantly women—who cannot offer collateral and thus cannot obtain loans from a normal commercial bank. Repayment of the loan is ensured by a group of guarantors, who are not entitled to receive loans themselves until the original borrower has repaid his or her loan. The idea has been replicated widely across the world. The founder of the Grameen Bank, Muhammad Yunus, was awarded the Nobel Peace Prize in 2006 for his pioneering work on micro-credit. More recent studies, however, have called into question whether micro-credit truly lifts most borrowers, particularly women, out of poverty or, like rotating-credit associations, is simply a survival mechanism.

Traditional civil society has no such clear boundaries, but fades into the larger society at one extreme and non-state forms of political authority on the other. In non-state societies, **governance** was an extension of the overall social organization, not the activity of specialized institutions.

The blurring of the lines between the society at large, more organized associations within it, and political authority is not completely a thing of the past, but can reappear in extreme situations of **state collapse**, as in Somalia (see Box 10.3).

Traditional civil society performed important economic activities that today are considered to be the responsibility of state authority. For example, long-distance trade was once organized and carried out through private, civil society networks that extended over long distances. States took over much of the responsibility for protecting trade routes and otherwise making large-scale economic activity more feasible. In places where the state has collapsed or is severely weakened, civil society is again taking on some of those functions. This has been the case in the

BOX 10.3 ISLAMIC COURTS IN SOMALIA

In the power vacuum created by the Somali state's collapse, and the failure of the United States and the United Nations to secure an agreement among warring clans and **warlords**, clan elders and ad hoc organizations tried to provide order and structure. Among these organizations were the Islamic courts, which sought to impose order and administer justice on the basis of a strict interpretation of **Sharia law**. First appearing in the early 1990s, these courts slowly organized into a Union of Islamic Courts. By 2006, the Islamic courts were well armed and competing for control over the country with an official, but powerless, government, which had emerged from negotiations backed by the **international community**.

Democratic Republic of the Congo (formerly Zaire) since at least the 1980s, for example.

Traditional civil society and the state in the contemporary world

Some traditional forms of civil society exist even in the industrialized countries and they pose no problem. On the contrary, they contribute to the reservoir of what Putnam (1993) calls 'social capital'. When traditional forms of civil society grow very strong as a result of the weakness or total collapse of the state, however, they can become highly problematic. Traditional civil society in the contemporary world is both indispensable and dangerous. Where the state is incapable, it can help people to survive and maintain a semblance of normal life under very difficult conditions. But in the absence of a strong state, civil society networks can also turn into a source of power and domination for an oligarchy, become estranged from the broader society, and thus prevent the rebuilding of the state and the introduction of democratic forms of governance (Migdal 1988: 24–41). In extreme cases, as in Libya after the overthrow of the Qaddafi regime, organizations that started as a result of citizens' efforts to overthrow a dictator have turned into armed militias that are a threat to citizens and to the central government.

The benign side of the reappearance of traditional civil society is apparent every day in countries in which government is unable to perform functions expected of a modern state. The government cannot fund schools for all children, and civil society responds by setting up alternative schools. (This also happens in some industrialized countries: the Charter School movement in the United States is a civil society response to the failure of many urban public school systems.) State collapse forces banks to close, and civil society responds by setting up informal systems. In the Arab world, the *hawala* system moves money rapidly and efficiently across continents and into remote villages. The formal economy cannot provide jobs for everybody, and civil society develops an informal sector that provides the livelihood of the majority of the population.

Another traditional civil society mechanism that becomes more prominent in **weak states** is **clientelism**. Instead of coming together in an organization to solve the problem they face collectively, people who cannot get what they need through formal state institutions, be it medical care and schooling, or justice through a corrupt court system, may turn to a powerful and rich individual for help. This person, the patron, will help them to get their children into school, to obtain the ration card necessary to receive subsidized food, and to make sure that their unlicensed small business will not be closed down by the police. The recipient of this largesse, the client, will repay the patron by giving his or her allegiance, voting for the patron if elections are held, or otherwise providing political support. **Patron–client relations** provide poor, powerless people with a useful form of access to power. However, they do so to the detriment of the development of modern institutions and forms of collective action that may lead to a long-term power redistribution (Nelson 1979).

There is also a much more malignant side to the reappearance of traditional civil society, because it can further undermine the failed state institutions for which it is trying to compensate. During the transition from apartheid in South Africa, a weakened government lost its capacity to enforce the laws that kept peddlers away from the business district of Johannesburg. Informal sector businesses took over the sidewalks, to the benefit of the people who were trying to make a living by selling vegetables and braiding hair on the street. But the informal marketplace also became the territory of criminal gangs, legitimate businesses were driven out, and the once thriving business district became a 'no-go' area.

And parts of the civil society that flourish because of the absence of the state may be hostile to efforts to revive it. The trading networks that form in war-ravaged countries respond to a need, but they can also become profitable organizations that resist the efforts of the new, stronger government to revive institutions. Vigilante groups, such as those that operate in many parts of Nigeria, are a civil society response to insecurity—but they tend to turn into criminal organizations that end up by preying on those they were supposed to defend. In extreme cases, the re-emergence of traditional civil society is a threat to the continued existence of the state or can challenge its reconstruction, as in Somalia recently and in Libya today.

The tension between traditional civil society and the state is also evident in the cultural domain. Traditionally, civil society has always been a major vehicle through which culture has been transmitted. In many countries, public education has deliberately sought to create a new culture, different from that transmitted by civil society and in many ways alien to it. A motivation for public education systems has always been the desire to create a new **national identity**, different and often hostile to the local identities transmitted by traditional civil society. In Turkey, under Kemal Ataturk, the state tried to impose secular values on a traditional society that upheld Islamic ones. This cultural conflict between states and traditional civil society continues today even in the most industrialized, democratic societies: it is evident, for instance, in the disputes in France over the right of Muslim girls to wear a headscarf in school, or in the United States in the battles over whether to teach the science-based theory of evolution in the so-called 'Bible belt', where many citizens accept the biblical idea that God created the world in six days about 6,000 years ago. In societies in which the state is weaker, or less determined to influence the culture, the battle is often won by civil society—the re-Islamization of culture in Egypt after decades of secular public education is a striking example (Wickham 2002).

KEY POINTS

- Traditional forms of civil society exist in all countries, but they do not necessarily perform traditional functions.
- When the state is weak, traditional civil society tends to be strong.
- Traditional forms of civil society help to alleviate certain problems created by the weakness of the state, but they can also prevent the strengthening of the state.

The Modern State and Civil Society as a Specialized Entity

The rise of civil society as an entity separate from the broader society and from the state is part of an overall process of specialization that has affected all social and political institutions, particularly in the later part of the twentieth century. This specialization of functions has been accompanied by a formalization of the organizations that discharge those functions.

Can the new, specialized, and professionalized organizations perform the three major functions expected of them, especially in developing countries—generation of social capital, representation of the interest and demands, and the provision of goods and, above all, services? The specialization of civil society alters the way in which civil society performs these functions in all countries, but raises particularly serious problems in developing countries.

Take first the widely held view that civil society organizations generate social capital, a concept first set forth by Putnam (1993) in a study of regional government in Italy, as an explanation of why the same institutions functioned differently in the north and south of the country. He observed that the inhabitants of the northern region shared a civic culture rooted in earlier experiences with self-government and sustained over the centuries by a rich associational life. These attitudes constituted the social capital that determined the way in which people viewed government and related to its institutions. This social capital was scarce in the southern regions, which had both a different historical experience and a dearth of associational life.

It is open to question to what extent the more specialized civil society organizations of today, with their professional staffs and narrow focuses, generate social capital. Professional, specialized organizations tend to have small, or even non-existent, membership and thus they do not reach many people. Even if they do, they engage them only on very specific issues. They probably do not inculcate in their members the attitudes of trust and cooperation that constitute social capital. Putnam argues that professional NGOs, even if devoted to democratic causes, contribute less to the social capital that supports democracy than seemingly irrelevant associations such as bowling leagues, or the charitable and social clubs once widespread in American towns. He even sees in the decreasing popularity of these organizations a harbinger of the decline of American democracy.

The problem is particularly acute in developing countries, where many NGOs have small memberships, focus on a narrow range of issues, and are highly dependent on foreign governments or international NGOs. Their contribution to social capital is highly questionable, particularly when compared to the social capital generated by more traditional social institutions (see Box 10.4). Such traditional institutions also teach values and attitudes, but not necessarily those extolled by Putnam as necessary for democracy. They may include, for example, extremely negative views of other ethnic or religious groups, deep distrust of all strangers, or demeaning attitudes towards women. The fact that the content of this social capital is different and may be contrary to democratic values does not alter the fact that it is deeply embedded in social relations and not easily erased, particularly by professional NGOs with weak social roots.

The second of the three functions attributed to civil society—the representational function—raises the question of whether or how far such groups can actually represent the society vis-à-vis the government. The simple answer is that specialized civil society organizations do not represent society as a whole in any country. But in developing countries and within nondemocratic international institutions, civil society organizations do broaden the range of interests that are expressed. Yet they do so in a lopsided way that favours groups with the capacity to organize and to access resources, even if their ideas are not widely held.

In well-established democracies, the problem of representation is solved by the existence of elected officials, freely chosen by the voters to represent their interests. Organizations of civil society are simply one among many types of organized interest group that put pressure on the elected officials to adopt the policies they favour. Professional NGOs are numerous and hold a variety of conflicting positions, as already stated, and compete for influence with a lot of other groups, including paid lobbies; thus they cannot advance a credible claim to represent the interests and the will of the entire population.

But in many developing countries representative institutions are often weak, and elections fall short of being free and fair; as a result, civil society organizations may more credibly claim to represent voiceless citizens. Civil society organizations also have a degree of credibility when they claim to speak for unrepresented constituencies in international institutions, which are designed to represent states, but provide no formal channels through which popular demands can

---

BOX 10.4 THE CONUNDRUM OF ISLAMIC CHARITIES

Since alms-giving (*zakat*) is one of the five pillars of Islam, Muslim countries have extensive webs of Islamic charitable organizations. Islamist movements and political parties have built on this charitable tradition to reach out to the population, providing educational and health services while spreading their religious and political message. Islamist movements, in other words, build on the social capital of Muslim societies. This creates a conundrum for liberal democracy advocates in Muslim countries and their Western supporters: social capital favours Islamist organizations, while liberal organizations struggle to put down roots outside intellectual circles.

---

be expressed. Because lack of popular representation is a real problem in many developing countries and in international organizations, NGOs' claims that they voice the voiceless have won a degree of acceptance in recent years, and have even gained them a place at the table in many policy discussions.

The issue of whether NGOs should be consulted despite their lack of representativity remains highly controversial and is unlikely to be resolved soon. As long as countries do not have truly democratic institutions, the voice of NGOs adds an element of pluralism to the political system, and the distortions created by this imperfect form of representation may be an acceptable price for such a broadening of the political process. On the other hand, there is an element of risk in mandatory consultations with organizations that are not representative and, above all, not accountable to the people in whose name they claim to speak.

The third function performed by modern, professional civil society organizations is the provision of goods and services to the population. Many voluntary organizations provide a wide range of assistance—from the very basic, survival-oriented food distribution or provision of emergency shelter, to the funding of research on rare diseases or the formation of support groups for people facing an almost infinite variety of problems. In this field, too, there are considerable differences between the importance of this civil society in industrial and less-developed countries, as well as in the issues raised by the existence of these organizations. On the one hand, these civil society organizations are much more numerous, better organized, and more capable in the industrialized countries. In developing countries, they are usually highly dependent on external funding, and very often find themselves in a subordinate position to the more affluent international NGOs that can access with greater ease money from rich countries and international organizations.

On the other hand, professional NGOs delivering goods and services often have a more important role in developing countries compared to that of richer counterparts in the industrialized West. In the poorest countries, for example, the assistance provided by NGOs is the main form of assistance available to the population, while in the richer countries NGOs supplement, rather than replace, the safety net provided by the government. This gives the foreign organizations that provide the funding for activities in developing countries a role that is often more important than that of the government. In extreme cases, the imbalance between the capacity of a developing country's government and that of the foreign and domestic NGOs operating there becomes dramatic and can hollow out the role of the government. To illustrate, in Afghanistan between January 2002 and March 2003, foreign donors channelled US$296 million in assistance through the Afghan government and US$446 million through international NGOs (see Box 10.5).

BOX 10.5 THE DANGER OF INTERNATIONAL CIVIL SOCIETY

The policy of donors funding two civil services—the government bureaucracy at an average wage of [US]$50 per month and a parallel bureaucracy of their own at [US]$500 per month—draws talented people out of government in the short term and fundamentally undermines the creation of a sustainable state in the medium to long term.

(Ashraf Ghani, Governor of the Bank for the Islamic State of Afghanistan, speaking to World Bank Governors, 3 October 2004)

KEY POINTS

• Professionalized and specialized civil society organizations generate little social capital.

• Specialized civil society organizations are not truly representative, but they broaden the range of interests expressed in the political process.

• Professional organizations can play a crucial role in the provision of services.

Civil Society and the State in the Developing World

Relations between state and civil society, both in its traditional and modern forms, are quite complex in the developing world, more so than in industrial countries. Political systems are undergoing change in many countries, some states are still consolidating or conversely are on the verge of failure, modern civil society is a recent construct, and traditional forms of civil society are still making adaptations to a changed social and political environment. As a result, relations between state and civil society are in flux. In consolidated democracies, the relationship is more stable and thus more predictable.

Civil society organizations relate to state institutions and officials in one of three different ways: they ignore them and try to avoid their control; they oppose them and work for their replacement; or they seek to influence their policies. The pattern of avoidance is most often found in countries in which the state is incapable of delivering services or other **public goods**. Civil society organizations give up on the state and seek to provide essential public goods on their own. Some of these activities are benign, for example the organization of alternative self-help schools for children neglected by the public system. Others are quite problematic: for example, in countries in which the police force is incapable of ensuring a minimum of security for citizens, vigilante groups sometimes degenerate into protection rackets or become predatory. The organizations of civil society that flourish in the space left by a failing state are unregistered and unlicensed, often illegal. In terms of structures, they thus fall into the category of traditional civil society, although the functions that they perform are a response to contemporary problems created by state collapse and/or political repression.

When the state is capable of performing its functions, but the government is repressive and unresponsive, civil society organizations are more likely to take an antagonistic position. Some civil society organizations that take on an opposition role are simply fronts for political parties, deliberately set up to circumvent donors' rules against funding political organizations. As mentioned earlier, in some countries, civil society organizations have strong party links; in others, civil society organizations turn into opposition groups after trying to influence the government and discovering they cannot do so. The example from Zimbabwe cited above illustrates this point very well. Organizations that see themselves as guardians of universal principles—human rights organizations, for example—are particularly likely to turn antagonistic when the government continues to violate those principles. Civil society groups that oppose the government can be organized as professional NGOs, or along less formal lines as broad **social movements** or loosely structured networks. Such a broad, loosely structured alliance of hundreds of small local organizations, or 'civics', formed in South Africa during the 1980s. The existence of this elusive hydra was crucial in convincing the apartheid regime that peace could not be restored by repressive measures and that a political solution was necessary.

Finally, the relationship of civil society to state and government can be a cooperative one. This is the ideal promoted by democratization programmes. There are various forms of cooperation. Civil society organizations, which possess a degree of expertise in their specialized area, lobby the government to promote specific policy reforms and even provide the government with the expertise to implement the reforms, such as by helping to write legislation. Women's organizations, which are not usually seen as particularly threatening by governments although they may antagonize conservative social forces, are adept at this advocacy role. For example, they helped to craft legislation in Uganda that expanded landownership rights for women, as well as a new divorce law more favourable to women in Egypt.

Another form of cooperation between government and civil society is found when the government contracts out the delivery of services to non-profit NGOs. This is rarer in developing countries than in Europe because it requires strong governments, capable of establishing a regulatory framework and providing supervision, and strong civil society organizations capable of delivering complex services. The existence of a weak government on one side and strong international NGOs, often backed by large amounts of foreign money, gives rise to the common complaint that, in such conditions, international NGOs de facto make policy, further weakening the government and undermining its capacity.

The relationship between state and civil society in developing countries is rarely an easy one. This explains why many governments see civil society organizations as dangerous enemies to be tightly controlled.

In democratic countries, setting up and registering an NGO is an easy process, and regulations aim above all at preventing abuse of tax-exempt **status** or the misuse of donations. By contrast, in many developing countries, NGOs are subject to complicated regulations aimed at suppressing groups that aspire to an advocacy role, instead of merely dispensing charity. An important issue that emerged in the 1990s in some countries is whether organizations of civil society should be allowed to receive foreign funding. Most governments welcome foreign funding of charitable organizations—for example groups that provide assistance to AIDS orphans in Africa; foreign funding of advocacy organizations, on the other hand, is very controversial.

KEY POINTS

- When the state is repressive, civil society organizations are usually antagonistic to it.

- When the state is weak and incapable of delivering services, civil society organizations seek to ignore the state and avoid its control, rather than to press for reforms.

- When the state is strong and civil society organizations are well developed, relations tend to be cooperative and constructive.

Civil Society and Democratization

The rapid transformation of the term 'civil society' from an obscure concept known to a few scholars to one that finds its place in all discussions of political transformation is a result of the rapid spread of democracy assistance initiatives that followed the end of the cold war. However, by the end of the 1990s, it was clear that many so-called democratic transitions had led at best to the formation of semi-authoritarian regimes rather than democratic ones (Ottaway 2003). Furthermore, the reform process was losing momentum almost everywhere (Diamond 1996). Nevertheless, democracy promotion abroad remains on the political agenda of most industrial democracies. And leaders in the developing world, including many with no democratic credentials and no visible intention of acquiring them, embraced the rhetoric of democracy.

The concept of civil society became an important part of all discussions of democratization for reasons grounded to some extent in theory—as discussed earlier—and to a larger extent in pragmatism. In order to provide democracy assistance, aid agencies had to break down the abstract idea of democracy into concrete component parts that could be supported with limited amounts of aid. Civil society was such a component, and a particularly attractive one. Developing civil society meant promoting government by the people and for the people. And when civil society was defined as a narrow set of professional NGOs, it was also an entity to which assistance could be easily provided.

Non-governmental organizations are easy to organize and cheap to fund; small grants go a long way. Professional NGOs were also a new type of association in many countries. Without roots in the traditional civil society and the culture of their countries, and highly dependent on outside funding, professional NGOs were easy to train and influence to conform to the funders' concept of what civil society should do. With donor support, NGOs multiplied rapidly in all regions of the world, displaying remarkably similar characteristics. This made the aid agencies' job of supporting civil society easier. It also raised the question of whether these organizations were truly addressing the specific challenges of democratization in their countries.

Many studies of the donor-assisted civil society have reached the conclusion that pro-democracy NGOs tend to be quite isolated from the society at large. For instance, this was a nearly unanimous conclusion of the contributors to *Funding Virtue* (Ottaway and Carothers 2000), with the only exception being two experts on the Philippines, where the growth of civil society was an indigenous process that owed much less to foreign assistance. This suggests that donor support is an important contributor to the isolation of civil society organizations. Many professional NGOs have small or no membership. They are often exclusively urban organizations with little reach in the countryside—only the best organized are able to extend their reach through networks of less formal community-based organizations (CBOs). Exchanges (often called 'networking') among the NGOs from different countries provide an opportunity for organizations to discuss their problems and to learn from each other, but they also contribute to creating a special international NGO world, the inhabitants of which talk to each other more easily than they do to their compatriots. These observations do not call into question the genuine commitment of many NGO leaders to democracy, human rights, or other causes. They do call into question, however, the capacity of these so-called organizations of civil society to influence their societies.

Democracy NGOs have other problems worth mentioning briefly. One is the opportunism that exists in the NGO world alongside genuine commitment: when assistance is available, setting up an NGO can simply be a way of making a living. **Corruption** also exists in the NGO world, which is unsurprising in view of its very rapid growth (see Chapter 15). And many, as mentioned earlier, become partisan organizations affiliated with political parties. These problems are tangible, but also inevitable, to some extent, and not particularly worrisome unless they are extremely widespread. They are simply part of the inevitable imperfection of the real world.

What is more worrisome is whether the growth of a small professional civil society actually contributes to democratization, and whether the attention lavished on these organizations has led to the neglect of organizational forms that might have greater popular appeal and greater outreach within the population. Democracy promoters recognize the weakness of the NGOs that they support and they equate it with the weakness of civil society. And yet, in many of the countries in which the organizations officially designated as civil society are weakest, for example in many war-torn African countries, informal civil society organizations have proven very resilient in trying to address the most severe difficulties created by state collapse. In their search for a society that is civil by their definition and assistable in terms of its formal characteristics, aid providers may have marginalized groups with a proven record of effectiveness.

Arab countries, with their contrast between a vast Islamic civil society and their struggling official civil society, illustrate the problem particularly well. In Egypt, the world of Islamic civil society is large and multifaceted. It includes charitable groups, organizations that provide free-of-charge medical services that the state has stopped delivering, organizations that offer some educational opportunities for students underserved by failing public schools, and groups that provide textbooks for university students who cannot afford them. It also includes organizations with political goals that do not satisfy the principles of liberal democracy, and terrorist groups that can only be defined as uncivil.

This Islamic civil society is well rooted in the society at large. Even organizations that are by no means traditional, but which represent a contemporary and (from a religious point of view) aberrant response to contemporary problems, can cast themselves as part of a well-established tradition. They are certainly better rooted in the society than the modern, professional, pro-democracy NGOs favoured by donors. But the new donors' civil society espouses the values of liberal democracy, while the more traditional Islamic civil society is at best ambiguous on this point. In the end, neither an isolated modern civil society nor a well-rooted Islamic one are good vehicles for democratic transformation.

An additional issue concerning the role of civil society in democratization has arisen recently in the context of the uprisings that have taken place in a number of countries—events that are often referred to as the 'Arab Spring' or the 'Arab awakening' (see Chapters 8, 11, and 14). The issue is that of the impact of large scale participation by unorganized citizens on democratization and deserves more discussion than it has received so far, because this form of mass civil society participation can have an extremely positive impact, but also has a darker side.

In Tunisia and Egypt, civil society participation in the form of sustained mass demonstrations over a period of weeks brought down two extremely well-entrenched authoritarian regimes with remarkably little bloodshed. These uprisings represented civil society involvement at its best, showing the determination of ordinary citizens to reclaim their rights from repressive regimes and the strength that ordinary people can muster with a minimum of organization, relying largely on social media and word of mouth.

Fast forward two years (at time of writing) and the darker side of mobilized civil society is also becoming apparent, particularly in Egypt, where the transition has been more difficult. Mass demonstrations have changed subtly from the actions of citizens taking responsibility for their own future to partisan affairs by rival political organizations to whip up support for their own goals outside the formal political process. Not much seems wrong with these partisan demonstrations, until we reflect on the fact that the **exploitation** of large crowds by political parties outside a legal political process was one of the means used by fascist and Nazi parties in gaining, and then holding on to, power. In no Arab country at present have the attempts by political parties to mobilize crowds for their own purposes reached alarming proportions. But it is important to keep the lessons of history

clearly in mind: mass civil society participation can be a positive means of forcing change on unmovable authoritarian regimes, but it can never become a means to govern a country democratically. In the long run, participation has to be filtered through institutions and legal processes, although in the short run and in specific historical circumstances direct mass participation can open the way to democratic transformation. (Samuel Huntington in *Political Order in Changing Societies*, 1968, offers a good discussion of participation and institutionalization.) The problem is to understand when direct participation starts turning from a positive phenomenon into the beginning of a new and dangerous authoritarianism.

KEY POINTS

- The difference between traditional organizations well rooted in the society, relatively close to the population, but not necessarily democratic or official, and the civil society recognized by international democracy promoters may be starker in the Muslim world than elsewhere at this time, but is found in all parts of the developing world.

- Democracy requires a large, active, democratically oriented civil society, but what is found in most countries is a bifurcated situation: an official civil society—small, democratic, but essentially elitist; and a less formal, traditional civil society—large, popular, well rooted, but of dubious democratic credentials.

- How to combine the democratic commitment of the former to the popular roots and outreach of the other is a major conundrum for democratization.

Conclusion

The chapter started with an acknowledgement of the ambiguity of the concept of civil society and of its lack of definitional clarity. It ends on the same note, but with a normative addendum. Not only is the concept of civil society an imprecise, ambiguous one, but it must also be accepted as such. The more strictly the concept is defined, the less it helps us to understand how people come together voluntarily to address problems that they cannot solve as individuals and which the state cannot, or does not want to, help solve for them.

It is, of course, possible to narrow down the definition closely. This is what the international development agencies do all of the time when they pick the organizations to support on the basis of the civility of their goals and the adequacy of their organizational structures. But what is gained in terms of clarity is lost in terms of the understanding of the society. First, the narrow definition loses sight of the many ways in which people in any society organize themselves to pursue their interests and satisfy their needs. It may reduce the effectiveness of any outside intervention, by focusing attention on groups that may be quite marginal to the society, but which happen to appear all-important to aid agencies. Second, a definition that separates a democratic, virtuous civil society, acting in the public interest, from a non-democratic, uncivil one, selfishly promoting narrow interests, is more normative than analytical. The idea of the common good and the public interest obfuscate the reality that all societies are made up of groups with different and often conflicting interests, and that all groups are equally part of the society, whether their goals conform to a specific idea of civility or not.

In conclusion, despite the caveat expressed at the outset, from an analytical point of view we need to accept that we cannot do better than accept that civil society comprises the entire realm of voluntary associations between the family and the state. It is a vast and complex realm. Voluntary associations take many different forms, ranging from small, informal self-help groups and ad hoc committees with narrow goals, to large, professional, and bureaucratic organizations with large budgets. In developing countries, civil society organizations perform a wide range of functions. At one extreme, there are narrowly focused groups that seek, for example, to provide support for AIDS orphans in a community or to raise money to improve the track that connects a village to the nearest highway. At the other, there are organizations tied into transnational networks with goals such as changing the World Bank's outlook on the construction of dams or delivering humanitarian assistance to populations in need. Many voluntary associations in developing countries try to provide services the state is unable to deliver. Others form to help citizens to resist pressure from predatory governments. Organizations that citizens develop voluntarily are not always 'civil' in the normative sense of the word. The realm of civil society comprises organizations that promote human rights and vigilante groups that prey on the people whom they are supposed to protect. While it is tempting to narrow the definition of civil society to organizations with commendable goals, this is not helpful. If we want to understand how people come together to defend their interests or to pursue their goals, we need to accept the diversity, the complexity, and in many cases the flaws of the associational realm that has become known as 'civil society'.

 QUESTIONS

1. Boundaries between civil and political society, clear in theory, often become blurred in practice. Is this a problem?

2. How can traditional forms of civil society persist in modern states, and what benefits and drawbacks do they offer to politics and development?

3. Should we be concerned about the potential negative repercussions of an empowered civil society for a weak state?

4. Can civil society organizations make up for weakness of political parties?

5. Is the development of a modern civil society sector a precondition or conversely an inevitable effect of democratization?

6. Should Western non-governmental organizations try to strengthen modern civil society groups in the developing world, and if so, how can they do this without putting their legitimacy at risk?

7. Mass participation by relatively unorganized citizens opened the way to democratic transformation in Tunisia and Egypt, but it facilitated the rise of fascism and Nazism in Europe. When is mass participation positive and when is it dangerous?

FURTHER READING

Edwards, M. (2009) *Civil Society* (Cambridge: Polity Press) Updated version of the original 2004 edition, dwelling mostly on the practice rather than the theory of civil society. Addresses the recent challenges from persistent oppressive regimes and developments in the economic market.

Florini, A. M. (ed.) (2000) *The Third Force: The Rise of Transnational Civil Society* (Washington DC: Carnegie Endowment for International Peace) Case studies of the role of transnational networks of civil society, including the global anti-corruption movement, human rights movement, organizations for democracy and against dam-building, and for environmental sustainability.

Hann, C. and Dunn, E. (eds) (1996) *Civil Society: Challenging Western Models* (New York: Routledge) A critical account that argues for a broader perspective on civil society.

Kasfir, N. (ed.) (1998) *Civil Society and Democracy in Africa* (London: Frank Cass). A critical view of conventional Western attitudes towards civil society in Africa.

Nelson, J. (1979) *Access to Power: Politics and the Urban Poor in Developing Nations* (Princeton, NJ: Princeton University Press) A wide-ranging empirical assessment of political participation by the urban poor in many developing countries, which downplays their revolutionary potential.

Ottaway, M. and Carothers, T. (eds) (2000) *Funding Virtue: Civil Society Aid and Democracy Promotion* (Washington DC: Carnegie Endowment for International Peace) A critical examination of civil society aid, drawing on cases in Africa, Asia, the Middle East, and Latin America.

Ottaway, M. and Chung, T. (1999) 'Debating Democracy Assistance: Toward a New Paradigm', *Journal of Democracy*, 10(4): 99–113 A cautious view of international 'democracy assistance' to civil society, and to elections and parties too.

Putnam, R. (1993) *Making Democracy Work: Civic Traditions in Modern Italy* (Princeton, NJ: Princeton University Press) A seminal work on social capital.

Wickham, C. R. (2002) *Mobilizing Islam: Religion, Activism, and Political Change in Egypt* (New York: Columbia University Press) A highly acclaimed analysis of the role of cultural identity, political economy, mobilization, and organization in political Islam in Egypt.

WEB LINKS

http://business.un.org/en   Links to the ways in which the United Nations system works 'in partnership' with civil society on issues of global concern.

http://www.carnegieendowment.org/publications/index.cfm   See *Middle Eastern Democracy: Is Civil Society the Answer?* by Amy Hawthorne. A critical examination of the question.

http://www.civilsocietyinstitute.org   The Civil Society Institute is an advocacy group 'committed to improving society with breakthrough thinking and creative action'.

http://www.grameen-info.org   The website of Grameen Bank Organization, including articles about micro-credit by its founder Muhammad Yunus.

http://www.ids.ac.uk/ids/   The site of the civil society and governance research project at the Institute of Development Studies, University of Sussex, which examines the interplay of civil society and governments in twenty-two countries. Funded by the Ford Foundation.

http://www.imf.org/external/np/exr/cs/eng/index.asp   The International Monetary Fund's Civil Society Newsletter provides regularly updated information on the IMF's collaborative efforts with civil society groups around the world.

http://www.imf.org/external/np/exr/cs/index.aspx   The International Monetary Fund's Civil Society website.

http://www.lse.ac.uk/collections/CCS   The Centre for Civil Society at the London School of Economics is 'a leading, international organisation for research, analysis, debate and learning about civil society'.

http://www.un.org/en/civilsociety/index.shtml/   The United Nations and Civil Society site explains the different ways in which the United Nations interacts with and promotes the development of civil society.

 For additional material and resources, please visit the Online Resource Centre at:
http://www.oxfordtextbooks.co.uk/orc/burnell4e/

11

Social Movements and Alternative Politics

Siri Gloppen

Chapter contents

Overview

Clarifying the concepts 'alternative politics' and 'social movements', the chapter shows how different forms of social movements have emerged and been influential during different periods, and introduces the main theoretical perspectives about why this is so and how we should understand this phenomenon. Turning to past and present social movements and alternative politics in the developing world, it distinguishes between three categories: movements concerned with democracy and governance; movements concerned with identity politics; and movements concerned with social justice. Current examples of each type show how they operate, and their strengths and challenges. The examples will also show that these categories are by no means mutually exclusive and that each movement may include a number of different concerns. Turning to the increasing globalization of social movements, we discuss how this affects, and is affected by, social movements in the developing world. The last part of the chapter asks what makes social movements successful and shows how this is answered in the literature.

Introduction

Throughout the **developing world**—and beyond—new forms of political participation challenge and transform established political **institutions**. Authoritarian rulers and democratically elected leaders alike are facing **social movements** and civic uprisings, as well as a range of strategies that aim to influence **governance** from below and to strengthen the accountability of ruling elites. Demonstrations for **regime change** in Cairo's Tahrir Square, anti-**corruption** movements in India, Inuit communities' demands for climate justice, and Andean indigenous peoples' struggle for constitutions respecting the rights of Mother Earth are very different forms of activism, yet share important commonalities. Rather than aiming for political office, these movements seek to alter the way in which the political system itself operates—sometimes by using parts of it (for example the courts) as instruments for change. In contrast to militant revolutionary movements, they aim to change the system in non-violent ways. They are often loosely organized, without clear leadership or organizational structures, which some see as a value in itself. And they increasingly rely on new information technology to mobilize and generate pressure, locally and globally. This chapter aims to show how social movements in the developing world and 'bottom-up', alternative **politics**, supported by new technology and globalized networks, can deepen democracy—but it also exposes the challenges inherent to sustaining such movements over time.

Social Movements and Alternative Politics

'Alternative politics' describes the burgeoning field of political activity that emerges 'from below', in the sense that it centrally involves ordinary people, as opposed to political elites, and takes place outside of formal politics and established political channels, such as parties, elections, and parliamentary politics. This includes one-off protests and riots, Facebook campaigns, and flash mobs, as well as long-term social movements pursuing social justice and political change.

A social movement can be defined as a loosely organized, but sustained, collective campaign in support of a social goal—typically a change in society's structure or values—that (mainly) acts outside institutional and conventional channels. While going beyond a single riot or protest, social movements mainly employ such non-conventional ways of participating in order to influence authorities to grant their demands. They may engage in conventional lobbying or challenge authorities in court, but social movements are essentially about collective action. The degree of organization may vary from loosely organized movements to well-defined and clear hierarchies, but even in organized movements participants are defined by their common ideology or goal rather than formal membership. Thus they cannot be equated with formal organizations such as unions or **nongovernmental organizations** (NGOs). However, unions and NGOs often participate in and organize movements—and social movements may develop into political parties, NGOs, or other formal organizations. The goals of social movements are radical in the sense that they pursue ideals challenging the status quo. The authority that they challenge may be the **regime** itself, as in the 'Arab Spring', or cultural norms, for example related to **gender** or race (Goodwin and Jasper 2003; Snow et al. 2004; Amenta et al. 2010).

Charles Tilly saw the early growth of social movements as a result of broad economic and political changes in the nineteenth century, including the spread of parliamentary politics, capitalist market economies, and the growth of the proletariat. Early social movements include the British abolitionist movement, and the labour and socialist movements of the late nineteenth century, which led to the formation of communist and social democratic parties and organizations. Typical of 'old social movements' is their focus on issues of economic and social justice.

In the 1960s and 1970s, so-called 'new social movements' erupted, including the civil rights movement, the women and gay liberation movements, the environmental movement, anti- (Vietnam) war movements, the student movement, and general cultural revolt. These movements were seen as 'new' in orientation, organization, and style. While 'old' social movements typically recruited from the working class, focused on economic issues and labour conflict, directed their attention towards the state, and aimed for economic redistribution to benefit particular groups, the 'new' movements expressed universalist concerns, often in the name of morality and universal rights. 'New' movements were generally composed of people who shared a concern for social issues rather than a material interest. And the ideological orientation was more towards identity and lifestyle concerns. Their repertoire of action was to a greater extent outside institutionalized politics; it was diverse, on the streets, and made use of symbols. They orientated themselves more toward **civil society** than the state, and depended on mass media and new information technology to get their message out. To avoid being de-radicalized and co-opted, what Michels (1962) famously termed 'the iron law of oligarchy', these movements have sought to avoid highly organized structures and bureaucratic organizations (Pichardo 1997; Nash 2010).

In reality, the differences between the 'old' and 'new' movements are less clear. Already in the eighteenth and nineteenth centuries, unconventional direct action was prevalent among social movements. And contemporary social movements range from highly organized and hierarchical women's groups, to the loosely organized Occupy Wall Street protests of 2011–12. They regularly interact with governments and some movements have transformed into political parties. Non-materialist movements in which the role of identity was essential have existed from the early nineteenth century (**feminist**, nationalist), while contemporary movements such as the Occupy movement have an 'old', materialist focus on economic justice and redistribution (Calhoun 1993; Pichardo 1997).

KEY POINTS

- 'Alternative politics' is political activity 'from below', outside of formal political channels, such as protests, riots, Facebook campaigns, and social movements.

- 'Social movements' are loosely organized, but sustained, collective campaigns in support of a social goal that (mainly) acts through alternative politics.

- 'Old social movements' typically focus on redistribution, and economic and social justice; 'new social movements', on non-material issues, values, and identity—but in practice the distinction is blurred.

The Origins of Social Movements

Why do people choose to engage in social movements and alternative politics rather than use normal political channels? Explanations have shifted. In the nineteenth and early twentieth centuries, many social scientists dismissed social movements as primitive actions by the irrational 'crowd'. 'Collective behaviour' theories were influential until the 1960s. Based on a pluralist conception of politics, in which all relevant interests could and should be expressed in the political marketplace, collective behaviour theorists saw no need or role for movements acting outside of conventional politics. Social movement participation was explained by social strain, leading to psychological stress, and pushing individuals into acting not to attain a specific goal or outcome, but merely to manage psychological tensions (McAdam 1982).

With the many social movements of the 1960s and 1970s (civil rights, peace, and women's **emancipation**, among others), scholars increasingly recognized that those engaging in alternative politics were acting rationally. Influenced by the works of Mancur Olson (1965) and others, 'resource mobilization' theories focused on movement participants' active and rational choices to participate. In their famous article 'Resource Mobilization and Social Movements: A Partial Theory', Zald and McCarthy (1979) introduce the notion of the social movement organization steering the movement, aggregating resources and operating like a firm competing for support within a social movement 'industry'. Within a movement, there may be many different organizations, each offering a different direction. These theories take as a given that, at any time, there are a sufficient number of discontented people in society and that what matters is the resources available to the various organizations; the more resources they acquire, the more mobilization they are able to produce (Goodwin and Jasper 2003).

Later, scholars recognized the importance of the political environment for social movements, using the concept of the 'political opportunity structure' to explain why mobilization occurs in some situations and not in others (McAdam 1982; Kitschelt 1986; Kriesi et al. 1995; Jenkins et al. 2003). The core idea is that, to understand why and how social movements mobilize, attention should be focused not (only) on the social movements themselves and their resources, but (also) on their environment, and the barriers and opportunities that they face in reaching their aims. Some see the political opportunity structure narrowly in terms of possibilities for accessing state power (Kitschelt 1986); others employ a dynamic conception of political opportunities, including alliance structures and which party is in power (Kriesi et al. 1995). This helps to explain fluctuations in mobilization within a country and why protest waves occur suddenly.

Another key concept used in explaining social movement mobilization is 'framing'. Framing processes give meaning to the actions of a movement, drawing on shared cultural understandings. This is important in mobilizing supporters, forming common identities, and garnering support, as well as for demobilizing antagonists (Benford and Snow 1988). Contemporary political theories of social movements often integrate framing, resource mobilization, and political opportunity structure perspectives. Careful framing identifies opportunities that may spur mobilization. And by perceiving the political structure more in terms of opportunities than constraints, and in terms of mobilizing resources, social movements may in fact create new opportunities, in which case the framing becomes a self-fulfilling prophecy (McAdam et al. 1996; Benford and Snow 2000).

KEY POINTS

- Early 'collective behaviour' theories explained mobilization as expression of grievances and deprivation.
- 'Resource mobilization' theories focused on people's active, rational choices to participate and the organization's own ability to mobilize resources.
- 'Political opportunity structure' theories focus on barriers and resources in the environment to explain why mobilization occurs.
- 'Framing' gives meaning to movement actions, and is important in mobilizing supporters and forming common identities.
- Scholars often combine resource mobilization, political opportunity structure, and framing perspectives.

Social Movements and Alternative Politics in the Developing World

The scholarly literature has traditionally focused on social movements in Europe and the Americas, but there is also a long history of social movements in the developing world. Of immense historical importance is the rise of strong national liberation movements during colonial rule in Latin-America, Asia, and Africa, which played crucial roles in struggles for national independence and in many cases turned into political parties, profoundly shaping the **post-colonial state**. The remainder of the chapter focuses on some

significant contemporary social movements in the developing world. These fall into three categories:

- movements focusing on *democratization* (aiming to change the regime or the nature of the state, continuing the tradition of the anti-colonial struggle);
- movements with a focus on *identity politics* (indigenous rights, rights of woman); and
- movements aiming to organize the disadvantaged in a struggle for *social justice* and redistribution of resources, locally and globally.

Social Movements and Democratization

The most spectacular social movements in the developing world in recent years were those demanding regime change in North Africa and the Middle East in early 2011—often referred to as the 'Arab Spring'.

The Arab Spring: from Tunisia to Egypt and beyond

On 17 December 2010, Mohamed Bouazizi, a 26-year-old street vendor, lit himself on fire outside a municipal building in the Tunisian town of Sidi Bouzid. His source of income, a wooden cart and a few pounds of fruit, had been confiscated by a local police officer, who claimed he lacked the required permit. Bouazizi went to the town governor's office to complain, but was turned away. Humiliated and frustrated, he chose self-immolation as his ultimate act of protest.

Tensions had been rising steadily in Tunisia under the authoritarian rule of President Zine al-Abidine Ben Ali. The secular and Western-oriented regime pushed market-based economic development and women's rights, but also brutally repressed civil society. Political opponents, independent journalists, secular activists, and Islamists faced harassment, torture, and imprisonment. An all-pervasive security apparatus monitored the population, employing a variety of legal and economic measures to silence dissenting voices. Aside from being denied political and civil rights, Tunisians faced rising food prices, staggering unemployment, and corruption at all levels of the government administration. In this context, Bouazizi's suicide became a symbol for wider political despair and economic dislocation, triggering a wave of protests (Freedom House 2012).

Hours after Bouazizi set himself ablaze, hundreds of people assembled to express solidarity, and to protest against police abuse and economic hardship. Some recorded the event on their mobile phones and posted videos to the Internet. The television network Al-Jazeera picked them up and broadcast them back to Tunisia, where the national media ignored the protests. Facilitated by mobile phones, international satellite television channels, online blogs, and social media such as Facebook and Twitter, protesters in Sidi Bouzid managed to get news of what was happening out. The dramatic story travelled fast, sparking demonstrations throughout Tunisia. Some protests turned violent and were met with severe police repression, but despite police violence and curfews, the rioting continued to escalate and soon reached the capital city, Tunis, where a rally of some 1,000 jobless university graduates was brutally dispersed by security forces on 27 December.

The Tunisian regime strengthened Internet censorship and online surveillance, and hacked into social media networks and blogging accounts. Several bloggers and web activists were arrested, but Tunisians found ways in which to work around the censorship and continued to post videos online. When Bouazizi died on 4 January 2011, the protests evolved into a popular uprising. Dozens of people were killed as the police cracked down on demonstrators—infuriating Tunisians, who responded by heightening the protests, which evolved into a direct challenge to the regime, and was dubbed the 'Jasmine Revolution' in Western media. The president attempted to end the crisis by promising not to seek re-election in 2014, but new large-scale demonstrations were organized across Tunisia. Hundreds of thousands joined and, crucially, the military sided with the people.

On 14 January, confronted with the largest anti-government demonstration that Tunis had ever seen, Ben Ali dissolved the government, declared a state of emergency, and fled the country with his family. In October 2011, Tunisia held its first free elections since independence to elect a Constitutional Assembly; in December 2011, the Assembly adopted a provisional Constitution and elected Moncef Marzouki as the President of the Republic.

Young Tunisians were key actors in Tunisia's revolution. They joined forces with civil society groups, trade unions, lawyers, teachers, leftists, **human rights** groups, Islamists, and opposition parties to put an end to Ben Ali's corrupt regime. After a few weeks of demonstrations, a cross-section of the Tunisian society participated in the uprising, which some commentators have called a 'Facebook revolution'. The use of communication technologies and the Internet has been widely credited as contributing to the successful mobilization and coordination of the movement (Howard and Hussain 2013).

For other dissatisfied citizens living under authoritarian rule, the success of the Tunisian revolt proved an emotional spark. Popular protests spread like wildfire from one Arab country to another, shaking nearly the entire region. On 7 January 2011, protests broke out in Algeria; on 12 January, in Lebanon; on 14 January, in Jordan; on 17 January, in Mauritania and Sudan; by 25 January, a revolution was under way in Egypt. In Yemen, a major demonstration was held on 27 January, and on 14 February an anti-government rally was organized in Bahrain. On 15 February, thousands of Libyans protested after the government arrested a human rights attorney. The rioting continued to spread and reached Kuwait on 18 February, Morocco on 20 February, Iraq on 25 February, Western Sahara on 26 February, Saudi Arabia on 11 March, and then Syria on 18 March (MacQueen 2013).

In Egypt, popular discontent had brewed for years under the military-backed authoritarian regime of President Hosni Mubarak. In the early 1990s, deterioration in living conditions and the lack of a political outlet fuelled an Islamist insurgency. The authorities responded by jailing thousands of suspected militants without charge and by cracking down on political dissent. Although the armed infrastructure of Islamist groups had been largely eradicated by 1998, the government continued to restrict political and civil liberties. In December 2004, Kifaya (meaning 'Enough'), an informal movement encompassing a broad spectrum of secular and Islamist activists, held the first-ever demonstration calling for President Mubarak to step down. Protests continued in 2005, but were met with a heavy-handed response (Beinin and Vairel 2011).

The Egyptian government sought to expand access to the Internet as an engine of **economic growth** and did not engage in substantial Internet censorship. Instead, it relied on its all-pervasive security apparatus, typically employing methods such as intimidation, legal harassment, detentions, and surveillance of online dissidents (Freedom House 2012). Despite these efforts to silence dissenting voices, hundreds of thousands of Egyptians continued to participate in online groups and to discuss issues of common concern in social media. In 2008, a Facebook group expressing solidarity with protesting textile mill workers attracted 70,000 followers and eventually coalesced into a political movement known as the 'April 6 Youth Movement'.

In June 2010, the 28-year-old web activist Khaled Said was beaten to death by Egyptian police officers in an Internet café in Alexandria. Said's brother posted a photograph of the disfigured corpse online, sparking widespread public demonstrations. The young Egyptian Google executive Wael Ghonim created a Facebook page entitled 'We are all Khaled Said', which was joined by hundreds of thousands in Egypt and globally. Encouraged by the Tunisian protests, the April 6 Youth Movement and Wael Ghonim called for supporters to gather in front of the Egyptian Ministry of Interior to protest against police brutality. Instrumental in mobilizing for protest was 26-year-old student Asmaa Mahfouz. On 18 January, she posted a video blog of herself on Facebook and urged the Egyptian people to join her a week later in Tahrir Square to bring down Mubarak's regime (Beinin and Vairel 2011).

On 25 January 2011, the 'Day of Revolt', organizers used mobile phones and landlines to disseminate information about the location and time of the demonstration. Protests erupted throughout Egypt, with tens of thousands of protesters coming together in Cairo and other cities across the country. They were joined by members from Islamic movements, such as the Muslim Brotherhood and the Salafists, and by Christians, secularists, intellectuals, and trade unionists, representing a broad cross-section of the Egyptian society. The Mubarak regime responded with brute force, deploying police and hired thugs to assault protesters, and shutting down the Internet. During the first few days of the revolt, Egyptian security forces detained a number of activists, bloggers, and Facebook group administrators. However, the protests continued.

On 28 January, hundreds of thousands of protesters throughout Egypt, burning symbols of Mubarak's rule, clashed with riot police and security forces. Military presence in Cairo increased and President Mubarak made a televised speech promising to dissolve the government. Clashes between antigovernment protesters and Mubarak's supporters broke out in Tahrir Square, resulting in several injuries and deaths. In the following week, Mubarak first announced that he would remain in office to ensure a peaceful transition of power, and then promised to transfer powers to the vice president, but the number and intensity of demonstrations continued to escalate.

On 11 February 2011, millions took to the streets demanding an end to Mubarak's thirty-year rule. After eighteen days of nationwide protests, in which around 800 Egyptians were killed and several thousand injured, the president stepped down. The Supreme Council of the Armed Forces took over, promising an orderly transition to civilian rule. Nationwide celebrations followed, but the transitional period turned out to be long and troubled. Only in June 2012 did Mohamed Morsi of the Muslim Brotherhood's Freedom and Justice Party become Egypt's first elected president. On July 3, 2013, the Egyptian army chief removed President Morsi from power and suspended the constitution after ongoing public protest against Morsi's rule.

During 2011, the 'Arab Spring' forced rulers to step down in Tunisia, Egypt, Libya, and Yemen. Tunisians, Egyptians, and Libyans have chosen new leaders in democratic elections. Two years on at the time of writing, however, the revolutions remain incomplete. In both Tunisia and Egypt, opposition groups united in the struggle against dire socio-economic conditions, corruption, and police brutality have divided over how to proceed. Both countries have repeatedly seen violent clashes between rival political factions and police crackdowns on protests. Liberals and secularists worry that the countries' new Islamist-dominated governments will attempt to curb personal liberties and the rights of women. The future of the revolutions depends on how these tensions are resolved.

The Arab uprisings of 2011 demonstrate the power of framing. When Bouazizi set himself on fire in Tunisia, activists succeeded in framing this as an act of sacrifice for the suffering of the nation, turning it into a powerful mobilization tool in a situation ripe with discontent. The Tunisian revolt, in turn, broke the dominant, immobilizing frame wherein democratic change was seen as impossible in the Arab world, unleashing forceful mobilization elsewhere in the region. It also demonstrated how conditions for social mobilization have radically changed as a result of new communication and information technology, thus altering the political opportunity structure of activists. Manuel Castells, in his book *Networks of Outrage and Hope: Social Movements in the Internet Age* (2012), shows how new technology not only altered the speed of the process and the ability to spread information, but also the structure of mobilization, under which networks made formal organization

BOX 11.1 LIBERIA: THE WOMEN OF LIBERIA MASS ACTION FOR PEACE

In 1989, civil war erupted in Liberia. Forces led by Charles Taylor launched a guerrilla insurgency against the country's military regime. The conflict escalated as a result of fractionalization among rebel groups and the intervention of foreign powers. More than 150,000 lives were lost before the warring factions signed a peace agreement in 1995 and agreed to hold elections. Taylor won and assumed presidency in 1997, but the peace was flawed. In 1999, civil war broke out again. By 2003, anti-Taylor rebels controlled two-thirds of Liberia, more than 200,000 had died in the conflict, and one in three Liberians had been forced to leave their homes. Opposition and government soldiers alike looted villages, raped women, and recruited children to fight.

Social worker Leymah Gbowee decided to bring women from her church together to pray for peace. They recruited hundreds of Christian and Muslim women, and formed the Women in Peacebuilding Network to secure peace through the collective action of women across ethnic and religious divides. Using the radio to spread the word, Gbowee called upon women to gather at a fish market in the capital Monrovia, past which

President Taylor's motorcade drove every day. In April 2003, the Women of Liberia Mass Action for Peace staged their first public protest. Dressed in white and carrying banners, thousands of women danced and sang for peace. They rallied at the fish market for months and declared a sex strike—denying sex to their men until they would stop the violence.

The women succeeded in forcing a meeting with President Taylor and made him promise to attend peace talks. Gbowee led a delegation of women applying pressure on the factions during the peace process. The women staged a sit-in, blocking all doors and windows to prevent delegates from leaving the peace talks without a resolution. In August 2003, an agreement was reached.

Liberian women became a political force, contributing greatly to the end of the civil war and aiding in bringing about democratic elections in 2005, including by registering voters and setting up polling stations. Their grass-roots campaign led to the election of President Ellen Johnson Sirleaf, the first woman elected as head of state in Africa (Fuest 2009; Gbowee and Mithers 2011).

---

redundant and succeeded in bringing diverse groups together in forceful action. The question is whether the network character and lack of formal organization is also part of the reason why the movement for change so quickly fragmented once the regimes fell.

Women played an important role in the Arab uprisings. The role of women is also pronounced in other social movements demanding political change in the developing world, as illustrated by the Women of Liberia Mass Action for Peace (see Box 11.1). Here, political changes were pursued and achieved by a movement specifically composed by women, using strategies that underscored women's agency and social power. It thus served two goals: political change towards a more peaceful and democratic Liberia; and the empowerment of women.

Alternative politics to further democratization in the developing world is not always about regime change. We also see efforts to deepen democracy and to improve the functioning of existing systems.

India: the 2011 Anti-Corruption Movement

With a population of 1.2 billion, India is the world's largest democracy. Except for a brief authoritarian interlude in 1975–77, she has maintained her democratic institutions since gaining independence from British colonial rule in 1947. India's democratic success runs counter to theories suggesting that democracy is unlikely to survive in poor countries with high levels of social diversity. But while India's democracy has been remarkably stable in terms of peaceful transfers of power through elections, it is flawed by government inefficiency and corruption. Corruption is omnipresent, ranging from the bribes that ordinary citizens pay to get a complaint recorded at the local police station, to high-profile corruption scandals surrounding government contracts. Although politicians and civil servants are regularly caught engaging in corrupt behaviour, a great deal goes unpunished. This has made many Indians cynical about the workings of their democracy (Kohli and Singh 2013).

In 2011, following a string of major corruption scandals, anti-corruption activists began to coalesce into a new national movement, which gained momentum across the country and galvanized public attention, through the use of social media and protests by high-profile Bollywood stars. The primary goal was to convince the government to institute an independent ombudsman to investigate and prosecute corruption cases. Parliament had proposed the creation of such an institution in the draft Lokpal Bill of 2010, but the activists found it to be ineffective and drafted their own version, the Jan Lokpal Bill (Ganguly 2012).

In April 2011, controversial veteran activist Anna Hazare began a hunger strike to induce parliament to include civil society in the drafting of the Lokpal Bill. The 74-year-old's 'fast to death' campaign attracted enormous media attention, triggering demonstrations of solidarity across India. About 150 people reportedly joined in the fasting. The global campaigning organization Avaaz promoted Hazare's campaign on its website and set up a petition to support the anticorruption movement. In 36 hours, 500,000 people had signed the petition. The English-language newspaper *The Times of India* called Avaaz a key player in the movement (see Box 11.2).

Four days into the fasting, the government agreed to create a joint committee of state and civil society to draft an effective bill. But as the government and the anti-corruption movement continued to disagree over the content, Hazare embarked on a second hunger strike in August—then a third one in December. The latter ended when the Lokpal Bill was passed in the lower house of parliament, but as of early 2013 the Lokpal Bill is still not final.

The 2011 anti-corruption movement tapped into public anger over corruption, managing to mobilize from diverse groups and bring together strands of the Indian middle class rarely gathering around the same cause. Towards the end of 2011, however, the protests slowed down. Hazare announced new hunger strikes in 2012, but did not draw the crowds marking the start of his campaign. Whether the India against Corruption movement will endure remains to be seen. After a split, it has spawned a non-affiliated political party,

the Aam Aadmi Party, launched in November 2012 (Ganguly 2012).

The Arab Spring and India's anti-corruption movement are testaments to how social media is changing conditions for social mobilization, and how local activists are able to use technology to gain exposure and force by linking to global networks. But they also illustrate the transient nature of global public attention and how difficult it is to sustain pressure without a more solid organizational structure.

Social Movements and Identity Politics

Social movements organizing around issues of identity and recognition, values, and world views have proliferated since the 1960s. The developing world has seen mobilization for gender equality and sexual rights—including in places where the opportunity structure seems closed. The Women to Drive campaign in Saudi Arabia (see Box 11.3) illustrates the importance in such contexts of 'acts of everyday resistance'. Private and 'apolitical' acts are framed in ways that imbue them with a broader meaning and political force, contributing towards building new identities.

Indigenous people, particularly in Latin America, have formed social movements to demand recognition for their identity, their rights to land and resources, their cultural autonomy, and public recognition of their legal norms. They challenge dominant conceptions of development and value, and prevailing political and social establishments. In the next section, we look more closely at two cases: Bolivia and Brazil.

On 8 March 2008, Wajeha al-Huwaider marked International Women's Day by posting a 3-minute clip of herself on YouTube. The video showed al-Huwaider behind the wheel of a car, pleading with the Saudi Interior Minister to lift restrictions on women driving in the ultra-conservative kingdom. Women to Drive is a campaign by Saudi women, who are denied more rights by the regime than men, for the right to drive motor vehicles on public roads. The Arab Spring inspired a more intensive campaign. From 17 June to late June 2011, some seventy cases of Saudi women driving were documented in videos uploaded onto Facebook and other social media.

Agarwal et al. (2012)

Bolivia: indigenous mobilization and the Law of the Rights of Mother Earth

Two-thirds of Bolivians consider themselves to be of indigenous descent—the highest proportion of any Latin American country. Yet wealthy urban elites, mostly descendants of Spanish colonialists, dominate political, economic, and cultural life. In the 1990s, Bolivia's long-excluded indigenous population mobilized.

A broad-based movement of indigenous people, peasants, and workers calling for nationalization of gas resources and a new constitution led to the 2005 presidential election victory of former cocoa farmer Evo Morales. They pushed for transformation of the country's legal framework towards greater recognition of indigenous rights, beliefs, and legal norms. The 1999 Constitution defines Bolivia as a pluri-national state, according more rights to the indigenous majority. It gives greater local autonomy, enshrines government control over key resources, and reflects a deep ecological concern (Boyd 2012).

Bolivia suffers serious environmental problems associated with mining, soil erosion from overgrazing and poor cultivation methods, deforestation, melting glaciers, loss of biodiversity, and water pollution. This has sparked deep concern and mobilization among indigenous groups, who see not only threats to their livelihood, but also deep violations of the sacred in nature. In 2010, in line with the new Constitution, the Bolivian legislature passed one of the most radical environmental laws ever created: the Law of the Rights of Mother Earth.

The law was originally developed by Pacto de Unidad, an alliance of grass-roots organizations, drawing on the indigenous view of the *Pachamama* ('Mother Earth') as a sacred home on which humans intimately depend. Nature is granted comprehensive legal rights—including the right to life, biodiversity, freedom from genetic modification, and restoration from the effects of human activity. The Law of the Rights of Mother Earth gives legal personhood to the natural system, and imposes responsibilities on the state, individuals, and organizations to respect its inherent rights. An ombudsman is authorized to oversee implementation of the law and Bolivians might bring to court those infringing on the integrity of Mother Earth.

The law is ground-breaking, but it remains to be seen whether it will prompt real change in a situation in which industries such as mining contribute a large portion of Bolivia's gross domestic product (GDP). Still, the law is a testament to the new importance of indigenous movements in Bolivia, after 500 years of political and economic marginalization.

The developments in Bolivia link to broader indigenous rights and climate justice movements in Latin America, and globally. Disappointed by the outcomes of the 2009 UN Climate Change Conference in Copenhagen, an alternative conference was held in Cochabamba, Bolivia, in April 2010. Around 30,000 people attended the event, and conference topics included a Universal Declaration on the Rights of Mother Earth and the establishment of a Climate Justice Tribunal.

Here, alternative and institutional politics intertwine as social movements engage in a range of alliances and strategies, including in party politics. Local and global processes intertwine, with local activists drawing strength from international connections and ties. Different causes intertwine, as indigenous activism and ecological movements link non-material issues of identity, values, and world views with material demands. The latter comes out even more clearly in the case of Brazil.

Brazil: indigenous protests against the Belo Monte Dam

In the 1970s, Brazil's military dictatorship planned to build gigantic hydroelectric dams on the Xingu River in the Amazon to provide cheap electricity for power-intensive industries, but shelved the plans as a result of controversy regarding the location of the dams on indigenous land. Brazil's elected civilian government revitalized the proposal in 1989, attempting to construct a six-dam setup. Concerned with the potential flooding of their land, local Kayapó Indians sought to stop the dam construction, successfully mobilizing international allies, the media, celebrities, and foreign governments.

The Brazilian government went back to the drawing board. To deal with soaring energy demands, plans were made to build more than sixty large dams in the Amazon Basin—among them Belo Monte, the third largest dam in the world. This project affected a smaller area than previous proposals, and was presented as ecologically and politically sound. However, the dam complex was to dramatically divert the flow of the Xingu River, creating drought and destroying vast areas of pristine rainforest.

Realizing that the dam would force thousands of their tribe members to relocate, local social movements along the lower Xingu united and organized numerous non-violent protests. In 2010, the Brazilian indigenous peoples of the Amazon released an Indian Declaration against Belo Monte. Nevertheless, the government gave the go-ahead to construct the dam complex.

The licensing process and the dam's construction have been mired in court battles. The Ministério Público (government prosecutors acting in the public interest) filed numerous lawsuits against the Belo Monte and, in 2012, Brazil's Supreme Court ordered work on the dam suspended until indigenous groups are properly consulted. But the battle is not over. Worries remain that if the dam is approved, it will create precedent for future destruction of rivers of the Amazon. Indigenous groups living near the Xingu River fear that they will lose both the means to sustain their livelihoods and their ancestral history. Helped by social media and websites such as Facebook and Twitter, their struggle continues to receive considerable international attention.

The fight against the Belo Monte dam has much in common with struggles in other parts of the world where invasive infrastructure projects affect indigenous land and destroy livelihoods of poor people. Most well known are perhaps India's social movements fighting against the Narmada Dam and other mega-projects displacing large numbers of people (Nilsen and Motta 2011). Again, 'new' social movement issues of indigenous identity, ecology, and alternative development intertwine with 'old' attention to social justice and economic redistribution. And we find a similar mix of traditional social movement strategies, such as protests and demonstration, and the use of formal channels, such as litigation—and alliances between local and transnational activists. Several transnational activist networks and NGOs have indigenous activism related to dam and river projects as their focus, and their importance should not be underestimated.

The discussion so far has shown the importance of material concerns and social injustice for social activism in the developing world, both for movements aiming for political change and for identity-based movements. We now turn to contemporary social movements for which such 'old' concerns are the core concern and demand.

KEY POINTS

- Identity concerns are central to social movements in the developing world, but often combine with material demands.
- Saudi women mobilized for gender equality by posting videos on the Internet of themselves driving cars. Such acts of everyday resistance are particularly important where political opportunity structures are constrained.
- Bolivia's indigenous people mobilized for 'rights of Mother Earth'—and for their own identity and material rights. They have done so by linking to global movements for indigenous rights and environmental justice.
- In Brazil and India, mobilization against large dams combines identity politics and material concerns, effectively mobilizing local, as well as transnational, activists.

Social Movements and Social Justice

That social movements in the global South have material resources and social justice as central concerns is no surprise in a situation marked by widespread poverty, and vast social and economic inequalities, both internally in developing countries and globally. South Africa is one of the most unequal countries in the world, and has a long tradition of social movements and activism, with struggles against racial discrimination spanning more than a century.

South Africa: the shack dwellers' movement (*Abahlali baseMjondolo*)

When Nelson Mandela was elected president of South Africa in 1994, it marked the end of nearly fifty years of **apartheid**. A new constitution promised to protect the human rights of all South Africans—including their social and economic rights—in a situation in which the rights of the majority black population were severely curtailed, residential areas segregated, and political power (and valuable land) reserved for the white minority.

The African National Congress (ANC) won the elections in a landslide, promising redistribution of land to black South Africans. But, once in power, it adopted a range of neoliberal policies that did not benefit the country's poorest and only a small fraction of the land was redistributed. The gap between rich and poor has widened.

It is estimated that one in ten South Africans live in shack settlements. Living conditions are often abysmal, with poor housing infrastructure, and lack of electricity and water supply, as well as overcrowding. The Kennedy Road settlement in Durban is among the most notorious. In 2005, the local government promised settlers a nearby plot for housing, but then sold the land to a local industrialist. Outraged by the betrayal, thousands of shack dwellers took to the streets, physically blocking the plot. This sparked one of the most prominent social movements in post-apartheid South Africa—*Abahlali baseMjondolo* (meaning 'Shack dwellers')—which has mobilized tens of thousands of members in more than sixty settlements. Their key demand is that the social value of urban land should take priority over its commercial value. Through methods ranging from street protests to election boycotts and litigation, *Abahlali* campaigns for quality housing and basic services to shack settlements, and for the expropriation of private land for public purpose (Mitlin and Mogaladi 2013).

The South African police violently repressed the shack dwellers' movement in the mid-2000s, but this declined after the repression was reported in the media and drew international condemnation. By using online and mobile tools to spread word of their successes, upcoming events, and ongoing efforts, *Abahlali* has built links with similar movements and garnered international support.

In October 2009, *Abahlali* won a major legal victory when the controversial Slums Act of 2007 was declared unconstitutional (Mitlin and Mogaladi 2013). The Provincial Government passed the Act to legalize the eviction of shack dwellers and to eradicate slums, allowing for mass evictions without the provision of suitable alternative accommodation. The South African Constitutional Court found the law to be in conflict with the Constitution, and struck it down.

Abahlali focuses on social justice concerns at the local level: the lack of material conditions for a decent life and broken promises to deliver basic services. It provides a structure to which people in the community can turn in emergencies and which can help to pressure local authorities on a daily basis. But it also addresses the laws, policies, and ideologies that underpin the system. *Abahlali* is organized around open mass assemblies and elected community-level committees. Rallies, workshops, and youth camps are held to mobilize and educate members, and a secretariat is elected at annual general meetings. It also engages formal government institutions, such as courts, and it has links to formal organizations locally and globally—links that help to secure both attention and resources.

Another South African social movement, the Treatment Action Campaign, shares with *Abahlali* the focus on material concerns and social justice, but it is more institutionalized, with a broader global reach.

South Africa: the Treatment Action Campaign

South Africans found themselves faced with the worst **HIV/AIDS** epidemic in the world, and a president, Thabo Mbeki, who refused to follow the recommendations of medical research and provide anti-retroviral treatment to those affected. This spurred the growth of a broad social movement, the Treatment Action Campaign (TAC). Joining together gay activists, academic lawyers, churches, and community activists, the TAC engages in a wide range of activities—from marches to policy research, advocacy, and litigation—and undertakes an extensive programme of health information. The TAC has repeatedly taken the government to court to push for provision of treatment for people living with HIV and AIDS, focusing on vulnerable groups such as pregnant mothers and prisoners, but with a view to universal programmes, and has been instrumental in the development of new policies. It has also taken pharmaceutical companies to court and succeeded in lowering drug prices (Yamin and Gloppen 2011).

Beyond being an influential force in South Africa's political landscape, the TAC has played a very important role internationally, particularly in the fight for cheaper drugs. It is also an inspiration to movements elsewhere and a voice in transnational activist networks (Gloppen and Roseman 2011). Its concern is not only with the local problems, but also the international economic system producing these inequalities, such as the international World Trade Organization (WTO) and the rules for protection of intellectual property and patents—that is, the Agreement on Trade-Related Aspects of Intellectual Property Rights (TRIPS).

The New Globalization of Social Movements

The TAC is thus part of a profound process of social movement **globalization**. Throughout this chapter, we have seen how social movements in the developing world connect with activists and organizations elsewhere, and use this to mobilize attention and resources. Social movement networks and exchanges across borders are not new. The anti-slavery movement, the women's suffrage movement of the nineteenth century, and the international labour movement were not confined within national borders. But the possibilities for cross-border exchanges between activists have increased enormously with the explosion of new media technologies (Nash 2010).

There is also a globalization of the focus of attention, with a stronger attention to global justice and the global processes producing global poverty and inequality, and unsustainable development. This is evident both in organizations such as Attac (see Box 11.4), and events such as the World Social Forums, bringing together the **global justice movement**, consisting of diverse movements and organizations sharing a critical perspective on the nature of economic globalization, and dominant models of development. Central actors include *Via Campesina* (meaning 'family farmers' international'), Christian movements advocating international debt relief (Jubilee 2000), and environmentalists concerned with climate change (Friends of the Earth), as well as youth and student groups, trade unions, peace groups, and development-focused think tanks.

Social movements in the developing world are important in this process, but critics argue that rather than bringing out critical voices from the global

> ### BOX 11.4 ATTAC
>
> Attac (that is, the Association pour une Taxation des Transactions financieres pour l'Aide aux Citoyens, or the Association for the Taxation of Financial Transactions and Aid to Citizens) is a global organization that originally fought to introduce taxes on foreign exchange transactions (a 'Tobin tax'). Since its formation in France in 1998, the organization has spread worldwide to more than forty countries and works on a range of issues. Its major focus is the regulation of financial markets, the closure of tax havens, and fair trade. Although politically independent, Attac is associated with the causes of the international left.
>
> Stockemer (2011)

South, it has become mainly a vehicle for northern NGOs and intellectuals. More generally, it is important to ask whether local activists in the developing world always benefit from their global ties. Perhaps it is the other way around: that they risk having their struggle hijacked by transnational activists in search of a cause. This brings us back to the question of what it is that makes a social movement successful.

> ### KEY POINTS
>
> - Social justice is a major concern for social movements in the developing world.
> - *Abahlali* mobilizes South African slum dwellers to push government authorities to change living conditions for the worst off, enlisting international support.
> - The Treatment Action Campaign mobilizes for treatment of HIV/AIDS, taking on the South African government, as well as global pharmaceutical companies and trade regimes.
> - Attac and the World Social Forums illustrate the increasing globalization, both in scope and focus, of social movement mobilization.

What Makes Social Movements Successful?

When trying to understand what makes some social movements more successful, we must first ask what we mean by 'success'. This must obviously be seen in light of the particular aims pursued, but we should keep in mind that a social movement may produce diverse outcomes, including internal outcomes, shaping the identities of participants, as they (indigenous people, women, gay people, shack dwellers) increasingly see themselves as rights-holders due equal concern and respect. Other outcomes are external, affecting public policies or the regime.

Gamson (1975) defined success as consisting of two components: being accepted as someone representing legitimate interests, who should be at the table when decisions are made; and the introduction of new advantages. Amenta and Young (1999), and Amenta et al. (2010) distinguish between: low-level benefits, which are short-term, easily revoked, and often symbolic, demonstrating to the public that something is being done; mid-level advantages, which are institutionalized, recurring, and often more substantial; and high-level successes (such as the right to vote for particular groups), which are substantial, hard to revoke, but also more difficult to obtain. The goods obtained may be material (public spending) or they can 'be less tangible, such as new ways to refer to a group' (Amenta et al. 2010: 290). Rodriguez-Garavito (2010) similarly distinguishes between symbolic and material effects.

To identify a movement's goals and intentions, and whether it has succeeded and had an impact, presents substantial methodological challenges. This is also because the social transformations that they ultimately seek often are long-term processes. These factors have led scholars to focus on intermediate 'outputs', 'outcomes', or 'impact', rather than ultimate 'success'.

The literature seeking to explain why some movements succeed emphasizes different factors. Some focus on internal aspects of movements, including the degree of disruption that they are able to cause, threatening the interests of elites, gaining media attention, and thereby promoting the movement's message. However, by being too disruptive, a movement may alienate moderate supporters or fractionalize, providing opportunity for states to bargain selectively with parts of the movement, thereby reducing its mobilizing potential.

As our examples show, social movements struggle to maintain mobilization and pressure over time. This has led to a long-standing debate in the literature on whether it is good for social movements to institutionalize (Della Porta and Diani 2006). In their influential book on *Poor People's Movements*, Piven and Cloward (1977) argued that poor people have limited chances of getting their voices heard through regular channels of interest aggregation such as elections or interest groups. Their only chance is to disrupt elites and

to threaten their privileges through unconventional means, such as demonstrations or sit-ins. If movements institutionalize (cooperating and regularly interacting with the state), it can lead to co-option, and the movement can fail, because it has fewer resources than other more powerful interests. A co-opted or institutionalized movement can lose its power to disrupt and its solidarity; the leaders may prioritize the sustainability of the organization and demand less radical change.

Others argue that conventional tactics complement alternative politics, and that the relationship between state and the movement may be one of both cooperation and conflict at the same time. Research shows that people participating in protest activities are also more likely than others to participate in conventional politics such as voting (Goldstone 2003). Movement members may become 'institution activists' and contribute to producing policies that further the goals of the movement (Suh 2011). Social movement organizations may also oscillate between protest activities and regular participation. Links between social movements and conventional politics are thus in practice often very close.

How movements protest—that is, their tactical repertoire,—also matters for success. Novel and surprising tactics makes success more likely, as they are prone to spur interest among potential supporters and the media, and authorities may not know how to respond. Shorter and Tilly (1974) argue that strikes were much more successful during the 1830s, when they were novel, than during the 1960s, when they were considered a routine part of protest. Employing a varied tactical repertoire is also useful, as is increasing the size of the movement, getting more people into the streets. Size is theoretically linked to success in at least three ways: it attracts more attention from media; it signals stronger opposition to politicians who may fear that it may hurt them electorally if they do not respond to the movement; and it increases movements' disruptive powers (Morris 1993).

If success were all about the movement itself, one could establish thresholds of participation or disruption at which success would be guaranteed. However, this is not the case. Even big and innovative movements fail. This led authors to pay attention to the political environment, such as the nature of the state structures and the existence of allies, referred to earlier as the political opportunity structure (McAdam 1982; Kitschelt 1986). More open states give more room for movement influence, while states with stronger implementation capacity potentially give more effective influence.

National and international allies are also seen as important for social movement success. Political opposition parties may be eager to support movements in order to gain new voters and allies among decision-makers may carry the movement's demands into the institutional arena (Giugni 2004: 120).

Social movement research increasingly pays attention to the interactions between the movements and their environment—known as a 'political mediation approach') (Amenta et al. 2010). Here, social movement success is seen to depend both on internal aspects of movements, what they are and do (resources, agency, strategic choices), and on external factors (barriers, potential allies)—and, most crucially, on the fit between the two, or, in other words, how well suited the strategies of the movement are to the social and political environment in which they operate.

KEY POINTS

- Social movements' success should be understood in relation to their goals, but also internal effects on participants should be considered. Such outcomes may be symbolic, as well as material.

- Some scholars explain social movements' success by the movements' internal characteristics; others, by the nature of their environment; yet others combine the two in a political mediation approach.

Conclusion

Alternative politics in the developing world is a diverse field, spanning YouTube activism for women's rights, disruptive mass demonstrations, and highly institutionalized social movements. Some movements seek to change the nature of the political regime; others focus on social injustice, or demand respect for their group identity, norms, and world view. But often the aims combine and mix. The Women of Liberia Mass Action for Peace is also about women's rights and about livelihoods. *Abahlali* seeks social justice for slum dwellers, but its struggle is also about slum dwellers' identity and broad social transformation. Indigenous peoples of Latin America struggle for respect for their culture and norms, but also for material rights to land and resources, and for constitutional change.

Social movements in the developing world are increasingly global, in terms of scope, mode of operation, and focus. New technology links them to activists elsewhere, and enables effective mobilization of support locally and globally. This carries enormous potential. Social media enables effective mobilization across diverse groups with few resources, spectacularly demonstrated by the Arab Spring revolutions. And global networks may generate instant pressure. The challenge is to convert this into sustained pressure.

? QUESTIONS

1. What are 'old' and 'new' social movements? How does this distinction relate to social movements in today's developing world?

2. Why are some social movements more successful?

3. What does it mean to say that social movements are 'globalized'?

4. What has social media meant for alternative politics in the developing world?

5. Using social movement theory, how would you explain the Arab Spring?

6. Is institutionalization inevitable for movements in the long run?

≋ FURTHER READING

Amenta, E., Caren, N., Chiarello, E., and Su, Y. (2010) 'The Political Consequences of Social Movements', *Annual Review of Sociology*, 36: 287–307 Gives a good overview of the consequences of social movements, and when and how they succeed.

Della Porta, D. and Diani, M. (2006) *Social Movements: An Introduction* (Malden: Blackwell) A thorough introduction to social movement research.

Dobson, W. J. (2012) *The Dictator's Learning Curve: Inside the Global Battle for Democracy* (New York: Doubleday) An intriguing book, written by renowned journalist William Dobson, about how movements learn from each other in the battle for democracy.

Nilsen, A. G. and Motta, S. C. (2011) *Social Movements in the Global South: Dispossession, Development, and Resistance* (London: Palgrave) Shows how contemporary popular struggles and social movements in Africa, South Asia, Latin America, and the Middle East politicize development in an age of neoliberal hegemony.

Stokke, K. and Törnquist, O. (2013) *Democratization in the Global South: The Importance of Transformative Politics* (Basingstoke: Palgrave Macmillan) The book looks to Nordic social democracy for insights into how democracy can be deepened in the Global South and made to serve the interests of working people without sacrificing economic growth.

🌐 WEB LINKS

http://www.abahlali.org   Website of *Abahlali baseMjondolo*, the shack dwellers' movement in South Africa.

http://amazonwatch.org   Website of Amazon Watch, a non-profit organization aiming to protect the rainforest and advance the rights of indigenous peoples in the Amazon Basin; contains information about legal struggles and cases of social mobilization.

http://messagefrompandora.org/   The film *A Message from Pandora* (2010) documents the battle to stop the construction of the Belo Monte dam in the Brazilian Amazon.

http://nvdatabase.swarthmore.edu/   The Global Nonviolent Action Database provides information about hundreds of cases of non-violent action.

http://www.dearmandela.com   The film *Dear Mandela* (2011) follows three young activists in the shack dwellers' movement in South Africa.

http://www.internationalrivers.org   Website of International Rivers, an organization working to halt destructive river infrastructure projects in the global South, address the legacies of existing projects, and improve development policies and practices.

http://www.praythedevilbacktohell.com   The documentary film *Pray the Devil Back to Hell* (2008) tells the story of Women of Liberia Mass Action for Peace.

http://www.tac.org.za/   Website of the Treatment Action Campaign in South Africa.

http://www.theguardian.com/world/interactive/2011/mar/22/middle-east-protest-interactive-timeline   This timeline was a significant source for the events of the Arab Spring.

For additional material and resources, please visit the Online Resource Centre at:
http://www.oxfordtextbooks.co.uk/orc/burnell4e/

PART 3
State and Society

The heading of Part 3 reverses the order of the two terms contained in the previous part to signify that Part 3 focuses chiefly on the **institutions** of state and their importance to society. In **politics**, institutions matter. The state is not merely one among many political institutions, but historically has been the pre-eminent focus of attention. In the modern world, under the impact of rapid social, economic, technological, and other changes taking place at the global, regional, and sub-state levels, the exact nature, role, and significance of the state are continually evolving. Questions related to states' capacity, and how power is exercised and checked through mechanisms of accountability, are key concerns of our chapters on **governance** and democracy.

This part has two main aims. The *first* is to explore the idea of the state in a **developing world** context and how, if at all, it differs from the state in more developed countries. Among other things this must involve some reference to past history. Can one framework accommodate all of the varieties of state formation? And what is most distinctive about the politics of countries characterized by endemic violent conflict or trying to emerge from **state failure**?

The *second* aim is to show how the governance capabilities of states and even more so the kind of political **regime**—the relationship between the institutions of government and society—have become a major focus for political inquiry. In at least some developing countries, there have been significant changes in the last few decades. This part is essential for enabling us to address important questions about how far the state in the developing world can be held responsible for addressing (or failing to address) fundamental developmental issues—and for determining whether it is equipped to resolve issues, including those affecting the economy, welfare, the environment, and **human rights**. For instance, what is the relationship between democracy, or democratization, and development? Is there a specific sequence in which these must arise? And how is power exercised and checked once a government is in office?

While Part 3 ranges over these issues, the more detailed policy matters that are bound up with them will comprise the substance of Part 4—which is best consulted after or alongside the material in Part 3. The illustrations in Part 3 are widely drawn from around the developing world. By comparison, case studies of countries selected to illustrate specific issues and themes can be found in Parts 5– 8. For example, while Chapter 22 includes a case study of post-Saddam Iraq, Chapter 20 on Pakistan and Chapter 23 on Mexico offer contrasting trajectories of political regime transformation. Readers are encouraged to consult the relevant case studies alongside the chapters in Part 3. In addition, for more extended discussion of the concept and debates about democratization and the contribution that party politics specifically makes to politics in developing countries, readers are recommended to visit the Online Resource Centre, where there is a comparative examination of the role of political parties specially written by Vicky Randall.

12

Theorizing the State

Adrian Leftwich

Chapter contents

Overview

Any explanation of successful and failed states in the developing world requires an understanding of the provenance, characteristics, and functions of the modern state as it evolved in what is now the developed world. This chapter first explores the nature of institutions and, in particular, the modern state as a set of political institutions of rule, geared to the organization and continuous management of economic development. Second, it analyses the emergence and features of the state in what is now the developed world. Third, it investigates the transportation of the modern state to the now developing world and the consequences of that. The central argument is that the characteristics of any state, anywhere, are largely defined by its evolving relations with the economy and society that it reflects, and both represents and dominates, in its historical, regional, and international context. Political processes in many developing countries are moving towards the establishment of state institutions of rule that may provide more stability and effectiveness for economic development and greater participation for citizens in decision-making processes. But the process is very difficult, slow, and uneven, and according to some, the process may be challenged by globalization.

Introduction: Political Institutions and the Modern State

Human societies cannot endure, prosper, or—especially—develop without broadly agreed and appropriate rules and conventions governing the conduct of social, economic, and political affairs, and about how human and other resources are to be used and distributed. Such sets of rules are what political scientists mean by **institutions** (see Chapter 3). Essentially, institutions direct and constrain human interaction. All societies have them; they must. The different institutional spheres often overlap (and sometimes conflict to produce undesired outcomes), and include social institutions (governing social interaction and behaviour), economic institutions (the customs, rules, and procedures governing economic behaviour, ranging from silent barter to rules governing stock-market behaviour), and political institutions (governing relations of power and authority).

The *forms of rule* expressed in different political systems, or *polities*, have varied widely. For instance, some polities initially involved only very basic forms of localized village headship or leadership; others, perhaps starting with such local and limited forms of rule and power, subsequently evolved at different speeds into steeper and more extensive hierarchies of centralized control and power over an increasing territorial space. The emergence of centralized polities (which some theorists refer to as 'early states') sometimes expanded over wide areas to encompass other societies so that they came to constitute what have been called 'centralized bureaucratic empires'.

However, the immense range of historical political systems that have given institutional expression to the different forms and distributions of power has shrunk dramatically since the sixteenth century, when one type of polity emerged in Europe and came to be the dominant political form of the contemporary world: the *modern state*. Although it varies in its forms, the characteristics of the modern state need to be distinguished from earlier polities, or 'non-modern' states, such as ancient city-states, feudal states, pre-modern, early modern, or absolutist states, or even 'princely states'.

The emergence of the modern state in Europe was a largely endogenous process, occurring within the geography and history of particular regions in the course of conflict, competition, and, especially, consolidation among them. To illustrate, in late fifteenth-century Europe, there were some 500 independent political units, but by 1900 this had shrunk to about twenty-five. And from within this history of European state formation, there developed, from the fifteenth century, outward thrusts of discovery, conquest, and control, loosely called 'imperialism' and 'colonialism'. These imperial processes carved out new 'countries' (which, in most cases, had not existed beforehand), they established new institutions of rule in the form of the colonial state (which either suppressed or used, and sometimes transformed, existing institutions of rulership), and drew such countries (or parts of them) into different kinds of largely subordinate economic relations with the metropolitan countries of the increasingly dominant 'West'.

KEY POINTS

- The emergence of specialist political institutions and organizations represents the differentiation of political systems or polities from other institutional spheres.

- The most recent and dominant form has been the modern state, the origins of which were primarily European.

- This form was carried outwards by European imperialism and colonialism, and imposed on diverse societies, or adopted and adapted by them. The external provenance of the state in many developing countries has been a critical factor in shaping and influencing their particular forms and the **politics** associated with them.

The Modern State

Traditional polities

The modern state was the product of slow evolution from prior political systems, or polities, but by the nineteenth century its central features were clear. The German sociologist Max Weber (1964) theorized those features of the 'modern' state that distinguished it from prior 'traditional' institutions of rule, or systems of authority. These earlier forms, he suggested, like the 'patrimonial' form of authority as he called it, were characterized by two overriding features.

First, there is the absence of any sharp distinction between the *rulers* and the *institutions of rule*. This was typical of the absolutist rule of some European monarchs well into the eighteenth century, as well as elsewhere in East Asia and Middle America. For instance,

Louis XIV, King of France in the mid-seventeenth century, made the point with great effect when he is alleged to have said to the *parlement* of Paris in April 1655, '*L'État c'est moi*' ('I am the state').

The second defining feature of traditional forms of rule was the relative absence of open, meritocratic entry, autonomy, independence, and security of tenure for the officials who surrounded the rulers. Unlike officials in the ideal-typical bureaucracy of the modern state, they were essentially the personal staff of the ruler, often paid by him or her, and with the more or less explicit requirement of personal loyalty to him or her rather than to the state or its constitution.

Defining the modern state

Many characteristics and functions distinguish the modern state. But it was the development of institutions of rule and governing that were formally separated from not only the rulers and the officials who ran them, on the one hand, but also the citizenry, on the other hand, that was central in the shift from 'traditional' forms of rule and authority to the modern state. The modern state consists of a set of **public institutions** and other public organizations that, together, define and implement the legitimate and hegemonic control, use, and distribution of power over a given sovereign territory and people. This definition identifies all of the key elements of the modern state.

- *Public institutions*   The institutions of the modern state are all 'public', and include the constitutional arrangements, laws, regulations, and other formal conventions that stipulate how formal power is achieved, used, and controlled, and which provide for the legal framework within which social, economic, and political life carries on.

- *Public organizations*   Whereas institutions are best understood as rules, laws, and constitutions, the *organizations* of the state are those agencies of rule and implementation, including 'the government', the legislature, the courts, civil service, army, and police, plus any state-owned agencies. All of these institutions and organizations in the modern state are formally differentiated from other institutions (especially private and non-state institutions) and individuals, and also from the incumbents of the offices and the citizens or subjects over whom they exercise authority.

- *Sovereignty and hegemony*   The institutions of the modern state and its laws have authority over a particular demarcated geographical area, and apply, in theory, to everyone within its territory.

- *Formal monopoly of violence*   The modern state has a monopoly of the legitimate use of violence and it is, or should be, the dominant agency of rule and law, whether democratic or not—in principle, superordinate over all others. In practice, in the course of their history, most modern states have struggled at times to achieve that dominance (Bates 2001). And some, until very recently, have continued to do so. An example is the Peruvian state's battle to subdue the *Sendero Luminoso* guerrilla movement, which exercised considerable power over parts of the country in the 1970s and 1980s.

- *Impartial bureaucracy*   The bureaucracy is (theoretically) impersonal, impartial, and neutral, and does not make law. But in practice policymaking is much more complex and, increasingly, specialist bureaucratic input into policymaking is the norm. Nonetheless, the central characteristic that distinguishes the modern state from prior forms of rule is the principle, at least, of *relative* independence and autonomy of the public service from both the elected political elites and parties, and also from the public. Moreover, the offices of state officials, whether constitutional monarchs, presidents, ministers, legislators, judges, police, or civil servants belong to the state, not to them personally. It is a fundamental assumption of the modern state that these public offices and powers should not be used for *private* gain by their incumbents (what would normally be called **corruption**). Occupancy of such offices should entail no powers of private **patronage** nor be used for the support of any particular private client base (**clientelism**), whether personal, regional, ethnic, or economic. (This is the essence of the concept of **good governance** that we discuss in Chapter 15.)

The modern state: imperatives, functions, and challenges

As the modern state consolidated and proliferated through the nineteenth and twentieth centuries, more countries began to adopt its broad template as their system of rule. For example, many Latin American countries adopted and adapted from France, and (to a lesser extent) the United States, in shaping their constitutions as they gained independence from Spain and Portugal between 1811 and 1900.

But the really central point is that the modern state emerged in the course of the 'great transformation' from agrarian to industrial societies (mainly in Europe), and in the consequential requirements for appropriate institutional and regulatory frameworks and functions to facilitate and extend this. It was both product and agent of that transformation. Indeed, it is essential to understand that the fundamental defining role and function of the modern state has been to promote, organize, protect, and sustain this economic and social transformation to industrialism—and beyond into the 'post-industrial' era. In the nineteenth and twentieth centuries, the histories of the now industrial powers, and the more recent modern history of the contemporary **developing world**, show that successful and effective modern states and successful economies go hand in hand, as do 'failed' states and failed economies. This process of state formation was, of course, intensified through the competitive economic, military, and other forms of nationalism that it promoted, and by the turbulent socio-political changes associated with the economic transformation. And, by the early twentieth century, four critical issues had come to confront the modern state: defence against external attack and internal security; the promotion and protection of the economy; democratization; and the associated demand for state provision of welfare. The manner in which each state dealt with them acted to define its character and its relations with the society that it claimed both to represent and to manage.

First, with regard to defence, the period 1850–1939 saw an intensification of what has been called 'despotic power'—that is, the power to control and suppress—as opposed to 'infrastructural power'—the power to penetrate and transform society (Mann 1986: 169–70; Weiss and Hobson 1995; Scott 1998). But, second, as indicated earlier, national economic development also was central to the emergence and defence of the modern state, and was closely associated with the competitive nationalisms of the nineteenth century. Thus successful modern **economic growth** and successful modern states with influence that extends beyond their borders have been inextricably linked. And there is nothing that sums this up better than

the slogan 'National Wealth, Military Strength' (often translated as 'rich country, strong army') adopted by the new post-Meiji elites in Japan after 1870.

In pursuit of these goals, most of today's leading industrial economies used state-directed industrial, trade, and technological policies (Chang 2002: 58 *passim*) to get ahead, to stay ahead (as in the case of Britain), or to catch up, as Germany, Japan, and the United States began to do in the nineteenth century. Three broad strategies, or models, were used (although each contained a variety of distinctive forms).

- The Anglo-American and Western European model involved the state ensuring four prime conditions for the promotion of private, market-driven growth, as argued by Douglas C. North (1990): securing property rights; establishing a fair and efficient judicial system; setting out an open and understood system of rules and regulations; and facilitating market entry and functioning (although at times state action has gone much further than this, as in the Depression years in the United States and in post-war reconstruction in Europe).

- The Soviet model of top-down industrialization was pioneered from the 1920s, and involves pervasive state ownership, control, and management of the economy, and the mobilization by the state not the market of resources (including human ones) in pursuit of transformative objectives.

- The third model is essentially the East Asian model of the **developmental state**, pioneered in Japan after 1870, and especially after the 1920s, which has been replicated in some other countries such as Korea and Taiwan (Leftwich 1995). This involved a much closer symbiosis between state and private sector (see Chapter 24), and has sometimes been called 'managed capitalism' or 'governing the market'.

Modern states in the developing world have sought to adopt modified versions of these three different strategies in their pursuit of economic growth through industrialization. Crucially, however, successful intervention along any of the strategic paths has occurred only where the appropriate political coalitions and distributions of power underpinning the state have allowed, rather than hindered, growth-promoting institutions and strategies. This has been one of the key differences between the older 'modern states' and the new 'modern states' of the developing world.

With regard to the challenges of democratization and redistribution, Huntington (1991) identified three great 'waves' of democratization (between 1828 and 1926, between 1943 and 1962, and from 1974 to the present day). In each, dominant state elites (almost always male-dominated) responded to democratic pressures in different ways, hence shaping the character of the polity depending on whether and to what extent they saw their interests being threatened by such demands. Where democratic progress continued—as in the extension of the suffrage to women—the associated deepening and extension of **civil society** had the effect of redistributing some political power through the forms of electoral, bargaining, and consultative processes. Moreover, the growth of powerful and increasingly well-organized labour movements in particular meant that few states in the developed world could ignore the demand for redistributive programmes, for example through taxation policy, welfare provision (health, old age, and education, for instance), and wage-level agreements. In consequence, those societies managed effectively by modern states are mainly characterized by levels of income inequality far less extreme than in many parts of the developing world (see Chapter 6).

KEY POINTS

- Modern states are the public political institutions and organizations of rule that are, in principle, differentiated and distinct from both the rulers and the ruled.

- The modern state emerged, evolved, consolidated, and was borrowed as the set of centralized institutions and organizations of rule, the central function of which was to manage national transitions from agrarian to industrial society, and to sustain economic growth.

- Historically, the modern state has been characterized typically by its public institutions and organizations, its sovereignty and hegemony, its formal monopoly of legitimate coercion (violence), and its theoretically impartial bureaucracy.

- Although different states adopted different strategies, successful economic growth and stable states have without exception been inextricably linked.

- In promoting economic growth and development, modern states have had to provide defence, and ensure law and order, respond to demands for a more inclusive

set of civic and democratic rights, and manage some redistribution of resources through tax and welfare arrangements.

- The broad strategy adopted in the pursuit of economic growth has depended crucially on the character of the political forces and coalitions underpinning state power, which in turn has influenced the achievement of developmental goals.

The State in the Developing World: Provenance and Forms

Most of the conditions and capabilities associated with the state's emergence in the now developed world have been largely absent in the developing world. In short, the formation of modern states in colonial and post-colonial contexts was not geared to the development of institutions and organizations of rule directed at promoting economic growth or transformative development, as occurred in Europe and elsewhere, whether on a capitalist, socialist, or mixed-economy basis. Moreover, most of the challenges that those earlier states had to meet—especially those of democratic pressures, and redistributive and welfare demands—have thus far exceeded the capability of many of the newer states. And, crucially, apart from some very important exceptions, this is explained by the quite diverse political forces and coalitions formed during or after the colonial era and which set up, inherited, adapted, or battled for control of the institutions of the modern state. Simply stated, these political forces, representing varying kinds of socio-economic elites and interests, seldom had the interest, the will or the power to establish or encourage growth-promoting institutions in accordance with any of the three models sketched earlier. This is why so many states in the contemporary developing world have been associated with weak or uneven developmental performances. But before proceeding further, two important introductory points should be made.

First, the problems facing these states are, in principle, no different from those that faced states and societies in the developed world, although they may differ in timing and context. These problems have been (and remain) essentially those of how to establish and sustain the institutions of rule that promote economic development, within or outside democratic polities, whether state-led or market-led, in the face of increasing pressures for democratization and redistribution, in a globalizing political economy.

Second, the kinds of modern state institution in post-colonial developing countries varied widely and were everywhere shaped by the interaction of four main factors: the nature of the pre-colonial polities; the economic purposes of colonial rule; the characteristics of the colonial state institutions and the socio-political groups that dominated them; and the manner of incorporation of pre-colonial political processes and institutions in the systems of colonial and post-colonial rule. Accordingly, the contemporary developing world is at least as diverse as were those societies in which the modern state emerged. Nevertheless, there are some major, common underlying themes too.

The modern state in the developing world: provenance

While the modern state in the now developed world grew largely through complex *internal* political processes in the course of the great transformations from agrarian to industrial societies, most states in the developing world owe their existence (and indeed their very borders) to the geographical definitions and institutional impositions of the colonial era. With few exceptions, the provenance of states in the developing world has largely been *external*, and few of them developed endogenously from prior local polities and systems of rule. In Asia, the exceptions include China, Korea, Japan, and Thailand, where some continuity can be traced back to prior local (absolutist, monarchical, and imperial) systems and institutions of centralized rule, as in Egypt and Ethiopia in the case of Africa. In Latin America, the main pre-colonial political institutions, especially the great centralized tribute-extracting empires of the Aztecs (Mexico) and the Incas (Peru), were extinguished by the Spanish conquest from the early sixteenth century, although cultural legacies remain even today.

Although the patterns of colonial state institutions varied widely across time and space (Young 1994: 244–81), they everywhere left very important influences on the politics and state structures after independence. Everywhere, and almost without exception, the project of colonial rule and control was undertaken initially for the benefit of the metropolitan countries or their particular interests (see Chapter 2).

Colonial states: imposed borders and the institutional patterns of rule

External design and imposition of 'national' boundaries

Perhaps the most far-reaching influence and impact has been the external shaping of geographical boundaries and institutional structures, the most dramatic illustration being the **scramble for Africa**, which produced the national boundaries of Africa today (see Box 12.1). Of course, there were no 'countries' with formally defined 'national' boundaries before this in Africa: political boundaries were often vague and porous. What there were, however, was a wide range of 'multiple, overlapping and alternative collective identities' (Berman 1998: 310), expressed in an equally wide range of institutional political arrangements. Such was the artificiality of the new, imposed boundaries that some 44 per cent of those still existing today are straight lines (Herbst 2000: 75), representing lines drawn cartographically on open maps. There was almost no indigenous definition of geographical boundaries, nor were any major 'national' movements, or 'nationalist' sentiments, involved in establishing the boundaries of modern African nation-states. The Latin American experience was not much different, in which the new states were carved from the huge vice royalties of the colonial system of rule in the course of the

---

> ### BOX 12.1 THE COLONIAL IMPACT IN AFRICA
>
> In Africa, large tracts of land were claimed by European powers as their possessions, either as colonies or protectorates, or, as in the case of King Leopold of Belgium, as private property in the form of the Congo Free State. The distribution arising out of the powers' scramble for Africa was formally recognized by their representatives at the Congress of Berlin, 1884–85. In all of this, Britain, France, Germany, and Portugal paid no regard to the enormous differences among the different African societies, which ranged from small-scale, self-governing, hunting-and-gathering bands to large, hierarchical political systems, as in the empires of Mali, Ghana, and Songhay in West Africa. Peoples with diverse cultures, religions, languages, and political systems who had previously lived alongside one another, sometimes peacefully and sometimes in violent conflict, but without formal boundaries, were now pulled together into entirely artificially created 'nation-' states.

struggles for independence in the nineteenth century. Led largely by the conservative *criollos* (colonial-born Spaniards or Portuguese, as in Brazil), the new states in consequence expressed political and socio-economic relations that even today reflect deep and profound inequalities between a small (and very rich) elite and a large (and very poor) mass, illustrated particularly well by Brazil (a former Portuguese possession), now one of the most unequal societies in the world.

In Asia, a similar pattern occurred and the Indian subcontinent provides the best example, where British rule brought diverse ethnic and religious communities—often tense with communal rivalries, not to mention more than 500 princely states—together in colonial India. But at independence the country was divided between India and Pakistan, with East Pakistan (later to become independent as Bangladesh) being separated by a great chunk of India from West Pakistan. Indonesia emerged from Dutch rule as an improbable 'nation-state' of about 13,000 islands stretching for some 3,500 miles from west to east, containing diverse linguistic, cultural, and religious communities (see Figure 21.1 in Chapter 21). Cambodia, Korea, Thailand, Myanmar, and to some extent Malaysia have been notable exceptions to this pattern, each reflecting closer lineages with some historical polity.

Extractive, rather than developmental, purposes of rule

The purpose of imperial rule was not developmental in the manner of the emerging modern states of Europe. On the contrary, all of the major colonial powers (and often the early private companies that acted for them) saw the extraction of riches, raw materials, and taxes as their primary objective.

External design and imposition of the institutions of rule

In trying to understand the problems and failures of many states in the developing world, it is fundamental to recognize that these extractive purposes shaped the kind of institutions of rule, which in turn formed the foundations for the states after independence. In so far as the institutions of colonial rule can be termed 'colonial *states*' (Young 1994), they were essentially states of extraction, and not aimed at promoting and organizing national economic development. With the exception of Japanese rule in Korea (Kohli 2004), no colonial institutions of rule bore any resemblance to any of the three models sketched earlier in the chapter. In short,

BOX 12.2 THE EXTRACTIVE NATURE OF IMPERIAL RULE

The Spanish conquistador and conqueror of Mexico, Hernando Cortés, in the sixteenth century, is reputed to have said: 'I came to get gold, not to till the soil, like a peasant.' In Indonesia, the 'culture system' of the Dutch, first under the Dutch East India Company and then through formal colonial rule, required Indonesians to deliver set amounts of spices to the authorities. Likewise, the ruthless requirements of King Leopold's Free State in the Congo demanded that rubber and ivory be collected, on pain of often cruel punishment of villagers (amputation of hands or feet was not unknown). Elsewhere throughout colonial Africa, raw materials, such as palm oil, beeswax, wild rubber, cocoa, and later tea, plus diamonds, gold, and copper, flowed back to Europe.

throughout the colonial world and until well into the twentieth century, the institutions of colonial rule and control were authoritarian, elitist, and geared to maintaining high levels of extraction for the benefit of the metropolitan powers (see Box 12.2).

Intensities and paradoxes of colonial institutions

The institutions of colonial rule displayed something of a paradox. At the centre, power was generally held very firmly as 'despotic' power—that is, the capacity to deploy force and coercion (Mann 1986: 169–70) to suppress and control. Challenges to colonial rule were usually put down with sometimes spectacular brutality, commonly with the assistance of locally recruited indigenous police and soldiers. The real locus of despotic power was largely confined to areas of economic or strategic importance, such as the cities, mines, plantations, or ports.

Yet there was seldom much infrastructural power (Mann 1986: 169–70)—that is, the capacity to penetrate, administratively, the length and breadth of the country, and to use that capacity to facilitate programmes of economic change and development (Migdal 1988). For example, large areas of non-urban Latin America, in the Amazon and the Andes, and especially in the huge rural hinterlands of countries such as Mexico, Brazil, and Argentina, although formally under Spanish or Portuguese colonial rule, remained far beyond effective control of the centre, and were run in effect by the *patrons* and *hacendados* of the great estates and the emerging *caudillos*, the local strongmen (a type of control termed **caudillismo**). The same was true for much of sub-Saharan Africa and large parts of South-East Asia. This lack of infrastructural power should not be at all surprising, given that the central purpose of European colonial rule was extractive, not developmental or transformative, and that much of colonial rule was done on a very limited budget and with a minimal administrative presence. But this dearth of infrastructural power of the colonial state created a legacy that still characterizes many new, modern states in the post-colonial world, while despotic power—protecting the new elites that took over after independence—remained pronounced in urban centres.

Because of weak infrastructural power, all colonial **regimes** came to depend on local-level 'bosses', 'big men', brokers, or oligarchs, some of whom derived their power originally from their traditional positions (such as the *caciques* of Latin America and the—sometimes artificially created—'headmen' or 'chiefs' in colonial Africa). The net overall effect of this was generally to constrain the emergence of effective modern states capable of establishing national institutions and organizations of rule for the promotion of national economic development. Indeed, the weakness of its infrastructural penetration required the central organizations of the state always to bargain and deal with the local brokers—often later institutionalized in federal political systems after independence, as in India and Nigeria and Brazil—thereby establishing complex, reciprocal networks of political influence and patronage in and around the institutions of the state, and hence imposing serious constraints on their capacity and autonomy (Barton 1997: 49; Kohli 2004). This is illustrated in Parry's description of the legacy of colonial rule in Latin America:

❝ This is *caudillismo* or *caciquismo*: the organisation of political life by local 'bosses' whose power and influence derives from personal ascendancy, family or regional association. In most countries the concentration of formal authority at the centre, the weakness of lawfully constituted provincial and local authority, leave wide scope for the activities of such people. The real effectiveness of central government may depend upon the nature of the bargain which it can strike with those who wield local influence and power; while the prestige of the *cacique* (local boss) may be enhanced by the 'pull' which he can exert in the capital. **❞**

(Parry 1966: 371–2)

Patron–client relations and the politics of the new states

This particular 'organization of political life' was the context within which patterns of patronage and

patron–client relations became so pervasive in the post-colonial world, frustrating the emergence and consolidation of the institutions of the modern state. Patron–client relations have typified human polities, before the modern state, almost everywhere. As discussed in Chapter 3, the basic characteristic of the institution of patron–client relations is an unequal power relation between patrons ('big men', in African terminology), who are powerful, rich, and high in **status**, on the one hand, and clients ('small boys', in African terminology), who lack power, wealth, or status, on the other hand. The patron–client relationship is reciprocal, but uneven, in that the patron has control of, or access to, resources and opportunities that he (it is usually a male) can provide for the client in return for deference, support, loyalty, and (in the context of post-independence electoral politics) votes. Patrons have an interest in maintaining their client base by being good 'big men'—that is, by delivering the goods—while clients (depending on the particular pattern of the relationship) may have some freedom to move from one patron to another from whom they might expect a better deal.

Clearly, the rules defining the institution of patronage are entirely at odds with the rules underpinning the modern state, and bear a striking resemblance to the pre-state European institutions of patrimonial rule, discussed by Weber. But as societies in the colonial world achieved independence from metropolitan powers and as attempts were made to build modern states, the principles and practices of patronage quickly established themselves in the interstices of the new institutions of rule, from top to bottom, thereby weakening state capacity and undermining its autonomy. Thus in Latin America, even under the 'bureaucratic-authoritarian regimes' of the 1960s and 1970s, whether on the left or the right politically, the regimes were constrained by the immense regional and local power of the old bosses, oligarchies, and political elites, in country and town, who could contain, if not derail, reform even under the toughest of military regimes, as in Brazil after 1965. And in Africa, where **patrimonialism** pre-dated the colonial impact and where, at independence, the commercial, capitalist, or landed classes were small and weak, it was almost inevitable that the resources of the state would be the target that competing groups would seek to capture, in order to feed and fuel their patronage links to 'friends and followers', whether of a regional, kin, or ethnic character. It was little different in much of South and South-East Asia during and after the colonial period.

Only in those few cases in which revolutionary political movements seized state power and largely crushed prior elites and dominant classes, as in Cuba and (North) Vietnam, has the power of patronage been contained, although it has sometimes reappeared. Other exceptional cases in which electorally or militarily dominant elites have taken over and pursued national economic growth for purposes of national defence—the classic recipe for state formation and consolidation—include the developmental states of South Korea, Taiwan, and Singapore (at which we look later in the chapter).

The State in the Developing World: Characteristics, Features, and Types

State characteristics in the developing world

Public institutions

One of the central characteristics of the modern state is that its institutions and organizations of rule are, or should be, essentially 'public', not owned or treated as their private domain by their incumbents. But one of the greatest problems in establishing modern states in the developing world has been to liberate public institutions and organizations from the private control of political leaders or from their 'capture' by special interests (Hellman et al. 2000). The combined effects of patrimonial rule and patronage have been to distort the neutrality of public institutions and to erode the independence of public organizations—whether they are policymaking bodies, courts, bureaucracies, armies, or other state-owned agencies. The net effect has often been the informal **privatization** of public organizations, in so far as they have been used to advance the private interests and clients of (usually) long-standing civilian or military leaders who have become heads of state. Essentially, this private use of public office and resources is the core definition of corruption. Certain heads of state—for instance Presidents Marcos and Suharto in the Philippines and Indonesia, Presidents Mobutu and Kenyatta of Zaire and Kenya, and Presidents Batista, Duvalier, and Somoza of Cuba, Haiti, and Nicaragua—might quite easily have repeated the view of Louis XIV, *'L'État c'est moi'*. (See Chapter 15 for an extensive discussion of the varying causes, forms, and responses to corruption in developing countries.)

Sovereignty, hegemony, and the monopoly of violence

Many states in the developing world have had great difficulty in establishing their hegemony and maintaining sovereignty within their borders. This is not only because of the power of local, private, or regional 'bosses' or 'influentials', but also because the **legitimacy** of the state has been commonly challenged by various groups (ethnic, religious, cultural, or regional), which do not wish to be part of it, or by political opponents who refuse (for good or bad reasons) to accept the incumbent regime. Also, secessionist, irredentist, and civil wars have plagued the modern states of the developing world from Peru to the Philippines, and from Angola to Afghanistan.

The earlier generation of modern states also faced these **nation-building** challenges. For instance, state education policy in nineteenth-century France had as one of its prime concerns the building of a sense of **national identity** and unity. Indeed, such issues persist to this day, as demonstrated in Basque separatism in Spain and Quebecois nationalism in Canada. However, such challenges have arguably been much more severe in the developing world. While this chapter has not identified nation-building itself as one of the core imperatives of the modern state, it must nonetheless be recognized that failure to achieve some degree of national, or multinational, integration and cohesion will jeopardize the state-building project. In effect, it is in Africa that the greatest incidence of conflicts of this kind and the adverse consequences are to be found. But there are many examples from elsewhere, such as Sri Lanka's long-running conflict between the Ceylonese majority in the south and the Tamil minority in the north. Moreover, Indonesia struggled for many years to hold on to East Timor. Guerrilla movements, both urban and rural, have challenged the hegemony and legitimacy of a number of Latin American states since the 1960s. Many states in the developing world cannot claim a formal monopoly of violence, a characteristic that marks them off sharply from most states in the developed world, although not all of those have in recent years been free from all violent internal conflict, as Northern Ireland and Spain illustrate. In some societies, the collapse of the centre and the proliferation of non-state sources of violence, and hence civil conflict, have produced a series of failed or **collapsed states** (Rotberg 2004), as in Somalia, Afghanistan, and Cambodia at various points in their recent history.

Elsewhere, there are states characterized by what scholars such as Ross (1999) referred to as the 'resource curse'. This refers to states sometimes described as '**rentier states**', in which a major part of state revenues are derived from such sources as taxes (hence rents) on companies involved in the extraction of some valuable natural resource, such as oil (classically), or diamonds or copper. It is argued that at least two consequences may flow from this dependence on resource revenues: first, it undermines democracy or democratization by reducing the state's need to be accountable to its citizens; and second, as occurred in Sierra Leone, the presence of such resources (diamonds) can fuel intense conflict between groups determined to control the trade or the state in order to capture the rents, which further weakens and sometimes simply destroys the central power and authority of an already weak **post-colonial state**.

Thus, weakened from within by internal conflict and held down by low rates of economic growth, many states in the developing world have found it difficult to maintain sovereignty. Poor countries, especially, find it harder to maintain their sovereign independence in the international arena than rich countries. Economic strength not only provides for defensive (or offensive) military capacity, but also reduces dependency and increases bargaining capacity in relations with public

institutions such as the World Bank, the International Monetary Fund (IMF), and foreign governments, and with sources of private investment and finance. In particular, where foreign aid inflows form a significant part of government expenditure, de facto sovereignty is seriously reduced as aid donors come to apply increasingly stringent conditions. As a percentage of central government expenditures, aid contributions have varied among less-developed countries, leading some countries to have lower degrees of aid dependency. These countries have been better able to maintain a grip on their own policymaking, although this has not meant that they have escaped entirely high levels of debt, another element that impacts on sovereignty.

Impartial bureaucracies

The pervasive legacy of patron–client relations, the culture of patrimonialism within the state, the absence of democratic accountability (even in its limited electoral form), low levels of economic growth, the power—and wealth—of special private interests through 'state capture', limited and often aid-dependent state budgets, low pay, high levels of state involvement in the economy, and hence much opportunity for discretionary bureaucratic decisions have all contributed to the undermining of bureaucratic impartiality in many developing countries. Moreover, bureaucratic continuity in much of Latin America has been constrained by the politics of the appointive bureaucracy, a system whereby incoming governments are able to dismiss (often many thousands of) bureaucrats (especially senior ones), and appoint their 'own' men and women (Schneider 1999: 292–4). Corruption, too, erodes state capacity to pursue coherent and consistent policies of economic growth, undermines development, and institutionalizes unfairness. By discouraging political elites from taking the tough decisions that development requires and by disabling the bureaucratic institutions of the state from carrying out effective implementation, the consequences for development can be severe. The difficulties in achieving appropriate forms of land reform in many developing countries offer a prime example, of which President Bhutto's failed attempts at land reform in Pakistan in the 1970s provides an excellent case study (Herring 1979).

Effective and developmental states

Despite this generally bleak picture of state characteristics in the developing world, there has also been a small group of *effective states* that must be mentioned. Chile, for instance, is generally perceived as having enjoyed an effective state for long periods of its history. Such states—whether democratic or not, and pursuing a wide range of economic policies—have usually been successful in promoting growth, reducing poverty, and enhancing overall welfare, even where their civil and **human rights** have not necessarily been good (although in some, such as Chile today compared to under President Pinochet's rule, it has improved greatly in the last fifteen years with deepening democratization). Described more generally as 'developmental states' (Woo-Cumings 1999), these states have taken both democratic and non-democratic forms, as well as pursued both formally socialist and non-socialist paths. While most examples have been concentrated in East or South-East Asia (such as South Korea, Taiwan, Singapore, Malaysia, China, and Vietnam), there are some non-Asian examples, including Botswana, Mauritius, and perhaps Cuba, and other recent borderline cases such as Ethiopia and Rwanda (see Chapter 15). But in all cases, whether officially capitalist or socialist, democratic or non-democratic, the effectiveness of these states has been driven by political dynamics that have concentrated sufficient power, autonomy, capacity, and (sometimes) accountability at the centre to ensure the successful achievement of their developmental goals.

KEY POINTS

- States in developing countries vary greatly, but in many, institutional and political legacies blur the boundaries between public institutions and private interests.

- Establishing organizations to monitor and control these boundaries have been difficult where there is no political will or capacity to do so.

- Many states in the developing world have found it difficult to maintain hegemony within their own territory, to protect their sovereignty, and to achieve a monopoly of violence.

- Impartial bureaucracies are less common in the developing than in the developed world.

- Patrimonialism and patronage, low levels of pay, and pervasive opportunities for discretionary behaviour all contribute to varying, but sometimes intense, patterns of corruption, thereby subverting the central purpose of the modern state: the promotion of economic growth and welfare.

- Both high levels of aid and rents from major extractive industries may undermine democratic processes.

The State in the Developing World: Facing the Challenges

The central function of the modern state has been to establish the institutional framework and organizational capacity for the promotion, management, and maintenance of economic transformation and growth, and especially the shift from agrarian to industrial society, and all of the social and political complexities that this has entailed. The effective elimination of patronage, the de-institutionalization of corruption, the clear differentiation of private and public interests and institutions, and the establishment of relatively impartial bureaucracies have always and everywhere been both condition and consequence of national economic growth, managed directly or supervised indirectly by the organizations of the state. In the course of its evolution, the modern state has also had to respond to the challenges of democratization and the associated demands for redistributive welfare measures, and has done so more or less successfully in the more developed economies in the course of the twentieth century.

The same cannot be said of many parts of the developing world in which many states have not yet been able to organize or manage economic transitions along the lines of any of the three main models outlined earlier. Instead, where attempted, industrial capitalisms have been distorted by excessive state regulation, corruption, and the sorts of general weakness where social and economic classes would normally be expected to demand change. Elsewhere, revolutionary socialist, 'forced march', state-led, economic transformations, and the state institutions of rule and management that they have required—of the kind that occurred first in the Soviet Union after 1917 and then in China after 1949, where the political forces that backed it were strong—have generally failed too. And the extraordinary symbiotic marriage of state and market, typified by various forms of the developmental state that have promoted economic progress in countries as different as South Korea, Taiwan, Singapore, Malaysia, Thailand, Mauritius, Botswana, and most recently China and Vietnam (Leftwich 1995), has simply been impossible to replicate elsewhere. It is the particular constellation of social, economic, and political forces that explains the success of these states, and not whether they happen to be democracies or not. In all cases, they illustrate the axiom that successful and effective modern states and successful economies go hand in hand.

Until the 1980s, few states in the developing world qualified as consolidated democracies. There were important exceptions: India, Jamaica, Venezuela, Costa Rica, Mauritius, and Botswana are but some, although many would question whether they all counted as *liberal* democracies (Burnell and Calvert 1999). This is because, in much of the developing world, conflicts—of class, regional, religious, or ethnic groups—have been so sharp that achieving consensus about rules of the political game has proved to be impossible. Different groups tend to prefer rules that would protect or advance their own particular interests and limit or reduce the interests of others. Second, many, although not all, of the conflicts have been about distributional issues: land, jobs; income; welfare support. Where economic growth has been slow or negative, it has simply proved impossible (even if desired) to meet such demands. Elsewhere, especially in Africa, cycles of military coup and counter-coup (although declining, but far from absent, since the 1990s) have been symptomatic of rival factions—ethnic, political, religious, or regional—seeking to gain control of the state, and hence its resources and opportunities, in order to feed their clientelistic chains. This again illustrates a central theme of the chapter. The modern state in the developed world has been compatible with democratic (at least electoral) politics only where it has ensured that economic growth could subsidize a steady (if slow and sometimes intermittent) increase in the broad welfare of the majority. The more the state has been able to do that, the more robust has been its legitimacy and the more consolidated has its democracy become.

KEY POINTS

- Most states in the developing world have experienced great difficulty in overcoming the challenges of economic growth, democratic claims, and re-distributional demands.

- Many states in the developing world have been unable to establish the institutions and organizations of rule that would permit economic growth according to capitalist, socialist, or developmental state models.

- In the absence of economic growth and in the presence of profound inequalities, states in the developing world have found it impossible to absorb and institutionalize democratic demands.

- Many states in the developing world have found it impossible to deliver improved human welfare through re-distributional means.

The State in a Globalized Developing World

A central question to theorizing the state is how **globalization** affects developing states and their policies, and whether these states can keep their sovereignty in an ever more interdependent world. Our understanding of what globalization means for the state has evolved from sweeping claims that sovereignty is seriously threatened, to more complex, nuanced, and even ambiguous perspectives.

For some analysts the triumph of economic neo-liberalism inevitably means that the state has less freedom to deviate from a narrow range of market-friendly economic policies. The political implication may be that, in democracies, electorates face restricted scope to make meaningful choices between alternative programmes for economic management and welfare provision; socialism is no longer a viable option. To be credible, political parties must occupy the centre ground, in a context in which the centre of gravity has itself moved to the right. This may reduce the state's ability to respond to the challenges mentioned in this chapter and hamper its sovereignty as policies are 'dictated' by supranational institutions. However, other commentators claim that the reality is less straightforward because of the difference that domestic political institutions and political agency still can make, such as through mediating the impact of external linkages and events. Weiss (2005: 346) even goes so far as to argue that, rather than a loss of state power, there has been structural and political entwinement—a mutual reinforcement of contemporary global networks and the domestic structures of nation-states. She argues that globalization is actually reinforcing and, in some important respects, augmenting the role of territorially based institutions, while at the same time altering the power distribution among different institutions of state and government departments as a result.

As one part of this scenario, professional technocrats in the government bureaucracy are being empowered vis-à-vis elected politicians. The executive too may gain in power relative both to the legislature and municipal institutions, owing to the growing importance of working with regional and global **governance** institutions, although in some large countries, such as India and Brazil, international financial institutions and transnational corporations now also deal directly with city and provincial administrations, circumventing the central government. In relation to poor, aid-recipient nations, critics have argued that, within central government, the power of finance ministries and central banks increases relative to spending ministries, in consequence of having to agree terms and conditions of borrowing with external creditors, and because aid donors have moved towards offering general budget support instead of emphasizing direct project and programme assistance.

Although globalization may have fuelled economic growth in countries such as China and India through increased trade, the same may not be the case for smaller countries, especially in Sub-Saharan Africa. According to Moore (2011), globalization influences the ways in which state revenue is obtained. New revenue opportunities, such as natural resources rents, illicit drug trade, foreign aid, or tax havens, are facilitated by globalization. Indeed, globalization may divert attention from promoting growth towards personal enrichment for political elites.

Overall, then, Phillips (2005: 102) observes that while a 'mainstay of the globalization-state debate, in both orthodox and critical perspectives, is the contention that states are increasingly centralized, insulated and "technocratic", and accountable primarily to global market forces rather than national societies', this should not be applied absolutely or uniformly. Instead, what is called a 'transformationalist approach' argues not only that states are undergoing variegated processes of adaptation and transformation, but also that the state may be critical to the 'authoring' and propulsion of globalization (Phillips 2005: 95). And although the international political economy literature has tended to focus its attention mainly on the developed world (Phillips 2005: 107–8; Mosley 2005: 357), the transformationalist approach equally applies to developing countries. Thus, for example, Mosley (2005: 357), in her account of government autonomy and cross-national diversity, drew attention to the differences in social policy between Chile and Mexico, which she explained by referring to domestic political alliances, the organization of the poor, and competitiveness of the political party system.

So while, for developing countries, the state's role in economic governance is said to be 'about how to incorporate societal actors in order to gain the capacity to formulate and implement efficient economic policies' (Kjaer 2004: 148), the *type* of intervention by the state and the specific policies that it pursues are no less significant than the actual amount of state intervention in markets that globalization allows or brings

about (Phillips 2005: ch. 4). Even where strong convergence towards standard neoliberal solutions does take place in the process of policy formation, intrinsically domestic features such as **neo-patrimonialism** and clientelism can make an enormous difference to the way in which policies are actually implemented and to their eventual outcomes.

> ### KEY POINTS
>
> - Globalization, in the sense of globalizing economic **neoliberalism**, is said to reduce state sovereignty.
> - It is also seen to foster states that are increasingly centralized, technocratic, and domestically unaccountable.
> - However, more recent 'transformationalist' accounts stress the variability in states' experience of, and responses to, globalization, in developing as well as developed countries.

Conclusion

Strong, stable, and effective states are inconceivable without strong economies. And strong economies are inconceivable without the institutional framework established by the state to enhance growth and welfare, whether capitalist or socialist. All examples of sustained economic growth and development have required effective states to make (and to adjust and adapt) appropriate institutions and organizations of rule, and to facilitate the coordination of the public with the private institutions. Market-oriented models would not have been successful in the West without pervasive state support in the form of investment in human and infrastructural capital, the raising of taxes, the regulation of commerce, the establishment of judicial and legal systems, and welfare provision—and much more. Top-down, state-led, Soviet-style, post-revolutionary industrialization, likewise, has also required appropriate institutions and organizations for success, as have the complex developmental states of East Asia. But in each and every case, behind the state and the institutions of development that it has created or facilitated has been a coalition of political and social forces willing and able to establish, maintain, and adapt those institutions. The problem, however, has been that the politics underpinning states in many developing countries have made them inept, disjointed, and divided agencies of economic growth, and hence have done little to promote human welfare or the reduction in poverty.

With the collapse of the bipolar world, the processes of globalization have accelerated. If such processes do indeed stimulate capitalist growth, then political forces will also gather momentum and help to build modern states based on the template of their European precursors. Instead of being the agents and beneficiaries of patronage and corruption, such forces will become the agents of their destruction, and of the creation of both the public and private institutions of rule that promote economic growth. In short, they will become much more like the states of the developed world. For sure, this will not happen everywhere; nor will it happen quickly or simultaneously. Nonetheless, such developments will bring into politics other popular social forces—sometimes based on the classical coordinates of class; sometimes, ethnicity; sometimes, religion; and increasingly, **gender**. They will use the new democratic space to demand social and welfare reforms that will constitute new challenges for the state, and, in the process, transform it, as in the case of gender inclusion and equality. How each will respond and adapt remains uncertain, and will depend on the shifting coalitions of power and resistance that such politics will create. But what is certain is that the political science of the modern state in the developing world, and elsewhere, has not by any stretch of the imagination reached its terminus.

? QUESTIONS

1. In what ways, if any, has the largely external origin of many states in the developing world influenced their form and function?

2. To what extent did the different colonial economic institutions influence the character and capacity of the colonial and post-colonial states?

3. How would you distinguish between the rules that govern institutions of patronage and institutions of bureaucracy?

4. Good governance presupposes effective states. But can either be achieved without the political will and political processes to keep them in place?

5. Identify some of the different types of state found in the developing world and compare their distinguishing characteristics, illustrating your answer with examples.

6. How may globalization pose a threat to state sovereignty in the developing world?

FURTHER READING

Bates, R. H. (2008) *When Things Fell Apart: State Failure in Late-Century Africa* (Cambridge: Cambridge University Press) This compact account charts and explains the causes and conditions of state failure in Africa.

Fukuyama, F. (2004) *State Building: Governance and World Order in the Twenty-First Century* (London: Pantheon Books) A concisely and elegantly written account of the complexities and dimensions of effective states and how they are built.

Kohli, A. (2004) *State-Directed Development: Political Power and Industrialization in the Global Periphery* (Cambridge: Cambridge University Press) An excellent comparative account of states and development in South Korea, Brazil, India, and Nigeria.

Leftwich, A. (1995) 'Bringing Politics Back in: Towards a Model of the Developmental State', *Journal of Development Studies*, 31(3): 400–27 Outlines a model of the developmental state.

Migdal, J. S., Kohli, A., and Shue, V. (eds) (1994) *State Power and Social Forces* (Cambridge: Cambridge University Press) Explores the relations between social and political forces and state power and capacity in a number of developing countries.

Rodrick, D. (2011) *The Globalization Paradox: Why Global Markets, States and Democracy Can't Coexist* (Oxford: Oxford University Press) A provocative argument about the fundamental 'trilemma' posed by the parallel projects of democracy, national determination, and economic globalization.

Woo-Cumings, M. (ed.) (1999) *The Developmental State* (Ithaca, NY: Cornell University Press) Explores the conditions and characteristics of developmental states.

Young, C. (1994) *The African Colonial State in Comparative Perspective* (New Haven, CT: Yale University Press) One of the finest accounts of the colonial state and its legacy, with insightful comparative observations.

WEB LINKS

http://www.crisisstates.com/   Many publications and research projects on crisis states in the developing and transitional world, based at the London School of Economics and Political Science.

http://www.foreignpolicy.com/   Use this site to navigate to the failed state index of journal *Foreign Policy*, funded and published by the Carnegie Endowment for International Peace, which includes quantitative measures for state strength and weakness.

http://www.gsdrc.org/   Website of the Governance and Social Development Resource Centre at the University of Birmingham, offering access to many papers, publications, and guidance concerning institutional aspects of states and governance in the developing world.

http://www.transparency.org/   Website of Transparency International, offering important and interesting information on global corruption plus the annual Corruption Perception Index for all countries and allowing navigation to the annual Global Corruption Report.

http://www2.ids.ac.uk/futurestate/   Work and publications of the Centre for the Future State, at the Institute of Development Studies, University of Sussex, which promotes research on how public authority can be strengthened and reconstituted to meet the challenges of the twenty-first century.

For additional material and resources, please visit the Online Resource Centre at:
http://www.oxfordtextbooks.co.uk/orc/burnell4e/

13
Violent Conflict and Intervention

Astri Suhrke and Torunn Wimpelmann

Overview

This chapter examines patterns of organized, violent conflict in the developing world since the onset of decolonization. It also discusses shifts in how scholars and policymakers have understood such conflicts, how these understandings have informed the international peace-building regime that developed in the 1990s, and the new forces that shaped the patterns of conflict during the first decade of this century.

Introduction: Decolonization and its Aftermath

In retrospect, it seems remarkable how few of the 100-plus transfers of authority associated with decolonization in Africa and Asia were violent. The transition from colonial rule to independence mostly took the form of widened political participation, enabling the colonial rulers to disengage formally, yet retain some influence. In some cases, however, the transition was violent. A key variable was the willingness of the colonial power to leave peacefully, which in turn was heavily influenced by the nature of the colonial political economy. The existence of plantation economies with a sizable number of white settlers seemed to predispose the transition towards a violent resolution, as Aristide Zolberg et al. (1989) write, and as evident in Indochina, southern Africa, and Kenya—possibly because plantations are immobile property that is difficult to divide or transfer. Plantation economy by itself was not a necessary condition however, as the long and perhaps extraordinarily violent war over Algeria's independence from France demonstrated. India was another exception, where decolonization entailed an extremely violent partition (see Chapter 2).

In Indochina and Southern Africa, wars over decolonization were transformed almost seamlessly into continued wars that lasted for several decades, as we shall see later in this chapter. In several other post-colonial countries, peace was fragile and punctured by renewed strife. While the new states were amalgams of populations separated by 'artificial' boundaries drawn by the colonial powers, the post-colonial elites mostly accepted these boundaries as given and very rarely went to war to dispute them. Rather, conflicts arose in relation to identity **politics** within the state, sometimes involving separatist demands, and in revolutionary struggles to capture the state and to reshape the social order in line with socialist visions and **liberation theology**.

Conflicts related to ethnicity or 'identity politics' followed several patterns (see Chapter 7). Polities with 'ranked' or 'hierarchical' ethnic systems (Horowitz 1985), in which distinctions between ethnic groups coincided with those between the ruler and the ruled, appeared particularly fragile. The ex-Belgian colonies of Rwanda and Burundi experienced early and repeated ethnically directed violence between Hutu and Tutsi. In Rwanda, the ruling Hutu majority attacked the Tutsi minority; in Burundi, the pattern was reversed. The violence started soon after independence and continued with some regularity in both countries until 1990, when an army of Tutsi in exile invaded Rwanda from neighbouring Uganda and sparked a civil war that culminated in the **genocide** of Tutsi in Rwanda in 1994. The colonial legacy that hardened and reified ethnic distinctions was partly to blame, but so were the organization of politics, intensified competition over land, and the reinforcing effect of each cycle of violence in the creation of mutually exclusive and separate communities (Banégas 2008).

Ethnically directed violence against minorities also occurred as part of state formation and **nation-building** policies, a phenomenon known from European history as well. Thus Uganda's President Idi Amin in 1972 forcibly expelled the country's Indian minority, a move that enabled him to seize the assets of a prosperous trading group and, perhaps more importantly, harness an African **national identity** as a source of **legitimacy** for his rule. In much of South-East Asia, Chinese trading minorities were vulnerable to nationalistic restrictions, as well as mob violence, when conflicts over the ethnic political order spilled into the street, as in Malaysia and Indonesia.

Communal conflict involving ethnic groups that were geographically separated generally placed the periphery in opposition to the centre over autonomy or separatist demands. While expressed in ethnic terms, secessionist conflicts typically reflect concurrent economic and political grievances or ambitions. Secessionist conflicts were common in early post-colonial Africa and Asia, for example the Outer Islands rebellion in Indonesia in 1957–58, the secession of the Katanga province from Congo in the early 1960s, and Biafra's quest for independence from Nigeria in the 1960s. In the Biafra conflict, the pictures of starving children in besieged rebel territory made a lasting imprint on Western images of the state of newly independent African countries.

However, the solid consensus among post-colonial governments against redrawing colonial boundaries ensured that very few secessionist struggles succeeded. Strong vested interests in the principle of sovereignty were one factor. There was also deep suspicion that ex-colonial powers were supporting would-be secessionist movements for economic gains and to demonstrate that the new governments were incapable of governing. The role of Belgian mining interests (*Union Minière*) in the secession of Katanga from Congo became a cause célèbre, causing a major civil war that sparked other secessionist offshoots and threw Congo into a long period of political turmoil. When the Katanga crisis finally ended in 1963, the Organization of African Unity (OAU) passed a resolution at its Cairo meeting in 1964 that explicitly called for 'respect for borders at the time of independence'. For a long time, the only two exceptions were the separation of East Pakistan (which became Bangladesh in 1971) and Eritrea's separation from Ethiopia in 1991. Much later, South Sudan split off from the rest to become a separate state after repeated wars, a peace agreement (2005), and a referendum (2011).

Conflicts over the political and socio-economic order that pitted revolutionary **social movements** against the old elites appeared in some cases to be a continuation of the independence struggle, as in southern Africa and Indochina. In Latin America, where decolonization had taken place in the early and mid-nineteenth century, struggles over the social order followed different trajectories. In Central America, agrarian protest developed into armed liberation fronts that, in the 1970s and 1980s, challenged the established landed oligarchy and their grip on the state. In South America in the same period, the armed forces seized power in Argentina, Brazil, Chile, and Uruguay to quell what they perceived as national security threats from leftist and communist forces, including urban guerrillas, the Tupamaros, in Uruguay. These conflicts became hardwired into the cold war and will therefore be discussed next.

KEY POINTS

- Post-colonial secessionist struggles occurred, but colonial borders mostly held.

- Independence struggles in South-East Asia and southern Africa were transformed into protracted cold war conflict, with devastating effects on the local societies.

Social Order Conflicts and the Cold War

By definition, conflicts over the social order have local roots. Above and beyond the particular local dimensions of the social order conflicts of the 1970s and 1980s, however, was a common element that added coherence and destructive intensity: the conflicts interacted with an especially severe phase of the cold war and this had important consequences. Conflicts over social change became expressed in the dominant discourse of the time—revolutionary socialism versus liberal democracy—which linked them to the ideologized power struggle between the United States and the Soviet Union. Recognizing that direct conflict between themselves would be mutually and totally destructive given their nuclear parity, the superpowers instead intervened competitively in the periphery. Local conflicts in what was then the 'Third World' became wars by proxies, enabling local protagonists to receive military, economic, and political support.

In this logic, the United States supported military **regimes** in South America to crush actual or suspected leftist movements, and in Chile helped to overthrow the democratically elected government of Salvador Allende in 1973. Washington supported anti-communist rebels in Nicaragua (the *contras*), and provided military, economic, and political support to the governments of Guatemala (see Chapter 26) and El Salvador to defeat the increasingly broad-based opposition to the oligarchy, and the iniquitous and

repressive social order that it represented. The Soviet Union provided material support to the other side, in particular Cuba. As the lone communist outpost in the region, Cuba served as a funnel for general assistance to rebel movements on the left, while leaders such as Fidel Castro and Che Guevara were sources of inspiration.

In Africa, a similar pattern developed. The South African **apartheid** regime and the still white-ruled Rhodesia actively helped to fight the US wars of proxy in Angola, Namibia, and Mozambique. On the other side, Cuba sent doctors, the Soviet Union provided massive economic and military aid, and sympathetic independent African governments extended sanctuary for fighters and refugees. The result was an intricate web of interaction between local, regional, and international actors, and their respective interests, as illustrated in the case of Mozambique (see Box 13.1). It was a self-reinforcing dynamic that served to sustain violence on the local level and increase systemic hostility between the superpowers.

Even a more indirect backdrop of large power rivalry could fuel local violence on an unprecedented scale, as demonstrated in the case of Indonesia in 1965.

BOX 13.1 THE WAR IN MOZAMBIQUE

A socialist national liberation movement, the Mozambican Liberation Front (FRELIMO), had been in the vanguard of the long independence struggle against the Portuguese and formed the first independent government in 1975. Its policy of radical socialist change, however, alienated many traditional farmers, antagonized the Catholic Church, and sharpened divisions between the northern and the southern regions of the country. When the government also denounced apartheid and colonialism, it alienated external forces as well. Neighbouring white-ruled Rhodesia sponsored a rebel force, the Mozambican National Resistance (RENAMO), receiving backing from the South African government and, in the background, the United States. The main reason for the US engagement was the active support given to the Mozambican government by the Soviet Union, which provided direct budget support and virtually all of its military equipment. The war between the government and RENAMO forces lasted for fifteen years, causing enormous death, destruction, and displacement, and a post-war population of *mutilados* who had been crippled, maimed, or tortured. The rebels had targeted the destruction of schools and health centres in order to undermine popular support for the government, leaving only a skeletal structure when the war ended.

President Sukarno, who had led the independence struggle against the Dutch, had ruled with few serious challenges to his power for almost a decade, but by the early 1960s two other main forces had emerged: the Communist Party of Indonesia (PKI); and the army. The delicately balanced tripod collapsed in 1965, in a context of rising international tension between the United States and the main communist powers. China was accused of using the PKI as a fifth column and an instrument of global communist expansion, while the United States was increasing its military engagement in Vietnam to prevent the 'dominoes' from falling to communism throughout South-East Asia. Against this background, the Indonesian armed forces set in motion a massive operation to physically eliminate the PKI. At least half a million people were killed, many in private vendettas that occurred in the wake of the purge. The next president, General Suharto, abrogated the previous foreign policy of non-alignment and Indonesia became a main recipient of US military aid, as well as economic assistance from the International Monetary Fund (IMF) and the World Bank (see also Chapter 21).

The most destructive of these local-cum-cold-war dynamics occurred when the superpowers moved from supporting wars of proxy in the **developing world** to engage with their own troops on the ground. In Indochina, the United States became heir to the failed French attempt to prevent the Vietnamese from gaining independence after the Second World War. The French withdrew in 1954, leaving a country divided between a northern part ruled by the Vietnamese Communist Party and a southern part ruled by a staunchly anti-communist Catholic elite. To shore up the south, the United States gradually increased its own troop commitments to fight what successive US governments and its close allies considered to be the forces of global communism, thus giving the war a world-historical significance, as well as testing the **status** of the United States as a superpower.

The Vietnam War also spilled over into Laos and Cambodia, in the latter case setting in motion a chain of events that produced the Khmer Rouge and its social revolution. Seeking to turn Cambodia back to 'year zero', the Khmer Rouge rule in Cambodia (1975–79) cost between 1 million and 2 million lives (in a population of around 7 million) as people useless to the revolution were killed or succumbed to its rigours. The excesses were stopped by another military intervention (led by a rival Khmer faction supported by

neighbouring Vietnam), but ignited a new civil war as the Khmer Rouge and other Khmer factions fought on from sanctuaries in neighbouring Thailand.

A mirror image of the disastrous Indochinese developments appeared in Afghanistan, where a local communist party, the People's Democratic Party of Afghanistan (PDPA), seized power in April 1978 and proceeded to launch a radical revolutionary programme. The Afghan revolution violently eliminated its enemies, brooked no compromise with established landed elites and religious leaders, and sparked a counter-revolutionary movement of *mujahidin* ('holy warriors') who assembled across the border in Pakistan. By late 1979, the Soviet Communist Party, which had close 'fraternal relations' with the PDPA and long-time interest in securing its strategic and economic foothold in Afghanistan, decided to send its own troops to impose greater order. The result, predictably, was an escalation of the war as the resistance movement gathered force, now very significantly helped by the United States, its allies, and China (which by this time was locked in a deep conflict with the Soviet Union). After a decade of fighting a losing war, the Soviet Union withdrew its forces in 1989, but peace did not come to Afghanistan. The resistance movement now split into warring factions, which started a civil war of their own in the early 1990s, the excesses of which enabled the Taliban to gain power as a force of order and justice.

KEY POINTS

- The cold war intensified conflicts over the social order in Africa, Asia, and Latin America, leading to '**proxy wars**'.

- Conflicts involving the troops of one or the other superpower directly were most destructive, as in Indochina and Afghanistan.

The Nature of Conflicts in the Post-Cold-War World

The end of the cold war gave decisive momentum to peace negotiations dealing with some of the most stubborn and difficult wars of proxy. Between 1991 and 1994, peace talks commenced or were concluded in Angola, Cambodia, El Salvador, Guatemala, and Mozambique; of these, only the Angola Accords collapsed. The peace settlements—based in all cases on compromises between the contending parties— signalled the end of the era of revolutionary struggles, and also the end of unfettered power of landed oligarchies and military dictatorships. With the collapse of the Soviet bloc and the consequent blow to the status of state socialism, liberal democracy and the market economy became dominant paradigms for social change and foreign assistance.

Yet hopes that the 1990s would inaugurate a new world order without wars were not vindicated. The number and overall severity of conflicts, as measured by battle-related deaths, decreased overall, but varied by region (Human Security Report 2005). The Americas remained relatively peaceful, as measured by number of violent conflicts; there was a steady decline of even small wars in east and South-East Asia, and in central and south Asia the data showed no clear trends. In sub-Saharan Africa, however, the numbers climbed steeply. Civil war erupted in Liberia (1989) and Sierra Leone (1991), in both cases lasting for a decade or more. The Democratic Republic of the Congo (DRC) was the scene of almost continuous war from 1996 to 2003, followed by subsequent, smaller wars. In Angola, a temporary peace in 1992 collapsed, followed by low-level renewed war until 2002. In the Horn of Africa, unrest continued.

What forces were driving these conflicts? The surface manifestations seemed chaotic, with military factions mobilized along clan, tribal, or ethnic lines, fighting for no clear political agenda apart from capturing the state. In the DRC, neighbouring states intervened in the fighting as well; at one time, three states were supporting the government and three more were supporting the rebels. With the end of the globalized struggle between communism and capitalism, analysts struggled to understand the nature of these and other conflicts in the developing world. The explanations focused variously on ethnicity and tribalism, the structure of resources, **state failure**, poor **governance**, and rapid democratization. New analytical approaches to the study of conflict were generated as well (see Box 13.2). Some analysts argued that the wars of the 1990s were qualitatively different from previous wars, marked by extraordinary violence against civilians, the force of ethnicity, and the internationalized structure of funding (Kaldor 1999). The claim of newness in relation to violence against civilians was decisively refuted (Kalyvas 2001), but other features were more novel.

The 'new wars' and their causes

The Balkan wars, the Rwandan genocide, and the war in Somalia were at the forefront of international attention in the first half of the 1990s. The importance of ethnicity in the first two cases, and of a related social dimension (clan) in Somalia, served to revive the notion that ethnicity was a principal driver of conflict. All cases were, of course, more complex. In Somalia, for instance, the state—which equated with the **patronage**-based rule of President Siad

---

BOX 13.2 STUDYING THE PROCESSES OF WAR

The study of the social and economic processes of war became more important, partly as an entry point to understand the post-war order. Some scholars focused on how wars were organized and financed, on how illegal or shadow 'war economies' functioned and sustained themselves. One result was to question conventional and rigid distinctions between war and peace as discrete phenomena. Anthropologists and other social scientists studied war (and other forms of violence) as a social process, conditioned by and understandable only in its social, economic, and political contexts (Richards 2004). Rather than seeking to identify discrete causes of war (such as ethnicity, poverty, profit-seeking, or state failure), these studies examine the historical conditions that enabled and shaped conflicts in particular ways.

In this perspective, if there was something fundamentally new about the wars after the cold war, it was linked to changes in the historical settings that shaped the way in which conflicts were fought. For instance, the need for new sources of funding gave rise to 'war economies' as rebel parties engaged in resource accumulation, which attracted 'conflict entrepreneurs' and often took on a logic of their own. Some governments raised militias in order to fight wars on the cheap. As the discipline and cohesion of national armies disintegrated, warfare decentralized, often intersecting with local conflict dynamics. Militias were mobilized with appeal to tribal and **ethnic identities**. Demobilized military personnel also found jobs as mercenaries in conflict elsewhere. Many former soldiers of the South African apartheid-era army, for instance, went to work for private military companies in countries such as Sierra Leone and Angola.

Barre—had imploded when the cold war ended and Siad Barre lost his principal source of patronage from the superpowers, which previously had competed for a strategic foothold in the Horn of Africa. Absent the central state, a protracted, clan-based struggle for power ensued, with varying degrees of violence. In Afghanistan, the Soviet withdrawal and subsequent loss of financial support for Najibullah's government led to its gradual, but definitive, demise, opening the way for a civil war among the former resistance fighters that now divided largely along ethnic lines, between Pashtun, Tajik, Uzbek, and Hazara.

The importance of natural resources as a source of conflict was highlighted in relation to the wars in Africa, where the availability of diamonds, timber, and rubber helped to finance the warring factions. Taking the point much further, some analysts claimed that contemporary wars were largely driven by the search for profit; the real purpose of war was not to win, but to engage in profitable crime under the cover of warfare (see Box 13.3). The most elaborate and influential formulation of this claim was made by a World Bank/Oxford University economist, Paul Collier. Using statistical analysis, Collier argued that civil wars were driven by individual, economic 'greed', rather than by political and social collective grievances. Collier's economic model is derived from rational choice theory, in which the self-interested, cost–benefit-calculating individual is the starting point for explaining social behaviour. In this model of war, the existence of primary resources suggests ready availability of lootable goods, which makes

rebellion a profitable undertaking, and poverty reduces the opportunity cost of war. A large number of unemployed and uneducated young men provide a pool of likely soldier-entrepreneurs. The most important exit from the perpetual conflict that traps African countries, therefore, is rapid **economic growth** and diversification (Collier et al. 2003).

The 'conflict trap' model was a more specific version of the long-standing theme in Western liberal discourse to the effect that economic **underdevelopment** causes conflict. As such, it fed into the stock of policy-oriented knowledge that informed the peace-building interventions from the 1990s and onwards (see later in the chapter). Other analysts were critical, however (Cramer 2006). There were concerns about assumptions and methods. A low level of education, for instance, might mean young males were ready to join a rebel army in order to make a living ('greed'), or that angry young males were joining to claim their social rights ('grievance'). The unstated, but obvious, policy implications of the model were decidedly conservative: if rebels are driven only by personal greed, by implication they have no claim to political legitimacy.

Analysts drawing on fieldwork from Africa drew yet different conclusions. Young, unemployed men were indeed readily mobilized for war, but not simply for reasons of profit; rather, rebellion was a response to a crisis of the state, manifested in lack of employment and educational opportunities, and widespread **corruption** and malgovernance, which generated widespread discontent. The absence of recognizable ideological claims or organizational cohesion

BOX 13.3 SIERRA LEONE'S 'BLOOD DIAMONDS'

In 1999, a Canadian **non-governmental organization (NGO)**, Partnership Africa Canada, published a report on the ongoing war in Sierra Leone, claiming that mining and sales of local diamonds had been the cause of widespread death, destruction, and misery for almost a decade in this small West African country. The level of violence in Sierra Leone, the authors argued, could have been sustained only by the diamond trade. The report further claimed that the rebels were less interested in winning the war than in maintaining a profitable trade under the cover of warfare. The report received worldwide attention and eventually led to a global certification system (the 'Kimberley process') that traced the origin of diamonds in order to stop diamonds mined by rebels from reaching the world market.

The focus on diamonds, however, risked reducing the war, and particularly the rebel movement Revolutionary United Front (RUF), to a simple greed for profit that obscured its political dimensions. In reality, the conflict was rooted in political exclusion and deteriorating living conditions, which had been a mobilizing factor for many rebel soldiers. The wartime diamond economy, moreover, did not represent a radical departure from peacetime practices in trade and production. A regional network of illicit trade and production in diamonds had existed for decades before the war. The RUF and other factions tapped into and sometimes altered these structures, often entering into alliances with established traders, miners, and exporters. Many of the actors in Sierra Leone's diamond industry thus remained the same throughout war and peace.

consequently did not mean that African rebel movements were apolitical (Keen 2012).

Another serious limitation on the economic interpretation of the 1990s conflicts in Africa was its strongly internalist perspective, which did not adequately reflect the changes in the international setting. While the end of cold war patronage forced both governments and rebels to find other means of financing their wars, the looting and trading of valuables were made possible by the international demand for diamonds, timber, and coltan, and big profits brought home by international traders. More generally, it is clear that the increasingly deregulated global economy in the post-cold-war world, which has accelerated global trade, communications, and financial transfers, also enabled the emergence of networks for arms trade, money laundering, and drug trafficking to generate instability in the South. The industrialized world has been slow to recognize this, if at all; rather, the dominant reaction in the North has been to interpret instability as a symptom of underdevelopment. The supply of arms is a case in point. Cheap and light weapons, partly pilfered from ex-communist-army stockpiles, are readily transported to conflicts spots in the South by a large, global network of arms traders. The United Nations' efforts to introduce international regulations on conventional arms trade have long been stymied by the main arms suppliers—above all, the United States. The change of government in the United States in 2009 opened a door, however. In October 2009, the UN General Assembly for the first timed resolved without opposition that its members would start negotiations on a 'strong and robust' arms trade treaty. As a first step towards global, treaty-based restrictions on the supply of arms, the Resolution signalled new constraints on international processes that fuel local violence.

> ### KEY POINTS
>
> - The end of the cold war made space for the settlement of many protracted conflicts, notably in Cambodia, Guatemala, El Salvador, and Mozambique.
>
> - New wars erupted, however, leading analysts to search for explanations in 'wars for profit' financed by natural resources, underdevelopment, state failure, and poor governance.
>
> - Claims that these 'new wars' were qualitatively different from 'old wars' were disputed.

New Forces

The attacks on Washington and New York on 11 September 2001 ('9/11') triggered a globalized, US-led military offensive against militant Islamic movements and their supporters. For students of contemporary history, it was a case of déjà vu. Instead of a rival superpower, the West faced a loosely structured network of militant Islamists; otherwise, the conflict dynamic was familiar from the cold war. Conducted mainly in the Middle East, South-West Asia, and the Horn of Africa, the 'war on terror' became an international, deeply ideologized construct that penetrated and distorted local conflicts, shored up local clients, demonized the adversary and—typically—produced more violence.

Militant Islam and the 'war on terror'

The first and principal front in the 'war on terror' was Afghanistan, which the United States invaded in 2001 to destroy al-Qaeda and its local Taliban allies. At the time, the Taliban regime controlled some 90 per cent of the countryside, partly through 'franchise' to local leaders, while the main Afghan opposition had regrouped in the north. This 'Northern Alliance' partnered in the US-led invasion and was rewarded with prominent positions in the new government installed in Kabul. Conflicts among the Afghan factions soon surfaced, however, partly on ethnic grounds. More serious was the revived insurgency led by the Taliban, who had regrouped in the mountainous border area between Afghanistan and Pakistan. By 2005, much of the south-eastern part of the country had become a war zone. By the end of the decade, the insurgency had spread to north and central regions as well, drawing support on the way from ethnic groups other than the Taliban's Pashtun core.

The international forces, known as the International Security Assistance Force (ISAF) and placed under North Atlantic Treaty Organization (NATO) command in 2003, were gradually increased to reach almost 150,000 by the end of the decade. The force level was comparable to the Soviet military presence at its peak during the 1980s. The Taliban and associated militant groups fought back, using 'asymmetrical warfare' such as suicide bombings and attacks on civilians to achieve their declared aim of driving out the 'infidel' invaders, defeating the 'puppet' government, and restoring Afghanistan as an Islamic emirate. The movement had sufficient support, both locally and from the de facto sanctuary enjoyed in Pakistan, to seriously challenge the government and the international forces. As it became increasingly obvious that the war was not winnable, but rather had spread to create havoc in Pakistan's border areas, the international coalition prepared to withdraw. The year 2014 was fixed as the date for final withdrawal of ISAF combat troops, leaving only a smaller Special Forces contingent to work with the Afghan security forces. Meanwhile, efforts were under way to open talks with the Taliban to lessen the uncertainties facing Afghanistan in the future (Suhrke 2011).

The 9/11 attack on the United States gave the Bush administration a pretext to invade Iraq, where Saddam Hussein had kept a fractured polity together primarily by fear and repression. Not surprisingly, violent sectarian struggles erupted in the wake of the invasion that brought down Saddam Hussein and dismantled the central coercive instruments of the state—the Ba'th Party and the army. Fighting among the Iraqis followed mainly ethnic or sectarian lines. Kurds, Sunni, and Shi'a fought each other, while US occupation forces supported by a newly re-established Iraq army and militias fought those who opposed the occupation regime, and later its Iraqi successor, or were suspected of working with al-Qaeda. In the process, Iraq became a magnet and nesting place for assorted militant jihadists, just as Afghanistan had been in the 1980s. By the end of 2011, all US troops had withdrawn from Iraq, but internal conflict continued as a low-grade sectarian civil war, punctuated by horrific bombing episodes and de facto ethnic cleansing as minorities fled neighbourhoods for greater safety among kin (see Chapter 22).

Local conflicts elsewhere were brought into the orbit of the 'war on terror' as well. The Philippine government received US assistance to help to defeat Muslim rebel movements that had been fighting for autonomy in the Muslim minority areas in the southern islands for a long time. In Somalia, the emergence of local Islamist bodies (the Islamic Courts Union) provoked an invasion of Ethiopian forces in December 2006, assisted by the United States. A new, 'moderate' Somali government was installed to help to deny Islamic militants the use of Somalia as a sanctuary. The government controlled little territory beyond the capital, however, while militant, undefeated factions of the Islamic Courts formed a new, hard-line movement (Al-Shabaab) to fight the government and

its international supporters. In Yemen, the US government worked with the ruling head of state to defeat militant Islamists who opposed the government, and who reportedly had links with international **terrorism** and al-Qaeda. To ensure full coverage of the African continent in the new security paradigm, in 2008 the US government established a separate command for the area (Africa Command).

The focus of Western governments on the dangers of international terrorism in the years immediately post-9/11 meant support for seemingly stable governments even if their stability, as in the Arab Middle East, rested on a heavy hand of repression. Again, the parallel with the cold war is striking: Western states then supported repressive regimes in Latin America, Asia, and Africa in the name of fighting communism (and Soviet policy was the reverse mirror image). The new fear of terrorism after 9/11 also focused attention on 'state failure' as a source of conflict in the developing world and generated large international programmes for assistance to 'state-building'.

State failure, state-building, and failing at building states

From the early 1990s and onwards, the concept of 'state failure' had figured as a particular understanding of underdevelopment. Early formulations were built around the divergence between *de jure* and de facto status. Robert Jackson argued that many countries in the developing world have *de jure* status—that is, they are formally recognized in the international systems as states—but lack de facto statehood—that is, the capacity to perform basic functions associated with the modern state, above all providing security and basic services for development. As a result, they are only 'quasi-states' (Jackson 1990).

The 9/11 attack and US response caused a spike in the concept's popularity in Northern policy discourse as a diagnosis of severe underdevelopment in the South that had international security implications. The UN Secretary-General, Kofi Annan, lent the weight of his office to the idea that failed states represented an international security threat. A major UN report issued in 2004 described a world of 'new and evolving threats. . . threats like nuclear terrorism, and State collapse from the witch's brew of poverty, disease and civil war' (United Nation 2004: 1). Partly as a result, state-building also became a core component of the international peace-building regime that was increasingly institutionalized as the new century opened (see later in the chapter).

A veritable industry of lessons and practices in international assistance to 'state-building' soon appeared. A number of Northern think tanks and institutes constructed indexes of 'failed', 'fragile', or 'collapsed' states. Somalia and the DRC often led the list; Afghanistan and Haiti were frequently cited as well. A large 'how to' literature appeared on the basic concepts, sequences, strategies, and tools with which to reconstruct states after misrule or upheavals. Main topics were how to create authority and legitimacy, institute public financial management, establish an effective and accountable civil service, and reform the police, among other things. The high level of ambition was captured in the title of one widely cited book, *Fixing Failed States* (Ghani and Lockhart 2008).

A critical literature developed as well. So-called 'failed states', it was noted, were a very diverse group. Some, such as Haiti, hardly represented a threat to international order at all (see Box 13.4). Some presumptively 'failed states' seemed to manage through grass-roots governance and local authority structures, as Somalia did in one period (Menkhaus 2006–07). The term suggested the causes of failure were all internal, had derogatory connotations, and was overtly normative by taking an idealized Western state as its model.

'People power'

The popular uprisings in the Middle East in the late 2010 took most analysts by surprise, although in retrospect the historical logic appears reasonably clear (Joffe 2011). Autocratic and repressive regimes in the Arab states had long been maintained by a coercive state apparatus, coated by a culture of fear, financed by oil and foreign aid, and buttressed by US and European support in the name of international stability—first against communism, and after 9/11 against militant Islam. Yet corrosive forces were at work. Responding to demands for market reforms by the World Bank and the IMF in the early 2000s, the Egyptian and Tunisian

---

BOX 13.4 HAITI: FAILED STATE—FAILED BY WHOM?

Haiti has long suffered from an excess of **despotic power** and a deficit of **infrastructural power** (see Chapter 12), and in that sense was a 'failed state' well before the term was invented. The absence of effective public services of any kind—notably, security, health communication, water supply, and public administration generally—was cruelly exposed by the severe earthquake in January 2010 that flattened much of the capital.

The lineages of this state go back to French colonialism. A slave revolt in 1804 made Haiti the first black-led **post-colonial state** in 1804, but in 1915 the country was invaded by the US Marines. A twenty-year occupation was followed by the ruthless dictatorship of François 'Papa Doc' Duvalier and his son, 'Baby Doc', whose thirty-year rule laid the foundation for another rebellion. In the late 1980s, peasants, farmers, and urban poor mobilized around Father Jean-Bertrand Aristide and his liberation theology of social justice. On the other side were Haiti's tiny economic elite of reconstituted plantation owners, other landowners, and merchants, with strong links to the army. The struggle between these forces shaped the Haitian state from Aristide's first election as president in 1990 until he was forced out in 2004. International support for Aristide was premised on a restructuring of the patrimonial and bloated Duvalierist state through liberalization and downsizing. Aristide, however, viewed the state as an instrument for radical redistribution of wealth and did not comply. He also failed to transcend the despotic state of the Duvaliers, using violence to maintain his power and alienating the masses he once had

mobilized (Dupuy 2007). In the end, he was defeated by the combined efforts of the Haitian elite, the United States, and France, and whisked out of the country on a US plane. Subsequent governments failed to reduce Haiti's desperate poverty and inequality—about 1 per cent of the population controls almost half of its wealth (Carillo 2007))—and some 9,000 UN peacekeepers struggled to maintain order amid pervasive crime and the presence of numerous violent gangs.

More fundamentally, critics argued that the 'state-builders' mistakenly saw the state as a system—an empirically observable, functional organization—autonomous and separate from society (Heathershaw 2011). Attempting to transplant a model Western state into a wide range of different contexts was fundamentally misguided; it failed to recognize that 'the state' was, in fact, a name for a set of political relations that had emerged historically and were unique in each context. Imposing a formal **institutional** design in the hope that such relations would materialize was likely to fail and could well be counterproductive. Instead, external 'state-builders' needed to understand the elite settlements that underpinned a given political order, and recognize that foreign aid and military assistance influenced such elite settlements in important, but often unpredictable and undesired, ways. This perspective, in turn, generated renewed interest in 'elite bargains' as a way in which to reduce conflict in undemocratic, or what one influential source called 'limited access', societies (North et al. 2009).

governments started to **privatize** and deregulate the economy. Not surprisingly, the immediate benefits of reforms were captured by a narrow elite, who ostentatiously displayed the wealth gained from lucrative new business holdings. The other side of this kind of 'crony capitalism' was deepening inequality and poverty. In Egypt, for instance, the privatization of the textile mill industry saw tens of thousands of workers lose their jobs. Additional demographic pressures produced huge unemployment, particularly among youth, and a sharp rise in the absolute number of poor. The annual Arab Human Development Report, published by the United Nations Development Programme (UNDP), documented the nature and sources of growing structural inequality. At the same time, **globalization** of communications helped to empower and connect discontented masses with an emerging social infrastructure of protest. The coercive state's dependence on control of information was broken.

As in the much earlier decolonization process already discussed, the popular uprisings in the autocratic states in the Arab Middle East in 2010–11 followed two main trajectories. In Tunisia and Egypt, the old regimes were overthrown rapidly and with little bloodshed. In both cases, the army effectively stood aside to let the paternalistic regimes fall. Erstwhile allies—above all the United States, but also the United Kingdom and France—did the same. The uprisings, after all, spoke with the voice of 'the people' and the autocrat's fall was quick (in Egypt, Hosni Mubarak stepped down after eighteen days of demonstrations). For the West, aligning with the popular forces, moreover, seemed the surest way in which to prevent militant Islamists with an international jihadist agenda from gaining strength.

Two years on at time of writing, it was still too early to determine how deeply the uprisings would alter the authoritarian practices of the state. This was particularly the case in Egypt, where the new, democratically elected president faced continued unrest, as well as accusations of failing to address state repression and continuing authoritarian rule. Nonetheless, the fact that popular mobilizations had succeeded in bringing down powerful heads of state in two countries was a powerful corrective to the widespread representation of the Middle East as a region somehow unsuited for democracy.

Events in Libya and Syria, however, showed the limits of 'people power' (see Chapter 11). In Libya, the opposition was weakened by regional and ethnic divisions, while Islamists, workers, and **civil society** lacked the organizational core that had underpinned the Egyptian uprising. It took a seven-month NATO aerial bombardment campaign led by Britain and France to bring down the Qaddafi regime in late 2011. In Syria, demonstrations starting in 2011 developed into a protracted and devastating civil war. The army stood firmly by the regime, society was divided along ethnic and sectarian lines, and NATO did not intervene directly. Western hesitation reflected several concerns. Arms aid to the rebel Free Syrian Army, it was feared, could fall into the hands of international jihadists. In the United Nation, Russia supported Bashir al-Assad's government and strongly opposed an international intervention, and the regional political scene was extraordinarily complex. (For a further discussion of the Syria conflict, see the Online Resource Centre.)

The international peace-building regime

The end of the cold war had opened up space for new forms of international activism. The Western world took a renewed interest in ending conflicts and building peace in the developing world, but also found greater opportunities for military intervention, whether reflecting humanitarian concerns or other interests. A reinvigorated UN engaged itself early to make, secure and build peace. The organization was involved in all of the major peace negotiations that took place in the aftermath of the cold war and laid the foundation for what developed into an international peace-building regime.

Then UN Secretary-General Boutros Boutros-Ghali defined the agenda in a 1992 document called *The Agenda for Peace*. During the next two decades, the international peace-building regime expanded massively. In 2012, the UN had twenty-nine active peace operations around the world, most of them multidimensional with a wide range of military, political, economic, and legal support functions. A UN Peace-building Commission had been established to closely direct and monitor peace-building in select countries. Traditional development agencies had reshaped some of their activities as peace-building and launched programmes early in post-war transitions. Both the World Bank and the UNDP established special organizational units to deal with post-conflict or conflict-prevention programmes. For donor agencies, international NGOs, and humanitarian and development organizations, peace-building represented a massive growth industry.

'Peace-building' gradually came to mean a standardized package of post-war aid, designed to provide security in the initial phase after the war ended, to promote and monitor demilitarization of the ex-belligerent armies and factions, to assist the return of refugees, to help to restart or kick-start the economy, to help to re-store or reform political institutions and the holding of democratic elections, to promote the establishment of **rule of law**, and to strengthen institutions to establish and monitor **human rights**, sometimes including ac-countability mechanisms for war crimes and massive human rights violations perpetrated during the conflict. The package was developed by the major donors and aid agencies, the international financial institutions (the World Bank, the IMF, the regional development banks), and the UN specialized agencies (especially UNDP, the World Food Programme, or WFP, and the United Nations High Commissioner for Refugees, or UNHCR), as well as the UN Secretariat. It was further streamlined by international organizations such as the Organisation for Economic Co-operation and Development (OECD), which started harmonizing guidelines for aid from the rich, industrialized states to peace-building activities.

Economic and political liberalization were also ad-vocated by Western governments and international or-ganizations as a foundation for a more peaceful world. The idea of democracy as a cornerstone of peace was celebrated in triumphalist terms by Western policy-oriented scholars. In the words of a co-founder of the American *Journal of Democracy*:

❝ The experience of this century offers important les-sons. Countries that govern themselves in a truly demo-cratic fashion do not go to war with one another . . . [they] do not 'ethnically' cleanse their own populations . . . [they] do not sponsor terrorism . . . [they] do not build weapons of mass destruction to use on or to threaten one another . . . [They] form more reliable, open and en-during trading partnerships . . . [they] are more environ-mentally responsible because they must answer to their own citizens. ❞

(Diamond, cited in Paris 2004: 35)

The proposition underpinned Western support for democratization, which was a pillar in the emerging international peace-building regime. The social sci-ence literature was more sceptical, noting that while established democracies tend to be internally peaceful and not to wage war on each other, the road to a full democratic stage is statistically speaking paved with violence and unrest (Hegre et al. 2001). In the peace-building communities, this simply meant that more must be done to stem the forces of violence in the course of building states, democracies, and post-war economic reconstruction for development. If, as much

of the literature claimed, the causes of war were to be found in poorly functioning state institutions, eco-nomic stagnation and unemployment, lack of democ-racy, or ethnic polarization, then peace-building had to remedy these conditions. That meant, first, helping to provide security, and then assisting in creating strong, yet democratic political institutions, a modern national army, a justice sector reflecting the rule of law, rapid economic growth in a market economy, and privatiza-tion if the state had been a major economic actor.

How do we assess the impact on peace of this di-verse and vast set of activities? Quantitative studies suggest that the post-conflict package tends to stabilize peace at least in the sense of preventing a relapse into full-scale war (Doyle and Sambanis 2006). Historical analysis of the capacity of the UN system to meet the enormous challenges of peace-building confirms that peace operations usually have stabilizing functions, but note problems of legitimacy and effectiveness (Berdal 2009; Sisk 2013). Case studies can be marshalled on either side of the balance sheet. Critics stress that intrusive missions often have counter-productive ef-fects and that the 'liberal peace' paradigm, which has framed peace-building for the past two decades, has an inbuilt potential to generate conflict. Both the eco-nomic and political marketplace are structured around competition, which in the typically unsettled condi-tions of countries emerging from internal strife can ignite violence (Newman et al. 2009). Liberalization before institutionalization is a recipe for conflict, as an oft-cited study concluded in 2004 (Paris 2004), and not only in post-war situations, as the Egyptian govern-ment was to realize when liberalizing the economy.

A much more radical critique claims that the basic function of peace-building is to manage the effects of economic exclusion of the developing world that threaten Western interests in the form of refugee flows, transnational crime, epidemic diseases, and ter-rorism. As formulated by Mark Duffield (2001), peace-building in this perspective is a security intervention by the developed world to control and contain the global poor, thereby preserving the present interna-tional power structure.

The end of peace-building as Westernization?

The people-powered uprisings in the Middle East had been self-consciously nationalistic in asserting their rights to define the political transformation. Even the

Libyan transitional regime did not invite a large-scale Western or UN-led peace-building mission, only a limited UN mission to assist primarily with the technicalities of the first post-Qaddafi elections. Western governments were mainly concerned to secure stocks of high-grade weapons in the unsettled condition that prevailed after Qaddafi. Western businesses interests and development contractors lined up for concessions and contracts financed by the country's oil revenues. This was no place for the standardized peace-building package introduced by foreign donors and aid organizations elsewhere. The same applied in Egypt and Tunisia, where Western governments had been discredited by their strong support for the fallen autocrats, and Islamist political parties were moving to the forefront.

Among the major Western governments, there was likewise a declining enthusiasm for major intervention and subsequent state-cum-peace-building missions. The experiences from Iraq and Afghanistan demonstrated the enormous problems involved, while financial crisis and economic austerity in the United States and the European Union accentuated the economic costs. The rise of the BRIC states—Brazil, Russia, India, and China—indicated that Western aid and policy paradigms would be challenged also in the peace-building sector.

Yet it seemed premature to announce the end of peace-building as a Western-led project to remake unstable or war-torn countries in the South in the mould of liberal democracy and market economies. Concerns expressed in the 2011 World Development Report of the World Bank were symptomatic. The report presented the South as a deeply violent place, torn not only by conventional civil wars, but also violence of all kinds, from drug trafficking to urban gangs. While some figures and claims were questionable, the overall message was clear: the rich and powerful states in the North and the international financial institutions must remain involved, and must maintain a long-term commitment to deal with the twin problem of security and development in the turbulent parts of the world.

Nevertheless, the need for adjustments in strategy was recognized. The new flavour had been anticipated in the UN Secretary-General's 2009 report on peace-building (United Nations 2009), which emphasized the importance of local context and local ownership. The report set the tone in the wider international peace-building community. Recognizing that the wholesale transformation of war-torn countries according to a universal template had the marks of hubris, peace-builders scaled down the ambitions and refocused on local non-state actors. Building on authority structures such as customary law, community or tribal police, and local elders to create hybrid forms of governance made more sense (Boege et al. 2009). But new departures ignited another debate in the literature. 'Hybridization', critics said, might mean support for oppressive groups and resemble the **indirect rule** of colonial times when customary 'chiefs' were empowered by imperial governments. Those favouring the new paradigm countered that pragmatism was better than dogmatism; Western peace-builders should dispense with preconceived models and focus on 'what worked' for the people in question.

KEY POINTS

- International sources of conflict in the developing world have changed. The US-led global 'war on terror' interacted with local tension in much of the Muslim world, particularly in Iraq, Afghanistan, Pakistan, and the Horn of Africa.

- Uprisings in the Middle East demonstrated the strength, but also the limits, of 'people power'. Global forces shaped the causes and trajectories of the uprisings.

- After the end of the cold war, international peace-building became an increasingly standardized package, which included economic and political liberalization, administrative reform and institution-building, and the holding of elections.

- Shortcomings of peace-building interventions generated search for corrections, with more attention to local context and ownership.

Conclusion

This chapter has surveyed different phases of conflict in the developing world, starting with the independence struggle. The decolonization itself was a major driver of violence, although far from all transfers of power took a violent form. The decades of the cold war saw local conflict dynamics shaped in decisive ways by the ideological and political competition between the communist and the capitalist world, with devastating effects on local societies. Continued violence in developing countries in the post-cold-war period raised new questions about the causes of these wars, including their relationship to natural resource **exploitation**, 'failed states', and poor governance. Yet also these wars were profoundly shaped by global political and economic developments, only more subtly. During the 1990s, novel international interventions in the form of 'peace-building' emerged as a concerted strategy to manage violence. The international peace-building regime was largely premised on the assumption that the main causes of conflict in the developing world were internal—in other words, a function of their underdevelopment. As this chapter has shown, however, the international setting of internal conflict is critically important, and an internalist perspective alone can therefore not be the basis for sound analysis and appropriate response.

? QUESTIONS

1. What were the most important factors determining whether colonized countries experienced a peaceful or violent transition to independence?

2. In what ways did the cold war impact on violent conflict in the developing world?

3. Was there a shift in the nature and patterns of conflict in the developing world after the end of the cold war, and if so, how can it be explained?

4. What are the potentials and limitations of 'people power' to change political systems?

5. What are the strengths and weaknesses of Western-led peace-building interventions?

6. How has the global 'war on terror' impacted on political change in affected regions of the South?

≋ FURTHER READING

Cramer, C. (2006) *Civil War is Not a Stupid Thing: Accounting for Violence in Developing Countries* (London: Hurst & Co) Critically examines the assumptions that violent conflict is inimical to development.

Kaldor, M. (1999) *New and Old Wars: Organised Violence in a Global Era* (Cambridge: Polity Press) Develops the argument that wars after the cold war are fundamentally different from previous wars.

Keen, D. (2012) *Useful Enemies when Waging Wars is More Important than Winning Them* (New Haven, CT: Yale University Press) Explores why civil wars—whether internationalized or not—are so numerous and protracted in the contemporary world.

North, D. C., Wallis, J. J., and Weingast, B. R. (2009) *Violence and Social Orders: A Conceptual Framework for Interpreting Recorded History* (New York: Cambridge University Press) Seeks to explain why societies that control violence through exclusive elite pacts are less developed than societies based on open access and competition.

Paris, R. (2004) *At War's End* (New York: Cambridge University Press) Critically assesses the impact of economic and political liberalization on post-war peace-building.

Zolberg, A., Suhrke, A., and Aguayo, S. (1989) *Escape from Violence: Conflict and the Refugee Crisis in the Developing World* (New York: Oxford University Press) Examines the nature of conflict in the developing world before and during the cold war.

⊕ WEB LINKS

http://www.hsrgroup.org/human-security-reports/human-security-report.aspx   Focusing on people rather than states, the Human Security Reports examine global and regional trends in wars and other forms of organized violence.

http://www.un.org/peace/peacebuilding   For UN Peacebuilding Commission efforts to garner international support for nationally owned and led peace-building efforts.

For additional material and resources, visit the Online Resource Centre at:
http://www.oxfordtextbooks.co.uk/orc/burnell4e

14

Democratization

Peter Burnell and Lise Rakner

Chapter contents

Overview

The 1980s and early 1990s saw a wave of change embracing political liberalization and democratization in Latin America, Africa, and Asia. However, by the new millennium, many doubts and reservations began to surface, and attention turned to the quality of democracy, democratic erosion, and authoritarian persistence. We now understand that the fall of repressive authoritarian regimes does not necessarily procure lasting and consolidated democracy. This chapter elucidates the idea of democratization, summarizes recent trends, and compares understandings of democratic consolidation. Relations between democratization and development provide a central theme, not least because of worries that social and economic problems can undermine democratic progress. Finally, the chapter discusses how domestic and international factors interact to affect politics generally, and processes of democratization more specifically, inside developing countries.

Introduction

Democracy is an essentially contested concept. The long history of theorizing about its meaning provides few certainties about what 'democratization' means. Democratization refers to a process of change; most writers conceive of it as a journey without end. In a widely used metaphor, Huntington (1991) characterized the extension of democracy beginning around 1974 as the '**third wave of democracy**', the two earlier waves (1828–1926 and 1943–62) each being followed by a reverse wave. For some countries, the experience has been attempted re-democratization following earlier democratic failure(s). Examples include Argentina's return to elected civilian rule in 1983 and Uruguay, which had military-controlled civilian government from 1973 to 1985. Ghana, now resembling a stable liberal democracy, made successive earlier attempts to re-establish elected civilian government following military rule in 1966–69, 1972–79, and 1981–92.

Regime Transformation, Democracy, and Democratization

Democratization is not a unilinear movement from political authoritarianism to democracy. Simple dichotomizations of **regime** types are an oversimplification. Different kinds of authoritarian regime exist: monarchy, as in some Gulf states; personal dictatorships; military-bureaucratic rule; and *de jure* one-party states, as in Tanzania and Zambia before the 1990s (see Brooker 2009). Authoritarian and semi-authoritarian regimes can enjoy a measure of **legitimacy** in the eyes of citizens. They draw on such sources as religious beliefs, as in theocratic Iran and Saudi Arabia, nationalism, and anti-imperialism, as in China and Cuba for example. Also a conviction may exist that the status quo serves personal security and material well-being better than the likely political alternatives, which could mean social conflict and political instability. Invidious comparisons with political experiments elsewhere may strengthen the conviction. Turmoil in post-Saddam Iraq bolstered conservative instincts in neighbouring Jordan and Syria. Even so, a plausible claim—especially following the 'Arab Spring'—is that no competing political ideology to democracy currently shows itself capable of achieving comparable acceptance throughout the world, although some rivals still have strong roots in some places, including certain Islamist political beliefs. Ottaway (2009) argues that even socialism no longer presents a potent global ideological challenge, notwithstanding the persistence of other kinds of *political* challenge to democratization.

Similarly, authoritarian breakdown can produce a variety of possible outcomes: protracted civil war came to Angola and Mozambique following independence; 'warlordism' and the state's disintegration overtook Somalia in the 1990s; or the installation of a different kind of authoritarian regime or a diminished subtype such as **competitive authoritarianism**, in which elections are being held although formal democratic **institutions** are routinely violated (Levitsky and Way 2010). After the end of the third wave of democratization in the 1990s, almost 90 per cent of all countries hold regular and competitive elections. However, many elections are held in authoritarian conditions under which the incumbent manipulates the electoral process (see Box 14.1); Robert Mugabe's Zimbabwe provides an example. Regime transformation can lead to several distinct intermediate hybrid types, prefaced by labels such as 'competitive' and 'electoral', as well as 'proto-', 'semi-', 'quasi-', 'limited', 'partial', 'defective', 'low-intensity', and so on—all examples of what Collier and Levitsky (1997) called 'democracy with adjectives'. In large countries and/or federal systems, democratic unevenness can occur across provinces or municipalities.

BOX 14.1 THE GROWTH AND SURVIVAL OF HYBRID REGIMES

Although, after the end of the cold war and third wave of democratization, the language and institutions of democracy were adopted by most countries, the actions of many regimes remain undemocratic and, as a result, they are referred to as 'hybrid' regimes. Hybrid regimes combine democratic procedures with authoritarian practices (Diamond 2002; Howard and Roessler 2006). They are especially prevalent in the **developing world** and have multiplied over the past twenty years (Schedler 2006). Despite an initial assumption that hybridity was a step on the path to democracy, many such regimes—Venezuela for example—have shown a surprising longevity, and ability to survive and prosper. Many of the democratic challenges experienced in hybrid regimes are tied to manipulation of democratic institutions, such as elections, oversight committees, parliaments, and courts.

BOX 14.2 DAHL ON DEMOCRACY

Citizens must have unimpaired opportunities to formulate their preferences, signify them and have them weighted equally. This requires certain institutional guarantees: freedom to form and join organizations; freedom of expression; right to vote; eligibility for public office; right of leaders to compete for support; alternative sources of information; free and fair elections; institutions for making government policies depend on votes and other expressions of preference.

(Dahl 1971: 2–3)

Democracy (from the Greek for 'rule by the people') has been called an inherently debatable and changeable idea. Yet ideas resembling the model of polyarchical democracy (**polyarchy**) advanced by the American political scientist Robert Dahl in the 1970s (see Box 14.2) have dominated much of the democratization discourse, at the expense of deliberative and **emancipatory** or more radical social ideas. Polyarchy centres on two main pillars: public contestation and the right to participate. Liberal democracy, which is akin to polyarchy, is the most commonly cited yardstick for judging the progress of democratization, and is generally believed to avoid the **fallacy of electoralism**. Diamond (1996), a prominent contributor to the literature, usefully distinguished between 'liberal democracy', in which there is extensive provision for political and civic pluralism, as well as for individual and group freedoms, and mere '**electoral democracy**', in which civil freedoms are less prized and minority rights are insecure, although elections could be largely free and fair.

How do we know which countries are democracies? Many scholars consult Freedom House ratings of freedom. Freedom House is a US non-profit organization that conducts annual evaluations of political rights and civil liberties throughout the world. It defines democracy, at minimum, as a political system in which people choose their leaders freely from among competitors who are not chosen by the government. Freedom is the chance to act spontaneously in a variety of fields outside the control of government and other centres of potential domination. Democracies are judged either free or partly free, as measured along a seven-point scale (1–2.5 = free; 3–5 = partly free; 5.5–7 = not free). Although the

Freedom House methodology has attracted criticism, the ratings are widely used for depicting global trends in democratization, and making national and intertemporal comparisons. They are convenient and accessible; alternatives such as the Polity IV codings, the dichotomous democracy score of Alvarez et al. (1996), and the Ibrahim Index of African Governance are also instructive, but not flawless.

Trends

The data indicate that, following a dramatic initial increase in democracies during the 'third wave', the number of liberal democracies levelled off by the early 1990s. While some countries such as Vietnam were never caught up in the tide, several emerging democracies soon began to show signs of democratic backsliding or 'hollowing out'. Freedom House data suggest that, by 2012, many countries were seeing freedom erode even while remaining within the same category, such as 'partly free'. The year 2012 was the seventh consecutive in which there was an overall decline in freedom in the world ratings, leading some scholars to warn about the possibilities of a growing authoritarian backlash (Puddington 2013).

KEY POINTS

- The dichotomy of authoritarian and democratic regimes ignores the variety of non- or pre-democratic regime types and different possible outcomes of political transition.

- As an idea, democratization is beholden to the fact that the very meaning of democracy itself is contested.

- Democratization's progress in the developing world has been uneven and, since 2005, has seen a slight decline on average. There are, however, differences both within and between regions, with North Africa now showing some progress.

Democratization as Process

Conceptual distinctions between political liberalization, democratic transition, and democratic consolidation are commonplace, but there is no necessary or inevitable sequence of events. As a prelude to 'political

BOX 14.3 THE JASMINE REVOLUTION AND ARAB UPRISINGS

The protests in Tunisia in December 2010 (see Chapter 11) sparked Tunisia's 'Jasmine Revolution'. The authoritarian regime of President Zine El Abidine Ben Ali was ousted and the uprisings in Tunisia set off the Arab uprisings—a revolutionary wave of demonstrations and protests in the Arab world that gathered momentum in the spring of 2011. Popular uprisings in Egypt, Libya, Syria, Yemen, and other Arab countries forced regimes that have ruled for decades without showing any inclination towards democracy to make concessions or to resign. The outcomes so far vary significantly. The Arab uprisings highlight both the uncertainties and diversity with regards to the democratization effect of political openings. While the authoritarian regimes in Tunisia, Egypt, and Libya fell after struggles involving various degrees of force, bloody conflicts were, at time of writing in mid-2013, still raging in Syria (see the Online Resource Centre for a case study on the Syrian conflict), and to a lesser extent in Bahrain and Yemen. Elsewhere, in Morocco, Jordan, and partly in Algeria, political concessions were made by the (semi-)authoritarian regimes, but popular discontents continue. So far, rich Gulf states such as Saudi Arabia have been much less affected.

opening', authoritarian breakdown can happen in different ways—gradual or sudden, violent or peaceful—and may range from moderate to absolute. It can be brought about by pressure from below or by concessions from the incumbent autocrat. Most often, it is a combination of the two, as highlighted by recent events in the Arab uprisings (see Box 14.3). 'Political liberalization' usually refers to a top-down process: political leaders aim to maintain power for themselves, reluctant to accept that institutionalized uncertainty over electoral outcomes should be the determining principle of who governs (and the possibility of alternation in office that implies). Liberalization advances political freedoms less than some civil liberties. In contrast, democratization introduces arrangements for genuinely competitive elections. Liberalization can become stalled, rather than lead on to democratization; it can also go into reverse. Conversely, largely free elections might be introduced without first establishing the **rule of law**, full executive accountability, and the flourishing **civil society** that are so important to democracy (see Chapter 10)—or what has been called '**democratization backwards**'. This occasions what

Zakaria (1997) called 'illiberal democracy', citing Iran and President Fujimori's Peru as examples. Liberalization and democratic openings can also happen simultaneously, when authoritarian collapse is sudden and complete, as in **apartheid** South Africa. Rulers who at first allow some liberalization without intending to embrace democracy may lose control of the momentum, overtaken by demands for full democratic opening.

A related distinction made by some analysts is that democratization 'emerges from below', and involves political, although not necessarily violent, struggle, in contrast to some of the earliest 'third wave' cases of re-democratization in Latin America, in which **pacted transitions** were negotiated by the political elites. So there is not just one, but several different routes to democratic reform; evidence about which ones provide the most durable change is mixed. Pro-democratic alliances that bridge different elements within the ruling elite and include civil society activists offer an optimum combination.

Democratic consolidation

Just as there can be political transition without transition to democracy, so there can be democratic transition without democratic consolidation. Conversely, democratic decline need not lead to full-blown autocracy. But how do we recognize democratic consolidation? Answers range from equating consolidation with longevity to democratic 'deepening' or qualitative improvements in such indicators as the rule of law, minority rights, and **gender** issues (see Chapter 9). Schedler (1998) recommended restricting consolidation to 'negative' notions: avoiding democratic breakdown or democratic erosion. Put differently, democratic consolidation means an expectation of regime continuity—and nothing else. A minimal definition like this maximizes the number of developing countries qualifying for democratic consolidation. More demanding accounts that rest on democratic 'widening'—the incorporation of democratic principles in public *and* private spaces in economic and social arenas such as the family—impose criteria that few countries satisfy. Somewhere in between lie accounts that draw heavily on the people's political attitudes and perceptions, an example being an Afrobarometer study (2009) of popular views about the supply of democracy in twenty African countries between 1999 and

2008. This found unconsolidated hybrid systems and one consolidating autocracy (Lesotho), but no consolidated democracies (defined as a sustained balance between popular demand and perceived supply at levels of 70 per cent and more). Botswana came closest. While the literature's concern with what makes for 'good democracy' (or conversely, 'defective democracy') can look premature for countries whose regime is still in political transition (Egypt for example), some developing world democracies such as South Africa compare favourably with Organisation for Economic Co-operation and Development (OECD) democracies in terms of female political representation—surely an important indicator of democratic quality.

More significant for democratic consolidation than simple longevity may be the ability to withstand shocks—whether generated at home or abroad, either directly such as in an attempted military coup or indirectly through dramatic deterioration in the economic climate. India's democracy, for example, shows great resilience in the face of **terrorist** provocations. One hypothesis is that democratic deepening strengthens resilience. However, if a new democracy has yet to be put to the test, can we know whether it is consolidated and whether expectations of continuity are justified? And what counts as a sufficient test? For some countries in southern Africa and the Sahel, the growing food insecurity that could come from climate change may well threaten political stability and democracy's survival in the coming years.

A more easily applied notion of consolidation is the double turnover test suggested by Huntington (1991: 266–7). This requires that a party that took office after a democratic election should relinquish office after losing a comparable election without seeking to resist or overturn the result. This would exclude Botswana, rated by Freedom House as a fully fledged democracy, but where the Botswana Democratic Party has yet to lose an election since gaining independence (1966). A more persuasive view sees consolidation as being achieved once democracy has become the only game in town. This requires a permanent attitudinal shift, not just a temporary behavioural accommodation. On that basis, Venezuela, after 1958 one of Latin America's longest continuous democracies, failed the test in 2002, when the army briefly deposed the elected president, Hugo Chávez. Ironically, President Chávez's return and accumulation of power until his death on 5 March 2013 had many critics doubt Venezuela's democratic

credentials, notwithstanding the continuing electoral cycle (in 2012, Freedom House rated Venezuela only partly free, with a deteriorating trajectory). Chávez's oil-funded **populist** and left-leaning pretensions that lambasted US imperialism may help to explain his popularity, but successive institutional changes signalled reduced executive accountability.

Many scholars regard legitimacy as one of democracy's most distinguished properties. For Diamond (2002), democratic consolidation is legitimation. Legitimacy is like reinforcing glue: it helps democracy to survive shocks. Indeed, we could say that a democracy truly consolidates when it ceases to rely on 'performance legitimacy' (acceptance grounded on meeting society's material wants or needs), and achieves principled or 'intrinsic legitimacy' (grounded in respect for democracy's fundamental values, as well as adherence to the procedures that these inform—free and fair elections for instance). Intrinsic legitimacy shelters democracy against such failings as weak developmental performance, India's experience for many years following independence. In a settled democracy, discontent with the performance of government is exacted on the government, by peacefully removing it from office at the polls. So far, public support for many of Africa's new democracies appears to have weathered economic hardship (Bratton et al. 2004). But, in Latin America, one view is that neither populist demagoguery nor the military pose the main threat to democracy now, but rather a 'continuing mediocre performance—the inability of democratic governments to meet the most important needs and demands of their citizens' (Hakim 2003: 122). This becomes more potent when combined with popular perceptions of bad **governance** and high-level **corruption** (see Chapter 15).

In conclusion, the conceptual baggage of democratic transition and consolidation may be too rigid a framework for analysing what, in reality, are multifaceted, multidimensional, and multidirectional processes of political change. In practice, these may resemble variable geometry: some of democracy's ingredients could be moving in one direction (possibly at different speeds); others may move in the opposite direction (again at different speeds); yet others may be standing still. For example, a stable competitive party system may emerge even as civic activism decreases from the heights that successfully brought down an autocracy.

KEY POINTS

- A minority of developing countries are liberal democracies, although many more approximate to electoral democracies.

- Democratic consolidation has been defined in different ways, with implications for which developing countries qualify. The quality of democracy is as important as its longevity.

- The idea of democracy assessment offers a potentially powerful tool for both comparative analysis and self-assessment.

- We must not exaggerate democratization's usefulness as a lens through which to examine **politics** in the developing world; other political variables such as the strength of the state and quality of government are very important.

BOX 14.4 RUSTOW'S METHODOLOGICAL PROPOSITIONS

- The factors that keep a democracy stable may not be the ones that brought it into existence; explanations of democracy must distinguish between function and genesis.

- Not all causal links run from beliefs and attitudes to action; the flow can be in both directions.

- The genesis of democracy need not be geographically uniform; there may be many roads to democracy.

- The genesis of democracy need not be temporally uniform; different factors may become crucial during successive phases.

- Correlation is not the same as causation; a genetic theory must concentrate on the latter.

- Not all causal links run from social and economic to political factors; the flow can be in both directions.

- The genesis of democracy need not be socially uniform; even in the same place and time the attitudes that promote it may not be the same for all politicians and citizens.

Source: Rustow (1970: 346)

Explaining Democratization

Explaining how democratization occurs and why it takes particular forms generates considerable debate. Explanations of consolidation can be expected to diverge from democratic transition. Similarly, the reasons that illuminate stalled transition could differ from those that explain a democracy's collapse, which may connect to **state failure**, or authoritarian persistence through military or one-party regimes that do not shy away from oppression, as did Myanmar's until very recently.

One approach to explaining different experiences with democratization emphasizes the impact of historical, political, and other legacies, and **path dependence** (see Chapter 3). At its most elaborate, path dependence claims that the nature of the pre-existing regime and the mode used to change it influence the sequel, and ultimately can determine a new democracy's chances of survival. This confirms why it is important to distinguish between types of authoritarian and semi-authoritarian regime, and hybrid regimes too, in order to establish if there were any previous, failed attempts to democratize. Like much theorizing about democratization, path dependence provides more valuable insights for some countries than for others (see Box 14.4). Failure to incorporate women on anything like equal terms in the power structures that emerge following civil conflict, even when they contributed significantly to the freedom struggles, is not unusual, but can often be explained by in-depth historical and sociological analysis.

One of the most durable ideas is that national unity 'must precede all the other phases of democratization' (Rustow 1970: 351). By 'national unity', Rustow (1970: 351) meant that 'the vast majority of citizens . . . must have no doubt or mental reservation as to which political community they belong to'. Some developing countries, Iraq for example, appear to lack this simple condition. Indeed, transition to democracy may be cherished as a means to manage or resolve violent and endemic conflict between groups, but the route taken to introduce democracy can itself occasion increased (violent) domestic conflict. Minorities harbouring fears of a majority tyranny may be stirred to demand national self-determination for themselves. Sri Lanka's history has been one of both democracy and long-running civil war between the Sinhalese and Tamil separatists in the north. The Tamils were defeated militarily in May 2009, but the prospects for liberal democracy in Sri Lanka remain unclear. President Rajapaksa won the elections in 2010, which were deemed by others not free and fair owing to the abuse of state resources and harassment of the opposition by the ruling party. The emergency laws used during the military conflict expired in 2011, but other laws still give the Sri Lankan state extensive powers to detain and control the political opposition.

More broadly, the literature explaining democratization can be distinguished into accounts emphasizing structure and accounts that dwell on agency. The first investigates the 'conditions', and even preconditions, whereby democratic trends are facilitated or actively promoted, or frustrated; the second focuses on process, highlighting the role of actors. The impact of actors may be greater at key turning points, such as democratic transitions or their timing, than over the long haul. The important role played by institutions broadly defined (see Chapter 3) must be recognized too. All things considered, democratization is perhaps best understood as a complex interaction that links structural constraints and opportunities to institutions and the shaping of contingent choice (Karl 1990).

Socio-economic conditions

Lipset's seminal article on the social requisites of democracy first published in 1959 (revisited in 1994) presents a powerful theory of the positive relationship between socio-economic **modernization** and the persistence of stable democracy. 'Requisites' are not *pre*requisites or *pre*conditions: shared prosperity does not have to be established in advance. Democratic transition can occur amid poverty and economic backwardness. But the idea that material progress enhances the chances of extending democratic longevity continues to be strongly supported by developing world evidence. It is very relevant to democracy's future prospects in parts of the Middle East. In contrast, where economic misfortune persists, and especially where the burdens that women endure are compounded by the existence of many female-headed households, the drawbacks for democracy and its quality in poor societies are particularly evident.

More social scientists began to investigate seriously the possibility that development could be the dependent variable; they started treating democracy as the independent or 'causal' factor (see Box 14.5). The idea that certain sorts of freedoms, notably economic freedoms, are beneficial to wealth creation goes back a long way, to Adam Smith (1723–90). But for many years the view that developing countries face a **cruel choice** proved very persuasive. Either countries could do what was necessary to develop their economies, mainly by concentrating on saving and investing to expand the productive capital stock, or they could emulate the

> ### BOX 14.5 THREE VIEWS ON DEMOCRACY AND DEVELOPMENT
>
> - Democracy is too conservative a system of power. It has a bias towards consensus and accommodation that cannot promote radical change in the system of wealth that is essential to establishing developmental momentum, especially in late developing societies. A truly **developmental state** needs more insulation from society (and world market forces) than democracy allows (Leftwich 2002).
>
> - Developing countries differ from the West in that democratic contestants do not have to compromise with capitalists; instead, they capture power for their own enrichment. This **rent-seeking** behaviour by politicians destroys the chances of development (Khan 2002).
>
> - Powerlessness and poverty go together. Democratic models might empower the poor and serve development, such as by attacking the corruption that benefits only a few (Grugel 2002).
>
> *Source:* Adapted from Leftwich (2002)

political systems of the West. The former requires government to take unpopular decisions, most notably restraining current consumption. Authoritarian regimes that are well insulated from social pressures have an advantage. In contrast, the structure of political incentives posed by competitive party politics appears biased towards raising popular expectations about immediate consumption and public welfare spending. Politicians running for office will promise 'jam today', at the expense of doing what is needful for 'jam tomorrow'. In the long run, economic decline beckons—the experience of Argentina for much of the 1980s and 1990s, culminating in a spectacular financial crisis in December 2001.

The moral seemed to be that democracy is a luxury that poor countries can ill afford. Only after development has progressed beyond a certain threshold does sustainable democracy appear more viable. The term **'wealth theory of democracy'** captures the idea. The dramatic economic performance of East Asian 'tiger' economies such as Taiwan and South Korea (see Chapter 24) in the cold war era, followed by successful democratic transition, conforms to this general theory. Critics, however, point to examples of developing world democracies such as Mauritius (since independence in 1968) and Costa Rica (a democracy since 1899, with only brief interruptions in 1917 and 1948) that have a generally good record of economic and social development. East Asia's examples of an undeniably successful deployment of the authoritarian model, which are continued today by Vietnam and China (see Chapter 28), are perhaps the real exceptions. But some regimes in Sub-Saharan Africa, such as Ethiopia and Rwanda, are now following this authoritarian state-led growth model. Rising prosperity does not guarantee transition to democracy. In oil-rich **rentier states** (see Chapter 12), such as those in the Gulf, and Equatorial Guinea and Angola in Sub-Saharan Africa, the manipulation of rent-funded public spending by authoritarian regimes looks quite durable. But this 'resource curse' seems not to apply where democracy is already established, as Botswana, blessed with diamond revenues, as well as income from cattle-raising, illustrates.

The significance of development for democratization

There is much statistical evidence that democracies can survive even in the poorest nations especially *if* they can generate development with widely distributed benefits, while meeting certain other conditions (Przeworski et al. 1996). But what is it about modernization and development that is so significant for democratization? Is it primarily a matter of resources, or a case of transforming attitudes, values, and patterns of behaviour, or the changes in class structure that come with capitalist development in particular? Or does the connection have more to do with development's integration of society into global structures and norms? Different theories emerge from concentrating on different aspects.

- Democratic institutions are expensive, and demand high organizational commitment and public involvement that affluent, well-educated societies can more easily provide. Technological and economic progress improves the physical infrastructure of political communication.

- Social modernization erodes old values that inculcate deference to traditional authority and generates self-confidence; people come to see themselves more as citizens than subjects. This increases the constituencies for rational-legal authority. Pragmatic values sympathetic to the politics of compromise and consensus lying at the heart of the 'democratic way' supplant non-negotiable values such as exclusive ethnic loyalties

that divide society. Integration into the global economy also brings exposure to the liberal and democratic values already enjoyed elsewhere (the 'demonstration effect').

- There is a well-known aphorism: 'No bourgeoisie, no democracy.' Development breaks the exclusive power of feudal landlords. Capitalist development creates a plurality of potential centres of power and influence independent of the state. A property-owning middle class has a vested interest in checking the arbitrary use of executive power; it has the economic means and know-how to organize pressure for the redistribution of power. There is a caveat, however: **economic growth** can widen the economic inequalities that sustain inequalities of power. Middle-class elements will defend an illiberal or undemocratic regime if they believe it serves their interests, for instance by providing stability. Prosperous Singapore, judged only partly free by Freedom House, is an example.

- Industrialization and urbanization help an organized working class to mobilize mass support to demand rights for ordinary people. Thus Rueschemeyer et al. (1992) disavow that democracy is created solely by the bourgeoisie, emphasizing instead the progressive role of the working class, acting together with middle-class elements. The relevance of this insight grows as more developing countries in Asia and Latin America become prominent industrial manufacturers.

The ambivalent relationship of market economy and democratic polity

A frequent assumption is that the market constitutes a necessary, but not sufficient, condition of democracy: there have been authoritarian regimes with market economies (President Pinochet's Chile, for example), but no examples of non-market democracies. In reality, the relationship is ambivalent. As Beetham (1997) explained, there are some negative effects associated with the virtues of the market; even its positive points must be qualified (Box 14.6). This issue can be reformulated in terms of the effects on democracy's quality. Thus, for example, for Rueschemeyer (2004: 89): 'To deepen democracy in the direction of greater political equality requires systematic and strong policies promoting social and economic equality. The quality

BOX 14.6 POSITIVE AND NEGATIVE CONNECTIONS BETWEEN DEMOCRACY AND THE MARKET

Positive connections

- The more extensive the state, the more difficult it is to subject to public accountability or societal control.

- The more that is at stake in elections, the greater is the incentive for participants to compromise the process or reject the outcome.

- Market freedoms and political freedoms are mutually supportive: both require the rule of law and ensuring it for one ensures it for both.

- Sovereignty of consumer and voter both rest on the same anti-paternalist principle.

- Market economy is necessary for long-term economic growth, which assists durable democracy.

Negative connections

- Independence of the market from the state distances the economy from democratic control.

- Free market competition intensifies socio-economic inequalities, which produce political inequalities and compromise democratic institutions.

- Market dispositions undermine the integrity of the democratic public sphere: market choices prevail over political choices; the logic of private self-interest colonizes the public sphere.

Source: Beetham (1997)

of democracy, then, depends on social democracy, on long-sustained policies of social protection and solidarity.' This is especially pertinent to countries such as Brazil and South Africa, which historically are among the most unequal of all societies, and even to India, where a substantial middle class develops alongside a large number of extremely poor people.

Political culture

The perceived significance of **political culture** dates from Almond and Verba's *The Civic Culture: Political Attitudes and Democracy in Five Nations* (1965). 'Political culture' embodies the attitudes, beliefs, and values that underlie a political system. For Almond and Verba, 'civic culture' supports democracy. After years during which the concept came under fire, democratization

scholars now agree that sustainable democracy requires a special set of values such as tolerance, mutual respect, and a willingness to trust in fellow citizens (**social capital**), not just acquaintance with democracy's procedures. Observers pore over the public attitude surveys such as Latinobarometer and Afrobarometer (2009); analysts dissect discrepancies between support for democracy generally, and dissatisfaction with the particular institutions and political leadership specifically (Doorenspleet 2009).

The principal constituents of a democratic political culture and relations among them and their requisites are all contested. For instance, it was once thought that the Protestant ethic made famous by the German sociologist Max Weber is more favourable to democracy than are Roman Catholicism and Confucianism, yet evidence from Latin America and Asia now refutes this. An especially topical debate is over whether it is the Muslim world, not the Arab world, that offers relatively inhospitable terrain for democracy. Attitudes towards women's rights and female equality are quite critical here: the political advancement of women generally in Muslim countries seems especially difficult, but not impossible (see Chapter 9). Progress depends as much on overcoming culturally and historically embedded forms of disadvantage as on reforming the institutions of government, such as introducing female quotas in legislative representation (Cornwall and Goetz 2005).

If something like civic culture is essential to democracy, is it a prerequisite or can it be allowed to develop later, and if so, what can bring it about? This not only raises the idea of civic education, but also sparks other questions about whose culture is most important, particularly in democratization's early stages: the elite level or the mass? One argument is that the primary threat to new democracies comes from the people in power, especially 'old generation' politicians who assume democratic pretensions reluctantly and without conviction, Kenya's President arap Moi being an example. Bermeo's (2003) argument, drawing on Europe and the Americas in the 1960s and 1970s, is that small elite coalitions, not the ordinary people, bear major responsibility for democratic failure. This seems to be borne out by broader developing world experience, especially where high-level corruption and the jealous possession of power by a few (as in Zimbabwe), and great institutional or class-based privilege (as with Guatemala's military and wealthy elite) persist unchanged.

Institutional crafting

Chapter 3 introduced institutional perspectives on politics in developing countries. Clearly, institutional design can have significant consequences for the distribution of power generally, and democracy's quality and sustainability specifically. Formal organizational changes may barely affect the way in which things actually work, if inherited **informal institutions** or patterns of behaviour such as patron–clientelism are impervious to change and prevent the economic advance that might otherwise flow from formal democratic transition, as Lewis (2009) argues with respect to Africa. Moreover, as Chapter 13 suggests, tensions between crafting democracy's institutional architecture, on the one hand, and the larger imperatives of peace-building and state-(re)building or their requisites, on the other, can quickly surface in societies needing to escape internal violence. The recent troubled history of Iraq and Afghanistan are illustrative.

Two institutional concerns that have attracted special attention in new democracies are, first, the balance of power and mutual oversight among the executive, legislature, judiciary, and other constituents of a 'self-restraining state', and second, elections and party systems. A self-restraining state embraces multiple institutional mechanisms for making government accountable (see Schedler et al. 1999). Latin American experience implies that presidentialism is more likely to be unstable than parliamentary democracy when combined with vigorous multi-partyism, but others (see, for instance, Kapstein and Converse 2009) warn against simple correlations and re-emphasize that what matters most is the effectiveness of strong institutional constraints on executive power.

O'Donnell (1994) proposed the category '**delegative democracy**', much cited in a Latin American context. It rests on the premise that whoever wins election to the presidency behaves as if he or she is entitled to govern as he or she thinks fit—constrained only by the hard facts of existing power relations and constitutional limits, which he or she may try to remove or relax. O'Donnell distinguished between 'vertical accountability' and 'horizontal accountability'. The former makes government accountable to the ballot box and could even be extended to more direct forms of societal accountability, through the activities of civil society (see Chapters 10 and 11) and judicial power to enforce the rule of law—even, indeed especially,

against democratically elected governments. Horizontal accountability, more generally, tends to be weak in delegative democracies and virtually non-existent in illiberal non-democracies.

> **KEY POINTS**
>
> - Different dimensions and phases of democratic change require their own explanation.
>
> - Economic development may be one of the best guarantors of durable democracy, especially if the benefits are widely distributed, although the reasons are contested.
>
> - The relationship of market-based or capitalist development to democratization is ambivalent.
>
> - Institutional and cultural perspectives on democratization are complementary to more economistic explanations.

International Dimensions of Democratization

The end of the cold war and collapse of Soviet power help to explain the increase in agitation for political reform in the developing world from the late 1980s, although democracy's return to Latin America was already well advanced. Now, however, we see the growing economic and financial engagement of China (and India) with developing countries (see Chapters 28 and 29), and in international forums both China and Russia defend the principles of state sovereignty and non-interference in the internal politics of countries. These developments mean that growing attention should be paid to examining how domestic and international factors interact to affect politics inside developing countries.

External influences can work in many ways, such as by example, persuasion, and more direct involvement. The active engagement of prominent Western democracies in international democracy support is now well established, but the United Nations too has become a major actor as in arranging practical support to the staging, monitoring, and observing of elections, especially valuable in new states and post-conflict situations. The United Nations Development Programme (UNDP) is a substantial funder of projects in democratic governance. In 2005, the UN launched a Democracy Fund, with India as a major sponsor, investing in civil society initiatives especially.

According to the Inter-American Democratic Charter of 2001: 'The peoples of the Americas have a right to democracy and their governments have an obligation to promote and defend it.'

The Charter:

- reflects the political will and collective commitment of the Americas' democratic nations, and defines what the OAS member countries agree are democracy's essential elements;

- responds directly to a mandate from the region's heads of state and government, who stated at the 2001 Summit of the Americas that the hemisphere needed to enhance its ability to strengthen democracy and respond when it is under threat;

- establishes procedures for when democracy has been ruptured, as in a coup, or is seriously altered and at risk; and

- identifies how democracy can, and should, be strengthened and promoted in the hemisphere.

Under the terms of the Charter, OAS member states may seek advisory services or assistance from the OAS to strengthen their electoral institutions and processes.

Source: OAS Charter

The influence exerted by developments within a region should not be ignored either. Several regional organizations have undertaken to encourage—and defend from domestic attack—democratic institutions, values, and practices in their member states. In Latin America, the Organization of American States (OAS) sets out to uphold the Inter-American Democratic Charter (see Box 14.7). The OAS helped Venezuela to restore democracy after the 2002 military coup. And the African Union's (AU) New Partnership for Africa's Development (NEPAD) established the African Peer Review Mechanism (APRM), with a view to advancing both economic and democratic governance of member states. This has yet to prove that it can make much impact, especially in a very important state such as Nigeria.

The role of the West has been discussed widely with regard to international **democracy promotion** in the developing world. Levitsky and Way (2010) claim that the degree of linkage that a country has

to the Western world, as well as the degree of leverage that Western countries hold over the country is important for understanding democratization processes. They claim that leverage without linkage through interest and knowledge is not enough. In terms of how the West utilizes their leverage, two approaches stand out: one attaches democratic, **human rights**, and governance **conditionalities** to offers of development aid and other concessions such as trade concessions; the other provides technical, financial, material, and symbolic support to democracy projects and programmes involving political parties, civil society, legislatures, and other institutions—namely, **democracy assistance**. By and large, governance conditionalities have been found to be ineffective when faced by determined opposition. Democracy assistance, now worth over US$5 billion worldwide, has a mixed record. Although support to elections has long been considered insufficient, building durable capacity in civil society too encounters difficulties (see Chapter 10): external involvement can easily compromise the independence of **non-governmental organizations (NGOs)**, as has long been found in the world of international development cooperation. A growing number of authoritarian and semi-authoritarian governments obstruct external assistance to pro-democracy groups and human rights campaigners. Sudan, for example, denied access to assorted foreign humanitarian workers.

A third alternative, the coercive imposition of democracy, is largely discredited. In fact, the conflating of democracy promotion with **regime change** understood as ousting governments by force, as in Afghanistan (2001) and Iraq (2003), is believed to have harmed the cause of international democracy promotion. It gave authoritarian rulers a reason to stir nationalist sentiment and to utilize anti-imperialist rhetoric against even non-coercive democracy promotion from outside. The current mood is that the legitimacy and credibility of international involvement have lost ground: a conscious re-labelling of democracy 'promotion' as 'support' is one response. But this state of affairs is probably linked to the loss of momentum that worldwide democratization per se experienced before the 'Arab Spring', even if the connections between the state of democratization and the state of democracy promotion, and the direction of causality, are exceptionally difficult to establish (Burnell and Youngs 2009).

Democratization's significance for international development

The idea of a 'cruel choice' between democracy and development no longer carries much weight. Many authoritarian regimes—especially weak and fearful autocracies, and some rentier states— badly misman-aged their economic and financial affairs, not least because of inadequate accountability. In contrast, party-based democracy can provide a more responsi-ble approach where the parties judge that their elec-toral fortunes over the long run will be influenced by how they perform in office. Democratically elected governments can possess the legitimacy to take tough, but necessary, economic decisions. Accountability makes the gross abuse of public resources less likely: corruption surveys, such as those from Transparency International, find that democracies generally are less corrupt, although significant variations exist across democracies (see Chapter 15 for further discussions of the links between regime type and corruption). To the extent that the sustained poverty reduction required for **human development** will happen only if poor people are empowered, the equal political rights and civil liberties that liberal democracy should bestow look more conducive compared to concentrating power in very few hands. A virtuous circle is possible: society exerts political pressure for an expansion of so-cial and economic opportunities, which then improve the prospects for stable democracy.

That said, our understanding of democratization's benefits for economic growth and development urges caution, and remains very imperfect (Williams et al. 2009). In particular, democratization appears to offer no surety for a progressive redistribution of wealth and incomes (Bermeo 2009a). A shrewd insight claims that attempts to reduce economic inequality espe-cially by populist leaders utilizing populist measures may come to threaten democracy's durability more than does inequality itself, especially if the measures actually damage the economic prospects of the poor in the long run (Bermeo 2009a: 33). Furthermore, as the processes of democratization are not unilinear, it is important to remember that just because an authoritarian regime has broken down, there is no guarantee that a democratic regime will follow; as dis-cussed earlier in this chapter, a 'hybrid' regime might be the outcome. Hybrid regimes often perform less well than more stable authoritarian regimes in terms of both development and economic growth (see

Chapter 15). However, this does not mean that democ-ratization and democracy are hostile towards growth and development; rather, it highlights the importance of knowing what we are comparing.

Globalization, democracy, and democratization

Inconsistencies in the West's support for democracy worldwide and the spotlight placed on democratic development inside developing countries may both look like sideshows in the presence of increased **globalization** and its effects.

Globalization can be understood as processes whereby many social relations become relatively de-linked from territorial geography, so that human lives are increasingly played out in the world as a single place. Economic globalization is only a part, albeit a very important part. Globalization diminishes the value of conventional democratic models if it makes state-bound structures less tenable. This has been said to be particularly true in parts of the developing world in which weak or ineffective states and poor govern-ance abound. In a globalizing world, the human forces that most influence people's lives are increasingly transnational and supraterritorial; in contrast, democ-racy is historically rooted in, and remains confined to, the borders of the national state.

Powerful agencies of global governance are shrink-ing the space available for national political self-determination. These agencies are not themselves democratically accountable. They have the advantage of specialized technical knowledge of complex global issues that many small and poor countries can only envy. The science of, and international negotiations on, climate change are illustrative.

Second, the political space in which self-rule remains an option is increasingly penetrated by various non-accountable external actors, estab-lishing local branches or subsidiaries, and forming domestic linkages and alliances that capture the policy processes. Transnational business provides many ex-amples. Again, small and poor states with political and bureaucratic weaknesses are among the most vulner-able. International democracy assistance has been said to make the world a safer place for capitalism, which critics believe retards the genuine empowerment of ordinary people.

Third, economic globalization renders states, gov-ernments, and political regimes more vulnerable to weaknesses in the international financial system, and to gyrations in world trade and capital flows, such as those dating from the collapse of 'sub-prime' housing loans in the United States, in 2007–08. According to the International Monetary Fund (IMF) and World Bank's *Global Monitoring Report 2009: A Development Emergency* (2009), some of the poorest countries were hardest hit by these events precisely because they are now more connected with world trade than before. Yet, unlike Britain or the United States, they cannot borrow heavily abroad to fund unexpected financial deficits. For example, South Africa entered recession in mid-2009 for the first time since 1992. The longer-term effects on democratization, together with damage done to the very idea of democracy through association with crisis-prone, market-led financial and economic models, can only be speculated on. India's democracy weathered the storm and resumed impressive economic growth quickly.

There are also counter-arguments that suggest that globalization has some worthwhile benefits for democratization in the developing world. First, the international spread of human rights and other democratic values is itself a part of globalization. This process is furthered by the increased opportunities for social networking and popular mobilization that come from revolutions in information technology, international communications, and transportation—highly visible signs of globalization. Descriptions of the Arab Spring as 'Facebook revolutions' illustrate the point. Globalization forces political openness, which threatens authoritarian regimes. Some developing countries now help to disseminate values central to democracy, through membership of organizations such as the OAS, or subscribing to bodies such as the UN Democracy Fund and International IDEA, although their more active support for democracy abroad is limited by their animus against anything that might resemble colonial or neo-colonial interference.

Second, if globalization can be made a more powerful force for economic progress, and especially if development's benefits can be shared equitably, then the prospects for *stable* democracy increase.

Third, democracy is predicated on there being some measure of state capacity, if only to counter the many physical, economic, and other challenges. States that are made stronger by the resources generated by globalization and improved governmental effectiveness can then respond more generously to society's material demands. As meaningful choices become possible, voting for political leaders gains more point.

Fourth, there is the globalization of civil society, which offers vehicles for people to try to influence supranational institutions even where nationally rooted public structures such as parliaments and political parties look incapable. Global networks help local civic actors in their struggles to open up political space at home; local actors draw support from regional and global cooperation when endeavouring to stand up to powerful international institutions—civic coalitions from small island states calling for action on climate change being an example. Yet the democratic accountability of such civil society organizations is often questionable and the unequal capacity to shape agendas—often dominated by Northern-based civic actors—is a matter for concern. Nevertheless, an increased role for global civil society features prominently in reflections on how a more democratic international order could emerge (for example Scholte 2011).

KEY POINTS

- The jury is still out on the potency of democratization to bring about socio-economic conditions that could underpin new democracies.

- There are many different routes by which the international environment can influence democratization in developing countries. Only some are supportive, some are unintentional, and their effects vary among countries.

- From a democratization perspective, globalization invites us to think not only about how to make the political space more democratic, but also about how to restore power to the political.

- Globalization has undermined some authoritarian regimes, but could pose longer-term threats to democracy.

Conclusion

Key issues at the heart of contemporary debates about democratization in developing countries include: what is democratization? How much progress has there been? Is a reverse wave under way? What explains democratic developments, and the influences that determine forwards and backwards movements? What are democratization's relationships to development? And how important is the international environment? This chapter has argued that the meaning of democratization, like democracy itself, is contested.

And while most developing countries have undergone political change over the last two decades or so, the number of new consolidated or stable liberal democracies is modest. In many countries, competing analytical frameworks such as **nation-building** and state-building may offer greater insights into their current-day politics.

Attention has turned away from explaining democratic transition (transitology) and describing democratic consolidation (consolidology), and towards specifying a democracy's quality, identifying democracies' hazard rates (the probability that they will decay), and explaining authoritarian persistence. Regime typologies have been enriched by the proliferation of hybrid regimes. There is a chicken-and-egg conundrum of how to sort out democratization's apparent requisites from its possible consequences.

Thus it is important to establish how economic circumstances and external forces influence democratization's fortunes, and how much is determined by political choices (decisions and non-decisions) and institutional initiatives. In the long run, development appears to favour democracy, but there are reservations about the full effects of the market, and global capitalism in particular, especially where popular aspirations for **human security** and human development are thwarted. Although substantial economic inequality appears not to be a barrier to democratic durability, it can reduce democracy's quality.

A comprehensive assessment of the possibilities for democratic self-rule and progress to date must take account of the international relationships of developing countries. As will be discussed further in Chapter 15, 'governance', which is closely connected with matters intrinsic to the classification of types of political regime, embraces a larger set of political issues that have now come to the fore.

? QUESTIONS

1. How do concepts of democratic consolidation and democracy's quality help us to understand politics in developing countries?

2. Does the existence of poverty explain the persistence of hybrid regimes?

3. Are there democratic alternatives to Western-style liberal democracy in the developing world?

4. Should building democracy be a priority in conflict-prone societies in which the state is weak?

5. How do democratic developing countries achieve legitimacy?

6. What explains the recent Arab uprisings and will they lead to stable democracy?

7. Should globalization be seen as promoting or impeding democratization?

≋ FURTHER READING

Beetham, D., Bracking, S., Kearton, I., and Weir, S. (2002) *International IDEA Handbook on Democracy Assessment* (The Hague/London/New York: Kluwer Law International) A foundation guide to how to assess democratic achievement, which can be supplemented with more recent guidance from the International IDEA website.

Bermeo, N. (2009a) 'Does Electoral Democracy Boost Economic Equality?', *Journal of Democracy*, 20(4): 21–35 A compact survey of arguments and evidence pertaining to a relatively neglected, but important, issue.

Brooker, P. (2009) *Non-Democratic Regimes*, 2nd edn (Basingstoke: Palgrave Macmillan) The most accessible source on the state of the remaining non-democracies during and after the 'third wave' of democratization.

Burnell, P. and Youngs, R. (eds) (2009) *New Challenges to Democratization* (New York and Abingdon: Routledge) Assesses linkages between challenges to democratization and challenges to international democracy support.

Cornwall, A. and Goetz, A. M. (2005) 'Democratizing Democracy: Feminist Perspectives', *Democratization*, 12(5): 783–800 A critical review of the issues.

Rustow, D. A. (1970) 'Transitions to Democracy', *Comparative Politics*, 2(3): 337–63 A seminal article on how democratic transitions come about.

Waylen, G. (2007) *Engendering Transitions: Women's Mobilization, Institutions and Gender Outcomes* (Oxford: Oxford University Press) A valuable corrective to the gender-blind approach of much democratization literature.

Williams, G., Duncan, A., Landell-Mills, P., and Unsworth, S. (2009) 'Politics and Growth', *Development Policy Review*, 27(1): 5–31 Surveys current understanding of the connections between political change and economic growth.

Democratization (edited in the UK) and the *Journal of Democracy* (edited in the United States) are two well-known journals, the second publishing an annual digest of the latest Freedom House survey.

WEB LINKS

http://www.afrobarometer.org   The site for national public attitude surveys on democracy, markets, and civil society in Africa.

http://www.freedomhouse.org   The site of the US-based Freedom House, which includes access to its annual comparative measures of freedom.

http://www.idea.int   The site of the multi-member International Institute for Democracy and Electoral Assistance (Stockholm), and its democracy research and promotion activities.

http://www.latinobarometro.org   The site for national public attitude surveys in Latin America.

http://www.ned.org   The site of the Washington-based, non-governmental National Endowment for Democracy, which houses the International Forum for Democratic Studies.

http://www.nepad.org   The official site of the New Partnership for Africa's Development, including documents representing the African Union's formal commitment to democratization among member states.

http://www.oas.org   The site of the Organization of American States, containing statements on themes such as strengthening the democratic commitment and protecting human rights.

http://www.un.org/democracyfund/   Includes the UN Secretary-General's 'Guidance Note' applying to all UN democracy promotion activities.

http://www.undp.org/governance   Presents the UNDP's work on democratic governance.

For additional material and resources, please visit the Online Resource Centre at:
http://www.oxfordtextbooks.co.uk/orc/burnell4e/

15
Governance

Lise Rakner

Overview

Governance and debates about good governance became central to the development discourse in the early 1990s. Following from this, measurements of governance became key features of international foreign aid as part of aid conditionality. The good governance agenda and the indices developed to assess governance have been criticized for being too encompassing, and for not adequately separating between how power is obtained (the input side of politics) and how power is exercised once in office (the output side of politics). Building from the previous chapter on democracy, in this chapter, governance is understood as the *interplay* between the input and output sides of politics. Two key features of governance capacity are assessed: the ability of a regime to tax and to curb corruption. Presenting recent debates about the developmental state, the chapter concludes with a discussion about the links between democracy and governance.

Introduction

The last chapter discussed how power is obtained (democratization); in this chapter, the focus shifts to discuss the concept of **governance**—or, put differently, how power is exercised and checked once a government is in office. The chapter begins with a discussion of the concepts of governance and **good governance**. The starting point for the governance debate dates back to the 1990s and the observed deficit of **politics** in the development debates. However, while a consensus emerged arguing that governance is important in its own right, and as a means for achieving equitable and sustainable growth, what governance is, how it differs from democracy, how it relates to the development processes, and what elements of the governance agenda that are most conducive to development have remained issues of debate on which no clear conclusions have been reached. According to Payne (2005: 55), the word governance 'is probably second only to globalization in use and abuse'. Governance as it has evolved may be understood as a fairly elaborate theory about how power is exercised and checked, through mechanisms of accountability, whereas democracy is about how power is attained through electoral processes and participatory **institutions**. However, in much of the literature on good governance reforms, this distinction is blurred. The chapter argues that the proliferation of governance assessments developed by various international agencies and governments underlines the lack of consensus about the concept of governance.

According to Francis Fukuyama (2013: 1), the comparative literature especially related to developing nations has so far paid too little attention to the institutions that accumulate and use power. Building on a key concept of statehood discussed in Chapter 12, that of impartial bureaucracies, the chapter moves on to discuss key factors that define quality of government in the **developing world**. Two central features of good governance are discussed: the capacity of a government to extract taxes from its citizens; and the ability to control **corruption**. The chapter shows that states that 'earn' income by taxing their citizens will need to be accountable to their citizens and need to develop capable state bureaucracies, whereas a state that derives its revenue from rents such as natural resources and aid may not be required to answer to its citizens to the same extent, or to build the same administrative capabilities. Similarly, the ability of the government to curb corruption is considered a key feature of quality of governance. In the last section, the chapter discusses whether quality of governance, understood as what politicians do when in office, can be separated from how policymakers obtain power, and is related to the issue of democracy.

Governance and Good Governance

Governance has an economic dimension that usually refers to property rights, transparency of economic transactions, freedom of information, and public sector management. The political dimension of governance is usually taken to mean government **legitimacy**, **human rights**, rule of law, and government accountability (Grindle 2010: 2). A common denominator in most understandings of governance is a focus on institutions (formal and informal) and 'rules of the game' (Hyden et al. 2004). *Good* governance, then, involves positive features within these institutions, often drawn from Western institutions.

The majority of empirical analyses looking at links between government and development find that improved governance has a significant and positive impact. The finding that good governance is associated with development success has been given as a rationale for promoting a wide range of reforms from public financial management, property rights, and political **regimes**, to public administration. There are, however, still many unanswered questions about which types of institution positively influence development and therefore should be supported. Both China and Vietnam have a number of 'non-conducive' governance features linked to authoritarian governments, high levels of corruption, and insecure property rights; yet both states have achieved **economic growth** linked to reduced levels of poverty and improved public services in areas of education and health.

Governance and aid conditionality

Disappointing results for economic **conditionality** in the 1980s prompted the World Bank to identify poor governance in developing countries and weak governance, rather than simply too much government, as major problems. In the 1990s, the Bretton Woods institutions wove good governance into the fabric of conditionality and then into criteria for **aid selectivity**. At the outset, the World Bank, in its idea of good governance, focused on such qualities as transparency, fiscal accountability, and sound management of the public sector—in short, economic governance. Other actors, including foreign ministries in the West and bilateral aid agencies, quickly expanded the agenda towards political governance, bringing in issues of democracy and human rights in general, and political pluralism and free and fair elections specifically. However, even in the narrower definitions employed by the World Bank, the concept of governance came to include issues to do with the distribution of power in society, and between state and society, or what we refer to here as the 'input' side of politics. The World Bank embraced the rule of law, a capable judiciary, and freedom from corruption among its governance objectives, and has devoted considerable support to help to build national capacities in these areas.

Governance indicators

The study *Governance Matters* of Kaufmann et al. (2009) (see Box 15.1) proceeds from a definition of governance as the traditions and institutions that determine how authority is exercised in a country. This includes the process by which governments are selected, held accountable, monitored, and replaced, as well as the capacity to formulate and implement sound policies effectively, and the respect of citizens and the state for the institutions that govern economic and social interactions among them. Now covering 212 countries and territories, and compiled from thirty-five data

sources and thirty-three different organizations, the most recent findings are displayed in *Governance Matters VIII: Governance Indicators for 1996–2008* (Kaufmann et al. 2009). The data fall into six dimensions: voice and accountability; political stability and absence of violence/**terrorism**; government effectiveness; regulatory quality; rule of law; and control of corruption. The research overall confirms that good governance is correlated with better development, and claims to find a large causal effect running from improved governance to better development outcomes and not the other way around. The findings also support beliefs that good governance significantly enhances the effectiveness of development assistance. While useful for cross-country and over-time comparisons, the methodology cannot say much about the specific institutional failures responsible for poor governance in particular settings, to which in-depth studies of individual countries must add more light.

The *Governance Matters* project is not the *only* source of information and analysis. The United Nations Development Programme (UNDP) Governance Centre in Oslo has, since 2008, carried out a Global Programme on Capacity Development for Democratic Governance Assessments and Measurements. This seeks to build on its existing Governance Indicators project—a project that set out to be more sensitive to **human development**, and to raise the profile of pro-poor and **gender**-sensitive indicators in particular, in a more country-contextualized way than other leading studies of governance. From a UNDP perspective, governance is the exercise of

---

BOX 15.1 *GOVERNANCE MATTERS VIII*: SOME LEADING FINDINGS

- Good governance can be found at all income levels. Developing countries such as Chile, Botswana, Uruguay, Mauritius, and Costa Rica score higher on certain dimensions such as government effectiveness, rule of law, and control of corruption than do countries such as Greece or Italy.

- Since 1998, countries showing substantial improvements have included: Ghana, Indonesia, Liberia, and Peru for voice and accountability; Rwanda, Algeria, Angola, and Sierra Leone for political stability and absence of violence/terrorism; and South Korea, Rwanda, and Ethiopia for government effectiveness. Regulatory quality in Iraq has improved, as has control of corruption in Tanzania.

- Since 1998, Zimbabwe and Thailand deteriorated in terms of voice and accountability, and Zimbabwe declined in respect of most other governance dimensions as well. Government effectiveness and regulatory quality both deteriorated in Bolivia, as has rule of law in Venezuela, and voice and accountability in Iran.

- Change does not always proceed in parallel across dimensions. Nigeria has, for example, recorded improvement in voice and accountability, but worsening of political stability and violence.

- The quality of governance globally has not improved much over the past decade.

Source: Kaufmann et al. (2009).

economic, political, and administrative authority to manage a country's affairs at all levels. Programmes funded by the UNDP for strengthening institutions of democratic accountability such as parliaments and judiciaries, along with support for decentralization and e-governance, are present in around 130 countries. They help with developing nationally owned processes for assessing and monitoring democratic governance, which is considered a priority. This last ambition travels in the direction of recent research on a World Governance Assessment first trialled by Hyden et al. (2004), for whom political notions of governance must be ascribed at least as much importance as economic notions.

Governance for Hyden et al. (2004) refers to the formation and stewardship of the informal and formal rules that regulate the public realm, the arena in which the state, and not simply economic and societal actors, interact to make decisions. They see governance more as a matter of behavioural disposition than of technical capacities. Crucially, the subjective opinions of 'local stakeholders' in the developing countries—experts from the government, civil servants, legislators, lawyers, representatives of media, and **civil society** organizations including trade unions, religious groups, business people, and academics—must be consulted over defining what governance means and how it is measured. In fact, increasing the relevance of governance assessments to national stakeholders in recipient countries is now emerging as a theme in international development cooperation, in the wake of the Paris Declaration on Aid Effectiveness of 2005, which brought together views from both sides of the international aid relationship and gave emphasis to, among other things, the principle of ownership. In the meantime, some of the more notable findings reported from the Hyden et al. (2004) study of sixteen countries support the theory that successful democratization enhances the quality of governance, while also showing that not every country with a high governance score is very democratic. Just as significant, increase in autocracy was found not to bring improvement in governance quality.

Other research projects that collect data on bureaucratic quality include the Bertelsmann Transformation Index and the Varieties of Democracy project. The Quality of Government Institute has developed a set of measures of quality of governance for 193 countries worldwide, based on expert surveys focusing on the level of a state's impartiality.

Alternative understandings of good governance

The foregoing discussion demonstrates that for, the Bretton Woods institutions, as well as for foreign ministries providing development assistance, good governance has become a concept that encompasses a large number of qualitative assessments, relating both to how power is obtained and what leaders do when in power. As can be seen with the concept of Hyden et al. (2004), governance is very broad and represents an ideal of what a democratically elected government should do when in power. Owing to the vastness of the concept of governance and all of the dimensions to which it refers, arguably it is difficult—if not impossible—for developing countries to implement all of the changes that the good governance agenda prescribes. Therefore Grindle (2007), among others, has argued that it is necessary to distinguish the governance needs of poor and middle-income developing countries. Grindle argues for degrees of good governance or 'good-enough governance', finding that the list of required institutions for development is simply too costly to sustain for the poorest developing nations. According to Grindle, good-enough governance implies paying attention to the particular context of a developing state before assigning a list of priorities. She presents a hierarchy of governance priorities, which gives an indication as to what should be a priority given the particular context of a country. For example, in a **collapsed state**, the best form of governance may be to ensure personal safety and conflict resolution first, ignoring accountability and responsiveness for the time being (Grindle 2007).

In a similar manner, Rothstein and Teorell (2008) criticize many definitions of good governance in that they are too encompassing. According to the two authors, the wide definitions blend *access* to power and *exercise* of power—or the input and output sides of politics. As an alternative, they define governance as the government's ability to enforce rules and to deliver services, regardless of whether that government is democratic or not. For Rothstein and Teorell (2008: 170), quality of government is when government acts impartially, which is defined as arising when, 'implementing laws and policies, government officials [do] not take into consideration anything about the citizen/case that is not beforehand stipulated in the policy or the law'. This firmly puts the output side of politics at the forefront. But their 'quality of government' concept still relates to how state (institutions) and society interact. When we now turn to discuss two key determinants of good governance, the ability to extract revenue and to control corruption, the discussion will show that, in practice, it is difficult to separate the input and output sides of politics.

KEY POINTS

- The governance debate was initiated in the late 1980s, linked to the observed deficit of politics in the development debates.

- Over the past decade, aid donor interest in governance has become progressively more intense and focused. In relation to this, donors are also increasing efforts into producing qualitative and quantitative governance assessments.

- While there is general agreement that governance is important for achieving equitable and sustainable growth, what governance is and which elements of the governance agenda that are most conducive to development remain debated.

- Global trends in governance overall show no great improvement, but evidence from individual countries shows that it is possible to make significant improvements over fairly short periods.

- Some authors contend that good governance is best understood as the degree to which government exercises power in an impartial manner.

Measuring Governance as Capacity: The Role of Taxation

The question that is still not adequately answered is what causes good governance and quality of government? In the governance literature, one of the most central elements signalling and influencing quality of government is its ability to generate revenue—or how a state taxes its citizens. Margaret Levi (1988: 1), emphasizing the centrality of taxation to state-building and state capacity, notes that 'the history of state revenue production is the history of the evolution of the state'. The history of modern state formation is closely tied to revenue creation and tax (see Chapter 12). American revolutionaries in the eighteenth century rallied around the slogan 'No taxation

without representation', and history repeatedly shows how, when rulers have been in need of increasing taxes, they have agreed to constraints making them more accountable to their citizens (Tilly 1990). The need for the elite to raise revenues through taxes has often been put forward as a historically important reason for the development from authoritarianism to democracy, because states that do not need to generate taxes from its citizens are postulated to be more autonomous from the people and thus less likely to democratize (see Box 15.2). Moore (2007) argues that if governments do not depend on taxes to finance public services and state operations, they have little incentive to build political and organizational capacity to negotiate and collect revenue, and spend it, effectively. The likely outcome of such a situation is arbitrary and poor governance.

Taxation influences government capacity in two ways. First of all, collecting taxes demands governance capacity regardless of how taxes are collected and what forms of revenue are extracted. This gives governments incentives to develop such administrative capabilities. Second, taxation is considered central to the quality of governance as a key instrument for influencing economic and social redistribution through progressive taxation. Simply put, lacking the ability to raise revenues effectively, states are not able to provide security and basic services or foster economic development (Bräutigam et al. 2008; Fukuyama 2013).

Taxation in the developing world

Tax extraction can be measured both by the percentage of taxes to gross national product (GNP), as well as by the nature of taxation—in other words, whether it is based on income or wealth, or more indirect taxation. Figure 15.1, focusing on the relationship between taxation and development as indicated by countries' Human Development Index (HDI) and total tax revenue as a percentage of gross domestic product (GDP), suggests that the ability to extract revenue is positively associated with higher development. The countries in the upper right-hand corner of the scatter plot diagram are the most developed and show substantially higher levels of tax extraction than the lesser developed countries. This suggests a strong relationship between tax extraction and development. Table 15.1 shows that the ten least-developed countries exhibit substantially lower levels of tax extraction (with an

BOX 15.2 COMPARING TAXATION AND ACCOUNTABILITY IN ETHIOPIA, GHANA, AND KENYA

Challenging a strict separation between the input and output sides of politics in relation to good governance, there are strong mechanisms that link taxation and pressures for increased responsiveness and accountability. This can happen through direct tax bargaining with citizens, leading to particular instances of political reform. Additionally, tax resistance by citizens may create indirect pressures for change and reform. Finally, taxation may become a catalyst for strengthening civil society organizations. The political context influences which of these mechanisms becomes most prevalent.

In Ghana, an open political system, numerous instances of direct tax bargaining have taken place and the willingness to pay taxes seems highly related to the popularity of governments. When unpopular governments have attempted to increase revenue, citizens have undermined these measures by tax evasion or labour unrest, forcing changes (such as in 1999–2000, when increasing financial problems led to defeat in the presidential elections). Tax bargaining also directly increases government responsiveness, which can be seen when, during 1999 and 2003, increases in VAT rates caused public protests, to which governments responded with promises to commit these tax revenues to specific popular social reforms.

Kenya, a less institutionalized political system, has experienced few such direct instances of tax bargaining. More indirect resistance to taxation by unpopular governments has, however, occurred more frequently. Unpopular governments were increasingly made fiscally weak by the explicit tax evasion of businesses linked to the opposition. This was seen in 2002 when the Moi government was ousted, and a more liberal and responsive government was put in place. Furthermore, businesses, whose profit was hurt by post-election violence in 2007–08, threatened to withhold tax revenues if the government did not find a solution to the problem.

The autocratic shape of modern Ethiopia has given citizens little bearing on revenue-raising. One example of tax bargaining exists nevertheless. In 2005, the government tried to introduce a tax on businesses, which provoked wide public outcry. In response, the government set up a commission to evaluate the fairness of the tax and, after the election, the government reduced taxes, increased participation in the assessment, and created new public forums for consultation about tax collection and expenditure.

Source: IDS (2010)

---

average of 13.5 per cent) than the ten most-developed countries (which average 33.2 per cent of tax revenue as a percentage of GDP). As Figure 15.1 shows, most developing countries struggle to collect taxes effectively and few developing countries have succeeded in creating a tax system with high levels of capacity. The tax systems of most developing countries are characterized by regressive and distortive taxation (Bräutigam et al. 2008). Moreover, tax administration is weak, often characterized by extensive evasion and corruption, and often disregards the informal sector. This is considered detrimental for governance, because states lose out on substantial revenue, tax compliance within the formal sector may decrease, and people in the informal sector remain disengaged from an unresponsive state (Joshi and Ayee 2008: 187–8).

Considering the importance of taxation for development, it is perhaps surprising that taxation has played a rather limited role in terms of foreign development aid and aid conditionality. According to Bräutigam et al. (2008: 2), the Bretton Woods institutions have tended to focus more on cutting expenditure than on raising revenue. Since the 1990s, however,

especially the International Monetary Fund (IMF), but also regional organizations and bilateral governments, have started to emphasize tax reform, and in particular the need to reform tax administration as a means for developing countries to increase revenue. From here, it follows that the ideas that shape tax reforms in developing countries today are heavily influenced by the norms of the Bretton Woods institutions. This suggests a significant *contrast* regarding revenue collection and state-building between developed and developing nations: the role of external actors, such as the IMF, has no counterpart in the historical models of how taxation has shaped governance capacity (Mahon 2004: 25). Fjeldstad and Moore (2008) find that the donor-initiated tax reforms intended to enhance governance capacity have done little for the developing nations. They argue that revenues lost to the global drive for trade liberalization for most developing countries have not been restored through other areas of tax reform such as value added tax (VAT).

Fjeldstad and Moore (2008) go on to argue that a taxation challenge that has received too little attention from political actors, donors, and civil society in

Table 15.1 Tax revenue as a percentage of GDP for the least- and most-developed countries

Ten least-developed countries 2011[1]	HDI score 2013[1]	Tax revenue as percentage of GDP 2013[2]	Ten most-developed countries 2013[1]	HDI score 2013[1]	Tax revenue as percentage of GDP 2013[2]
Niger	0.304	13.3	Norway	0.955	42.8
DRC	0.304	18.9	Australia	0.938	26
Mozambique	0.327	18.1	United States	0.937	24.8
Chad	0.340	5.2	Netherlands	0.921	38.2
Burkina Faso	0.343	7.8	Germany	0.920	36.3
Mali	0.344	14.6	New Zealand	0.919	31.3
Eritrea	0.351	*	Ireland	0.916	28
CAR	0.352	9.3	Sweden	0.916	45.8
Guinea	0.355	14.7	Switzerland	0.913	29.8
Burundi	0.355	20.1	Japan	0.912	28.8

* No data could be provided for Eritrea

Note: CAR = Central African Republic; DRC = Democratic Republic of Congo

Sources: [1]Human Development Report (UNDP 2013); [2] Heritage Foundation (2013)

developing countries is that of widening the tax base. This is particularly relevant in terms of incorporating the informal sector into the tax net. Developing nations often display low tax levels under which large sectors of the **informal economy** escape the tax net. Illustrating this, in 2006, just over 80 per cent of the Zambian workforce was engaged in some form of economic activity in the informal sector. The tax base in Zambia is thus currently focused on a relatively few wealthy businesses, as well as public employees, who contribute with the lion's share of all direct taxes. This is negative because the state is not able to generate enough revenues to provide public services such as schools, roads, and health facilities. Furthermore, the fact that only a fraction of the population is included in the tax net may suggest that the government is only to a limited extent held accountable by Zambians for the spending of revenue.

But a given level of taxation does not necessarily translate into the efficient use of tax revenues. In developing countries depending on aid transfers, revenues can be wasted on poor administration or corruption. As a result, tax reform has been considered as a governance reform, in particular by the Bretton Woods institutions. Tax reforms have often

focused on simplifying taxes and repealing those that are hard to collect and easy to hide. Perhaps the most prominent reform of tax administration has been the creation of semi-autonomous revenue authorities, independent from finance ministries, and manned by highly professional and well-paid professionals. According to Fjeldstad and Moore (2008: 239), the more than thirty autonomous revenue authorities that have emerged in the last two decades in the developing world have helped to **privatize** tax collection. The problem with the autonomous revenue authorities in some developing countries is that autonomy in practice has hidden the fact that the revenue authorities in fact are answerable only to one person: the president. The Uganda Revenue Authority (URA), for example, was initially very successful in terms of collecting more revenue more efficiently. But after a period the performance stalled and observers link this to the fact that the URA in practice was directly accountable to President Museveni (Therkildsen 2004). In contrast, the South African Revenue Services (SARS), which has succeeded in increasing the level of taxation, has tended to work very closely with all relevant state agencies, including the Treasury (Fjeldstad and Moore 2008: 253).

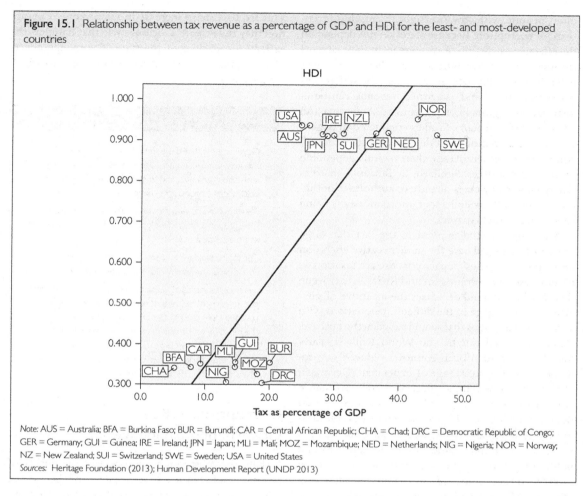

Figure 15.1 Relationship between tax revenue as a percentage of GDP and HDI for the least- and most-developed countries

Note: AUS = Australia; BFA = Burkina Faso; BUR = Burundi; CAR = Central African Republic; CHA = Chad; DRC = Democratic Republic of Congo; GER = Germany; GUI = Guinea; IRE = Ireland; JPN = Japan; MLI = Mali; MOZ = Mozambique; NED = Netherlands; NIG = Nigeria; NOR = Norway; NZ = New Zealand; SUI = Switzerland; SWE = Sweden; USA = United States

Sources: Heritage Foundation (2013); Human Development Report (UNDP 2013)

The difference between earned and unearned revenue

In Chapter 12, we saw that some developing states are described as '**rentier states**' because major parts of state revenues are derived from taxes on companies involved in the extraction of some valuable natural resource, such as oil, diamonds, or copper. However, contrary to taxes extracted from individuals and businesses (indirect and direct), rents on natural resources are considered to undermine governance and state capacity, and even to fuel intense conflict between groups determined to control the trade or the state in order to capture the rents. This further weakens, and sometimes simply destroys, the central power and authority of an already weak **post-colonial state**. Moore (2011: 1759) argues that 'political authorities which enjoy revenue that does not have to be "earned"

politically are more likely to abuse their power and govern badly'. Referring to the 'resource curse', it is hypothesized that governments that do not depend on levying taxes on the population, but which get the bulk of their revenue from oil or other natural resources are often unresponsive and unaccountable to their people (Ross 1999). The argument is that, as oil revenue accrues to a small number of big companies and central states, states become independent of citizen-taxpayers and thus in effect become unresponsive to them. There are therefore few incentives to promote broad economic responsiveness outside of the oil sector. Instead, the revenues can be used to buy off opposition and to fund repressive internal security. Oil may also attract foreign military and political support that can disrupt internal dynamics. Furthermore, revenues from natural resources are often opaque with low oversight, increasing incentives for corruption. Because states do not depend on the effective extraction of revenue from their citizens through an effective bureaucracy, they have fewer incentives to build such institutions. The differences between 'earned' and 'unearned' revenue can be illustrated by regional comparisons of Argentina and Tanzania (Moore 2007). Studies conducted in Argentina show that regions that depend on citizens for income are more democratic than regions depending on natural resources. Similarly, in Tanzania, in areas where people pay taxes directly to authorities not indirectly to local tax collectors, more money is being spent directly on taxpayers.

A number of studies point to the fact that large levels of foreign aid have the same negative effects on developing countries' capacity to extract taxation as natural resources. Bräutigam and Knack (2004) argue that development aid decreases the incentive of governments to engage in the difficult negotiations with various social groups that would broaden the tax base. Research carried out by the World Bank similarly found that aid to African countries reduced government revenue by an average of 10 per cent (Devarajan et al. 1999). However, the effect of aid on governance is not clear. According to Moore (2011: 1771), we do not have conclusive evidence that aid makes countries less interested in increasing tax revenues, but aid does seem to weaken and fragment local administrative and political institutions—a tendency fuelled by the large increase in the number of aid channels, leading to a 'dispersal of the attentions, energies and resources of recipient governments'.

When states do not collect taxes from their citizens, these citizens may have few incentives to control the government and their spending. Kjaer (2004) notes that there is considerable controversy over the extent to which the payment of taxes in developing countries can be seen as a 'quid pro quo' for better services. Public services that are deemed faulty, as in the case of corruption, can serve as an excuse for underpayment, which again leads to worse services. In order to break such vicious governance cycles, proper incentives must be put into place, including incentives for public servants to work more effectively and for punishing underpayment. One such example was the creation of National Revenue Service (NRS) in Ghana during the 1980s. The most corrupt were dismissed, pay was increased, and a performance bonus linked to the total amount of revenue collected was introduced.

This led to a sharp increase in tax revenue. Corruption may thus create a vicious cycle that hampers the extractive capacities of the state. The malign effects of corruption on governance are the topic to which we turn next.

KEY POINTS

- Governments that depend on taxes to finance public services have clear incentives to build capacity to negotiate and collect revenue, and to spend it effectively, which *may* in turn lead to good governance.

- Taxation is positively associated with development, measured by human development indices and tax revenue as a percentage of GDP.

- The main challenge in many developing nations is to find cost-efficient ways in which to tax the informal sector.

- It is necessary to distinguish between revenue as 'earned' and 'unearned'. States that receive the bulk of their revenue from natural resources or aid do not depend on the effective extraction of revenue from their citizens through an effective bureaucracy and have fewer incentives to build efficient bureaucracies.

Corruption: A Key Governance Challenge

Perhaps the most important aspect of the quality of government is absence of corruption and, because of this, low levels of corruption is often used as a proxy for good governance (Rothstein 2011). Rose-Ackerman (2004: 1) defines corruption as the 'misuse of public power for private or political gain'. Corruption can be explicitly illegal, as in the case of bribing officials, or it can be on the border between legal and illegal. Rose-Ackerman distinguishes between two different kinds of corruption: one relates to administrative corruption and concerns, for example, using bribery and favouritism to lower taxes, to escape some form of regulation, or to win low-level procurement contracts; the other refers to a situation in which the state itself can be characterized as serving the interests of small segments of business or politicians—a situation in which the state is captured. Moreover, one can distinguish between 'grand corruption', relating to large-scale projects that generate massive rents, and 'petty corruption', such as bribing a police officer to escape a fine or a health worker to get faster treatment (see Box 15.3).

BOX 15.3 CORRUPTION IN SOUTH SUDAN

South Sudan became independent on 9 July 2011, emerging from decades of civil war. The country faces myriad governance and poverty challenges, as well as continued hostilities with Sudan. According to a recent report by the U4 Anti-Corruption Resource Center (Mores 2013), citizens commonly face demands for bribes in their dealings with government institutions to access basic public services. The latest Transparency International Global Corruption Barometer found that, among those respondents who have had contact with nine **public institutions** (police, education, judiciary, medical services, land services, tax revenue, customs, registry and permit), 66 per cent reported paying bribes in the past twelve months. The citizens' experience with corruption is especially high in dealing with the police (where 47 per cent of those in contact with the police reported paying bribes), registry and permit services (46 per cent), the judiciary (43 per cent), and land services (41 per cent). Southern Sudanese overwhelmingly reported that they paid bribes in order 'to avoid a problem with the authorities' (40 per cent) or 'to speed things up' (33 per cent).

Source: Transparency International (2011)

High levels of corruption are associated with more unequal distribution of income. And while there is a general consensus among economists and policy analysts that corruption is a universal problem, the worst effects are felt in developing nations. Just as high levels of taxation are positively associated with development, corruption appears negatively associated with development, when measured by the Human Development Index (see Figure 15.2 and Table 15.2). The costs of corruption for developing countries were highlighted by the UN Secretary-General in his 2009 statement to the International Anti-Corruption Day:

66 When public money is stolen for private gain, it means fewer resources to build schools, hospitals, roads and water treatment facilities. When foreign aid is diverted into private bank accounts, major infrastructure projects come to a halt. Corruption enables fake or substandard medicines to be dumped on the market, and hazardous waste to be dumped in landfill sites and in oceans. The vulnerable suffer first and worst. 99

(Ki-moon 2009)

Corruption affects welfare and growth in developing countries by means of a range of mechanisms. Perceptions of, as well as experience with, corruption discourage business, investments, and growth. Foreign investment seems to be lower in corrupt societies and corruption distorts firms' production decisions, such as where to produce and where to purchase supplies. Corruption also increases budgetary costs of **public goods** and services, because informal payments—that is, 'kickbacks'—bring up costs. Owing to corruption, public development projects become more costly and affect development in a negative way. As discussed earlier, weak and corrupt tax collection agencies and tax evasion also affect revenue generation. Moreover, as a result of leaks out of the system, service delivery and **human capital** are negatively affected by corruption. In Indonesia, for example, at least 18 per cent of rice distributed to the poor through a social safety net programme was lost as a result of corruption (Olken 2006: 856).

An argument in the development literature nevertheless holds that, in the context of cumbersome and pervasive regulations, corruption may actually *foster* development and growth (Bardhan 1997: 1322). Political scientist Samuel Huntington (1968: 386) argued that: 'In terms of economic growth, the only thing worse than a society with rigid over-centralized dishonest bureaucracy, is a society with rigid, over-centralized, honest bureaucracy.' However, improved empirical data and information about corruption and its effects on economic growth has largely refuted these claims, and there is increasing evidence that the economic costs of corruption are substantial. As argued by Gray and Kaufmann (1998: 8): 'Instead of corruption being the "grease" that lubricates the "squeaky wheels" of a rigid administration, it fuels the growth of excessive and discretionary regulations.' The costs of corruption are not only related to money, but can also prove detrimental for public trust. Corruption threatens democracy by corroding rule of law, democratic institutions, and public trust in leaders. For the poor, women, and minorities, corruption means even less access to jobs, justice, or fair and equal opportunity. According to Rothstein (2011), corruption may adversely affect democratic legitimacy, and install lower levels of interpersonal trust and belief in the political system among citizens, which may have wider governance consequences. High levels of corruption may also increase the likelihood of protracted conflict (see Chapter 13). When public trust plummets,

Figure 15.2 Relationship between corruption and development in the ten least and ten most corrupt countries

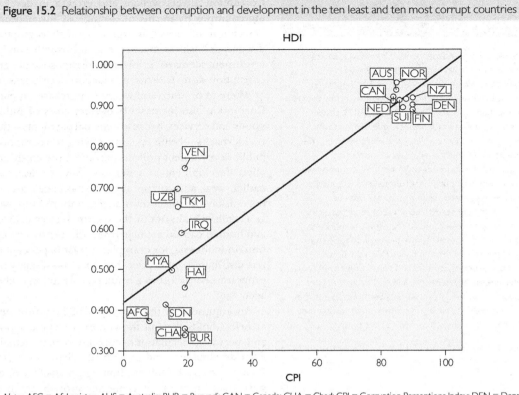

Note: AFG = Afghanistan; AUS = Australia; BUR = Burundi; CAN = Canada; CHA = Chad; CPI = Corruption Perceptions Index; DEN = Denmark; FIN = Finland; HAI = Haiti; HDI = Human Development Index; IRQ = Iraq; MYA = Myanmar; NED = Netherlands; NOR = Norway; NZL = New Zealand; SDN = Sudan; SUI = Switzerland; TKM = Turkmenistan; UZB = Uzbekistan; VEN = Venezuela

Sources: Human Development Report (UNDP 2013); Transparency International (2013)

Table 15.2 The ten most corrupt and least corrupt countries with corresponding HDI figures

Ten most corrupt countries	TI (2012)	HDI (2013)	Ten least corrupt countries	TI (2012)	HDI (2013)
Afghanistan	8	0.374	New Zealand	90	0.919
Sudan	13	0.414	Finland	90	0.892
Myanmar	15	0.498	Denmark	90	0.901
Turkmenistan	17	0.698	Sweden	88	0.916
Uzbekistan	17	0.654	Singapore	87	0.895
Iraq	18	0.590	Switzerland	86	0.913
Burundi	19	0.355	Norway	85	0.955
Chad	19	0.340	Australia	85	0.938
Haiti	19	0.456	Netherlands	84	0.921
Venezuela	19	0.748	Canada	84	0.911

Sources: Human Development Report (UNDP 2013); Transparency International (2013)

affecting the scope of government interventions, this again may affect political stability.

The causes of corruption

Corruption in developing countries is widespread not because people are different, but because conditions are ripe (Gray and Kaufman 1998). The basic causes of corruption are scarce public benefits, low wages, job insecurity, high levels of inflation, presence of natural resources and foreign owned companies, and monitoring difficulties. Such a public benefit may be access to a particular service or having a law not apply to one's case (a traffic fine, for example). When rents are high and it is relatively easy to keep payoffs secret, opportunity for corruption is ripe. Corruption will also thrive where there are inadequate and ineffective controls. But within a country, the level of corruption may vary greatly between sectors. In Ghana, for example, almost 50 per cent of citizens claim to have paid bribes when interacting with police, whereas only 5 per cent have done so when dealing with the health sector (Rose-Ackerman and Truex 2012: 53). Corruption will occur when the illicit benefits outweigh expected costs (Rothstein 2011). A problem with corruption, in particular for developing countries, is that it has a tendency of feeding on itself: the more corruption there is in society, the less formal and informal punishment of corrupt behaviour, and thus the easier it is for someone to commit corrupt acts. High levels of corruption affect development in a negative manner, just as low development may increase corruption, creating a vicious cycle in which weak underlying economic conditions facilitate corruption (Rose-Ackerman 2004: 10).

The negative effects of corruption are illustrated in Figure 15.2, showing that the most corrupt countries in the world, as measured by the Corruption Perceptions Index (CPI), are also among the least developed and that the least corrupt are also the most developed. As the scatter plot diagram shows, corrupt countries record consistently lower development scores than the least corrupt. The least corrupt countries are found among the most developed countries, and vice versa. As can be seen, however, among the most corrupt countries, there are strong variations regarding the level of development. This suggests that although corruption may be detrimental to development, even highly corrupt countries may experience economic growth. Although this does not tell us if one leads to the other, it shows that the two concepts correlate substantially. Underlying the argument that corruption pervades a vicious development cycle, high inequality also spurs corruption. A range of other historical and social factors influences governance and corruption. For example, corruption is considered to be more prevalent in countries with higher ethnic fragmentation, in nations with few Protestants, and in societies characterized by Socialist or French legal origin.

Reforms to reduce corruption

Considering the negative effects of corruption for the development of state capacity and services in the developing world, it is not surprising that curbing corruption has, since the 1990s, been a central concern for the Bretton Woods institutions and bilateral governments, as well as international **non-governmental organizations (NGOs)**. Reflecting the broad definition of governance applied by the Bretton Woods institutions and bilateral governments, as discussed earlier, efforts to enhance oversight and transparency are considered key factors for reducing corruption. International aid agencies have put large sums of money into anti-corruption. Anti-corruption work involves preventing corruption by building transparent, accountable systems of government, and strengthening the capacity of civil society and the media (Cremer 2008). Corruption indices have become useful tools for drawing media attention to the problem of corruption (see Box 15.4). A common starting point has been the establishment of anti-corruption commissions, which sometimes have investigative functions; in other instances, anti-corruption agencies have awareness-raising and public education functions as their main purpose. The value of such commissions is debatable and many have suggested that they have had a limited effect in battling corruption (Doig et al. 2007).

Recent research shows that although corruption is rampant, and has detrimental consequences for governance and development, it is possible to reduce corruption. Because corruption and bad governance in many cases benefit a select few high up in the hierarchy, there is reason to believe that they will oppose such efforts. This leads to the question of whether it is really possible to separate good governance and the capacity to provide services in a just and equitable manner from the question of accountability and democracy. We will turn to this debate in the next section.

BOX 15.4 MEASURING CORRUPTION

Until the early 1990s, few empirical studies of corruption existed owing to lack of data. Since then, a number of corruption indices have emerged based primarily on assessments by experts and businessmen collected by a variety of organizations. Two often-used measures of corruption, Transparency International (TI) and World Government Indicators (WGI), are based on the perceptions of experts and surveys of the perceived level of corruption. They are based on a so-called 'poll of polls', meaning that they take the average of numerous polls and combine them. Since the data will always contain some degree of uncertainty, one should be careful to conclude that there are significant differences between countries that have similar scores (Kaufmann et al. 2010). However, as the distance increases, it will become more meaningful to speak of a real difference. For example, the difference between Somalia and Myanmar is negligible; the difference between Somalia and Denmark, however, is not. The perception-based indicators can nevertheless be problematic, because they may be measuring mere inferences by experts rather than actual levels of corruption—that is, if an expert believes a country to be democratic, then he or she may infer from this that corruption should be low, which will in turn validate the theory that democracy leads to less corruption (Treisman 2007).

KEY POINTS

- The absence of corruption is often used as a proxy for good governance and is understood as the misuse of public power for private or political gain.

- Research on corruption has improved and expanded rapidly in the last two decades because of better data. Recent research largely agrees that corruption is negatively associated with development, as measured by the Human Development Index (HDI).

- Corruption adversely affects democratic legitimacy, and leads to lower levels of interpersonal trust and belief in the political system among citizens, which may have wider governance consequences.

- Corruption indices have become useful tools for drawing media attention to the problem of corruption.

- International aid agencies have invested significant resources in anti-corruption strategies through building transparent, accountable systems of government, and strengthening the capacity of civil society and the media.

The Relationship between Democracy and Governance

Do democracies in the developing world do a better governing job than autocracies? In other words, is there reason to expect that democratic states provide better services because they are more legitimate and depend on the consent of citizens? When the World Economic Forum met in Davos in January 2013, hundreds of economic experts from around the globe agreed that the biggest challenge facing the world is the increasing income gap between rich and poor. This income gap is not only between countries, but also currently many developing countries are experiencing dramatic income disparities between various groups. Against this background, some scholars have questioned whether democracy is a luxury that poor and developing countries can ill afford, and argued that policymakers should be more concerned with the quality of government and the public services that governments provide its citizens.

Civil liberties and democracy are often seen as the antidote for developmental deficiencies owing to the possibility of voicing one's opinion and holding officials accountable. The foregoing discussion about reforms to curb corruption and to enhance revenue collection indicates that many of the successful reforms to improve governance involved enhancing the voice of citizens and accountability of the political elites toward the citizens. This suggests that, in reality, it is difficult to separate the output side from the input side of politics when discussing governance reform in the developing world. The distinction is necessary, however, if we want to understand whether democracies perform better than autocracies. Scholars working within the concept of quality of government emphasize this distinction. The empirical evidence regarding the relationship between democracy and governance performance is not entirely conclusive. Many quantitative studies seem to indicate that democracy has a negative impact on governance in the early phases of democratization processes (Charron and Lapuente 2010: 244). Quality of government appears to be highest in highly democratic countries, medium-high in strongly authoritarian regimes, and lowest in semi-democracies or what Chapter 14 referred to as 'electoral democracies' (Bäck and Hadenius 2008). This suggests a curvilinear relationship between democracy and quality of governance, meaning that, at low levels of democracy, a democratization process may in fact decrease the quality of governance, such as in Peru under Fujimori (McMillan and Zoido 2004). Charron and Lapuente (2010) further find that, at low levels of economic development, democracy may have a negative effect on the quality of governance, whereas at higher levels of economic development, democracy will have a positive effect. As politicians aim to get re-elected, they will be responsive to citizen demands. At lower levels of economic development, citizens' demands will be more centred towards short-time consumption rather than long-term investments, which is not conducive to good governance. As economic development increases, citizens will be increasingly patient and concerned about future gains, and therefore favour more long-term investments. This also shows that the input and output sides of politics are intrinsically linked. Theoretically, a democratic country should be more open and transparent, and it should be easier to hold politicians accountable. However, autocratic countries may, to a much larger degree, crack down on corruption, thereby increasing the costs of corruption. Accordingly, in a democracy, the

risks of getting caught are possibly higher and the possibility of bottom-up control is higher. In an autocracy, the risks of getting caught are lower, but the top-down punishment (that is, the cost) is potentially much larger. If corruption is more prevalent in economically underdeveloped countries, can one expect corruption to decline automatically as a country develops economically? Or is corruption actually such an impediment to growth that one first has to solve the corruption issue before economic development can start?

Partly as a result of these adverse effects of democratization, or partial democratization that primarily focuses on partially free elections at regular intervals, some scholars, notably linked to the African Power and Politics project, have argued that, since they can be detrimental to development, competitive elections should not be considered as an important part of a developmental process (Kelsall and Booth 2010; Therkildsen and Bourgouin 2012; see Box 15.5). According to Kelsall (2012), introducing multiparty democracy in neo-patrimonial states can lead to increased **clientelism** and more short-sightedness as politicians aim to get elected and secure their share.

BOX 15.5 DEVELOPMENTAL PATRIMONIALISM

'Developmental **patrimonialism**' is a term that describes *centralized* rent management under which economic transformation is favoured over political participation (Kelsall 2011: 80). Drawing on experiences of certain East Asian countries such as South Korea and Indonesia, it has recently been utilized to analyse the African context. Two countries, Rwanda and Ethiopia, have exhibited such traits. Both countries are characterized by centralized, top-down patron–client networks controlled by the government, which have permitted putting in place far-sighted industrial policies for rent maximization, leading to high economic growth (Kelsall 2012: 679). Close and cooperative relations between politicians and business interests have furthermore helped government to focus on economic areas that are underdeveloped. In Rwanda, the ruling Rwandan Patriotic Front (RPF) has tight control over the Crystal Ventures holding company, which has started ventures in many underinvested areas such as telecommunications (Booth and Golooba-Mutebi 2012). The Endowment Fund for the Rehabilitation of Tigray (EFFORT) is the Ethiopian equivalent. It has invested extensively in a range

of areas, from cement manufacture to textiles (Kelsall 2012: 680). All board members are from the ruling party, the Ethiopian People's Revolutionary Democratic Front (EPRDF). However, individual EPRDF members have not been enriched directly by rents; rather, rents are managed strategically to secure political stability and economic growth (Vaughan and Gebremichael 2011: 36). However, it is questionable how sustainable such regimes are, especially when it comes to successions. Other countries having gone through this sort of development before have often failed to keep growth for an extended period of time. These leaders should not be seen as more benevolent than other political leaders. In fact, by 'making the pie grow', rent collection in the long run can be increased. Moreover, they may see such policies simply as the best way in which to keep themselves in power. Developmental patrimonialism is less likely to occur in democracies, and may indeed come at high costs in terms of civic and political liberties, and both Rwanda and Ethiopia remain highly autocratic (with Freedom House scores of 5.5 and 6.0, respectively).

KEY POINTS

- It is difficult to separate the output side from the input side of politics when discussing governance reform in the developing world.

- The empirical evidence on whether autocracies or democracies perform better in terms of delivering services to its populations is not conclusive. Some studies indicate that democracy has a negative impact on governance in the early phases of democratization processes.

- Some scholars argue that since competitive elections can be detrimental to development measured as governance capacity, they should not be considered as an important part of a developmental process.

Conclusion

In this chapter, we have seen that governance emerged as a key concept during the early 1990s. For international development organizations, the governance concept provided an opportunity to address social issues and government reform without 'meddling' with internal affairs or politics. A common denominator in most understandings of governance is a focus on institutions (formal and informal) and 'rules of the game'. However, the concept of governance has also come to embrace the concept of democratization, with a strong emphasis on state–society relations. Owing to the vastness of the concept of governance

and all of the dimensions to which it refers, it is very hard for developing countries to implement all of the changes that are prescribed. Therefore some scholars have proposed an emphasis on 'good-enough governance', focusing on the minimal conditions of governance necessary in order to ensure political and economic development. Building from here, scholars have claimed that definitions of good governance are too encompassing, making it impossible to establish what it exactly is. Emphasizing quality of government and the need for a government to act impartially, recently scholars have argued for a concept of governance that puts the output side of politics at the forefront.

However, as the discussion in this chapter has shown, when emphasizing two central elements of state capacity—the ability to tax and to curb corruption—in reality it is not easy to separate the concept of governance from the question of how power is obtained (democratization). The discussion has indicated that both the ability to generate revenue and that to minimize corruption are closely linked to how state institutions and societies interact. Do democracies perform better than autocracies in terms of providing quality of public services? The evidence is inconclusive. The lesson learned about governance is that an essential condition for successful outcomes is that there is a domestic drive for development and that aid supports such a domestic drive. But if the political environment is unfavourable to providing effective leadership, governance reforms will have limited effect.

 QUESTIONS

1. Discuss the merits of the 'good-enough government' argument. Can it be argued that some aspects of governance are more important than others?

2. Why is there such great variation in respect of 'good governance' experienced by different countries in the developing world?

3. Why and in what way is a government's ability to extract taxes related to governance?

4. In what way does corruption present an obstacle to development?

5. Might foreign aid create the same type of dependency as the one stemming from natural resource rents, with the same consequences?

6. In what way can a country avoid bad governance when finding abundant natural resources? Is it dependent on the 'goodwill' of rulers or might some kind of institutional framework help to prevent bad governance?

FURTHER READING

Doornbos, M. (2006) *Global Forces and State Restructuring* (Houndmills: Palgrave Macmillan) Essays on issues relating to globalization, governance, and the state in developing countries.

Grindle, M. (2007) 'Good Enough Governance Revisited', *Development Policy Review*, 25(5): 533–74 Challenging the conventional understanding of good governance, Grindle shows how 'good enough governance' may be more appropriate for many developing countries.

Harrison, G. (2005) 'The World Bank, Governance and Theories of Political Action in Africa', *British Journal of Politics and International Relations*, 7(2): 240–60 A critical analysis of the World Bank's governance agenda and prospects for reform in Africa.

Hyden, G., Court, J., and Mease, K. (2004) *Making Sense of Governance: Empirical Evidence from Sixteen Developing Countries* (Boulder, CO:Lynne Rienner) A comprehensive assessment informed by extensive evidence covering half the world's population.

Kaufmann, D., Kray, A., and Mastruzzi, M. (2009) *Governance Matters VIII: Governance Indicators for 1996–2008*, World Bank Policy Research Working Paper No. 4978, available online at https://openknowledge.worldbank.org/bitstream/handle/10986/4170/WPS4978.pdf?sequence=1 The latest publication compiling global World Governance Indicators.

Kaufmann, D., Kraay, A., and Mastruzzi, M. (2010) *The Worldwide Governance Indicators: Methodology and Analytical Issues*, World Bank Policy Research Working Paper No. 5430, available online at http://papers.ssrn.com/sol3/papers.cfm?abstract_id=1682130 Gives an introduction into the methodology behind the widely used World Governance Indicators.

Moore, M. (2004) 'Revenues, State Formation, and the Quality of Governance in Developing Countries', *International Political Science Review*, 25(3): 297–319 Explores the implications of fiscal sociology for governance in the developing world's rentier states.

Moore, M. (2011) 'Globalisation and Power in Weak States', *Third World Quarterly*, 32(10): 1757–76 A comprehensive and thought-provoking article about the implications of globalization for governance in weak and small states.

Treisman, D. (2007) 'What Have We Learned about the Causes of Corruption from Ten Years of Cross-National Empirical Research?', *Annual Review Political Science*, 10: 211–44 This article provides readers with a thorough critique of common measures of corruption.

WEB LINKS

http://cpi.transparency.org/cpi2012/results/   The Transparency International Corruption Perceptions Index (2012).

http://info.worldbank.org/governance/wgi/index.asp   The World Bank World Governance Indicators Project.

http://kellogg.nd.edu/projects/vdem/index.shtml   Site for the Varieties of Democracy Project.

http://www.bti-project.org/home/index.nc   Site for the Bertelsmana Transformative Index.

http://www.institutions-africa.org/   Site for the African Power and Politics project.

http://www.odi.org.uk/wga_governance/About_WGA.html   Site for World Governance Assessment.

http://www.oecd.org/   Site includes the Paris Declaration on Aid Effectiveness (2005), a shared vision of aid relations by international donors and developing world partners, including the idea of ownership by partners.

http://www.qog.pol.gu.se/   Site for the Quality of Government Institute.

http://www.u4.no   Provides anti-corruption material, including applied research, through an extensive web-based resource centre, based in Bergen, Norway.

http://www.undp.org/oslocentre/   Provides information on the UNDP's Global Programme on Democratic Governance Assessments.

http://www.unodc.org/unodc/en/treaties/CAC/   Site for the United Nation Convention against Corruption (UNCAC).

http://www.worldbank.org/wbi/governance   The World Bank Institute's site on governance and its activities in support of governance capacity-building.

For additional material and resources, please visit the Online Resource Centre at:
http://www.oxfordtextbooks.co.uk/orc/burnell4e/

PART 4
Policy Issues

In this part, several major policy domains in development are examined. The themes do not concern developing countries only; in all of the developing regions, they represent notable challenges to both state and non-state actors at the present time. Our concern is not with 'development', per se, or as a universal concept, although the increasingly holistic way in which development tends to be understood these days inevitably has implications for the presentation here. Rather, this part again has two main aims.

First, it aims to show how states, like other major actors in the economy and society, are confronted by certain key issues in development and face seemingly inescapable challenges. States in particular have to entertain large decisions that involve political risks and impose considerable administrative burdens, concerning such matters as economic development, welfare, the environment, and **human rights.** However, as Chapter 19 on security amply illustrates, for example, we cannot understand the precise nature of the issues simply by seeing them through the lens of concerned actors in the West. All of the policy issues must be viewed against the background of the local context in the developing countries. This can differ dramatically from one country and social group to another.

A *second* aim is to show the different ways in which governments and non-governmental actors and international bodies determine their responses, by comparing different strategies and their likely consequences. Here, the relevance of international influences to the way in which policy agendas are formed and often to policy implementation is undeniable, but nevertheless should be examined critically. The object of Part 4 is to illuminate the policy process, while necessarily being limited in how much detail it can convey about the policy substance. What choices really are open to developing countries and just how much scope for exercising choice independently have they experienced to date? Does state action necessarily offer the most appropriate way forward? Does 'one size fit all', or does the evidence suggest that the political response can embody distinct national and subnational frameworks for defining problems, devising solutions, and implementing a course of action?

Readers are encouraged to read the introductions to Parts 5–8 and to consult relevant case studies alongside the chapters in Part 4.

16

Development

Tony Addison

Overview

This chapter discusses development policy objectives, noting how these have changed over the years, with a more explicit focus on poverty reduction coming to the fore recently. It also examines the relationship between economic growth and poverty reduction. The chapter then discusses how to achieve economic growth, and then moves on to the big question of the respective roles for the market mechanism and the state in allocating society's productive resources. The chapter then discusses how economic reform has been implemented and the political difficulties that arise. It also considers the importance of transforming the structure of economies and the new global development landscape, including changes in development finance. The chapter concludes that getting development policy right has the potential to lift millions out of poverty.

Introduction

There are nearly 1.3 billion people living in extreme poverty today, defined as having less than US$1.25 per day on which to survive (see Table 16.1). This is nearly a quarter of the population of the **developing world**. The situation in sub-Saharan Africa is especially desperate: nearly half of the population is poor and the number in poverty has grown. Hunger accompanies malnutrition, as do ill-health and low

Table 16.1 Extreme poverty, 1981–2008

	Number of people living on less than US$1.25 a day (m)			Share of people living on less than US$1.25 a day (%)		
	1981	1996	2008	1981	1996	2008
East Asia and Pacific	1096.5	639.7	284.4	77.2	35.9	14.3
China	835.1	442.8	173.0	84.0	36.4	13.1
Eastern Europe and Central Asia	8.2	18.2	2.2	1.9	3.9	0.5
Latin America and the Caribbean	43.3	53.6	36.8	11.9	11.1	6.5
Middle East and North Africa	16.5	12.3	8.6	9.6	4.8	2.7
South Asia	568.4	630.8	570.9	61.1	48.6	36.0
India	428.7	463.4	445.0	59.8	47.2	37.4
Sub-Saharan Africa	204.9	349.4	386.0	51.5	58.1	47.5
Total	1937.8	1704.0	1289.0	52.2	34.8	22.4

Sources: Chen and Ravallion (2012: Table 2); PovcalNet, http://iresearch.worldbank.org/PovcalNet/index.htm

life expectancy. Yet set against this grim picture there has also been considerable progress—notably in East Asia, where extreme poverty is a fraction of its level thirty years ago, with China being an outstanding success (see Table 16.1). Even in South Asia, which has the largest numbers of poor people of all of the main regions, both the percentage and the number of people in poverty have fallen substantially over the last decade.

Looking at **economic growth**, many East Asian countries have grown at rates that are historically unprecedented. Whereas it took Britain—the world's first industrial nation—fifty-four years to develop from a low per capita income economy to a middle-income economy, it is estimated that it took Hong Kong, Singapore, and Taiwan (the 'tigers') only ten years to achieve middle-income **status** (Parente and Prescott 2000). China has been growing at annual rates of around 9 per cent and India's growth has accelerated as well, and their demand for oil and other commodities has pushed up global commodity prices to the benefit of sub-Saharan Africa (which remains overwhelmingly dependent on commodity exports), as well as Latin America (where commodities still have a large export share). But while growth in sub-Saharan Africa has risen in recent years, the region has performed very badly for much

of the period between 1980 and 2000 (with notable exceptions, such as Botswana and Mauritius). Latin America achieved steady, if unspectacular, growth in the period up to the late 1970s, but then went into deep recession during the debt crisis of the 1980s (described by Latin Americans as the 'lost decade'). Latin America recovered in the 1990s, but then underwent another bout of turbulence (with a spectacular economic collapse in 'star reformer' Argentina), before strong commodity earnings once again pushed up growth (especially in Brazil and Chile). Lastly, oil wealth raised living standards in the Middle East and North Africa, but this region has, with only a few exceptions, largely failed to achieve economic diversification and to provide employment for a growing and young population, an important contributor to the 'Arab Spring' (see Table 16.2).

In sum, the developing world today presents a very mixed picture: very fast growth and poverty reduction in much of Asia; growth after long-term decline in sub-Saharan Africa, but high poverty and largely undiversified economies; growth after considerable economic volatility in Latin America; and often disappointing performance in North Africa and the Middle East, despite often abundant natural resources. Growth fell over 2008–09 as the world entered its worst economic recession

Table 16.2 Economic growth in terms of average annual GDP per capita (%)

	1980–89	1990–99	2000–09	2010–11
Low income	0.04	0.25	2.88	3.85
Middle income	1.45	1.91	4.54	5.87
Lower middle income	1.92	1.71	3.89	4.86
Upper middle income	1.52	2.22	5.02	6.49
Low & middle income	1.35	1.78	4.39	5.70
East Asia & Pacific	3.33	1.92	2.62	4.36
Europe & Central Asia	1.70	1.46	1.54	1.83
Latin America & Caribbean	−0.19	1.20	1.80	4.18
Middle East & North Africa	−1.59	2.09	2.30	2.88
South Asia	3.08	3.30	4.83	6.03
Sub-Saharan Africa	−0.69	−0.56	2.02	2.32
High income	2.36	1.86	0.94	1.76

Source: World Bank World Development Indicators (2013)

since the 1930s (see Chapter 4), although the larger 'emerging economies' (Brazil, China, and India) experienced less of a slowdown than first feared and many of the smaller economies have come through largely unscathed by the crisis in comparison to earlier global economic shocks (Africa especially). Climate change could reduce economic growth in countries that are vulnerable to flood or drought, thereby increasing poverty, especially in regions that are already environmentally stressed. Therefore differences between developing countries could widen in the future.

What role has development policy played in these different outcomes? What policies are most important for accelerating development? Is the development past a guide to the development future? What lessons can we transfer across countries? As Nobel Laureate Robert Lucas (1988) says: '[T]he consequences for human welfare involved in questions like these are simply staggering. Once one starts to think about them, it is hard to think about anything else.' And thinking about development policy has changed over time. On some issues, there is now considerable agreement about what needs to be done. But many issues remain deeply controversial, with starkly contrasting viewpoints.

KEY POINTS

- Nearly 1.3 billion people live in extreme poverty, about a quarter of the developing world's population.

- Poverty is falling in Asia, but remains high in sub-Saharan Africa and significant in Latin America.

- Asia continues to grow fast, sub-Saharan Africa is growing again, and Latin America's economies are now stronger.

Defining Development Policy Objectives

Much of today's debate is centred on poverty reduction as the primary objective for development policy. People differ as to how to define 'poverty': economists typically favour monetary measures, using data collected from household surveys of incomes and expenditures. If the household falls below a defined poverty line, then it is classified as poor. However, not all countries have the data to define poverty in this way, so measures of the 'dollar a day' (now US$1.25 to reflect the rise in the cost of living) variety are often used to calculate the global and regional aggregates.

Non-monetary measures of poverty are increasingly used—measures such as infant mortality, life expectancy, and literacy—and people vary in how well they are doing across these different dimensions. Some may have a rising income, but remain illiterate, for example, and women often do worse than men, reflecting **gender** discrimination (in access to education and jobs, for example). People in chronic poverty suffer from multiple deprivations, making it very difficult for them to ever escape, and poverty is passed down the generations: the children of the chronically poor generally remain poor when they become adults (Chronic Poverty Research Centre 2008). The **Millennium Development Goals (MDGs)**, which were adopted by the world's leaders in the UN Millennium Declaration of September 2000 as guiding principles for the international development community, reflect the multidimensional view of poverty. The larger and faster-growing economies, such as Brazil, China, and Indonesia, stand the best prospects for MDG success, whereas 'failed states', such as Afghanistan and the Democratic Republic of Congo (DRC), will most likely fail. But this is not to say that significant progress cannot still be made in areas such as child-killer malaria, in relation to which there are major initiatives and funding.

In the early days of development policy, during the era of decolonization from the late 1940s through to the 1960s, poverty reduction was often more implicit than explicit in development strategies. These tended to focus on raising gross domestic product (GDP) per capita by means of economic growth—it being assumed that poverty reduction would then follow, more or less, from growth. Early development thinkers emphasized raising output, in particular increasing overall labour productivity (output per person) by shifting labour from sectors in which productivity is low to sectors in which it is high. This led to a concentration on industry, which was seen as the dynamic sector, while many policymakers saw smallholder agriculture as hopelessly backward and unproductive. Crudely put, industrialization and urbanization became synonymous with development in the minds of many policymakers from the 1940s to the 1960s. This was reinforced by what appeared, at the time, to be the successful example of the Soviet Union—a country that achieved large-scale industrialization from the 1930s onwards. Aid donors enthusiastically supported big infrastructure projects, especially when these benefited the commercial interests of their own countries.

Income per capita is an *average* measure of a country's living standard and there can be a wide *variation* around this mean. This variation—the inequality of income—exhibits substantial differences across countries, reflecting differences in the distribution of wealth (land, other property, and financial wealth) and **human capital** (peoples' skills and capabilities, which are partly a product of their education and which make them more productive). The differences in turn reflect country-specific histories of colonization, war, and policies.

Some people worry about inequality more than others (see Chapter 6). Quite apart from the ethical dimension, and social stability and the implications for democratic development (see Chapter 14), high inequality makes economic growth less effective in reducing poverty. A Latin American landowner with millions of hectares will benefit much more from agricultural export growth than a smallholder eking out a living on just a few hectares. Put differently, high-inequality societies need to grow a lot more quickly to achieve the same amount of annual poverty reduction as low-inequality societies.

So countries need to protect and build the assets of the poor, particularly their human capital, as well as the **natural capital**, such as the soils, forests, and fisheries, on which their livelihoods depend. Providing primary education, basic health care, water, and sanitation will not only raise the **human development** of poor people, but will also raise their productivity. This will help them to diversify their livelihoods in both self-employment (for example from dependence on subsistence agriculture, and into cash crops and micro-enterprises) and wage employment (the poor will earn more as skilled workers than as unskilled workers). Asset *redistribution* may also be necessary to build the assets of the poor. Often, this applies particularly to land and its transfer from the rich to the rural poor. Asset redistribution is much more challenging politically and large-scale redistributions tend to be associated with political revolutions.

In these ways, economic growth will start to become more pro-poor and each percentage point of growth will deliver more poverty reduction. This is not to say that all of the poor are in a position to benefit from growth; the chronically poor, who suffer from multiple deprivations, may be elderly or so sick that they are unemployable, and the illiterate are the least attractive to employers even in a growing economy. Many of the chronically poor live in remote regions far from the main economic centres, and even strong economic growth can bypass them. For the chronically poor, it is important to use the additional public revenues generated from growth, collected through the tax system, to finance more social protection. State-building is therefore vital to achieving poverty reduction through public programmes.

Awareness of what holds poor people back came to the fore in the 1970s, in part because of disillusion with the outcomes of the first development decades. The high hopes of decolonization proved to be largely illusory in Africa, and poverty persisted in Latin America notwithstanding growth. This led to a radicalization of the development debate, with **dependency theory** much in vogue. In addition, by the 1970s, there was much more evidence from academic research on the determinants of poverty, and how poverty responds to economic and social change. This led to a reconsideration of the earlier view that smallholder agriculture was un-dynamic, and a new emphasis on the talents of poor people as farmers and micro-entrepreneurs. Development professionals began to see new ways of helping the poor to build their livelihoods and, for the first time, the knowledge of the poor themselves came to be valued. The World Bank began to move away from its traditional emphasis on lending to physical infrastructure and towards poverty reduction, particularly through agricultural development, the principal livelihood of the world's poor.

Note that a direct focus on poverty reduction has a sharper political dimension than a focus on growth in a development strategy. For a start, the poor may be poor because they have very little, if any, political voice. This is true of many of the rural poor in sub-Saharan Africa, for instance, and is evident in the way in which development strategies often ignored them or, perversely, taxed them (see Bates 1981). Politicians need to expend very little political capital when they talk about economic growth being 'like a tide that raises all boats'. But when it comes to spending public money, basic pro-poor services are often left behind, after services that prioritize the needs of more vocal, and more effectively organized, non-poor groups. A general **urban bias** against the rural areas was evident in much of post-independence Africa. Vocal and wealthy interests can effectively control the legislatures that determine the pattern of public spending and taxation (as in Central America), and the political power that accompanies wealth is another reason why many people worry about high inequality. When economic crisis strikes, governments often let the burden of adjustment fall on the meagre services that actually benefit the poor. However, some governments do more for poor people than others, and there are substantial differences in outcomes for poverty and human development across countries at similar levels of per capita income. Vietnam is one such success story (see Box 16.1). Moreover, within countries, different regions often spend very different amounts on pro-poor services, reflecting the operation of local political factors: for instance, in India, the state of Kerala is an outstanding success.

BOX 16.1 THE VIETNAM SUCCESS STORY

Vietnam, a country with a population of 84 million and which suffered a devastating war from the 1950s to the 1970s, is Asia's best-performing economy after China. Vietnam is also one of the world's success stories in poverty reduction. Poverty has fallen from 58 per cent of the population in 1993 to under 20 per cent today.

The key to this success has been the construction of a vigorous export economy, the creation of more opportunities for small enterprises, and investment in agriculture. Exports have expanded rapidly, enabling the economy to diversify, with considerable foreign investment especially following a 2000 bilateral trade deal with the United States that opened up the latter's market to Vietnamese exports, thereby encouraging US multinationals to establish factories employing Vietnam's cheap and abundant labour. This trend accelerated after

Vietnam's accession to the World Trade Organization (WTO) in 2007.

Following the end of the war in 1975 and the country's unification, the Hanoi government extended Marxist central planning, with its heavy restrictions on private enterprise, to the country's capitalist south (which had lost the war). The economy performed badly under this system, with hyperinflation and a sharp fall in living standards being the main results. Tentative reform began in the 1980s, with a move from collectivized agriculture to a market-orientated smallholder system, and gathered pace with the adoption of the *Doi Moi* ('new changes') strategy in 1986. Reform intensified in the early 1990s as financial pressures grew with the drying up of aid from the Soviet Union, Vietnam's old cold war ally. The government restored macro-economic stability, liberalized restrictions on

BOX 16.1 THE VIETNAM SUCCESS STORY (continued)

small private enterprises, and sought out foreign investment. However, the government is far from relinquishing all control over the economy and there are still many state-owned enterprises; these account for 40 per cent of GDP in what is officially called a 'socialist-orientated market economy'.

Export manufacturing has led to more urban jobs and urban poverty has fallen substantially. Vietnam has gone from a country of food shortages to become a leading exporter of rice and coffee, resulting in increased incomes and a diversification of livelihoods in rural areas. But poverty remains stubbornly high in less advantaged regions such as Vietnam's Central Highlands, where many of Vietnam's ethnic minorities live. They constitute 15 per cent of the total population, but 40 per cent of the poor.

Vietnam's rapid economic growth is therefore not delivering enough benefits for these people, who need better education and health care, and more investment in transport and communications infrastructure, to improve market access.

Vietnam is a success, but its economic growth has come from a very low level of per capita income, reflecting the impact of the long war and the economic crisis of the immediate post-war years. Its government administration is very bureaucratic, **corruption** is a problem, and the Communist government's grip on power is threatened by the economy's opening-up and the accompanying increased flow of ideas and information from abroad. Vietnam therefore faces some tough challenges ahead in maintaining the momentum of its success.

KEY POINTS

- Poverty reduction has become a more explicit objective of development policy, and economic growth is now seen as more of a means to an end, rather than a final objective in itself.

- Growth is important to reducing poverty, but not all poor people benefit from growth and the chronically poor often miss out.

- Effective states are necessary to achieve development objectives, particularly in providing pro-poor services and infrastructure.

Markets and States

Achieving growth is far from easy, especially in countries that are landlocked and distant from markets (Bolivia and Niger, for example), subject to tropical diseases (West Africa in particular), and with climates and terrain that make them vulnerable to floods or droughts (Bangladesh and Africa's Sahel zone). Some countries therefore start with more favourable prospects for growth than others. But the prospects for growth also very much depend upon the design of development strategy, and particularly on the state's role.

Most people agree that states have an important role to play in protecting property rights, enforcing contracts, and defending their citizens against external aggression. Economists have emphasized the importance of the first two of these in providing a favourable climate for investment and for reducing the transaction costs of market exchange, both of which facilitate growth.

However, beyond a core set of **public goods**, such as law and order, and defence, people start to disagree about how much economic and social infrastructure the state should provide (public versus private education and health care, for example). And people often have radically different views about how far (if at all) the state should intervene in market mechanisms to set prices, control quantities, set standards, and regulate producers or act as a producer itself. Much of the debate about development strategy can be reduced to differences in views about what is the appropriate level of state provision, and whether the state should mostly leave the market alone or intervene extensively.

These different viewpoints partly arise from different perspectives on how markets work. Much disagreement centres on how well market mechanisms yield poverty reduction—or, indeed, whether markets sometimes work against poor people, making them poorer. Market optimists favour light regulation to let the market deliver the economic growth that best reduces poverty. Market pessimists favour state intervention, arguing that market outcomes reflect power and that this is often unfavourable to the poor (monopolies prevailing in unregulated markets, for example).

But people differ over the appropriate role for the state because they also hold different views over what constitutes the 'ideal society'. Nearly everyone agrees that an ideal society must achieve absolute poverty reduction, but some people favour state action to reduce overall income inequality as well. Others are vehemently opposed to such egalitarian ideas, citing individual freedom, including the right to accumulate wealth. Also controversial are the ability of market mechanisms to yield economic growth, and whether a higher (or lower) growth rate will result from state intervention in the market mechanism.

Market optimists will favour a minimal state: one that provides protection for property rights, together with public goods that the market either does not supply or undersupplies, such as defence or transport infrastructure. In contrast, people who are pessimistic about the market's ability to deliver their ideal society will favour a more active state, but their conceptualization of what the state should do can vary considerably. At one extreme is central planning (practised by the former Soviet Union), under which society's productive factors are allocated according to a plan without reference to market prices, and under which state ownership of enterprises and property prevails (of which North Korea is one of the few examples left and even it has partially liberalized the economy). The 'European model' is at the other end of the scale of active states: continental European states provide very high levels of public goods and regulate the market 'in the public interest', but otherwise encourage a very vigorous private sector. The present difficulties in Europe illustrate the point that even the most successful models need renewal to cope with global economic change.

Views on state effectiveness have swung like a pendulum over the last fifty years. As countries came to independence, they built national planning apparatuses and wrote national plans. The Soviet Union's example was very influential in China, Cuba, and Vietnam, and so was the state planning that even the capitalist economies introduced during the 1940s and many retained afterwards.

However, by the late 1970s, this confidence in the state's abilities was starting to erode as growth slowed down as a result of policy failure in many (but certainly not all) countries that pursued state-led development, together with the first (1974) and second (1979) oil price hikes by the Organization of Petroleum Exporting Countries (OPEC), and the associated world recessions, which tested state capacities to breaking point. During this time, the International Monetary Fund (IMF) became very important in providing balance-of-payments support. Several of the oil exporters also borrowed heavily using their oil revenues as collateral (for example Nigeria, Mexico, and Venezuela) and they suffered macro-economic crisis when the world

oil price fell during the 1980s. The result was the debt crisis that stalled growth, especially in Latin America, for much of the 1980s (see Chapter 4).

The intellectual pendulum swung back (albeit with considerable resistance) towards the market mechanism in the 1980s and accelerated with the collapse of communism, and the start of the transition to market economies, in Eastern Europe and the Soviet Union. This was reinforced by the IMF and the World Bank, and their loan **conditionality** (often dubbed the '**Washington consensus**' on what constitutes good policy).

With so many of its client countries in deep distress, the World Bank was compelled to move beyond its traditional project lending and, in the 1980s, it started to provide balance-of-payments support through structural adjustment loans (SALs). They attempted to change the structure of economies fundamentally by introducing more market discipline on resource allocation. A SAL carried such policy conditionalities as: currency devaluation (to stimulate the supply of exports); the conversion of import quotas into import tariffs to reduce **rent-seeking** (and then tariff reduction in order to place more competitive pressure on inefficient infant industries); the removal (liberalization) of market controls in agriculture (to provide more incentives for farmers); and the reform of public expenditures and taxation (to shift more spending towards development priorities and to mobilize more public revenues to finance spending). The IMF's policy conditionality also included reducing the fiscal deficit to curb inflation, which reduced export competitiveness and economic growth.

Although World Bank and IMF adjustment lending was intended to deal with the immediate macroeconomic crises, it was also seen as a way of making poor economies more efficient and therefore better able to grow. Growth required a reduced role for the state in the productive sectors, as well as reduced controls on the private sector. Irrespective of the merits or otherwise of reform, countries in economic crisis had little alternative but to sign up to the conditionality, since private capital flows slowed dramatically with the onset of the debt crisis in the 1980s and official development flows became one of the few sources of external finance. This was especially true for the low-income countries.

The effects of reforms are never clear-cut. Many people oppose reform (*ex ante*) fearing a loss, even if this is not the case (*ex post*). Conversely, some people may gain a lot (for example those producing exports), but the gains are not immediate. Sometimes, a particular reform will benefit the majority of people, but if each person's gain is small, then they do not have much incentive to mobilize in support of reform, whereas the minority may stand to lose a lot and therefore has a much greater incentive to mobilize against reform. Reform can therefore stall even if, in aggregate, it benefits the majority. This is a good example of what Olson (2001) calls a 'collective action problem', which refers to the difficulties that arise in organizing a group of people to achieve a common objective.

Yet while the self-interests of elites or other small groups do often impede change, there are cases in which major reform programmes have been initiated and sustained despite elites having much invested in the status quo. Elite state actors may organize themselves into positions in which they profit from reform by investing in private enterprises that will benefit from liberalization, or by buying state assets on the cheap when they are **privatized**. Rulers may also initiate reform for reasons other than private financial gain. A concern for their reputation and legacy, patriotism, changing ideology, or a fear of more powerful neighbours are all drivers of elite behaviour.

Ruling elites in China, Vietnam, and now Myanmar all initiated reforms despite having strong interests in the unreformed system. India undertook significant economic liberalization in the early 1990s, reflecting domestic criticism of the long-standing strategy of planning and state ownership. China and Vietnam's liberalizations have also been largely motivated by shifts in view within their ruling elites, rather than external pressures from the IMF, World Bank, and other donors.

The backlash against liberalization

Although it is highly controversial, liberalization is straightforward in its implementation because the state simply withdraws, partially or wholly, from the market. But some reforms require a strengthening of state capacity and better **governance** for their success. This is especially true of revenue and public expenditure reforms (see Chapter 15). The state's capacity to mobilize tax and customs revenues, and then to spend these resources effectively on pro-poor services and development infrastructure, requires a capable, well-motivated, and corruption-free government administration, at both central and local levels.

However, the quality of civil services, together with their motivation, was in steep decline before reform began in many countries, especially in Africa where inflation eroded real wages in the public sector. Governments were therefore attempting to implement demanding changes with very limited institutional and human resources, and in some cases IMF fiscal conditionality weakened state capacities further. Reform breakdown and policy reversals are common. Zambia, for example, went through many donor-supported adjustment programmes that largely failed to achieve progress, notwithstanding there being greater political commitment by the government to this in the 1990s than previously. There is also a fierce debate on whether economic reform contributed to the breakdown of states and societies in countries such as Sierra Leone and Somalia (on conflict-prone societies, see Chapter 13).

So-called 'second-generation' economic reforms (privatization and financial reform, in particular) took place from the 1990s onwards in countries such as Ghana, Uganda, and Tanzania. Implementation of second-generation reforms was often problematic. For instance, privatization was often non-transparent in many cases, thereby transferring valuable assets to the politically connected. Financial reform was especially difficult. Asia's financial crisis in the 1990s and Africa's bank failures both highlight the need to build capacity for prudential supervision and regulation in central banks before major liberalization of financial controls. Tax reform and the construction of better systems of public expenditure management proved to be tough to implement.

Every shift in the intellectual debate sets up a counter-reaction, in part because proponents of the shift often overemphasize the likely benefits or are simply wrong. Thus, from the mid-1990s onwards, a reaction against market liberalization and privatization set in, owing to sharp increases in inequality during reform, rising concern over liberalization's social effects, and the mismanagement of privatization. The intellectual pendulum then began to swing back towards the state and its role.

Latin America experienced especially intense criticism of liberalization, reflecting the very mixed outcome from reform programmes in the 1990s. Governments in Argentina, Bolivia, Peru, and Venezuela rejected the Washington consensus, and extended state control over their mining and energy sectors to boost government revenues. The commodity price boom after 2000—the result of China's demand for commodities to feed its rapid economic growth—enabled many governments to pay off their debts, and the improved credit rating of Latin America's sovereign borrowers reduced the influence of the IMF and the World Bank upon which Latin America relied for financing in times of economic crisis.

In the 1990s, economists increasingly came to recognize the importance of institutions to making the market mechanism work well for development and poverty reduction (see Chapter 3). This included the World Bank and the IMF. The experience of the transition economies of the former Soviet Union was central to this heightened awareness of the importance of institutions, as were the difficulties with second-generation reform in Africa. High-quality **institutions** are needed, such as an effective legal system that protects property rights and reduces the costs of market transactions, making markets more efficient and investment easier. All of this illustrates the importance of building effective state capacities and improving governance (Chapter 15), to regulate markets in the public interest and to achieve improvements in the public goods that are essential to a well-functioning market economy, as well as for poverty reduction.

KEY POINTS

- The economic role of the state is one of the central issues dividing opinion on development strategy.

- An early emphasis on state-led development was eventually challenged by a market-liberal view, leading to widespread economic liberalization.

- Rising inequality led to a backlash against economic liberalization, especially when the fruits of the eventual growth were unequally distributed.

- Despite the rollback of the state, it still has many roles to play in providing public goods, as well as in regulating markets in the public interest

---

Achieving Structural Transformation

The structure of an economy—the division of economic activity and employment across agriculture, natural resource extraction, manufacturing, and services—is central to whether it can achieve fast and sustained economic growth, and to the impact of that growth on employment and poverty reduction. The

role of SALs in the 1980s and 1990s in trying to change the structure of the developing economy has been noted already. In this section, we discuss structural transformation in more detail, for it remains a central issue of development policy to this day, and, not surprisingly, there remain different views on the roles of the state and the market in achieving it. This is so even in low-income countries that have achieved better growth rates in recent years, for they mostly remain very undiversified economies and therefore vulnerable to shocks that hit their narrow range of economic activities, which is especially a concern in Africa where growth remains dependent on commodity exports. Diversification in economic activity is a key metric of success in structural transformation.

For market liberals, developing countries that follow their **comparative advantage** will reap higher living standards by trading as much as possible with the developed countries and with each other (see Chapter 4). Their export earnings can then finance imports of products in which they have a comparative *disadvantage*. The market-liberal story of trade is one of mutual gains from trade for both the developing and the developed worlds. Development policy seeking to change the structure of the economy is therefore best driven by the principle of comparative advantage.

For market liberals, comparative advantage also underpins their view of how trade contributes to economic growth, through **outward-oriented development**. Growth in developing countries' labour-intensive exports (their comparative advantage) will eventually bid up the price of labour (thereby contributing to poverty reduction) and encourage capital-for-labour substitution. The skill content of exports will also rise as educational investment builds human capital, allowing developing countries to start competitively producing what is presently made in the developed world. The state must assist this process through judicious public investment, in infrastructure for example, but it is the market that drives the process of structural transformation.

In the early years, many policymakers felt that such outward-orientated development would not yield much growth. Instead, many saw the domestic market as the main growth driver, and they favoured inward-orientated development and import-substituting industrialization (see Chapter 4). Producers who would benefit from protected markets also lobbied for the policy, and their influence increased over time as they used the **economic rents** associated with protection to fund sympathetic politicians and political parties, sometimes engaging in outright corruption. Critics of protection argue that rent-seeking comes to dominate the strategy, no matter how well intentioned initially, and this view underpinned the World Bank's efforts to open up economies in the 1980s.

In practice, the effects of lobbying and rent-seeking vary widely. They were at their worst in sub-Saharan Africa, where **weak states** were easily captured by powerful rent-seekers, and where the smallness of domestic markets made import substitution unviable without high tariffs and very tight import quotas, which encouraged massive evasion and smuggling. Criticism of India's 'licence Raj' led to economic liberalization in the early 1990s. even if India's growth was respectable, if undramatic, prior to liberalization. And import substitution achieved some 'learning by doing', facilitated by India's enormous domestic market, which gives domestic manufacturers larger economies of scale. South Korea's planning mechanism effectively contained rent-seeking, and export subsidies offset the disincentive to export production inherent in import protection. Since South Korea is an outstanding development success, it is difficult to believe that it would have achieved even higher growth without import protection (see Chapter 24).

Today's low-income countries enjoy advantages that South Korea and other past success stories did not—namely, a larger global market of middle-income and rich countries in which to sell their products and services, a greater range of foreign investment partners (which now include the large middle-income countries themselves, which have become investors in poorer economies), and a much larger menu of technologies to help them to do so. At the same time, the success of China in the low-cost end of the global manufacturing supply chain can make it harder for smaller developing countries to break into labour-intensive manufacturing, the traditional first step in structural transformation. It can be done, as Vietnam shows, but it requires a good strategy to guide policy and investments, especially in the infrastructure required to connect national economies into global value chains.

Countries therefore need the right strategy for today's global economy. Yet there is a continuing weakness in development strategy, especially when it comes to economic diversification and employment creation. In the early days after independence, most developing countries created national plans. Sometimes, those plans were unrealistic, but they did at least focus the technocratic minds of governments, and in East Asia they generally worked well. Africa's development plans were the least well articulated, but there were exceptions; in Botswana, successive national plans have guided the allocation of the country's substantial revenues from diamonds, enabling it to achieve more economic diversification.

The move away from such planning during the era of structural adjustment led to a dearth of hard thinking within countries about how to develop new economic sectors. Aid donors and many economists placed too much faith in the market's ability to generate diversification of economies away from traditional sectors—that is, to achieve change in economic structure.

A national plan that sets out how to use aid, other capital inflows, and domestic tax revenues for development will ideally set out objectives for both human development and economic growth, linked to investments that promise high returns: health investment for human development (and by improving human capital, this should help economic growth as well) and infrastructure investment for economic growth, to take two examples.

However, the MDGs agenda is almost entirely centred on the human development side of development strategy. Discussion around the 'post-2015 agenda' is now focusing more on economic development, especially job creation, but how is this best achieved? Market liberals would say 'leave it to the market', which will create the sectors that maximize growth and employment. Social entrepreneurs, such as Muhammad Yunus, founder of Bangladesh's innovative Grameen Bank, would say 'invest in micro-enterprises', especially through micro credit. One group of increasingly influential economists would say 'conduct randomized control trials' (RCTs), in a similar way to the randomized control approach to testing new medicines, to better understand what works— for example different approaches to education provision and microfinance—and then use evidence from successes to scale up to larger programmes (these proponents of RCTs being known as the 'randomistas') (Ravallion 2009). Each of these approaches shares a limited view of what the state should do: that it should largely confine itself to basic service delivery to achieve human development and that economic development is then to be driven by entrepreneurs, whether motivated by profit or wider social goals. Economic growth is then the resulting accumulation of many small-scale investments and successes.

However, East Asia still offers a bold vision that goes beyond this limited conceptualization of the state's role. The region's economic transformation is remarkable, defying the liberal view that states cannot be trusted to succeed when they move beyond providing public goods and protecting property rights. East Asia also challenges the randomistas, who argue that economists do not really know what produces economic growth. East Asia's transformation does not fit the social entrepreneur model either: states in partnership with the private sector created companies that eventually became very large-scale indeed—generating enormous numbers of jobs and in some cases becoming global brands (South Korea's Samsung and China's Lenovo are two examples).

East Asia's success is influential in the creation of what is known as the 'new structuralist economics'. This approach is also referred to as the 'new industrial policy', although the aim is to diversify the economy into sectors with higher value-added, which may be manufacturing, but also services (information technology for example), and agricultural crops with higher value-added than traditional subsistence farming.

One influential Chinese proponent of new structuralist economics, Justin Lin (2011), argues that the state should help private enterprise to create 'leading sectors'—sectors in which a more advanced economy already holds the lead, but where the gap is not too large for the poor country to leap. Footwear and other light manufacture such as toys are examples. Lin argues that older state-led strategies failed when countries tried to move into sectors in which there was too big a gap between the latecomer and the more advanced economies, resulting in the latecomer never becoming competitive enough to gain global market share, leaving enterprises requiring continued state help. The new structuralist approach shares with older strategies a view that markets are imperfect and will not deliver outcomes beneficial for rapid economic development without vigorous state action to overcome market failures that hold back private investment.

In contrast to the old paradigm of state-led development, the new structuralists see much less need for the state itself to own enterprises (and in this way it accepts much of the subsequent critique of state-owned enterprises). It is also more positive about the prospects for export growth than older state-led development, which tended to give much more emphasis to import substitution. It therefore incorporates elements of the market-liberal approach of SALs,

including an outward-orientated focus, but blends them with a strong, but careful, role for the state in helping private enterprise to find new leading sectors.

KEY POINTS

- Import substitution works much better in countries with large domestic markets and in which policy encourages export production as well.

- While the failure of many countries to achieve growth through import protection increased support for outward-orientated development, this too requires a well-designed strategy, particularly in creating new skills to sell in the global marketplace.

- The new structuralist economics that emerged out of East Asian success argues for the state to help private enterprises to create leading sectors, where the gap between the poor countries and the more advanced economies is not too large for the poor country to leap.

The Global Development Landscape

Low-income countries have to make development policy in the world as it is, not as they wish it to be. Until they can diversify their economies, they remain subject to high levels of risk; even the best development plans can be knocked off course by commodity price shocks and climatic shocks. Middle-income countries with diversified economies are more robust and have more possibilities to shape the world economy, especially when their economies are large, such as Brazil, China, and India. They can influence the global 'rules of the game' in finance, trade, and investment, and the international institutions that formulate and implement those rules.

Protectionism is still widespread in world trade despite the liberalization conducted under the auspices of the General Agreement on Tariffs and Trade (GATT) and WTO. The WTO's Doha Development Agenda negotiations, launched in 2001, remain in a state of deadlock, after a largely fruitless decade of talk. Trade protectionism reflects the balance of power between economies and economic blocs. Nowhere is this more apparent than in world agriculture. Rich countries pay large subsidies to their farmers and restrict imports from developing countries. This depresses the world prices of some major export earners for developing countries, notably cotton and sugar, thereby reducing the incomes of their farmers. Brazil has used the WTO to successfully challenge US protectionism, but the smaller and poorer countries lack the resources to defend their interests. They also find it difficult to access the markets of the larger developing countries such as India, which also protects its farmers from foreign competition (although this protection has recently been reduced). The developing countries do not always have common interests in world trade negotiations and they face powerful political bodies, such as the European Union, which are adept at protecting their interests.

Whereas the rules of the game governing global trade are slow to change, the last decade has seen rapid change in global development finance. The result has been increased power for the middle-income countries, a wider menu of external finance options for low-income countries and therefore greater scope for policy manoeuvre, and a reduction in the power of the rich world and the ability of aid donors to impose policy conditionality on low-income countries.

Development finance covers a wide spectrum from **official development assistance (ODA**—usually to governments) of varying levels of concessionality, ranging from grants to loans at rates lower than market rates, portfolio flows (commercial bank lending, flows into government and corporate debt, and company equities via stock markets), foreign direct investment (FDI, which, in contrast to portfolio flows, is longer term), and remittances by households to each other.

With their success in export markets, middle-income countries have built up substantial foreign exchange reserves. They were also motivated by the Asian financial crisis of 1997–98 when it paid to have large reserves to ward off speculative currency attacks (those that did not, such as Indonesia, fell into the care of the IMF). The reserves of the oil producers have risen along with global oil prices as well. All of this has given the middle-income countries substantial financial power in bond and equity markets worldwide, and is evident in their 'sovereign wealth funds' that invest globally, including FDI. They have put some of this new financial muscle into aid programmes, so that the emerging donors have become significant players in foreign aid over the last decade (see Chapters 28 and 29).

Low-income countries are benefiting from these new sources of commercial finance and foreign aid. The volume of remittances that they receive has also risen and is at least triple the amount of official development finance. South Asian countries benefit from the export of large amounts of labour to the wealthy Middle East and the resulting remittances home.

The sovereign debt of developing countries is currently in high demand, the result of hard-won economic reforms and high commodity prices. Expansionary monetary policy in the rich countries in the aftermath of the 2008 financial crisis has also driven down yields on rich country bonds to very low levels making the much higher yields on developing country bonds even more attractive to investors. In 2012, a bond issue by Zambia was oversubscribed, a remarkable turnaround for a country that was seen as a by-word for macroeconomic disaster in the 1980s. In 2013, Nigeria entered the JP Morgan emerging market Government Bond Index, a move that opened up its debt to purchase by pension funds and others in the developing world. At the same time, countries must be careful that they do not overborrow to the point at which they cannot service the debt in the event of, for example, a decline in commodity export earnings.

With a wider range of development finance now available, official aid is becoming less important to low-income countries as a group (with the exception of the small 'fragile states'). Many of the recipients are also tired of the complexity of aid, and the associated transactions costs that arise from the multiplicity of aid programmes and aid donors, each with its own procedures, and the lack of progress in rationalizing aid to make it more efficient despite successive attempts down the years.

Recipient countries have a great deal more room for manoeuvre with donors than in the era of structural adjustment, both because of the increased number of donors, but also because of the improvement in many recipient country economies. To a degree, they can play the traditional Western donors off against emerging donors such as China, and negotiate hard when they deal with the new donors. The ability of traditional donors to attach strict conditions to their aid has withered. In any case, traditional donors will provide aid to countries that are of strategic importance irrespective of whether these countries comply with any donor pressure on development policy. Ethiopia, Pakistan, and Afghanistan are such examples.

The recent graduation of countries from low-income to middle-income status (for example Ghana) as a result of sustained economic growth and the likely graduation of more in the near future (including Bangladesh over the next decade) also raises questions about the relevance of the international aid architecture, which was built around the objective of transferring resources from rich to poor countries. Whereas, at the turn of the millennium, some sixty-three countries were classified as low income, this number has now fallen to thirty-six (Sumner 2010). Yet many of the new middle-income countries still have large incidences of poverty, and since some of the new graduates to middle-income status have large populations (India, Nigeria, and Pakistan), this means that for the first time there are more poor people in middle-income countries than in low-income countries (Sumner 2010).

Graduation presents a difficulty in keeping foreign aid focused on poverty, because one of the largest sources of grant aid, the International Development Association (IDA), is reserved for low-income countries. More broadly, it can be asked: what is the added value of aid to middle-income countries that have rising revenues resulting from economic growth, which increases the size of their tax bases and therefore their ability to fund more pro-poor public spending? India illustrates how the world is changing. In the early 1990s, when India went through the balance-of-payments crisis that spurred eventual reform, it needed the World Bank and other official finance to ease its adjustment. Today, India has ample access to international capital flows. It also has a growing aid programme of its own (see Chapter 29). Yet it still has one third of the world's people living on less than US$1.25 per day. It would seem unfair for international aid not to help these people even if they live in a country now defined as middle income rather than low income. At the same time, while India now has more tax revenue to fund anti-poverty projects, its tax revenues in relation to the large numbers of people still in poverty mean that it is not yet in a position to fund all of its poverty reduction effort from domestic revenues or from borrowing. There is a case for traditional aid donors to remain engaged with countries even as they graduate to middle-income status. But the nature of that relationship will have to change.

KEY POINTS

- Low-income countries now have a wider menu of development finance options and greater scope for policy.

- The ability of aid donors to impose conditionality on low-income recipients has declined.

- With more countries moving from the low-income to the middle-income groups, aid needs to be rethought.

Conclusion

There are issues on which there is considerable consensus and issues regarding which deep controversy remains. That development policy must have an explicit focus on poverty reduction is one of the main areas of consensus in today's development policy community. In contrast to the period up to the 1970s, when it was thought that economic growth would automatically deliver poverty reduction, it is now recognized that pro-poor policies are necessary to maximize growth's benefits for the poor. Moreover, it is widely agreed that poverty reduction does not only entail higher incomes, but also improving human development indicators: poverty is a multidimensional concept. This implies improving the delivery of pro-poor services, particularly in basic health care, safe water and sanitation, and primary education, with a particular emphasis on delivery to rural areas (which contain high levels of poverty) and to women (see Chapter 9). Relatedly, it is widely agreed that the formation of human capital through better health and education is not only good for poverty reduction, but also contributes to growth by enabling diversification into skill-intensive manufactures and services. In this way, poor economies can seek to benefit from **globalization**.

Compared with the early years of development, there is now a greater recognition of the market's importance to growth. There is much less support for the state having a direct role in owning productive enterprises itself, and more of a focus on the private sector. Market liberals would still confine the state's primary role to protecting the property rights of private investors, large and small, and the provision of public goods that are underprovided by markets alone. They fear the rent-seeking associated with market regulation. Social entrepreneurs favour micro-enterprise, and support it through instruments such as **micro-credit**, with states building basic service provision rather than extensive state involvement in the productive side of the economy. Economists of a randomista persuasion are in favour of states scaling up support to basic services and livelihood projects, once they have learned more about the best means to do so from randomized control trials. They do not generally favour a larger-scale role for the state and are critical of economists with more ambitious roles for the state in driving growth.

Yet the success of East Asia has demonstrated a more active role for the state in the productive economy and the potential for state success in supporting the private sector to build leading economic sectors, especially for export products and services. In contrast to proponents of early state-led development strategy, the new structuralist economists see less of a role for the state in owning and operating enterprises itself, and less of a focus on import substitution (unless the domestic market is large enough to deliver economies of scale). They are aware of the problems of rent-seeking that state intervention in markets can create, but argue that institutions and mechanisms can be created to minimize the downside and maximize the upside of closer partnership between the state and the private sector.

Countries are now keener to attract private capital flows especially when they bring new technologies, as can be the case with foreign direct investment. Countries that were formerly considered to be poor debtors are now attracting international investor attention when they market their sovereign bonds. With more plentiful private capital available to them, they are much less dependent on foreign aid (reinforced as well in many cases by ample earnings from natural resource revenues). Aid donors are less important in driving development strategy than in previous years in most, but not all, countries. This throws more responsibility onto state effectiveness.

Getting development policy right has the potential to lift millions of people out of the misery of poverty. But making the right policy choices is not just a technical matter; it also requires careful political judgement about how to promote economic and social change in ways that stand the most chance of success, in an environment that—as the global financial crisis and recession of 2008–09, and the demands imposed by climate change show—is becoming ever more complex.

QUESTIONS

1. What are the main causes of East Asia's success in economic development? Can other countries adopt the East Asian model successfully?

2. How can poor people participate more fully in economic growth? How will their participation vary across developing regions?

3. If economic reform does yield significant benefits for growth and living standards, as its proponents argue, then why is it often so difficult politically?

4. What should be the role for the state in economic development and how might this differ across developing regions?

5. Why has Africa found it so difficult to achieve economic development and what can be done to improve Africa's performance in future?

6. What lessons does China's development success offer to other countries?

7. Does the new structuralist economics offer a better perspective on development strategy than the older state-led development paradigm?

8. Is it better to be a low-income country in today's global economy than it was in the global economy of fifty years ago?

FURTHER READING

Addison, T. (2003) 'Economics', in P. Burnell (ed.) *Democratization through the Looking Glass* (Manchester:Manchester University Press), 41–55 Examines how democracy affects economic performance, and contrasts democracy to autocracy in its development effects.

Banerjee, A. V. and Duflo, E. (2011) *Poor Economics: A Radical Rethinking of the Way to Fight Global Poverty* (New York: Public Affairs) A strong statement on the potential for randomized control trials to help to create better anti-poverty programmes.

Chronic Poverty Research Centre (2008) *The Chronic Poverty Report 2008–09* (London: CPRC) Discusses people who remain poor for much or all of their lives, and who benefit least from economic growth.

Collier, P. (2007) *The Bottom Billion: Why the Poorest Countries are Failing and What Can Be Done about It* (Oxford: Oxford University Press) An influential analysis of success and failure in development, including Africa.

Kanbur R. (2001) 'Economic Policy, Distribution and Poverty: The Nature of Disagreements', *World Development*, 29(6): 1083–94 A clear and balanced view of the contemporary poverty debate, and why people differ over growth's effects on poverty. Includes very useful comparisons between the differing viewpoints of the World Bank and non-governmental organizations on poverty.

Lin, J. Y. (2012) *The Quest for Prosperity: How Developing Economies Can Take off* (Princeton, NJ: Princeton University Press) A discussion of the new structuralist economics by an influential Chinese economist.

Pritchett, L. (2013) *The Folk and the Formula: Fact and Fiction in Development*, UNU-WIDER Annual Lecture No. 16, available online at http://www.wider.unu.edu/publications/annual-lectures/en_GB/AL16/ On the importance of state capability for development and poverty reduction, and the struggle to improve it.

Rodrik, D. (2003) *The Globalization Paradox: Democracy and the World Economy* (New York: W.W. Norton) A good place to start on different development strategies in relation to globalization and some of the political tensions involved.

Wade, R. (1990; repr. 2003, with a new introduction by the author) *Governing the Market: Economic Theory and the Role of Government in East Asian Industrialization* (Princeton, NJ:Princeton University Press) An authoritative assessment of how East Asia achieved its economic success, which challenges the market-liberal view and emphasizes the role of the state.

WEB LINKS

http://www.chronicpoverty.org   An international partnership of researchers and NGOs working on chronic poverty and its eradication in Africa, Asia, and Latin America.

http://www.eldis.org   Very easy-to-use site, with downloadable research papers, reports, and many links to other sites.

http://www.imf.org   The IMF posts reports on its member countries and agreements with governments (such as 'Letters of Intent'), which spell out in detail economic reforms. The IMF's annual reports on the state of the world economy are also widely read.

http://www.odi.org.uk   The website of the Overseas Development Institute (UK), an independent think tank on development issues. The ODI Briefing Papers provide authoritative insight into the latest development issues.

http://www.un.org/millenniumgoals   For progress towards the Millennium Development Goals (MDGs).

http://www.undp.org   The website of the United Nations Development Programme (UNDP), which is leading the UN's work on the Millennium Development Goals. The UNDP's annual Human Development Report can also be viewed at this site.

http://www.unrisd.org   The website of the United Nations Research Institute for Social Development (UNRISD). The UNRISD focuses on the social dimensions of development, as well as development's political aspects.

http://www.wider.unu.edu   The website of the United Nations University's World Institute for Development Economics Research (UNU-WIDER). The UNU-WIDER Working Paper series offers a wide range of viewpoints on economic development issues, particularly in the areas of poverty measurement and inequality.

http://www.worldbank.org/en/topic/poverty   The poverty reduction website of the World Bank discusses poverty measures and presents cases of success in reducing poverty.

For additional material and resources, please visit the Online Resource Centre at:
http://www.oxfordtextbooks.co.uk/orc/burnell4e/

17
Environment

Peter Newell

Chapter contents

Overview

This chapter explores how developing countries are managing the relationship between the environment and development. Often considered a threat to their economic development and prospects for growth, environmental issues have nevertheless come to feature centrally on policy agendas throughout the developing world. Driven by donors, public concern, and vocal environmental movements, responses to these issues have taken a number of different forms as they compete for 'policy space' with other pressing development concerns and are subject to changing thinking about the effectiveness of different policy tools to tackle environmental problems. This chapter explores these issues, connecting global agendas to national policy processes, explaining differences and similarities between how countries respond to these issues, and identifying patterns of continuity and change in the politics of environment in the developing world.

Introduction

From an issue on the periphery of the policy agendas of most developing country governments, the environment has assumed an important and rising **status** on the national political agendas of states in Africa, Latin America, and Asia. This shift results from a combination of pressures from global institutions, donors, and active citizen movements, and has evolved alongside a growth in both scientific understanding of environmental problems and rising levels of public concern, often generated by environmental disasters or conflicts. In particular regarding the issue of global warming, there is a growing recognition that development gains may be systematically reversed by extreme and unpredictable climate change, which impacts most directly on the world's poor, whose livelihoods depend on agriculture, fishing, and other productive sectors particularly vulnerable to changes in rainfall and temperature.

Yet the status of the environment as an issue on developing country agendas often remains precarious. Environmental issues in many areas of the world are only loosely embedded within national policy processes, incoherently related to wider economic and social agendas, and subject to displacement by issues that assume a greater priority for most countries. The theme of this chapter, then, is continuity and change. Most countries are operating in a context in which an increasingly globalized economy impacts more directly than ever before on the relationship between environment and development. Moreover, the **institutions** and structures of global environmental **governance** shape more strongly than ever before the nature of environmental policy within the **developing world**. At the same time, this is not a passive process. Global environmental agendas have to be grafted onto existing policy agendas, national priorities, and decision-making processes that, in many cases, are characterized by bureaucratic inertia, organized opposition to reform, and reluctance to realign priorities. Yet some 'rising powers' such as India and China have also become highly proactive in global policy deliberations on the environment, as well as seeking to capitalize economically on the growing demand for environmental goods and services in the global economy. At the same time, they have also become increasingly important players in global geopolitical competitions over natural resources in Africa and elsewhere.

The chapter is organized into five main sections. The first two sections sketch the increasingly important global context for debates about environment and development, and the links between them. Such links have been institutionalized through the growth of global bodies and areas of international environmental law produced through a series of United Nations (UN) negotiations. The third looks at policy processes at the national level: how these global agendas have been responded to and 'domesticated' by individual governments. This means tackling questions about what is unique about policy processes in developing countries and what extra challenges are associated with tackling environmental problems in these settings. The fourth section looks at the range of tools and strategies that developing countries have adopted in order to combat environmental degradation. This includes discussion about the shifting roles of governments, market actors such as businesses, and **civil society** in natural resource use management and protection. The fifth section explores probable future directions of environmental **politics** in the developing world, pulling together these patterns of continuity and change.

KEY POINTS

- The environment has assumed an important and rising status on the national political agendas of states in Africa, Latin America, and Asia.

- Yet the status of the environment as an issue on developing country agendas is precarious. It is often displaced by issues that assume a greater priority for most countries.

- We can observe a process of continuity and change. Environmental challenges are handled within existing national policy frameworks, but **globalization** has changed the relationship between environment and development, and the balance of power among the actors charged with delivering **sustainable development**.

Global Context

In an unequal and fragmented international society, it is perhaps not surprising that it has been very difficult to construct a global consensus about which environmental issues are most urgent. It is often assumed that differences of opinion on this issue fall along North–South lines, where developed countries are more concerned with global problems, such as climate change and ozone depletion, and conservation issues, such as whaling and forest protection, while developing countries attach greater priority to rural issues, such as desertification and soil erosion, and localized environmental threats, such as water pollution and air quality in cities. Even a cursory look at the politics of global negotiations on these issues suggests that these categorizations are, at best, only partially accurate.

First, we need to consider issues of causation and impact. Many of those people who contribute most to global environmental degradation are not those that will suffer its worst effects. While climate change will have global impacts, wealthier countries are better placed to adapt to its adverse consequences. Whereas the Netherlands can build sea defences against sea-level rise, Bangladesh does not have the resources to protect itself against widespread flooding of low-lying agriculturally important areas. Likewise, while Australians can use sun lotions to protect themselves from harmful ultraviolet rays that are stronger as a result of ozone depletion, many rural Chileans will not be able to afford the luxury. Yet it is the developed world that contributes to global environmental problems to a proportionally much greater extent. For example, 80 per cent of the world's climate-changing carbon dioxide is produced by less that 25 per cent of the world's population. One country alone, the United States, which makes up just 4 per cent of the world's population, is responsible for 20 per cent of global emissions, while 136 developing countries together account for 24 per cent. We should also recall, however, that exposure to environmental harm and culpability for causing it is highly uneven and differentiated within countries in which inequalities along class, **gender**, and racial lines are often magnified and exacerbated by global environmental change.

Second, the economic importance of natural resources to a country's economic development is a significant determinant of its position on a particular environmental policy problem, making it difficult for developing countries to form common policy positions. Brazil has traditionally resisted calls to view the Amazonian rainforests as part of the common heritage of humankind because of their strategic importance to the country's economic development. Many other developing countries, however, have called for this principle of **global stewardship** to apply to a range of common pool resources, such as Antarctica and the deep seabed, on the basis that if those resources are to be exploited, they should be for the benefit of all and not only those richer countries that are in a position to exploit them. Similarly, while the Alliance of Small Island

States (AOSIS), threatened by sea-level rise associated with global climate change, has strongly advocated controls on greenhouse gas emissions, the Organization of Petroleum Exporting Countries (OPEC) bloc, the economies of which are heavily dependent on the export of oil, have resisted such controls.

While some developing countries view environmental policy as an opportunity to secure additional aid and new forms of technology transfer, others feel threatened by agendas that appear to constrain their prospects for growth. The G77 bloc of least-developed countries—formed at the UN after a meeting of the United Nations Conference on Trade and Development (UNCTAD) in 1964, for the purpose of promoting the collective economic interest of Third World countries—has traditionally placed the responsibility for short-term action on climate change upon the North in the negotiations on the subject. But many Latin American and Asian countries have targeted opportunities to earn much-needed revenue from participating in projects under the Clean Development Mechanism set in train by the Kyoto Protocol concluded in 1997. This allows Northern countries to pay for emissions reductions through projects in parts of the developing world where it is cheapest to do so. The rapid growth of industrial power-houses such as India, China, and Brazil has further fractured the unity of the G77 bloc. It is increasingly difficult, in light of their rising contribution to the problem of global warming, (for example China is now the single largest emitter of greenhouse gases, although not on a per capita basis), for these countries to refute the need to adopt their own legally binding emissions reduction obligations. Countries such as the United States have made their cooperation in further negotiations contingent on these countries accepting cuts in their own future emissions. Indeed, the Bali Roadmap, negotiated in 2007, explicitly called for nationally appropriate mitigation actions from developing countries, and even those countries keen to agree a second commitment period for the Kyoto Protocol (beyond 2012)—as proposed at the Durban summit in 2011 to be put in place by 2015—accept the need to move beyond the division of commitments that underpins the current Protocol between Annex 1 (more industrialized countries) and Non-Annex 1 (developing countries) in the light of which countries are now emitting most greenhouse gases and will do so into the future.

Third, aside from areas in which core national economic interests may be at stake, global environmental institutions have played a key role in shaping the national

BOX 17.1 KEY GLOBAL ENVIRONMENTAL INSTITUTIONS

United Nations Environment Programme

- Created following Stockholm Conference on the Human Environment in 1972

- Initially conceived as clearing house of environmental data and research, and to set up demonstration projects

- No statute or charter to describe its function and role

- Governing Council of fifty-eight members elected by UN General Assembly on regional formula for four-year terms

- Council mandated to promote cooperation on environmental issues and to recommend appropriate policies

- Budget of only US$10.5 million a year from regular UN budget

- Depends on voluntary contributions from member countries for financing specific projects

- No structured system of dispute settlement

- Enforcement reliant on peer review and moral pressure

Commission on Sustainable Development

- Intergovernmental body; members selected from UN

- Composed of fifty-three members elected for three-year terms

- Meets annually

- Reports to Economic and Social Council (ECOSOC) of UN

- Purpose is to review progress at international, regional, and national levels in implementation of Rio ('Earth Summit') Agreements, such as Agenda 21, the Rio Declaration, and the Forest Principles

- It provides policy guidance, promotes dialogue, and builds partnerships with major groups

Global Environment Facility

- Key financing body for actions on climate change, biodiversity loss, ozone depletion, international waters, land degradation, persistent organic pollutants (POPs)

- Set up with a budget of US$1.3 billion prior to the Earth Summit as a global fund to oversee the financing of the Rio Agreements

- Has allocated US$9.2 billion, supplemented by more than US$40 billion in co-financing, for more than 2,700 projects in more than 165 developing countries and countries with economies in transition

- Three implementing agencies: United Nations Environment Programme (UNEP); United Nations Development Programme (UNDP); World Bank

- World Bank administers facility on day-to-day basis and is trustee of the GEF trust fund

- Decisions made by consensus; in case of dispute, decisions made on double majority basis

environmental policy agendas of many developing countries. Box 17.1 summarizes the mandates and key activities of some of the more prominent global environmental institutions. It is their access to financial resources and the mandate that they have to oversee the implementation of key global environmental accords that allows these bodies to play this role. As Box 17.1 shows, the Global Environment Facility (GEF) has responsibility for overseeing the transfer of aid and technology to developing countries in order to help them to meet their obligations under the Rio Agreements, for example on climate change and biodiversity conservation. The provision of aid and technology to developing countries to meet these commitments recognizes that these countries require assistance in making a contribution to global efforts to tackle forms of environmental degradation to which most currently contribute very little. Concern was expressed at the time of the UN Conference on Environment and Development in Rio in 1992 that aid for the implementation of these

international environmental agreements should be 'additional' to that which developing countries receive for other development purposes. This concern continues today in relation to calls for 'new and additional' finance for climate change mitigation and adaptation. Developing countries are concerned that, in a context of financial austerity in donor countries, and in the absence of clear benchmarks and effective tracking, it will be tempting for richer countries to divert or re-label **official development assistance (ODA)** intended for other development purposes as aid for climate mitigation and adaptation.

Increasingly, however, these institutions and the conventions that they seek to enforce have sought to facilitate the integration of environmental and developmental concerns rather than see them as competing issues. There has been a clear shift towards addressing development concerns that can be traced from the Stockholm Conference on the Human Environment in 1972 onwards (see Box 17.2). This prepared the ground

BOX 17.2 CHRONOLOGY OF ENVIRONMENT AND DEVELOPMENT ON THE INTERNATIONAL AGENDA

1972: Stockholm Conference on the Human Environment

- Created United Nations Environment Programme (UNEP)
- Established key principles of responsible global environmental stewardship
- Set in train global scientific cooperation

1980: Brandt Commission

- North–South: A Programme for Survival
- Addressing North–South elements more clearly: trade; debt; energy; food

1987: World Commission on Environment and Development

- *Our Common Future* (Brundtland Report)
- Birth of a concept: 'sustainable development'

1992: United Nations Conference and Development (UNCED)

- United Nations Framework Convention on Climate Change

- Convention on Biological Diversity
- Rio Declaration
- Statement of Forest Principles
- Agenda 21

2002: World Summit on Sustainable Development (WSSD)

- Agreement on water and sanitation (to halve the number of people without access to basic sanitation by 2015)
- Agreement on fisheries (plan to restore world's depleted stocks by 2015; to create marine areas around the world by 2012)

2012: Rio+20

- Produced a non-binding document called 'The Future We Want', which emphasized 'green growth' and the need to strengthen institutional frameworks for sustainable development as major themes, but failed to agree on new targets or concrete actions

for the famous Brundtland Report *Our Common Future* (1987)—which first coined the phrase 'sustainable development', defined as 'Development which meets the needs of the current generation without compromising the ability of future generations to meet their own needs'. The title of the Rio Conference that followed five years later encapsulated the rhetorical integration of environmental and developmental objectives: the 'United Nations Conference on Environment and Development'. Ten years on, the language of sustainable development was placed centrally in the naming of the follow-up to Rio, the 'World Summit on Sustainable Development' (WSSD) in Johannesburg in 2002. At the Rio+20 Summit in 2012, great emphasis was placed on the idea of a 'green economy' to promote the idea, once again, that growth could be green.

Despite this rhetorical shift, many developing countries and activists have been critical of the way in which certain issues have been actively kept off the agenda of these summits. The Rio Conference of 1992 attracted criticism for not addressing issues such as debt, terms of trade, or the regulation of multinational companies—issues that some developing countries

have sought to advance since the early 1970s, initially through the platform of the 'new international economic order'. The US delegation to the Conference fought hard to remove references to unsustainable levels of consumption in the Rio documents in 1992 and again in 2012, and concerns were raised during the WSSD at attempts to thwart the negotiation of a new convention on corporate accountability.

Rather than viewing environmental issues as stand-alone concerns, it is becoming increasingly clear that it is necessary to '**mainstream**' environmental concerns into the activities of leading development actors. As far back as 1987, the World Bank set up an environmental department; it now insists on detailed environmental impact assessments of all of its lending programmes. Yet it continues to draw fire for a perceived failure to mainstream environmental issues throughout its operations. For example, despite serving as the interim trustee of the Green Climate Fund, a report from the World Resources Institute found that less than 30 per cent of the World Bank's lending to the energy sector has integrated climate considerations into project decision-making and that, as late as 2007, more than 50 per cent of the World Bank's energy-sector portfolio did not include climate change considerations at all (World Resources Institute 2008). The World Trade Organization (WTO), for its part, has created a Committee on Trade and Environment. This first met in 1995 to look at the relationship between environmental standards and trade liberalization, although notably and controversially not the environmental impacts of trade. The emphasis has therefore been on defining the legitimate circumstances in which environmental and human health concerns can be invoked as exceptions to the normal obligations that countries assume through membership of the WTO, rather than the ecological cost of transporting greater volumes of goods across ever larger distances, for example. The question is whether environmental considerations should be allowed to drive decisions about which types of trade are desirable and necessary from the point of view of sustainable development, or whether all environmental measures that impact upon trade have to be compatible with WTO rules. For developing countries, one of the key concerns has been the growth in environmental standards that many fear will be used as barriers to trade and disguised forms of protectionism to protect Northern producers from competitive exports from the South. High-profile cases that have come before the WTO's Dispute Settlement Body (DSB), such as the Tuna–Dolphin disputes, have reflected this fear. In this case, the United States sought to ban yellowfin tuna imports from Mexico on the grounds that the nets being used by the Mexican fishing industry to catch tuna fish were also killing dolphins.

KEY POINTS

- There is now a wide range of global environmental agreements that developing countries have signed and are in the process of implementing.

- Although development issues have gained a higher profile in global environmental summits and agreements, there is still some concern that Northern countries continue to control the agenda.

- Countries' positions on these issues do not fall neatly along North–South lines, however, and key differences exist between developing countries on many high-profile global environmental issues.

- There have been moves towards mainstreaming environmental concerns into the lending practices of multilateral development agencies, but critics suggest these have not gone nearly far enough.

Environment and Development: An Uneasy Relationship

The relationship between environment and development is not an easy one, and many conflicts are subsumed under the convenient banner of 'sustainable development', the aims of which it is difficult for anyone to refute. Many have therefore questioned its value as an analytical concept, when it can be invoked so easily to justify 'business as usual' polluting activities. The term disguises conflicts over priorities between environment and development, gives few, if any, indications about which forms of development are sustainable, and is inevitably interpreted by different actors to mean different things. Fundamental conflicts over the causes and appropriate solutions to environmental degradation persist. These include the debate about the extent to which population growth is a cause of environmental degradation. Malthusian (after the eighteenth-century thinker the Reverend Thomas Malthus) analysis of resource degradation, popular in certain strands of 1970s environmental thinking (Ehrlich 1972), suggested that rapid increases in population were driving the planet towards ecological collapse because of the strain on natural resource systems. The influential 'limits of growth' report in 1972 of the Club of Rome suggested instead that unsustainable patterns of resource use would ultimately bring about ecological collapse because of the finite nature of the natural resource base upon which we all depend. Many developing countries and more radical environmental groups target overconsumption and affluence in Western societies, rather than population, as the key cause of the global environmental crisis.

Given this lack of consensus on the causes of environmental degradation, it is unsurprising that consensus eludes attempts to find appropriate solutions. Old conflicts in development over aid, trade, debt, and the role of technology get replayed through discussions about how to combat environmental degradation. Those believing that poverty leads people to use resources unsustainably have looked to ideas such as debt-for-nature swaps, whereby debt relief is provided in exchange for commitments to preserve areas of forest, as a way out of this cycle. This model informs current initiatives on reducing emissions from deforestation and forest degradation (REDD), and payments for ecosystem services (PES), which compensate host communities for the environmental service that they provide in preserving forests that act as important carbon sinks.

Critiques of the effects of aid and technology transfer on developing countries also get rehearsed in environmental debates. For example, it is alleged that technologies that are transferred as part of global environmental agreements are often out of date, inappropriate to local needs, and serve only as a subsidy to Northern producers of technologies for which markets no longer exist. In environmental terms, it is also argued that technologies are no substitute for tough action aimed at reducing unsustainable patterns of production and consumption, and that developed countries often prefer to transfer technologies to developing countries rather than take measures to address the source of environmental degradation in their own countries.

This, then, is the global historical and contemporary context that shapes the ways in which developing countries have been tackling environmental issues at the national level. The next section looks in more detail at the commonalities and differences in the ways in which developing countries have responded to these global environmental agendas, while grappling with their own unique environmental problems and development needs.

KEY POINTS

- The term 'sustainable development' disguises key conflicts over priorities between environment and development.

- There is little consensus on the causes of environmental degradation and the importance that should be attached to population growth in the South, as opposed to unsustainable consumption in the North.

- Fundamental disagreements arise concerning the role of aid, trade, and technology as appropriate solutions to environmental problems.

Policy Processes

Political diversity

It is impossible to make generalizations about environmental policy that would apply across the entire developing world. Although nearly all developing countries are involved in global negotiations on the aforementioned issues, the processes by which they translate those commitments into workable policies at the national level are very different. First, there is the issue of power. There is clearly a difference between countries such as China or India, with significant scope for independent action and power to assert their interests in global forums, and smaller and less powerful countries such as Uruguay or Zambia. This difference relates in part to the resources that can be committed to participating in global processes, which can be highly time-consuming and resource-intensive. Environmental negotiations take place all around the world and are therefore costly to attend, and to participate effectively in them requires a large delegation with access to scientific and legal expertise. Developing countries are often able to send only at most one or two government representatives to these negotiations, which are often run with parallel meetings that a small delegation cannot attend. But it is also about the leverage that countries wield. At critical moments, such as in the final hours of the Copenhagen Climate Change Summit in December 2009, it was larger developing countries such as Brazil, South Africa, India, and China that were invited to participate in a closed meeting to advance progress in the talks. They were the actors whose cooperation and support was most required.

But the degree of power that a country has in global economic terms and the extent to which it is aid-dependent also affects its vulnerability to pressure to take environmental action. Countries such as Mali and Ethiopia are highly dependent on aid. In Mali's case, the overwhelming majority of that aid comes from its former colonizer, France. Research programmes and policy priorities are therefore strongly affected by such bilateral financial ties. Countries such as Brazil, on the other hand, have a larger degree of discretion in determining policy positions, and they can draw on greater economic weight in trade and industrial terms to resist calls from the **international community** to do more to combat deforestation in the country.

Second, but related, are issues of capacity for the enforcement of policy. Many developing countries, such as India, have some of the most impressive legislative Acts on environmental issues in the world. But lack of resources and training, and the **corruption** of local pollution control officials, often conspire to delay implementation. Sometimes, the nature of the problem and the size of the country are the key constraints. For example, regulating the cultivation and trade in genetically modified (GM) seeds is almost impossible in a country the size of China and many instances of illegal growing of non-authorized seeds have been reported. Managing the transborder movement of GM seeds, as is required by the 2000 Cartagena Protocol on Biosafety (under the Convention on Biological Diversity), presents many problems for developing countries, where seed markets are often poorly regulated and even basic equipment with which to test movements of seeds across borders is unavailable. Where countries have a strong economic and developmental incentive to ensure active compliance, extra steps may be taken. Kenya is keen to be seen as an attractive tourist location for wildlife safaris. Because tourism provides a large source of revenue, officials have gone to controversial lengths to tackle the problem of illegal poaching of elephants and rhinos for their ivory and horns. These include shooting poachers and banning tribal groups from culling animals for food, even on their own ancestral lands.

Third, the degree of importance that will be attached to environmental concerns, at the expense of broader development goals, will reflect the nature of democratic politics in the country. The strength of environmental groups in a country, pushing for new policy and acting as informal 'watchdogs' of compliance with environmental regulations, will be determined by the degree of democratic space that exists within the country. Countries such as India and Mexico have strong traditions of active civil society engagement in environmental policy. India, for instance, hosts such globally recognized **non-governmental organizations (NGOs)** as the Centre for Science and Environment and its more research-oriented counterpart The Energy and Resources Institute (TERI), which are active in global policy debates, as well as domestic agenda-setting. In Singapore and China, by contrast, the avenues for policy engagement are few and tightly restricted. The scope and effectiveness of environmental policy will also be shaped by the extent to which the interests of leading industries are affected by proposed interventions. Where policy directly impinges on the interests of a particularly powerful industry, policy reform is often stalled or environmental concerns are kept off the agenda altogether. The close ties between logging companies and state officials that often have personal commercial stakes in the companies is an often-cited reason for the lack of progress

to reverse unsustainable logging in South-East Asia (Dauvergne 1997).

The way in which governments formulate and implement policy also reflects a broad diversity of styles of environmental policymaking. Each country has a unique history when it comes to its approach to regulation, the organization of its bureaucracy, and the extent to which public participation in policy is encouraged and enabled. The Chinese government is able to act decisively and in a 'command and control' fashion to sanction industries failing to comply with pollution control regulations. In India, the Supreme Court has played a decisive role in moving environmental policy forward, often in controversial circumstances, setting strict and sometimes unrealistic targets, for example for the phasing out of non-compressed-natural-gas (CNG) vehicles in Delhi. Other countries have a more reactive policy style, influenced by popular politics. In Argentina, the government had consistently failed to take action to protect a forest in the north of the country until football legend Maradona joined Greenpeace's campaign to protect the forest, prompting immediate government action.

Approaches to environmental policy also reflect the different ways in which knowledge, especially scientific knowledge, informs policy. Scientific knowledge does not provide a neutral and value-free guide to which environmental problems are the most serious or how they should be addressed. It is employed strategically by government officials to support their position within the bureaucracy, but can also change political practice and priorities by highlighting some areas of concern while ignoring others. The power of expert communities in this regard explains why developing countries have sought greater representation of Southern-based scientists in international environmental bodies providing advice to policymakers, such as the Cartagena Protocol on Biosafety's 'roster of experts' or the Intergovernmental Panel on Climate Change.

Given these factors, there is sometimes also a mismatch between the expectations contained in multilateral environmental agreements about the way in which commitments should be implemented and the realities of what is possible in many developing country settings. There is the problem of capacity, whereby the resources and skills to oversee micro-level implementation of environmental regulations emanating from central government to meet global commitments are often lacking. In addition, many agreements, including the Cartagena Protocol on Biosafety, specify the process by which national environmental frameworks should be designed, with respect to public consultation and participation. Yet many are poorly placed to set up meaningfully elaborate participatory processes for deliberative and inclusive decision-making across a wide range of issues, involving a cross-section of their societies. Democratic values are weakly embedded in many societies and publics in many places remain sceptical of interaction with official bodies, such that good global intentions may not translate well into local practice.

Common challenges

Despite these differences in the policy positions and policy styles that developing countries have adopted, it is worth highlighting some common challenges that nearly all developing, and of course many developed, countries face in the design and execution of environmental policy. First, there is the scale of resources required to tackle environmental problems. Undertaking scientific research and monitoring the enforcement of pollution control places large resource demands on developing countries in particular. International environmental agreements create new demands of governments for more regulation, more monitoring, and an efficient and effective bureaucracy to oversee these, often across multiple levels of governance right down to the local level. Despite the availability of global funds to support some of these activities (see Box 17.1), it remains difficult even for larger developing countries to meet these expectations.

Second, in spite of the efforts of active environmental movements within developing countries, as well as globally, it remains the case that political constituencies with a strong preference for more effective environmental policy are often very weak. The issue is not only that the beneficiaries of environmental policies are not present in policy debates (future generations) or not adequately represented (indigenous peoples for example), but also that political parties with strong commitments to environmental issues are not well developed in most parts of Asia, Africa, and Latin America. Conversely, the presence in Europe of green parties has served to keep environmental issues on the agendas of the main parties.

Where **social movements** have taken up environmental issues, they often touch on deeply sensitive issues—for example access to resources such as forests and water or land reform—bringing them into conflict with state elites. *Campesino* (peasant-based) movements in Latin America often incorporate environmental issues into broader campaigning platforms for land redistribution and greater levels of compensation for the appropriation of natural resources (see Chapter 11). Movements for environmental justice that oppose the location of often hazardous and highly polluting industries in poorer communities often frustrate the development ambitions of policy elites. The ability of movements to use environmental issues to advance broader political agendas serves to entrench the suspicion that many governments have of environmental agendas. Occasionally, however, governments see in environmental issues an opportunity to gain political capital on an issue of national concern. The Argentine government became locked in conflict with neighbouring Uruguay over pulp mills set up there, which it alleged are contaminating the Uruguay River that the two countries share. Argentina even initiated proceedings at the International Court of Justice in The Hague over the issue following large popular protests, despite claims that it hosts many equally polluting pulp mills within its own territory.

Third, it is important to recognize the global economic pressures that all countries face, but which developing countries face more acutely. Crushing debt burdens and the conditions attached to **structural adjustment programmes** (SAPS; see Chapter 16) often create incentives for economic activities that are highly destructive of the environment. Export-led growth patterns, which often require intensive use of land with heavy applications of chemical fertilizers, and the creation of export-processing zones (EPZs), the aim of which is to attract foreign capital to areas in which labour is cheap and environmental standards are lower, are indicative of this. Deteriorating terms of trade for timber, minerals, and agricultural produce also drive developing country economies, dependent on single commodities, to exploit that resource unsustainably. In the aftermath of the financial crisis in South-East Asia in the late 1990s, for example, timber producers increased exports to unsustainable levels to compensate for the losses that they incurred from depreciating national currencies.

The broader issue is what has been termed the 'race to the bottom' in environmental standards as developing countries compete to lower environmental regulations in order to attract increasingly mobile investors. The evidence for this is mixed.

Some argue that increased patterns of trade interdependence have the effect of raising standards as developing country exporters seek access to lucrative Western markets that require higher environmental standards (Vogel 1997). However, there are many examples of regulatory reforms not being introduced or not implemented for fear of deterring investors. For example, in response to pressure from soybean exporters in the United States, the Chinese government delayed plans to introduce a series of biosafety measures that exporters considered overly restrictive. In other cases, lack of environmental regulation has been used as a **comparative advantage** to attract environmentally hazardous production of substances, such as toxic wastes and asbestos, which were banned in richer countries. The desperation of many developing countries to attract investment on any terms therefore clearly both affects their ability to prioritize action on the environment and, in certain situations, will lead them to lower standards in order to attract mobile capital.

It is also the case that many developing countries have abundant natural resources that make them key locations for extractive industries. For years, activists have berated the mining industry for its environmental pollution, **human rights** violations, and displacement of indigenous peoples. The oil industry too has been accused of double standards when it operates in developing countries. The activities of firms such as Shell in Nigeria's Niger Delta and Texaco in Ecuador have attracted global attention as a result of activist exposure and high-profile legal actions against the companies (Newell 2001).

By way of response, many firms have developed corporate social responsibility (CSR) programmes to defend and promote their reputations, and to present themselves as a force for good. It is now commonplace for larger companies to claim that their companies incorporate sustainable development in their investment decision-making. This discourse is being picked up by export-oriented Southern-based multinationals and state-owned firms as they come under pressure from Northern corporate buyers and consumers to improve their own social and environmental performance. However, it remains the case that many of the drivers of corporate environmental responsibility, including government incentives, civil society watchdogs, and consumer and investor pressure, are currently underdeveloped in many parts of the developing world. Firms within

countries with strong trading ties to overseas markets in which compliance with tougher environmental regulations is expected will often have higher standards than many firms in parts of sub-Saharan Africa, for example, which are more isolated from such global pressures.

Fourth, the **underdevelopment** of the scientific expertise that underpins environmental policy is a characteristic common to many developing countries. While there are many international scientific research programmes on environmental issues and many international environmental agreements have panels or rosters of experts, the representation of scientists from developing countries is often low. There have been initiatives from UNEP to try to address this problem by ensuring, for example, that a percentage of scientists on such bodies are from developing countries. But the problem endures, and the implication is that the agendas of Northern researchers and their policy networks attract greater attention and resources than issues and concerns that are more pertinent to the developing world. This criticism has been levelled at the work of GEF, for instance, for being more responsive to the agendas of Northern bodies upon which it is dependent for funding than to the recipients of its capacity-building measures in the South. The World Bank (2000: 14) has also conceded that its' 'preference for big loans can easily distract regulators from confronting their communities' most critical pollution problems'.

KEY POINTS

- Despite facing similar international pressures to integrate environmental issues into development policy, the willingness and ability of developing countries to address environmental challenges is highly uneven.

- There are important differences in priorities, power and policy autonomy, resources and capacity, and policy styles between governments in the developing world, and in relation to the role of environmental and business groups in policy formulation and implementation.

- There are, however, many common challenges that developing countries face when it comes to environmental policy: weaknesses in enforcement capacity; economic vulnerability, which means that trade and aid leverage can be used to influence policy; and an underdeveloped knowledge base from which to develop environmental policy.

BOX 17.3 THE RIGHT TO WATER IN SOUTH AFRICA

- South Africa is the only country that recognizes the human right to water at the constitutional and policy level through its Free Basic Water policy.

- The Water Services Act of 1997 provides for a basic level of water for those that cannot pay. People are entitled to 25 litres of water free per day for personal and domestic use.

- There is, nevertheless, uneven access to water. Problems of capacity of local authorities to deliver on the commitment and financial constraints have led to undersupply and to people being cut off. This has led some people to get water from unprotected sources—leading to health problems.

- The government is also under immense pressure to introduce user fees and cost recovery in line with market-based approaches to water provision.

- Many people are also unaware of their constitutional right to water and therefore when their rights are violated.

- Although some legal cases have secured interim relief from disconnections by invoking the right to water, the onus on proving inability to pay rests with the water user and depends on his or her access to legal representation.

Source: Mehta (2006)

New Policy Instruments for Environmental Protection

We have already noted the different policy styles that developing countries around the world have employed in the design and implementation of environmental policy. It is also the case, however, that they have been affected by shifts in prevailing thinking about the most efficient and effective way in which to provide environmental goods, particularly an increased emphasis on the use of market-based mechanisms. This is not to suggest that strong **developmental states** are not, on occasion, able to intervene forcibly to close down polluting industry, or to overlook the important role of legal systems in driving environmental policy reform and in protecting the rights of citizens against their own government. Courts have been a key site for poorer groups to seek compensation for socially and environmentally destructive investments that have undermined their livelihoods (see Chapter 11). They have provided a venue in which to draw attention to grievances that have not been recognized elsewhere. Where successful, legal cases can uphold key rights to environmental information, ensure that environmental impact assessments are undertaken in advance of large industrial projects, or contest the forced displacement that is associated with infrastructural projects such as dams. In Nigeria, numerous cases have been brought against oil companies by communities seeking compensation for damage to land caused by oil spillages from company pipelines in the Niger Delta. Companies exploiting lower health and environmental standards in developing countries, providing their workers with less protection than their counterparts in the North, have also ended up paying large out-of-court settlements to victims of industrial hazards. More positively and proactively, poorer groups have also been able to use legal remedies to realize their rights to key resources such as water, which is a constitutional right in South Africa (see Box 17.3), or to access forests (Newell and Wheeler 2006).

Relying on legal remedies to tackle environmental problems is often inadequate, however. People frequently resort to the law only after the pollution has occurred. There are also limits to how poorer groups can use the law to their benefit. Poorer communities frequently lack the financial resources to bring a case. They lack the 'legal literacy' necessary to understand their rights under the law and how they can be realized. These problems of access are often compounded by long backlogs of cases and distrust in the independence of the legal system. There are many legal barriers to successfully demonstrating cause and effect between a polluting activity and evidence of damage to human health or the environment, particularly when poorer groups are exposed to such a range of hazards in their day-to-day lives.

State-based environmental regulation, in general, however, has been subject to sustained criticism from key development actors such as the World Bank on the grounds that it is inflexible, inefficient, and often ineffective at delivering the change in behaviour that it intends. Increasingly, the preference is for the use of the market as a tool for incentivizing positive action and deterring polluting activities. Examples of pollution charging in China, Colombia, and the Philippines show that pollution from factories has been successfully reduced when steep, regular payments for emissions have been enforced. Market tools such as labelling have also been accepted in many developing countries as a means by which to assure global buyers of the environmentally responsible way in which the product has been produced, as well as to facilitate consumer choice. For example, certification has been used in the forestry sector by the popular Forestry Stewardship Council (FSC) scheme. The World Bank, UNDP, and many regional development banks are also now active in setting up carbon markets throughout the developing world, as a way of accessing carbon finance and providing support to lower carbon development pathways.

Another general trend in environmental policy that is catching on in the developing world is the adoption of voluntary measures by industry. Codes of conduct among leading companies are now commonplace in the North, and many of those firms investing overseas are insisting that their suppliers and partners adopt them. The trend forms part of the rejection of the alleged inefficiencies and ineffectiveness of central government 'command and control' policy measures noted earlier. But it also reflects the preference of firms to set their own standards appropriate to their own circumstances in a way that avoids or pre-empts state intervention. In the environmental context, environmental management systems such as ISO 14001 created by the International Organization for Standardization (ISO) are increasingly popular. While, traditionally, such standards have tended to apply only to larger firms that can afford the compliance costs and those seeking access to developed country markets, small and medium-sized enterprises (SMEs) are increasingly seeking ISO certification in order to serve as subcontractors for ISO-certified enterprises. There are also sector-specific programmes such as 'Responsible Care' in the case of the chemical industry, which have been adopted in countries such as Mexico and Brazil in a process described as 'exporting environmentalism' (Garcia-Johnson 2000). It is clear, then, that global market pressures from buyers and consumers increasingly exercise as significant an influence on environmental policy practice in many parts of the developing world as the international agreements which governments sign up to.

As a reaction to the limitations of market-based and voluntary mechanisms, there has also been a growth in what has been termed '**civil regulation**' (Newell 2001): civil-society-based forms of business regulation. The increasing use of such tools as shareholder activism and boycotts, and the growth of watchdog groups such as OilWatch based in Nigeria, are illustrative of the trend. New forms of engagement in constructing codes of conduct and building partnerships between business and civil society also come under the umbrella of civil regulation. Concern has been expressed that many of these tools are available only to well-resourced groups with good access to the media and in societies with strong traditions of free speech. But there does seem to be evidence of these strategies being employed on an increasing scale in most parts of the global South. Strategies of resistance and exposure of corporate wrongdoing date from colonial times, but there has also been a notable proliferation in groups across the entire spectrum adopting them, ranging from confrontation to collaboration. Many of these groups are also increasingly globally well connected. This means that companies engaging in environmentally controversial activities in the developing world can also expect to face shareholder resolutions and embarrassing media publicity in their home countries. The Canadian company Tiomin, for example, has faced considerable pressure from activists in Canada over its mining operations on Kenya's coast, working with local NGOs such as CoastWatch.

It is unclear at this stage what the net effect of these forms of civil regulation will be on the environmental performance of investors in developing countries. The hope is that groups with the expertise and capabilities to plug gaps and weaknesses in systems of government pollution control and monitoring can play an important complementary role as informal regulators. One study of community-based regulation in Vietnam shows how this has been possible when 'the energies and actions of average community members and the responses of front-line environmental agencies' have been brought together (O'Rourke 2004: xvii). This may encourage firms to respect the environmental standards of the countries in which they operate to a greater degree than if they were not there, and so help to dissuade companies from adopting double standards when they operate in developing countries. The extent to which groups will be allowed to perform this role will depend on the strength of civil society in a given setting and the extent to which its activities are tolerated by the state. Issues of whom the groups represent and to whom they are accountable will also have to be faced if they are to be seen as legitimate actors in environmental policy.

KEY POINTS

- Many countries continue to use central government 'command and control' environmental policy measures.

- Despite their limitations, poorer groups have sought to use legal remedies to claim rights to resources, to contest planning processes, and to seek compensation for loss of livelihood.

- There has been a shift, however, in thinking about how best to tackle environmental pollution away from state-based approaches, towards the use of market instruments and voluntary approaches.

- Many companies in developing countries are seeking certification for their products in order to get access to Northern markets.

- In recent years, there has been a trend towards informal industry regulation by civil society groups. The long-term impact of this form of civil-society-based regulation will vary by country, and the extent to which such groups are able to address issues of their own accountability and representation.

Futures

Attempting to predict the likely future of environmental policy in the developing or developed world with any degree of accuracy and precision is a fruitless endeavour. It is, however, possible to identify certain patterns of continuity and change. We have seen how many developing countries face common challenges in terms of how to reconcile pressing development needs with environmental goals. Countries have inevitably responded in different ways that reflect, among other things, their political systems, the nature of their economies, and the level of civil society engagement. But we have seen similar problems of enforcement at the national level, constraints that arise from economic relationships of trade, aid, and debt, and conflicts between global, often largely Northern, environmental priorities and more pressing issues at the local level.

Through global processes of negotiation, increasingly integrated supply chains, and globally interdependent trading patterns, we have seen how pressures come to be exerted on developing countries to design and implement environmental policies in ways that reflect the priorities of Northern governments, businesses, and international organizations. Shifts in thinking about environmental policy, and what makes it more effective and efficient, are transmitted through donor lending and the global reach of transnational companies. These are the sorts of pressures that bring about conformity and harmonization in environmental politics in the developing world.

But there is much that is subject to change, such is the fragile and often ephemeral status of environmental issues on the policy agendas of countries the world over. The status of such issues is as vulnerable to the state of the world economy as it is to the health of the planet. Despite calls in the North for a 'green new deal' (increased public investment in new jobs and green technology in the wake of the financial crisis that started in 2008), government spending on environmental programmes notoriously goes down in times of recession as other issues assume a higher profile. The links between security and the environment continue to attract increasing attention. Resources such as oil and water are often cited both as a cause and a manifestation of geopolitical conflicts in the Middle East, for example, while the way in which drought exacerbated the conflict in Darfur has led some to call it, controversially, the world's first 'climate war'. Priorities shift according to global events as much as they reflect changes in domestic politics following changes of government. A realignment of donor priorities in the wake of these shifts may have a significant impact on resource allocations for environmental projects, or the extent to which some regions of the developing world come to be favoured over others on the basis of their strategic value to Western interests. Nevertheless, with or without donor support, developing countries face many environmental challenges of their own, including water pollution, land degradation, and urban air quality. It is often the human impact of these problems that attracts attention and acts as the driver for change. The increasingly high human cost of environmental degradation exacts an economic price: costs to health systems increase—levels of disease—and an unhealthy workforce is an unproductive workforce. Despite increasing acknowledgement of the human and developmental case for tackling environmental degradation, stark trade-offs between environmentally damaging investment and no investment at all continue to force governments to put profit before the needs of their own people or the planet. Global economic pressures from highly mobile companies and global economic institutions further load the dice towards investment and exports over the imperatives of sustainable development.

Sometimes, of course, environmental problems draw attention to themselves and demand action from governments. Floods in Mozambique, droughts in Ethiopia, and forest fires in South-East Asia, the intensity of which will increase as our climate changes, prompt short-term emergency measures. Rarely, however, do they initiate deeper reflection about the deeper causes of the crisis. Nevertheless, the increased incidence of such human-induced, yet seemingly 'natural', events may, more than any other single factor, serve to focus the world's attention on the environmental consequences of current patterns of development. They may come to act as a catalyst to more far-reaching action aimed at combating environmental degradation.

Conclusion

Developing countries face a range of often contradictory pressures from international institutions, market actors, and civil society regarding how to reconcile environmental protection with broader development goals. How they handle these challenges will be a function of both domestic political factors and global political influences. Access to diminishing supplies of resources such as oil and conflicts over water, exacerbated by climate change, will link environmental issues ever more closely to questions of national and international security. A key driver of policy responses will continue to be environmental disasters, which focus public attention on the impacts of particular types of development. The challenge is to harness this concern towards longer-term change aimed at tackling the causes of environmental degradation, rather than merely to address some of its immediate symptoms.

QUESTIONS

1. Why has the relationship between environment and development been so uneasy?

2. Is it still meaningful to refer to the global South in international environmental negotiations?

3. Discuss the relationship between environment and national and international security.

4. How far does climate change force us to rethink conventional models of development?

5. Under what circumstances might environment and development challenges be reconciled more effectively in the future?

6. Which institutional reforms could improve the international community's ability to promote sustainable development effectively?

FURTHER READING

Adams, W. M. (2008) *Green Development: Environment and Sustainability in the Third World*, 2nd edn (London: Routledge) Provides a detailed history of the concept of sustainable development, and the different ways in which it has been interpreted and applied in the mainstream and by its critics.

Bryant, R. L. and Bailey, S. (1997) *Third World Political Ecology* (London: Routledge) Provides a useful actor-based introduction to the key forces shaping environmental politics in the developing world, from business and multilateral institutions, to NGOs and the role of the state.

Elliott, L. (2004) *The Global Politics of the Environment* (London: Macmillan) Wide-ranging textbook that covers not only the global environmental agenda, but also issues of trade, debt, and aid, which bring together environmental and development agendas.

Keeley, J. and Scoones, I. (2003) *Understanding Environmental Policy Processes: Cases from Africa* (London: Earthscan) Drawing on research in Ethiopia, Mali, and Zimbabwe, this book examines the links between knowledge, power, and politics in understanding how environmental issues come to be framed and the consequences of this for how they are acted upon.

Newell, P. (2012) *Globalization and the Environment: Capitalism, Ecology and Power* (Cambridge: Polity) Emphasizes the centrality of politics and social relations to understanding the nature of the relationship between globalization and the environment, focused particularly on trade, production, and finance, and their environmental impacts, governance, and contestation.

Peets, R., Robbins, P. and Watts, M. (eds) (2010) *Global Political Ecology* (London: Routledge) Collection of essays, which provides theoretical perspectives from political ecology and political economy, and empirical case studies of a range of urban and rural environmental issues from the developed and developing world.

WEB LINKS

http://practicalaction.org/home   The site of Practical Action, UK (formerly known as Intermediate Technology and Development Group) contains details on the organization, its project and research work, and reports and publications on a range of environment and development issues.

http://www.acts.or.ke   The African Centre for Technology Studies, Nairobi, Kenya, provides useful studies, resources, and news items on issues such as agriculture and food security, climate change, and biotechnology.

http://www.cseindia.org   The site of the Centre for Science and Environment, Delhi, India, contains reports and details of campaigns on key environmental challenges facing India, although maintains a global focus too.

http://www.iied.org   The site of the International Institute for Environment and Development, London, UK, contains details on the latest research and publications produced by the Institute on a range of environment and development issues.

http://www.iisd.org   The International Institute for Sustainable Development, Winnipeg, Canada: among other useful databanks, this site gives access to the Earth Negotiations Bulletin, which provides updates on all of the leading international environmental negotiations.

http://www.steps-centre.org   This University of Sussex research centre on social, technological, and environmental pathways to sustainability produces research on a range of environmental and development issues. The site also provides access to the Eldis gateway from where searches for information and studies on particular environmental issues in specific developing countries can be undertaken.

http://www.twnside.org.sg   The site of the Third World Network, Kuala Lumpur, Malaysia, contains position papers, reports, and information updates from the network's members on issues such as trade, biotechnology, and climate change.

http://www.unep.org   The United Nations Environment Programme site is a mine of information about global environmental issues and the negotiations aimed at tackling them.

http://www.worldbank.org   Contains the World Bank's *World Development Report 2010: Development and Climate Change*.

For additional material and resources, please visit the Online Resource Centre at:
http://www.oxfordtextbooks.co.uk/orc/burnell4e/

18
Human Rights

Michael Freeman

Chapter contents

Overview

The language of human rights is a pervasive feature of contemporary international politics, but it is not well understood. This chapter offers an analysis of the concept, a brief account of its history, and a description of the international human rights regime. It proceeds to examine two persistent problems that arise in applying the concept to developing countries: the relations between human rights and development; and the relations between the claim that the concept is universally valid and the realities of cultural difference around the world. The idea of human rights derives from historical problems of the West. It is necessary to consider its applicability to the problems of developing countries in a world constituted by great inequalities of political power and wealth.

Introduction

The concept of '**human rights**' derives primarily from the United Nations Charter, which was adopted in 1945 immediately after the Second World War. The Preamble to the Charter declares that the United Nations (UN) was determined to 'reaffirm faith in fundamental human rights, in the dignity and worth of the human person, in the equal rights of men and women, and of nations large and small'. In 1948, the UN General Assembly adopted the Universal Declaration of Human Rights, which sets out a list of human rights 'as a common standard of achievement for all peoples'. The list includes such civil and political rights as those to: freedom from slavery, torture, arbitrary arrest, and detention; freedom of religion, expression, and association; and a number of economic and social rights, such as the rights to education and an adequate standard of living. These rights were intended to protect everyone from tyrannical governments like that of Nazi Germany and from the economic misery that was thought to have facilitated the rise of fascism.

Although the countries of Latin America, Asia, and Africa formed the majority of those that produced the Declaration, many of the world's people lived at that time under colonial rule and were thus excluded from this process. The concept of human rights was derived from a Western philosophical tradition and was shaped mainly by European historical experience. Colonialism was itself condemned for its human rights violations and, when worldwide decolonization brought many new states to the UN, the **post-colonial states** accepted human rights in principle, although their priorities differed from those of the West, emphasizing self-determination, development, economic and social rather than civil and political rights, and anti-racism.

Disagreements about which human rights should be legally binding led to the adoption of two UN human rights covenants in 1966: the International Covenant on Civil and Political Rights; and the International Covenant on Economic, Social and Cultural Rights. The UN's World Conference on Human Rights, held in Vienna in 1993, declared all human rights to be 'indivisible and interdependent'. Now, each covenant has been ratified by more than 80 per cent of the UN's member states.

The UN has adopted several more specialized conventions (see Box 18.1). There are also regional human rights conventions, although these do not cover the whole world, especially the Middle East and Asia. The European Convention on Human Rights was adopted

---

BOX 18.1 UNIVERSAL AND REGIONAL HUMAN RIGHTS REGIMES

Universal Declaration of Human Rights 1948

European Convention on Human Rights 1950

International Covenant on Civil and Political Rights 1966

International Covenant on Economic, Social and Cultural Rights 1966

International Convention on the Elimination of Racial Discrimination 1966

American Convention on Human Rights 1969

Convention on the Elimination of Discrimination against Women 1979

African Charter on Human and Peoples' Rights 1981

Convention against Torture 1984

Convention on the Rights of the Child 1989

---

in 1950; the American Convention on Human Rights in 1969; and the African Charter on Human and Peoples' Rights in 1981.

Many developing countries have poor human rights records. There are internal and external explanations of this. The internal explanations include poverty, ethnic tensions, and authoritarian government. Some of the internal problems of developing countries are legacies of colonialism. The external explanations include support for dictatorships by the great powers, especially during the cold war, and the global economic system, which many believe is biased against developing countries and thereby hinders their capacity to develop the **institutions** necessary to protect human rights. Since the end of the cold war, and the discrediting of the Soviet, state socialist model of development, **neoliberalism**—the ideology of free markets—has dominated global economics. Whether neoliberalism promotes respect for, or violation of, human rights is highly controversial. The Universal Declaration's conception of human rights, however, presupposed effective states and neoliberalism tends to weaken states, and especially their capacity to protect social and economic rights, such as those to health, education, and freedom from poverty. The harmful effects of such policies disproportionately affect women and children. Recently, following criticism of neoliberalism from many quarters, international economic policies have been modified, at least in theory, to address the problems of global poverty.

Developing countries have been vulnerable both to military coups and to ethnic conflict. Both are attributable, at least in part, to legacies of colonialism and both lead to serious human rights violations. While the dominant human rights discourse is highly *legalistic* and emphasizes legal solutions to human rights problems, social scientists have recently revived the concept of **civil society** (see Chapter 10) as a barrier to tyranny. Developing countries vary considerably in the strength of their civil societies, but some observers see civil society as the best hope both for development and the improvement of human rights protection. Human rights seem to require a balance between effective states and strong civil societies, which is difficult to achieve when resources are scarce.

In 1979, the authoritarian, Westernizing **regime** of the Shah was overthrown in Iran and an Islamic republic established. This stimulated challenges to dominant conceptions of human rights from the perspectives of Islam and other non-Western cultures. In the mid-1990s, government representatives and intellectuals from the economically successful countries of South-East and East Asia argued that human rights should be reinterpreted according to 'Asian values' in their societies. The critique of human rights from the standpoint of cultural diversity was thereby added to, and sometimes confused with, the critique from the standpoint of economic inequality. Following the financial crisis of 1997, talk of 'Asian values' diminished without disappearing altogether. Debates about Islam and human rights, however, increased, and became more intense after the **terrorist** attacks on the United States of 11 September 2001 ('9/11').

KEY POINTS

- The concept of human rights, promoted by the UN after the Second World War to combat dictatorship, was embodied in the UN Charter (1945) and the Universal Declaration of Human Rights (1948).

- At that time, people living under colonial rule were excluded from participating in the concept's elaboration; thereafter, new, post-colonial states accepted human rights in principle, but prioritized development-related rights.

- In the decades after 1948, the UN developed a large body of international human rights law.

- Many developing countries have poor human rights records for a combination of internal and external reasons, and many have also challenged dominant interpretations of human rights by appealing to their own cultural traditions.

The Concept of Human Rights

Human rights are rights of a special kind. The concept of 'rights' is derived from that of 'right'. Right is distinguished from wrong, and all societies have standards of right and wrong. 'Right' is sometimes called 'objective', because it refers to a supposedly objective standard. Many people would say that the prohibition of murder is objectively right. Rights are sometimes called 'subjective', because they 'belong' to individuals or groups, who are the 'subjects' of rights. Thus subjective rights are **entitlements** and differ from objective concepts such as 'right' by emphasizing the just claims of the rights-holder. The idea of subjective rights is often said to be distinctively Western and relatively modern.

Human rights are commonly defined as the rights that everyone has simply because they are human. Philosophically, this is problematic, because it is not clear why anyone has rights because they are human. A theory of rights is needed to justify this belief. Legally, it is also problematic, because some human rights are denied to some humans, for example the right to liberty is denied to those who have committed serious crimes. Politically, human rights are those rights that have generally been recognized by governments. The Universal Declaration provides us with an authoritative list of human rights, but it is difficult to distinguish precisely between human rights, other rights, and other social values. It may, however, be important to do so, because people increasingly claim as their human rights what may not be human rights, or may not be rights at all, but rather social benefits or merely what people happen to want.

The two 1966 Covenants distinguish between two categories of human right: civil and political rights, on the one hand; and economic, social, and cultural rights, on the other. Western governments tend to prioritize the first type; developing countries, the second. The distinction itself is, however, controversial: the right to property, for example, is often regarded as a civil rather than an economic right, which seems absurd. The Vienna Declaration (1993) sought to overcome the distinction by proclaiming that all human rights are 'indivisible'. This idea has become increasingly influential as the United Nations, its member governments, and international institutions, such as the World Bank, have come to recognize that neglect of human rights is at least sometimes a barrier to development. It is now also often said that there are three generations of rights: the two types already mentioned constitute the first and second generations; and there is a third generation, consisting of 'solidarity' rights, such as the right to development. These distinctions are also controversial, both because the reference to generations misrepresents the history of human rights, and because the meaning and value of third-generation human rights are questionable.

A brief history

Some say that the concept of human rights is ancient and found in all, or most, of the world's cultures. This claim usually confuses subjective rights with objective right. Notions such as 'justice' or 'human dignity' are found in many cultures. The idea of individual, subjective rights is more unusual and consequently more controversial.

Some scholars have argued that individual rights cannot be found before the late middle ages and did not become politically important until the seventeenth century in England. The concept of 'citizens' rights' is, however, found in ancient Greek and Roman thought. The modern concept of human rights derives from that of natural rights, which was developed in Europe in the late middle ages, and featured prominently in the political struggles of seventeenth-century England. Natural rights were derived from natural law and were known by reason. This idea burst onto the stage of world **politics** with the American and French revolutions in the late eighteenth century. In the nineteenth century, it fell out of favour, because it was thought to be unscientific and subversive of social order. The concept of human rights evokes that of natural rights, but differs in at least two important ways: first, it does without the controversial philosophy of natural law; second, it sees rights as social rather than natural.

Contemporary conceptions

The dominant conception of human rights today derives from its origins in Western **liberalism**, the philosophy that gives priority to individual freedom. Human rights are the rights of individuals and the individualism of the concept is often said to be alien to non-Western cultures. Western countries tend to favour an individualist conception of human rights, whereas developing countries tend to have a more collectivist conception. This distinction is often overstated, however, since the idea of individual rights is attractive to many non-Westerners, and Western countries balance individual rights with collective interests.

KEY POINTS

- Human rights are rights of a special kind: they are the rights that everyone has because they are human, or are those generally recognized as such by governments or international law.

- Distinctions between civil and political rights, on the one hand, and economic, social, and cultural rights, on the other , and among three generations of human rights have been subject to strong criticisms.

- Human, as distinct from citizens', rights are modern, deriving from the late medieval idea of natural rights, which fell out of favour after the French Revolution, but was revived by the UN in the form of human rights.

- The dominant conception of human rights is controversial in developing countries, because it is thought to express the Western philosophy of liberal individualism.

Human Rights Regimes

A regime is a set of rules and practices that regulate the conduct of actors in a specified field. Human rights regimes exist at international, regional, and national levels.

The UN system

The **international human rights** regime consists of a large body of international law and a complex set of institutions to implement it. Chief among these institutions was the UN Commission on Human Rights, established in 1946. Its members represented governments and it was criticized for political bias. In 2006, the UN replaced the Commission with the Human Rights Council. The Council has improved on the work of the Commission in some respects and has remained controversial in other respects. The UN employs independent experts as members of working groups, or as rapporteurs on specific themes (such as torture) and countries. The members of the committees that monitor the various treaties are also independent experts. **Non-governmental organizations (NGOs)**—consisting of citizen activists and experts—play an important role in providing information, and campaigning for the development and implementation of human rights standards. It is difficult to evaluate the effectiveness of the international regime, but the consensus of scholars is that it is rather weak.

Regional and national regimes

There are regional human rights regimes in Europe, the Americas, and Africa. The European is the most effective and the African, the least. Many scholars believe that the most important location for the protection of human rights is national law. The international regime is fairly effective in *promoting* human rights, but relatively ineffective in *implementing* them. Regional regimes are generally effective only when supervising relatively effective national regimes. Many national constitutions include human rights; these are most effective in countries that have democratic governments, independent judiciaries, and strong civil societies.

Legal regimes and power politics

Developing countries frequently complain that the international human rights regime is a smokescreen behind which powerful Western states pursue their interests. There is truth in this charge, but many governments of developing countries have terrible human rights records and this has in most cases probably hindered, rather than promoted, development. The powerful states of the West, and the UN itself, have been criticized both for not intervening to prevent human rights violations, as in the Rwandan **genocide** of 1994, and for intervening too forcefully or for dubious motives, as in Iraq in 2003.

> ### KEY POINTS
>
> - The human rights conduct of states is regulated, with varying degrees of effectiveness, by legal and political regimes at international, regional, and national levels.
>
> - The international human rights regime is fairly effective regarding promotion, but relatively ineffective regarding implementation; the European regime is the most effective regional regime, but human rights are best protected by national laws.
>
> - The international human rights regimes are predominantly legal and, behind them, international power politics dominates the human rights agenda, which, for developing countries, makes them matters of intense controversy.

'Human Rights Begin at Breakfast'

There is a widely held view that developing countries must give development priority over human rights. The fundamental intuition underlying this view is that starving people cannot benefit from, say, the right to free speech and that, without development, human rights are not possible—and perhaps not even desirable. 'Human rights begin at breakfast', Léopold Senghor, the former President of Senegal, is supposed to have said. Various arguments support this position. It is claimed, for example, that human rights—especially economic and social rights—are simply too expensive for poor countries. It is also maintained that human rights subvert social order and thus hinder development, especially in less-developed countries with problematic ethnic divisions. The government of Singapore, for example, has often made this argument. Even if this is not so, free societies tend to divert resources from savings and investment to consumption, and this slows down long-term development. Empirically, the so-called Asian 'tigers'—South Korea, Taiwan, Malaysia, and Singapore, in particular, and more recently China—are cited as examples of successful economic development under authoritarian rule. The idea that human rights are *necessary* for development—an idea commonly promoted by the West—is thereby falsified. Most Western countries developed their economies and human rights over long periods of time, and generally recognized human rights only when they had sufficiently developed economies to support them.

Conceptions of development

'Development' is often assumed to mean economic development, and economic development has often been measured by per capita income. Recently, however, development has been reconceptualized as '**human development**', with emphasis on the quality of life. The economic development of states is compatible with the misery of many people. The new conception of development sees human rights and development as *conceptually* overlapping. There is, for example, a human right to an adequate standard of living. If development is defined in terms of the standard of living, then human rights and development are positively correlated *by definition*. The new conceptualization has had practical implications: the United Nations Development Programme (UNDP), for example, has recently included the protection of human rights in its policies. This new conception of development has been closely associated with an increased emphasis on **gender** equality.

Are human rights and development interdependent?

The Vienna Declaration asserted that human rights and development are 'interdependent'. Is this true?

The arguments that restrictions of human rights are either *necessary* or *sufficient* for development are not well supported by the evidence. The arguments often rely on very selective use of case studies, especially from East Asia. South Korea and Taiwan achieved rapid economic development under authoritarian governments, but both developed into liberal democracies. Singapore has also been economically successful, with a so-called 'soft authoritarian' regime. Other cases are ambiguous. Some Latin American countries—such as Pinochet's Chile—had some **economic growth**, but also some economic setbacks, under authoritarian rule, while China has achieved rapid economic growth combined with serious human rights violations in recent years. Authoritarian regimes can sometimes achieve rapid economic development. Most repressive regimes, however, have failed to deliver development. This suggests that violating human rights as such does not explain economic development. The causal connection between human rights violations and development has never been established. Some countries that have combined economic development with restrictions of civil and political rights—such as South Korea, Singapore, and China—have relatively good records with respect to economic and social rights, such as education and health. Some development economists believe that democratic political rights and social rights, such as those to health and education, are conducive to success in development.

The relations between development and human rights may well be mediated by other factors, including the economic strategies adopted by governmental elites and the country's security situation. Taiwan, South Korea, and Singapore all faced external and/or internal security threats that made authoritarian government more likely, if not strictly necessary, and all were able to locate themselves favourably within the global economic system.

Respect for human rights is therefore not generally *necessary* for economic development and violation of human rights is certainly not *sufficient* for economic development. *Most countries that have persistently and seriously violated human rights have been unsuccessful in developing their economies.* The increasing political repression in Zimbabwe, for example, has been accompanied by economic collapse, and the former is certainly a cause of the latter. It is very difficult to generalize about the relations between development and human rights, however, and we should be very cautious about inferring policies for particular countries from generalizations, and, *a fortiori*, from the experience of selected countries.

Attempts to establish statistical relations between human rights and development in large numbers of countries have also produced inconclusive, and sometimes apparently contradictory, results. Famous Indian economist Amartya Sen has argued that the evidence suggests little correlation, positive or negative, between respect for civil and political rights and economic growth, and that the violation of such rights is not *necessary* to economic development. He reminds us that human rights have a value that is independent of development, in so far as we believe in 'the dignity and worth of the human person', and argues consequently that the available evidence is no barrier to the policy of pursuing development-with-human-rights. But if the relation between human rights and development is unclear, and developed states have far from perfect records in respecting human rights, then the most grave human rights disasters of recent years—such as the tyranny of Idi Amin in Uganda (1972–78), the mass killings by the Khmer Rouge in Cambodia (1975–79), the terror regime of Saddam Hussein in Iraq (1979–2003), and the genocide in Rwanda (1994)—have taken place in developing countries. Why is this?

Developing countries are mostly poor and are economically vulnerable to the power of rich states. This makes economic development difficult. Without economic development, the resources for implementing human rights are scarce. Paradoxically, where resources are not scarce (as in oil-producing countries, such as Nigeria, Saudi Arabia, Iraq, and Iran), the temptations of **corruption** and authoritarianism may also be great. This has come to be known as 'the resource curse'.

The achievement of independence from colonial rule, the ethos of the United Nations and world culture, and the spread of information and images through modern media of communication have raised expectations of economic progress among the peoples of the developing countries. Then, the persistent inability of governments to meet them has created widespread and intense social frustration, active opposition to governments, and consequent repression. These problems are aggravated in many developing countries by ethnic divisions. Although ethnic diversity does not necessarily lead to conflict and human

---

BOX 18.2 BARRIERS TO HUMAN RIGHTS IMPLEMENTATION BY DEVELOPING COUNTRIES

- Most developing countries are poor and cannot afford the full implementation of human rights.
- Most developing countries have little power in the global economic system, and are consequently vulnerable to the policies of powerful states and non-state actors that are often hostile to human rights.
- In the conditions of contemporary global culture and media of mass communication, under which the expectations of many people in developing countries for economic progress are high, the inability of governments to meet those expectations stimulates protest and repression.

- Most developing countries have ethnic divisions that predispose them to conflict in conditions of scarcity, and consequently to repression.
- Corrupt and incompetent government has been common in developing countries, and human rights violations are explained in part by the desire of corrupt rulers to remain in power.
- Many developing countries have had traditional cultures under which human rights enjoyed little place, and have developed a modern human rights culture only in a weak form.

---

rights violations, such divisions are difficult to manage where ethnicity is a potent source of competition and can therefore lead to serious human rights violations.

Developing countries should not be seen simply as dependent victims of domination by rich states, international institutions, multinational corporations, or global capitalism. They have some autonomy, however limited, as the success of the Asian tigers demonstrates. Corrupt and incompetent government has contributed to the economic failures of many developing countries, and human rights violations are partly explained by the desire of powerful and corrupt rulers to remain in power, as in China, Indonesia, Iraq, Saudi Arabia, Nigeria, and Zimbabwe, for example.

Most developing countries lack traditions of human rights (see Box 18.2). They may have traditional cultures with morally admirable features, such as mutual solidarity, and they may also have active human rights organizations—which are found throughout much of Asia, Africa, and Latin America—and even individual 'human rights heroes' (such as Aung San Suu Kyi in Burma/Myanmar). But, in contrast with Europe, the value of human rights may not be deeply embedded in the public culture of the society. Even where the government has ratified international human rights treaties and human rights are written into national constitutions, human rights may not be a strong feature of the **political culture**.

The Vienna Declaration maintained that democracy, development, and human rights were interdependent. This claim, however, oversimplifies a complex set of relations. Democracy is probably not necessary to development, but may improve its chances (see Chapter 14). The problem is that it is very difficult to establish democracy at very low levels of development. Empirically, democracies respect human rights better than do

other forms of government, but all democracies violate human rights sometimes, and so-called 'facade democracies', which hold formally fair and free elections, but exclude sections of the population from effective political participation, are likely to have fairly poor human rights records. The protection of human rights by legal institutions may run counter to the democratic will of the people. The human rights of suspected criminals, refugees, and ethnic and political minorities are particularly vulnerable to democratic violations, in both developed and developing countries. Finally, in developing countries with ethnic divisions and weak human rights traditions, the process of democratization itself may lead to serious human rights violations. Democratization played a role in ethnic conflict and genocide in Rwanda, for example. In both the Philippines and Indonesia, democratization has led to new forms of human rights violations, as space is made for ethnic demands that are met by repressive responses. The **war on terrorism** led to human rights violations

KEY POINTS

- It is commonly argued that development should have priority over human rights, although when development is defined by reference to the quality of life, it overlaps with the concept of human rights.

- Although the empirical relationship between human rights and development is not well understood, the available evidence suggests that it is weak. There are independent reasons for valuing human rights.

- Democracies generally respect human rights better than do authoritarian regimes, but sometimes violate them. The war on terrorism led to human rights violations by both democratic and authoritarian governments.

in some democracies, as well as in some authoritarian countries.

Universalism and Cultural Diversity

The Preamble to the Universal Declaration of Human Rights refers to 'the equal and inalienable rights of all members of the human family', and the Declaration proclaims itself to be 'a common standard of achievement for all peoples'; Article 1 states that all human beings 'are born free and equal in dignity and rights'. The Vienna Declaration reaffirmed the universality of human rights.

This universalism of human rights beliefs derives from the liberal Enlightenment doctrine of eighteenth-century Europe that the 'Rights of Man', as human rights were then called, were the rights of everyone, everywhere, at all times. This doctrine derived in turn from Christian teaching that there was only one God, and that the divine law applied to everyone, equally, everywhere, and at all times. One source of Christian philosophy was the Graeco-Roman theory of natural law, which taught that all human beings formed a single moral community, governed by a common law that was known to human reason. The philosophical school of the Stoics was the proponent of pre-Christian, natural-law philosophy. The natural-law philosophical tradition that runs from the Stoics through medieval Christianity to Enlightenment liberalism and the contemporary concept of human rights forms a powerful, although controversial, component of Western, and to some extent global, culture.

Cultural imperialism and cultural relativism

The belief that human rights are universal appears to conflict with the obvious cultural diversity of the world. Moral and political ideas, many people say, derive from culture, and different societies have different cultures. To impose human rights on everyone in the world is therefore intolerant, imperialistic, and unjustified. This moral logic may be supported by the *historical* claims that: first, the concept of human rights is a Western concept; and second, the West has a history of political, economic, and **cultural imperialism** that is not yet over. Some non-Western critics of human rights argue that not only is the concept of human rights alien to non-Western cultures, but also that its use by the West is part of a project of global political

and economic domination. The 2003 war in Iraq might be cited as an example of the use of human rights to legitimate political expansionism.

In the 1990s, a number of governments and intellectuals from East and South-East Asian countries that had achieved considerable economic success called into question the dominant interpretation of human rights by appealing to what they claimed were distinctively Asian values. This claim was somewhat puzzling, as the cultures of East Asia are extremely diverse, ranging from officially atheist China to predominantly Muslim Indonesia and Malaysia. One of the leading proponents of 'Asian values'—Dr Mahathir Mohamad, then prime minister of Malaysia—acknowledged that Asian values were similar to *conservative* Western values: order; harmony; respect for authority. The Asian values argument was partially acknowledged by the Vienna Declaration, which reaffirmed the universality of human rights, but conceded that 'the significance of national and regional particularities and various historical, cultural and religious backgrounds should be borne in mind'. Read literally, this statement is uncontroversial, for it would be foolish to interpret and implement human rights without bearing in mind the significance of these cultural differences. However, many Asian NGOs continued to affirm the universalist orthodoxy without qualification. Thus two different Asian approaches to human rights were produced during this controversy. Some human rights scholars and activists saw the appeal to Asian values as an ideological attempt to justify authoritarian government, but it did provoke a debate about how the universal values of human rights should be reconciled with the world's cultural traditions.

Much of the *moral* critique of human rights derives from the claim that it constitutes cultural imperialism, and relies on the intuition that imperialism is obviously wrong. If we ask *why* imperialism is wrong, however, we may say that it violates the rights of those who are its victims. If we next ask *which* rights of the victims are violated by imperialism, the most common answer is 'the **right to self-determination**'. At this point, the objection to moral universalism depends on a universal principle (the right to self-determination) and is therefore self-contradictory. If there is at least one universal right (the right to self-determination), there may also be others. It is difficult to argue that the right to self-determination is a universal right without accepting that the right not to be enslaved is also a universal right. This appeal to universalism does not necessarily justify the full list of rights in the Universal Declaration, but it does refute one common line of argument against universalism.

Another approach would be to reject all forms of universalism, and to rely on the claim that all moral principles derive from *particular* cultures, that particular cultures are *diverse*, that some cultures reject at least some human rights principles (gender equality is a common example), and that human rights are valid only within the culture of the modern West. On this view, there is a human rights culture. But it is only one culture among many and, because it derives from Western (secular) liberalism, it is not particularly appealing, still less *obligatory*, for those who, perhaps on the basis of their religious beliefs, subscribe to nonliberal moral and political codes. This argument has been proposed by some (but not all) Muslims, who believe that Islam requires submission to the will of God and that this must have priority over any secular obligations, such as those of human rights.

This argument avoids the self-contradiction of the anti-imperialist approach, but at a considerable cost. The first difficulty is that the argument that all actual moral principles are justified by the cultures of which they form a part is another universal principle that cannot be used against universalism as such without self-contradiction. The next difficulty is that if all principles are justified by their cultures, then imperialism would be justified by imperialistic cultures—a view that is anathema to critics of human rights universalism. They could argue that, according to the criteria of their culture, imperialism is wrong, but they could not show would-be imperialists why they should act according to these criteria. In practice, most critics of human rights universalism accept that racism is universally wrong and cannot be justified by racist cultures like that of **apartheid** South Africa. A further difficulty with the 'culturalist' conception of morality is that actual cultures are complex, contested, and overlapping. There are, for examples, many schools of Islamic thought; there are disputes about the requirements of the religion and Islamic ideas have mixed with other ideas in different ways in different societies. The idea of a homogeneous culture that justifies particular moral ideas is a myth. The world is full of a great diversity of complex moral ideas, some of which cohere in different ways, with different degrees of uniformity and solidarity, into patterns that are themselves subject to change, in part as the result of interaction with other cultures.

These arguments do not themselves provide a justification of human rights. Only a justificatory theory of human rights could do that, and any such theory is likely to be controversial not only between the West and the rest, but also within Western thought, and even among human rights supporters. They also imply no disrespect for culture as such. Culture provides meaning, value, and guidance to human life, and there is a human right to participate in the cultural life of one's community. They do show that cultures are not self-justifying, and that we commit no logical or moral error in subjecting actual cultures to critical scrutiny. **Feminist** human rights scholars have argued that the appeal to culture has often been made in an attempt to justify the oppression of women.

Islam, human rights, and the war on terrorism

The rise in oil prices in the early 1970s, the Islamic Revolution of Iran (1979), the persistence of corrupt, authoritarian governments, and extreme poverty in many Muslim countries, and the continuing Israel–Palestine conflict contributed to the development of fundamentalist Islamic parties and movements.

As Soviet troops withdrew from Afghanistan in 1988, Osama bin Laden, son of a rich Saudi businessman, who had recruited non-Afghans to support the Afghan resistance to the Soviet occupiers, formed al-Qaeda to continue a *jihad* (holy war) against the perceived enemies of Islam. In 1991, the forces of the secular Iraqi regime of Saddam Hussein invaded Kuwait, the population of which is almost wholly Muslim. A US-led force, acting with UN authority and based in Saudi Arabia, expelled the Iraqi invaders from Kuwait. Following this war, several attacks on US and other targets were attributed to al-Qaeda, culminating in the attacks of 9/11. The United States responded by invading Afghanistan, the extreme Islamic government of which, the Taliban, was believed to have protected al-Qaeda. President Bush declared a war on terrorism. The United States set up a detention camp in Guantanamo Bay, Cuba, where it held several hundred suspected terrorists without due process of law. Many countries introduced new anti-terrorists laws, which were criticized by NGOs for their neglect of human rights protections. After the United States and some of its allies invaded Iraq in 2003, many allegations of human rights violations by US troops became common. Allegations of torture by US forces in Afghanistan, Iraq, and at Guantanamo Bay, and charges of the 'rendition' (transportation) of suspects to other countries in which torture was common, were made by thoughtful and well-informed observers. Pictures of the mistreatment of Iraqi prisoners in the Abu Ghraib prison in Baghdad created an international scandal.

These events changed the context of the global human rights struggle, because the United States had become the only superpower; administration officials had, both in internal memoranda and public pronouncements, shown contempt for the UN, international law, and human rights. Many governments have used the war on terrorism as an excuse for increasing human rights violations. Although most Muslims oppose terrorism, the use of Islam by al-Qaeda to justify its actions, the widespread targeting of Muslims as suspected terrorists, the election of a hard-line Islamist president of Iran, the publication of cartoons highly offensive to Muslims in a Danish newspaper, and the circulation of an anti-Muslim film made in the United States all contributed to a crisis in the relations between Islam and the West. Human rights activists had to come to terms both with the war on terrorism and their own relations with Islam. There are many schools of thought within Islam, some incompatible with human rights in important respects (especially relating to the rights of women), while others seek reconciliation between Islam and human rights. Some experts believe that the question of Islam and human rights is not fundamentally one of religion, but of the political and economic problems of the Middle East. These problems derive in part, but by no means wholly, from the history of Western imperialist intrusions into the Middle East. The election of Barack Obama as US President in November 2008 was based in part on promises to end the human rights violations associated with the 'war on terror'. Expert observers generally believe that he has kept these promises only in part, although some of his proposed reforms have been obstructed by his political opponents.

Since December 2010, there have been widespread protests throughout the Middle East popularly referred to as the 'Arab Spring'. The motives, ideas, processes, and outcomes of these protests varied greatly from country to country. Appeals to human rights and democracy have been mixed with 'Islamist' aspirations, as well as with pragmatic political and economic demands. Although these protests overthrew some authoritarian governments and continue to threaten others, their outcomes, especially regarding human rights, remained uncertain at the time of writing (beginning of 2013).

KEY POINTS

- The argument that attempts to universalize human rights are imperialistic fails because it presupposes the universal right to self-determination.

- The argument that all values are relative to culture is unconvincing, because cultures are not self-justifying and hardly anyone believes that anything done in the name of culture is justified.

- The concept of human rights includes the right to practise one's culture, and thus human rights and culture may be compatible. Some cultural practices may, however, violate human rights standards.

- The rise of **political Islam** and the US war on terrorism have raised new challenges for the human rights movement.

The New Political Economy of Human Rights

Marxists have traditionally argued that human rights conceal real inequalities of wealth and power. The inclusion of economic and social rights in the list of human rights has been intended to meet this criticism, but its success has been very problematic. First, economic and social rights have been relatively neglected in international politics, compared with civil and political rights; second, great inequalities of wealth and power persist worldwide. Nevertheless, some attempts have been made recently to integrate human rights with development and to improve poverty-reduction strategies.

Globalization

'Globalization' is a contested concept in social science. Global trade is ancient and there is a dispute as to how it may have changed in recent times. However, whatever economic historians may say about global trends, it is obvious that we live in a dynamic, interrelated world that is changing rapidly in certain important respects. What is the impact of globalization on human rights?

Globalization has been opposed by a worldwide protest movement expressing diverse concerns, including world poverty, environmental degradation, and human rights. This has replaced, to a considerable extent, the earlier socialist movement opposing capitalism. The targets of this movement are primarily rich states, intergovernmental organizations dominated by the rich states (such as the World Trade Organization, or WTO), and multinational corporations (MNCs). The human rights movement has recently increased its concern about the role of MNCs in human rights violations, either directly (for example by the employment of child labour) or in collaboration with repressive governments. Issues of globalization, development, the environment, and human rights have often come together as MNCs seek to develop natural resources in ways that damage the environment (see Chapter 17) and local ways of life, and popular protests (see Chapter 11) are sometimes met by governmental repression.

The relations between human rights and globalization are complex, however. The idea of human rights claims to be universal, and the human rights movement seeks global reach and achieves it to some extent by global means of communication (especially now through the 'new social media'). Empirical research on the impact of MNCs on human rights in developing countries has produced mixed results according to the different research methods used. There is no doubt that some MNCs are involved in human rights violations in developing countries, but the only generalizations about the effect of MNCs on human rights in developing countries that are justified by the evidence are that the impact of MNCs can be positive and can also be negative, and no simple generalizations are valid.

Global capitalism is a dynamic process that probably has positive and negative consequences for human rights. There is also a global economic regime—consisting of organizations such as the G8, the G20, the World Bank, the International Monetary Fund (IMF), and the WTO—that attempts to regulate global capitalism and the economies of the developing countries. The World Bank and the IMF are powerful actors in the international economy, and have traditionally been unconcerned with human rights. Critics have alleged that their policies have often been very harmful to human rights, especially economic

and social rights. The World Bank has recently opened up a dialogue with NGOs and independent experts on human rights, but it remains to be seen whether this will change its policies significantly. The WTO is also accused of working to the disadvantage of the developing countries. The UN conception of human rights is a statist, social democratic idea, whereas the global economy, and the international financial institutions that are supposed to regulate it, are based on a neoliberal ideology that prefers vibrant markets and **weak states**. Recently, extreme neoliberalism has been somewhat modified by the belief that '**good governance**' and poverty reduction are necessary to development.

A new approach to globalization and human rights is based on the concept of '**human security**'. This idea first appeared in the 1994 UNDP Report, which defined human security as safety from a wide range of threats to human well-being, such as hunger, disease, and repression, as well as new threats, such as terrorism and climate change. The discourse of human security was intended to transform the familiar concept of state security—which was often used to violate human rights—to suggest that state security was best promoted by protecting the security of everyone. It was also intended to integrate humanitarian relief, development assistance, human rights promotion, and conflict resolution. The special vulnerability of women and children to the effects of conflict and poverty are often emphasized (see Box 18.3). The concept has been criticized on several grounds: it is too broad and vague to generate clear obligations; it repeats, while ignoring, the established concept of human rights; it threatens to replace the legal obligations of states to protect human rights with policy options to protect human security; it undermines the discourse of the international human rights movement; and, by switching the emphasis from rights to security, it may legitimate the violation of rights in the name of security. Nevertheless, the concept may include threats to human well-being not adequately addressed by human rights—such as climate change—and to persons not well protected by human rights law, such as those who are stateless. The concept of human security, carefully defined, could improve the concept of human rights and its implementation by connecting it systematically to problems—such as international crime, global finance, and climate change—which have not traditionally been addressed by the human rights movement (see Chapter 19 for further discussion).

BOX 18.3 HUMAN SECURITY: THE CASE OF DARFUR

It took three months for Fatouma Moussa to collect enough firewood to justify a trip to sell it in the market town of Shangil Tobayi, half a day's drive by truck from here. It took just a few moments on Thursday for janjaweed militiamen, making a mockery of the new cease-fire, to steal the $40 she had earned on the trip and rape her. Speaking barely in a whisper, Ms. Moussa, who is 18, gave a spare account of her ordeal. 'We found janjaweed at Amer Jadid,' she said, naming a village just a few miles north of her own. 'One woman was killed. I was raped.' Officially, the cease-fire in Darfur went into effect last Monday. But the reality was on grim display in this crossroads town, where Ms. Moussa and other villagers were attacked Thursday as they rode home in a bus from Shangil Tobayi. The Arab militiamen who attacked them killed 1 woman, wounded 6 villagers and raped 15 women, witnesses and victims said.

(*New York Times* correspondent, Lydia Polgreen, 12 May 2006)

Darfur is a region of western Sudan, about the size of France, with a population of approximately 6 million. After a long and brutal civil war between the Sudanese government and the Muslim north against the Christian south, a peace agreement was signed in January 2005. Darfur, composed of many ethnic groups, all Muslim, has suffered from extreme economic and social neglect since colonial times. The relative stability of Darfur was undermined by increased competition for diminishing land resources as a result of desertification, the emergence of a racist Arab ideology in Sudan, expansionist policies by Libya's Colonel Qaddafi in neighbouring Chad, and the intrusion of southern Sudanese rebels into Darfur. Darfurian self-defence organizations developed into a number of rebel forces. The Sudanese government sought to repress these rebellions by a savage counter-insurgency, called by some, including the US government, a 'genocide', employing Arab militias known as the *Janjaweed* (evil horsemen). A peace agreement was signed in Abuja, Nigeria, on 5 May 2006 by the Sudanese government and the largest rebel group, but not by other rebels. Estimates of those killed in the period 2003–06 range from 200,000 to 500,000, those displaced more than 2 million, and those suffering deprivation nearly 4 million. UN Secretary-General Kofi Annan compared Darfur to the Rwandan genocide of 1994. By July 2006, the UN and the European Union had passed various resolutions, a few rich countries had supplied some, but insufficient, humanitarian aid, and the peace agreement remained empty words. In the period 2006–09, the level of violence appeared to decrease, but according to some well-informed sources the humanitarian catastrophe remained.

KEY POINTS

- Marxists have criticized human rights for obscuring inequalities of wealth and power inherent in capitalism, while more recently the anti-globalization movement has criticized globalization's implications for human rights.

- Global capitalist institutions are quite frequently involved in human rights violations, but the general relations between global capitalism and human rights are complex.

- The global economic regime that seeks to regulate global capitalism almost certainly has a major impact on human rights, but the nature of this impact is controversial.

Conclusion

The concept of human rights became important in world politics only with the adoption of the United Nations Charter in 1945. Although it was derived from Western moral, legal, and political philosophy, it was declared to be universal. On the foundation of the UN Universal Declaration of Human Rights (1948), a large body of international human rights law has been elaborated. Most of this is legally binding on most states and the principles of the Declaration have been reaffirmed by all UN members. Nevertheless, international procedures for implementing human rights are weak, human rights violations are common, and the concept of human rights is not universally accepted as culturally legitimate.

The main question raised by human rights in the developing countries is the relationship between development and human rights. This is a complex issue. There is more than one definition of 'development' and some definitions include human rights. There is, however, a widespread view that some restriction of human rights is a precondition of development and that development should take priority over human rights. There is no doubt that some countries have achieved rapid rates of economic development while violating civil and political rights. However, most rights-violating countries have poor records of development. The relations between human rights and development are still not well understood, but the evidence suggests that, generally, factors other than human rights are more important in promoting or obstructing development. The case for violating human rights for the sake of development is therefore much weaker than it has often been thought to be. The view that human rights are necessary for economic development is, however, not well supported by the evidence. There are also strong reasons for respecting human rights independently of their relation to development. Recently, international efforts have been made to integrate human rights and development.

Developing countries are generally poor, which makes it difficult to fund the implementation of human rights. They may not want to do so because their governments are corrupt and unconcerned with human rights. They may not be able to because external agents—for example donor governments and/or international financial institutions—limit their capacity to do so by insisting on the reduction of state budgets.

The United Nations is right in seeing development and human rights as interdependent, not in the sense that each always helps the other, but rather in so far as improvements in each makes the achievement of the other easier. Crises of development are often accompanied by crises of human rights, as countries such as Somalia, the Democratic Republic of Congo, and Liberia show. Development success is good news for human rights—as South Korea and Taiwan illustrate—although the interests of elites and local cultures may limit human rights achievements, as in Singapore. Rwanda and Zimbabwe show that apparent initial success in development accompanied by human rights violations may lead to disaster for both human rights and development.

The process of globalization has been associated with the assertion of cultural difference. This has meant that the claim that human rights are universal, although reaffirmed by UN member states in 1993, is constantly challenged. Some of these challenges express the interests of the powerful, who are reluctant to allow a voice to dissenters. Others raise difficult questions about legitimating universal principles in a culturally diverse world. Debates about Asian values in the 1990s have been succeeded by debates about Islam and terrorism, but the underlying problems may be political and economic, rather than cultural or religious.

Arguments that the concept of human rights expresses the interests of the West or the rich are generally not convincing. Taking human rights seriously would benefit most the poorest and most oppressed. There is a danger, however, that Western states may discredit the concept by associating it with their own foreign policies motivated by their own interests. The cause of human rights will be damaged if it is, or is perceived to be, a new form of imperialism. Although human rights are now well established in great power politics, it may be that the best hope for their future lies with the increasing number of grass-roots movements in the developing countries.

? QUESTIONS

1. Is there now a global consensus on human rights?

2. What are the best arguments for human rights?

3. Evaluate the record of the UN Human Rights Council so far.

4. What are the main problems raised by the idea of the rights-based approach to development?

5. Can Islam be reconciled with human rights?

6. Is the idea of human rights an example of cultural imperialism?

7. What are the implications of human rights for global poverty reduction strategies?

8. Can poor countries afford human rights?

≋ FURTHER READING

Alston, P. and Robinson, M. (eds) (2005) *Human Rights and Development: Towards Mutual Reinforcement* (Oxford: Oxford University Press) A useful collection of essays on the integration of human rights and development.

Brownlie, I. and Goodwin-Gill, G. S. (eds) (2010) *Basic Documents on Human Rights*, 6th edn (Oxford: Oxford University Press) An authoritative collection of international legal texts.

Donnelly, J. (2013) *Universal Human Rights in Theory and Practice*, 3rd edn (Ithaca, NY: Cornell University Press) An excellent introduction to the international conception of human rights and the principal issues of human rights implementation.

Pogge, T. (ed.) (2005) 'Symposium: World Poverty and Human Rights', *Ethics & International Affairs*, 19(1): 1–83 Various approaches to the ethics of world poverty.

Forsythe, D. P. (2012) *Human Rights in International Relations*, 3rd edn (Cambridge: Cambridge University Press) An authoritative introduction to the topic.

Freeman, M. A. (2011) *Human Rights: An Interdisciplinary Perspective*, 2nd edn (Cambridge: Polity Press) A comprehensive introduction for social science students and law students who want a non-legal approach.

Howard-Hassmann, R. E. (2012) 'Human Security: Undermining Human Rights?', *Human Rights Quarterly*, 34(1): 88–112 Critical assessment of human security from a human rights perspective.

Office of the United Nations High Commissioner for Human Rights (2004) *Human Rights and Poverty Reduction* (New York/Geneva: United Nations) An influential analysis of the relations between human rights and development.

Sen, A. (1999) *Development as Freedom* (Oxford: Oxford University Press) A thought-provoking argument for the mutual relations between development and freedom.

Uvin, P. (2004) *Human Rights and Development* (Bloomfield, CT: Kumarian Press) A provocative critique of various attempts to integrate human rights and development.

WEB LINKS

http://www.amnesty.org   Amnesty International.

http://www.hri.ca   Excellent website for communication about, and among, human rights activists.

http://www.hrw.org   Human Rights Watch.

http://www.ohchr.org   The website of the Office of the UN High Commissioner for Human Rights, which is the best way into the UN human rights system.

http://www.unglobalcompact.org   Website of UN Global Compact, which coordinates international efforts for global corporate social responsibility, including human rights protection.

For additional material and resources, please visit the Online Resource Centre at:
http://www.oxfordtextbooks.co.uk/orc/burnell4e/

19

Security

Nicole Jackson

Overview

This chapter examines the contested concept of security and its application to issues in the developing world. The study of security today has widened to include far more than an examination of military issues and threats to states; it now includes a range of real and perceived threats to peoples, societies, regions, networks, and the global community. The topic generates scholarly debates about the definition of security and the impact of globalization on security issues. Two key security issues that concern us here are: violent conflict (including state and non-state) and international organized crime (including narcotic, human, and arms trafficking). To varying degrees, these issues pose threats to much of the developing world, and have provoked a wide range of local, regional, and Western policy responses. The challenge for both the developed and developing worlds is to adopt a more holistic approach to security policy, one that bridges the artificial divide between traditional security and development studies.

Introduction

'Security' is a highly contested term and there is considerable debate over its definition. The study of security has traditionally taken place within international relations, and especially in its subfield 'security studies'; only relatively recently has it been considered within development studies. In its more traditional form, the discipline of security studies examines military issues and the interplay among 'great powers'. It has therefore been criticized for being Western-centric, and for dismissing or marginalizing the weaker **developing world** and the so-called 'real threats' to its people and societies. However, 'security studies' is multidisciplinary and draws from various disciplines. Its focus is wide: it includes philosophical understandings about the nature of reality, normative questions, empirical studies, and detailed policy prescriptions.

The term 'security' is derived from the Latin *se* ('without') and *cura* ('care'), suggesting the absence of a threat. Security is the absence of threat—to the stability of states, regions, the global community, networks, and/or human lives. For a nuanced understanding of security, issues must be considered at different levels of analysis. There are many security issues in the developing world that threaten, to various degrees, peoples, societies, and states. They include violent conflict (state and non-state) and international organized crime (trafficking in persons, narcotics, and small arms). How these issues are perceived and acted upon form the subject of this chapter. These two issues are chosen for examination here because they are widely perceived to pose immediate and pervasive security concerns across the developed and developing worlds.

The chapter begins with an overview of major scholarly debates about security. It identifies key Western-defined security concepts that are applicable or useful to understanding the developing world. Debates over the definition of security are important because they can influence who decides what security means, what issues are put on the agenda, and how they are dealt with. The chapter then examines the impact of **globalization** on security issues. Today, many issues in one area of the world increasingly affect security in another. Globalization also allows the West to have a major influence on how security issues around the world are perceived and challenged (see also Chapter 13). The rest of the chapter is divided into two parts to examine violent conflict and international organized crime. Each section asks what the geographical distribution of the so-called threat is, considers who or what is threatened, and explores variations in perceptions and key policy responses.

Scholarly Debates about Security

Realists, who dominated the study of international relations from 1940 to 1990, defined security as 'national security'. To quote Stephen M. Walt (1991: 212), 'security studies may be defined as the study of the threat, use and control of military force'. The focus is on military threats to the state, and inter-state conflict. The traditional understandings of security emphasized states and their competition for power in the international system. States were perceived as primarily motivated by desire for military (and economic) power, rather than by ideas or ethics. Today, this understanding continues to underpin most governments' foreign policies. Meanwhile, the military-centric approach continues to be popular in some academic circles and is generally termed 'strategic studies'.

While there are a variety of nuanced realist theories, which explain and predict different events, they all tend to examine conditions that make the use of force more likely, its effects, and resulting policies. Structural realists stress the importance of the international system, while neoclassical realists focus on how power is also influenced by domestic variables and perceptions. **Conventional constructivists**, in turn, focus on security as a social construction, and stress the role of identity and norms.

After the cold war, new approaches in security studies proliferated, with the aim of challenging traditional realist theories. The debate began in response to the claim that the security agenda must be broadened to examine threats beyond state and military security. For example, in 1983, Buzan (1991) defined security as including military, social, economic, political, and environmental 'sectors' or dimensions.

Today, other threats to the security of states are termed non-traditional issues, or **non-traditional security threats** (that is, non-military). These issues include: environmental problems (ozone depletion and global warming); threats from nationalism; migration; international crime (narcotic trafficking, human trafficking); and disease, such as **HIV/AIDS** and severe acute respiratory syndrome (SARS). This expansion of the concept of security does not undermine the realist logic of traditional security studies, because the main focus is still on the state system. Nevertheless, many traditionalists argue that this widening makes the concept redundant, and dilutes the important task of analysing military threats and inter-state conflict. Other scholars within international relations ask *whose* security is threatened. And the reply is that it is not only states that are threatened.

These 'new security' scholars deepen the concept to include global, network, regional, societal, and individual security. There are many issues, such as wars, **terrorism**, crime, and health epidemics, each of which can affect security at many different levels. Threats also change over time; they vary depending on context, and the perceptions of peoples and states. Perceptions themselves may even be undefined or ambiguous. Security issues defined by the peoples and states in the developing world are often different from those defined by peoples and states in the developed world.

Concepts of security and the developing world

Security studies, as a discipline, is mostly Western-oriented and defined by Western theories (see Box 19.1). Although its practitioners increasingly note unique political and cultural conditions, they rarely draw on the rich variety of other philosophical traditions, such as Islamic thought, and Indian or Chinese philosophy. In the developing world, academic work on specific security issues tends to occur within traditional policy-oriented circles that are often dominated by strategic studies. However, this is changing as more scholars and practitioners recognize a misfit between wider international relations theory and developing world realities. Traditional security thinking, with its focus on sovereignty, inter-state war, and abstract theory, is increasingly confronted by the reality of interlinked political, economic, and social systems, and internal and transnational conflicts, particularly seen in the developing world.

Critical security studies, in its broadest sense, is a collection of approaches all united by dissatisfaction with so-called traditional security studies, and in particular its state- and military-centrism. Critical approaches range from conventional constructivists, through the Copenhagen and Aberystwyth schools, to feminist, neo-Marxist, and more radical post-modern positions. They can be positivist or **post-positivist**.

The Aberystwyth School of critical security studies differs from traditional security studies in its focus on the lives of people and in its concept of 'emancipation', or freedom (of people from threats), and concern with justice and **human rights**. It may be understood as particularly relevant to the developing world where the states themselves are often the source of the threat. Realists counter that the focus should remain on the state and that critical security studies impose 'a model of contemporary Western polities that are far

---

BOX 19.1 APPROACHES TO SECURITY STUDIES

- *Realism* Classical realists define security as national security. These traditionalists emphasize military threats to the state and inter-state conflict.

- *Modified realism* These scholars continue to emphasize the state, however some broaden the focus away from military threats, while others move the focus away from the 'great powers' towards the developing world.

- *Constructivism* Mainstream constructivists examine the role of ideas, identity, and other cultural factors in our understanding or 'construction' of security.
  - *Interpretive constructivists* examine the role of language in mediating and constraining social relations.
  - *Radical constructivists* maintain the linguistic focus but also examine power.

- *The Copenhagen School* The Copenhagen School broadens the security agenda to five 'sectors': military; political; economic; societal; and ecological. The state remains the referent object. Their '**securitization** framework' examines how language is used to construct threats.

- *The* **Aberystwyth School** These scholars conceptualize security not in terms of its relation with the state, but in terms of that with its people. Scholars attempt to identify victims of social exclusion and to evaluate strategies for their **emancipation**.

- **Post-structuralists** This broad group examines the social context in which security discourse is embedded.

- **Feminist** *perspectives* Feminists range from liberal to critical, but are united in their view that security has generally been presented as **gender**-neutral, when in fact it is infused with gendered assumptions and representations.

removed from Third World realities' (Ayoob 1995: 97). Critical social theory, however, has a different agenda from 'problem-solving' approaches. It studies how all knowledge is produced socially and aims to reveal the political behind seemingly neutral knowledge.

The **human security** perspective, with its focus on individuals and the protection of lives from critical and pervasive threats, also attempts to move the focus away from realist, state-centred concerns towards those that are more salient to the peoples of the developing world. It stresses the importance of people being secure inside states, and makes a connection between international peace and establishing human security. The 'broad' concept of human security, first outlined in the 1994 United Nations (UN) Human Development Report, argues that human security rests on two pillars: freedom from want; and freedom from fear. Even broader definitions of human security include, for example, food security, adequate shelter, security from poverty, and, for some, alleviation of 'threats to human dignity' and to 'cherished values'. Poverty is a central concern for most of those who adhere to a 'broad' or 'broader' approach to human security. For them, security is a priori about human beings, and they understand poverty and insecurity to be mostly synonymous. Others, however, argue that these definitions are too encompassing to be helpful in policy development. In contrast, they adopt a 'narrow' concept of human security focusing on freedom from violence, including the role of criminal and political violence on individuals. This focus on the individual leads to the favouring of non-coercive policy approaches ranging from preventative diplomacy and conflict management, to addressing the root causes of conflict.

The broad concept of human security has been considered by scholars in Asia and Africa, and even adopted in some regional security arrangements, for example the Association of South-East Asian Nations (ASEAN). Generally, however, the difficulty with putting the human security concept into practice is that its liberal focus on individuals and human rights appears threatening to many authoritarian leaders, and is contrary to the emphasis that many societies place on community and the state. Most states in the developing world are the providers of security, the power of which is predicated on the concepts of absolute sovereignty and non-interference in domestic affairs. At the theoretical level, recent scholars have tried to bring together narrow and broad approaches, or to reconcile state security with the narrow approach.

Feminists adopt many varied perspectives on security, however they are united in their understanding that security has generally been presented as gender-neutral, when in fact it is infused with gendered assumptions and representations. Liberal feminists, for example, are interested in notions of equality and tend to focus on questions of women's representations within the public sphere. Radical feminists focus more on notions of difference. Feminist perspectives on war have focused on the impact of war and conflict on women and men, their active roles in armed conflict, and how assumptions about masculinity and femininity figure in conflict and decision-making.

Other feminists focus on geopolitics and human security, and examine, for example: the shifting scales from households to national to international; the breaking down of dichotomies, personal and public, at the national and international levels; and the unequal and violent relationships in families, communities, and the transnational system. A notable consequence of the recent increase of scholarship and awareness about gender and security is the UN Security Council Resolution 1325 on women, peace, and security, adopted in October 2000, which states that women and girls are affected by armed conflict in different ways from men and boys, and argues the importance of incorporating a 'gender perspective' into peace operations. The details of these differences and how they should inform policy is, as we shall see later in the chapter, controversial.

Another Western-defined concept that has applicability to the developing world is 'securitization', defined as 'the move that takes **politics** beyond the established rules of the game and frames the issue either as a special kind of politics or as above politics' (Buzan et al. 1998: 23). The securitization framework highlights how language is used to construct threats. Although it is a helpful descriptive and explanatory tool, particularly in understanding how states elevate particular threats, again there are difficulties. It has been critiqued for its focus on the state and for the difficulties in putting this concept into practice. There are fears that securitization arguments (that is, the labelling of an issue as a security threat) could be misused by rulers for domestic purposes. For example, in Latin America, there is a widespread consciousness about how security rhetoric has been used by military governments in the past against their own people, and there is therefore distrust about how it may be applied. This has led some scholars to examine the opposite process of *desecuritization* (the act of moving an issue back into the political realm). Of course, more positively, securitization may also allow for the efficient handling of challenges, and the mobilization of support and resources. And for scholars, the application of this framework helpfully highlights key questions such as *who* can securitize or desecuritize, as well as the conditions and consequences of such actions.

Finally, within the developing world, new (and non-Western) thinking about security is being developed and put into practice. For example, China's multilateral cooperation and dialogue through the Shanghai Cooperation Organization (SCO) on a range of new security issues (such as terrorism and trafficking) demonstrates a unique type of cross-regional cooperative thinking and, to some extent, action on non-traditional security issues.

Globalization of security

The study of security has evolved largely in tandem with globalization. Globalization, understood as a state of interdependence, accelerated by advances in technology, trade, political relationships, transboundary communication, and movement of peoples, goods, and services, has created new channels for exercising power outside the state. The state is not about to disappear, but is confronted by new global forces, transborder flows (financial, population, environmental, viral), international **regimes**, and complex networks (media, criminal, terrorist). Thus globalization has heightened existing security priorities such as terrorism, organized crime, narcotic trafficking, and disease. Globalization can turn essentially local problems into regional or global security challenges. It allows issues and events in the developing world to reach the developed world, and vice versa.

This process should not be overstated, however. The interrelatedness of the world is not new; the degree is simply greater. Indeed, some scholars argue that regions are the appropriate level (as opposed to the global or local levels) at which to examine security issues. There is also a real danger that globalization is facilitating new forms of interaction (or power) that increasingly allow the West to dominate the security agenda, and to structure the way in which security issues around the world are perceived and challenged. This is of particular concern for the developing world,

and is reflected in the partial merging of security and development policy agendas.

The merging of security and development agendas?

There has been an increasingly vigorous debate among scholars and practitioners over efforts to link development and security agendas, for example over the controversial linking of development aid to the **war on terror**. A serious concern is that development goals based on humanitarian principles, poverty reduction for instance, have been increasingly subordinated to Western foreign and security policy objectives. Some countries well known for human rights abuses have been offered US aid to take a supportive position on the war on terror. Examples include Pakistan (see Chapter 20) and Uzbekistan. From the perspective of many development studies scholars, development concerns should not be subordinated to international security issues and the securitization of aid does not address real development issues.

Of course, the merging of security and development agendas is not new. During the cold war, development aid was linked with the geopolitical power struggles of the United States and the Soviet Union. Today, economic prosperity and growth are generally viewed as co-dependent on security, and linked as policy issues by many Western governments. **Underdevelopment** is, however, often viewed more in terms of the potential threat it poses to the security of powerful countries than in terms of the well-being of affected populations. Underdevelopment is thus considered by many Western governments and organizations as threatening national and global security, for example by fuelling illicit drug-trafficking or supporting the spread of terrorism. The World Bank report, *Breaking the Conflict Trap* (2003b), for example, controversially describes conflict and its associated security problems as a failure of development (see Chapter 13).

Realists would argue that Western governments have always linked their aid policies to their strategic interests, relatively neglecting countries of lesser economic or political interest to them. Countries deemed to be of direct interest at a particular time, for example Afghanistan, Iraq, and Israel, receive comparatively favourable consideration. However, recently there has also been a trend towards a more overt and instrumental securitization of the development agenda.

Violent Conflict: War and Terrorism in the Developing World

One of the key security issues in the developing world is violent conflict. Most of the world's poorest countries are suffering, or have recently suffered, from large-scale, violent conflict. Traditionally, security analyses of the developing world focused on inter-state wars, with a particular focus on the role of the colonizers or superpowers in fuelling the conflicts. However, since the end of the cold war, there has been an acknowledgement in the discipline that much of the violence in the world actually occurs within states, and that civilians have been the victims of violence perpetrated by both state and non-state groups (see Chapter 13). Therefore the previously dominant state-level of analysis is increasingly being supplemented by other levels—individual, regional, network, or global.

Traditional and non-traditional violent conflict

Traditional security studies examined violence between states. However, since the end of the cold war, the number of inter-state wars around the world has declined. Even in the region with the greatest number of ongoing inter-state wars, Central and West Africa,

many of these inter-state tensions and conflicts have arisen from spillovers of interethnic conflict and civil war, and are therefore different from traditional wars between states. For example, in former Zaire from 1998 to 2003, approximately 3 million people died in a civil war that ended up involving nine other countries: Angola; Zimbabwe; Namibia; Chad; Sudan; Uganda; Burundi; Rwanda; and Tanzania.

Scholars of traditional security studies quantify military power. The developing world spends a comparatively high proportion of its gross domestic product (GDP) on defence. Of course, military power is a double-edged sword. It may undermine, rather than enhance, a country's security. Arms expenditures divert resources and often form an enormous economic, as well as human, drain on a country. Moreover, when states become trapped in arms races that consume a great percentage of their resources, war may become more likely.

The primary focus of global arms sales is to the developing world. During the period 2004–11, the value of arms transfer *agreements* with developing nations comprised 68.6 per cent of all such agreements worldwide (Grimmett and Kerr 2012). From 2008 to 2011, the United States and Russia dominated the arms market in the developing world. In 2011, the United States ranked first in the value of arms deliveries to developing nations at US$10.5 billion, or 37.6 per cent of all such deliveries. The largest share of these agreements was with Saudi Arabia. Russia ranked second in these deliveries at US$7.5 billion, or 26.8 per cent. The top purchasers in the developing world were Saudi Arabia, India, and the United Arab Emirates (UAE).

Much of the developing world is also confronted with the traditional threat of the use of nuclear weapons. In October 2006, North Korea alarmed its regional neighbours and the great powers when it joined India, Pakistan, China, Israel, Russia, the United States, Britain, and France in the nuclear club. Since then, North Korea has test-fired short-range missiles and threatened a pre-emptive nuclear strike against the United States in response to UN sanctions (March 2013). Other potential members, who in the past have shown interest in developing a nuclear programme or who are suspected of pursuing nuclear ambitions, include South Africa, Brazil, Iran, and Venezuela.

While wars between states have been declining, intra-state conflict is common, particularly in the developing world. Internal security problems are pervasive in many areas of Asia, the Middle East, Latin

America, and especially Africa, where interethnic conflicts, insurgencies, and civil wars have been endemic and prolonged (see Chapter 13). In contrast to the traditional approach, the human security approach is helpful in stressing internal dynamics and the human costs of war. This includes issues such as child soldiers and landmines, which pose considerable threats to the lives of peoples of the developing world. The use of children in war is not new, but has been the subject of an increasing amount of public and policy attention. Children fight in almost 75 per cent of today's armed conflicts (Human Security Report Project 2005: 35). They have been used in terrorist operations in Northern Ireland, Columbia, and Sri Lanka. In looking at the data on the impact of wartime sexual violence on children, the Human Security Report 2012 finds it limited, but also shows that the majority of sexual violence against children is perpetrated by family members and acquaintances, and not by strangers and combatants.

The human security approach also highlights that the greatest human costs of war are not the battle deaths, but the 'indirect' deaths caused by disease, lack of access to food, clean water, and health care services. The lives of refugees, who commonly result from wars, are often at great risk—for example the 1.5 million refugees who fled the Rwandan **genocide** of 1994 into neighbouring Zaire (now the Democratic Republic of Congo), Tanzania, and Burundi. As of late July 2013, the two-year old civil conflict in Syria had resulted in about 100,000 deaths by some estimates and a massive refugee displacement into neighbouring countries, including Lebanon, Jordan, and Turkey (BBC News 2013).

Distribution of the conflicts and Western response

Overall, the number of active major armed conflicts has gone down. However, many small wars have erupted as others have died down, and currently many groups are rearming. Most violent conflicts in Asia, the Middle East, Africa, and Latin America are geographically separate and often unrelated. However, linkages within regions are common, as are ties with the developed world, particularly because of the involvement of great powers. The linkages with the developed world are often in a state of flux. For example, US and North Atlantic Treaty Organization (NATO) combat troops, engaged in **robust peacekeeping** in Afghanistan, are leaving by 2014. (Robust peacekeeping allows them much more leeway to make peace as opposed to keeping and monitoring it.) The total number of US troops that served in Iraq between March 2003 and December 2011 is over a million, and 4,487 US military personnel lost their lives. More than 110,000 Iraqis were killed over those years and millions displaced, largely by the ensuing sectarian struggle for power that continues today.

In 2012, the UN had approximately 114,000 personnel serving on fifteen peace operations led by the UN Department of Peacekeeping Operations (DPKO) on four continents. Since 1948, there have been a total of sixty-eight UN peacekeeping operations. The percentage of women deployed as civilians in peacekeeping operations is approximately 30 per cent (UN DPKO 2013). Three all-female UN police units have been deployed—Indians in Liberia, and Bangladeshi in Haiti and the Democratic Republic of Congo.

New technology continues to change the conduct of conflict and war. For example, US drones have played a crucial role in disrupting and eliminating military networks in the Middle East, Pakistan, and North Africa over the past decade (Drone Wars UK 2012). According to the US Government Accountability Office, the number of states that have acquired a complete drone system has grown from forty-one in 2005 to seventy-six in 2012. Over the next decade, there is projected to be US$80 billion in global spending for drones. This will increasingly affect developing and developed states, and in the near future drones may well be used by states and non-state groups to target neighbouring states or domestic threats. Based on the US precedent in which drones have lowered the threshold for dropping bombs, a real fear is that states may resort to force more easily and more often.

The **international community** perceives the need for a unified global agenda, rather than unilateral approaches, to resolve many of the violent conflicts. However, international action continues to be mostly limited and very selectively applied. Western approaches have ranged from outright neglect, through preventative measures, to (unilateral and multilateral) military intervention. From the perspective of most developing countries, international involvement—and in particular military intervention—is highly problematic and an infringement of their state sovereignty. They perceive the developed world as posing security threats to the developing world, in particular through the threat of military intervention, and the projection of Western or Northern power through the process of globalization. However, at other times, some states and non-state actors chastise Western states for not doing enough, for example in the case of Syria at the time of writing.

In this spirit, the Non-Aligned Movement (NAM), originally developed to combat colonialism and to avoid competing superpower alliances, has become increasingly influential. The NAM is made up of 120 developing countries that are increasingly concerned with reasserting their influence in a world largely still dominated by the United States, as well as by specific issues such as globalization, HIV/AIDS, and international crime. The continued challenge for the NAM is to move beyond anti-Western rhetoric and to gain world attention in order to effectively promote the interests of the developing world.

Gender and conflict

Recently, as mentioned earlier in the chapter, there have been attempts to bring a gendered perspective to the study of armed conflict, and this has led to a focus on the unique threats that women and girls face in conflict zones. There is, for example, more attention paid to the widespread phenomenon of wartime sexual violence. Although more men are killed in battle than women, we know that women are more vulnerable to sexual violence and predatory behaviour. The difficulty, however, is that there is little reliable data to help to determine whether sexual violence in war is increasing or not. This lack of reliable statistics also exists, for example, when we look at whether it is men or women who are more affected by 'collateral damage', war-exacerbated disease and malnutrition, or long-term psychological trauma. This means that policies relating to gender and conflict are rarely based on robust evidence, because good data is either not available or, where available, not accessible to non-specialists. It may also mean that many analyses underestimate the gender-based violence directed against males. According to the Human Security Report 2012, in the majority of countries in conflict, the reported levels of sexual violence may be lower than the mainstream narrative suggests. Moreover, the evidence that it suggests is that the level of sexual violence worldwide is likely declining, not increasing. The report also suggests that domestic sexual violence in war-affected countries is far more pervasive than the conflict-related sexual violence that is perpetrated by rebels, militias, and government forces, and which receives the overwhelming majority of media and official attention. However, some feminists have expressed concerns: they have argued that the evidence cited is selective, they have criticized the assumption that the incidence of sexual violence needs to be increasing for it to be regarded as a problem, and more broadly they have worried about how such report 'findings' might be used.

The securitization of terrorism in the developing world

Despite the variety of ongoing violence in much of the developing world, there was a shift of Western attention towards global terrorism after 11 September 2001 ('9/11'). Terrorism is an asymmetrical strategy available to weak actors seeking to level the strategic playing field. It is a tactic designed to achieve an objective (usually political) by using violence against innocent civilians to generate fear. Terrorism has been widely used in both the developed and developing worlds.

After 2001 and the beginning of the war on terror, the West focused particularly on transnational terrorist violence rather than other types of internal or interstate conflict. The declining capacity of some states to meet basic human needs and to enforce the **rule of law** was increasingly perceived to provide fertile conditions or training areas for global terrorist sympathizers. For example, in Afghanistan, some areas of Pakistan and Somalia, and other very weak or **collapsed states**, groups with links to al-Qaeda were commonly understood to have flourished, with some posing transnational threats. Western security concern has continued to focus particularly on organizations and groups at the network and global levels that are considered to require networked and global responses. Attention on Africa has especially increased in this regard.

While a causal relationship between poverty and terrorism has not been established, it is clear that non-state armed groups are able to exploit the dehumanizing conditions that result from poverty. The militarization of society, and the context of violent occupation and war, which characterize many developing states, can be used by terrorists to gather sympathy for violent acts against perceived oppressors and their supporters. Globalization has also provided them with new means to finance, carry out, and publicize attacks, as well as to forge alliances or networks with other groups around the world. Nevertheless, most terrorist actions remain localized. Non-state groups view terrorism as cheap and effective, and thus a weapon of choice for their wars against oppressive states. For example, until it was defeated by the Sri Lankan military in May 2009, the Liberation Tigers of Tamil Eelam (LTTE) had fought the Sri Lankan government since the 1970s with a well-organized terror campaign, pursuing objectives ranging from greater autonomy to complete secession.

When the war on terror became the West's first global priority in 2001, states with large Muslim populations and insurgency movements became priorities for US assistance. The United States substantially increased its foreign aid to Pakistan, India, the Philippines, Indonesia, and Uzbekistan as part of its anti-terrorism efforts. US military and security aid to Africa has since then also increased—and, as Bermeo (2009) argues, serves to undercut US efforts at **democracy promotion** too. The post-9/11 war on terror, by its very definition, took a primarily military approach consistent with traditional security. However, it is increasingly acknowledged by a variety of security actors that unless social, economic, and political contexts are addressed, and other tactics such as diplomacy and intelligence are deployed, these challenges will not disappear and could indeed escalate.

The West's perceived abuse of power and neglect of certain issues is felt strongly in the developing world. Just one example given of Western hypocrisy is when the United States and Britain provided military support for regimes with very poor human rights records (as in Uzbekistan), while preaching the need for democracy and human rights. Ironically, such hypocrisy creates fertile ground for organizations in the developing world that advocate terror and the rejection of the West, together with its agenda of **good governance** and democracy (see Chapters 14 and 15).

KEY POINTS

- Today, violence between states, the traditional subject of security studies, is less common than intra-state violence.

- Human security focuses on individual lives and the human costs of war.

- Violent conflict in the developed world is diverse, and specific to regions and particular states and localities.

- Western involvement in conflicts ranges from neglect to outright military intervention.

- New technologies, such as lethal drones used to counter terrorism, also provoke anti-Western sentiment.

International Organized Crime

International organized crime (IOC), a significant threat to peoples, societies, and states, is often overlooked when examining the developing world. However, the movement of illicit goods across borders is not new, and around the world organized crime has always presented a variety of threats. What is new today is the scale of the problem, and the growing power and capability of organized crime. International organized crime includes activities such as trafficking in narcotics, small arms, nuclear materials, and people, smuggling of illegal aliens, and money laundering. Few of these activities are confined to specific areas of the globe; rather, they have taken on a transnational character. The global aspect of the drug trade, for example, mirrors the global divisions of labour found in other economic realms, where production in the developing areas has risen largely to meet the demand in advanced industrial states.

Criminals have benefited significantly from globalization—that is, from the rise of information technology, the development of stronger political and economic linkages, and the shrinking importance of global distance. Globalization has expanded illegal markets, and increased the size and resources of criminal networks. Some IOC groups operate within strategic alliances, like firms; some work in globally coordinated networks; others have looser and more ad hoc affiliations. Global criminal organizations vary in terms of their cohesion, longevity, degree of hierarchical control, degree of penetration, and acceptance within society. International organized crime groups based in the developing world include, for example, the Triad gangs of Hong Kong, China, and various overseas ports, and the Colombian cocaine cartels.

Securitization of crime

Traditionally, crime has been categorized as an economic activity, a 'low politics' topic best suited to disciplines such as economics or criminology. However, it has become increasingly obvious that crime may threaten individual, societal, state, regional, and even global security. The network level is particularly relevant here, because while criminals often act in interconnected groups across borders, there is similarly a need for international cooperation (or networks) to counter them.

As described earlier, the determination by governments that an issue constitutes a security problem is generally driven more by realist, state-centred calculations than by humanitarianism. Drugs and arms are thus considered by states to be security issues in part because of their connection to violence. From a traditional standpoint, they may threaten the stability of governments. However, IOC also impacts on human security directly at the individual level in specific national, regional, or local contexts.

International organized crime poses a considerable challenge to states in the developed and developing world. At its most extreme, it can control territory, extract rents, provide services for local populations, and even wage war, as in Colombia and Afghanistan. It can also pose long-term structural damage such as the erosion of rule of law. The direct threat to state control is exacerbated by the relative weakness or low levels of political institutionalization of the state (as in Nigeria, Laos, and Tajikistan). Thus crime groups often work in 'ungoverned areas', but also may work in tandem with the state—a phenomenon termed 'state capture'. More generally, IOC erodes faith in democratic **institutions** depending on the degree to which criminality pervades the political, institutional, and financial infrastructure of the state—a significant problem in the post-Soviet states. Finally, IOC can undermine the state by destroying trust between people and state, eroding the tax basis and diverting resources.

International organized crime poses specific problems for developing countries. Crime is perceived as a sign of social instability, which may drive away foreign investment, foreign aid, and business. For example, in some African states, investment levels are low partly because of the perception that the rule of law does not prevail. International organized crime can also undermine the ability of a state to promote development. Finally, crime can harm social and **human capital**, and is associated with increased violence. It can have a far greater impact on human lives in countries in which the state is less able to intervene to protect individuals, for example in Brazil and South Africa.

Three key types of IOC that, to varying extent, impact on security at all levels of analysis are trafficking in persons, narcotics, and small arms.

Trafficking in persons

Trafficking in persons is a highly complex phenomenon that includes recruitment, movement, and **exploitation**. It is a threat to human security because, in its many forms, it violates human rights by depriving people of basic human dignity, and by jeopardizing individual and public health. Human rights violations include the lack of freedom of movement, and physical, sexual, or mental abuse. Trafficking in persons may also be perceived as a threat to global security because it is often part of a larger phenomenon of illegal migration and transnational organized crime.

There are many types of human trafficking: forced labour, including that of children (for example in South Asia, where people are forced to work in so-called 'sweat shops'); slavery (Sudan); selling of organs (Latin America and Asia); selling of orphans (for example following the December 2004 tsunami in South Asia). However, the most common and most lucrative is sex trafficking. Sex trafficking is global in scope, but particularly affects peoples in the developing world, from Tajikistan and Nigeria to Thailand.

Narcotic trafficking

Narcotic trafficking similarly affects, to varying extents, the security of peoples and states around the world. Traditionally, Asia and Latin America have been key source regions, while Europe and North America have been key regions of demand. However, overall narcotic consumption is increasing around the world. There is also evidence that transit states eventually become consumer and distributor states, as is currently happening in much of the post-Soviet Union and Africa.

Narcotic trafficking activity in places such as Colombia and Afghanistan damages economies, corrupts institutions, and affects regional stability and security. In spite of 2012 peace negotiations, Colombia epitomizes the security threats posed by crime. There, drug trafficking has represented a direct security threat to people, while criminal organizations, as well as violent political organizations such as the Revolutionary Armed Forces of Colombia (FARC) and National Liberation Army (ELN) in Colombia, have undermined the capacity of the government to rule the country. Narcotic trafficking also affects human security because individuals suffer the negative health effects of drugs such as cocaine and heroin, and the spread of HIV/AIDS associated with intravenous drug use. The United Nations Office on Drugs and Crime (UNODC) suggests that there were between 15.5 million and 38.6 million 'problem drug users' aged 15–64 in 2010 (UNODC 2012). Of course, different drugs pose unique problems for different regions. The report shows that there has been resurgence in opium and heroin production in Afghanistan, Myanmar, and Colombia after a fall in production in Afghanistan since 2007, and a shortage there resulting from crop failure in 2010. Demand has also increased resulting in higher prices.

Narcotic trafficking also tends to be associated with other types of crime. For example, in Colombia, incidents of murder and kidnapping are among the highest in the world, with between 2 million and 5 million people being displaced by guerrillas or kidnappers since the 1980s. Throughout Latin America, drug trafficking undermines **civil society** through pervasive **corruption** and intimidation of politicians, and through the breakdown of law and order (see Chapter 23 on Mexico).

Small arms trafficking

The third IOC security issue is small arms trafficking. At the end of the cold war, there was a surplus of weapons that became ready stockpiles for legal and illicit markets. Today, over two-thirds of the world's legitimate arms sales (and likely more of the illegal sales) are directed towards developing states. This both reflects and contributes to violence in the developing world. Worldwide, small arms and light weapons are responsible for the majority of direct conflict deaths. Many of the so-called 'new conflicts' that characterize the post-cold-war world tend to be fought using small arms and light weapons, and not conventional weapons or the threat of weapons of mass destruction (WMDs), which characterized the cold war.

The widespread availability of small arms has been a factor in facilitating and sustaining wars and violence, and is thus a concern to human and state security. In the developing world, small arms are inexpensive and widely available, which makes them very difficult to regulate. Their small size and the fact that they are relatively easy to use make them ideal for untrained combatants and children. They have thus contributed to the tragic growth in numbers of child soldiers, particularly in Africa.

The ability of developing countries to obtain an abundance of weapons has often been facilitated by great power struggles, through direct or illegal sales. During the cold war, rival powers armed regional antagonists such as India and Pakistan, Iran and Iraq, Israel and Syria, Ethiopia and Somalia. Most producers of arms are now selling them simply for commercial profit in many conflicts throughout the developing world and especially in Africa.

International policies

In the past, illicit trades and trafficking were most often perceived to be the responsibility of the state harbouring the clandestine transnational activities. Today, there is a broad consensus within the international community that many of these are regional or global security threats, and that the international community must be actively engaged to counter them. Criminal (and terrorist) networks are believed increasingly to pose distributed and mobile threats. There is often no obvious source that is easy to target and thus international cooperation is required to counter them effectively.

Some developing states are perceived by international organizations as having become transshipment regions for organized crime activities, and there is a fear that they are becoming safe havens for them. Overall, governments in developed and developing countries have obsolete tools, inadequate laws, ineffective bureaucratic arrangements, and ineffective strategies to deal with IOC. However, the situation in many developing countries is comparatively worse. There, power generally rests in the hands of a small group of elites who have ambiguous attitudes towards crime.

In this context, international organizations have taken steps to securitize (defined as 'push to the top of the political agenda') these activities. UN Conventions have been signed (see Box 19.2), but difficulties in implementation remain. As mentioned, another major challenge is that in many regions of the world

---

BOX 19.2 UN CONVENTIONS ON ORGANIZED CRIME

2000	UN Convention against Transnational Organized Crime
2000	UN Convention against Transnational Organized Crime: Protocol against the Smuggling of Migrants by Land, Sea and Air
2000	UN Convention against Transnational Organized Crime: Protocol to Prevent, Suppress and Punish Trafficking in Persons, Especially Women and Children
2001	UN Convention against Transnational Organized Crime: Protocol against the Illicit Manufacturing of and Trafficking in Firearms, Their Parts and Components and Ammunition
2003	UN Convention against Corruption

criminal groups are either tolerated, or more directly supported, by governments. International organized crime may pose **security dichotomies** for peoples and states: as well as the negative effects on individual and state security, trafficking activities may provide work for people when the state cannot help them, and may contribute to a state's economy, especially in times of crisis or transition.

The effectiveness of many of the policies initiated by the international community against IOC is questionable. The securitization of crime has meant that several specific strategies—in particular border management and law enforcement—have been adopted. These strategies are important, but limited. The most extreme examples of securitization include the use of special military forces in the 1990s by Britain and the United States in tackling South American drug cartels, and the use of NATO to counter trafficking in Afghanistan. The continuing flow of cocaine and heroin shows the limitations of such traditional security approaches.

Finally, once again, Western governments are generally not as interested in the root causes or the effects of crime on individuals (the human security approach), as they are in the effects of transnational or global crime on Western states and peoples. Western states are therefore often viewed as hypocritical by the developing world for exhorting them, for example, to do more to decrease narcotic trade, when the trade is largely driven by Western demand.

KEY POINTS

- International organized crime groups pose a variety of levels of threat to peoples, states, and regions in the developing world, as well as to the global community.

- International organized crime operates in transnational groups, demands transnational responses, and thus can be usefully considered at the network or global level of analysis.

- While trafficking in persons is predominantly a human security threat, narcotic and arms trafficking pose threats to individuals, societies, and states. All three types of trafficking are increasingly perceived by the international community as global security threats because of their real and perceived negative effects on Western peoples and states.

- International organized crime poses security dichotomies for developing states, in that their activities may be perceived, by states and peoples, positively as well as negatively.

Conclusion

Key issues in current debates about security and the developing world include the following.

- What is security?
- Are Western-defined concepts and approaches about security applicable to the developing world?
- What have been the ramifications of globalization on security issues?
- Are development goals based on humanitarianism increasingly subordinated to Western foreign and security policy objectives?

'Security' is a contested concept and this chapter argues that security must be examined through different levels of analysis. Today, the discipline of security studies increasingly includes not only state-centred analyses, and the study of military threats and inter-state conflict, but also intra-state conflicts and direct threats to individual lives. Critical security studies, including feminist, normative, and post-structuralist approaches, all question the concept of security and critique the realist/traditionalist approach. This chapter has adopted a comprehensive definition of security that entails examination at the individual, state, regional, network, and global levels.

Many security issues impact strongly on developing states. The two key issues examined in this chapter—violent conflict and international organized crime—affect security at many levels of analysis. Security threats are perceived differently in the developed and developing worlds. They change over time, depending on context, and on the perceptions of peoples and states. The developing world, similarly to the developed world, is not monolithic, and different issues affect different countries, areas, and regions.

Western states and organizations have often structured global priorities according to their own, generally traditionally defined, security interests. Those interests are mostly focused on the transnational effects of so-called threats to Western peoples and states, rather than on the issues that directly threaten developing states and their peoples. For example, the preoccupation with global terrorism after 2001 initially diverted attention and funding from many development issues, but this is changing and, among many states and organizations, there is now a renewed focus on them (and a greater focus on their relationship to terrorism).

From the perspective of many developing countries, the developed world itself poses many security threats, in particular the threat of military intervention and the projection of Western or Northern power through the process of globalization. Developing countries have limited means available to make their voices heard and little bargaining power. In the absence of a conventional military balance, some developing states with sufficient economic and technical capacity have sought weapons of mass destruction to level the playing field. Less well-off state and non-state actors turned to terrorism as a potential equalizer; others engage in 'bandwagoning' with the dominant power, or join regional organizations and the Non-Aligned Movement to pool resources and project a unified response. The dilemma for the developing world continues to be how to promote its interests effectively in a world in which few listen to its voices. The challenge for both worlds is to adopt a more holistic approach to security policy, one that bridges the increasingly artificial divide between traditional security and development studies.

? QUESTIONS

1. What are the key approaches to the study of security?

2. What is the impact of globalization on human security in the developing world?

3. What is the benefit of bringing a gendered perspective to the study of armed conflict?

4. Does the West's 'securitization' of terrorism have any specific implications for state security in the developing world?

5. How does international organized crime affect the security of peoples and states in the developing world? Explain with reference to either narcotic trafficking or human trafficking.

6. From a critical security perspective, explain how and why Western governments are not responding appropriately to security challenges in the developing world.

≋ FURTHER READING

Ayoob, M. (1995) *The Third World Security Predicaments: State Making, Regional Conflict and the International System* (Boulder, CO: Lynne Rienner) An important book examining security in the developing world from a state-centric perspective.

Chen, L., Fukuda-Parr, S., and Seidensticker, E. (eds) (2003) *Human Insecurity in a Global World* (Cambridge, MA: Global Equity Initiative, Asia Center, Harvard University) Examines global issues from the human security perspective.

Friman, R. and Andreas, P. (eds) (1999) *The Illicit Global Economy and State Power* (New York: Rowman and Littlefield) Offers a solid introduction to the subject of transnational organized crime.

Human Security Report Project (2012) *Human Security Report 2012: Sexual Violence, Education, and War: Beyond the Mainstream Narrative* (Vancouver, BC: Human Security Press) The HSRP produces ground-breaking reports that define human security as freedom from violence. They provide data and analysis about the effects of violence on peoples around the world.

Jackson, R. J. (2013) *Global Politics in the 21st Century* (Cambridge/New York: Cambridge University Press) This ground-breaking textbook explores the interrelations between globalization and new security challenges.

Kegley, C. W. Jr (ed.) (2003) *The New Global Terrorism: Characteristics, Causes, Controls* (Saddle River, NJ: Pearson Education) An excellent edited volume of major academic articles on non-state violence.

Pettiford, L. and Curley, M. (1999) *Changing Security Agendas and the Third World* (London/New York: Pinter) This thought-provoking book examines security from a developing world perspective, countering traditional international relations theory.

Tickner, J. A. (1992) *Gender in International Relations: Feminist Perspectives on Achieving Global Security* (New York: Columbia University Press) A ground-breaking book introducing feminist perspectives on global security.

United Nations (2004) *A More Secure World: Our Shared Responsibility, Report of the UN Secretary General's High Level Panel on Threats, Challenges and Change* (London: Stationery Office) This UN-commissioned report outlines the key security challenges facing the world today and gives proposals for their resolution.

WEB LINKS

http://first.sipri.org/ Facts on International Relations and Security Trends (FIRST) gives access to a large number of databases on traditional and non-traditional security issues.

http://www.crisisgroup.org/ Site of the International Crisis Group (ICG), a non-profit NGO that provides high-quality reports and briefs on deadly conflicts around the world.

http://www.humansecuritygateway.info/ The Human Security Gateway, an excellent research and information database on human security issues.

http://www.isn.ethz.ch/ The site of the International Relations and Security Network, which shares specialized information among international relations and security professionals worldwide.

For additional material and resources, please visit the Online Resource Centre at:
http://www.oxfordtextbooks.co.uk/orc/burnell4e/

PART 5
Regime Change

This section includes two chapters providing case studies of **regime change**. As Chapter 14 has described, during the 1980s and 1990s there was huge academic interest in, and hopes for, a seemingly global 'third wave' of democratization. The term 'democratization' itself was central to analysis of political change in developing countries, with the understanding that democratic **regimes** were emerging out of preceding authoritarian regimes, whether based on personal dictatorships, or single-party or military rule.

As time passed, it became clear that there was no irresistible tide of democratization-except perhaps in the very, very long run. There were still significant countries, even regions, largely untouched by this trend and at the same time, in many other countries, democratic beginnings were soon mired or corrupted, leading, as we have seen, to the coining of a range of neologisms indicating the different ways in which democracy had been compromised (for example '**electoral authoritarianism**').

Accordingly, the focus in Part 5 is on regime change—or indeed the limits to regime change—without any necessary prior assumption of an underlying democratization process. Here, we understand a regime as a form or system of government (as distinct from the individual governments that take or yield power within its terms). Regimes can be defined in formal terms, but for a fuller characterization we may need to consider less formal, underlying characteristics and continuities. Our case study chapters, on Pakistan and Indonesia respectively, enable us to explore and illustrate these different aspects of the theme of regime change, in contrasting circumstances.

In the case of Pakistan, as David Taylor relates, there has been an almost bewildering succession of regimes, in formal terms at least. Post-independence, early broadly democratic forms soon gave way to military, or military-bureaucratic, types of rule. There followed a brief and troubled quasi-democratic interlude in the 1970s, a decade of military rule under Zia, unstable democratic government through much of the 1990s, a further military coup led by Musharraf, and only from 2008 more freely contested government elections. Whilst on one level, then, Pakistan is characterized by regime instability, on another more profound level, according to Taylor, the military has remained a dominant force, either directly or indirectly, in its **politics**.

Indonesia appears to provide a contrasting case study. After more than thirty years of military-based rule under Suharto, democratic elections in 1998 ushered in a sustained era of competitive party politics. Edward Aspinall argues that Indonesia remains a democracy, albeit a 'fragile' one. The main perceived threat to democratic continuity, given the continuing underlying reality of Indonesia's geography and cultural diversity, is fragmentation or even national disintegration, but Aspinall suggests that decentralized, democratic government may prove better able to accommodate these centrifugal pressures than authoritarian rule.

20

Pakistan: Regime Change and Military Power

David Taylor

Chapter contents

Overview

Since its creation in 1947, Pakistan has struggled to develop a system of sustainable democratic government. She has experienced a succession of regime changes, alternating between qualified or electoral democracy and either military or quasi-military rule. But underlying apparent instability and regime change, a continuing feature has been the central role of the military in the political process. This pattern is in stark contrast to India, despite sharing the same colonial background. Ironically, the reintroduction of military rule has usually been welcomed in Pakistan as a relief from the factional disputes among the civilian political leaders and accompanying high levels of corruption. This chapter describes Pakistan's history of regime change and explains the military's persistent influence, culminating in the period of rule by General Pervez Musharraf, from 1999 to 2008. Figure 20.1 is a map of Pakistan and Box 20.1 provides an overview of key dates in Pakistan's history.

Introduction: From Independence to State Breakup in 1971

Pakistan's military forces (principally the army, which numerically and politically has always been the key player) have dominated the country for most of its history since independence. This has meant not only political power, but also the pre-emption of a substantial share of economic resources. According to International Institute of Strategic Studies estimates, defence expenditure was 3.16 per cent of gross domestic product (GDP) in 2007, a figure that has been declining in the past few years, but remains the highest in the region.

Figure 20.1 Pakistan

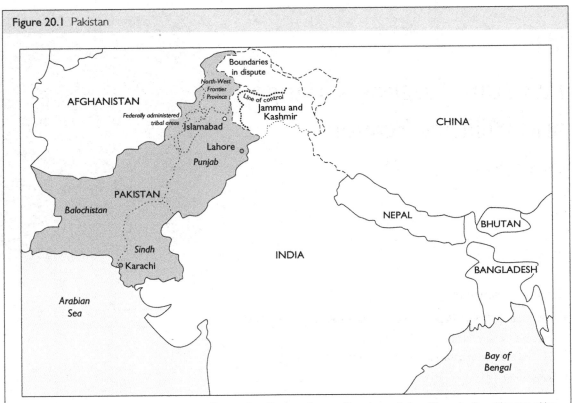

Note: Boundaries in the Kashmir region are in dispute. The use of specific nomenclature and boundary symbols on this map implies neither recognition nor non-recognition of the legality of the political regions or boundaries to which they refer.

BOX 20.1 KEY DATES IN PAKISTAN'S HISTORY

15 Aug 1947	Pakistan independence
11 Sept 1948	Independence leader Muhammad Ali Jinnah dies
Feb 1954	Pakistan joins a US-led cold war military alliance
Mar 1956	First Constitution passed (but never fully implemented)
Oct 1958	General Ayub Khan carries out first military coup
Febr 1960	Ayub Khan elected president through indirect election
Mar 1962	New Constitution passed
Sept 1965	Indecisive war with India
Mar 1969	Ayub Khan forced to hand over power to General Yahya Khan
Dec 1970	Elections give absolute majority to East Pakistan-based Awami League
Dec 1971	Indian intervention brings about defeat of Pakistan army and separation of Bangladesh
Jan 1972	Zulfikar Ali Bhutto, leader of the Pakistan People's Party (PPP), becomes president (later prime minister)
Apr 1977	General election returns Bhutto to power, but opposition launches agitation, claiming that the results were rigged
July 1977	Military coup led by General Zia-ul-Haq
Apr 1979	Bhutto executed
Dec 1984	Referendum gives Zia the basis to become president
Aug 1988	Zia killed when his plane is blown up
Nov 1988	Elections bring Benazir Bhutto (daughter of Zulfikar Ali Bhutto) to power

May 1998	Pakistan tests nuclear devices	Oct 2007	Musharraf stands down as Army Chief
Oct 1999	Military coup led by General Pervez Musharraf	Dec 2007	Benazir Bhutto assassinated
Apr 2002	Referendum makes Musharraf president	Feb 2008	Elections bring PPP back to power
Oct 2002	Elections bring to power the Pakistan Muslim League (Quaid) (PML(Q)), a party sympathetic to Musharraf	Aug 2008	Musharraf resigns as president succeeded by PPP leader, Asif Ali Zardari, widower of Benazir Bhutto
Mar 2007	Chief Justice of Pakistan suspended by President	Mar 2013	Elections won by Pakistan Muslim League; its leader, Nawaz Sharif, forms coalition government and becomes prime minister

Defence consumes almost as much as the total federal expenditure on social and economic development. The army (excluding paramilitary forces) is 550,000-strong, and many more depend on the army directly or indirectly for employment. Internationally, the image of Pakistan as a **garrison state**, although acceptable at times to the United States and other Western powers, has often created difficulties, for example the country's suspension from the Commonwealth after the 1999 military coup until 2004. A garrison state is a state maintained by military power and, in some definitions, is a state organized primarily around the need for military security.

The dominance of the military in Pakistan has been explained in different ways. Some analysts note the way in which Pakistan inherited a strong army from the colonial state; others see it as an aspect of a social order still dominated by landowning groups. The two arguments come together in the fact that the army has traditionally been recruited very heavily from rural areas of the Punjab—the most populous of the country's four provinces—and from adjacent areas of the North-West Frontier Province (renamed Khyber Pakhtunkhwa in April 2010), although the officer corps is increasingly coming from more urban and middle-class families, and efforts have been made to broaden the base of the rank and file. During the colonial period, the government took steps to ensure the soldiers' loyalty, for example through generous treatment in the allocation of land and through the racially based classification of Indians into martial and non-martial groups. The army thus tends to share a strong sense of Pakistan as a unitary state. Regional and international factors are also important, with Pakistan's long-running conflict with India over Kashmir and the cold war both influential in enhancing the role of the army.

When British India became independent in 1947, and was simultaneously divided into the two successor states of India and Pakistan, the armed forces were similarly divided. As a result of previous recruitment policies, Pakistan got more than its proportionate share of soldiers. It also inherited a social structure in which control of land and of the people who worked the land was the single most important basis of political power. Political parties were weak.

At first, the unchallenged authority wielded by Muhammad Ali Jinnah, who had led the Pakistan movement from its inception, kept tensions between provinces, and between locals and newcomers, in check. However, after his death in 1948, the country lacked political leadership of national standing. While popular leaders emerged in the eastern wing of the country (now Bangladesh), in the west (from where the army was recruited) provincial politicians battled for local control with little regard to national issues.

At the same time as Pakistan was facing difficulties in establishing stable structures of government, there was a belief that India's leaders had agreed to the partition of British India grudgingly and would miss no opportunity to sabotage its new neighbour. The distrust soon found a focus in the conflict over the princely state of Jammu and Kashmir. As a Hindu ruler with a powerful Hindu minority dominating the upper ranks of the bureaucracy, but with an overall Muslim majority, the Maharaja, Hari Singh, prevaricated over to which new state to affiliate. War ensued between India and Pakistan, until a truce under United Nations auspices was negotiated in August 1948.

The weakness of Pakistan's political institutions and perceived need for security against a more powerful India meant that the army as an institution became increasingly important in Pakistan's public life. The first Pakistani Commander-in-Chief of the army,

General Ayub Khan, became minister of defence for a period in 1954 and played a key role in bringing Pakistan into the US-led military alliance system that was constructed in Asia in the early 1950s. A complementary development was the assertion of the role of the bureaucracy and judiciary as guardians of the state in the absence of strong national leadership and in the face of challenges to the dominance of the established social order, in particular of the Punjab. While not identical, the social base of the army and the bureaucracy overlapped, and their perceptions of Pakistan were similar.

Under the Constitution that had been adopted in 1956, Pakistan's first parliamentary elections were due in 1958. To avoid the accession to power of H. S. Suhrawardy, an East Bengal-based politician, then President Iskander Mirza declared martial law. Shortly after, Ayub Khan assumed political control, sending Mirza into exile. Ayub Khan was able to obtain a judgment from the Supreme Court authorizing his rule. He also conducted a campaign against the political leaders whom he had displaced. Hundreds of politicians were disqualified from further political activity, on the grounds of **corruption**. This was complemented by an analysis of the situation that seemed to draw both on colonial assumptions and on some of the contemporary thinking in the United States, for example by the political scientist Samuel P. Huntington, about economic and political development. Pakistan was seen as a society that needed firm leadership if it was to enjoy healthy national development.

Building on this analysis, Ayub Khan initiated what was called the 'Basic Democracies' system, which brought around 80,000 local leaders and notables into **politics** on a non-party basis. As well as electing a National Assembly, they also formed an electoral college for the presidency and, in 1960, Ayub Khan was duly elected president. This enabled him to dispense with martial law and to formulate a new Constitution for the country—duly brought into effect in 1962. This defined Pakistan as a progressive Muslim state, pursuing policies that reflected a dynamic interpretation of religious values. In line with this, in 1961 Ayub Khan's government issued the Family Laws Ordinance, which introduced reforms in the area of marriage and divorce, significantly improving the rights of women. Although Ayub Khan eventually permitted the re-establishment of political parties in order to provide a safety valve, and in fact placed himself at the head of one of them so as to attract many of the local leaders who had dominated rural politics in the past, he was unable to cope with the increasing alienation of East Bengal, and in basic democrat and presidential elections held in 1964–65 he was unable to gain a majority there.

Growing discontent in both parts of the country, especially after an abortive attempt to seize Kashmir led to war with India in September 1965, paved the way for the then army chief, General Yahya Khan, to displace Ayub Khan in March 1969 and declare a fresh period of martial rule. He promised direct parliamentary elections, which were held in December 1970. East Pakistan, which held a demographic majority, voted overwhelmingly for the Awami League, led by Sheikh Mujibur Rahman; Zulfikar Ali Bhutto, a former protégé of Ayub Khan who had established his own Pakistan People's Party (PPP) in 1967, won convincingly in the west, but on a smaller scale. Sheikh Mujibur Rahman's insistence on his right to the prime ministership and on his power to write a constitution that would give full autonomy to the east was rejected both by the army and by West Pakistan's politicians, and in March 1971 the army deployed force to assert the authority of the (West) Pakistan state. Indian intervention led to a decisive military defeat for Pakistan, providing the opportunity for Bhutto to take over in the west and ushering in the creation of Bangladesh in the east.

KEY POINTS

- Pakistan has been dominated by the army since its creation in 1947. Social and political factors, as well as the cold war context, have contributed to this situation.

- Pakistan's state structures derive from the colonial period; the colonial army was recruited heavily from the areas of British India that became Pakistan in 1947, especially the Punjab.

- Because conflict with India, especially over Kashmir, has fostered insecurity, the army has been able to place its needs and requirements at the centre of political life.

- Ayub Khan, Pakistan's first military ruler following the 1958 coup, attempted to develop an alternative political structure based on mobilization of rural leadership.

- The unsuccessful 1965 war with India ultimately led to Ayub Khan's downfall. The failure of his successor, General Yahya Khan, over Bangladesh led to his displacement by a civilian politician, Zulfikar Ali Bhutto.

Unstable Government: 1971–99

The Bhutto era represented an attempt at a politics of **populism**, but by using the apparatus of the state to achieve his ends, Bhutto remained caught within its folds. The army, as an institution, remained a central actor, being used in 1974 to put down an internal rising in the province of Balochistan. The personalization of power by Bhutto alienated many army officers. In 1977, he faced a political crisis largely of his own making when he was accused by the opposition parties of rigging elections. Following three months of continuous agitation in the main cities, the army, headed by General Zia-ul-Haq (whom Bhutto had promoted ahead of more senior generals in the belief that he had no political ambitions), intervened and called for fresh elections.

Bhutto's evident popularity among his supporters persuaded General Zia to have him rearrested and the elections postponed. Bhutto was controversially arraigned on murder charges and executed in April 1979, although the judicial decision was not unanimous. A feature of the Zia period was the expansion of the armed forces' intelligence service, the Directorate of Inter-Services Intelligence (ISI). As well as managing Pakistan's involvement in the Afghan conflict, as a result of which it developed close links with selected Islamist leaders, for example Gulbuddin Hekmatyar, the ISI began systematically to monitor the activities of political parties. More generally, Zia gave strong encouragement to the growth of Islamist sentiment in the army, a shift most noticeable among the more junior ranks.

During the early 1980s, Zia pressed ahead with the Islamization of the country's institutions, for example introducing changes to the banking system to eliminate the payment of interest. One major series of initiatives that attracted worldwide attention was a redefinition of the legal position of women. Their standing as witnesses in legal cases was reduced to half that of men, and rules on pre- and extramarital sexual relations made more punitive in ways that especially disadvantaged women. In 1985, Zia felt strong enough to end the period of direct martial rule, reintroducing a heavily modified Constitution that gave the president sweeping discretionary powers. This had been preceded by a referendum that was widely regarded as bogus, but which enabled him to claim a five-year term as president. Elections held under the new Constitution on a non-party basis then allowed the choice of a traditional landlord politician, Mohammad Khan Junejo, as the prime minister. Nearly three years later, Zia dismissed the prime minister, claiming that Islamization was proceeding too slowly. Then, in August 1988, he was killed by a bomb planted on his plane. Many theories have been advanced, but it is still not certain who the perpetrators were.

After Zia's death, elections brought back to power the PPP under the leadership of Bhutto's daughter Benazir, and she alternated in office with the other major civilian political leader, Nawaz Sharif, whose power base lay in the Punjab and who had originally been inducted into politics by Zia. A major role was also played by the Muttahida Qaumi Movement, a party representing the Urdu-speaking population of Karachi and in whose creation Zia had again played a part. In eleven years, there were four elections. This might appear an interlude of democratic politics, with political parties competing for control of government, but throughout effective power was in fact shared between the political leadership, the army, and sections of the civilian bureaucracy. This uneasy arrangement produced constant difficulty. In 1993, a deadlock between the president, Ghulam Ishaq Khan, a former senior civil servant who had been close to Zia, and the then prime minister Nawaz Sharif, was eventually resolved through the intervention of the army chief, who insisted that both resign prior to new elections under a neutral, caretaker prime minister. Nawaz Sharif returned to power in 1997 and succeeded in amending the Constitution to restrict the powers of the president. He also forced General Jehangir Karamat, the army chief, to resign in 1998 and appointed as his successor General Pervez Musharraf, who was born in India and had come to Pakistan as a refugee at independence. Musharraf nevertheless reasserted the right of the army to take part in policymaking by unilaterally embarking on a military adventure in the Kargil district of Kashmir in 1999. The fighting—the most intense since 1971—was brought to an end through US diplomatic pressure and without any gains by Pakistan. This left the army and the government deeply suspicious of each other. In October, General Musharraf launched a military coup to prevent his own dismissal.

General Musharraf's Rule from 1999 to 2008

Coming after a period of instability, Musharraf began with substantial popular support. He promised action against the more notoriously corrupt politicians and bureaucrats, and seemed in tune with the aspirations of many of Pakistan's urban population for a more liberal lifestyle. He gained credit for a bold move to open up the electronic media to private ownership, although his willingness to support US intervention in Afghanistan after the **terrorist** attacks of 11 September 2001 ('9/11') was unpopular in many quarters. The question that he had to resolve, however, was how quickly to return to civilian rule while maintaining his own and the army's decisive power to intervene in areas that were deemed critical to national interests.

Musharraf's initial political move was to hold a referendum in 2002 to make himself president, but the exercise was seen as manipulated and lacking **legitimacy**. In another echo of previous military rulers' strategies, Musharraf also increased devolution of administration to the local level and matched it with non-party elections to local councils. Elections later in the year were fought on a party basis, but the leaders of the two main parties, who were both based abroad, were unable to participate directly. A breakaway faction of the Pakistan Muslim League (PML(Q)), known popularly as the 'King's Party', was able, with strong official support, to win a plurality of seats and form a government. The opposition refused to accept the legitimacy of constitutional changes introduced by presidential fiat and brought National Assembly proceedings to a halt for most of 2003. At the end of the year, a deal was struck with the main Islamist parties to allow some changes to be introduced, but, given Musharraf's own liberal leanings, this was a tactical deal (for the Islamists, the quid pro quo was a clear run for their government in the North-West Frontier Province) and served only to heighten the contradictions in his efforts to remain above civilian politics. It also acted as a brake on his efforts to reform the law on sexual offences, in which regard only a very modest measure could be passed in 2006. Both of the main political parties continued to demand that he leave office.

In March 2007, Musharraf took the dramatic step of suspending the Chief Justice of Pakistan, allegedly because of abuse of power, but in reality for fear that the Supreme Court would rule against him on key political and constitutional issues. The decision provoked nationwide protests led by the lawyers, and Musharraf's position began to weaken. In July, the Chief Justice was reinstated, but in November, Musharraf again imposed a state of emergency, enabling him to once more dismiss the Chief Justice. The assassination of Benazir Bhutto at the end of the year, apparently by Islamist militants, changed the political landscape yet again and the PPP won the elections that were eventually held in February 2008. In August, Musharraf was forced to resign and Benazir Bhutto's widower, Asif Ali Zardari, succeeded him. One major factor in this decision was the evident desire by General Kayani, the new army chief, to withdraw the army from direct political involvement.

One major reason for Musharraf's long survival was that he enjoyed the political and financial support of the United States; towards the end of his period in office, however, the United States put increasing pressure on him for a negotiated handover of power to civilian parties. Another reason for his survival was the relatively strong performance of the economy, buoyed by increased inflows of funds both from official donors, following Pakistan's strategic importance in the wake of 9/11, and from diaspora Pakistanis. Inflation was brought under control and industrial production picked up, although poverty levels remained stubbornly high.

While initially staunch in his support for Pakistan's long-standing positions on Kashmir, by 2001 Musharraf set in motion talks with India over Kashmir, partly in response to pressure from the **international community**, and perhaps partly in the hope that a breakthrough would win back much of the civilian electorate. However, these negotiations moved very slowly, largely because of India's reluctance to make matching concessions, and eventually proved fruitless.

A key challenge that Musharraf was unable to resolve was the rising tide of Islamist militancy. This had taken firm root in the 1980s, when, during the Zia period, militants had been encouraged, especially by the ISI, to fight against Soviet forces in Afghanistan and thereafter to become engaged in the Kashmir struggle. A network of religious schools (*madrasahs*) had developed, which trained a generation of fiercely committed young men willing to sacrifice themselves in a fight against what were perceived as oppressive and un-Islamic **regimes**. In July 2007, the government was forced to take military action to close down a mosque in the capital Islamabad that had become closely associated with an Islamist group. Fierce fighting led to at least 100 deaths, although the total may well have been higher. While the United States continually pressed the Pakistan government to take a tougher line, the political parties and public opinion generally were deeply suspicious of what was perceived as the West's anti-Muslim agenda.

KEY POINTS

- Musharraf enjoyed substantial support for his coup, seen as promising relief from corrupt and incompetent civilian governments.

- Musharraf responded to 9/11 by giving full support to the United States, although this was unpopular with some sections of the population.

- Like his predecessors, Musharraf sought to discredit existing political leaders and to build a party loyal to himself; he amended the Constitution to increase his discretionary powers as president.

- Musharraf's popular support declined steadily; he tried to divide the political parties, but in the end was unable to maintain his juggling act.

Conclusion

Pakistan has experienced frequent apparent **regime change**, generally oscillating between forms of more direct military rule and civilian rule with some element of competitive party politics. Since 2008, civilian rule has prevailed and, in March 2013, for the first time in Pakistan's history, a democratically elected government was allowed to complete its full term. Elections in May saw a high voter turnout and the coming to power at national level of a coalition led by Nawaz Sharif. To that extent, democratic transition may be advancing in Pakistan. The vision of Pakistan set forth by the country's founding fathers was essentially democratic, and even if army intervention has sometimes been tolerated as a necessary evil, the aspiration to achieve a stable, progressive democracy has always been widespread. Today, support for democracy is growing within the country's younger middle class, especially, but not only, in the major cities. But it would be premature to suggest that the military's political role is declining.

A discourse on politics has developed that is shared not only by the military, but also by some other sections of society. Politics as it has commonly been practised is conceived as an aspect of the 'feudal' phase of Pakistani history. To break its hold, the army may need to intervene to help the process along. The 'ordinary' Pakistani is a key figure in this discourse and is brought into politics through carefully tailored institutions from which party politics are excluded, at least on the surface. The acquisition by Pakistan of nuclear weapons in the late 1990s, carefully guarded by the army, has heightened the sense that the armed forces have a unique role to play in the survival of the state.

While the army leadership projects itself as the guardian of the national interest, it is often seen by others as primarily concerned with its own interests. Retired officers are frequently appointed to senior administrative positions and given preferential treatment, most significantly the allocation of prime rural and urban land. The armed forces, the army in particular, have major business interests, such as the Fauji (Military) Foundation, the profits of which go to support welfare programmes, primarily, but not exclusively, aimed at army veterans and their families. Nothing has changed in this respect in recent years.

A key challenge to the army since the beginning of the 2000s is the initiation of internal security operations against Islamic militant groups, some of whom have, since the end of 2007, fought under the banner of the Tehrik-i-Taliban Pakistan. In 2008-09, the army fought major battles in the Swat valley in Khyber Pakhtunkhwa before it could be recaptured from the militants. There has also been fierce fighting along the Afghan border. Army losses in these campaigns and the evident difficulty of bringing the insurgency under control are themselves worrisome, but more serious is the risk that they pose to the internal coherence of the army itself. Some members of the armed forces are evidently sympathetic to Islamist ideas, and also resent the actions of the Americans in Iraq and Afghanistan, especially the targeting of militants on Pakistani territory and the deaths of innocent bystanders in US drone attacks. The death of Osama Bin Laden at US hands in an army-dominated town near Islamabad was both an embarrassment and also, to many, a provocation. The possibility of a coup within the army (as against the pattern to date, whereby all four coups have been carried out by the army as an institution) cannot be ruled out.

Some army leaders believe that Pakistan cannot sustain a political system that does not give a major role to the armed forces. Turkey is often cited as a parallel example. Some civilians share this view, but many more reject it, especially in the smaller provinces. However, until there has been a lengthy spell of civilian rule under a prime minister or president who has the skills to wean the army away from its current set of assumptions without provoking a backlash, further direct or indirect military intervention in politics remains a constant possibility.

? QUESTIONS

1. What policies did the colonial state pursue that prepared the way for recurrent military intervention in politics after independence?

2. 'More apparent than real.' Comment on this assessment of frequent regime change in Pakistan.

3. Compare and contrast the political strategies of Generals Ayub Khan, Zia-ul-Haq, and Pervez Musharraf.

4. What have been the consequences for Pakistani society of prolonged periods of military dominance?

5. Assess the prospects for democratic consolidation in Pakistan over the next five years.

6. What factors constrain the Pakistan army's ability to repress Islamist militancy?

7. Is Pakistan likely to see further military interventions in the future, and if so, why?

FURTHER READING

Ali, T. (1983) *Can Pakistan Survive? The Death of a State* (Harmondsworth: Penguin Books) Highly critical analysis by a leading journalist and political activist.

Aziz, M. (2007) *Military Control in Pakistan: The Parallel State* (London: Routledge) A recent work that focuses on the extent to which the military intervenes to protect its institutional interests.

Cloughley, B. (2000) *A History of the Pakistan Army: Wars and Insurrections* (Karachi: Oxford University Press Pakistan) A history of the army that details its role at various stages of Pakistan's history. The author has known many of the key personalities involved.

Cohen, S. P. (2002) *The Pakistan Army* (Karachi: Oxford University Press) Based on extensive interactions with the Pakistan army's leadership, this carefully documented analysis of the history and development of the army is coupled with a discussion of its political attitudes.

Dewey, C. (1999) 'The Rural Roots of Pakistani Militarism', in D. A. Low (ed.) *The Political Inheritance of Pakistan* (Basingstoke: Macmillan), 255–83 The author is a historian of the Punjab, and relates the persistence of military influence to the army's embeddedness in the structures of power in rural society.

Jaffrelot, C. (ed.) (2002) *A History of Pakistan and its Origins* (London: Anthem Press) An up-to-date collection on different aspects of Pakistan's history and social structure. The contributions by the editor are especially valuable.

Jalal, A. (1990) *State of Martial Rule: The Origins of Pakistan's Political Economy of Defence* (Cambridge: Cambridge University Press) A detailed study of the process by which the Pakistan army became central to the Pakistan state. The author locates internal processes within the general cold war context.

Lieven, A. (2012) *Pakistan: A Hard Country* (London: Allen Lane) Written by a journalist-turned-academic, the book provides an up-to-date survey of the issues facing Pakistan.

Musharraf, P. (2006) *In the Line of Fire* (London: Simon and Schuster) General Musharraf's own (ghostwritten) account of his life and times.

Rizvi, H.-A. (1986) *The Military and Politics in Pakistan* (Lahore: Progressive Publishers) Detailed study of civil–military relations by a leading Pakistani scholar.

Siddiqa, A. (2007) *Military Inc.: Inside Pakistan's Military Economy* (London: Pluto Press) This work documents and analyses the extent of the Pakistan army's involvement in the civilian economy.

Talbot, I. (1998) *Pakistan: A Modern History* (London: Christopher Hurst) The most reliable of recent histories of the country. Talbot has a strong sense of the provincial roots of contemporary Pakistan.

WEB LINKS

http://countrystudies.us/pakistan/ A detailed US-based compilation of information on the history, economy, society, and politics of Pakistan.

http://www.sacw.net/ The South Asia Citizens Web is an independent space that provides exchanges of information between and about citizen initiatives in South Asia.

For additional material and resources, please visit the Online Resource Centre at:
http://www.oxfordtextbooks.co.uk/orc/burnell4e/

21

Indonesia: Redistributing Power

Edward Aspinall

Chapter contents

Overview

This chapter focuses on the crisis of 'national disintegration' in Indonesia in the years of democratic change that followed the collapse of President Suharto's authoritarian regime in 1998. After decades of militaristic and centralized rule, there was a sudden eruption of fragmentary and contentious politics based around ethnic, regional, and religious identities. Civil disturbances, inter-communal warfare, and separatist insurgencies occurred in several regions. Government leaders feared that decades of nation-building efforts were unravelling. This chapter surveys the historical experiences that led to this outcome, outlines the main dimensions of the crisis, and discusses alternative explanations for it. Some accounts pointed to the intractable nature of Indonesia's problems, ultimately deriving from the heterogeneity of the population and the 'artificiality' of the country's colonial origins, while others emphasized the role of the post-colonial state in generating ethnic tensions and violence. Figure 21.1 is a map of Indonesia and Box 21.1 provides an overview of key dates in Indonesia's history.

Figure 21.1 Indonesia

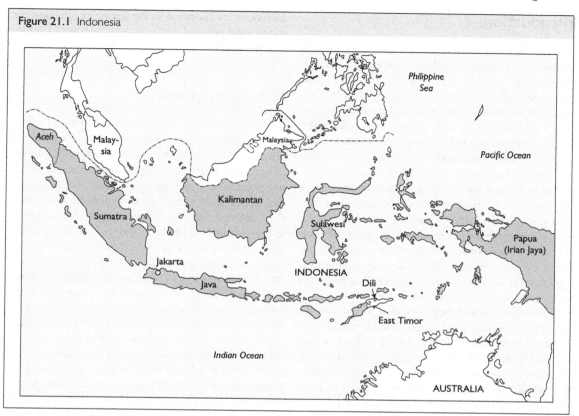

BOX 21.1 KEY DATES IN INDONESIA'S HISTORY

1942	Japanese military occupies the Netherlands East Indies
1945	Nationalist leaders proclaim Indonesian independence
1945–49	Independence revolution: armed conflict and negotiations with the Dutch
1955	Indonesia's first parliamentary elections produce a fractured political map
1959	President Sukarno dissolves parliament and establishes 'Guided Democracy'
1965	Failed coup attempt in Jakarta; army begins massacre of communists
1966	President Suharto's 'New Order' regime begins
1997	Asian financial crisis
1998	Nationwide student protests force resignation of President Suharto; B. J. Habibie takes over and initiates political reform
1999	Democratic elections; East Timor votes to become independent; major violence in Maluku and Aceh
2005	Helsinki peace agreement signed by Acehnese rebel leaders and government representatives
2009	Third post-Suharto democratic elections

Introduction

When President Suharto's military-based **regime** collapsed in 1998, hopes were high in Indonesia that the country was entering a new democratic era. These hopes were realized: over the following decade, a remarkably successful process of **regime change** took place such that, by the end of the first decade of the 2000s, Indonesia was being celebrated internationally as one of the democratization success stories of the preceding decade. However, democratization was accompanied by a surge of mobilization along ethnic and religious lines. In the worst instances, communal conflicts caused thousands of deaths. In three provinces, long-standing separatist movements re-emerged, leading to the independence of one province, East Timor, which became an internationally recognized sovereign state in May 2002. Many Indonesians began to fear that their country would break up.

Indonesia's political trajectory over recent decades mirrors broad trends in the **developing world**. The country has faced **nation-building** challenges similar to those experienced by other **post-colonial states**, and it has experimented with solutions resembling those tried elsewhere. In the post-independence years of the 1950s, Indonesia adopted a political format (parliamentary democracy) and a development strategy (economic nationalism and state-led industrialization) similar to those of many other African and Asian postcolonies. Also, as in many other newly independent states, democratic rule did not long survive the divisions unleashed by independence, social transformation, and the cold war. From the late 1960s, Indonesia approximated more to the model of authoritarian developmentalism pioneered by states in East Asia such as South Korea and Taiwan, albeit with a much weaker state.

As well as outlining the main trends, this chapter surveys the alternative explanations for the fragmentary pressures. With some simplification, it can be seen that there are two schools of thought. On the one hand are those who see fragmentation as virtually an inevitable product of Indonesia's great ethnic heterogeneity. In this view, the post-1998 violence was merely the latest explosion of tensions that first surfaced in the early post-independence years. President Suharto's authoritarian rule kept the lid on centrifugal forces, but once repressive constraints were removed, these forces reasserted themselves. A second set of explanations takes a less pessimistic view of Indonesian society, instead pointing to the disruptive effects of the state's own political and economic policies as causes of fragmentation.

Making Indonesia

A starting point for understanding Indonesia's post-1998 fragmentation is noting the great ethnic and religious diversity of the country. Indonesia consists of approximately 17,000 islands, about 6,000 of which are populated. There are more than 700 languages, and about 1,000 ethnic groups (depending on how they are defined). By far the largest ethnic group is the Javanese, at about 42 per cent of the population. Approximately 88 per cent of Indonesians are Muslims, alongside significant Christian, Hindu, and Buddhist minorities. While most Indonesian Muslims are Sunni, they are themselves divided, notably between 'traditionalists', who are followers of *ulama* (religious scholars) in rural areas, and the more urban 'modernists'. Like many post-colonial states, Indonesia is not heir to any long-standing pre-colonial polity (indeed, the word 'Indonesia' was not coined until the nineteenth century and became popular only in the early twentieth century). Instead, it was the Dutch colonialists who united the diverse societies of what is now thought of as Indonesia into a single colony, the Netherlands East Indies.

For scholars who argue that durable nations arise out of ethnic affinity or belief in common descent (for example Connor 1994: 90–100), it would follow logically that Indonesia is not a true nation-state. In fact, the Indonesian experience demonstrates the historical processes by which a sense of nationhood may arise and, over time, strike deep roots.

In the early twentieth century, a new Indonesian nationalist movement emerged, led by Western-educated elites. Early nationalist leaders stressed the need for unity among the diverse peoples of the archipelago. For example, they relabelled the Malay language (already a lingua franca in colonial times) as Indonesian, the 'language of unity'. Experiences of struggle and sacrifice during the early nationalist movement (c. 1912–42) and independence revolution (1945–49) popularized the ideal of Indonesian unity and sanctified it in blood. In the early years of independence, nation-building became the theme par excellence of the country's leaders, especially its first president, Sukarno.

However, the transition to independence was fractious. Elections in 1955 produced a parliament divided between secular-nationalists, communists, traditionalist Muslims, and modernist Muslims. Cabinets rose and fell in quick succession. Tensions between Muslims and secularists over whether the state should oblige Muslims to observe Islamic law caused deadlock in a constituent assembly. Armed revolts in several regions expressed regionalist, Islamic, and anti-communist urges. Rapid growth of the Communist Party threatened Indonesia's elites.

President Sukarno tried to overcome these divisions by a system of left-**populist**, but authoritarian, rule, which he labelled 'Guided Democracy' (1959–65). However, this system did not prevent polarization between the massive Communist Party on the left, and the military and its allies on the right. The military was ultimately victorious, cementing its triumph with the massacre of approximately 500,000 leftists in 1965–66. Subsequently, under Suharto's leadership, the military established an authoritarian regime, the 'New Order', which lasted from 1966 to 1998.

The New Order still focused on nation-building, but whereas Sukarno had tried to unify Indonesia by mobilizing and channelling popular passions, Suharto and the military tried to suppress them. They proclaimed that they aimed at 'accelerated **modernization**', which would eliminate 'primordial' divisions. They believed they had to limit political mobilization in order to create a stable environment for economic development. Indonesia experienced almost three decades of rapid growth. Gross domestic product (GDP) and income per capita tripled between 1970 and 2000, and the number of people inhabiting urban areas doubled to around 40 per cent of the total, with the proportion employed in agriculture falling by a third. The regime also encouraged national cohesion by pursuing economic integration, and propagating unifying national symbols and cultural habits. For example, it developed a **Pancasila** ideology, to which all citizens were expected to adhere, and expanded uniform national education for school students (Drake 1989).

Rapid economic and social change was not matched by political evolution. Suharto remained in power, ageing and inflexible. His regime still aimed to constrain, control, and repress popular pressures rather than to accommodate them. Political strains increased in the early 1990s, as speculation grew about presidential succession and rising social forces became more assertive. The collapse of the regime, however, was triggered not by **economic growth**, but by economic crisis. When the Asian financial collapse of 1997 hit Indonesia, it triggered student-led protests, which, in May 1998, forced Suharto to resign.

At this point, Indonesia did not seem to be facing fundamental crisis. The old authoritarian regime had collapsed under extreme pressure, but most Indonesians were optimistic that they could design a more democratic replacement. There had been separatist unrest in some provinces, but it had been militarily suppressed. Some communal violence accompanied rising anti-Suharto sentiment, but it was of secondary importance to the anti-Suharto protests, the leaders of which wanted to solve the country's national problems by introducing political reform (*reformasi*). Overall, their mood was optimistic.

KEY POINTS

- Indonesia is an ethnically diverse nation-state formed within the boundaries of the Dutch colony, the Netherlands East Indies.

- Early post-independence governments stressed nation-building, but faced difficulties in managing conflicts generated by the transition to independence.

- Suharto's New Order regime (1966–98) pursued authoritarian and centralized solutions to Indonesia's nation-building challenges, suppressing independent **politics** and emphasizing economic development.

- The collapse of this regime did not result from communal conflict.

Democratization and National Disintegration

Responding to popular discontent, post-Suharto governments pursued rapid democratization. Defying predictions, this process proceeded smoothly. The military withdrew from national political management. New political parties and **civil society** organizations multiplied. The press became one of the most free in Asia. Democratic elections were held in 1999, and again in 2004 and 2009, producing a fragmented political map (see Box 21.2).

In many regions, anti-government *reformasi* protests seamlessly gave way after Suharto fell to a new **localism**, meaning the tendency to prioritize local

BOX 21.2 FRAGMENTATION: INDONESIA'S PARTY SYSTEM

Major vote winners in post-Suharto legislative elections	1999 (%)	2004 (%)	2009 (%)
Secular nationalist parties			
Gerindra, Greater Indonesia Movement Party, personal vehicle for former General Prabowo Subianto			4
Golkar, the ruling party under Suharto's New Order regime	22	22	14
Hanura, People's Conscience Party, personal vehicle for former General Wiranto			4
PDI-P, Indonesia Democracy Party—Struggle, led by Megawati Soekarnoputri and heir to Sukarnoist nationalist traditions	34	19	14
PD, Democrat Party, personal vehicle for president Susilo Bambang Yudhoyono	—	7	21
Pluralist Islamic parties			
PKB, National Awakening Party, aligned with the main traditionalist Islamic organization, Nadhatul Ulama	13	11	5
PAN, National Mandate Party, aligned with the main modernist Islamic organization, Muhammadiyah	7	6	6
Islamist parties			
PPP, United Development Party, Islamic party first formed under the New Order	11	8	5
PKS, Justice and Welfare Party, party of puritanical, urban intellectuals	1	7	8

Source: Author's calculations taken from Komisi Pemilihan Umum (General Elections Commission), online at http://www.kpu.go.id

cultural, economic, and political interests and identities over national ones. Many demonstrators wanted to replace discredited local officials and voiced long-suppressed local grievances. Often, their protests were framed in terms of reassertion of local cultural identities. In some regions, there were demands that only *putra daerah* ('sons of the region') should obtain political posts, government contracts, or civil service employment. This process accelerated after the government of President Habibie (1998–99) introduced regional autonomy legislation, which devolved wide-ranging political powers and financial responsibility to several hundred district governments (Aspinall and Fealy 2003). In one of the world's most radical experiments in decentralization, political and economic power shifted massively to the local level.

In some places, localism took violent form. There were two main categories of violence. First, there was conflict *within* local societies, between rival religious or ethnic communities. Sometimes, this involved one-sided attacks on largely defenceless minority groups. A series of mob attacks against ethnic Chinese (a group

that makes up about 2 per cent of the population—the figure is disputed—but which is prominent in trade) coincided with the fall of Suharto (Purdey 2006). Violence in Kalimantan (Borneo) was directed largely against migrants from the island of Madura. Some hostile communities were more evenly matched. The worst inter-communal violence occurred in Maluku (the Moluccas), where the population was almost equally divided between Muslims and Christians, resulting in virtual civil war and some 5,000–6,000 deaths.

A second category of violence involved local communities confronting state authority. These conflicts mostly involved separatist movements fighting with (or being repressed by) security forces. The best-known case internationally was East Timor, which had long been a site of conflict and source of diplomatic difficulties for Indonesia. President Habibie unexpectedly allowed a vote on independence supervised by the United Nations (UN) there in 1999, prompting the military to organize militias to terrorize the population. They caused approximately 1,500 deaths during a wave of destruction after 78.5 per cent of the population voted for independence. Violence was worse in Aceh, in northern Sumatra, where a long-running insurgency reignited after Suharto fell. For a time, the guerrillas of the GAM (Free Aceh Movement) controlled much of the countryside. Between 1999 and 2005, approximately 7,200 persons were killed in the ensuing conflict and counter-insurgency operations. In Papua, the western half of the island of New Guinea, support for independence was also great among the indigenous Melanesian population, although here most independence supporters used non-violent means (Chauvel 2003).

Observers have offered many different explanations for post-Suharto disintegrative tendencies and violence. In general terms, the debates mirrored broader ones between advocates of primordialist and modernist interpretations of ethnic and nationalist conflicts.

First, some argued that violence reflected deep-seated, primordial, and even ancient identities and enmities. This view was mostly discredited among scholars (Mote and Rutherford 2001). However, it was popular among some journalists and commentators, who sometimes used the metaphor of the 'seething cauldron' to describe Indonesia. The second set of arguments held that post-Suharto violence stemmed instead from recent processes of economic development, social change, state formation, and repression. For example, they argued that popular support for independence in Aceh resulted from inequitable resource **exploitation** in the province under Suharto (Aceh had major natural gas reserves and had been a big contributor to national income) and from the military violence used to eliminate what had initially been a tiny separatist movement there (Robinson 1998). Analysts of violence in Maluku pointed to the accumulation of tensions in that province under Suharto, caused by migration and competition between Muslims and Christians for bureaucratic positions and economic resources, in conditions under which such tensions could not be resolved by democratic means (Bertrand 2002).

Examination of the extent and variety of post-Suharto violence makes the second group of explanations more convincing. Overall, the death toll in post-Suharto episodes of large-scale ethnic violence (approximately 20,000 in an overall population of 200 million), while very great, was far less than in many other recent internal conflicts in the developing world. The media concentrated on places where violence was worst and tended to overlook the fact that most regions remained peaceful. The image of a country on the verge of disintegration also loses force if we remember that it was in only three provinces (out of a total of twenty-seven in 1998) that there was significant support for independence.

Analysis of the three 'separatist provinces' (Aceh, Papua, and East Timor), however, requires us to qualify the view that disintegrative pressures arose only because of Suharto's authoritarianism. It is certainly true that repression under Suharto increased support for independence in each place. But repression in these provinces was also a *response* to popular resistance as much as being a cause of it. Aceh, for example, was not notably more militarized than other provinces prior to the establishment of the GAM in 1976. Understanding the origins of separatism requires us to extend our historical inquiry to before Suharto's rule, back to the colonial origins of Indonesia.

One distinguishing feature of each separatist province was that its mode of incorporation into the Indonesian nation-state produced a strong regional identity at least partly defined against Indonesia. East Timor was the obvious example: it had never been part of the Netherlands East Indies, but was instead a Portuguese colony. Against a backdrop of cold war tensions, Suharto's army violently invaded the territory in 1975, causing great loss of life. Many East Timorese never accepted the Indonesian presence, viewing it instead as an occupying power. Papua had been ruled by the Dutch, but it also had a distinct history. The Indonesian nationalist movement had not struck deep roots there in the early twentieth century. Crucially, when Indonesia became independent in 1949, Holland retained control over Papua and began to groom local leaders for independence. Following US pressure on Holland, Papua was incorporated into Indonesia in the 1960s, but by then most politically conscious Papuans imagined a future separate to Indonesia. Incorporation involved Indonesian military action and intimidation, causing lasting resentment. Aceh was different again: its population enthusiastically supported Indonesia's independence struggle in 1945–49, so much so that Aceh was the only part of their former colony that the Dutch did not dare to try to reconquer. As a result, Aceh's leaders had unfettered control over local affairs during that period. When Indonesia became independent, they lost much of that autonomy, causing bitterness and gradual evolution of a distinct identity. The GAM built on this resentment when it called for Aceh's independence.

Toward Reintegration

By 2003–04, Indonesia's new democratic system was consolidating. There were many elements of continuity between the old regime and the new democracy (notably many of the people operating the levers of state power in the government bureaucracy and in politics were the same as under the New Order, even if there was now competition for political office). However, political openness and electoral competition were becoming widely accepted as basic rules of the new democratic system. Importantly, for our purposes, the country no longer appeared to be on the verge of disintegration. The worst violence was passing: for instance leaders of the warring communities in Maluku reached a peace agreement in February 2002. Even in Aceh, GAM leaders agreed to give up their independence goal and signed an accord with the government in August 2005.

In part, the crisis ended because violence had simply exhausted itself. But the state's own response also contributed. The crisis had prompted two contradictory policy approaches from national elites. First, it had triggered toughening of views and a return to hard-line, even militaristic, policies in some instances. This reflected the view in some elite circles, especially in the military, that Indonesian unity was fragile and should be maintained with constant vigilance. After the 'loss' of East Timor, from 2000 post-Suharto governments once again suppressed separatist movements. In Papua, security forces harassed, arrested, and (in one case) assassinated pro-independence leaders, while in Aceh a full-scale military assault on rebels was launched in May 2003. Military and government leaders were adamant that such steps were needed to stop a domino effect whereby the separatist contagion would spread to other provinces. Critics argued that violent methods would fan separatist sentiment in the long run, as in the past. Yet the return to military solutions in the short term ended the sense of possibility

that had arisen in separatist provinces after Suharto fell. In Aceh, for example, GAM rebels abandoned independence partly because they realized that their guerrilla campaign had reached an impasse.

The return to hard-line policies was not the dominant response, however, and it does not provide the main explanation for how the crisis ended. Most of Indonesia's new leaders knew that Suharto's old centralized and authoritarian system could not be revived. Instead, they saw democratization and decentralization as means to ensure national survival, believing such policies would empower local communities to redress their own grievances. Even in Papua and Aceh, therefore, alongside military operations, the government offered concessions in the form of Special Autonomy laws (see Box 21.3). In most regions of Indonesia, democratization and the nationwide decentralization laws had the desired effect. Most local leaders no longer concerned themselves with challenging Jakarta, but instead busied themselves with local affairs.

This change does not mean that Indonesia experienced a sudden and miraculous transition to **good governance**, as some of the international agencies promoting decentralization had hoped. On the contrary, old elites adapted to the new system. In most regions, **corruption** proliferated, as local leaders used state funds to enrich themselves and their supporters. But the transformation did mean that the axis of political contention, including struggles to control economic resources, shifted from the national level to the regions. Localism still flourished, but not in ways that directly undermined the idea of Indonesia.

Although the crisis of the post-Suharto years has passed, the new dispensation raises other possibilities: not of sudden disintegration, but rather of gradual decline in national cohesion. Whatever ordinary citizens thought about the former regimes of Presidents Sukarno and Suharto, they could see that each articulated a clear set of national goals and had concrete ideas about how to achieve them. Evidence of nation-building was visible everywhere: ubiquitous mass mobilization under Sukarno; economic development, infrastructure projects, and ideological indoctrination under Suharto. A uniform national **political culture** was developing. Even today, there are still factors creating a sense of commonality (such as the national electronic media, especially television). Now, in a new era of decentralized politics, for the first time for fifty years there are also strong countervailing pressures. In one perspective, Indonesia is becoming

BOX 21.3 SPECIAL AUTONOMY IN ACEH AND PAPUA

Key Points of the Papua Special Autonomy Law 2001 and the Government of Aceh Law 2006

- Wide-ranging grant of powers, covering everything except foreign affairs, defence, security, judiciary, monetary and fiscal matters, and religion, which are retained by the central government

- Both provinces retain a larger share of natural resource revenues than other provinces, including from oil and gas (80 per cent for Papua; 70 per cent for Aceh)
- Both provinces may have their own symbols, including a flag and an anthem
- Establishment of **human rights** courts, and truth and reconciliation commissions

Papua	Aceh
Establishment of a Papuan People's Council, consisting of representatives of women, traditional communities, and religious groups; charged with ensuring that indigenous rights are upheld	Application of Islamic (Sharia) law to Muslims in Aceh; establishes a Sharia court with authority over both civil and criminal matters
Indigenous Papuans granted certain special rights, for instance only an indigenous Papuan may become governor	Establishment of a council of *ulama* (religious scholars) with special advisory powers
Provincial government charged with protecting customary law, land rights, and local culture	Independent candidates (that is, those not nominated by political parties) can run in elections for governor and district heads; formation of local political parties, to run in local elections from 2009

a patchwork of regions, in which local interests and dynamics predominate over national ones.

An example is the contest over the political role of Islam. In the 1950s, division over whether the constitution should require Muslims to observe Islamic law rent the body politic at the national level. After the fall of Suharto, Islamic parties made only token efforts to revive the national constitutional debate. Instead, by late 2006, several dozen local administrations had begun to introduce regulations that included elements of Islamic law (for example making the Islamic dress code mandatory for women) piecemeal. Secular-oriented groups tried to oppose such initiatives nationally, but failed to gain much traction in the regions concerned.

And yet it would be rash to pass a negative judgement on the future of Indonesia's national project. For many Indonesians, the new diversity produced by democratic politics and regional autonomy does not signify loss of national cohesion, but simply readjusts a political formula that had been tilted too far in favour of uniformity. Although localism is vigorous, many factors still underpin national unity, including widely shared pride in national history and symbols. Belief

that diversity is integral to Indonesian identity is itself a core element in Indonesian nationalism. Finally, certain safeguards have been built into Indonesia's new institutional framework to constrain disintegrative tendencies (for instance, to register for elections, political parties must prove that they have a broad national presence).

KEY POINTS

- Extreme post-Suharto fragmentary pressures and violence lasted for a brief period (approximately five years), and were followed by reconsolidation.
- State violence played a role in overcoming this crisis, especially in ending (at least for a time) separatist challenges.
- More significant were decentralization and democratization. These policies assuaged local grievances and encouraged regional elites to engage in local political processes rather than to challenge the central state.
- The major challenge facing Indonesia today is not dramatic disintegration, but gradual decline of cohesion.

Conclusion

Between 1998 and about 2004, Indonesia went through a dramatic process of regime change. Some scholars argue that this change has in some senses been superficial, by pointing to underlying continuity in the structures of social power that underpin the political system. Even so, there is wide agreement that the rules governing how political office is obtained and exercised have changed profoundly, and that civil liberties and elections are a central feature of the new system.

In some respects, Indonesia is still a fragile democracy. One particularly disturbing dimension of this period of regime change, and the focus of this chapter, was the crisis of national disintegration that coincided with it. Clearly, democratization was the enabling context for this crisis to take place; beyond that, we have discussed two sets of explanations for it—those that locate the source of these problems in the country's multi-ethnic make-up and its origins as heir to an artificial colonial state, and those that instead focus on grievances caused by state action, especially under the Suharto regime.

Indeed, it should be stressed that, while the country has great ethnic and linguistic diversity, Indonesia is no more artificial than any post-colonial, or indeed any other, modern state. Modern nation-states did not arise seamlessly from pre-existing ethnic communities, but were instead produced by long processes of state- and nation-building. In most cases, these processes involved force, as well as the creation over generations of political **institutions**, standardized education, and other mechanisms for generating national cohesion.

QUESTIONS

1. What is meant by 'fragmentation' in a country such as Indonesia? Are all forms of fragmentation equally damaging or dangerous?

2. Is it accurate to describe fragmentation pressures in Indonesia after 1998 as being a product of democratization?

3. Is it possible for an ethnically diverse country like Indonesia to experience regime change from an authoritarian to a democratic system without undergoing serious violence?

4. National political leaders in highly diverse countries often say that policies of decentralization will accelerate fragmentation. Are they correct?

5. May 'regime change' in developing countries such as Indonesia change structures of power and domination?

FURTHER READING

Aspinall, E. and Mietzner, M (eds) (2010) *Problems of Democratisation in Indonesia: Elections, Institutions and Society* (Singapore: Institute of Southeast Asian Studies) An account of the inner workings of Indonesia's post-Suharto democracy and of the major challenges confronting democratic consolidation.

Bertrand, J. (2004) *Nationalism and Ethnic Conflict in Indonesia* (Cambridge: Cambridge University Press) Overview of the ethnic conflicts that accompanied and followed the fall of Suharto. The author explains the grievances that motivated each conflict and links them to the broader institutional shifts associated with democratization.

Robison, R. and Hadiz, V. R. (2004) *Reorganizing Power in Indonesia: The Politics of Oligarchy in an Age of Markets* (London/New York: Routledge) An account of the democratic transition, emphasizing political economy and the preservation of elite authority and privilege.

Van Klinken, G. (2007) *Communal Violence and Democratization in Indonesia: Small Town Wars* (London: Routledge) Uses a sociological approach to explain six key episodes of post-Suharto communal violence.

WEB LINKS

http://cip.cornell.edu/Indonesia   Produced by Cornell University, *Indonesia* has, since the late 1960s, been the premier academic journal on Indonesian affairs.

http://www.insideindonesia.org   Australia-based quarterly magazine that focuses on human rights and political and environmental issues.

http://www.thejakartapost.com   Indonesia's premier daily English-language newspaper, complete with a useful search engine and archives.

For additional material and resources, please visit the Online Resource Centre at:
http://www.oxfordtextbooks.co.uk/orc/burnell4e/

PART 6
Fragile versus Strong States

Whereas the focus of Part 5 was on a country's **regime** or system of government, in Part 6 it is on the state. Whilst regime and state are closely linked concepts, 'regime' refers to the type of rule—for instance democratic or authoritarian—whilst the 'state' is more of a summary term for the assemblage of ruling institutions and organizations.

Referring back to Chapter 12, Adrian Leftwich argues that the modern state, including the state in developing countries, faces four kinds of challenge: defence against external attack and internal security; promotion and protection of the economy; democratization; and provision of welfare. All states have to deal with these challenges and, to the extent that they are able to do so, they may be described as 'strong' and 'effective', or 'fragile' and 'failing' (although, as Astri Suhrke and Torunn Wimpelmann caution us in Chapter 13, these labels need to be used sparingly and with care). As Leftwich sets out, various different 'types' of state have been identified in the **developing world,** such as the bureaucratic-authoritarian state, the patrimonial state, the democratic state, the **developmental state,** and the **rentier state.**

Different states, or types of state, have different kinds of strength and weakness. A 'repressive' state could be 'strong' or effective in terms of maintaining internal order, for instance, but much less so when it came to promoting economic development and welfare. There is also the question of whether certain state strengths or capacities are prerequisites for or more important than others. As related in Chapter 1, Samuel Huntington (1968) argued that 'strong' government, in the sense of internal order, was a precondition of economic and political reform. Leftwich, on the other hand, emphasizes economic strength: '... strong, stable and effective states are inconceivable without strong economies.'

The country case studies illustrate both the complexity of notions and assessments of state strength and weakness, and also the precariousness of state strength in practice. Nadje Al-Ali and Nicola Pratt focus on Iraq in the wake of the 2003 invasion. They argue that, under Saddam Hussein, the Iraqi state had been not so much strong as 'hard', or even 'fierce', with the emphasis on its capacity for repression. Despite constitutional reforms and democratic elections, violence and **corruption** have been hallmarks of post-Saddam Iraq; some have wanted to call it a 'failed state'. The authors argue, however, that the concentration of oil revenues and security forces in the hands of the executive under the prime minister are more reminiscent of Saddam's 'fierce state'.

Andreas Schedler describes how, in Mexico, something like a modern state was already emerging under Porfirio Diaz. Following a period of turbulence and revolution, the PRN/PRI (Institutional Revolutionary Party) emerged as the dominant force in government, at the head of a centralized patrimonial bureaucracy and enjoying a degree of **legitimacy**. A process of democratization culminated in defeat of the PRI in the presidential elections of 2000, but subsequently the Mexican state has faced a massive challenge to its internal sovereignty and security from organized crime, associated notably with the drugs trade, again leading some to argue that it is 'failing'.

Of the three countries presented in this section, South Korea comes closest to the notion of a 'strong state'. Peter Ferdinand describes the emergence of an almost 'textbook' developmental state, under General Park Chung Hee, featuring a close relationship between the state and industry in the interests of national development and defence. Even in this case, the state has faced a mounting challenge from social forces with democratization from the 1990s; it has failed to confront the entrenched power and associated corruption of the **chaebols** in the wake of the Asian financial crisis, whilst its international position is overshadowed by China and the continuing threat posed by North Korea.

22

Iraq: From Hard State to Failed State—or Fierce State?

Nadje Al-Ali and Nicola Pratt

Overview

This chapter explores whether Iraq is a failed state and how it arrived at that possible character-ization. It examines the period since the US-led invasion of Iraq in 2003, which led to the fall of the dictatorship of Saddam Hussein. It focuses on three areas: the reconstruction of Iraq's political institutions; post-invasion violence and security; and human and economic development. The chap-ter demonstrates how the failure to reconstruct political institutions capable of reconciling Iraq's different political groupings has weakened central government, increased corruption within state institutions, and fed into ethnic/sectarian violence. Consequently, the Iraqi state is failing to provide necessary services and infrastructure for economic and human development. However, in light of the centralization of political and military power in the hands of the prime minister, it would be more precise to argue that Iraq is a 'fierce state' rather than a 'failed state'. Figure 22.1 is a map of Iraq and Box 22.1 provides an overview of key dates in Iraq's history.

Figure 22.1 Iraq

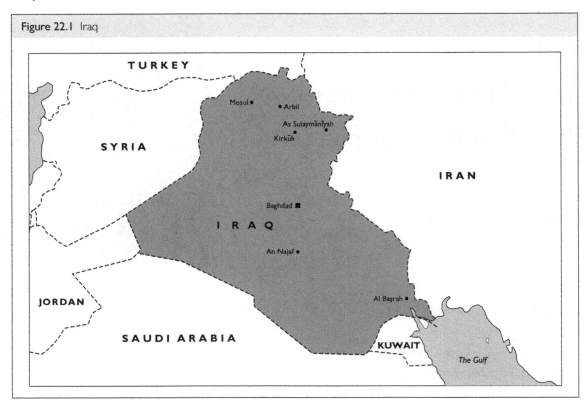

BOX 22.1   KEY DATES IN IRAQ'S HISTORY

1831–1914	Ottoman rule of Iraq	July 1979	Saddam Hussein becomes president
1914	British invasion of Iraq	1980	Following Iranian revolution, Iraqi government cracks down on Shi'a Islamist groups, including Da'wa Party; expels 40,000 Shi'a to Iran
1921	British install Faisal Ibn Husain al-Hashemi as first king of Iraq		
1932	Independence formally granted to Iraq by League of Nations	1980–88	Iran–Iraq War
July 1958	Military coup against monarchy and British presence; establishment of republic; 'Abdel Karim Qasim becomes prime minister	1988	Iraqi government wages Al-Anfal campaign, which includes chemical warfare, in Kurdish areas in northern Iraq, resulting in up to 60,000 deaths
Feb 1963	Military coup against Qasim by Ba'thists and Arab nationalists	Aug 1990	Iraq invades and annexes Kuwait; United Nations (UN) imposes strict sanctions regime against Iraq (until April 2003)
Nov 1963	President 'Abd al Salam 'Arif and allies sideline Ba'thists		
July 1968	Ba'thist military coup	Jan–Feb 1991	'Desert Storm'—US-led international military coalition forces Iraqi troops out of Kuwait by means of air bombardment of Iraq
1972	Nationalization of oil industry		
1974–75	Iraqi government puts down Kurdish revolt for greater autonomy in northern Iraq	Mar 1991	Iraqi government crushes popular uprisings in north and south of country; UN creates 'safe haven' in north; UN weapons inspections begin

May 1992	Elections in Kurdish areas	Jan 2005	Elections to Iraqi Transitional National Assembly
July 1992	Kurdish Democratic Party (KDP) and PUK (Patriotic Union of Kurdistan) form Kurdish Regional Government, but maintain respective areas of control	May–Sept 2005	Drafting of the Permanent Constitution
		Oct 2005	Referendum on the Permanent Constitution
		Dec 2005	Elections to the Council of Representatives
May–Aug 1994	Armed conflict between PUK and KDP	Feb 2006	Attack on the Al-Askari Mosque in Samarra escalates sectarian tensions and triggers widescale violence
Sept 1998	Fighting between PUK and KDP ended by Washington Agreement		
Dec 1998	'Operation Desert Fox'—air bombardment of Iraq by United States and Britain in retaliation for Iraq's non-cooperation with weapons inspectors	Sept 2006	Constitutional Review Committee formed
		Jan 2007	US President Bush announces the deployment of a further 30,000 US troops to Iraq (generally known as 'the surge')
Mar 2003	United States and Britain invade Iraq		
Apr 2003	US forces enter Baghdad; toppling of Ba'th regime	Feb 2009	US President Obama announces that all US combat operations in Iraq will end by 31 August 2010, and that he intends to fully withdraw all American troops by the end of 2011
1 May 2003	Coalition Provisional Authority (CPA) replaces Office for Reconstruction and Humanitarian Assistance (ORHA)		
		Apr 2009	Britain withdraws all troops from Iraq
23 July 2003	Establishment of twenty-five-member Iraqi Governing Council (IGC) (responsible for advising CPA)	Mar 2010	Elections to the Council of Representatives take place
8 Mar 2004	Signing of Transitional Administrative Law (laying out timeline for elections and constitution drafting)	Nov 2010	Irbil Agreement signed, enabling national unity government to be formed
		Dec 2011	Withdrawal of US forces
28 June 2004	Abolition of CPA and IGC, and handover of US power to Iraqi Interim Government		

Introduction

From its independence in 1958 until the imposition of international sanctions in 1990, Iraq benefited from a large and highly educated population (see Box 22.2 for demographic information), excellent infrastructure and welfare services, and a large and well-equipped army, paid for by significant revenues from the sale of oil. Yet this success came at a political price. The **regime** of former President Saddam Hussein (1979–2003) was one of the most authoritarian in the region and political dissent was brutally suppressed. According to the typology of late political economist, Nazih Ayubi (1994: 449), Iraq could be categorized as a 'hard state' and a 'fierce state', but not a 'strong state'.

Saddam Hussein came to power as the head of the Ba'th Party in 1979. He used techniques of power utilized by previous Iraqi regimes—exclusion of rivals, promoting communal mistrust, developing **patronage** networks, and the use of violence (Tripp 2002: 194). He privileged his extended clan, whilst also developing communal and tribal relations as mechanisms of patronage and coercion (Tripp 2002: 194). Opposition to the Ba'th Party came from various political tendencies, including communists, secular liberals, Arab nationalists, democrats, and Islamists, and cut across ethnic and sectarian lines, including many Sunni political dissidents. However, Kurdish nationalists and Shi'a **political Islamists** were particular targets of regime repression and crimes against humanity.

The US-led invasion of 2003 triggered a number of processes, some of which were intentional, but others of which were unintended, which have led some to label Iraq a 'failed state'. At the time of writing, the Iraqi state is certainly a paralysed state when it comes to providing essential services and security to

BOX 22.2 THE IRAQI POPULATION

Iraq's population, like other countries in the Middle East, is very young, with about 40 per cent of the population under the age of 15. Relatively high birth rates (about four per woman), as well as high death rates of adult males as a result of wars, violence, and political oppression over the past decades, has created not only a young population, but also a demographic imbalance between men and women. While no official statistics are available, estimates range between 55 per cent and 65 per cent of the population as female. The more recent violence linked to the invasion and occupation of Iraq has increased this demographic imbalance both in terms of age and **gender**. During 2006 and 2007, more than ninety civilians died violently every day (United Nations Assistance Mission for Iraq 2007). The number of civilian casualties remains significant, with around 4,000 civilians killed in 2010 and 2011, respectively (Iraq Body Count 2012). Men have been the main victims of these violent deaths.

In terms of ethnic and religious make-up, Iraq has historically been diverse and mixed. Shi'a Arabs make up the majority of the Iraqi population, followed by Sunni Arabs, Kurds (predominantly Sunni), Iraqi Turkmen, and Assyrian and Chaldean Christians, as well as Yazidis. Historically, Iraq also had a large indigenous Jewish population, the majority of whom migrated from Iraq in the 1950s and 1960s. Arabic (Iraqi dialect) is the most widely spoken language, followed by Kurdish, Turkish, Aramaic, Syriac, and Armenian. While the south has been predominantly Arab Shi'i and the north mainly inhabited by Sunni Kurds (there is also a minority of Shi'a Kurds called Faili Kurds), as well as Iraqi Turkmen and Assyrian and Chaldean Christians, central and southern Iraq has always been very mixed. Sectarianism, especially in its overt violent form, is predominantly a post-invasion phenomenon; Iraqis had been living as neighbours and even intermarrying for decades. However, since Saddam Hussein's assumption of the presidency in 1979, divide-and-rule tactics increased sectarian divisions inside Iraq (Farouk-Sluglett and Sluglett 2003). There is no doubt that Kurds and Shi'a bore the brunt of the atrocities committed by the regime (see Box 22.1). Yet Sunni Arabs in political opposition parties and, increasingly, even within the Ba'th Party were also subjected to arrests, torture, and executions, as were members of other minorities such as Chaldeans, Assyrians, Turkmen, and Mandeans if they were part of opposition groups, or at least suspected to be so. Based on accounts of Iraqis of different ethnic and religious backgrounds, social class played a more important role in terms of defining social difference (Al-Ali 2007). Post-2003, religious and ethnic minorities, such as Christians, Yazidis, and Mandeans, have been targeted and have fled the country in large numbers.

its citizens. However, it would be incorrect to claim that the Iraqi state is failing in its entirety. According to Toby Dodge (2012), Prime Minister Nuri al-Malaki (2006–) has built informal patronage networks and gained control over Iraq's sizeable security forces. Iraq is certainly no longer a 'hard state', as it was under the Ba'th regime. However, rather than a 'failed state', it may be more precise to characterize Iraq as a 'fierce state' once again (Ayubi 1994: 449).

Reconstructing Iraq's Political Institutions

On 20 March 2003, in the face of significant opposition, the United States, supported by Britain, launched a 'pre-emptive' military attack on Iraq in order to disarm the country of its weapons of mass destruction (WMDs) and end its support for international **terrorism**. Since then, the evidence for these claims has been largely discredited. The regime of Saddam Hussein was toppled on 20 April 2003; by 1 May 2003,

US President George Bush had declared the end of hostilities, designating Iraq a 'post-conflict' zone. Yet in reality Iraq was entering a new phase of conflict— one that has combined elements of anti-colonial insurgency with the 'new wars' of the post-cold-war period.

Before the invasion, the US administration of President George Bush had assumed that it would hand over power to an Iraqi government within a short time frame. However, shortly after the invasion, it became clear to the United States that this would not be straightforward. After decades of dictatorship, there were no local Iraqi leaders, except for the Kurdish parties in northern Iraq, and there was limited local acceptance of the former opposition in exile that were brought into Iraq with the coalition forces (Melia and Katulis 2003). With the aim of creating a government that would be legitimate in the eyes of the Iraqi population, the United States entered into discussions with Iraqi political and religious leaders. With involvement from the UN, a plan for the introduction of democracy to Iraq was agreed, which would begin with the drafting of a transitional constitution, followed by multiparty elections to a transitional assembly and the drafting of a new constitution, and ending with elections to a new legislature—the Council of Representatives. Indeed, a political process took place, more or less following the timetable agreed at the end of 2003. However, this process, despite its apparently liberal underpinnings and UN technical support, failed to engender a transition to democracy. Instead, it contributed to fostering perhaps even wider **corruption** and sectarianism within the political system than had previously existed.

Explanations of the failure of the post-invasion political transition may be divided between flawed implementation versus flawed design. The timing of the elections and the constitution-drafting process were too early and/or too hurried, thereby undermining possibilities for reconciliation and confidence-building amongst Iraq's different communities. There was little consultation with Iraqi **civil society** over the contents of the constitution, as had been practised in other post-conflict countries. In addition, the United States attempted to shape the transition process according to its strategic interests: initially marginalizing the Sunni population, which it regarded as the source of the anti-US insurgency (International Crisis Group 2004); and later, bringing unelected Sunni representatives in to the process in an attempt to dampen the insurgency (International Crisis Group 2005).

Arguments criticizing the design of the political transition cite the nature of the electoral system adopted for the transitional assembly, which resulted in underrepresentation for the Sunni population (many of whom had boycotted the elections) (Diamond 2004; Rubin 2004). There are also concerns that the UN, US, and other major donors attempted to implement what has become a standard post-cold-war liberal peace-building package with little recognition of the specific complexities of Iraq (Richmond 2009)—a country emerging from over a decade of sanctions, decades of dictatorship, and a recent war.

Post-invasion political institutions have proved ineffective in rebuilding the Iraqi state. Instead, the political system has helped to engender corruption and paralysis of decision-making. Most political parties do not represent different political ideologies or ideas, but rather ethnic/sectarian-defined communities. Attempts at power sharing within the cabinet, through the allocation of ministerial posts to different parties

in proportion to seats in parliament, has become an opportunity for asset-grabbing and zero-sum **politics**, rather than cooperation. This has greatly delayed the formation of governments following different rounds of elections, presenting obstacles to effective decision-making.

The political issues that have continued to divide Iraq's parties mainly along ethnic/sectarian lines concern the distribution of political power, territory, and resources—namely: the exploitation of oil resources and distribution of oil revenues; defining the boundaries of Iraqi Kurdistan, which has become what Denise Natali (2010) calls a 'quasi-state'; federal arrangements; the de-Ba'thification law; and reintegration of former insurgent fighters (the latter two issues predominantly affecting Sunnis). (For more details, see International Crisis Group 2008.) In addition, since 2011, there have been growing popular demonstrations against the central government and the Kurdistan Regional Government, protesting against corruption and poor services, whilst Iraq's Sunni community has protested against discrimination by al-Malaki's government.

Most worrying for the future of Iraq has been the possibility of return to dictatorship under Prime Minister Nuri al-Malaki (Dodge 2012). When first appointed in 2006, al-Malaki was perceived to be a compromise candidate, who was too weak to govern and deal with the many challenges ahead. Yet he managed systematically to marginalize political rivals and to control state institutions, particularly the security services and the intelligence services (Dodge 2012). Al-Malaki instrumentalized the Justice and Accountability Commission charged with 'de-Ba'thification' to increase sectarian sentiments and to sideline political competition, particularly from Sunni politicians. Even when, in the 2010 elections, a plurality of the electorate voted for the opposition Al-Iraqiyya coalition, al-Malaki managed to outmanoeuvre them to retain his post and his powers (Dodge 2012; International Crisis Group 2012). Increasingly, civil society associations, journalists, and women's rights activists, who are expressing dissent and opposition to corruption, lack of transparency, and lack of proper infrastructure, have come under attack by the regime. Arrests, harassment, imprisonment, torture, and even executions have become almost everyday occurrences in this new 'fierce' state, just as they were during the time of Saddam Hussein (Jamail 2012).

KEY POINTS

- Following the overthrow of the Ba'th regime, the United States helped to establish a multiparty democracy through the organizing of elections and the drafting of a constitution. Post-invasion political institutions helped to politicize ethnic/sectarian differences and exacerbate corruption in state institutions.

- Power-sharing arrangements in government increased conflict between the major parties, rather than encouraging cooperation, and paralysed decision-making by politicians.

- Ineffective political institutions have paved the way for the re-emergence of dictatorship and rampant **human rights** abuses under the leadership of Nuri al-Malaki.

Post-Invasion Violence and Security

There are several causes of the violence and lawlessness that broke out following the US-led invasion. Several writers point to the failure of the United States and its allies to send sufficient troops to Iraq to maintain law and order following the ouster of the Ba'th regime (for example von Hippel 2004; Dodge 2005). According to Larry Diamond (2004), a senior adviser to the Coalition Provisional Authority (CPA), the United States exacerbated the security problem as a result of 'two strategic miscalculations': the de-Ba'thification policy, which removed people from government on the basis of their membership of the Ba'th Party—regardless of their past conduct; and the dissolution of the Iraqi army, which may have pushed some Iraqis towards the insurgency, whilst depriving the CPA of help in restoring order.

Much of the violence in post-invasion Iraq was initially directed against the US-led occupation, including the multinational forces and Iraqi police force, as well as Iraqi and foreign civilians working for Iraqi state institutions and foreign agencies. This insurgency was made up of different groups (mainly Iraqi, with some foreign fighters) that combined, to different degrees, patriotic and political Islamist motivations. Their aim was to eject US forces from Iraq and to protect the unity of Iraq (International Crisis Group 2006). The surge in US troop numbers in 2008, combined with divisions between insurgent groups over tactics, and the arming of Sunni militia (called the 'National Council for the Awakening of Iraq') in the fight against 'al-Qaeda in Iraq' dampened anti-US insurgency-related

violence in early 2009. The US troops were withdrawn at the end of 2011. Despite the huge build-up of Iraqi security personnel, the deadly targeting of civilians, particularly Christian and Shi'i worshippers, has continued, suggesting that al-Qaeda continues to operate in Iraq.

In 2006–08, sectarian violence by different militia groups—either those linked to political parties in government, such as the Badr Brigade, Mahdi Army, and Peshmerga, or other neighbourhood militia—resulted in daily deaths on the streets of Baghdad and other cities in central Iraq, with individuals being summarily executed and their bodies dumped in sewage plants, irrigation canals, or even in the middle of the street (Abdul-Ahad 2006). The majority of killings occurred on a 'tit-for-tat' basis between Shi'i and Sunni groups. During this period, more than 40,000 families were displaced as minorities were 'cleansed' from neighbourhoods, particularly in Baghdad, to make them religiously homogeneous. After 2008, sectarian violence significantly decreased. However, ethnic and sectarian tensions have continued, because they are endemic to the existing political arrangements. In 2013, central government and Iraqi Kurdistan troops faced off over disputed territory along the border of the Iraqi Kurdistan region.

Ten years after the invasion of 2003, Iraq became once again a heavily militarized country and society. This is despite the United States' initial aims to demilitarize Iraq to prevent it from threatening the security of its neighbours, particularly Kuwait, which Iraq invaded in 1990, but also its own population. The United States spent more than US$19 billion to train and equip the new Iraqi armed forces, topped up by more than US$16.6 billion from the Iraqi government (International Institute for Strategic Studies 2008:226). The Iraqi Ministry of Defence's budget rose yearly after 2003 and, by 2013, Iraq emerged sixth in terms of world rankings for military spending (CIA 2013).

Whilst men constitute the majority of victims of violence, the lack of security impacts upon women in particular ways. Women have been abducted by criminal gangs, raped, beaten, and their bodies dumped, or they have been sold into prostitution. If they manage to survive the ordeal, the stigma attached to rape deters women from reporting cases of sexual violence, since they could be killed by their families in order to protect their 'honour'. As a result of the security situation, many women have stopped going to work or university and young girls have been pulled out of school.

KEY POINTS

- The sources of violence in Iraq are multiple and have included the insurgency against the US-led occupation, al-Qaeda, sectarian violence, and general lawlessness and organized crime.

- In 2008, the United States managed to decrease the violence through a surge of troops and arming Sunni tribes to fight al-Qaeda. However, sectarian tensions and al-Qaeda bombings have continued.

- The re-militarization of the Iraqi state and huge numbers of Iraqi security personnel have not managed to eliminate the relatively high incidence of violent deaths in Iraq.

- Women are affected in particularly negative ways by continuing violence and insecurity.

Human and Economic Development

Following the invasion and thirteen years of economic sanctions, which both had a devastating impact on human and economic development, Iraq was in dire need of rebuilding and humanitarian assistance. However, reconstruction was undermined by a range of factors. The first few years after the downfall of Saddam Hussein were punctuated by changes in state personnel. Many experienced Iraqi civil servants were either dismissed from their jobs as part of the de-Ba'thification orders or fled the country as a result of the widespread violence. Meanwhile, staff were hired and fired with the changes in interim governments in the first few years following the invasion. In many cases, the political parties dominating national politics used state institutions to build up networks of patronage and nepotism, rather than hiring the most competent people to implement much-needed reconstruction (Al-Ali and Pratt 2009: 66). Slow disbursement of funding owing to the dire security situation, as well as lack of expertise, also contributed to undermine reconstruction. These factors were exacerbated by the widespread use of US contractors, rather than local companies, to undertake the rehabilitation of essential services and infrastructure. They became a target for insurgent attacks, as well as often inflating costs, whilst failing to achieve their objectives (Herring and Rangwala 2006; Al-Ali and Pratt 2009).

In line with notions of liberal peace-building, the CPA attempted to dismantle Iraq's state-dominated economy and establish a free market. It promoted neoliberal economic reforms, such as liberalizing prices and removing subsidies. However, some critics have argued that such reforms undermined, rather than supported, economic reconstruction and **human development** (Herring and Rangwala 2006). As a result of price liberalization, food prices increased considerably after 2004, leading to malnutrition amongst the poorest households. According to one report, over 10 per cent of children below the age of 5 in nine districts suffer from acute malnutrition (Agency for Technical Cooperation and Development et al. 2010: 7).

There has emerged a significant problem of corruption within Iraq's state institutions. A report by international watchdog Transparency International (2005: 87) claimed as early as 2005 that Iraq could 'become the biggest corruption scandal in history'. The corruption ranges from petty bribery of civil servants, which was already increasingly common under the sanctions regime, to the misuse of millions of dollars of reconstruction funds owing to a lack of oversight by donors or by Iraqi institutions. Under Prime Minister al-Malaki, corruption has become entrenched and endemic throughout the Iraqi state. In 2009, it was estimated that 10 per cent of the central government's revenues were lost through corruption (cited in Dodge 2012: 162). Meanwhile, al-Malaki has hindered anti-corruption cases (International Crisis Group 2011).

As foreign troops have largely been withdrawn, international aid and the commitment to sustainable recovery for the country has almost stopped. Officially, Iraq has become a 'middle-income country' (World Bank 2012), yet the Iraqi government has so far been unable to develop the economy beyond the oil sector or to ensure the basic needs of its population. Iraq's economy remains heavily dependent on its oil industry and has so far failed to diversify. In 2011, oil revenues reached approximately US$83 billion, and oil and gas accounted for about 60 per cent of GDP, 99 per cent of exports, and over 90 per cent of government revenue (IAU 2012). Yet the Iraqi government has had only very limited success in translating macro-economic gains into an improved standard of living for the Iraqi population (Index Mundi 2013).

Only 45 per cent of the population has access to clean drinking water; food prices and food insecurity have risen; the health system is overburdened, and in need of both equipment and professional staff; education is inadequate at all levels, from primary school to universities, and illiteracy and school drop-out rates are high (Agency for Technical Cooperation and Development et al. 2010). Poverty and unemployment remain serious problems throughout the country. Over 20 per cent of Iraqis are living under the poverty line—that is, on less than US$2 per day—while unemployment stands at about 15 per cent, with women and youth particularly hard hit (Agency for Technical Cooperation and Development et al. 2010). Years of insecurity, violence, and lack of protection have seriously affected the health and well-being of Iraqis, particularly children, women, and internally displaced populations, as well as disabled people. The ongoing political violence, lawlessness, militarization of society, and increased authoritarianism continue to generate insecurity, and seriously hamper human and economic development.

KEY POINTS

- Iraq had already experienced a humanitarian crisis and deterioration of infrastructure as a result of thirteen years of economic sanctions.

- While national security has been high on the agenda, **human security** has been neglected.

- Lack of expertise, neoliberal economic reforms, widespread corruption, and poor security have been obstacles to economic reconstruction and human development.

- Iraqi society continues to experience a humanitarian crisis.

Conclusion

Since the toppling of the Ba'th regime in April 2003, Iraq has faced multiple challenges that are interconnected and unresolved. The political process, rather than encouraging cooperation, has contributed to conflict and failed to resolve key issues about the future of the country. The ongoing violence, as well as the weakness and corruption of Iraq's government, have presented huge obstacles to the economic reconstruction process, thereby impacting upon human and economic development. Simultaneously, the failure of human and economic development feeds grievances against the government and the political process more generally.

The experience of Iraq illustrates the complex relationship between the political process, law and order, and socio-economic development (Burnell 2009). It also underlines the significant role played by external actors, particularly the United States, in shaping the post-conflict reconstruction process. US belief that **democracy promotion** and neoliberal economic reforms were the panacea to Iraq's problems has yet to be proven correct. Finally, the Iraq case emphasizes the need to pay attention to informal and unofficial channels of patronage and **clientelism** in order to understand the workings of the state. Iraq's failing political institutions and state institutions suggest that Iraq is indeed a failed state; the ability of the prime minister to control oil revenues and the large security forces to concentrate power in his hands makes Iraq a 'fierce state'. In both scenarios, the consequences for Iraq's citizens are grim.

? QUESTIONS

1. Is the term 'failed state' useful in understanding the Iraqi state since 2003?

2. What are the sources of ethnic/sectarian conflicts in Iraq?

3. Why have Iraqis been unable to rebuild their country to the levels of development experienced before 1991?

4. Is Iraq heading again towards dictatorship?

5. How do Iraqis' views of the previous regime shape their views of how post-invasion Iraqi institutions should be crafted?

6. To what degree have the international community's post-conflict reconstruction measures contributed to Iraq's problems since 2003?

FURTHER READING

Abdullah, T. A. J. (2003) *Short History of Iraq* (London: Pearson-Longman) A concise, insightful, and rigorous history of Iraq since the Iran-Iraq war by a well-respected Iraqi intellectual.

Al-Ali, N. (2007) *Iraqi Women: Untold Stories from 1948 to the Present* (London/New York: Zed Books) An accessible modern history of Iraq told through the voices of different Iraqi women.

Al-Ali, N. and Pratt, N. (2009) *What Kind of Liberation? Women and the Occupation of Iraq* (Berkeley, CA: University of California Press) Exploration of US reconstruction efforts in Iraq after 2003, focusing on their impact on women and women's activism.

Dodge, T. (2013) *Iraq from War to New Authoritarianism* (London: International Institute for Strategic Studies) An incisive and insightful analysis of the major challenges facing post-invasion Iraq, with a focus on Iraq's remilitarization and the rise of a new authoritarian regime.

Farouk-Sluglett, M. and Sluglett, P. (2003) *Iraq since 1958: From Revolution to Dictatorship* (London/New York: I. B. Tauris) Provides the political, social, and economic background to some of the key developments in the post-invasion period.

Fawn, R. and Hinnebusch, R. (eds) (2006) *The Iraq War* (Boulder, CO: Lynne Rienner) A collection that explores the international dimensions of the invasion of Iraq, including the reasons why the United States went to war, and the impact of the war on international and Middle East regional relations.

Haddad, F. (2011) *Sectarianism in Iraq: Antagonistic View of Unity* (London: Hurst & Co) An insightful and nuanced discussion of sectarianism based on empirical research in Iraq.

Herring, E. and Rangwala, G. (2006) *Iraq in Fragments: The Occupation and its Legacy* (London: Hurst & Co) A detailed account of political developments in Iraq during the first few years following the invasion, focusing on the ways in which the US occupation shaped political outcomes.

Tripp, C. (2002) *A History of Iraq* (Cambridge: Cambridge University Press) A history of modern Iraq that focuses on the development of Iraqi state structures and their implications for how politics has played out. A very important background to understanding post-invasion developments.

WEB LINKS

http://gulfanalysis.wordpress.com/ Iraq and Gulf Analysis: a periodic commentary on Iraqi politics by Reidar Visser of the Norwegian Institute of International Affairs

http://iwpr.net/programme/iraq Institute for War and Peace Reporting, Iraq programme.

http://www.crisisgroup.org/en/regions/middle-east-north-africa/iraq-iran-gulf/iraq.aspx International Crisis Group reports on Iraq.

For additional material and resources, please visit the Online Resource Centre at:
http://www.oxfordtextbooks.co.uk/orc/burnell4e/

23

Mexico: Transition to Civil War Democracy

Andreas Schedler

Overview

With a population of more than 115 million, a vast and heterogeneous territory, and an extended common border with the United States, Mexico commands the attention of international policymakers. In the last two decades of the twentieth century, the big challenge of the country was political democratization. A decade afterwards, it is organized criminal violence. In the presidential elections of 2000, the victory of conservative opposition candidate Vicente Fox sealed the end of more than seven decades of uninterrupted hegemonic party rule. It culminated a protracted process of democratization by elections. Yet, as its fledgling democracy was struggling to find its way, Mexico slid first imperceptibly, then dramatically, into a situation of civil war. It suffered a pandemic escalation of violence related to organized crime. The democratization of the Mexican state was followed by serious challenges to its internal sovereignty (see Chapter 12). This chapter analyses this double transition: the country's incremental and largely peaceful transition to democracy, followed by its sudden descent into civil war. Figure 23.1 shows a map of Mexico and Box 23.1 provides an overview of key dates in Mexico's history.

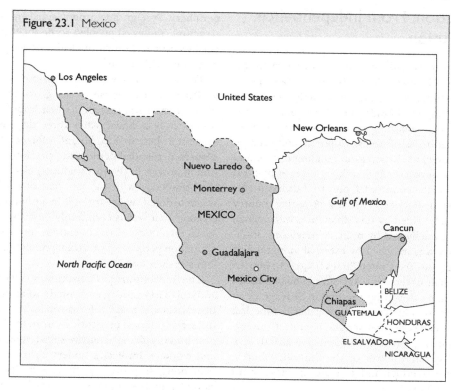

Figure 23.1 Mexico

1810–21	War of Independence against Spain
1846–48	War between Mexico and the United States
1857	New Republican Constitution
1876–1910	Presidency of Porfirio Díaz
1910–20	Mexican Revolution
1917	New Constitution (still in force)
1929	Foundation of the National Revolutionary Party, later changed to Institutional Revolutionary Party (PRI)
1934–40	Land redistribution, social reforms, and oil nationalization under President Lázaro Cárdenas
1982	Debt crisis
1988	PRI presidential candidate obtains a bare majority in 'earthquake election' among allegations of fraud
1990	Foundation of the Federal Electoral Institute (IFE)
1994	North American Free Trade Agreement (NAFTA); Zapatista rebellion
1996	Crossing the democratic threshold: 'decisive' electoral reform
2000	Opposition candidate Vicente Fox, from the conservative National Action Party (PAN), wins the presidency
2006	Felipe Calderón preserves the presidency for the PAN; deepens and extends the 'war on drugs'; descent into civil war
2012	Enrique Peña Nieto from PRI wins presidential election

Introduction: From Independence to Revolution

As Mexico reached independence from Spain after a decade of war in 1821, it faced the triple challenge of redefining its political **regime**, constructing a modern state, and laying the foundations of a capitalist economy. Failure in establishing a regime—in institutionalizing accepted rules of access to power and exercise of power—precluded success in building a state and developing a market. In its first thirty years of political independence, the country fell prey to the vicissitudes of **caudillismo**. Between 1821 and 1850, the country was (nominally) ruled by fifty different governments, most of them delivered by military rebellions. Internal instability was matched by external vulnerability. In the war against the United States (1846–48), Mexico lost around half its territory. At home, civilian **politics** was increasingly driven by the major cleavage common to most of nineteenth-century Latin America: conflict between conservatives and liberals. Conservatives sought to protect the inherited political, economic, and cultural power of the Catholic Church. Liberals strove to limit it and to create an autonomous sphere of secular politics.

The developmental dictatorship under Porfirio Díaz (1876–1910), while harshly repressive, brought an unprecedented measure of stability and institutional **modernization**. Having taken power by a coup, General Díaz proceeded to set up an early variant of **electoral authoritarianism** (see Box 23.2). Regular (indirect) presidential elections confirmed his continuity in power. At the same time, something like a modern state started to take shape, with a central government, a national military, and a permanent bureaucracy extending its reach to the country's periphery. Foreign investment aided by public infrastructure (railways) enabled some incipient, dependent industrialization through the development of an extractive enclave economy.

The Mexican Revolution (1910–20) is customarily explained as a response to the growing impoverishment of the rural masses. Its first impulse, however, was entirely political. After three decades of developmental dictatorship, liberal reformer Francisco I. Madero demanded democratic elections and alternation in power. In the 1911 (indirect) elections, he won the presidency with 99.3 per cent of total votes. He was murdered two years later in a military coup. The ensuing civil war is commonly described as the first social revolution of the twentieth century, and about 1.4 million people out of a total population of 15.2 million lost their lives.

The revolutionary Constitution, enacted in 1917 and still in force today, enshrined a mixture of political **liberalism** and social reformism. It copied almost the full set of political **institutions** from the US Constitution, and stipulated extensive social rights for peasants and workers. Ironically, under subsequent one-party hegemony, it proved ineffective in its procedural, as well as in its substantive, aspects. It worked neither as an effective institutional constraint on politics nor as an effective policy programme.

KEY POINTS

- During much of the nineteenth century, Mexico's difficulties in institutionalizing a political regime frustrated its efforts at state-building and economic development.

- Revolutionary civil war in the second decade of the twentieth century led to a new constitution, the liberal restraints and social aspirations of which were rendered ineffective by subsequent hegemonic party rule.

BOX 23.2 ELECTORAL AUTHORITARIANISM

Electoral autocracies display a nominal adherence to the principle of democratic rule, while denying democracy in practice. They hold regular multiparty elections, yet constrain and subvert them so deeply as to render them instruments not of democracy, but of authoritarian rule. Modern examples are Indonesia under Suharto and Russia under Putin (see Chapter 14).

The Foundations of Electoral Authoritarianism

Post-revolutionary politics continued to be disorderly and violent. The bullet, alongside the ballot, enjoyed acceptance as a valid currency for gaining and losing public office. Violent protest, military rebellion, and the physical elimination of adversaries remained common. But regular elections took place at all levels, although nothing resembling a structured party system existed. Politics remained a game of elite competition mediated by force, not by formal institutions.

The crisis of presidential succession in 1928 marked a turning point. After the assassination of President Elect Alvaro Obregón, outgoing President Plutarco Elías Calles announced his intention to institutionalize the revolutionary government. In 1929, he founded the National Revolutionary Party (PRN) as an umbrella organization of all revolutionary leaders, factions, and parties.

Twin institutionalization

The PRN was to pacify electoral disputes by providing a transparent mechanism of electoral coordination: it would select winning candidates from among the 'revolutionary family', reward their followers, and crush their opponents. By the mid-1930s, the PRN had centralized candidate selection by dissolving local parties and prohibiting the immediate re-election of deputies. Within a few years, what was initially a loose alliance of local factions established itself as a centralized hegemonic party that was to rule Mexico for the rest of the century.

Before quitting power peacefully in the 2000 presidential elections, the successor party of the PRN, the Institutional Revolutionary Party (PRI), was the longest-ruling political party in the world. It had clearly excelled in fulfilling its original mission of pacifying and stabilizing the country. How did the PRI achieve this extraordinary success in party and regime institutionalization? Like all institutions, it had to achieve two basic objectives: 'stability' and 'value' (Huntington 1968). The former is a matter of expectations; the latter, one of evaluations. People had to know that the PRI was there to stay, but they had to value it, too.

The institutional infrastructure

Over seven decades, the PRI sustained a regime that looked as exceptional as its longevity. In essence, it rested upon three institutional pillars: a hierarchical state party; state corporatism; and electoral gatekeeping.

On the first, the hegemonic party operated as a big 'linkage mechanism' that turned the Mexican state into a unitary hierarchical organization. By controlling all branches and levels of government, the hegemonic party effectively cancelled the constitutional distribution of state power. It annulled the horizontal division of power between the executive, legislative, and judicial branches, as well as the vertical division of power between central government, federal states, and municipalities. The fusion between state and party granted almost unlimited powers to the president, who acted as the supreme patron at the peak of a **clientelist** pyramid—the Mexican state.

The state in turn controlled **civil society** by co-opting and corrupting potential dissidents and opponents. The party patronized and domesticated labour unions, peasant organizations, and popular movements by incorporating them into tightly controlled corporatist arrangements. It kept business people content with subsidies, market protection, and informal access to power.

Electoral autocracies like the PRI regime reproduce and legitimate themselves on the basis of periodic elections that show some measure of pluralism, but fall short of minimum democratic standards. Their violations of liberal-democratic norms may be manifold (see Schedler 2013), and post-revolutionary Mexico had nearly all of them in place: limitations of civil and political liberties; restrictions on party and candidate registration; discriminatory rules of representation; electoral fraud; **corruption**; and coercion—as well as an incumbent enjoying close to monopolistic access to media and campaign resources.

The ideological infrastructure

Following Sartori (1976), scholars commonly portray Mexico's post-revolutionary regime as 'pragmatic' authoritarianism. True, the PRI did not institute a mobilizational dictatorship that tried to coerce its subjects into ideological uniformity. Its relative tolerance of pluralism, however, should not be mistaken for the absence of ideology. Its revolutionary nationalism was not a mere echo chamber. Actually, the PRI was able to create what Antonio Gramsci called 'cultural hegemony'. The state party defined lasting coordinates of **national identity**—the national history, national foes and heroes, national symbols and rituals, and last, but not least, the promise of progress and justice. Its ideology—a combination of liberalism, nationalism, and the corporative defence of the welfare state—continues to define the terms of national political correctness.

The Structural Bases of Regime Change

The relationship between economic development and political democracy has been subject to intense debate (see Chapter 14). But although for a long time a democratic underachiever, Mexico seems to confirm the elective affinity between socio-economic and political modernization.

Societal transformation

Not unlike Porfirio Díaz—even if less personalistic, repressive, and exclusionary—the PRI established its own version of developmental dictatorship. Especially during the 'Mexican miracle' between 1940 and 1970, it achieved steady rates of **economic growth** and expanding public services. Notwithstanding the economic crises that erupted at each presidential succession from 1976 to 1994, seven decades of modernizing authoritarian rule by the PRI produced profound societal transformations. At the end of the revolution, Mexico was a poor, rural country with no more than 16.5 million inhabitants. At the turn of the century, it had grown into an urban middle-income country with almost 100 million inhabitants. Although about half of the population still counts as poor and the country displays one of the most unequal income distributions in the world, societal modernization was bound to create strong pressures for democratization. Societal pluralism could hardly be contained within the confinements of a single party. In addition, the structural dissociation between a hegemonic party and a complex society was deepened by economic mismanagement and crisis.

Economic crises

After 1970, a mixture of structural disequilibria and performance failure pushed Mexico into periodic economic recessions. Each presidential succession from 1976 to 1994 was marked by economic crisis. The oil boom and external debt first postponed, and then aggravated, the big crash that hit the country in 1983. In retrospect, the debt crisis of the early 1980s was the starting point of democratization. There was nothing inevitable about it, however. Neither structural incongruence nor cyclical stress translate smoothly and automatically into democratizing progress. During the 1970s and 1980s, the talk of the day was about *crisis*. Anything seemed possible, including a return to the violence of the past. It was only in the late 1980s that this diffuse sense of alarm receded. Actors and analysts started talking about democratic *transition*, and started playing the game of peaceful, incremental political democratization.

Democratization by Elections

Under electoral autocracies like the PRI regime, elections are not 'instruments of democracy' (Powell 2000), but battlefields of democratization. Unlike democratic elections, manipulated elections unfold as two-level games in which parties compete for votes at the same time as they struggle over basic rules. Democratization 'by elections' ensues when opposition parties succeed at both levels, when they manage to undermine both pillars of authoritarian rule: its popular support, as well as its anti-democratic institutions (Schedler 2013). Mexico's emergent opposition parties—the right-wing National Action Party (PAN) and the left-wing Party of the Democratic Revolution (PRD)—were able to start such a self-reinforcing spiral of rising competitiveness and democratic reform. As they turned into serious contenders, they were able to remove successive layers of authoritarian control through negotiated electoral reforms.

Electoral competition

Historic turnout figures indicate that the hegemonic party's capacity for electoral mobilization was modest. Its official election results, by contrast, were impressive. Until 1982, all Mexican revolutionary and post-revolutionary presidents were elected by acclamation (except for 1946 and 1952, when they faced relatively popular splinter candidates). Plurality elections prevented opposition parties from winning legislative seats until the early 1960s. In 1963, the PRI introduced some element of proportional representation to keep the PAN in the electoral game, yet without jeopardizing its two-thirds majority—a condition to enact constitutional changes.

In the wake of the 1982 debt crisis, however, the governing party's hegemony began to crumble. First, the PAN started to win, and to defend its victories, in a series of post-electoral confrontations, at the municipal and state levels in northern Mexico. Then, in the 1988 presidential election, the performance of PRI dissident Cuauhtémoc Cárdenas shattered the image of PRI invincibility at the national level. His followers continue to think that he actually won the contest, being denied victory only by blatant electoral fraud. Afterwards, opposition parties conquered more and more sites of subnational power, at the same time as they strengthened their presence in the bicameral national legislature. In 1997, the official party lost its absolute majority in the Chamber of Deputies, inaugurating a period of divided government. Finally, in 2000, PAN candidate Vicente Fox won the really big prize in Mexican politics—the presidency.

Electoral reform

The rising competitiveness of the party system made possible (and was made possible by) profound changes in the institutions of electoral **governance**. Today, vote-rigging and the state control of elections belong to the past. Within less than a decade, Mexico effectively remodelled its electoral institutions. The electoral reforms added up to a veritable institutional revolution within the (self-denominated) regime of the institutional revolution.

The new electoral system rested upon three institutional columns: a new independent election body; the judicialization of conflict resolution; and comprehensive oversight by parties. Mexican parties decided to delegate the organization of elections to a permanent and independent election management body, the Federal Electoral Institute (IFE), founded in 1990. Electoral reformers also set up a new system for the judicial resolution of election disputes: the Electoral Tribunal of the Judicial Power of the Federation (TEPJF) now has the last say in all electoral disputes, national as well as subnational. Finally, parties institutionalized a 'panoptic regime' of surveillance that allows them to monitor the entire electoral process closely, step by step.

KEY POINT

* Mexico's democratic advance resulted from the interplay between democratizing reform and increasing interparty competition.

Transition to Civil War

With the 2000 alternation in power, Mexico turned into a 'normal' Latin American democracy operating in the context of a **weak state** and an unequal society. Like most democracies in the region, it has faced serious challenges of consolidation, deepening, and performance. Yet one dramatic development has blown up all expectations of democratic normality: the country's vertiginous descent into civil war.

The escalation of violence

In 2006, after a close and contentious election, conservative Felipe Calderón assumed the Mexican presidency amidst a lingering security crisis. During the Fox government, violent competition between drug-trafficking organizations (so-called 'cartels') had been provoking more than 1,000 homicides per year, with a rising tendency (see Figure 23.2). In the academic literature, we speak of 'civil war' when confrontations between armed groups within a state cost a minimum of 1,000 'battle-related deaths' per year.

Although it had not been an issue during the election campaign, President Calderón decided to make the combat against drug cartels the defining policy of his presidency. It was to turn into its defining failure. Heavily relying on military support, Calderón essentially escalated the one-sided strategies pursued by his predecessors: bolstering the security apparatus without strengthening the justice system, drawing the military into police functions without subjecting it to oversight, chasing down cartel leaders without dismantling cartel networks, pursuing drug trafficking while giving

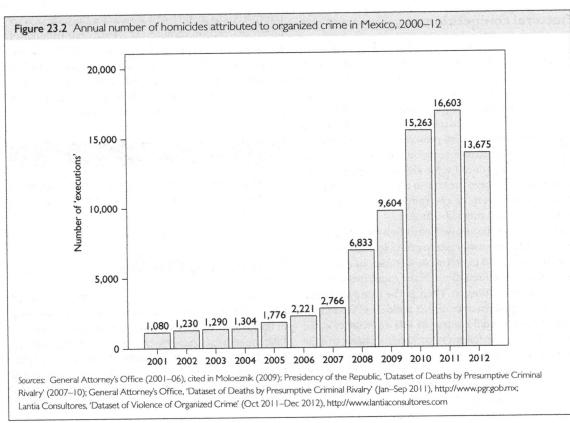

Figure 23.2 Annual number of homicides attributed to organized crime in Mexico, 2000–12

Sources: General Attorney's Office (2001–06), cited in Moloeznik (2009); Presidency of the Republic, 'Dataset of Deaths by Presumptive Criminal Rivalry' (2007–10); General Attorney's Office, 'Dataset of Deaths by Presumptive Criminal Rivalry' (Jan–Sep 2011), http://www.pgr.gob.mx; Lantia Consultores, 'Dataset of Violence of Organized Crime' (Oct 2011–Dec 2012), http://www.lantiaconsultores.com

traffickers a licence to kill each other, conducting massive arrests of suspected criminals while lacking the capacity of subjecting them to fair and effective trials, and seeking mass confiscations of drug money and arms while lacking serious strategies against money laundering and the importation of arms.

Policy incoherence permitted the creeping civil war to escalate, qualitatively as well as quantitatively. In qualitative terms, modes of assassination moved towards demonstrative cruelty, routinized and ritualized. In certain parts of the country, the public display of tortured, dismembered, and decapitated bodies became part of ordinary life. In quantitative terms, the number of annual homicides attributed to criminal organizations shot up from more than 2,000 in 2006 to more than 15,000 in 2010. In 2011, these figures reached a peak. In the subsequent year, they declined for the first time (see Figure 23.2). We do not know yet whether this constitutes the beginning of a trend. Besides, data problems are massive. Thousands of people have 'disappeared' after forced abductions. According to official figures, more than 26,000 individuals were reported 'missing' during the Calderón administration.

The morphology of war

It is true that the new Mexican civil war is not a classical civil war in which ideological insurgencies strive to topple state power. It is a prototypical 'new' civil war, fought for material gain, not social justice. Its societal protagonists strive to evade or capture the state as much as to confront it. Moreover, the war is not one, but many. Its major lines of conflict run between criminal enterprises. The Calderón administration routinely attributed 90 per cent of drug-related assassinations to informal justice (the 'settling of scores') between criminal organizations. This figure was merely impressionistic, not to say propagandistic. Only 10 per cent of victims are innocent, it said; the rest are guilty. In what amounted to a tacit **privatization** of the death penalty, their cases were not prosecuted.

While the war involves various interacting 'non-state' conflicts, it also contains elements of 'one-sided' violence predatory criminals unleash against civilian actors. Organized homicides have only been the tip of the violent iceberg. As criminal organizations have diversified their activities, the country has seen the dramatic expansion of violent crimes such as kidnapping, human trafficking, and extortion (mafia-like protection rackets).

The Mexican state, of course, is a warring party, too. In theory, it is the monopoly holder of legitimate violence; in practice, it commits criminal violence on a large scale. International **human rights** associations coincide in diagnosing 'widespread grave human rights violations committed by the military and police' (Amnesty International 2012: 234). In part, these violations are expression of state *abuse*. They are the non-intended, but inevitable, consequence of acting with brute force, little intelligence, and no oversight in an 'irregular war' characterized by endemic problems of information (see Kalyvas 2006). In part, illegal state violence is a symptom of state *collusion*. Public officials are known to collaborate with criminal organizations (see, for example, Human Rights Watch 2013: 29–33).

Not the entire state apparatus is at the service of criminal organizations, of course. During the Calderón administration, more than 2,500 security officials and more than 200 military personnel were murdered by criminal organizations. The 'collateral damages' to democracy have been massive, too. Dozens of mayors, former mayors, and candidates have been assassinated. Civil society activists have been intimidated and murdered. Seventy-four journalists and media-support workers have been killed between 2007 and 2012, making Mexico one of the most dangerous places for journalism and political activism (Molzahn et al. 2013: 30).

Explaining organized violence

Why has Mexico turned, within a few short years, into a 'violent democracy' (Arias and Goldstein 2010), a democracy besieged by civil war? Some might say that there is no puzzle to be explained. Mexico's plunge into societal violence has been a process of Latin American 'normalization'. Today, the country's homicide rate of 18.6 per 100,000 inhabitants lies close to the regional average of 15.6 (data for 2010 by Organization of American States 2012: 18). But even if we were prepared to habituate ourselves to a new level of 'structural' violence, we would still want to explain its recent surge. One set of arguments points to rising access to the *material resources* necessary to wage a civil war.

(a) *Money* The trade with illegal drugs is a lucrative business. It creates the wealth that permits criminal 'oligarchs' (Winters 2011) to organize their violent self-defence. While the tradition of drug production and trade in Mexico reaches back to the late nineteenth century, the market received a massive expansionary shock in the closing decades of the twentieth century, when cocaine trafficking routes shifted from the Caribbean to Mexico. Illicit wealth sustains the organization of violence. Yet the private organization of violence also produces wealth. According to estimates, less than half of the income of so-called drug cartels derives from actual drug sales. The rest comes from other violence-based illicit activities, some market-oriented, others predatory.

(b) *Arms* Since the late 1990s, Mexican drug cartels have been engaged in a kind of subnational armament race, expanding and professionalizing their structures of defence and repression. Given the porousness of the border and the free availability of small weapons on the US market (even more so since the ban on assault weapons was lifted in 2004), they have enjoyed unlimited access to means of destruction.

(c) *Personnel* The Mexican drug industry is estimated to employ about half a million people. An unknown number of professionals of violence work in the paramilitary branches of criminal organizations—as bodyguards, kidnappers, torturers, killers. Common clichés of poor young men who have nothing to lose suggest that the cartels' proletarian reserve army is unlimited—which may or may not be true. We know little about the identity and recruitment of killers. Up to now, though, labour supply for the Mexican killing field has been abundant.

A second set of explanations points to the *field of actors*. Both the state and organized crime have gone through processes of *fragmentation*. In the 'good old times' of hegemonic peace, state officials and criminal organizations institutionalized corrupt exchanges: the former agreed to tolerate illicit enterprises; the latter, to pay for official protection and follow certain rules of conduct. These 'state-sponsored protection rackets' (Snyder and Durán-Martínez 2009) have broken down. Both sides have been destabilized by the multiplication of actors. On the one side, the spread of electoral competition replaced hegemonic party discipline by party pluralism at all levels of the political system. On the other side, the governmental strategy of leadership decapitation destabilized the entire system of criminal actors. It fractured all relationships: within cartels, among cartels, and between cartels and the state. It provoked the 'disorganization' of organized crime. In 2006, six major transnational drug cartels were operating in Mexico. Four years later, it was twice as many. In addition, more than sixty local criminal organizations had sprung up, developing any kind of activity that organized violence can render profitable, from mass kidnapping to private protection. The destabilization and multiplication of violent actors intensified violence within cartels (succession crises), among cartels (market competition), against the state (self-defence), and against society (predation).

The demand shock of the cocaine boom explains what made the war ignite; the structural availability of money, arms, and personnel, what has made it feasible; and the fragmentation of actors, what made it escalate. Together, these bundles of factors explain why the war is likely to go on for the long haul.

KEY POINTS

- Already, at the official inauguration of its democracy in 2000, Mexico faced a creeping, low-intensity civil war between drug cartels. Ignited by the cocaine boom of the 1990s, it was also fuelled by structural factors: easy access to arms and recruits.

- During the presidency of Felipe Calderón (2006–2012), societal violence escalated. Almost 70,000 assassinations attributed to criminal organizations were registered during his term. Tens of thousands of individuals were reported missing. Dozens of mayors, journalists, and civil society activists were murdered.

- While strengthening the security apparatus, the government did little to strengthen the justice system. Its strategy of leadership decapitation destabilized the field of criminal actors. It intensified violence among cartels, between cartels, and against the state.

- The state has been a victim, as well as an agent, of criminal violence. Abuse of power, as well as collusive behaviour, have been widespread. At the local level, the boundaries between state and crime have often been blurred.

Conclusion

At the turn of the twenty-first century, after traumatic experiences of instability and violence, followed by seven decades of authoritarian stability, Mexico finally seemed to have found a way of reconciling political stability and democracy. After the tranquil alternation in power of the year 2000, democracy seemed to be blessed by instantaneous consolidation. The democratic consensus within the political elite seemed firm. No anti-system actors were threatening the fledgling democracy.

Today, after only two presidential terms, the picture looks much less encouraging. Rather than direct challenges to democracy, direct challenges to the state have arisen. Once again, the country has descended into the hell of massive fratricidal violence. The Mexican state is not a failed state. There are many things that it manages to accomplish rather well and there are vast regions, including the capital city, that have been spared the fall into the abyss of public insecurity. Yet both the state and democracy have come under siege. They are damaged and debilitated.

Within the current security crises, the PRI, the former authoritarian hegemon and grand champion of peace and order, has returned to national power. While former President Calderón chose to dramatize criminal violence, President Peña Nieto (2012–) seems to be betting on its normalization. We do what we can, he conveys to the national public, so stop worrying and turn to other issues. Controlling violence and building the democratic **rule of law** are complex, long-term projects. For them to happen, though, they require more than democratic delegation, more than trust in competent governance. They require that civil society assumes its part in the containment of civil war. In the closing years of the previous presidency, popular mobilization introduced significant changes in public policy and discourse. Unless citizens are willing and able to sustain their critical activism, Mexico is likely to institutionalize the subversive coexistence of civil war with formal democracy.

QUESTIONS

1. What were the central political and economic challenges of post-independence Mexico?

2. How do you account for the institutional and ideological foundations of Mexico's post-revolutionary authoritarianism?

3. How did Mexico's socio-economic modernization in the twentieth century create pressures for political democratization?

4. Which were the core features of 'democratization by elections'?

5. Which are the main features of the internal war that drug cartels wage among themselves and against the Mexican state? How does it affect the quality of Mexican democracy?

6. Why did this new civil war emerge? Why did it escalate? Why is it likely to persist in the near future?

FURTHER READING

Escalante, F. (2012) *El Crimen como Realidad y Representación* (Mexico City: Colegio de México) An insightful analysis of the treatment of violence in the Mexican public sphere.

Greene, K. F. (2007) *Why Dominant Parties Lose: Mexico's Democratization in Comparative Perspective* (Cambridge: Cambridge University Press) A theoretical and empirical analysis of hegemonic party demise in Mexico.

Grillo, I. (2011) *El Narco: Inside Mexico's Criminal Insurgency* (New York: Bloomsbury Press) A succinct recount of historical drug trafficking and contemporary drug violence in Mexico.

Guerrero, E. (2012) 'La Estrategia Fallida', *Nexos*, 1 December, available online at http://www.nexos.com.mx/?P=leerartic ulo&Article=2103067 A balanced criticism of the Calderón presidency by one of the most prominent security analysts.

Human Rights Watch (2011) *Neither Rights nor Security: Killings, Torture, and Disappearances in Mexico's 'War on Drugs'* (New York: HRW) One documentation among several of human rights abuses by Mexican security agencies.

Molzahn, C., Rodriguez Ferreira, O., and Shirk, D. A. (2013) *Drug Violence in Mexico: Data and Analysis through 2012* (University of San Diego, CA: Trans-Border Institute) A data-rich discussion of organized criminal violence in Mexico.

Ríos, V. (2012) 'Why Did Mexico Become So Violent? A Self-Reinforcing Violent Equilibrium Caused by Competition and Enforcement', *Trends in Organized Crime*, 16(2): 138–55 An empirical analysis of spiralling violence in Mexico.

Schedler, A. (2007) 'Mexican Standoff: The Mobilization of Distrust', *Journal of Democracy*, 18(1): 88–102 A resumé and critical analysis of the 2006 post-electoral conflict.

Turati, M. and Rea, D. (eds) (2012) *Entre las Cenizas: Historias de Vida en Tiempos de Muerte* (Mexico City: Sur+ Ediciones) Narrative accounts of civic initiatives in a context of uncivil violence.

Valdez Cárdenas, J. (2012) *Levantones: Historias Reales de Desaparecidos y Víctimas del Narco* (Mexico City: Aguilar) Narrative accounts of organized violence from the perspective of victims.

WEB LINKS

http://justiceinmexico.org   News and data on violence and the rule of law in Mexico by the Trans-Border Institute, University of San Diego

http://movimientoporlapaz.mx   Movement for Peace, Justice and Dignity, founded by Javier Sicilia, with links to other societal initiatives against violence

http://www.democracy-violence.net   An international research network on democracy and violence (available from January 2014)

http://www.presidencia.gob.mx   Mexican presidency

For additional material and resources, please visit the Online Resource Centre at:
http://www.oxfordtextbooks.co.uk/orc/burnell4e/

24

South Korea: Strong State, Successful Development

Peter Ferdinand

Overview

In 1945, the Korean peninsula was freed from Japanese colonial rule by the United States and the Soviet Union. It was divided into two states—one communist in the North; one capitalist in the South. In 1950, North Korea (the Democratic People's Republic of Korea, or DPRK) invaded the South (Republic of Korea, or ROK). In three years, more than a million people died as a result of the conflict and it devastated the Korean economy. In 1961, it left per capita income in the South, at approximately US$92 per year (in nominal terms), among the lowest in the world. By 2008, that figure had risen to around US$19,115. In 1995, it became only the second Asian state after Japan, and the second former colony anywhere, to be admitted to the Organisation for Economic Co-operation and Development (OECD), just after Mexico. In 2009, the ROK became the first former aid recipient to join the OECD's Development Assistance Committee (DAC). This makes it one of the success stories of economic development, in which the state itself played a central role. Figure 24.1 is a map of South Korea and Box 24.1 provides an overview of key dates in South Korea's history.

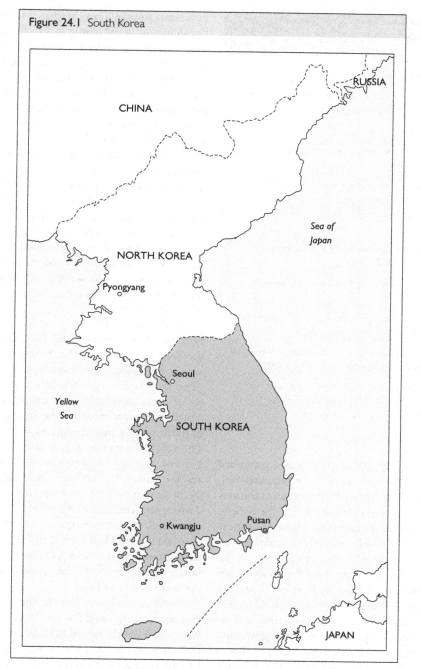

Figure 24.1 South Korea

Introduction: Historical Sources of National Strength

Four legacies from before 1953 contributed to the drive for national economic development, especially after 1961: social traditions; the traditional 'vortex' of centralization; the impact of Japanese colonialism, partition, and civil war; South Koreans' perception of their place in the East Asian region and the world.

First, South Korea has the distinct advantage of being ethnically homogeneous. Out of the current population of nearly 49 million, only 20,000 Chinese

BOX 24.1 KEY DATES IN MODERN KOREA'S HISTORY

1910	Colonized by Japan
1945	Creation of two separate independent Korean states in the north and the south
1950–53	Korean War
1961	General Park Chung Hee seizes power in South Korea
1987	Democracy re-emerges as General Roh Tae Woo allies with former oppositionist Kim Young Sam to form the Democratic Liberal Party and rule through it
1992	Kim Young Sam becomes the first civilian president since 1961
1997	Asian financial crisis; Kim Dae Jung is elected president
2002	Roh Moo Hyun's election as president marks rise of new political generation
2007	Lee Myung Bak is elected president from the Grand National Party (inauguration February 2008)
2012	Park Gyeun-hye (daughter of Park Chung Hee) is elected president from the Saenuri Party (formerly Grand National Party)

living there with Korean nationality are not considered ethnic Koreans. Although the civil war generated millions of refugees and separated families across the new border, there has been no contestation of the right to exist of a Korean state. No significant group in society wanted to leave. The only unresolved business was: which Korean state should represent the whole of the Korean nation? This has meant that ethno-nationalism has been the dominant kind in Korea (Chapter 7), although this has led to considerable ambivalence in South Korean society about the state of their 'fellow' Koreans in the North, especially among those who still have relatives there. It is striking, for example, that in the United Nations General Assembly South Korea votes the same way as North Korea more often than it does with the United States (Ferdinand 2013).

Also, over the centuries, Confucianism became the dominant ideology of social organization. Over half of the population of the Republic of Korea (ROK) now are either Christian or Buddhist, but principles of Confucian social organization are deeply embedded in Korean society. These respect a hierarchy of relationships within the family, in which everyone knows their obligations towards everyone else, as the basis for a well-ordered society. The patriarchal head of the family was entitled to absolute respect; so too was the emperor or ruler. Filial piety—the devotion of the son to the father—was the core relationship. The word for 'state' (guk'ka) in Korean is an amalgam of 'nation' and 'family', as it is in Chinese.

Second, an early analysis of South Korean **politics** identified a 'vortex' of centralization as the dominant dynamic determining Korean political development into the modern era. This meant the dominance of the court (in imperial times) and the capital (Seoul) over the rest of a country of villages—that is, a lack of intermediate social organizations. Traditionally, Korea was polarized between rulers and the mass of society. There was weak horizontal organization (Henderson 1968). This enhanced the potential power of the new state.

Third, colonialism launched Korean **modernization** and development. Until the twentieth century, the Korean peninsula—the 'hermit kingdom'—was a poor backwater, largely ignored by its neighbours. After 1910, Japanese colonialism introduced a wider set of regional relations and industrialization in the North, but in consequence the Japanese occupied all of the important managerial and administrative posts. The colonial experience generated a very powerful sense of patriotism among Koreans, both in the North and the South. The injustices that had been inflicted by the Japanese—their treatment as inferiors—created a strong unifying factor. Nevertheless, a small middle class of Korean entrepreneurs emerged. After 1945, they laid the foundation for Korea's indigenous industrialization drive in the South. Korean business corporations (the *chaebol*) came strongly to resemble the pre-war *zaibatsu* of Japan.

Fourth, a hunger to remake the country after the civil war underpinned the development drive in both North and South, where both felt overshadowed by their near neighbours China and Japan, and respective superpower protectors. The social whirlwind of the civil war, followed by land reform, had the effect of eroding social support for traditional elites, even if habits of deference persisted. Support could be transferred to the modernizing state.

Nevertheless, historical experience left challenges, as well as potential strengths. The civil war bequeathed a legacy of political turbulence and social mistrust, as well as the legacy of a northern border that was as arbitrary as those of former colonial states in Africa (see Chapter 12). Some in the South had collaborated with occupation by the North and resentments persisted. The victors exploited their victory to distribute spoils to their supporters, which encouraged **corruption**. The economy stagnated. The nationalist President Rhee Syngman (in Korean, the surname comes first) was widely regarded as corrupt and, in 1960, he attempted to rig elections again, only to be overthrown by popular demonstrations led by students. In turn, this led fairly swiftly to a military takeover led by General Park Chung Hee, who ruled the country until his assassination in 1979. It was President Park who laid the foundations for Korea's 'take-off'.

KEY POINTS

- Following independence, Korean society possessed many traditional elements that contributed to national unity.

- This unity provided a core strength for national development.

- Yet the civil war also left a concomitant legacy of division and mistrust.

- It took the efforts of presidential strongman Park Chung Hee to impose the order that served as the basis of national development.

The Korean Developmental State: Dictatorship, Development, and National Restoration

Under the banners of national reconstruction and anti-communism, the Park Chung Hee **regime** set out to make the country 'rich and strong'. The main goals were economic development, but President Park packaged this in an even bigger project of 'national restoration' to match what had happened in Japan in the nineteenth century. He justified prioritization of national economic development, arguing that 'the Asian peoples want to obtain economic equality first and build a more equitable political machinery afterward' (Jones and Sakong 1980: 43).

Generals dominated government until 1992. This meant that development and industrialization were pursued as much for purposes of national defence against an ever-threatening North as for improving

living standards. For example, in 1973, the regime set up a national shipbuilding industry; Korea is now the world's largest shipbuilder and Hyundai the largest shipbuilding company. General Park imposed what has subsequently been termed a '**developmental state**' (see Chapter 12). Its main features have been described as: a nationalist agenda; state direction of finance for priority development projects; an effective and technocratic bureaucracy; a partnership between state and business; authoritarianism; and favourable international circumstances (Woo-Cumings 1999: 1–31). The major development decisions were formulated by the Economic Planning Board (EPB), founded in 1961. For the next fifteen years, the economy grew even more quickly than 'planned'.

A key factor was the state's '**embedded autonomy**' (Evans 1995): aimed at developing capitalist enterprises, the state was insulated from excessive pressure from those interests. The military's political domination helped. During the 1960s and 1970s, a solid, more merit-based, bureaucracy was created, replacing the political appointees of the 1950s. This was accompanied by what has been called a 'hardening' of the state's structures and operating practices (Myrdal 1968). Myrdal (1968: 66–67) said that, in 'soft' states, 'policies are often not enforced, if they are enacted at all', whereas in 'hard' states, 'the success of planning for development requires a readiness to place obligations on people in all social strata to a much greater extent . . . [and] requires . . . rigorous enforcement of obligations, in which compulsion plays a strategic role'. The Korean military strengthened the state apparatus: between 1960 and 1970, the number of state officials nearly doubled, from 240,000 to 450,000 (Kohli 2007: 89), and relied on trusted businessmen for economic success. To use the title of the book by Kim (1997), it was a case of *Big Business, Strong State*. Some companies had been established under the Japanese. Others took advantage of the new opportunities created by a shortage economy that ran on permits and licences. They were able to accumulate business empires, the most successful building *chaebol*—that is, business groups or conglomerates.

The *chaebol* were family-based companies with cross-holdings of shares in subsidiaries. They benefited from government favouritism; financing remained the preserve of state banks. General Park was able to direct the nation's economy and initiate industrial projects by summoning the thirty top business leaders for meetings within one room; cartels were encouraged to form

Table 24.1 South Korea's average annual growth rate of gross domestic product (GDP) (%)

1950–59	1960–69	1970–79	1980–89	1990–99	2000–08
5	8.5	9.5	9.4	5.4	4.8

Source: World Bank, *World Development Report* (various years); EconStats.

and compete among themselves. Individual *chaebol* were compensated for government-induced financial losses (Lee 1997). However, as Kim emphasizes:

66 The story of South Korea's remarkable economic achievement is not simply that the state summarily reformed itself and gave marching orders to the private sector and that the private sector complied. The success was in part due to the private sector, which went over and beyond the state's mandate and actively took advantage of the favorable economic environment created by the state. . . . Those *chaebol* that grew most rapidly did more than simply invest in sectors that the state had recommended; they employed their shrewd entrepreneurial skills. 99

(Kim 1997: 123)

Most crucially, where businesses before 1961 grew primarily through **rent-seeking**, afterwards they were forced to focus on production.

A few families grew exceedingly rich and were also widely resented (Eckert 1990). In 1989, the Ministry of Finance estimated that, in each of the ten largest *chaebol*, the main family held roughly 50 per cent of all of the shares, whether directly or through cross-holdings (Janelli 1993: 84). The relationship between the regime and leading *chaebol* was one of both mutual support and vulnerability, with the balance of power gradually tipping towards the *chaebol*, although government kept control of financial resources, thereby stunting the development of an independent financial sector. Debt-to-asset ratios of *chaebol* soared, but few, if any, thought about the likely consequences until the financial crisis of 1997. The government also tightly controlled the labour unions; memories of the civil war and military service, and fear of communist infiltration, were all invoked to strengthen **legitimacy** (Janelli 1993).

Korea followed Japan in concentrating upon full employment policies to raise welfare, rather than introducing a welfare state for which there was no popular demand, in part because of the Confucian tradition of family obligations. Large construction and infrastructure policies, rather than welfare programmes, were used to stimulate economic activity when the business cycle turned downwards.

To sum up:

66 Park re-created the cohesive-capitalist state inherited from a colonial past and used it with a vengeance to push industrialization. Renewed contacts with Japan and the availability of Japanese capital and technology proved indispensable for these efforts. Within this framework, Park engineered a growth-oriented alliance of state and capital, recorporatized labor, and used economic nationalism to exhort the entire society into the service of economic advancement. 99

(Kohli 2007: 123)

According to the World Bank, average annual per capita growth in gross national income (GNI) between 1960 and 1995 was around 7.5 per cent (see Table 24.1).

KEY POINTS

- An intensive period of economic development and industrialization between 1961 and 1979 created a powerful business sector, but also solidified business dependence upon the state.

- From the early 1980s onwards, successive administrations tried to shift support towards small and medium-sized businesses, but were stymied by the entrenched power of the *chaebol*, upon which the government became increasingly dependent to deliver national prosperity.

Development Policies

In 1953 the economy was still overwhelmingly agricultural. The first task, land reform, was accomplished relatively easily because larger landowners were tarred with

Table 24.2 Gross domestic savings as a percentage of South Korea's growing GDP

1960	1970	1980	1990	2000	2008
2	16.2	20.8	36.1	33	30.1

Sources: World Bank, *World Development Report* (various years); EconStats

the brush of having collaborated with the Japanese. The second priority was rebuilding the country—a nationalist project, the execution of which created rents for businessmen who supported the government.

The government also strongly encouraged large-scale savings, by imposing punitive taxes on expensive consumer imports, and periodically mobilized the media to urge people to be 'patriotic' in their spending. The results were impressive (see Table 24.2) and the savings were channelled towards government-determined investment priorities.

Initially, the government pursued **import-substitution industrialization** (ISI—see Chapter 4), as much for reasons of national security as for the prevailing orthodoxy of development economics. In 1965, however, the government was forced to change strategy, as the United States reduced its aid to Korea to pay for the Vietnam War. Korea reacted by concentrating more upon exports, with the blessing of the United States and increasing access to world markets. The selective targeting of industries for national development succeeded handsomely; by the early 1970s, the government was sufficiently confident to introduce a policy to develop heavy and chemical industries (HCI). Following a temporary setback from oil price shocks, exports to the United States doubled between 1985 and 1988. Also, Korean corporations were now able to tap international financial markets for investments.

As Korean industry began to catch up with technologically more sophisticated international competitors, it also began to distance itself from government direction. The *chaebol*, now frequently obtaining cheaper funds abroad than from the government, increasingly began to talk of 'economic democracy'—autonomy from state interference.

KEY POINT

- South Korea's adoption of a state-led strategy for development has been outstandingly successful.

The Emergence of Democracy: Stronger Society, Weaker State, but Swelling Corruption

During the 1990s, Korea turned into a functioning multiparty democracy, which withstood the Asian financial crisis of 1997–98 without any attempt by the military to regain control. In elections in 1997, power changed hands from one party to another for the first time, and peacefully, allowing Kim Dae Jung, a veteran oppositionist to the military's rule, to become president.

Political reform can be attributed in part to pressure from the labour movement and students, followed by white-collar workers, in part to increased pressure from the US administration, and in part to a greater willingness of later military leaders to make compromises. Until the late 1980s, it was commonly said of Korea (and other countries in the region) that democracy was an alien, Western concept. Yet the military leaders never abolished the national legislature, and they tried to enhance their legitimacy by organizing their own parties and winning elections—although President Park did declare himself 'president for life' in 1972.

Such was the country's economic development in the 1980s that, in 1988, gross domestic product (GDP) exceeded US$3,000 per capita—the threshold beyond which, for Huntington (1996b: 7–8), military coups scarcely succeed. Even in 1980 the overwhelming majority of the population said that they felt 'middle class' (Choi 1997: 106), although still heavily dependent on state largesse. There was no permanently active **civil society** counterposed to the state—something that only began to appear in the 1990s, as much a consequence of democratization as a cause.

However, the owners of *chaebol* were becoming restive about state control, feeling better equipped than government bureaucrats to determine development strategy. As Moon (1994) puts it, the relationship was becoming increasingly 'unruly'. Yet the main catalysts for change were workers and students. The labour unions saw democracy as essential to asserting their members' interests, after decades of repression. And although students benefited from the massive expansion of the education system made in response to Confucian values and the needs of a more technologically advanced economy, they were less deferential to their elders than previous generations. There were also far more of them. By the late 1980s, there were 1.4 million university students; in 1960, when students brought down Rhee Syngman, there were only 101,000. Repression by the riot police and the army alienated parents, especially middle-class ones. And organized religion became a more potent factor in democratization. Christianity attracted many more believers among the newly urbanized. By the mid-1980s, roughly a quarter of the population had converted to Christianity. Both Protestant and Catholic churches openly challenged the military leaders, and became the chief forum for political protest in the early 1980s.

In 1980, students in Kwangju City took to the streets to show solidarity with striking industrial workers. The riot police reacted with force, leading to at least 240 deaths. The regime survived the crisis, but as the eyes of the world fixed on Korea and its preparations to host the 1988 Olympic Games, a new crisis emerged: in 1987, General Park Chung Hee provoked widespread public anger and street protests by nominating General Roh Tae Woo as the next president. White-collar workers also joined in. President Reagan specifically telephoned President Park to warn against bloodletting. So the authorities embarked upon protracted secret negotiations, at the end of which Roh Tae Woo agreed with the leader of the largest opposition party, Kim Young Sam, to form a new party, with the understanding that Kim would become president after Roh. They called the new merged party the 'Democratic Liberal Party', deliberately echoing the name of the Liberal Democratic Party that had ruled Japan for more than thirty years. They hoped to inaugurate a similar period of conservative ruling-party dominance.

The 1990s saw democratic consolidation. The military withdrew from politics. Kim Young Sam replaced Roh Tae Woo as president and launched an anti-corruption campaign. Military officers were accused of misappropriating public funds, which harmed the image of the armed forces. The two preceding presidents, Chun Doo Hwan and Roh Tae Woo, were sentenced to long prison terms for massive corruption and responsibility for the Kwangju massacre. To break the tradition of over-centralization, Kim introduced elected institutions for local government, which in turn provided opportunities for the parties to extend their activities and to create additional posts to reward party members. But because political habits change slowly, this increase in elected officials also increased the amount of 'consideration' needed to achieve 'favourable' decisions. So while Korea remained a comparatively 'hard' state, democracy made it somewhat softer and more opaque.

In 1995, Kim led Korea into the OECD, which many pro-democracy activists had long advocated as a means by which to strengthen the democratic basis of politics, as well as to entrench a more market-oriented approach to economic management. Nevertheless, Kim's term of office ended in ignominy; the hopes of creating a hegemonic ruling party were dashed and Kim Dae Jung replaced Kim Young Sam. He in turn promised to deepen democracy and root out corruption. He guided Korea's responses to the Asian financial crisis that engulfed the country in 1997–98, but then his term of office ended ignominiously too, with two sons arrested on charges of corruption.

Korean politics was beginning to undergo a generational transformation, as leaders who had dominated the opposition movement for thirty years left the scene. The new president, Roh Moo Hyun, also from Kim Dae Jung's party, was in his 50s and offered electors a fresh start. He appointed other newcomers to national office. But his presidency ended in yet further ignominy amid allegations of corruption, which drove him to commit suicide in 2009.

KEY POINTS

- Economic development reconfigured social forces and gradually constrained military rule. Then a changing external environment acted as a key catalyst in South Korea's transition to democracy.

- Democratic consolidation has yet to witness a marked decrease in high-level corruption.

Conclusion: Travails after Achieving Development

By 2010, South Korea had the fifteenth largest economy in the world. Along with Mexico, it was even touted by Goldman Sachs as one of the four largest and most promising states among the 'next eleven' for further economic success and for foreign investors—that is, as having the potential to join the largest economies in the world (Wilson and Stupnytska 2007). Nevertheless, there was a widespread underlying sense of political malaise. In the World Values Survey carried out at the end of the 1990s, admittedly in the aftermath of the Asian financial crisis, only 17 per cent of ROK respondents said that they were 'very proud' to be Korean. Only 27 per cent believed that 'most people can be trusted' (although the world average was only 28 per cent) (Inglehart et al. 2004: Tables G006, A165). According to Lee (2011: 402), despite the ethnic homogeneity, 'Korea suffers from endless conflict and chaos, and Korean society is fractured by small, competing, and unyielding special interest groups'. Despite the **Gini coefficient** of household incomes of 0.31 in 2010, which made the ROK twenty-ninth in the world and more equal than most European states, Koreans still widely complained about inequality. Despite all of the development that has taken place, the average Korean worker still works the largest number of hours per year of any country in the OECD—that is, more than was worked by workers in Britain, the United States, and Japan in 1970 (Ferdinand 2012: 152). Its politics are still dominated by men. Standards of living have still not caught up with those of the developed West. And in years to come these problems are likely to be exacerbated by generational conflicts of interest, as Korean society ages rapidly.

To a significant extent, this fretfulness reflects the ambivalence that many Koreans still feel about the place of the *chaebol* and their family owners in Korean society, especially their cosy relationship with the state, and it is a lingering legacy of the Park Chung Hee era. It was a source of pride that China took the *chaebol* as a template for reform of its state-owned enterprises at the end of the 1990s. However, the widespread Korean perceptions of interlocking corruption in these companies and the state has fuelled popular cynicism (Kang 2002), even though in Transparency International's 2012 Corruption Perception Index (CPI), the ROK was ranked only forty-fifth out of ninety

(Transparency International 2012). Most of all, it suggests that the state is either not strong enough, or not willing enough, or both, to deal with it. Kang (2002) graphically expresses the relationship between political and business elites as one of 'mutual hostages': each is dependent on the other. Ever since the 1980s, the Korean government has declared an intention to bring about a rebalancing of the economy by reducing the weight of the *chaebol*, and increasing that of small and medium-sized enterprises (SMEs), yet it never happens. After the Asian financial crisis, Koreans accepted the severe austerity imposed by the liberal Kim Dae Jung administration in part because it promised to do something about the *chaebol*. Yet the ensuing corruption scandals persuaded the electorate that little had changed, and it led to the electoral victory in 2007 of Lee Myung Bak from the conservative Grand National Party in part because he was a former chief executive officer of a *chaebol*. People hoped that he would run the country and the economy more successfully, because he would be able to get government and business to cooperate. Yet, at the end of his term, he had an even lower approval rating than his predecessors. And then, in 2012, as much out of nostalgia for the dynamism of the Park Chung Hee era as out of belief in her platform of policies, they elected Park's daughter, Park Geun-hye, as president from the same party (now called the Saenuri Party), with the highest proportion of votes of any candidate since democracy was introduced in 1987.

Lastly, for all of its successes, the ROK has not grown into a self-confident rising power in the world like the BRICS (that is, Brazil, Russia, India, China, and South Africa). Partly, this reflects its regional perspective, in that it has traditionally seen itself as a 'prawn among whales' (that is, China, Russia, and Japan) in northeast Asia; partly, it reflects anxiety over China's recent rapid rise and its very touchy relations with Japan. It reflects fear of the unpredictable, and now nuclear-capable, North Korea just across the border and also the sobering experience of the Asian financial crisis, a bitter reminder of the difficulty for even a 'strong' state like Korea's of insulating its economy. It is still fundamentally dependent on the United States to defend it in case of invasion, yet its leaders have always harboured doubts about the unconditional willingness of the United States to come to its aid. So although the ROK is now a member of the OECD and has even signed a landmark free-trade agreement with the United States, it is less a global 'player' than, say, Mexico.

? QUESTIONS

1. What were the main features of Korea's developmental state?

2. In what ways was the state strong and society weak?

3. How far has this changed?

4. How far has Korea abandoned the developmental state, and why?

5. Which was more important in the transition to democracy in Korea, long-term socio-economic change or short-term political crisis?

6. Why is it so difficult to stamp out corruption in politics in Korea?

🌐 FURTHER READING

Amsden, A. H. (1989) *Asia's Next Giant: South Korea and Late Industrialization* (Oxford: Oxford University Press) Examines how and why Korea got prices 'wrong', and yet achieved dramatic economic growth.

Eckert, C. J. (1990) 'The South Korean Bourgeoisie: A Class in Search of Hegemony', *Journal of Korean Studies*, 7: 115–48 Outlines the rise of the families owning *chaebol*.

Evans, P. (1995) *Embedded Autonomy: States and Industrial Transformation* (Princeton, NJ: Princeton University Press) Focuses on a key element of the developmental state.

Henderson, G. (1968) *Korea: The Politics of the Vortex* (Cambridge, MA: Harvard University Press) A very influential early attempt to theorize politics in Korea.

Janelli, R. L. (1993) *Making Capitalism* (Stanford, CA: Stanford University Press) The internal life of a Korean *chaebol* based on extended fieldwork.

Jones, L. P., and Sakong, I. (1980) *Government, Business and Entrepreneurship in Economic Development: The Korean Case* (Cambridge, MA: Harvard University Press) A revealing early account of the key role of government in Korean development.

Kim, E. M. (1997) *Big Business, Strong State: Collusion and Conflict in South Korean Development, 1960–1990* (Albany, NY: State University of New York Press) An excellent analysis of this key relationship during Korea's high-growth period.

Pirie, I. (2005) 'Better by Design: Korea's Neoliberal Economy', *Pacific Review*, 18(3): 355–74 A good and provocative summary of the changes in Korean political economy after the Asian financial crisis.

Shin, D. C. (1999) *Mass Politics and Culture in Democratizing Korea* (Cambridge: Cambridge University Press) The best single account of the emergence of Korea's democracy.

Shin, D. C. and Park, C.-M. (2008) 'The Mass Public and Democratic Politics in South Korea', Y. Chu, L. Diamond, and A. J. Nathan (eds) *How East Asians View Democracy* (New York: Columbia University Press), 39–60 Updates the previous work.

Woo-Cumings, M. (ed.) (1999) *The Developmental State* (Ithaca, NY: Cornell University Press) Outlines the basic principles and their realization in various countries around the world.

〰 WEB LINKS

http://english.yonhapnews.co.kr/   The main news service in Korea.

http://englishdp.tistory.com/   The liberal-left opposition party, the Democratic Party.

http://international.ohmynews.com/   The English-language version of a citizen journalist website.

http://www.acrc.go.kr/eng_index.html   Anti-Corruption and Civil Rights Commission

http://www.kdi.re.kr   Korean Development Institute.

http://www.korea.net   The South Korean government's official homepage.

http://www.koreaherald.com/   The *Korea Herald* (Seoul).

http://www.nec.go.kr/engvote/main/main.jsp   National Electoral Commission.

http://www.saenuriparty.kr/web/eng/index.do   The main conservative party, Saenuri.

 For additional material and resources, please visit the Online Resource Centre at:
http://www.oxfordtextbooks.co.uk/orc/burnell4e/

PART 7
Development and Human Rights

This part highlights the relationship between development and **human rights** in two different empirical contexts—namely, Nigeria and Guatemala. As earlier chapters have shown (Chapter 16 on development and Chapter 18 on human rights), there is a somewhat ambiguous relationship between these two concepts. A strong argument has been made that development is more feasible in strong states where human rights are limited. Some have made the claim that economic development is more likely in states that limit human rights, especially related to civil and political rights. Human rights should become an integral part of **governance** later on in the development process, because it is simply too expensive for poor countries to implement the necessary reforms. However, as Chapter 18 further illustrates, the main empirical basis for such claims has come from a few well-discussed cases in South-East Asia, such as South Korea and China. There is no conclusive evidence that violations of human rights in any case will *lead* to development, but, as the previous examples show, there is no clear-cut positive relationship between human rights and development either.

However, in many cases, the two concepts are also overlapping. Development is increasingly defined more broadly than solely economic development. When **human development** is discussed, it is clear that human rights play an integral part. Additionally, human rights are not exclusively related to civil and political rights. By including aspects related to economic and social rights, it becomes apparent that the two concepts are closely linked.

With regard to the relationship between development and human rights, Nigeria presents an interesting puzzle. Nigeria is a very oil-rich country, but has not been able to translate its immense natural resources into sustainable economic development and respect for human rights. As a result, Nigeria is an example of 'resource curse' in that tremendous riches have resulted in an undiversified economy served by a corrupt elite (as discussed in Chapter 15 on governance). Ethnic and religious tensions, a result of colonialism, have been exacerbated by disastrous economic development, which has in turn led to a deteriorating human rights situation and intense violence. Although **civil society** remains strong, the country is mired by bad governance, low development, and a worsening security context.

In Guatemala, human rights abuse and **underdevelopment** seem to go hand in hand. The civil war that tormented the country for several decades left several hundred thousand dead. The peace treaty achieved in 1996 was by many seen as a welcome respite and hopes were high. However, as the chapter shows, the security situation leaves much to be desired, and the country exhibits one of the world's highest murder rates and a high degree of underdevelopment. Because the state has failed to prevent, and has often even encouraged, human rights abuses, the system of formal democracy is not well regarded by Guatemala's citizens. Civil society has remained weak and unable to check the gross human rights violations. Development, both economic and otherwise, has been hampered by the security situation.

25

Nigeria: Human Rights, Development, and Democracy

Stephen Wright

Overview

Nigerian governments have struggled to promote human rights in the face of significant ethnic, regional, and religious divisions, and have not produced the level of economic development commensurate with the country's vast earnings from natural resources. Military governments ruled the country for a total of almost thirty years, curtailing many political and civil rights, but there is hope that the successive civilian governments of President Olusegun Obasanjo (1999–2007), President Umaru Yar'Adua (2007–2010), and President Goodluck Jonathan (2010—) have consolidated democracy, even though significant societal and human rights problems remain. Despite these problems, Nigeria continues to promote a forceful external presence in the continent, shaped by its demographic size as Africa's largest country, as well as by its significant petroleum and natural gas exports. Figure 25.1 is a map of Nigeria and Box 25.1 provides an overview of key dates in Nigeria's history.

Introduction

The West African state of Nigeria has suffered, since its independence from Britain in 1960, with chronic political instability, resulting in the longest period of unbroken civilian rule being the most recent, since 1999. Prior to colonial rule, the territory that was to become Nigeria consisted of numerous empires, but British colonists gradually absorbed these into three administrative regions.

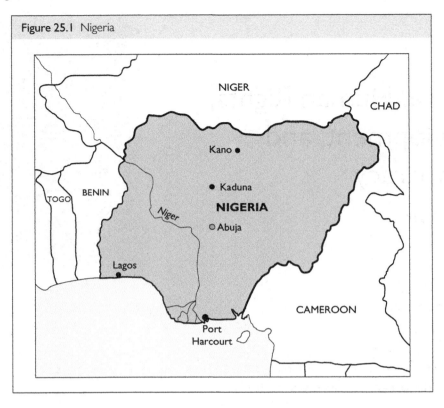

Figure 25.1 Nigeria

BOX 25.1 KEY DATES IN NIGERIA'S HISTORY

1914   Britain pulls together various territories into the colony of Nigeria

1960   Independence from Britain

1966   Two military coups end the first civilian republic

1967   The start of the three-year civil war over Biafran secession

1976   Murtala Muhammed assassinated; Olusegun Obasanjo takes over as military head of state, supervising a transition to civilian rule

1979   Second civilian republic inaugurated, under President Shehu Shagari

1983   Military coup on New Year's Eve ushers in sixteen years of military rule

1985   Ibrahim Babangida takes over in palace coup; postpones multiple attempts to return to civilian government

1993   Moshood Abiola wins the presidency, but elections annulled by Babangida; later that year, Sani Abacha seizes power in a coup

1999   Following the death of Abacha in 1998, a new transition is undertaken that elects Obasanjo to the presidency and a new civilian republic begins

2007   Umaru Yar'Adua elected president in a disputed election; the first successful civilian transfer of power

2010   Following Yar'Adua's death, Vice-President Goodluck Jonathan is appointed president and wins the subsequent elections in April 2011

In turn, these regions were amalgamated into the colony of Nigeria in 1914, although each maintained a strong degree of identity and separation. Tensions between the three regions deepened in the 1950s, as ethnicity became a political vehicle in the jostling for power in a post-independent Nigeria. This struggle to manage ethnic tensions has been a constant feature, and has significantly contributed to the country's instability and **human rights** difficulties.

Instability

The British installed a parliamentary democracy in Nigeria prior to their departure in 1960, but this imported system could not function effectively in the highly combative political environment. The first of many military *coups d'état* took place in January 1966, sweeping the civilians from office. A second coup later in the year slid the country towards a brutal civil war between 1967 and 1970, during which as many as 3 million civilians died. Despite efforts to ease ethnic and religious tensions—notably by breaking up the three powerful administrative regions into smaller units, eventually ending up with thirty-six internal states—instability remained. The civilian government installed in 1979 barely lasted four years before the military swept back and a despotic era of military rule emerged with severe abuses of human rights. This period ended in 1999, when the civilian government of President Olusegun Obasanjo (himself a former military head of state) was elected to office. His re-election in 2003 was considered a hopeful sign of a maturing democratic system, although the election of President Umaru Yar'Adua in 2007, which was widely perceived to have been manipulated, cast a shadow over such progress. Obasanjo had attempted to change the Constitution in 2006 to allow him to contest a third term in office, but was defeated by the Senate in a victory for political rights. He then went on to muscle Yar'Adua into office in arguably the most corrupt election in Nigeria's history. Yar'Adua's three years in office were undermined by ill health and, in the last three months, he was absent from the country in hospital in Saudi Arabia, but refused to cede power to his vice president, Goodluck Jonathan. Such chicanery, shaped largely by elite and ethnic concerns, made a mockery of the Constitution, but a semblance of stability resumed after Yar'Adua's death. All of this is indicative of the challenge of building democracy and human rights in a severely fractured state.

Regional influence

Nigeria's prominence in the West African region stems largely from two key factors: population and petroleum. Ethnicity politicizes the census process and makes an accurate headcount problematic, but the population is estimated to be around 160 million, a little under a sixth of the continent's total population, and places the country as the world's eighth largest. By 2025, it is predicted to be the world's fifth largest. Geological good fortune enabled Nigeria to be a prominent producer and exporter of oil and gas, making Nigeria's the largest economy in the region (equal to the other West African states combined), and one of the largest in Africa. Currently, Nigeria stands as the world's eleventh largest producer of oil and the sixth largest in the Organization of Petroleum Exporting Countries (OPEC), with 4 per cent of the world's proven reserves.

Nigeria has been the leading member of the Economic Community of West African States (ECOWAS) since its founding in 1975. All of Nigeria's neighbours are former French colonies, and ECOWAS is perceived in Nigeria as an attempt to check French influence in the region. During its almost forty years, ECOWAS has attempted to improve trade and movement of people within the region. Official trade figures remain low, around 10 per cent of total trade, whereas unofficial (illegal) trade has flourished, with the porosity of the Nigerian borders being an important contributory factor. The control of trade policy and routes provides a major avenue for **corruption** by elites.

Nigeria has taken up leadership causes on behalf of the continent as a whole. During the 1960s and 1970s, these focused upon non-alignment, African independence, liberation in southern Africa, and economic rights. After 1980, as economic problems weakened Nigerian leverage, the country's global impact was less certain. During the 1990s, Nigeria's position as Africa's proclaimed 'champion' was further undermined by the rise of South Africa, which was a stronger economic power and which, in Nelson Mandela, had a leader who far surpassed in stature Nigeria's despotic military leaders. Nigeria's isolation peaked during the mid-1990s, when minor sanctions were imposed by the West and Nigeria was suspended from the Commonwealth. Nigeria's failure to democratize until 1999 also served to undermine its **legitimacy** to lead.

The new civilian era opened up by the election of Obasanjo helped to restore some credibility, and also to repair frayed relations with the United States, the European Union, and the international financial institutions. Investment in the oil and gas sectors increased considerably, although they had not been affected much during the 1990s. Nigeria played an important role in helping to establish the New Economic Partnership for Africa's Development (NEPAD) in 2001, a major development initiative for the continent in partnership with the United Nations and industrialized countries. Nigeria also benefited from the United States' strategy to lessen its dependence upon Middle Eastern oil, and today some 40 per cent of Nigeria's oil exports go to the United States.

KEY POINTS

- British colonization created a 'new' country of Nigeria, the people of which had lived separately prior to colonial rule, but where ethnic differences were accentuated.
- Nigeria's population is the largest in Africa.
- Nigeria has significant influence in West Africa and tries to shape African political initiatives.

The Political Economy of Oil

Transformation of the economy

At independence, agriculture dominated the economy. The British had created export production of single crops for each region—groundnuts in the north, palm oil in the south-east, and cocoa in the south-west. Oil production, focused in south-eastern Nigeria, began in earnest in the 1960s and proved to be a contributing factor in the country's civil war. Once peace was attained, oil production accelerated rapidly, contributing to an economic boom in the 1970s, helped significantly by soaring prices after 1973. Agriculture quickly lost its prominence as oil revenues contributed more than 90 per cent of export revenues, a figure that has remained fairly constant ever since. Massive development schemes were started, including dams, roads, airports, universities, and hospitals, but some of these projects were of more political significance than economic benefit to the country.

The combination of oil wealth and a large consumer population led to considerable foreign investment and tighter inclusion in the global political economy. By the end of the 1970s, Nigeria utilized its growing diplomatic and economic **status** to pursue important foreign policy initiatives, notably working for the 'liberation' of Zimbabwe and South Africa, and attempting to represent the views of developing countries in their call for a transformed and more egalitarian global political economy. Its true economic clout, however, was somewhat of an illusion, as subsequent events showed.

Elusive development

The hopes and ambitions of the 1970s were undermined after 1980 by a series of events. The most important of these was the glut of oil in world markets, which contributed to the collapse of Nigerian revenues. An economy distorted by the oil bonanza was now undermined by the rapid bust of the market. Development projects quickly became expensive white elephants and import dependence racked up large national debt. Oil revenues had not only been squandered, but were siphoned off to corrupt civilian and military elites, taking billions of dollars out of the development process. Oil sucked investment from other areas of the economy, as Nigeria became a textbook example of the 'resource curse'. The governments of the 1980s, civilian and military, were forced to relinquish their outspoken role in world **politics**, and to take up the very different challenge of seeking structural adjustment funding and debt support from the World Bank and International Monetary Fund (IMF). These adjustments, particularly affecting health care and education, created a harsh impact on large swathes of the Nigerian population, undermining social and economic rights.

The 1990s was arguably the most difficult decade in Nigeria's political and economic development. Continuing low oil revenues served to debilitate social and **human development**. Infrastructure and transport crumbled, despite efforts at **privatization** and liberalization of critical sectors following World Bank and IMF orthodoxy. External debt rose to a level of US$34 billion, then the largest in Africa. Compounding the problem was the country's military leader between 1993 and 1998, General Sani Abacha, whose brutal rule and suppression led to Nigeria's ostracism from many international bodies for heinous human rights abuses.

The election of Obasanjo in 1999 helped to stabilize the economic environment. His initial attempt to crack down on corruption brought some limited success. Obasanjo was able to pay down the country's debt considerably, and facilitated large investment inflows into the oil and gas sectors. His willingness to concede to the demands of Western countries and corporations brought a respite within the global arena, but did little to promote economic justice or development to the majority inside Nigeria. The policies of his successors have also done little to transform the economy. In 2012, according to the United Nations, Nigeria ranked 156 out of 187 countries in terms of its human development, with average life expectancy just 52 years.

Current political economy challenges

Many challenges remain to promote a more balanced, stable, and equitable political economy. These include massive economic inequalities, alongside huge unemployment, poor levels of human development, and a rampant abuse of economic rights. Diversification away from a dependence upon oil and multinational corporations has not occurred, and is unlikely in the foreseeable future. This reality weakens genuine efforts to seek true economic development and the promotion of economic rights. The thorny problem of revenue allocation within Nigeria still pits local communities against the federal government, most notably in the oil-producing areas of the delta region, where an insurgency has been led by the Movement for the Emancipation of the Delta (MEND), the members of which feel cheated out of a greater share of resources. The government's response (allegedly in collusion with some of the oil corporations) has tended to be very violent, undermining **human security** and disrespecting rights, even though a truce declared in October 2009 with MEND, followed by the Yar'Adua and Jonathan (who is from the region) administrations, has helped to curb some of those excesses.

Corruption continues to undermine genuine economic development and a fairer economic system. The World Bank estimated in 2012 that Nigeria had lost some US$400 billion in oil revenues to corruption over the previous four decades. Lucrative contracts remain in the hands of patrimonial elites. Transparency International ranks Nigeria 139 out of 176 countries in its 2012 Corruption Perceptions Index (CPI). The gross domestic product (GDP) per capita stands at only US$1,280. The more democracy is pursued, the more entrenched and resistant the forces of corruption appear to be.

KEY POINTS

- The mainstay of the Nigerian economy is oil, accounting for about 90 per cent of export revenue.

- Nigeria is tightly linked into the global political economy and this relationship has significant implications for economic policy inside the country.

- The 2000s witnessed a slight upturn in macro-economic conditions, partly helped by the presence of civilian government, although still with ethnic divisions and economic inequalities.

Social Change, Democracy, and Human Rights

Social and religious fabric

Nigeria is made up of a complex mosaic of ethnic, regional, and religious identities, all of which have served at some time or other to undermine the country's stability. British colonialism forged together a country of disparate people, and also helped to create a heightened sense of **ethnic identity** and competition. The three regions—north, west, and east—of colonial Nigeria contained a single dominant ethnic group in each—Hausa, Yoruba, and Igbo, respectively—who increasingly viewed politics as a battle for resources between the ethnic groups, and as a struggle to undermine the political and economic rights of their opponents. The fledgling federal state at independence could not contain this animosity, and the early experiment in democracy was brought to an abrupt halt with the 1966 military coup. Tensions between these three powerful ethnic groups form only a part of the story. Minority ethnic groups, particularly from the centre of the country and the country's oil belt, have increasingly become a major factor in politics. Superimposed upon this ethnic tension is religion. A rough division sees the country divided into a Muslim north and a Christian south, although the reality is much more complex. Religious differences have become increasingly politicized, and the establishment of Sharia (or Islamic) law in twelve northern states exacerbates an already tense situation and appears to threaten religious freedom and civil rights for Christians in those states. Such religious tensions are also exacerbated by severe economic deprivation, poverty, and disaffection across the country. Religious riots, normally led by unemployed and alienated youth, killing hundreds at a time, are now commonplace. These provide a problem that no Nigerian government has been able to solve and has often led to repressive retaliation by security forces.

The most recent manifestation of these problems is the emergence of the radical Islamic group, Boko Haram (meaning 'Western education is bad/sacriligous'), in the north (see also Chapter 8). Drawing strength from radicalized and unemployed youth, this organization has resorted to terror tactics, with bombings and assassinations in government offices, international agencies (such as the UN compound in Abuja), Christian churches, and other random attacks. In February 2013, for example, the organization killed nine aid workers innoculating children against polio. The overall death toll since 2008 from its actions is estimated at 3,000. Boko Haram's actions have certainly threatened human security within Nigeria, and undermined political and civil rights. Actions by security forces, however, have not necessarily respected human rights either, and these actions continue to undermine broad civil and political rights. Although this is often viewed as a religious issue, a strong case can be made to explain this in terms of the failure to provide economic rights and development across broad areas of northern Nigeria, and also as an indictment of government corruption and the country's weak position within the global political economy.

Political institutions and parties

Since 1960, Nigeria has had just less than thirty years of military government, four different constitutions and republics, both parliamentary and presidential forms of government, at least eight governments overthrown by the military, and numerous different sets of political parties. The internal federal structure has evolved from three regions to thirty-six states in an effort to undermine the strength of regional and ethnic politics (and to offer more politicians the opportunity to extract wealth). In this environment of experimentation and instability, it is little surprise that democratic **institutions** and structures of government have found it difficult to establish themselves. It is fair to say that Nigeria's political elites, both civilian and military, have not provided a stable polity and predictable political and civil rights.

At independence, Nigeria was bestowed the **Westminster model** of government. This failed to contain the conflicts between government and 'opposition', which were exacerbated by the struggle between the fledgling federal government and established ethnically driven regional governments. With hindsight, this system perhaps operated effectively for only two or three years, but it lingered until the 1966 military coup. Military governments ruled for all but four years between 1966 and 1999, and ranged considerably in capability and probity. Political parties were proscribed during much of military rule, undermining political rights and freedoms, and little progress was made in solving the social, ethnic, and religious problems facing the country. The civilian Second Republic (1979–83) was, like the first, dominated by northern power groups, and fizzled out in extreme corruption, ethnic bias, and electoral fraud before being swept from office on New Year's Eve 1983. This republic was very much fashioned upon the American presidential model, with an executive president, a Senate, and a House of Representatives, and was adopted for the Fourth Republic in 1999.

The 1990s proved to be the darkest period of political development, as the federal government became the personal plaything of one leader, Sani Abacha. In elections for the Third Republic in 1993, results pointed to a win by Chief Moshood Abiola, a Yoruba Muslim businessman. Alarmed at the possible consequences to their interests, the military government under Ibrahim Babangida annulled the elections, and transferred power to a military and civilian coalition that lasted a few months before being overthrown by Abacha. When Abiola returned from exile in 1994, he was detained by Abacha, and eventually died in prison (his wife was assassinated). Plans for a return to civilian government were repeatedly postponed, as civilian political leaders were hand-picked and dropped by Abacha. By 1998, Abacha had manipulated the political process to the extent that he was the sole presidential candidate of all five parties allowed by his **regime**. This was arguably the pinnacle of state repression and human rights abuses in the country's political history. Upon Abacha's surprise death, yet another transition was started, and a new slate of political parties created. The success of Obasanjo, a former military head of state who had been imprisoned for three years by Abacha, indicates the residual power of military leaders in the political process. In 2003, the presidential election was contested by two former military heads of state, Obasanjo and Muhammadu Buhari.

The April 2007 presidential election provided the first-ever transfer of power from one civilian government to another—a stunning statement about the frailty of political and civil rights in the country. Tensions within the ruling People's Democratic Party (PDP) were rife during Obasanjo's second term, with the president and vice president Atiku Abubakar trading barbs and, by 2006, each calling for the other's resignation. Abubakar accepted the presidential nomination from the opposition Action Congress in December 2006, sparking further conflict. The PDP selected a relatively unknown governor from the northern state of Katsina, Umaru Yar'Adua, to be its presidential candidate, probably because Obasanjo hoped to maintain his influence over party and country. The 2007 elections were marred by widespread fraud and violence, as Yar'Adua was guided into office. He largely continued Obasanjo's policies, although in a more subdued, low-profile manner, primarily because of his poor health. The uncertainty regarding the constitutional transition of power from Yar'Adua to Jonathan underlines the fragility of the system. The 2011 elections, although more peaceful than those of 2007, again polarized the country on north–south lines.

Civil society

Despite long periods of oppressive rule and human rights violations, **civil society** groups have remained active and strong promoting civil rights. The media have been outspoken during even the darkest times, and help to maintain a healthy dialogue about national and local policies. The universities have also played a strong role in voicing opinions about governments and policies, and student and faculty protests and strikes are common. Similarly, trade unions are relatively well organized and not afraid to take action when their interests are threatened, and judges strive to maintain their independence. During the Abacha administration, repression of these groups was at its maximum, with many jailed without trial, but large numbers fought back against the regime, often from exile. Human rights and democracy organizations flourished, and worked with external groups to maintain pressure upon the regime. Unfortunately, these groups were sometimes divided upon ethnic lines, but nevertheless indicated the strength and vitality of civilian society, resisting blatant oppression. Prominent Nigerian writers such as Chinua Achebe, Ken Saro-Wiwa, and Wole Soyinka were also important in maintaining pressure upon the corrupt

regimes. With such a vibrant civil society, one perhaps might expect significant advances in the political arena in terms of **good governance** and accountability. Unfortunately, to date, this has not fully transpired.

Women's groups are also well represented in civil society, although their focus is often shaped along regional and ethnic lines. For example, the Federation of Muslim Women's Associations in Nigeria (FOMWAN) focuses upon education and health within an Islamic framework. Nationally, women's groups argue that they are worse off than in pre-colonial times, because their economic and political rights have been usurped by men. Few women reach the highest rungs of politics, especially in the north of the country. A UN report in December 2009 stated that only 10 per cent of women are tested for HIV, and that 90 per cent of pregnant women with HIV are not accessing treatment. Much work still needs to be done to improve the status of women, even though they do play significant roles within the formal and informal economies.

KEY POINTS

- Significant political experimentation with institutions and structures of government has occurred, but with only modest success in containing societal strains.

- Civil society groups have maintained a consistently strong role in promoting human rights in Nigerian political life.

- The re-election of Obasanjo in 2003, and the election of Yar'Adua in 2007 and Jonathan in 2011, give hope to the idea that the cycle of military rule has been broken.

Conclusion: Human Rights and Development

Probably the best way in which to describe Nigeria is as a country of unfulfilled promise. Despite its demographic size and economic potential, the country has been dogged by numerous political, social, economic, and human rights problems. Development in the Nigerian context does appear to be linked to the need for improving political and human rights. Successive democratic elections after 1999 provide optimism that the country has finally turned away from military government and may be moving closer to pursuing better development targets. Large inflows of foreign investment into the oil and gas sectors indicate economic strength, even though significant economic inequalities remain and the country still holds a position of vulnerability within the global political economy.

Corruption, however, remains endemic and fraud is an important element found in all elections. Ethnic and religious intolerance and violence remain problematic and undermine human security, with sucessive governments showing only small gains and often resorting to violence against these groups. Violent unrest in the critical oilfields spells problems unless this can be resolved. Human development indicators remain relatively poor. Democracy's quality is flawed and its future not yet secure.

Many of these problems are not new, and Nigeria has weathered them quite effectively to date. But there has been scant progress over five decades in solving these endemic rights issues. Significant problems exist in consolidating civil, political, economic, and religious rights, with human security also under threat. Nigeria is often seen as a bellwether for other African countries, and so how it develops is of vital importance to the West African region, if not to the continent as a whole.

? QUESTIONS

1. Was the breakdown of the new Nigerian state in the early 1960s almost inevitable? Why?

2. Is national cohesion essential for development in Nigeria?

3. To what extent has oil benefited or detracted from development in Nigeria? Is there a 'resource curse'?

4. How effective are civil society groups in promoting democracy and human rights in Nigeria?

5. Does the transition of power from one civilian government to another confirm that democracy is entrenched in Nigeria today?

≋ FURTHER READING

Balogun, M. (2009) *The Route to Power in Nigeria* (New York: Palgrave Macmillan) An empirical analysis of failed leadership in Nigeria.

Campbell, J. (2011) *Nigeria: Dancing on the Brink* (Lanham, MD: Rowman and Littlefield/Council on Foreign Relations) An assessment of contemporary Nigeria through the eyes of a recent US ambassador to the country.

Cunliffe-Jones, P. (2010) *My Nigeria: Five Decades of Independence* (New York: Palgrave Macmillan) A journalist's account of Nigeria.

Falola, T. and Heaton, M. (2008) *A History of Nigeria* (Cambridge: Cambridge University Press) An overview of the historical development of Nigeria, and the legacies of history faced today.

Iliffe, J. (2011) *Obasanjo, Nigeria and the World* (Woodbridge: James Currey) A focus on Olusegun Obasanjo's role in Nigeria's political life since the 1960s.

Maier, K. (2000) *This House Has Fallen: Midnight in Nigeria* (New York: Public Affairs) A more informal account of the political and social demise of Nigeria during the 1990s.

Okonta, I. and Oronto, D. (2003) *Where Vultures Feast: Shell, Human Rights, and Oil* (London: Verso) An account of oil issues in the Nigerian delta.

Smith, D. J. (2007) *A Culture of Corruption: Everyday Deception and Popular Discontent in Nigeria* (Princeton, NJ: Princeton University Press) An examination of the methods and impact of corruption in Nigeria.

Soyinka, W. (1996) *The Open Sore of a Continent: A Personal Narrative of the Nigerian Crisis* (New York: Oxford University Press) The Nobel laureate's bitter account of the failings of the Abacha regime.

Wright, S. (1998) *Nigeria: Struggle for Stability and Status* (Boulder, CO: Westview Press) An analysis of Nigeria since independence, focusing upon domestic instability and efforts to promote a strong external policy.

WEB LINKS

http://www.onlinenewspapers.com/nigeria.htm   Offering access to numerous news sources.

http://www.newswatchngr.com   *Newswatch* magazine.

http://www.ngrguardiannews.com   *The Guardian* (Lagos) newspaper.

http://www.vanguardngr.com   *Vanguard* news media.

For additional material and resources, see the Online Resource Centre at:
http://www.oxfordtextbooks.co.uk/orc/burnell4e/

26

Guatemala: Enduring Underdevelopment

Rachel Sieder

Overview

This chapter examines Guatemala as a persistent case of underdevelopment, defining development in terms of social, economic, cultural, and political rights. It argues that the roots of Guatemala's underdevelopment lie in its domination by external powers, and historical patterns of state formation and economic accumulation premised on acute social and cultural inequality, violence, and impunity. The 1996 peace agreement represented an attempt to reverse historical trends, to 'engineer development', and to secure the human rights of all Guatemalans. Some key development indicators have improved since the 1990s, but basic human rights, security, and development continue to be denied to most Guatemalans. The final section signals the main contemporary causes of the country's persistent underdevelopment: a patrimonialist and predatory state underpinned by a strong, conservative private sector, a weak party system, the continued influence of the armed forces and counterinsurgency logics, and the entrenched presence of transnational organized crime. Figure 26.1 is a map of Guatemala and Box 26.1 provides an overview of key dates in Guatemala's history.

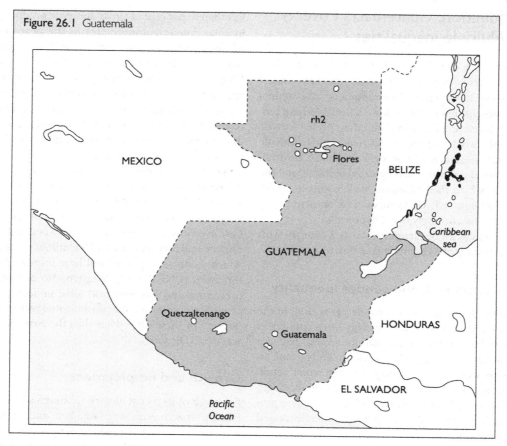

Figure 26.1   Guatemala

1944	Forced labour abolished; universal male suffrage introduced
1952	Agrarian reform law approved
1954	Democratically elected government of Jacobo Arbenz overthrown in coup backed by US Central Intelligence Agency (CIA)
1960	First guerrilla insurgency
1978–83	Height of counter-insurgency war; 100,000 civilians killed or disappeared 1981–83
1984–85	Military oversee guided transition to elected, civilian government
1990	Oslo Accord between government and Unidad Revolucionaria Nacional Guatemalteca (URNG) establishes framework for national peace negotiations
1994–96	United Nations mediates peace process; agreements reached on human rights, indigenous rights and identity, resettlement of displaced populations, clarification of human rights violations, agricultural modernization, and reform of the military and the state
1996	Final peace settlement signed
1999	United Nations Truth Commission finds Guatemalan state guilty of acts of genocide during armed conflict; recommends prosecutions
1999	Frente Repúblicano Guatemalteco (FRG), led by former dictator Ríos Montt, wins presidential elections
2007	Social democrat candidate Álvaro Colóm wins presidential elections
2011	Former military intelligence chief Otto Pérez Molina wins presidential elections

Introduction: Guatemala's Poverty and Multiple Inequalities

The influence of rights-based approaches to development (see also Chapter 18) in recent years has ensured that our understanding of 'development' and '**underdevelopment**' has become more holistic. Where previously development was measured simply in terms of economic variables, today assessments tend to include composite measures of the socio-economic, cultural, and political rights enjoyed by its inhabitants, and the extent to which their inclusion, well-being, and security are guaranteed. Thinking on development policy has evolved accordingly (see Chapter 16).

Guatemala can be characterized as a country with persistent underdevelopment (see Box 26.2).

Ethnic, regional, and gender inequality

Economic differences between different regions of the country and between ethnic groups—in a country in which indigenous people constitute around half the population—are huge. The predominantly rural indigenous areas of the country have the worst conditions of poverty, health, education, and land shortages (see Box 26.3). Government spending on welfare provision is lower in rural areas, although it has increased in recent years.

Guatemala is classified as a middle-income country, but has a long history of low social spending. This is partly accounted for by historically low rates of tax collection: Guatemala's tax coefficient remained at less than 10 per cent of gross domestic product (GDP) in 2012, despite commitments in the peace accords of 1996 to increase it to 12 per cent by 2002. (For the significance of taxation for good government, see Chapter 15.) Public spending on education, health, and infrastructure improved somewhat after the mid-1990s, but remains very low by regional standards (CESR-ICEFI 2009). The legacy of **gender** and ethnic discrimination is evident in literacy statistics: although literacy rates for women improved between 1989 (when 67.5 per cent of women were literate) and 2006 (when 84.8 per cent of women were in this category), women still lag behind men (91.4 per cent of whom are literate), and indigenous women in the rural areas have even lower literacy rates (at 68.9 per cent). However, overall literacy rates and the number of years for which students stay in school have improved during the 2000s (UNDP 2008). Women also occupy more precarious and less well-paid jobs: in 2006, 75.7 per cent of women worked in the informal sector and 53.4 per cent of these earned less than the basic minimum wage (UNDP 2008).

Growth and employment

For much of its recent history, Guatemala has enjoyed relative macro-economic stability and reasonable growth—an annual average of 2.7 per cent between 1986 and 2007. Growth reached 5.7 per cent in 2007, but declined subsequently as a result of the global economic crisis. Nonetheless, with one of the highest population growth rates in the region (around

---

BOX 26.2 KEY DEVELOPMENT INDICATORS FOR GUATEMALA

UN Human Development Index	0.574 (131 out of 187 countries)*
UN Human Poverty Index (HPI-1)	19.7% (76 out of 135 countries)
Gini index	55.1
Share of national income of top quintile of population	60.3%
Share of income of bottom quintile of population	2.9%
Percentage of population in poverty	50.9%
Percentage of population in extreme poverty	15.2%
Numbers of people living in poverty	6.6 million (of total population of 13 million)

Sources: UNDP (2008, 2010); * http://hdrstats.undp.org/en/countries/profiles/GTM.html

BOX 26.3 KEY INEQUALITY INDICATORS FOR GUATEMALA

Percentage of overall population in poverty	50.9%
Percentage of indigenous population in poverty	73%
Percentage of non-indigenous population in poverty	35%
Percentage of indigenous population in extreme poverty	26.4%
Percentage of non-indigenous population in extreme poverty	7.3%
Percentage of rural population in poverty	74.5%
Percentage of urban population in poverty	27%
Percentage of rural population in extreme poverty	24.4%
Percentage of urban population in extreme poverty	5%

Source: UNDP (2008)

2.6 per cent per annum), income per capita growth rates were significantly lower (and even negative during the 1980s), averaging around 1 per cent annually over the past fifty years. Economic development has not generated sufficient low-skilled jobs to absorb the poor. Consequently, between 700,000 and 1 million Guatemalans are forced to migrate for seasonal harvest work. Working conditions for migrant workers are extremely tough: they are often paid less than the minimum wage, and have little or no access to health and educational facilities. In recent years, the structural crisis of coffee and sugar markets (two of Guatemala's main agro-exports) has drastically reduced national and regional employment opportunities for migrant workers, and the numbers of those attempting to reach the United States as illegal migrants increased. Poor families increasingly rely on dollar remittances from family members working in the United States, which represent around 10 per cent of overall GDP. In 2009, average annual remittances per person were around US$300, compared with an average for Latin America and the Caribbean of around US$100 (UNDP 2010).

Democratic disenchantment

Like most of Latin America, Guatemala is now formally a democracy. However, while respect for political and **human rights** has undoubtedly improved compared to the 1980s, these rights are still far from secure and democracy remains fragile. Since restoration

of electoral rule in 1986, elections have become freer and fairer, and an increasingly broad spectrum of political opinion has been represented at the polls, particularly following the successful conclusion of a negotiated settlement to the armed conflict in December 1996. During the 1990s and 2000s, decentralization and electoral reforms increased opportunities for citizen participation in municipal government. Yet Guatemalans' levels of political participation and faith in the institutions of government are low compared to other countries in the region. Voter turnout is comparatively poor and regional public opinion surveys, such as the Latinobarometer, regularly find that Guatemalans have some of the lowest regard for democratic norms in the region. One explanation is chronic impunity and citizen insecurity: Guatemala has one of the highest homicide rates in the region and extremely high levels of so-called common, especially violent, crime. Crime and gender-based violence are a common occurrence for many citizens, particularly the poor. Between 2007 and 2009, the number of violent deaths was between 45 and 49 for every 100,000 inhabitants—more than double the annual average during the thirty-six years of the armed conflict (UNDP 2010). The judicial system is weak, impunity is routine, and those responsible for criminal acts are rarely prosecuted. Respect for indigenous peoples' rights was a cornerstone of the peace accords (see later in the chapter), but despite some advances, progress has been extremely slow. For most Guatemalans, democracy clearly has yet to deliver.

KEY POINTS

- Guatemala has among the highest rates of poverty and inequality in Latin American and Caribbean.

- In 2009, 50.9 per cent of the population lacked sufficient income to meet their minimum subsistence requirements.

- Indigenous people, rural inhabitants, women, and children are amongst the poorest and most disadvantaged sectors of the population.

- Despite relative macro-economic stability, tax collection and social spending rates over the last three decades have been low.

- A return to **electoral democracy** occurred in 1986, but citizen disenchantment with democratic performance is high.

Patterns of State Formation

Guatemala's economic fortunes were built on agro-exports and based on a highly exploitative form of rural capitalism, which in turn was reflected in authoritarian and exclusive forms of **politics** and development. The dispossession of indigenous people from their historic lands began with Spanish colonization in the sixteenth century and accelerated during the late nineteenth-century coffee boom. The capitalist planter class in Guatemala relied on forced wage labour, becoming increasingly dependent on the coercive power of the central state, dominated by the armed forces, to ensure its supply of workers. Economic downturns necessitated repression by the military to quell wage demands and to ensure profitability margins. Ruling elites did not view the poor and particularly the indigenous as citizens, but rather as subjects to be disciplined, controlled, and 'civilized'. Race and class discrimination were mutually reinforcing and underpinned the economic system.

The cold war: reform reversed

Between 1944 and 1954, reformist governments were elected, following a coup by junior military officers. The administration of Juan José Arévalo (1944–51) introduced universal male suffrage, abolished forced labour and indentured servitude, and sponsored progressive labour and social security legislation. The more radical government of Jacobo Arbenz (1952–54) introduced an agrarian reform law in an effort to stimulate agricultural production and to address rural poverty.

However, the expropriation of large, underutilized estates and their distribution to landless peasants angered both rich landowners and the US-based United Fruit Company, one of the largest landowners in Guatemala. United Fruit conspired with US President Eisenhower's administration and elements of Guatemala's armed forces to overthrow the reformers, accusing the Arbenz government of communist sympathies. In 1954, Guatemala gained the dubious distinction of being the second country subject to a CIA-sponsored 'cold war coup' (Iran being the first in 1953).

Following the overthrow of Arbenz, the Guatemalan armed forces were supported by the United States within the regional framework of counter-insurgency training. The state became increasingly dominated by the military, which by the 1970s had become a powerful economic actor in its own right. Espousing a virulent anti-communism, the private sector relied on the army to repress workers' demands for improved wages or better working conditions. Delegating the business of government to the military, it nonetheless exercised a permanent veto on social reform.

Insurgency, counter-insurgency, and genocide

Such acute socio-economic and political exclusion contributed to the emergence of a guerrilla insurgency in the 1960s. This was brutally repressed by the army. State violence increased throughout the 1970s, targeting trade unionists, social activists, and reformist politicians, reaching a peak in the early 1980s when de facto military **regimes** fought an all-out war against the civilian population to stamp out a second guerrilla insurgency. This involved hundreds of army-led massacres, 'scorched earth' measures, the forced displacement of thousands of Guatemalans, mandatory paramilitary 'civil patrols' for all indigenous men in the countryside, and the militarization of the entire state apparatus; it constituted one of the most extreme cases of state repression in twentieth-century Latin America. In total, during thirty-six years of armed conflict, some 200,000 people were killed (2 per cent of the 1980 population), nearly a quarter of whom 'disappeared'. Another million were displaced, either internally or into Mexico. In 1999, the United Nations found that the Guatemalan state was responsible for over 90 per cent of gross human rights violations documented throughout the armed conflict, and was guilty of acts of **genocide** against the indigenous population between 1981 and

1983. This massive destruction of human and **social capital** had significant negative consequences for Guatemala's development prospects.

Electoral democracy and peace negotiations

In the mid-1980s, the military returned the country to civilian rule in a 'guided transition' to democracy designed to improve the country's standing before the **international community**, while perpetuating effective control by the armed forces over national affairs. Presidential elections held in 1985 were won by the centre-right Christian Democrat Party; a new Constitution was adopted in 1986. Yet political parties remained weak and fragmented, the influence of the military was undiminished, and state-perpetrated political repression of political opponents and trade union and human rights activists continued.

The armed conflict was not resolved until December 1996, when the pro-business sector government of President Alvaro Arzú signed a definitive peace settlement with the insurgent Unidad Revolucionaria Nacional Guatemalteca (URNG), bringing nine years of stop–start peace talks to a successful conclusion. The final phase of the negotiations was overseen by the United Nations and, after 1994, an on-site UN mission was charged with verification of the accords. Through its sponsorship of the peace settlement, the international community became highly involved in attempts to kick-start development in Guatemala.

KEY POINTS

- Guatemala's republican history is characterized by authoritarian rule, coercive rural capitalism, and racist discrimination.

- A reformist democratic regime was overthrown in 1954, at the height of the cold war, by a US-backed military coup.

- In response to guerrilla challenges, the armed forces militarized the state and used extreme violence against the civilian population.

- The country returned to elected civilian government in 1986, but the military continued to dominate politics and repress opponents.

- Thirty-six years of civil war finally ended with a UN-sponsored negotiated settlement in 1996.

The Peace Accords: A Turning Point?

The peace accords aimed not only to end the armed conflict formally, but also to reverse the country's historically exclusionary pattern of development. They comprised thirteen separate accords, involving four main areas:

- the resettlement of displaced populations, the reincorporation of former guerrillas, and reconciliation regarding past violations of human rights;

- an integrated programme for **human development**, which mandated a 50 per cent increase over five years in health and education spending;

- goals for productive and **sustainable development**, including market-led reform of the agricultural sector; and

- **modernization** of the democratic state, including reduction in the role of the armed forces, strengthening the **rule of law**, and increasing **civil society** participation, particularly in implementing the accords themselves.

Three cross-cutting elements were emphasized: the rights of indigenous communities; commitments regarding the rights and position of women; and greater social participation. The international community pledged more than US$3.2 billion in aid—over 60 per cent as grants to implement the accords.

Lack of domestic commitment

The peace accords constituted important achievements in their own right, but implementation was slow and uneven. Given the country's violent past, and history of socio-economic and ethnic and gender exclusion, meeting the comprehensive goals of the peace settlement was bound to be challenging. However, lack of commitment by key domestic actors further constrained prospects for success. While the international community and civil society organizations backed the agreements, the commitment of the main political parties, the military, and the private sector to the settlement was weak. The powerful and conservative private sector staunchly defended its privileges blocking land and tax reforms, despite the more progressive stance of certain reformist elements within the business community.

Implementation: a mixed record

Other aspects of the peace settlement were more successful. The guerrillas were reincorporated into civilian life—the ceasefire was not breached and the URNG became a political party. Displaced and returned refugee populations were resettled, although many complained of being allocated poor land and of insufficient access to credit. A UN-led truth commission was completed in 1999, a major achievement that signalled army responsibility for gross violations of human rights and recommended legal prosecutions. Yet despite the efforts of human rights organizations to secure justice, impunity remains the norm. (In May 2013, former dictator Ríos Montt was convicted of genocide in a historic ruling, yet the country's Constitutional Court subsequently accepted an appeal by the former dictator's lawyers which may lead to the verdict being overturned.) Attacks have occurred against human rights organizations and indigenous communities struggling to secure prosecutions for human rights violations carried out during the armed conflict. And in recent years social protest has been increasingly met with repression, particularly when communities protest against the negative effects of large-scale development projects such as mining or hydroelectric dams. Spending on health and education did increase in the 2000s, and a number of important structural reforms were implemented, particularly in education. However, this has not yet had an appreciable impact on social indicators. The global economic downturn in 2000–01, combined with the fall in agro-export prices, severely hampered even the limited development plans for the rural sector set out in the peace accords. The rural poor continue to lack access to land. In some cases, large landowners made a healthy profit from the peace funds provided by the international community by selling unproductive lands at inflated prices to the national peace fund. Landless peasants settled on these lands found that they were unable to feed themselves and were saddled with debt repayment obligations that they could not meet.

Human Security and Development

Since the end of the armed conflict, insecurity has worsened; homicide rates have climbed, as have other indicators of crime, such as violence against women. In contrast to the period of the armed conflict, human rights violations are increasingly perpetrated by private agents rather than by state forces. In general, judicial and police authorities fail to investigate, try, and punish crimes, and ordinary Guatemalans lack faith in the ability of the state to guarantee the rule of law and human rights. Organized crime is an increasingly important source of capital accumulation, and transnational criminal networks have penetrated politics, the private sector, and government in the post-war period (Grupos de Poder en Petén: Territorio, política y negocios, 2011; Panner & Beltrán, 2010).

A patrimonialist state and weak party system

In addition to private sector intransigence, the failure to modernize the state and the weakness of democratic institutions provide clues to Guatemala's continuing underdevelopment. The internationally prescribed formula of institutional strengthening and 'civil society strengthening' contained in the peace accords failed to transform an exclusive, **patrimonialist** state into a **developmental state** (see Chapters 3 and 12). This reflects the balance of political forces and inherent difficulty of changing historically entrenched patterns. The nature of Guatemala's party system is both cause and effect of the patrimonialist state.

During the 1990s, a core nucleus of political parties on the right and centre-right of the political spectrum contested elections, signalling a degree of stability of the party system, but these parties continued to be dominated by personalist politics within the private sector. Some centre-left parties, including the former guerrilla URNG, gained ground after 1995, but command a negligible share of the vote.

In general, political parties tend to be dominated by powerful individuals who campaign on the strength of their personal, **clientelist** networks, rather than by programmatic coherence or the representation of different groups in society. Subject to continuous division and fragmentation, many are little more than electoral alliances of convenience to support the interests of one or another economic sector. In the absence of congressional majorities, governments are forced to rely on opportunistic coalitions between the different parties. Party discipline is extremely lax, elected deputies often switching their allegiance during their term of office, and clientelism is rife. In broad terms, two blocs currently dominate Guatemalan politics. The first is a **populist** coalition of forces that relies on clientelist networks, particularly in the rural areas. This loose alliance represents a new economic elite linked to sectors of the military and organized crime. In the early 2000s, the political vehicle for this bloc was the right-wing populist Frente Republicano Guatemalteco (FRG), led by former military dictator Ríos Montt. In the latter part of the decade, that bloc dominated the government of Social Democrat Alvaro Colóm, which held power between 2007 and 2012. The opposing bloc, dominated by traditional private sector interests and multinational companies, was represented by the governments of Oscar Berger (2003–07) and former General Otto Pérez Molina (2013–). Despite election promises to get tough on crime and increase employment, the record of all post-war governments on security and development has been dismal.

Military power, weak civil society, and continued human rights abuses

The armed forces largely retained their power following the peace settlement. Troop numbers were reduced during the late 1990s, but the military budget increased and the army has again been employed in public security functions, directly contravening the peace accords. The police remain weak, corrupt, and underfunded.

Serving and former military officers form part of a network of so-called 'parallel powers', which has influence within the highest spheres of government. These mafia-style networks are implicated in **corruption** scandals, organized crime, and maintaining impunity for those guilty of gross violations of human rights. Police and army units are implicated in extrajudicial executions and so-called 'social cleansing operations', including one notorious massacre of prison inmates in 2006. A UN Commission to investigate abuses by clandestine groups operating in the country was finally approved in late 2006, in part in response to consistent failure of the Guatemalan state to tackle this problem effectively. In 2009, the UN Secretary General extended the mandate of the Commission to 2011, but efforts to secure prosecutions were stymied. Civil society organizations have become more vocal advocates of government transparency and accountability in recent years, but violence and intimidation against rights activists continue, and popular awareness of the historically high costs of dissent means that Guatemalan civil society remains comparatively weak. Indigenous Mayan organizations gained a national presence after the early 1990s, and promoted important national and local development initiatives, but their influence has declined as formal politics has been colonized by clientelist interests and organized crime. According to the framework for peace negotiations, all reforms to the Constitution had to be approved by Congress and then passed by a majority in a national referendum. A poll held in May 1999 (with a turnout of less than 20 per cent) rejected a package of constitutional reforms that included the official recognition of Guatemala as a multicultural and multi-ethnic nation-state. Elements of the private sector campaigned vociferously against recognition of indigenous peoples' rights, arguing that it would lead to 'reverse discrimination' and **balkanization** of the country. Unlike other Latin American countries with large indigenous populations—for example Bolivia or Ecuador—multicultural reforms of the state have been relatively limited to date. Guatemala has ratified the International Labour Organization (ILO) Convention No. 169 on the rights of indigenous and tribal peoples, but has failed to honour its international commitments to respect indigenous rights. Conflicts over large-scale infrastructural developments in indigenous regions—such as gold mining and hydroelectric dams—have led to increasing violent clashes in recent years.

In spite of the end of the armed conflict, the human rights situation in Guatemala remains bleak. High levels of violent crime, continued impunity, and the ineffectiveness of the police and the judiciary mean weak civil rights protection. The growth of rival armed gangs linked to drug trafficking during the 1990s worsened the security situation for ordinary Guatemalans. Tough-on-crime policies against gang members have failed to generate significant improvements. Male homicide rates are amongst the highest in Latin America and the Caribbean; violent murders of women also increased in the 2000s, leading campaigners to talk about 'femicide'. More than 5,000 murders a year are committed in Guatemala—more than during the final years of the armed conflict; most are never investigated. United Nations officials have accused the Guatemalan government of fostering a culture of impunity and have pointed to the costs of violence for development: the United Nations Development Programme for Guatemala estimated in 2006 that violence cost 7.3 per cent of GDP, costs that were associated with health care, lost production, and public and private security.

Conclusion

Guatemala is a **predatory state**, rather than a developmental state. The US-supported derailing of the reformist administration of Jacobo Arbenz produced one of the most violent and authoritarian regimes in the region. The state lacked autonomy and was effectively colonized by powerful private interests. During the cold war, it was supported by the regional superpower under the aegis of anti-communism. Despite transition to electoral rule two decades ago, such predatory tendencies have not disappeared; indeed, many now point to the increasingly mafia-style operation of the Guatemalan state.

The peace process of the 1990s provided an important space for reorienting historically exclusionary patterns of development. However, without the political commitment of the most powerful domestic actors, international pressure, and the support of civil society, organizations were unable to secure such a shift. Guatemala today is a weak and illiberal democracy: the population may enjoy suffrage or political rights, but civil rights are not enforced, and the rule of law is routinely flouted by powerful actors within and outside government. Historical patterns of ethnic and economic exclusion, combined with the legacy of extreme levels of state violence against the civilian population, mean that citizen participation is relatively weak. The strength and conservatism of the private sector, its historic reliance on the armed forces, and the systematic persecution of the left and centre-left has engendered a particularly weak and venal political class and party system, constituting another impediment to development. More progressive elements secured a foothold during the 1990s, but they face powerful opposition and seem unable to consolidate effective parties capable of winning elections.

Finally, long-term structural factors have not favoured the Guatemalan economy. Historically reliant on a particularly exploitative form of rural capitalism, the private sector has largely failed to adapt to new global conditions despite the relative decline of traditional agro-exports. High commodity prices have helped to secure macro-economic stability, but the historic lack of investment in **human capital** remains a serious impediment to future economic development. Prevailing economic policies have proved singularly incapable of generating greater development and equality.

?   QUESTIONS

1. Critically examine Guatemala's performance in terms of rights-based measures of development.

2. Was the peace agreement successful in fulfilling its goals? Why, or why not?

3. In what ways does the deteriorating security situation impede development?

4. Are the main causes of underdevelopment in Guatemala largely economic or mainly political?

FURTHER READING

Center for Economic and Social Rights (CESR) and Instituto Centroamericano de Estudios Fiscales (ICEFI), (2009) *Rights or Privileges? Fiscal Commitment to the Rights to Health, Education and Food in Guatemala. Executive Summary*, available online at http://www.cesr.org/downloads/Rights%20or%20Privileges%20Executive%20Summary%20final.pdf An insightful source on social and economic rights in Guatemala.

Grandin, G, Levenson, D. T., and Oglesby, E. (eds) (2011) *The Guatemala Reader: History, Culture, Politics* (Durham NC: Duke University Press) A good historical overview of the Guatemalan case.

United Nations Development Programme (2007) *Human Development Report 2007–2008*, available online at http://hdr.undp.org/en/reports/global/hdr2007-2008/ Good data source on political and economic developments in Guatemala.

— (2008) *Guatemala: ¿Una Economía al Servicio del Desarrollo Humano?*, Guatemalan National Report on Human Development 2007–08, available online at http://hdr.undp.org/es/informes/nacional/americalatinacaribe/guatemala/name,3430,es.html Supplies good information on the current human rights situation in Guatemala.

— (2010) *Guatemala: Hacia un Estado para el Desarrollo Humano*, Guatemalan National Report on Human Development 2009–10, available online at http://hdr.undp.org/es/informes/nacional/americalatinacaribe/guatemala/name,20685,es.html An updated and informative data source.

WEB LINKS

http://hdr.undp.org/en/reports/national/latinamericathecaribbean/guatemala/name,3430,en.html   United Nations Human Development Report for Guatemala 2007–08.

http://web.worldbank.org/WBSITE/EXTERNAL/COUNTRIES/LACEXT/0,,contentMDK:20525480~pagePK:146736~ piPK:146830~theSitePK:258554,00.html   World Bank Guatemala Poverty Assessment—navigate from here to the World Bank Guatemala Poverty Assessment (GUAPA) 2003.

For additional material and resources, please visit the Online Resource Centre at
http://www.oxfordtextbooks.co.uk/orc/burnell4e/

PART 8
South–South Relations

Over the past few years, increasing attention has been given to the development of stronger South–South relations. The international scene is changing. Through country case studies of Brazil, China, and India, this part shows how new powers claim their place in international **politics**, and present challenges and opportunities for other developing countries and developed countries alike. These three countries form part of the BRICS (along with Russia and South Africa), which are all emerging economies challenging the economic and political hegemony of traditional Western powers. They are becoming increasingly significant global partners and, in 2009, the BRICS called for a greater voice for developing countries in international financial institutions. This is not to say that these countries are homogenous in any way; their economies, incentives, and political systems all differ. They do, however, present a challenge to the old North–South divide.

Brazil has emerged as a regional, as well as a global, power. Through her chapter, Leslie Armijo shows how Brazil has striven to play a bigger role on the international scene. This is seen through the active campaigning for continental integration in which Brazil has played an important role by means of several initiatives. Brazil has also conducted an active foreign policy on a global scale, linked to trade, climate, finance, and nuclear proliferation. The increased prominence of Brazil on the international scene can also be explained by increasing relative capabilities compared with Western countries.

China's relations with other developing countries have been given significant attention. Deborah Bräutigam displays how, by means of foreign aid, economic cooperation, **soft power** (such as the Confucius Institutes), and more importantly trade, China aims to be seen as a responsible global power. More precisely, China wants to secure territorial integrity and sovereignty, and to prevent Taiwan from gaining international standing. It also wants to be seen as a leader of developing countries, although not a threatening one. Lastly, it wants to secure a stable political environment in order to provide economic development. Many people voice fears that this international engagement resembles a form of new colonialism, because it revolves around importing cheap raw materials and exporting cheap manufactured goods.

The final chapter shows how India and other developing countries are becoming bigger players in the international foreign aid **regime**. Emma Mawdsley contends that, until recently, foreign aid was mainly seen as stemming from Western, developed countries. Recently, however, many non-traditional donors have either appeared or come to attention. A central feature of aid from southern partners is that it comes with few **conditionalities**. India started its foreign aid activities in the 1950s. The main reason for such an early commitment was a willingness to create regional goodwill among hostile neighbours, to provide energy security, and to create relations of solidarity with developing countries, and a resulting increasing international stature. The paradox here remains that even though India increases its international efforts and decreases its own dependence on aid, a large part of its population still remains very poor. As with traditional development partners, there are also mixed motivations behind the involvement of India in foreign aid.

27

Brazil as a Global Player?

Leslie Elliott Armijo

Overview

Brazil is a big country. With a landmass similar in size to that of continental United States, and a population of 197 million and gross domestic product (GDP) of US$2.5 trillion in 2011, Brazilians make up half the population and generate over half the economy of South America. In the eyes of much of the world, as recently as the early 1990s, Brazil remained a 'banana republic', with annual price inflation over 1,000 per cent and chaotic politics, including a president who resigned in 1992 in order to avoid impeachment over allegations of corruption. Yet Brazil today has a large and growing presence on the international scene, as a member of the BRICS group comprising Brazil, Russia, India, China, and South Africa, a key player in international climate forums, an active participant in the major economies' Group of 20 (G20) (see Chapter 5), and since 2010 a creditor of the International Monetary Fund (IMF). Governed in recent years by a moderately left-leaning coalition under Presidents Luíz Inácio 'Lula' da Silva (2003–10) and Dilma Rousseff (2011–), Brazil is a stable democracy, with a growing middle class, and a policy and business elite eager to expand their country's influence in the world. Brazilian leaders cherish their foreign policy autonomy and have enthusiastically embraced 'South–South' diplomacy under both Presidents Lula and Dilma—both universally referred to by their given names in Brazil. Nonetheless, Brazil remains a fundamentally Western and liberal power, whose policies bear a family resemblance to those of today's major advanced industrial countries. Figure 27.1 is a map of Brazil and Box 27.1 provides an overview of key dates in Brazil's history.

Figure 27.1 Brazil

BOX 27.1 KEY DATES IN BRAZIL'S HISTORY

1500	Portuguese explorer Pedro Alves Cabral, seeking a passage to India, instead encounters Brazil
Mid-17th c.	Sugar exports, worked with coerced labour, dominate Brazil's economy
1550–1866	Nearly 5 million enslaved Africans disembark in Brazil, almost half of all slaves brought to the Americas
1808	Fleeing Napoléon, the Portuguese court relocates to Brazil
1821–89	Independent Brazilian kingdom, evolving toward constitutional monarchy. Slavery ended in 1889
1889–1930	Brazil becomes an oligarchic republic, whose economy depends on coffee exports
1930–64	Urban populist government, dominated by President Getúlio Vargas until his suicide in 1954
1964–84	Modernizing military rule, including high growth period 1967–73, known as the 'Brazilian miracle'

1985	Peaceful transition to civilian, democratic rule	2009	Brazil joins Russia, China, and India to form the
1988	First truly democratic constitution adopted		BRICs, adding South Africa (to become the
1994–95	*Real* Plan economic policies end decades of recurrent high inflation		BRICS) in late 2010

Introduction: A Brief History

The Portuguese colonized lightly populated Brazil, first arriving at the turn of the sixteenth century. Three centuries later, Brazilian elites took advantage of the Napoleonic Wars to declare independence from the European power in 1822. The new country constituted itself as a monarchy, ruled by a prince of the Portuguese royal family, thus avoiding the bloody wars among rival *caudillos* that spawned seemingly endless conflicts in much of newly independent Spanish-speaking Latin America throughout the nineteenth century. African slaves provided much of the labour in its primary-product export economy. Brazil's Princess Isabel announced the abolition of slavery in 1889, the final straw that led local elites to overthrow the monarchy. Thereafter, regionally based landowner coalitions ruled Brazil, under rules of political competition that were sometimes democratic, although often not, through the mid-twentieth century. By the time of the Second World War, Brazil had significant industrial centres and an activist international diplomacy. Brazilians remain proud of having been the only Latin American country to participate as a combatant in the war, which it entered on the side of the Allies, and to have been a founding member of the United Nations.

In the latter half of the twentieth century, Brazil struggled with the challenges of the military in **politics** and democratization (see Chapter 14). After twenty years in power, the army peacefully relinquished political power in 1985. Brazil today is a democracy with a federal, bicameral, and presidential system. Under the military, Brazil pursued import-substituting industrialization (see Chapter 4). The big economic policy successes since democratization have been ending multi-digit annual inflation (in 1995), reigniting growth (beginning in 2000), and reducing Brazil's horrendous income inequality (see Chapter 6). In 1991, 40 per cent of Brazilian households were poor and 20 per cent indigent (extremely poor), but by 2009 the respective figures had fallen to 16 and 6 per cent (IPEA 2013).

Brazil in the Western Hemisphere: Active Pursuit of Continental Integration

Since its return to democratic government in 1985, Brazil has sought closer ties abroad, particularly with its South American neighbours. Of the eleven other states in South America, Brazil directly borders all but Chile and Ecuador. The early twenty-first century has seen three differing hemispheric integration projects being pursued simultaneously, one favoured by the United States, one by Venezuela, and the third by Brazil. Brazil has cooperated just enough with the US-led project, which reflects a more politically and economically conservative vision of regional cooperation, and with the Venezuela-led project, which is explicitly socialist and leftist, to remain on reasonably good terms with both countries.

The United States' integration vision

Since the late 1980s, a major US foreign policy goal in the Western hemisphere has been to bring the legal frameworks of all of the hemisphere's countries into economic regulatory convergence with the generally pro-free enterprise and business-friendly rules prevailing in the United States. The United States seeks open trade and lower barriers to foreign direct investment (FDI), especially in sectors such as banking, insurance, utilities, and other services, which many countries historically have reserved for locally owned firms, often state-owned enterprises. The United States also strongly favours a legal framework by which disputes between transnational corporations, often headquartered in the United States, and host country firms and governments would be adjudicated in administrative courts run by the World Trade Organization (WTO), instead of in courts in the host countries, which US experts fear will be biased against foreign investors. The many democratic transitions throughout the hemisphere in the 1980s led US officials—who tend to equate democratic politics and laissez-faire economics–to hope that their international economic vision would be shared by their neighbours.

Following the implementation on 1 January 1994 of the North American Free Trade Agreement (NAFTA) among the United States, Canada, and Mexico, the United States organized a meeting in Miami of all of the hemisphere's leaders except Cuban President Fidel Castro, inaugurating an annual process known as the 'Summits of America'. Through these summits, the United States hoped to promote a Free Trade Area of the Americas (FTAA), featuring 'deep' economic integration, similar to that of NAFTA. The proposed FTAA would include very liberal rules governing international trade and capital flows, yet would not seek political integration, collective decision-making, or region-wide citizenship or immigration rights.

Brazil's role in the annual Summits of the Americas has been to push for negotiated tariff reductions in goods, while opposing 'deep integration' of the regulatory framework for such arenas as foreign investment, intellectual property, and government procurement. Alternatively, Brazil argued, if the FTAA were going to include the rules governing foreign investment, as desired by the United States, then it also should include new rules on agricultural and commodities trade, historically excluded from trade negotiations owing to opposition from the advanced industrial countries, who are afraid of harm to their domestic farm sectors. In the end, Brazil, Argentina, and Venezuela all made clear their disinterest in the FTAA, for which formal negotiations continue, but which most observers consider permanently stalled. The United States turned to its second-best strategy of signing bilateral free trade or investment treaties with smaller and/or more pro-US countries.

The Brazilian and Argentine project

Meanwhile, Brazil and Argentina pursued their own vision of regional integration, which was sub-continental, and later continental, in scope rather than hemispheric. Following their countries' respective returns to democracy in 1983 and 1985, Presidents Raúl Alfonsín of Argentina and José Sarney of Brazil initiated talks on creating a regional customs union. Both politicians realized that it would be easier to establish civilian control over the military if generals on either side of their common border were denied the excuse of a threat from the other country as a ruse to maintain power. In 1991, the presidents of Argentina, Brazil, Paraguay, and Uruguay formally inaugurated the Common Market of the South (MERCOSUR), initially only a forum for negotiating multilateral tariff reductions, but later a fully fledged regional integration organization, complete with a nascent, although relatively powerless, parliament (PARLASUR). Created in 2004, PARLASUR is only advisory, but has the long-term goal of 'establish[ing] mechanisms to facilitate the incorporation of MERCOSUR norms into the laws of the five member states'. Venezuela joined MERCOSUR in 2012, while Chile, Bolivia, and Peru are associates.

Since 2000, the Brazilian, Argentine, and other governments have pushed for the transformation of MERCOSUR into a continent-wide organization promoting both economic integration and political collaboration. In 2000, then Brazilian President Fernando Henrique Cardoso had organized the first summit of all South American heads of states, inviting not only the leaders of Latin American countries, but also those of Dutch-speaking Suriname and English-speaking Guyana. In 2004, the twelve leaders created UNASUR, the Union of South American Nations.

One difference from the NAFTA/FTAA project, which focuses on liberalizing and harmonizing economic regulation, is that the South American integration process envisions closer political, as well as economic, ties among members. UNASUR builds on two existing multilateral economic groupings in South America—MERCOSUR and the Andean Community (CAN), a free trade agreement among Colombia, Peru, Bolivia, and Ecuador—and will, for the time being, use their existing institutional infrastructure. To many observers' surprise, in 2007, Brazil and Venezuela further announced the formation of the South American Defense Council (CDSA) under UNASUR auspices. Colombia, the most consistently politically conservative large Latin American country, almost did not join, as a result of ongoing tensions with its neighbour Venezuela, South America's most left-leaning country. However, personal diplomacy by senior Brazilian and other officials kept the negotiations and **institutions** alive, and in March 2009 the CDSA held its first meeting, with representatives of all twelve member states in attendance. This does not mean that CDSA is a mutual aid treaty, much less an agreement to mount joint operations;

thus far it is a joint political process, ostensibly to discuss common and relatively apolitical defence concerns such as coordinated responses to natural disasters and pandemics, and airline safety, as well as to facilitate intraregional defence procurement, the latter a significant potential benefit for Brazil's large defence industry.

The Bolivarian Alliance

The third regional integration vision is that of a mutual aid union of socialist and popular-progressive Latin American and Caribbean states. The Bolivarian Alliance of Latin America (ALBA), grew out of the Venezuela–Cuba Peoples' Trade Agreement (TCP) of December 2004, and pointedly excludes the hemisphere's capitalist hegemons, the United States and Canada. Bolivarian initiatives have been funded by Venezuelan government petroleum earnings, and thus far ALBA has attracted as additional members only smaller states of the Andes and circum-Caribbean, including Bolivia and Ecuador in South America. Among the late Venezuelan President Hugo Chávez' most cherished projects was a new multilateral development bank in South America to be known as the Banco del Sur ('Bank of South'), conceived as an alternative to the 'capitalist' and 'imperialist' Inter-American Development Bank (IDB), headquartered in Washington, DC. Although all four original MERCO-SUR countries joined the talks to create the Banco del Sur, with Brazil and Argentina joining Venezuela in pledging financial support, as of early 2013 there were no concrete results.

Brazilian diplomacy

Among these alternatives, Brazilian leaders have played an assertive diplomatic game. For example, Lula's foreign minister, Celso Amorím, in senior government positions in every administration since the early 1990s, was politically and stylistically moderate, while deputy foreign minister and later strategic affairs minister, Samuel Guimarães, was left-leaning, confrontational, and given to asserting that Brazil did not 'need permission' from the United States or anyone else in choosing its foreign policy positions. Their partnership yielded some progress in the president's political agenda of maintaining cordial relations across the political spectrum of their neighbours. Brazil has resolutely and publicly opposed overt coups or

questionably legal impeachments against an elected head of state, even a clearly flawed one, as in Honduras in 2009 or Paraguay in 2012, but has been loath to criticize lesser anti-democratic moves by incumbent leaders, such as actions by Venezuelan President Chávez to reduce press freedoms.

An example of Brazil's energetic diplomacy in the hemisphere is the innovative drug policy initiative of former Brazilian President Fernando Henrique Cardoso (1995–2002). Along with former presidents Ernesto Zedillo of Mexico and César Gavíria of Colombia, Cardoso co-chaired a seventeen-member commission of Latin American notables, funded entirely by private foundations. The Latin American Commission on Drugs and Democracy (LACDD) argued for decriminalization of marijuana, and a focus within Latin America on confronting the drug-cum-criminal gangs terrorizing many cities, while de-emphasizing eradication of drug crops in the countryside (LACDD 2009). This initiative is in the early stages, but represents innovative Latin American public policy collaboration, even when this directly challenges US policy orthodoxies.

In sum, the United States' foreign economic policy goal for the Western hemisphere is for an extension of something like the NAFTA southwards, a hope that has seemed unrealistic since 2004. Venezuela and Cuba would like a political alliance of left-leaning Latin American and Caribbean developing countries to assert itself against the United States and Canada, but have not been able to inspire any of the larger, more influential states to join with them. Brazil, which occupies a middle ground in terms of economic ideology, has initiated or enthusiastically participated in a host of new regional initiatives, many of which aim to strength South American economic, but also political, integration. In the judgement of some analysts, as of the end of the first decade of the twenty-first century, these new multilateral organizations as yet amounted to little (Malamud 2011). Other observers see their construction as significant even in the absence of joint policymaking or explicit regulatory convergence.

It is hard or impossible to imagine these outcomes in the absence of activist leadership by South American presidents, particularly in Brazil, and of democratic transitions throughout South America, which have allowed resolution or at least calming of numerous border and other disputes, many of them decades-old.

Key Global Issues for Brazil

This section summarizes Brazilian foreign policy initiatives in four global issue arenas: trade; climate; financial **governance**; and nuclear proliferation.

Trade

As noted earlier in the chapter, Brazil participated in the FTAA negotiations, but also acted to try to construct its own groupings, such as MERCOSUR. Similarly, in early 2003, Brazilian leaders joined other 'Southern' counterparts to form the India, Brazil, South Africa (IBSA) process in order to seek joint negotiating positions at the WTO, despite the structural differences in their economies.

Brazilian leaders have clear preferences for their own national trade strategy. While they accept that trade promotes growth, which they intensely desire, they also would prefer to have an export surplus, and a substantial and rising share of exports that is manufactured goods rather than primary products such as food and natural resources. Brazil usually has a trade surplus, particularly when global commodity prices are high, as they have been since the early 2000s. In 2009, China overtook the United States to become Brazil's single most important trading partner, which generated angst in Brazil. In the view of Brazilian policymakers, the main problem with trade with China, and Asia more generally, is that these countries purchase mainly raw materials such as soybeans or iron ore, while selling Brazil mainly manufactured goods—a pattern that Brazilian leaders fear could undermine their industrial base and lessen future growth. The share of manufactured and semi-processed goods in total Brazilian merchandise exports fell from 69 per cent in 2003 to only 50 per cent in 2012. Trade concerns provide one reason for Brazil's political focus on strengthening regional ties: over 80 per cent of Brazilian exports to Latin America and the Caribbean in 2012 were industrial products—as compared to only about 20 per cent to Asia.

Climate

A second multilateral issue arena has been that of negotiations over cutting greenhouse gas (GHG) emissions and other climate issues. The Amazon River Basin, the vast majority of which is in Brazil, contains the world's largest rainforest, a hugely important global carbon sink. Beginning in the late 1980s, Brazil became the principal target of global ecological campaigners, mostly from the industrialized world, who condemned its high and rising rates of deforestation, associated with gold prospecting by poor migrants and especially with the illegal, but mostly unpoliced, burning of huge swathes of virgin forest for cattle ranches (see Chapter 17).

Yet, in the twenty-first century, Brazil began to claim the mantle of being a 'green' energy power (Harvey 2010). Its own energy matrix minimizes GHG emissions. Brazil is a world leader in the production and use of biofuels. Its sugar-cane ethanol is the world's most efficiently produced, and all new cars since the late 1990s have been engineered to run on a gasoline–ethanol mix. Currently, over half of Brazil's total energy used comes from renewable sources, and over 70 per cent of electricity from hydropower.

Moreover, via a two-track process of beginning to enforce its own environmental laws and the development of concrete proposals for multilateral solutions in global negotiations—formally known as the United Nations Framework Convention on Climate Change (UNFCCC)—Brazil has become an active and respected participant in the global climate **regime**. In 2004, for example, Brazil attempted to mediate between the advanced industrial countries (whose view has been that countries whose pollution is absolutely largest and/or growing fastest, such as China and India, must make the largest cuts), and developing countries, who understandably demand that per capita energy consumption should first become more equal worldwide (Friman 2006). At the December 2010 UNFCCC negotiating round in Copenhagen, an informal meeting of leaders of the United States and the BASIC countries (Brazil, South Africa, India, and China) generated a non-binding accord including the first concrete promises of cuts by both developed and developing countries (see Chapter 17).

In the most recent period, Brazil's policies again have become more problematic in the eyes of environmentalists, who claim that the federal government's plan to expand hydropower, as through construction of the huge Belo Monte dam on the Xingu River, a major tributary of the Amazon, will have very negative implications for both local habitat and the livelihood of nearby indigenous groups. While hydroelectric power is renewable, it nonetheless incites controversy. The other significant shift is that Brazil has suddenly become wealthy in fossil fuels. In 2006, prospectors found the first of several enormous underwater oil fields off the Rio de Janeiro coast. If these 'pre-salt' finds are fully confirmed, Brazil will become one of the top ten countries worldwide in terms of petroleum reserves. As the current administration—and almost any plausible alternate—is more committed to rapid **economic growth**, which it views as essential for poverty reduction, than to maximizing its green credentials, we may expect increasing conflicts, involving both Brazilians and external actors, over new dams and deep-sea drilling.

Finance

A third international realm in which Brazilian governments are desirous of leaving their mark is that of global financial and economic regulation, although this could not happen before Brazil's own economy was sufficiently well-run for the country's financial experts to be respected abroad. Brazil's strong private banks now compete with Spanish banks to be the leading financial institutions in Latin American markets. Yet a place in the significant global governance clubs is not something that the global economy's major powers hand out easily. Instead, Brazil and other emerging powers have been invited into the tent only as the G7 countries have come to recognize that they need these countries' cooperation.

The Asian financial crisis of 1997–99 led to the founding of two new multilateral organizations—the Financial Stability Board (FSB, initially the Financial Stability Forum) and the financial Group of 20 (G20, also known as the large economies' G20)—as multilateral bodies to consider reforms of the global financial architecture. The FSB was sited at the Bank for International Settlements (BIS) in Basel, and for the first decade it had only two developing country members, the financial entrepôts Singapore and Hong Kong. The FSB quickly developed into a multilateral body for detailed technical consultations among regulators, issuing numerous arcane, but influential, reports. The financial G20 was more representative than the FSB, but influenced public policy less. The financial G20

included the G7 major industrial democracies, Australia, the European Union, and most of the larger developing economies, including Brazil, Mexico, and Argentina in Latin America (see Chapter 5). After issuing a cautious report on needed reforms of the global financial architecture, the financial G20 seemed destined for obscurity.

Then the worldwide financial crisis of 2008–09 provided the shock that elevated the financial G20 to global significance. Following the September 2008 crash of Lehman Brothers investment bank, economic policymakers in Washington, DC, abruptly recognized that the balance of global financial and economic capabilities had shifted toward developing countries, particularly in East Asia. The only appropriate multilateral group available was the financial G20. The United States asked President Lula da Silva, the 2008 financial G20 president, to convene the first G20 heads of state summit in Washington, DC. By late 2009, the summits, negotiations, communiqués, and commitments on coordinated macro-economic stimulus packages of the G20 had overshadowed those of the wealthy democracies club, the G7. In early 2009, the international financial crisis also provided the impetus for four large emerging economies to organize themselves as the BRICs (Brazil, Russia, India, and China), later adding South Africa to become the BRICS. The BRICS have pressed for increased voice for themselves and others in global financial organizations such as the International Monetary Fund (IMF).

Nuclear proliferation

In the early 1990s, Brazilian President Fernando Collor da Mello ceremoniously buried a casket symbolizing the secret nuclear weapons development programme of Brazil's military government in the 1970s. Although Brazil now has credibly renounced all intentions to produce nuclear weapons and is a party to the Non-Proliferation Treaty (NPT), successive governments have refused to participate in the full range of its additional inspection protocols, to the intense annoyance of the United States, for whom the NPT is the litmus test of 'responsible' international behaviour by emerging powers. Brazil, although without any regional military worries, and firmly democratic, capitalist, and culturally 'Western', nonetheless views its nuclear independence as a key indicator of foreign policy autonomy. In 2010, during the ongoing war of words and economic sanctions between Iran and the West, Brazil and Turkey attempted to broker a face-saving compromise: allowing Iran to store spent nuclear fuel in Turkey, as a guarantee that it would not be secretly enriched to make weapons. When the United States and European Union angrily rejected the proposed deal, President Lula da Silva backed down, noting that Brazil did not approve of economic sanctions on Iran, but would 'abide by international law' (Fleischer 2010). While this episode was hardly a success for Brazilian diplomacy, it clearly illustrates the country's efforts to be seen as a global player. Brazil's unprecedented cooperation with Turkey, also an emerging power, fellow democracy, and financial G20 member, was facilitated by their leaders' sense of occupying a common position in the global system.

KEY POINTS

- Since the country's democratic transition in 1985, Brazilian leaders have taken a much more active role in global diplomacy, cooperating with other emerging powers including India, South Africa, China, Russia, and Turkey.

- Brazil's negotiating positions already have altered outcomes in the global regimes for trade and climate change.

- Although Brazil wishes to maintain an independent stance vis-à-vis the United States, Brazil is nonetheless a Western, liberal, and capitalist power.

Toward Global Multipolarity?

This chapter's preceding sections have emphasized assertive Brazilian diplomacy and the presence of plausible foreign partners among other emerging powers in both the region and the world. A third reason that Brazil has become more globally visible than before is its relatively greater command of material capabilities than in the past. The majority of Brazilian opinion leaders are convinced that the world is becoming more multipolar, and that Brazil is thus objectively entitled to a greater voice in global affairs.

There are many possible ways in which to suggest that relative capabilities among sovereign states may be shifting. Table 27.1 shows a shifting distribution of 'hard power' capabilities among the major traditional powers of the G5 (France, Germany, Japan, Britain, and the United States) and large emerging powers, including Brazil. The Contemporary Capabilities Index (CCI) is computed as the mean of each country's annual share in world totals of six types of material resource that arguably are useful for exerting international influence: production of goods and services (gross domestic product, or GDP); population; fixed plus mobile telephone subscriptions (as an indicator of technological access); industrial value-added (an indicator of technological development); global

Table 27.1 Contemporary Capabilities Index			
	1995	2003	2010
Traditional powers			
United States	15.7	15.1	13.1
Japan	8.3	7.7	5.2
Germany	4.5	3.0	2.1
France	2.8	2.5	2.0
United Kingdom	2.8	2.5	2.0
Emerging powers			
China	6.5	11.2	14.0
India	3.7	4.5	6.3
Russia	3.0	2.5	2.7
Brazil	2.0	1.7	2.6
Mexico	0.9	1.3	1.1

foreign exchange reserves (an indicator of financial power); and world military spending (Armijo et al. forthcoming). The CCI undoubtedly understates the true international influence of the wealthy democracies such as the G5, because it excludes crucial '**soft power**' resources such as institutionally determined influence in global governance organizations and possession of an internationally attractive language, culture, educational system, or political system (Nye 2005). Nonetheless, it is noteworthy that the BRICS countries—especially, but not exclusively, China—have increased their relative command of material resources very dramatically, while the G5's share has been drifting downwards.

KEY POINTS

- In terms of material power resources and influence, Brazil was not a global power in the twentieth century.

- In the early twenty-first century, Brazil aspires to become a major international player.

Conclusion

Brazil has become more consequential on the world stage over the past twenty years, as judged by the frequency with which it is routinely included in regional and global governance summitry. Following terminology initially introduced by Kenneth Waltz (1979), one may take a 'first image' (leadership) view of Brazil's current prominence, noting that Brazilian diplomacy has been indefatigable and occasionally clever. A 'second image' (domestic politics) approach, equally plausible, highlights political and economic changes within Brazil, as well as the fact that many other emerging powers worldwide also are now functioning, politically stable countries, and that many of them are mass democracies—all changes that should render agreements among them easier and more credible. Alternatively, it may be international relations' 'third image' (the systemic balance of capabilities) that explains the most about why Brazil can now claim a seat in many influential global forums that previously were closed to it. Whatever the reasons, Brazilian leaders increasingly see themselves as players on a global stage.

? QUESTIONS

1. Many Brazilian policymakers aspire to have their country considered a major power. Is this a reasonable goal?

2. Can Brazil be the 'environmental power' for the twenty-first century? Why?

3. Compared to China, India, and Russia, Brazil is geographically situated in a peaceful, unthreatening neighbourhood. What difference might this make to its foreign policy positions?

4. Does Brazilian cooperation with countries such as China, Venezuela, and Turkey threaten the United States?

FURTHER READING

Burges, S. W. (2009) *Brazilian Foreign Policy after the Cold War* (Miami, FL: University Press of Florida) A full-length treatment of contemporary Brazilian foreign policy available in English.

de Lima, M. R. S. and Hirst, M. (2006) 'Brazil as an Intermediate State and Regional Power: Action, Choice, and Responsibilities', *International Affairs*, 82(1): 21–40 A review of Brazilian diplomacy through the early 2000s from two eminent Brazilian experts.

Fausto, B. (1999) *A Concise History of Brazil* (Cambridge: Cambridge University Press) A scholarly, yet highly readable, summary of Brazilian history since colonial times.

Font, M. A. and Randall, L. (eds) (2011) *The Brazilian State: Debate and Agenda* (Lanham, MD: Lexington Books) Focuses on various public policy issue arenas, from state reform to the economy.

Kingstone, P. and Power, T. J. (eds) (2008) *Democratic Brazil Revisited*. (Pittsburgh, PA: University of Pittsburgh Press) Rigorous political analysis of problems in Brazilian democratic consolidation.

Love, J. L. and Baer, W. (eds) (2008) *Brazil under Lula: Economy, Politics, and Society under the Worker-President* (New York: Palgrave Macmillan) Further views of contemporary Brazilian issues, edited by an eminent historian and well-known economist.

Weyland, K., Madrid, R. L., and Hunter, W. (eds) (2010) *Leftist Governments in Latin America: Successes and Failures* (Cambridge: Cambridge University Press) Analyses Brazilian leftist governments since 2003 in comparative perspective.

 WEB LINKS

http://topics.nytimes.com/top/news/international/countriesandterritories/brazil/index.html   Brazil news archive, *New York Times*.

http://wilsoncenter.org   The home page of the Woodrow Wilson International Center for Scholars; offers access to the Brazil Center for centrist news and opinion.

http://www.cfr.org/region/index.html   The portal of the United States' Council on Foreign Relations, an independent think tank, closely representative of the 'foreign policy establishment' in Washington, DC.

http://www.cipamericas.org   News and views from the left-leaning investigative journalists of the Americas Program at the Center for International Policy.

http://www.coha.org/   News and views from the left-leaning investigative journalists at the Council on Hemispheric Affairs.

 For additional material and resources, please visit the Online Resource Centre at:
http://www.oxfordtextbooks.co.uk/orc/burnell4e/

28
China and the Developing World

Deborah Braütigam

Overview

China's rise as a world power marks the coming of age of a country that has, in recent years, been considered part of—and yet different from—the rest of the developing world. China's South—South relations are shaped by the nature of the Chinese state: a highly capable, developmental state that uses an array of instruments to promote its interests. In addition to foreign investment and commercial loans, the Chinese have developed 'soft power' tools with which to engage other developing countries. Chinese ties are shaped by long-standing foreign policy principles, including non-interference in the internal affairs of others, equality, and mutual benefit. China's need for raw materials and resources, the political imperative of reassuring other developing countries that China's rise will not pre-empt their opportunities, and China's embrace of globalization and the growth of its own multinational companies also condition its ties with other developing countries. Some applaud the rise of China as an investor and financier, noting that China provides an alternative to the Washington consensus. Others worry that Chinese competition, and lower concern for environmental, social, and governance standards, may set back progress in other developing countries. Figure 28.1 is a map of China and Box 28.1 provides an overview of key dates in China's history.

Figure 28.1 China

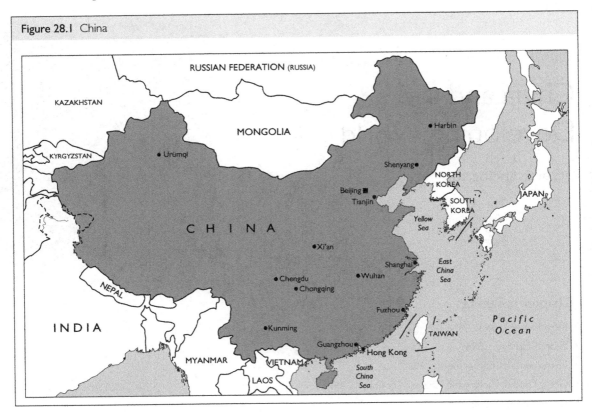

BOX 28.1   KEY DATES IN CHINA'S HISTORY

1949	Founding of the People's Republic of China (PRC)	1979	One-child policy imposed
1950	China intervenes on North Korea's side in Korean War	1982–83	Chinese premier Zhao Ziyang visits eleven countries in Africa
1955	Bandung Afro-Asian Conference in Indonesia	1989	Tiananmen Square demonstrations violently suppressed
1958–59	Great Leap Forward		
1959	China sends troops to suppress revolt in Tibet, tightening control	1989	Taiwan begins diplomatic offensive
		1993	China begins to import oil
1960	Soviet Union withdraws aid and advisers from China	1996	President Jiang Zemin state visit to six African countries, the first Chinese president to visit Africa
1962	Border war with India over Tibet		
1963	Chinese premier Zhou Enlai visits ten African countries		
		1997	Britain returns Hong Kong to China
1966–76	Cultural Revolution led by Mao Zedong and the 'Gang of Four'	2000	Forum on China–Africa Cooperation (FOCAC) established
1972	War with Vietnam (February–March)	2004	President Hu Jintao state visit to Brazil, Argentina, Chile, and Cuba
1976	Tanzania–Zambia Railway opens		
1978	Chinese pragmatists win over radicals; economic reforms begin	2005	President Hu Jintao pledges US$10 billion finance for Millennium Development Goals (MDGs)

2006	Beijing Summit of FOCAC; forty-four African heads of state participate	2012	China Central Television (CCTV) Africa launches in Nairobi, Kenya
2008	Beijing hosts summer Olympics; unrest in Tibet	2013	President Xi Jinping visits Russia and three African countries (Republic of Congo, South Africa, and Tanzania) on first foreign trip
2011	Exxon discovers oil in South China sea; regional disputes escalate		

Introduction

At least since the founding of the People's Republic of China (PRC) in 1949, the Chinese have considered themselves to be part of the **developing world**. China lost portions of its territory to the colonial ambitions of others, suffered armed invasion and revolution, and endured more than a decade as a failed state in the 'warlord period' between 1916 and 1928. Yet China's history as a developing country is also quite different from most other parts of the global South.

China has been an effective regional power in the past. The roots of its capable state bureaucracy can be traced back to the third century BC. China has long had the capacity to extend its reach far beyond its borders. Agriculture was relatively productive and well beyond the level of subsistence, while manufacturing was fairly well developed in areas such as Shanghai, even before the Second World War. Although, after 1949, China was subjected to political sanctions and trade embargos, it has never been dominated by foreign multinational corporations, grown dependent on foreign aid, or felt the weight of external pressure to liberalize its economy or to democratize.

In recent decades, as China has moved to regain its historic prominence as a centre of world trade, culture, and political influence, these differences have helped to shape the framework for its contemporary South–South engagement. In addition, China is both a centralized **developmental state** in the mode of Japan or South Korea, and a socialist country still undergoing economic liberalization. This tension means that while Beijing continues to plan its overseas engagements and has many tools with which to promote its interests, it no longer exercises complete control over state-owned companies and provincial governments. It has even less influence with the growing number of private Chinese and Hong Kong firms operating overseas (Gill and Reilly 2007).

Chinese foreign policy is influenced by the 'five principles of peaceful coexistence' (see Box 28.2). These principles emphasize sovereignty, non-interference in each other's internal affairs, non-aggression, equality, and mutual benefit. With some notable exceptions, such as Chinese support for left-wing rebellions abroad during the Cultural Revolution (1966–76), or sporadic clashes along the borders with the former Soviet Union, Vietnam, and India, Chinese leaders have shied away from political or military intervention overseas and promoted non-interference as a standard that prizes sovereignty over newer norms such as universal **human rights** or the '**responsibility to protect**' (R2P).

Too weak to stand as a counterweight to the hegemony of the Soviet Union or the Western powers during the cold war, China emphasized the equality of nations as promised by the United Nations and advocated multilateral forums for international negotiations concerning the rules of world order. Concerned about the vulnerabilities and inequalities associated with dependence on the Soviet Union during the 1950s, and with a relatively small budget for external assistance, China emphasized economic cooperation and mutual assistance, rather than the one-way transfer of resources through foreign aid. However, as China grows in power and influence, and as Chinese loans and investments are put at risk in politically tense environments, assumptions of equality, and the principles of mutual benefit and non-interference, are increasingly difficult to maintain.

BOX 28.2 FIVE PRINCIPLES OF PEACEFUL COEXISTENCE (1954)

1. Mutual respect for each other's territorial integrity and sovereignty

2. Mutual non-aggression

3. Mutual non-interference in each other's internal affairs

4. Equality and mutual benefit

5. Peaceful coexistence

China's South–South partnerships today build on a substantial history of foreign aid and economic cooperation, new instruments of **soft power**, and skyrocketing increases in trade, loans, and investment over the past decade. This involvement with other developing countries has at least four overarching goals.

(1) China aims to preserve its own sovereignty and territorial integrity. This security concern also helps to explain why Chinese assistance has always been concentrated in Asia, particularly in the countries on its border: North Korea, Cambodia, Burma, and Pakistan, for example.

(2) China has long used economic diplomacy to counter efforts by its breakaway province of Taiwan to gain international standing. This explains Beijing's emphasis on the 'One China' policy: a consistent practice of cutting off formal ties with all countries that give official diplomatic recognition to the government in Taiwan as 'China'.

(3) China wants to maintain its long-standing role as a leader among developing countries, while assuaging fears that its rise will threaten other countries. Knitting together regional groupings, ratcheting up communications and assistance, and building up the tools of public diplomacy are part of this effort.

(4) Finally, Beijing is keen to create a stable global environment that will allow China to focus on its own economic development. This includes secure access to raw materials, new markets, and opportunities for Chinese companies overseas.

KEY POINTS

- China considers itself to be a developing country, yet there are many differences between China's history and that of others in the global South.

- China is a developmental state and has many instruments with which to reach its national goals. But as China liberalizes its economy, it has less control over its companies and their behaviour overseas.

- The five policies of peaceful coexistence influence Chinese foreign policy and economic cooperation. These stress non-interference in internal affairs of other countries and mutual benefit.

A Brief History

Ethnic Chinese traders and labourers have ventured abroad for many centuries, settling in dense communities in South-East Asia, and establishing 'China-towns' in many other parts of the developing world. During most of its imperial history, however, the Chinese state was uninterested in venturing abroad, with the exception of the voyages of the Muslim Admiral Zheng He who travelled to Africa between 1418 and 1433.

In the mid-nineteenth and early twentieth centuries, the Chinese lost portions of their territory: the island of Taiwan to Japan; Macao to Portugal; Hong Kong to Great Britain. The last imperial dynasty ended in 1911 with the founding of the Republic of China (ROC). Battles with warlords between 1916 and 1928 gave way to a civil war between the ROC and the Chinese communists. In 1949, with the communists close to victory, the government of the ROC fled to the island of Taiwan, where it remains today. The United States intervened in the conflict by sending the Seventh Fleet to patrol the waters between Taiwan and the mainland. The United States was also able to muster enough international support to keep the ROC (that is, Taiwan) in China's Security Council seat at the United Nations until 1971.

At first, the Chinese communists had close ties with the Soviet Union, which sent advisers and helped to build China's economy. Deteriorating ties led Moscow to cut its assistance in 1960, just as the Chinese had begun to back away from the Great Leap Forward (1958–59), a disastrous effort to mobilize the population to create collective farms, rural mines, and rudimentary, small-scale industries. More than 20 million Chinese are believed to have died as a result of the Great Leap, combined with several natural disasters.

At the same time, the break with the Soviet Union helped China to solidify a role as part of the 'Third World'—not in the capitalist camp, but not in the Soviet camp either. The origins of this idea of non-alignment can be traced to the 1955 Afro-Asian Solidarity Conference in Bandung, Indonesia, at which Chinese leaders met with those from India, Egypt, and others just emerging from colonialism. Bandung helped mark out a space for countries that wished to avoid the two cold war camps. The five principles of peaceful coexistence proposed by China's premier Zhou Enlai were later espoused by the Non-Aligned Movement (NAM), even though there were notable exceptions: China's 1962 border war with India sparked by the Chinese military's suppression of the Tibet uprising, for example.

During the 1950s and even in the 1960s, Chinese engagement with other developing countries emphasized advancing the cause of socialism. When Zhou Enlai visited Africa in 1964, he declared the continent 'ripe for revolution'. Chinese assistance to communist North Vietnam, locked in combat with the United States, took up 40 per cent of China's aid budget during this period. However, the goal of regaining China's seat in the United Nations (UN) became an equally important objective. This required assuaging the fears of non-socialist countries in places such as Africa. Aid was an important tool in China's economic diplomacy. In 1975, four years after winning its seat back in the UN, China had aid programmes in more African countries than did the United States (Bräutigam 2011). In contrast, Chinese ties are newer in Latin America, a legacy of the cold war and of American hegemony. Chile, under socialist president Salvador Allende, was the first Latin American country to switch diplomatic ties from Taipei to Beijing (in 1972). Taiwan retained diplomatic ties with much of Central America until very recently.

In the late 1970s, under reformist leader Deng Xiaoping, the Chinese began a long road of gradual economic reforms. In 1982, Chinese premier Zhao Ziyang embarked on a trip to eleven African countries to discuss what China's economic reforms would mean for its relationships on the continent. Instead of aid, he said, China would now emphasize 'South–South cooperation' in a diversity of forms. It would experiment, beginning with joint ventures, construction projects, and other forms of engagement aimed at mutual benefit and practical results.

Nearly thirty years later, Chinese companies were making headlines with multibillion-dollar business deals in developing countries. China's relationship with other developing countries had evolved a great deal. The world had begun to see a small group of powerful countries—Brazil, Russia, India, and China—as the 'BRICs' (see Chapter 5): not as developed as the West and Japan, but not 'Third World' either (Glosny 2010: 129). Being part of this group allowed China to follow Deng Xiaoping's advice: 'Keep a low profile and be patient.'

KEY POINTS

- Like many other developing countries, China suffered colonial incursions, periods as a failed state, and civil war during the twentieth century.

- After the founding of the People's Republic of China in 1949, the Chinese communists broke away from the Soviet Union and tried to build a non-aligned movement.

- In the 1970s, aid shifted from being primarily a tool to support other socialist countries to being primarily a tool to win diplomatic recognition.

- As China shifted toward the market, its overseas engagement began to stress business opportunities and economic cooperation.

Instruments of Engagement

Although it attracted little notice until after the millennium, Chinese business engagement in Asia, Africa, and elsewhere in the developing world had been steadily growing since the 1990s. As that decade began, Chinese construction companies were already starting to win contracts in countries around the world. In a separate trend, in 1993, China's oil imports exceeded its oil exports for the first time (Downs 2007). By the end of the 1990s, it was clear that South–South cooperation would need to be vastly increased if China were to find the new markets and access to resources required to sustain its rapid **modernization**.

Following in the footsteps of Japan and other developmental states, the Chinese established new instruments to meet these goals. The China Export Import Bank (China Eximbank), set up in 1994, offered preferential government loans to facilitate trade and investment, particularly in poorer countries. It would also manage a new foreign aid instrument: low-interest (concessional) loans. The China Development Bank (CDB), set up in 1994, primarily to serve development needs within China, gradually began to support China's efforts to go global. In 2006, the CDB set up the China–Africa Development Fund, an equity fund targeted to reach US$5 billion, to promote Chinese investment. The CDB has also extended very large lines of credit to Chinese companies active overseas. The telecoms company Huawei, for example, received a US$10 billion line of credit in 2004 and another US$20 billion in 2009.

Beijing also began to set up new regional organizations to boost political, cultural, and economic ties. The Forum on China–Africa Cooperation (FOCAC) was established in 2000, and the Shanghai Cooperation Organization (SCO) emphasizing mutual security concerns, in 2001. The SCO comprises China, Russia, Uzbekistan, Kazakhstan, Kyrgyzstan, and Tajikistan. Forums were founded for the Caribbean, Portuguese-speaking countries, Arab states, and the Pacific Islands. These have many similar features, often including promises of aid, trade benefits, and debt relief.

Free trade agreements (FTAs) are another instrument of Chinese economic engagement. As of 2013, China had finalized six bilateral FTAs, with Singapore, New Zealand, and four developing countries: Chile, Costa Rica, Pakistan, and Peru. In addition, the Association of South-East Asian Nations (ASEAN) countries have a joint FTA with China.

The selection of regions for engagement reflected three goals:

(1) the drive to secure access to resources, in particular oil;

(2) the diplomatic isolation of Taiwan and the protection of Chinese interests in the many small countries in Africa, the South Pacific, and the Caribbean, where the competition with Taiwan remained a factor; and

(3) promoting business—for example, business networks in the Portuguese-speaking Chinese enclave of Macao were enlisted to give Chinese companies an important **comparative advantage** in concluding deals with countries such as Brazil.

Soft power

In addition, China's soft power expanded. Just as the French promote their language and culture and influence through the Alliance Française, and the Germans through the Goethe Institutes, so the Chinese have been setting up Confucius Institutes to teach the Chinese language and to sponsor cultural events. Between 2004 and 2012, more than 500 Confucius Institutes have been established in 108 countries. Since 1963, more than seventy-three countries have hosted Chinese medical teams, which spend two years offering traditional Chinese and Western medical treatments in local hospitals before returning to China. Between 2006 and 2012, university scholarships for African students were to increase from 2,000 to 5,500 per year. The Chinese

established a Youth Volunteer Programme in 2002, sending the first volunteers to countries on China's border: Laos and Burma. In 2006, Beijing pledged to send 300 youth volunteers to Africa. Between 2005 and 2011, some 17,000 young Chinese volunteers and language teachers were working in 117 countries.

As they moved up in international influence and power, Chinese leaders also became increasingly visible as benefactors in multilateral situations. For example, in a speech at the United Nations in September 2005, Chinese President Hu Jintao made a pledge to provide US$10 billion in finance for the **Millennium Development Goals (MDGs)** and training opportunities in China for 30,000 people from developing countries. The Chinese joined the African Development Bank in 1985 and the Inter-American Development Bank in 2009. In 2007, after many years as a recipient of World Bank assistance, China became a donor to the World Bank.

China's effort to position itself as a 'responsible power' was reflected in its unprecedented response to the Indian Ocean tsunami disaster in 2004 and the Pakistan earthquake in 2005. Chinese humanitarian aid that year came to about US$250 million—half from the government, and half from Chinese **non-governmental organizations (NGOs)** such as the Red Cross, and the private sector (Qi 2007: 5). Although Chinese humanitarian aid has been more modest since then, China has continued to provide emergency aid to countries around the world, sending earthquake disaster relief to Haiti in 2010 and tsunami relief to Japan in 2011, as well as humanitarian assistance to both Libya and Syria in 2012.

Arms and peacekeeping: China's military presence

Chinese arms in world export markets and the emergence of Chinese peacekeepers are two other sides of Chinese involvement in the developing world. Small arms made in China have been a feature of most conflicts in the developing world in recent years. Yet the restructuring of China's defence industry and the divestiture of enterprises formerly owned by the military means that it is difficult to track the dimensions of this trade. Beijing has not published information on its export of arms, while arms traders have sometimes mislabelled shipments of Chinese arms as agricultural equipment in order to slip past arms embargoes (Taylor 2009: 126). It is likely that more than half of China's arms exports go to Asia, with Africa receiving about 17 per cent. China is estimated to be third behind France and Russia as a supplier of arms to Africa (Taylor 2009: 119–20).

Although Chinese spokesmen insist that they respect the UN arms embargo on southern Sudan, military equipment of Chinese make has been recovered from sites in the troubled province of Darfur. In 2008, on the eve of landlocked Zimbabwe's controversial presidential election, South African unions in the port of Durban refused to unload the *An Yue Jiang*, a ship carrying arms intended for the Mugabe government, in power since 1980. In 2011, the Chinese foreign ministry admitted that state-run arms companies had negotiated arms sales to Libya, reportedly totalling more than $US200 million.

This portrait of China as arms supplier to rogue **regimes** is offset by another picture: China's role as a supplier of United Nations peacekeepers. More than 17,390 Chinese peacekeepers have served nineteen UN peacekeeping missions. At the end of 2011, according to UN figures, some 1,924 Chinese were serving in the UN police or military missions, mainly in Lebanon, Sudan, Liberia, and the Democratic Republic of the Congo. Of UN Security Council members, China ranks as the top supplier of UN peacekeepers. In 2009, responding to a sharp rise in attacks by Somali pirates on ships moving through the Arabian Gulf, the Chinese dispatched two naval ships to help to escort merchant vessels through the troubled waters. The Chinese navy coordinates with the United States and other countries whose ships also patrol the Arabian Gulf.

A growing assertiveness by China's navy has troubled several of its neighbours in the South China Sea, where Vietnam, the Republic of China (Taiwan), the Philippines, Malaysia, Brunei, and China have a series of overlapping claims to small islands, including the Spratly and Paracel archipelagos. These remote islands are primarily fishing grounds, but the relatively unexplored area is believed by some to have significant potential for oil and gas.

KEY POINTS

- Chinese policy banks were established to provide finance to meet government objectives. This follows the 'developmental state' model pioneered by Japan.

- China set up a number of regional organizations as strategic forums for interaction. Soft power and China's military presence also increased.

Going Global: Fuelling the Chinese Economy

Above all, China's growing partnerships with other developing countries today are based on economic interests. China's rapidly growing economy and position as the 'world's workshop' require raw materials and markets. Since 2001, under the 'Going Global' policies, Chinese companies have expanded their efforts to diversify their markets and to assure a supply of raw materials to the Chinese economy. Chinese firms are encouraged to invest abroad, helping Chinese industries at home to move up the value chain, and to shift away from labour and energy-intensive manufacturing. The Chinese state also wants a select group of its companies to become global leaders.

Trade is central in this effort. In 2004, visiting Latin America and the Caribbean, and in 2006, during a large summit of African leaders in Beijing, Chinese President Hu Jintao announced targets of US$100 billion in trade by 2010—with both regions. China succeeded early. In 2000, trade between China and Africa was only US$10.5 billion, and in Latin America, US$12.2 billion. By 2011, African trade surpassed US$160 billion and in Latin America, US$242 billion. This surge was partly a result of high prices for natural resources, stimulated by China's growing demand. However, in both regions, Chinese exports made up nearly half of this trade, demonstrating the success of Chinese companies in diversifying their markets. In Africa, some small-scale Chinese traders are competing with African traders in local markets, leading to complaints.

Chinese banks have ratcheted up their loans in developing countries, and some of these large loans are linked to natural resource exports. In Brazil, newly discovered oil deposits locked between layers of deep-sea salt beds required billions for state-owned Petrobras to unlock. The CDB offered Petrobras a line of credit of US$10 billion to be repaid by regular exports of oil (valued at the market price). In 2010, Venezuela signed a similar CDB oil-backed line of credit, for US$20 billion over ten years. Researchers identified over US$75 billion in lending commitments from Chinese banks in Latin America, since 2005, although these are not all resource-backed (Gallagher et al. 2012). The Democratic Republic of the Congo signed a deal in 2008 with a Chinese consortium to develop a copper/

cobalt mine. Output from the mine was expected to repay US$3 billion (and possibly more) worth of infrastructure (roads, rail, hospitals, water systems, universities), to be built mainly by Chinese companies. War-torn Angola has received at least US$10 billion in similar oil-backed infrastructure credits from China Eximbank and the Industrial and Commercial Bank of China since 2004, while in 2010 Ghana signed an agreement worth US$3 billion with the CDB, to be repaid in oil.

From resource-backed construction deals like these and by winning contracts financed by the World Bank, other donors, and African governments, Chinese companies have earned billions of dollars in recent years: US$36.1 billion in Africa; US$51.0 billion in Asia and the Middle East; and US$103.4 billion worldwide in 2011 alone. Many of these construction contracts were secured by telecoms companies such as Huawei, as the Chinese state helped them to profit by assisting Africans to bypass the era of fixed-line telephones and jump directly into wireless.

KEY POINTS

- The 'Going Global' policies involve trade diversification, secure access to raw materials, overseas investment, and contracting, and the building up of Chinese multinational corporations.

- Chinese trade has risen enormously, reaching US$160 billion in Africa and US$242 billion in Latin America in 2011.

- Chinese banks have made very large, long-term loans, many linked to repayment in natural resources. In Africa, some of these loans pay for much-needed infrastructure.

Controversies

Chinese engagement with other developing countries is more controversial than that of any of the other BRICs. Some worry that large new loans will exacerbate debt burdens. Particularly in Latin America and Africa, critics charge that Chinese economic engagement replicates 'colonial' patterns: exports of manufactured goods and imports of raw materials. Chinese textiles, plastic products, and other simple manufactured goods threaten the weak industrial sectors in some countries. Colombia imposed tariffs on Chinese textiles and South Africa asked China for temporary voluntary export restraints. While Chinese demand benefits commodity exporters through higher prices, Chinese goods have provided devastating competition for many manufacturers. To counter the political frictions caused by these trade patterns, the Chinese have announced programmes such as the planned construction of at least ten overseas economic zones, in which Chinese companies will be encouraged to invest in manufacturing.

Social and environmental complaints about Chinese companies are common. Many Chinese companies, particularly in Africa, use Chinese nationals for management and technical positions—on average, about 20 per cent of employment in a project or investment will be Chinese. In 2008, at least 140,000 Chinese were officially working in Africa and these numbers have been rising steadily (Ministry of Commerce, PRC, 2009). Others have criticized Chinese companies' low environmental, safety and labour standards. In one infamous case, an explosion in a Chinese-owned factory killed more than fifty Zambian workers. Poor work conditions have led to strikes and host government reprimands, from Peru to Papua New Guinea. Chinese companies are blamed for overfishing in the coastal waters of other developing countries, or for illegal timber harvesting. In 2005, Chile banned Chinese fishing trawlers from its ports, while coastal African countries have raised similar concerns. The rise of Chinese private companies, provincial firms, and increased independence for non-state actors (including Hong Kong companies) means that Beijing now has fewer levers with which to control the actions of its companies overseas (Gill and Reilly 2007).

Finally, **civil society** groups in developing countries and in the global North (along with northern governments) charged that Chinese policies of aid and commercial engagement with 'no strings attached' propped up rogue regimes in places such as Sudan, Myanmar (Burma), and Zimbabwe. The Chinese response is that active engagement works better than embargoes, that they abide by sanctions when imposed by the United Nations, and that their diplomats have played constructive roles in getting warring parties to agree to peace talks over thorny issues such as the Darfur rebellion in oil-rich Sudan. They also point out that, when it is convenient for them, Western companies and governments themselves engage with many reviled regimes.

Conclusion

Beijing is careful not to position China as the leader of the developing world. At the same time, Chinese leaders want their country to be seen as a 'responsible power', the rise of which will provide more opportunities than threats to other developing countries. As it grows wealthier, Beijing does not want to replicate the familiar 'North–South' relations based on foreign aid. And yet it runs the risk of being seen as reproducing 'neo-colonialism' through patterns of trade and investment based on raw materials and low-level manufactured goods. Because China's engagement with other developing countries has grown so rapidly, it is difficult to find more than anecdotal evidence of the impact of China's ties on **governance**, debt, environment, employment, or social standards. This makes it challenging to find balanced and accurate analysis, but it also means that the field is open for evidence-based research on an important new phenomenon.

KEY POINTS

- Chinese patterns of trade in many developing countries often follow 'colonial' patterns, with China exporting manufactured goods and importing raw materials.

- Concerns raised about Chinese companies overseas include their tendency to employ Chinese in management and skilled labour roles, and low social and environmental standards.

- China's policy of investment and aid without political conditions means that it actively engages some pariah regimes, such as Sudan, Zimbabwe, and Myanmar (Burma).

- Western reporting on Chinese economic engagement is often inaccurate. Misinformation travels quickly through cyberspace, lingering on websites without being corrected.

QUESTIONS

1. China is a quintessential 'Westphalian' power, believing strongly in state sovereignty. As China grows in power, is it more likely to follow existing global rules or will it create new rules?

2. Is China's rise a threat—or an opportunity—for other developing countries? Why?

3. What kind of evidence would we want to see in order to answer question 2?

4. Is China's effort to increase its attractiveness (soft power) likely to succeed in other developing countries?

5. Should China become more like the more developed countries in its pattern of aid and economic engagement? Why, or why not?

FURTHER READING

Bräutigam, D. (2011) *The Dragon's Gift: The Real Story of China in Africa* (Oxford: Oxford University Press) A comparative introduction to Chinese aid and economic engagement in Africa. Tackles the myths and misunderstandings, as well as the dimensions of engagement and how it works.

Nathan, A. J. and Scobell, A. (2012) *China's Search for Security* (New York: Columbia University Press) Focus on China's relations with its immediate neighbours, as well as other states in Asia and beyond.

Strauss, J. C. and Armony, A. C. (eds) (2012) *From the Great Wall to the New World: China and Latin America in the 21st Century* (Cambridge: Cambridge University Press) A special issue of *China Quarterly*, this book provides a comprehensive look at China's engagement in Latin America.

WEB LINKS

http://mqvu.wordpress.com/   Exporting China's Development to the World—a comprehensive website and blog by an international team of anthropologists, who research China's development engagement around the world.

http://www.chinaafricarealstory.com   China in Africa: The Real Story—a website and blog exploring Chinese aid, investment, and economic engagement in Africa.

http://www.chinadialogue.net/reports   China Dialogue focuses on China, environment, food security, and development issues.

http://www.thedialogue.org/chinaandlatinamerica   The Inter-American Dialogue, China Program, website, devoted to Chinese engagement in Latin America.

For additional material and resources, please visit the Online Resource Centre at:
http://www.oxfordtextbooks.co.uk/orc/burnell4e/

29

India as a 'Post-Colonial' Development Partner

Emma Mawdsley

Overview

Many countries of the global South have established 'development cooperation' policies and pro-grammes with other low- and middle-income countries. A few started as long ago as the 1950s, while others are more recent entrants to the field. Often bundled closely with trade, investment, and diplomatic agendas, such South–South partnership includes debt relief, concessional loans, grants, humanitarian assistance, technical support, and educational and training provision. Until recently, most Western commentators on foreign aid and development largely overlooked these (so-called) 'non-traditional' donors, but they are now firmly on the radar. The '(re-)emerging' donors and development partners raise a series of opportunities and challenges for the main-stream aid community, while the direct and indirect impacts of their development cooperation programmes have profound implications for the world's poor, and for the politics of development. This chapter outlines the main trends and issues of South–South development cooperation, using India as a case study. Figure 29.1 is a map of India and Box 29.1 provides an overview of key dates in India's history.

Figure 29.1 India

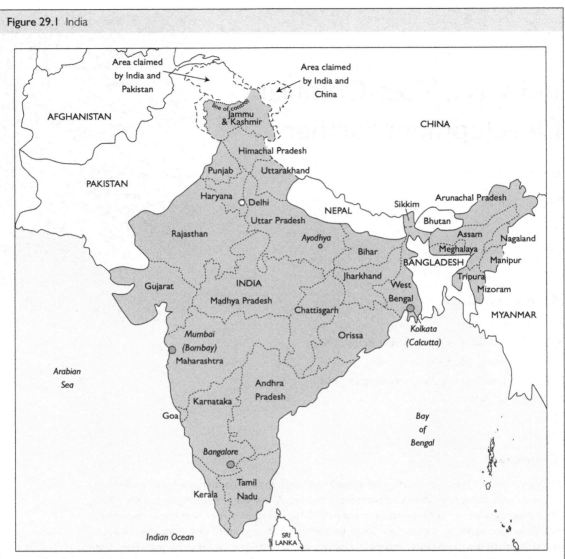

Note: Boundaries in the Kashmir region are in dispute. The use of specific nomenclature and boundary symbols on this map implies neither recognition nor non-recognition of the legality of the political regions or boundaries to which they refer.

BOX 29.1 KEY DATES IN INDIA'S HISTORY

1857	'Revolt', 'Mutiny', or 'First War of Independence' is suppressed	1920–22	Civil disobedience movement against British rule is launched by Congress, led by Mahatma Gandhi
1858	India comes under direct rule of the British Crown, which takes it over from the East India Company	1947	India achieves independence, but country is violently split by the Partition; East Pakistan (later Bangladesh) and West Pakistan (later Pakistan) are also created out of the former colony; Jawaharlal Nehru becomes independent India's first prime minister
1885	Indian National Congress is formed by emerging nationalists		

1949–52	Constitution of India is drawn up, declaring it to be a secular, federal republic	1998	Bharatiya Janata Party (BJP), a Hindu nationalist party, wins national elections; controversial nuclear tests carried out shortly afterwards
1962	India loses a short border war with China, despite earlier declarations of friendship	2000	India's population reaches 1 billion
1964	Jawaharlal Nehru dies	2006	Hu Jintao visits India, the first Chinese president to do so for a decade
1966	Indira Gandhi, Nehru's daughter (no relation to Mahatma Gandhi), becomes prime minister, leading the ruling Indian National Congress Party	2007	Launch of India's first commercial space rocket
1971	Third war with Pakistan, this time over the secession of East Pakistan to form Bangladesh	2008	Closer US–India ties signalled by a nuclear deal
		2009	Indian National Congress, with Manmohan Singh as prime minister, re-elected to central government
1984	Indira Gandhi assassinated; her son Rajiv Gandhi elected prime minister	2011	India joins the United Nations Security Council as a non-permanent member
1989	Congress loses the national elections to a coalition of other parties	2012	Manmohan Singh offers line of credit to Burma in the first official visit by an Indian prime minister since 1987
1991	Major economic reforms implemented by Prime Minister Narasimha Rao mark a decisive shift towards neoliberalism		

Introduction

Over the last few decades, India has not been only a recipient of foreign aid (at one time, the largest recipient in the world), but also a 'donor' of concessional loans, grants, technical assistance, peacekeeping forces, humanitarian assistance, debt relief and so on. This chapter explores how and why a country that still has more absolutely poor people than the whole of sub-Saharan Africa gives development assistance to countries in Asia, Africa, and beyond. It will start with a brief introduction to the issue of the '(re-)emerging' development actors and then move on to a more detailed analysis of India's development cooperation.

The 'Rising Powers' as Development Actors

Commentators tend to disagree—often virulently—about every conceivable aspect of 'mainstream' foreign aid, including stated and real motivations, effective and appropriate modalities, desirable recipients, direct and indirect impacts, and much more. The depth and range of disagreement is not surprising given the enormous complexity of the global foreign aid architecture, the vast range of actors—from

the World Bank, to bilateral aid agencies, to global **non-governmental organizations (NGOs)**, right down to small grass-roots local organizations—and its multiple, contingent, and often conflicting stated rationales—humanitarian, developmental, commercial, and geopolitical. But what almost all of these contending evaluations share is a dominant geographical imaginary that views foreign aid as given by rich industrialized countries to poorer countries. Until recently, with few exceptions, Western analysts almost entirely overlooked the large number of other countries that offer official 'development assistance' to other poorer countries. Six (2009) suggests that this represents a form of amnesia concerning these 'Other' donors. However, this is a situation that has changed rapidly, and large numbers of (so-called) 'non-traditional' donors and development partners (see Box 29.2 for a discussion of terminology) are now very much on the agenda.

The DAC donors

The Organisation for Economic Co-operation and Development (OECD) is made up of thirty-four countries, all of which are relatively industrialized and high income. Of these, twenty-seven are members of the Development Assistance Committee (DAC), while the twenty-eighth member is the European Commission

BOX 29.2 TERMINOLOGICAL DILEMMAS

'Emerging' or 'new' donors? Some countries are only recently embarking upon development assistance programmes (for example Thailand), but many have a long history of development partnership (for example Saudi Arabia, Vietnam, and Poland).

'Post-colonial' donors? In some ways, this is an attractive term, because it explicitly reverses **orientalist** binaries that set up the North as giver and the South as receiver. However, if the term is used in the sense of 'countries that were once formally colonized but which are now independent', it is not universally accurate.

'Non-DAC' donors (NDDs)? Although accurate, as a residual category (that is, something that is defined by what it is *not*),

this term appears to promote the centrality of the Development Assistance Committee (DAC) of the Organisation for Economic Co-operation and Development (OECD): what unites all of the other donors is their non-DAC **status**, suggesting a peripheral location, or even an unfulfilled aspiration. It does not signal the active critique of DAC ideologies and practices, and the wider discontent with the dominant structures of foreign aid, felt by many around the world, and especially within the global South. Moreover, many NDDs are cautious about the label of 'donor', with some firmly rejecting it. 'Donor' is burdened with associations of paternalism, hierarchy, and neo-colonial interference. Similarly, some reject the term 'foreign aid', preferring 'development assistance'.

(see Box 29.3). All are Western, with the exception of Japan (which at one point was the largest aid donor in the world) and, since January 2010, South Korea. The DAC has traditionally acted as a powerful forum for formulating dominant aid policies and practices around the world.

Many Southern, Gulf, and Central/East European states have been development partners for decades, and in some cases, quite substantial donors. In 1978, for example, the Organization of Petroleum Exporting Countries (OPEC) donors alone provided one third of all official foreign aid. Current calculations suggest that the NDDs contribute around 12–15 per cent of 'foreign aid', although extreme difficulties with both definitions, and the availability and robustness of data, mean

BOX 29.3 DAC AND NON-DAC DONORS

DAC members

Australia, Austria, Belgium, Canada, Czech Republic, Denmark, European Commission, Finland, France, Germany, Greece, Iceland, Ireland, Italy, Japan, Luxembourg, Netherlands, New Zealand, Norway, Poland, Portugal, Slovac Republic, South Korea, Spain, Sweden, Switzerland, United Kingdom, United States

Main non-DAC donors/development partners

Brazil, Bulgaria, China, Cuba, Cyprus, Estonia, Hungary, India, Israel, Kuwait, Latvia, Lithuania, Malta, Mexico, Romania, Russia, Saudi Arabia, Slovenia, South Africa, Taiwan, Thailand, Turkey, United Arab Emirates, Venezuela

that this can be estimated only with considerable caution. Although dwarfed by the DAC total, this is still a significant absolute and relative amount. Moreover, for some recipient countries, aid from the (re-)emerging development partners constitutes a high proportion of the total—notably, the Occupied Palestinian Territories and North Korea. Another way of looking at it is to compare absolute amounts with those of DAC donors. The OECD-DAC (undated) calculated that, in 2011, Saudi Arabia provided more **official development assistance (ODA)** than fifteen DAC donors, and China, more than eight DAC donors. The growing numbers of Southern donors was starkly demonstrated after the Indian Ocean tsunami of 2004, when more than seventy countries offered humanitarian assistance.

Today's (re-)emerging development partners have a variety of historical ties and contexts for their development assistance. In the post-war era, a large number of communist countries provided various forms of development assistance to other communist countries and to 'friendly' **regimes**, including Vietnam, Yemen, and Indonesia, amongst others. The Arab OPEC donors significantly expanded their development cooperation **institutions** following the oil price rises of the 1970s. Driven by regional geopolitical and economic considerations, and shaped by Islamic cultures of charitable giving, some have been substantial donors for more than forty years.

The historical lineages of other donors lie in more specific interests. For example, the origins of Taiwan's foreign aid activities are highly specific to its competition with the People's Republic of China (PRC) for diplomatic recognition, but they also reflect its achievement of rapid and very successful industrial development and **economic growth**, and the view that it has valuable experiences to share.

It is notable that it is only in the last few years that the broader development community has really woken up to these 'other' development actors. What has jolted Western academics and policymakers out of their amnesia in the last few years has much to do with the growing role and presence of China (Bräutigam 2009). China is a major, long-standing development assistance partner to many countries, and its growing development partnership activities actively complement its wider economic, diplomatic and geopolitical ambitions (see Chapter 28). The recent visibility of these other donors/partners has also been driven by Venezuela's substantial aid programme under Hugo Chávez, which was openly constructed as a challenge to US hegemony, as well as simply the growing numbers of development actors. Furthermore, in 2004, ten new states joined the European Union. Most had previous experience of foreign aid during the socialist period, but they are now in the process of re-establishing their aid institutions and policies in compliance with the Union's norms and standards (Lightfoot 2008).

We can now observe within the heavily Western-dominated 'global' foreign aid architecture, including DAC, its member states, the World Bank Group, and various United Nations bodies, a huge new interest in this more diverse set of development actors. This chapter offers a case study of India as a 'post-colonial' development partner. India is obviously not representative of these 'new' partners—they are simply too diverse in their origins, histories, interests, capabilities, ideologies, and cultures—but what we sacrifice in breadth, we gain in some depth through this case study.

KEY POINTS

- There is no easy way in which to capture or categorize the diversity of the (re-)emerging development partners.

- Although they have historically contributed a significant share of official 'aid', Western academic and policy analysts have tended to overlook their roles and activities—something that is now changing rapidly.

- South–South development cooperation is not the same as 'foreign aid'. It usually includes 'aid' and 'aid-like' flows and activities, but is frequently explicitly bundled and blurred with investment, trade, and diplomatic agendas.

India and South–South Relations

Over the last sixty years, India has been at the centre of a series of attempts to contest the ordering of the world along the economic and political hierarchies established during the colonial period, which deepened in the period after the Second World War. India was a key architect of the Non-Aligned Movement (NAM), for example, which had its origins in the 1950s and which insisted on the sovereign right of the newly decolonizing nations to resist subordination to the cold war giants. At the Bandung Conference of 1955, the principles of South–South solidarity were set out as: mutual respect for territorial integrity and sovereignty; mutual non-aggression; mutual non-interference in domestic affairs; equality and mutual benefit; and peaceful coexistence. Although aid was never a major aspect of the NAM, these discourses of non-interference and mutual benefit remain the stated values underlying much South–South development cooperation programmes (although, like other aspects of NAM, practices sometimes depart from principles).

Over the last ten or fifteen years, sustained high economic growth (albeit very socially and regionally uneven in its rewards) has enabled India to put greater financial and diplomatic weight behind these assertions of global stature. Whereas, in the first few decades of independence, India had to mobilize other strengths—Prime Minister Nehru's charisma and the exercise of 'soft power', India's size, its ability to play off the United States and Soviet Union, and its technological and scientific strengths—now its growing wealth, and the confidence of its increasingly assertive middle classes and elites, are underpinning a new vigour in its foreign policy (Raja Mohan 2004). During the 1990s and twenty-first century, for example, India has been a controversially disruptive voice in the World Trade Organization (WTO), demanding a better deal for developing countries. However, despite claims to Third World leadership:

    ❝ India's foreign policy has always exhibited a dichotomy between principle and practice: an ideological opposition to formal institutionalized discrimination in the international system—such as UNSC [United Nations Security Council] permanent membership and nuclear weapon status in the Nuclear Non-Proliferation Treaty—has gone hand-in-hand with a pragmatic willingness to seek the best possible deal for India within a hierarchical international system that is not egalitarian. ❞

(Sahni 2007: 23)

This would suggest that India's claim to leadership, and to South–South partnership and solidarity, must be critically and carefully appraised in all arenas, including its development cooperation efforts. Singh (2007: 10), for example, argues that 'ever since economic liberalization started in 1991 India's foreign policy has been increasingly driven towards finding export markets, and attracting foreign capital and technological know-how', and observes the growing place of development cooperation in facilitating these trends. As this chapter will argue, while there are indeed many potential direct and indirect benefits from India's development cooperation efforts, it would be naive to see these as necessarily positive simply by virtue of India's post-colonial status and rhetoric of developing country solidarity, as some less critical commentators claim.

> ### KEY POINTS
>
> - India has long positioned itself as a leader of the **developing world**, and has been an active and sometimes effective challenger of neo-imperialistic hierarchies that characterize the current world order.
>
> - India's strategic imperatives (as with any other state) mean the pursuit of its interests may sometimes elide, and sometimes clash, with the interests of other Southern states, and groups within them.

India as a Development Assistance Partner

After independence in 1947, India was very quickly targeted by both the United States and the Soviet Union as a potential cold war ally, although over the succeeding decades the United States was to turn much more strongly to India's neighbour and rival, Pakistan. Even so, both offered substantial amounts of aid to India and it became one of the largest aid recipients in the world. Despite this status, India rapidly took on a donor mantle, starting in the 1950s with its northern Himalayan neighbours, Nepal and Bhutan. As well as funding infrastructure development, India assistance included the provision of technical experts in a wide range of fields to partner countries, and the offer of scholarships and training. Despite budget constraints, Nehru was determined that India would invest in science and technology, and to that end he made sure that scarce funding was directed towards universities and research institutions—expertise that India has been able to deploy abroad. In 1964, India created the Indian Technical and Economic Cooperation (ITEC) scheme. The scheme supports projects, deputations of experts, and study tours, but its main focus is on providing training programmes in areas as diverse as small and medium-sized enterprises (SMEs), rural credit programmes, food processing, textiles, information technology, and women's entrepreneurship. The scheme now runs in 156 countries and, through it, the Indian government offers about 4,000 placements a year.

What explains India's early entry into donor activities? Clearly, it was in part motivated by the desire to create regional goodwill, especially given the hostile embrace of West Pakistan (now Pakistan) and East Pakistan (now Bangladesh) following Partition in 1947. Moreover, after Sino–Indian friendship crumbled (the nadir being the 1962 border invasion), India wished to promote strong and stable buffer states between itself and China. Thus India looked to secure regional allies, and its development cooperation played some part in that. A second incentive was energy security, which helps to explain the early focus on hydropower projects in Bhutan and Nepal. A third motivation arose from India's desire to take its place in the world not only as a regional, but also as an international, power. Being a development partner helped to build relations of solidarity with other newly independent countries, and signalled India's aspirant status to international stature.

India's own technological achievements continue to be reflected in its development cooperation profile. One of its current flagship technology transfer programmes is the pan-Africa e-network. The scheme aims to provide facilities for tele-education, tele-medicine, and network video conferencing for heads of state in all fifty-three members of the African Union (AU). The network will also connect fifty-three learning centres, ten super-speciality hospitals (three of which are in India), fifty-three other hospitals, and five universities (two in India). India has committed at least US$100 million to this scheme. Other forms of development assistance include debt write-offs, and a substantial set of contributions to food aid and peacekeeping personnel. The pursuit of 'soft power' continues to be a major incentive for development cooperation, as a resurgent India acts as a key player in the growing challenge to current hegemonies.

Development assistance, in other words, can be a useful means of promoting good diplomatic relations around the world.

However, the last few years have witnessed some significant changes in the modalities of India's development cooperation. In particular, lines of credit are becoming an increasingly favoured route of channelling development assistance. These are a form of state-sponsored subsidy for Indian or recipient country firms (or governments), and are intended to facilitate the development of trade and investment. Lines of credit are often tied to the purchase of Indian goods and services. Since 2003, these have been managed by the Export-Import Bank of India, which is managed indirectly by the Ministry of Finance. The Ministry of Commerce is also playing a growing role—indicative of the increasingly economically strategic profile of Indian aid. India's development cooperation is evidently being increasingly leveraged to support commercial and trade objectives. Mutual benefits with 'partner' countries are entirely possible within this new dispensation—being strategic does not necessarily undermine effectiveness, just as being altruistic does not necessarily achieve positive change—but the claims to a 'win–win' scenario are not always substantiated.

The changing geography of Indian development cooperation is also suggestive of its increasingly strategic intent. After Asia, Africa has long been a major destination for India's developmental assistance, with the anglophone Commonwealth countries historically the favoured partners. However, one of the interesting shifts in India's engagement with Africa has been its growing interest in West Africa (Singh 2007). While India has had long linkages with Nigeria and Ghana, it has tended to have less diplomatic affinity and trade relations with francophone countries. What has changed is the growing demand for resources—above all oil—and the search for investment opportunities. Reflecting these new imperatives, in 2004 the 'Techno-Economic Approach for Africa-India Movement' (TEAM-9) initiative was launched by the government of India, together with eight resource- and energy-rich West African countries.

India also contributes to regional and global development institutions, and is now a net creditor to the International Monetary Fund (IMF), and a major contributor to the World Food Programme and to UN peacekeeping forces. In the last few years, India has also engaged in development cooperation with other donors, although so far only in a limited number of arenas—notably Afghanistan, in which it is a member of the Afghanistan Donors Group. India was also one of the 'Group of Four' (G4), together with Australia, Japan, and the United States, which coordinated the post-tsunami emergency relief response in 2005. One area in which there has been little change to date has been that of NGOs and other **civil society** organizations. Aside from the Indian Red Cross, India has not yet sought to make use of NGOs as a channel for development funding and assistance. The government has an uneasy relationship with its own NGO community, and in the past has appeared reluctant to devolve any overseas functions in this direction—although this may be something that changes in the next few years.

India has also been involved in emerging pressures on the global architecture of foreign aid. In 2007, for example, India helped to promote the creation of the Development Cooperation Forum in the United Nations Economic and Social Council (ECOSOC), which, unlike the DAC, represents a grouping of donors *and* recipients, and which seeks to identify *mutually* acceptable principles and priorities. India, like other (re-)emerging development partners, has signalled its independence from dominant aid ideologies and practices, deliberately articulating different principles of development engagement. Thus, in 2003, India announced that it no longer needed the assistance of the majority of its own donors, although they are still able to fund NGOs in India, under government supervision and through multilateral organizations. The remaining donors (Germany, Japan, Russia, Britain, the United States, and the European Union) are subject to considerable scrutiny and direction from the government, and in 2012 a timeline for the end of British aid to India was agreed. India has recently paid off its debts to fifteen bilateral funders, and large parts of its debt to the Asian Development Bank and the World Bank. However, the paradox of India's own vast levels of poverty remains unresolved. For some commentators, India's development cooperation is all about diplomatic and commercial support for the 'rising power' constituency of India—the politicians, policymakers, and increasingly affluent middle classes who benefit most from its booming neoliberal economy and increasingly assertive global presence. At present, these benefits appear not to be trickling down to the mass of India's poor. Questions are also being raised about who benefits from Indian development cooperation in recipient countries. In some cases, it certainly supports wider 'development' benefits; in other cases, Indian development assistance appears to be providing financial and technical support for land grabbing and resource extraction that benefit donor and recipient elites, while often displacing and exploiting poor and marginalized peoples (Rowden 2011).

KEY POINTS

- India has a long history of development assistance in Asia and Africa, in some cases dating back to the 1950s.

- India argues that it differs from Western donors in that it promotes 'genuine' partnership and mutual benefit.

- Many commentators suggest that the motivations for Indian development assistance are increasingly tilting from promoting South–South solidarity and diplomatic alliances, towards more commercial and resource-oriented needs. However, these are not necessarily mutually exclusive.

- The benefits of India's development cooperation are shared unevenly, domestically and abroad.

Conclusion

Political analysts of foreign aid are becoming increasingly aware of the opportunities and problems raised by the diverse set of 'non-traditional' development partners. For their supporters, these (re-)emerging development actors represent a break from, and alternative to, the discredited intentions and outcomes of Western-dominated foreign aid. As Woods (2008: 1220) suggests:

> **"** In Africa and elsewhere, governments needing development assistance are skeptical of promises of more aid, wary of conditionalities associated with aid, and fatigued by the heavy bureaucratic and burdensome delivery systems used for delivery of aid. Small wonder that the emerging donors are being welcomed with open arms. **"**

However, despite claims by some to a selfless postcolonial solidarity, there is no doubt that the NDDs share the complex mix of motivations that characterize Western donors—humanitarian, geopolitical, and commercial. The differences between them reside more in the modalities and discourses of NDD foreign aid. The relative lack of **conditionalities** is key here: no **structural adjustment programmes (SAPs)** or insistence on '**good governance**' accompany the bulk of NDD assistance. Supporters argue that this more honest relationship represents genuine partnership, as opposed to what many see as the hollow use of the term by the World Bank and others, allowing partner countries to benefit much more from investment in training opportunities, infrastructure development, trade growth, and local investment. Critics, on the other hand, fear that the NDDs will contribute to an unravelling of the fragile process towards greater transparency, effectiveness, and well-targeted antipoverty efforts.

Most analytical attention is understandably directed at China, but India, like other NDDs, provides a fascinating example of a challenge to Western-dominated institutions, practices, and ideologies of foreign aid. The **politics** of the developing world is changing, and development cooperation is one constituent element and reflection of this, bringing new challenges and opportunities for poorer peoples and poorer countries around the world.

 **QUESTIONS**

1. What will be the impacts of the (re-)emerging development actors on humanitarian intervention, longer-term development, poverty reduction, and economic growth in poorer countries?

2. What will be the impacts of these donors and development partners on the existing architecture of foreign aid—the ideologies, policies, and practices of the dominant institutions?

3. What part will 'non-traditional' development assistance play in the changing global geographies of economic and geopolitical power that are taking place and predicted to accelerate?

4. What challenges do these shifts imply for theorizing politics and development in a new global era?

FURTHER READING

Agrawal, S. (2007) *Emerging Donors in International Development Assistance: The India Case*, Partnership in Business and Development Working Paper, available online at http://www.idrc.ca/EN/Documents/Case-of-India.pdf   A useful summary of Indian development cooperation, but should be read with more up-to-date work by Chaturvedi (see below) and others.

Chaturvedi, S., Fues, T., and Sidiropoulos, E. (2012) *Development Cooperation and Emerging Powers: New Partners or Old Patterns?* (London: Zed Books) Includes a chapter on India.

Manning, R. (2006) 'Will "Emerging" Donors Challenge the Face of International Co-operation?', *Development Policy Review*, 24(4): 371–83 A view on the emerging donors from the former director of DAC.

Mawdsley, E. (2012) *From Recipients to Donors: Emerging Powers and the Changing Development Landscape* (London: Zed Books) A comprehensive and accessible account of the 'rising powers' as development actors.

Woods, N. (2008) 'Whose Aid? Whose Influence? China, Emerging Donors and the Silent Revolution in Development Assistance', *International Affairs*, 84(6): 1205–21 Critically summarizes the 'emerging donors' and the response of the 'traditional' donor community.

WEB LINKS

http://ssc.undp.org/   Homepage of the United Nation's special unit for South–South cooperation.

http://www.africa-union.org/root/au/Conferences/2008/april/India-Africa/India-Africa.html   Website for the Africa–India Forum Summit.

http://www.oecd.org/dac/aidstatistics/trackingtrendsbeyondthedac.htm   Based on DAC definitions of 'ODA', provides calculations of all DAC and some key non-DAC donor contributions.

For additional material and resources, please visit the Online Resource Centre at
http://www.oxfordtextbooks.co.uk/orc/burnell4e/

Appendix A

Case Study Countries: Basic Indicators

	Population 2012, million[1]	Average annual population growth 2000–11, %[2]	GNI 2011, US$bn, PPP[2]	GNI per capita 2011, US$ PPP[2]	GDP per capita growth 2011, %[2]	% of population on less than US$1.25 a day, PPP (Most recent)[2]	GINI index (most recent)[2]	HDI value 2012[1]	Political rights 2012–13[3]	Civil liberties 2012–13[3]
Brazil	198.4	1.1%	2,245	11,420	1.8%	6.1%	54.7	0.73	2	2
China	1,353.6	0.6%	11,270	8,390	8.8%	11.8%	42.1	0.699	7	6
Guatemala	15.1	2.5%	70	4,760	1.3%	13.5%	55.9	0.581	3	4
India	1,258.4	1.5%	4,492	3,620	4.9%	32.7%	33.9	0.554	2	3
Indonesia	244.8	1.2%	1,091	4,500	5.4%	18.1%	35.6	0.629	2	3
Iraq	33.7	2.8%	123	3,750	6.8%	2.8%	30.9	0.59	6	6
Mexico	116.1	1.3%	1,919	16,720	2.7%	0.7%	47.2	0.775	3	3
Nigeria	166.6	2.5%	372	2,290	4.7%	68%	39.7	0.471	4	5
Pakistan	180	1.9%	507	2,870	1.1%	21%	30	0.515	4	5
South Korea	48.6	0.5%	1,489	29,920	2.9%	n/a	31.6*	0.909	1	2
UK	62.8	0.6%	2,255	35,950	−0.0%	n/a	40.8*	0.875	1	1
US	315.8	0.9%	15,211	48,820	1.0%	n/a	36*	0.937	1	1

* Old data from 1998–2000

Note: GNI = gross national income; GDP = gross domestic product; PPP = purchasing power parity; HDI = Human Development Index

Sources: [1]UNDP (2013) Human Development Report; [2]World Bank (2011); [3]Freedom House (2012)

Appendix B

Case Study Countries: Gender-Related Indicators

	HDI rank 2012[1]	GDI rank 2012[1]	Maternal mortality 2010, deaths per 100,000 live births[1]	Female population with at least secondary education (most recent), % ages 25 and older[1]	Male population with at least secondary education (most recent), % ages 25 and older[1]	Labour force participation rate women 2011, % ages 15 and older[1]	Labour force participation rate men 2011, % ages 15 and older[1]	Women seats in parliament 2012, %[1]	Total fertility rate[2]
Brazil	85	85	56	50.5%	48.5%	59.6%	80.9%	9.6%	1.8
China	101	35	37	54.8%	70.4%	67.7%	80.1%	21.3%	1.6
Guatemala	133	114	120	12.6%	17.4%	49%	88.3%	13.3%	3.1
India	136	132	200	26.6%	50.4%	29%	80.7%	10.9%	2.6
Indonesia	121	106	220	36.2%	46.8%	51.2%	84.2%	18.2%	2.2
Iraq	131	120	63	22%	42.7%	14.5%	69.3%	25.2%	3.5
Mexico	61	72	50	51.2%	57%	44.3%	80.5%	36%	2.3
Nigeria	153	n/a	630	–	–	47.9%	63.3%	6.7%	5.3
Pakistan	146	123	260	18.3%	43.1%	22.7%	83.3%	21.1%	3
South Korea	12	27	16	79.4%	91.7%	49.2%	71.4%	15.7%	1.2
UK	26	34	12	99.6%	99.8%	55.6%	68.5%	22.1%	1.9
US	3	42	21	94.7%	94.3%	57.5%	70.1%	17%	2

Note: HDI = Human Development Index; GDI = Gender-related Development Index

Sources: [1]UNDP (2013) Human Development Report; [2]World Bank (2013)

Glossary

Aberyswyth school Differs from traditional security in its focus on the lives of people, and its concept of emancipation and concern with justice and human rights.

aid selectivity Determining aid allocations between countries on the basis of demonstrable commitment to pro-developmental policies and institutions rather than on the basis of future promises or conditionalities.

apartheid An Afrikaans word meaning 'separateness', in South Africa expressed as the official government policy of racial segregation between 1948 and 1989.

ascriptive identities Groupings to which people belong by birth rather than by choice.

autonomy of politics/political autonomy The extent to which politics, as a level or sphere of social life, is determined by economic and/or social/cultural dimensions of society, or is able independently to impact on those dimensions.

balkanization Referring to the breaking up of a region or country into small territorial units, often as a means to 'divide and rule'.

caste A system of social stratification characterized by hereditary status, endogamy, and social barriers sanctioned by custom or law.

caste associations Organizations to represent the interests of a caste group or cluster of closely related caste groups, largely confined to India.

caudillismo Historically referring to the organization of political life in parts of Latin America by local 'strongmen' (*caudillos*) competing for power and its spoils.

chaebols The family-based business groups or conglomerates, many of them with cross-ownership, that have been South Korea's primary source of capital accumulation.

Christian democracy The application of Christian precepts to electoral politics.

civic nationalism Involving unity among citizens of an autonomous state.

civil regulation In the environmental arena, referring to a range of activities undertaken by civil society actors aimed at creating new frameworks of expectation and obligation for companies.

civil society A term highly contested, concerning the realm of voluntary citizen associations that exists between the family and the state, enjoying independence of the latter and seeking to influence public policy without aspirations to public office; **modern civil society** comprises formal, professionalized nongovernmental organizations typical of the late twentieth century; **traditional civil society** is organized more informally, and may follow patterns with deep and enduring roots in history and society.

clash of civilizations Referring to Samuel P. Huntington's prediction that, after the end of the cold war, international conflicts would increasingly have cultural characteristics, most notably setting the Christian 'West' against the mostly Muslim, mostly Arab, 'East'.

clientelism/clientelist Referring to the exchange of specific services or resources (usually publicly funded) between individuals in return for political support such as votes, and essentially a relationship between unequals.

collapsed state *See* **state collapse**.

commodification The transformation of something into a commodity to be bought and sold on the market.

comparative advantage The economic theory that countries should specialize in the production and export of those goods and services in which they have a *relative* production cost advantage compared with other countries.

competitive authoritarianism A kind of 'illiberal democracy' in which formal democratic institutions are widely viewed as the principal source of political authority, but rulers violate the rules so strikingly that the regime fails to meet conventional minimum standards of democracy.

conditionality/conditionalities Referring to the attachment of policy and/or other conditions to offers of financial and other assistance, with the possibility of aid sanctions for non-compliance.

conventional constructivists Examine the role of ideas, identity, and other cultural factors in our understanding or 'construction' of security.

corruption Involving the private use of public office and resources, and generally considered illegal.

critical security studies Refers to approaches united by dissatisfaction with the so-called 'traditional' security studies, and in particular its state- and military-centrism.

cross-conditionality Exists where one lender makes its aid offers conditional on the recipient meeting conditions laid down by one or more other lenders.

cruel choice Jagdish Bhagwati's term for the dilemma that he believed faced developing countries: either concentrate on economic development, or emulate the political systems of the West.

cultural imperialism The domination of vulnerable peoples by the culture of economically and politically powerful societies.

decentralized despotism A pattern of colonial and post-colonial government identified by Mahmood Mamdani (1996) as arising from the colonial practice of indirect rule.

delegative democracy According to Guillermo O'Donnell, resting on the premise that whoever wins election to the presidency is thereby entitled to govern as he or she thinks fit, constrained only by the hard facts of existing power relations and a constitutionally limited term of office.

democracy assistance Comprises largely consensual and concessionary international support to democratic reform chiefly by way of specific projects and programmes, such as civil society capacity-building endeavours.

democracy promotion Encompasses a wide range of approaches including not only democracy assistance, but also diplomatic pressure and, in some accounts, much more coercive forms of intervention of which democratization is the stated goal.

democratic peace theory The claim that democracies do not go to war with one another.

democratization backwards Describing situations in which largely free elections are introduced in advance of such basic institutions of the modern state as the rule of law, full executive accountability, and a flourishing civil society.

dependency theory An argument that the weak structural position of developing countries in the international capitalist system influences important variables in their political life, as well as explains their failure to achieve stronger development.

despotic power The power to control and suppress (as Michael Mann has called it), as opposed to **infrastructural power** (that is, the power to penetrate and transform society).

developing world A term conventionally referring to the predominantly post-colonial regions of Africa, Asia, Latin America and the Caribbean, and the Middle East, perceived to be poorer, less economically advanced, and less 'modern' than the developed world.

development administration A field of study aimed at providing an understanding of administrative performance in the specific economic and cultural contexts of poor, non-Western societies.

developmental state According to Adrian Leftwich, concentrating sufficient power, autonomy, and capacity at the centre to bring about explicit developmental objectives, whether by encouraging the conditions and direction of economic growth or by organizing it directly; its hallmarks include a competent bureaucracy and the insulation of state institutions from special interests in society—in other words, the state enjoys **embedded autonomy**; while there are significant differences among the cases commonly cited as examples of the development state, the most successful examples in East Asia have tended to be authoritarian.

direct democracy Exists where citizens can vote directly on public policy and decide what is to be done on other important political issues, through devices such as referenda.

eco-colonialism An argument that the imposition of environmental conditions on financial and economic support for developing countries restricts their development.

economic growth The rate of growth in a country's national output or income, often measured by its gross domestic product (GDP) or gross national product (GNP), and often presented on a per capita basis.

economic rents Incomes derived from the possession of a valuable licence or permit, particularly for the import of foreign goods.

electoral authoritarianism/autocracy In which elections are an instrument of authoritarian rule, an alternative to both democracy and naked repression.

electoral democracy A fairly minimalist conception of democracy that highlights electoral competition and a degree of popular participation, but understates the civil liberties and some other distinguishing features associated with liberal democracy.

emancipation In international relations theory, comes from the Aberystwyth School of **critical security studies** that defines security in terms of 'emancipation' or freedom of people from threats.

embedded autonomy According to Peter Evans, characterized by the relative facility of the developmental state to transcend sectional interests in society, providing a sound basis for pursuing national industrial transformation.

entitlements Justified rights or claims belonging to individuals or groups.

equality of outcome An approach that aims to make people equal whatever their original differences.

ethnic identities Socially constructed identities that follow when people self-consciously distinguish themselves from others on the basis of perceived common descent and/or shared culture; many, but not all, such identities are politicized.

ethnic morphology Refers to the form and structure of groups.

ethno-national identities Defining the nation in ethnic terms, attaining unity through the merger of ethnic and national identities, and demanding autonomy for ethnic nations.

ethnopolitical identities Those ethnic identities that have been politicized—that is, made politically relevant.

evaluation research Research into the outcomes of programme intervention or policy change.

exploitation Defined by the *Oxford English Dictionary* as, 'a situation in which somebody treats somebody else in an unfair way, especially in order to make money from their work'.

extents of freedom In Amartya Sen's terminology, the capabilities or the *freedom* to achieve whatever functionings an individual happens to value.

extractive state The idea that the extraction of the nation's (natural resource) wealth for the benefit of its ruler(s) becomes the primary goal of the ruler(s).

extraversion A theory of African political behaviour developed by Jean-François Bayart (1993) that argues that, historically, the relatively weak development of the continent's productive forces and its internal social struggles made African political actors more disposed to mobilize resources from their relationship with the external environment.

failing state A state that is failing in respect of some or all of its functions without yet having reached the stage of 'collapse'.

fallacy of electoralism Privileging electoral contestation as if that were a sufficient condition for democracy to exist.

fatwa A religious edict issued by an Islamic leader.

feminism/feminist Comprising recognition and action on women's common bonds and inequalities between men and women.

garrison state A state maintained by military power and, in some definitions, a state organized to secure primarily its own need for military security.

gatekeeper state A term coined by the African historian Frederick Cooper (2002) to denote a form of state focused on controlling the intersection of the territory with the outside world, collecting and distributing the resources that that control brought.

gender Referring to ideas about male and female, and the relations between them as social constructions rather than the product of biological determinants only.

genocide Referring to deliberate extermination of a social group selected on grounds of culture, ethnicity, or race.

Gini coefficient A commonly used measure of inequality (household income or consumption): the higher the figure, the more unequal the distribution.

global justice movement A loose, increasingly transnational network of non-governmental and social movement organizations opposed to neoliberal economic globalization, violence, and North–South inequalities; they support participatory democracy, equality, and sustainable development.

global stewardship Referring to resources that are said to be part of the common heritage of humankind and should be managed for the benefit of all.

globalization A highly contested term, defined in different ways that range from increasing global economic integration, in particular international trade, to processes whereby many social relations become relatively delinked from territorial geography and human lives are increasingly played out in the world as a single place.

globalization theory Focusing on a process of accelerated communication and economic integration that transcends national boundaries, and increasingly incorporates all parts of the world into a single social system.

good governance Originated in World Bank discourse to mean the sound management of public affairs with a bias towards neoliberal conceptions of the state's role in the economy, but went on to acquire broader connotations sharing many of the ideas and institutions associated with democracy, and hence democratic governance.

governance An omnibus term with a variety of meanings that reflects its usage in diverse disciplines and practices ranging from new public management to international development cooperation, and spanning institutions at both the local and the global levels; best defined contextually, and best understood with reference to both the objective and normative purposes of the definer, as exemplified in, for instance, the similarly wide-ranging, but nevertheless contrasting, accounts offered by the Governance Matters Project of the World Bank and the World Governance Assessment,

which lies closer to the thinking of the United Nations Development Programme.

Hindu caste system A complex and ancient, although evolving, system of social stratification in which people's caste status is determined at birth.

HIV/AIDS Refers to human immunodeficiency virus, a retrovirus that infects cells of the human immune system; it is widely accepted that infection with HIV causes AIDS (acquired immunodeficiency syndrome), a disease characterized by the destruction of the immune system.

human capital Referring to the knowledge, skills, and capabilities of individuals.

human development According to the United Nations Development Programme, about freedom, well-being, and dignity of people everywhere; the UNDP's Human Development Index measures longevity, educational attainment, and standard of living.

human rights Either the rights that everyone has because they are human or those generally recognized as such by governments or in international law.

human security An emerging paradigm that links development studies and national security, and which is defined as the protection of human lives from critical and pervasive threats; a wide-ranging version claims that human security is 'freedom from want'—extreme poverty precludes real security; more narrowly, human security is 'freedom from fear'—the emphasis is on safety from violence, including wars and violent crime.

Ikhwan The brethren, religious followers of *Wahhabism*.

import-substitution industrialization (ISI) Referring to the economic strategy of protecting the growth of manufacturing industry by reserving the home market for domestic producers ('infant industries'), through introducing barriers to imports.

indirect rule A mode of rule developed especially, although not only, by Britain under which the colonial power allowed native rulers and chiefs to exercise limited authority.

informal economy Referring to employment and wealth creation that is not captured by the official data, offering opportunities for people who are unable to participate in the formal economy; governments find it difficult to regulate and tax the informal sector.

informal institutions Rules and procedures that are created, communicated, and enforced outside the officially sanctioned channels; they may undermine, reinforce, or even override the formal institutions.

infrastructural power The power to penetrate and transform society.

institutions Collections of (broadly) agreed norms, rules, procedures, practices, and routines, either formally established or written down and embodied in organizations, or as informal understandings embedded in culture.

intentional institutional design Refers to situations in which political institutions are deliberately, consciously, and explicitly designed or reformed, often with a particular object in view.

international community A loose term denoting the main Western powers and the international organizations in and over which they exert considerable influence, for example in the United Nations.

international human rights regime A large body of international law and a complex set of institutions to implement it.

legitimacy A psychological relationship between the governed and their governors, which engenders a belief that the state's leaders and institutions have a right to exercise political authority over the rest of society.

liberal imperialism The idea that powerful advanced Western states should intervene, if necessary by force, in other countries to spread good government and liberal democratic values.

liberalism A political philosophy that gives priority to individual freedom.

liberation theology A school of theological thought with widespread influence in Latin America beginning in the 1960s, which explores the relation between Christian theology and political activism in the areas of poverty, social justice, and human rights.

localism The tendency to prioritize local cultural, economic, and political interests and identities over national ones.

mainstreaming In the context of gender and environment, infusing public policies with a gender or environmental focus.

majlis A traditional tribal forum for male elders that has evolved into an institution for consultation between ruler and ruled (Saudi Arabia).

micro-credit The provision of small loans to poor people who cannot obtain normal commercial credit for entrepreneurial activities.

Millennium Development Goals (MDGs) Established by the United Nations Millennium Declaration (September 2000) in the following eight areas: to eradicate extreme poverty and hunger; to achieve universal primary education; to promote gender equality and to empower women; to reduce child mortality; to improve maternal health; to combat HIV/AIDS, malaria, and other diseases; to ensure environmental sustainability; to develop a global partnership for development.

modern civil society *See* **civil society**.

modernization Referring to a complex set of changes in culture, society, and economy characterized by urbanization, industrialization, and, in some cases, secularization, although one response to it may be religious revival.

modernization revisionism A critique of modernization theory, centred on its oversimplified notions of tradition, modernity, and their interrelationship.

multi-ethnic or multicultural national identities Defining the nation in terms of several ethnic or cultural identities contained within citizenship, political interaction, and an overarching national identity in an autonomous state.

nation-building Referring to building a sense of national belonging and unity.

national identities Inherently political, emphasizing the autonomy and unity of the nation as an actual or potential political unit.

natural capital Comprising nature's free goods and services.

neoliberalism Stressing the role of the market in resource allocation and a correspondingly reduced role for the state, together with integration into the global economy; aspects of the neoliberal agenda are exhibited in the **Washington consensus** associated with the Bretton Woods institutions.

neo-patrimonialism Combining patrimonialism and legal-rational bureaucratic rule, which gives formal recognition to the distinction between the public and the private.

new institutional economics (NIE) An approach that focuses on the way in which society's institutions affect economic performance.

new protectionism Referring to the measures of developed countries to reserve their domestic markets for home producers by means of non-tariff barriers such as imposing environmental standards.

newly (or new) industrialized(izing) countries (NICs) Referring to those developing countries primarily, but not exclusively, in East Asia (also sometimes called 'dragon', or 'tiger', economies) that experienced dramatic industrialization soonest after 1945.

non-governmental organizations (NGOs) Organizations that operate in civil society and are not part of government or the state (although they may sometimes be dependent, in part, on government for funding).

non-traditional security threats Non-military issues such as environmental problems, threats from migration, international organized crime, and disease.

non-violent action Refers to methods of political action that do not involve violence or the threat of violence against living beings; instead, they involve an active process of bringing political, economic, social, emotional, or moral pressure to bear in the wielding of power in contentious interactions between collective actors, through methods such as protest demonstrations, marches, civil disobedience, and land occupations.

official development assistance (ODA) Comprising resources transferred on concessional terms with the promotion of the economic development and welfare of the developing countries as the main objective.

ontological equality The assumption that all people are born equal.

orientalism Referring to Edward Said's (1995; 1978) influential account of Western dominance of the East and how images of the Orient (the 'other') helped to define the West as its contrasting image.

outward-oriented development Looking to the global economy as a driving force for economic growth, through the creation of a favourable policy environment for exports.

overpopulation Referring to birth rates that exceed death rates, producing growth that is difficult to sustain with the given resource base.

pacted transition In which transition to democracy comes about by agreement among political elites integral to the precursor regime.

Pancasila The official ideology of Suharto's Indonesia, enjoining belief in a supreme being, humanitarianism, national unity, consensus democracy, and social justice.

path dependence Claiming that point of origin, the method of change, and choices made or not made along the way significantly influence the outcome and final destination.

patriarchy Referring to the ideology and institutions of male rule, male domination, and female subordination.

patrimonialism Treating the state as the personal patrimony or property of the ruler (hence 'patrimonialist **state**'), and all power relations between ruler and ruled as personal relations.

patron–client relations Connecting **patronage** and **clientelism**.

patronage The politically motivated distribution of favours, intended to create and maintain political support among groups.

political culture Embracing the attitudes, beliefs, and values that are said to underlie a political system.

political Islam Refers to a political movement with often diverse characteristics that, at various times, has included elements of many other political movements, while simultaneously adapting the religious views of Islamic fundamentalism or Islamism.

politicide Referring to extermination of political enemies.

politics On a narrow understanding, a kind of activity associated with the process of government and, in modern settings, also linked with the 'public' sphere; on a broader understanding, it is about 'power' relations and struggles not necessarily confined to the process of government or restricted to the public domain.

politics of order A critique of political development theory that focused on the need for strong government and political order.

polyarchy Robert Dahl's influential idea of democracy that rests on the two pillars of public contestation and the right to participate.

populism A political ideology or approach that claims to be in the interests of 'the people'.

post-colonial state A state that came into being as a consequence of the dissolution of the European colonial empires.

post-positivists Referring to those who reject the idea that the world can be studied in a value-free way.

post-structuralism/post-structuralist Sometimes also referred to as 'post-modernism', a broad philosophical approach that questions the epistemological foundations of 'rational' enlightenment thinking.

predatory state Close to the idea of an **extractive state**, one that exploits the people for the benefit of the rulers and holds back development.

privatization The transformation of something that is communally or publicly owned to private property.

process conditionality Refers to the requirement of the poverty reduction strategy process that a government formulates (pro-poor) development policy itself through the consultation of local stakeholders, civil society in particular, so as to secure 'local ownership', in principle thereby avoiding the failings of conditionality.

pro-natalism/pro-natalist Referring to policies or values that motivate high birth rates.

proxy wars Conflicts carried out on behalf of, and supported by, the great powers, as was often the case in developing areas during the cold war era.

pseudo-democracy Existing where there is not a sufficiently fair arena of electoral contestation to allow the ruling party to be turned out of power.

public goods Goods, such as defence, which, if supplied to anybody, are necessarily supplied to everybody, as a consequence of which the market is unlikely to provide them in sufficient quantity.

public institutions The institutions of the modern state are all 'public' institutions and include 'the government' and legislature, the courts, the civil service, the army and the police, plus any state-owned agencies.

realists In international relations theory, include classical realists who define security as national security; they emphasize military threats to the state and inter-state conflict.

regime A set of rules and practices that regulate the conduct of actors in a specified field (as distinct from political regime understood as a system of government).

regime change Came to be applied to the practice of removing a government by external force, as in the military invasion of Afghanistan and Iraq to topple the Taliban and Saddam Hussein's government, respectively; some opponents of international intervention in developing countries choose to identify it with the aspirations behind democracy promotion and democracy assistance from the West.

religio-politics Political activity with religious dimensions.

rentier state A state the income of which takes the form primarily of rents from a resource such as oil, or from foreign aid, rather than from taxing the subjects, which gives it high autonomy from society and may restrain citizens from demanding democratically accountable government.

rent-seeking Referring to the pursuit of gains (**economic rents**) to be derived from control over scarce goods or services—a scarcity that might be artificially created for the purpose.

responsibility to protect Refers both to states' responsibility to protect their own citizens and the international community's responsibility to engage in humanitarian intervention when a state fails in its responsibilities.

right to self-determination The claimed right of a distinct group of people to determine their own political, economic, and cultural destinies.

robust peacekeeping Used by the North Atlantic Treaty Organization (NATO) to define the new type of peacekeeping in which its troops in Afghanistan are engaged, under which they have more leeway to make peace, as well as to undertake peacekeeping and monitoring functions.

rule of law The idea that all citizens, including the lawmakers and all other government officials, are bound by the law and no one is above the law.

scramble for Africa The late nineteenth-century territorial expansion of European powers in Africa, leading to the Congress of Berlin (1884–85), which formally adopted the division of the new colonies and protectorates.

secularization The gradual diminution of the influence of religion on public affairs; **liberal secularism** advocates separation of church and state, with the second power being dominant and no one religion having official priority.

securitization Occurs when an issue is presented as posing an existential threat to a designated object, traditionally, but not necessarily, the state; the designation of the threat in this way is used to justify the use of extraordinary measures in response.

security dichotomies Refer to a duality of perceptions, a division into two contradictory understandings of a security issue—one negative and one positive.

Sharia law Islamic religious law, incorporated to varying degrees in the legal systems of states with large Islamic populations.

social capital Referring to social networks, norms, and trust, which enable participants to function more effectively in pursuing a common goal; arguably, high levels are valuable both for political and economic cooperation.

social movements Loose networks of informal organizations that come about in response to an issue, crisis, or concern, and which seek to influence social and other public policy, such as environmental policy, often through using direct action, which may or may not employ violence.

societal collapse Occurring where the fabric of linkages and feedback mechanisms between state and society and within society are irreparably ruptured.

soft power In its original formulation by Joseph Nye Jr, the ability of a country's culture, ideals, and policies to influence others by attraction and without deliberate resort to bribery or coercion.

soft state Gunnar Myrdal's term for states with low enforcement capacity, such as those with lax bureaucracy and corruption.

state–church relations The interactions in a country between the state and the leading religious organization(s).

state collapse Occurring where a functioning state system ceases to exist.

state failure Indicating a less-than-complete collapse of the state system.

stateless societies Societies that do not have a state, but which may still enjoy a measure of social and economic order.

status A quality of social honour or a lack of it, which is mainly conditioned by, as well as expressed through, a specific style of life.

structural adjustment programmes (SAPs) Designed to shift economic policy and management in the direction of the **Washington consensus**, sometimes leading to more narrowly focused sectoral adjustment programmes, and often associated with structural adjustment loans (SALs) from the Bretton Woods institutions and other aid donors.

subsistence economy Referring to activity outside the cash economy for barter or home use.

sustainable development A disputed term, which was defined by the Brundtland Report (1987) as development that meets the needs of the present without compromising the ability of future generations to meet their own needs; environmental degradation is minimized while ecological sustainability is maximized.

terrorism A tactic designed to achieve an objective (usually political) by using violence against innocent civilians to generate fear.

third wave of democracy Samuel P. Huntington's term for democratization in the late twentieth century.

traditional civil society See **civil society**.

transaction costs The costs of doing business in a market economy, including the cost of finding market information, as well as the costs incurred when parties to a contract do not keep to their agreement.

ulema Islamic clergy or body consisting of those educated in Islam and **Sharia law**, with the function of ensuring the implementation of Islamic precepts.

underdevelopment Lack of development, according to dependency theory, which is a consequence of capitalist development elsewhere.

unequal exchange The idea that international trade between developed and developing countries is an instrument whereby the former exploit the latter and capture the greater part of the benefits.

unsecularization A global religious revitalization.

urban bias Bias in public policy and spending against the rural areas in favour of urban areas or urban-based interests, owing to their greater political influence.

war on terror(ism) The term given by the United States and its allies to an ongoing campaign with the stated goal of ending global terrorism; launched in response to the 11 September 2001 ('9/11') terrorist attacks on the United States.

warlords Powerful regional figures possessing coercive powers, inside a country.

Washington consensus The term applied to a package of liberalizing economic and financial policy reforms deemed essential if Latin America (and subsequently other parts of the developing world) are to escape debt and rejuvenate their economic performance; quickly became attached to the policy approach in the 1990s of the Bretton Woods institutions especially—namely, the International Monetary Fund

(IMF) and World Bank; the central elements are fiscal discipline, reorientation of public expenditures, tax reform, financial liberalization, openness to foreign direct investment, privatization, deregulation, and secure property rights.

weak states According to Joel Migdal, states lacking the capability to penetrate society fully, to regulate social relations, to extract and distribute resources, or to implement policies and plans.

wealth theory of democracy Claiming that the prospects for stable democracy are significantly influenced by economic and socio-economic development.

Westminster model Referring to the institutional arrangement of parliamentary government bequeathed by Britain to many of its former colonies.

women's (or gender) policy interests Referring to official decisions or practices in which women have a special stake because of need, discrimination, or lack of equality.

women's policy machinery Units within government such as women's bureaux, commissions of women, ministries of women, and women's desks.

References

Abdelal, R., Herrera, Y., Johnston, I., and McDermott, R. (2009) 'Identity as a Variable', in R. Abdelal, Y. Herrera, I. Johnston, and R. McDermott (eds) *Measuring Identity: A Guide for Social Scientists* (New York: Cambridge University Press), 203–236.

Abdul-Ahad, G. (2006) 'Inside Iraq's Hidden War', *The Guardian*, 20 May.

Acharya, A. (1999) 'Developing Countries and the Emerging World Order', in L. Fawcett and Y. Sayigh (eds) *The Third World beyond the Cold War* (Oxford: Oxford University Press), 78–98.

Adeney, K. and Wyatt, A. (2004) 'Democracy in South Asia: Getting beyond the Structure–Agency Dichotomy', *Political Studies*, 52(1): 1–18.

Afrobarometer (2009) *Neither Consolidating nor Fully Democratic*, Briefing Paper No. 67.

Agarwal, N., Merlyna, L., and Wigand, R. T. (2012) 'Online Collective Action and the Role of Social Media in Mobilizing Opinions: A Case Study on Women's Right-to-Drive Campaigns in Saudi Arabia', *Public Administration and Information Technology*, 1(1): 99–123.

Agency for Technical Cooperation and Development, Antares Foundation, Danish Refugee Council, Handicap International, Internal Displacement Monitoring Centre, International Rescue Committee, Italian Consortium of Solidarity, Knowledge for Iraqi Woman Society, Kurdistan Civil Rights Organization, Medecins du Monde—France, Mercy Corps, Mercy Hands, Muslim Aid, Muslim Hands, NGO Coordination Committee for Iraq, Premiere Urgence, and War Child (2010) *Fallen off the Agenda? More and Better Aid Needed for Iraq Recovery*, Policy Brief, available online at http://www.internal-displacement.org/8025708F004CE90B/(httpDocuments)/A2FF9602D6790D28C1257760004A4910/$file/More+and+Better+Aid+Needed+for+Iraq+Recovery+-Brief.pdf

Ahluwalia, P. (2001) *Politics and Post-Colonial Theory: African Inflections* (London: Routledge).

Ake, C. (1996) *Democracy and Development in Africa* (Washington DC: Brookings Institution).

Alavi, H. (1979) 'The State in Post-Colonial Societies', in H. Goulbourne (ed.) *Politics and the State in the Third World* (London: Macmillan), 38–69.

Alavi, H. (1988) 'Pakistan and Islam: Ethnicity and Ideology', in F. Halliday and H. Alavi (eds) *State and Ideology in the Middle East and Pakistan* (New York: Monthly Review Press), 64–111.

Alden, C. (2007) *China in Africa* (London: Zed).

Al-Ali, N. and Pratt, N. (2009) *What Kind of Liberation: Women and the Occupation of Iraq* (Berkeley, CA: University of California Press).

Allison, R. and Williams, P. (1990) *Superpower Competition and Crisis Prevention in the Third World* (Cambridge: Cambridge University Press).

Almond, G. and Bingham Powell, G. (1966) *Comparative Politics: A Developmental Approach* (London: Little, Brown).

Almond, G. and Verba S. (eds) (1965) *The Civic Culture: Political Attitudes and Democracy in Five Nations* (Newbury Park, CA: Sage Publications).

Alvarez, M., Cheibub, J., Limongi, F., and Przeworski, A. (1996) 'Classifying Political Regimes', *Studies in Comparative International Development*, 31(2): 3–36.

Amenta, E. and Young, M. (1999) 'Making an Impact: Conceptual and Methodological Implications of the Collective Goods Criterion', in M. Giugni, D. McAdam, and C. Tilly (eds) *How Social Movements Matter* (Minneapolis, MN: University of Minnesota Press), 22–41.

Amnesty International (2012) *Amnesty International Report 2012: The State of the World's Human Rights* (London: AI).

Anderson, B. (1991) *Imagined Communities: Reflections on the Origin and Spread of Nationalism*, rev. edn (London: Verso).

Arias, E. D. and Goldstein, D. M. (eds) (2010) *Violent Democracies in Latin America* (Durham: Duke University Press).

Armijo, L. E., Muehlich, L., and Tirone, D. C. (forthcoming) 'The Systemic Financial Capabilities of Emerging Powers', *Journal of Policy Modeling*, Special issue.

Aspinall, E. and Fealy G. (eds) (2003) *Local Power and Politics in Indonesia: Democratization and Decentralization* (Singapore: Institute of Southeast Asian Affairs).

Avaaz (2013) 'About Us: Our Community', available online at http://www.avaaz.org/en/community.php

Ayers, A. J. (2009) 'Imperial Liberties: Democratisation and Governance in the "New" Imperial Order', *Political Studies*, 57(1): 1–27.

Ayubi, N. (1995) *Overstating the Arab State: Politics and Society in the Middle East* (London: I. B. Tauris).

Bacevitch, A. (2011) 'The U. S. Withdrawal from Iraq Marks the End [of] America's Great Expectations', *Washington Post*, 11 December, available online at http://www.washingtonpost.com/opinions/the-us-withdrawal-from-iraq-marks-the-end-of-american-supremacy/2011/12/12/gIQAStpTyO_story.html

Bäck, H. and Hadenius, A. (2008) 'Democracy and State Capacity: Exploring a J-Shaped Relationship', *Governance*, 21(1): 1–24.

Banégas, R. (2008) 'Introduction: Rethinking the Great Lake Crisis, War, Violence and Political Recomposition in Africa', in J.-P. Chrétien and R. Banégas (eds) *The Recurring Great Lakes Crisis: Identity, Violence and Power* (London: Hurst), 1–26.

Bank for International Settlements (2010) *Triennial Central Bank Survey: Report on Global Foreign Exchange Market Activity in 2010* (Basel: BIS).

Bardhan, P. (1997) 'Corruption and Development: A Review of Issues', *Journal of Economic Literature*, 35(3): 1320–46.

Barton, J. R. (1997) *A Political Geography of Latin America* (London: Routledge).

Bastian, S. and Luckham, R. (eds) (2003) *Can Democracy Be Designed? The Politics of Institutional Choice in Conflict-Torn Societies* (London: Zed).

Bastos, S. and Camus, M. (2003) *Entre el Mecapal y el Cielo: Desarrollo del Movimento Maya en Guatemala* (Guatemala: FLASCO).

Bates, R. H. (1981) *Markets and States in Tropical Africa: The Political Basis of Agricultural Policy* (Berkeley, CA: University of California Press).

Bates, R. H. (1989) *Beyond the Miracle of the Market: The Political Economy of Agrarian Development in Kenya* (Cambridge: Cambridge University Press).

Bates, R. H. (2001) *Prosperity and Violence: The Political Economy of Development* (New York: W. W. Norton).

Bauer, P. T. (1981) *Equality, the Third World and Economic Delusion* (London: Methuen).

Bayart, J.-F. (1993) *The State in Africa: The Politics of the Belly* (London: Longman).

Baylis, J. and Smith, S. (eds) (2001) *The Globalization of World Politics*, 2nd edn (Oxford: Oxford University Press).

Bayly, S. (1999) *The New Cambridge History of India, IV.3: Caste, Society and Politics in India from the Eighteenth Century to the Modern Age* (Cambridge: Cambridge University Press).

BBC News (2008) 'Profile: Mercosur—Common Market of the South', available online at http://news.bbc.co.uk/1/hi/world/americas/5195834.stm

BBC News (2013) 'Syria Death Toll Now above 100,000, says UN Chief Ban', 25 July, available online at http://www.bbc.co.uk/news/world-middle-east-23455760

Beddoes, Z. M. (2012) 'For Richer, for Poorer', *The Economist*, 13 October, available online at http://www.economist.com/node/21564414

Beetham, D. (1997) 'Market Economy and Democratic Polity', *Democratization*, 4(1): 76–93.

Beinin, J. and Vairel, F. (2011) *Social Movements, Mobilization, and Contestation in the Middle East and North Africa* (Stanford, CA: Stanford University Press).

Benford, R. and Snow, D. (1988) 'Ideology, Frame Resonance, and Participant Mobilization', in B. Klandermans (eds) *International Social Movement Research* (Greenwich: Jai Press), 197–217.

Benford, R. and Snow, D. (2000) 'Framing Processes and Social Movements: An Overview and Assessment', *Annual Review of Sociology*, 26: 611–39.

Berdal, M. (2009) *Building Peace after War* (London: The International Institute for Strategic Studies).

Berger, M. (1994) 'The End of the "Third World"?', *Third World Quarterly*, 15(2): 257–75.

Berman, B. (1998) 'Ethnicity, Patronage and the African State: The Politics of Uncivil Nationalism', *African Affairs*, 97(388): 35–341.

Bermeo, N. (2003) *Ordinary People in Extraordinary Times: The Citizenry and the Breakdown of Democracy* (Princeton, NJ: Princeton University Press).

Bermeo, N. (2009) 'Democracy Assistance and the Search for Security', in P. Burnell and R. Youngs (eds) *New Challenges to Democratization* (London and New York: Routledge), 73–94.

Bertrand, J. (2002) 'Legacies of the Authoritarian Past: Religious Violence in Indonesia's Moluccan Islands', *Pacific Affairs*, 75: 57–85.

Beynon, J. and Dunkerley, D. (eds) (2000) *Globalization: The Reader* (London: Athlone Press).

Bhalla, S. S. (2002) *Imagine There's No Country: Poverty, Inequality and Growth in the Era of Globalization* (Washington DC: Institute for International Economics).

Billig, M. (1995) *Banal Nationalism* (London: Sage).

Birmingham, D. (1995) *The Decolonization of Africa* (London: UCL Press).

Boege, V., Brown, A., Clements, K., and Nolan, A. (2009) 'On Hybrid Political Orders and Emerging States: What is Failing—States in the Global South or Research and Politics in the West?', *Berghof Handbook Dialogue Series*, 8: 15–35.

Booth, D. and Golooba-Mutebi, F. (2012) 'Developmental Patrimonialism? The Case of Rwanda', *African Affairs*, 111(444): 379–403.

Boserup, E. (1989) *Women's Role in Economic Development*, rev. edn (London: Earthscan).

Boyd, D. R. (2012) *The Environmental Rights Revolution: A Global Study of Constitutions, Human Rights, and the Environment* (Vancouver, BC: UBC Press).

BP (2009) *Statistical Review of World Energy 2009*, available online at http://www.bp.com

Brahm, E. (2007) 'Uncovering the Truth: Examining Truth Commission Success and Impact', *International Studies Perspectives*, 8(1): 16–35.

Bratton, M. and van de Walle, N. (1994) 'Neopatrimonial Regimes and Political Transitions in Africa', *World Politics*, 46(4): 453–89.

Bratton, M. and van de Walle, N. (1997) *Democratic Experiments in Africa* (Cambridge: Cambridge University Press).

Bratton, M., Mattes, R., and Gyimah-Boadi, E. (2004) *Public Opinion, Democracy and Market Reform in Africa* (Cambridge: Cambridge University Press).

Braunstein, E. (2006) *Foreign Direct Investment, Development and Gender Equity: A Review of Research and Policy* (Geneva: United Nations Research Institute for Social Development).

Bräutigam, D. (2009) *The Dragon's Gift: The Real Story of China in Africa* (Oxford: Oxford University Press).

Bräutigam, D. and Knack, S. (2004) 'Foreign Aid, Institutions, and Governance in Sub-Saharan Africa', *Economic Development and Cultural Change*, 52(2): 255–85.

Bräutigam, D., Fjeldstad, O.-H., and Moore, M. (2008) *Taxation and State-Building in Developing Countries: Capacity and Consent* (Cambridge: Cambridge University Press).

Brown, J. (1985) *Modern India: The Origins of an Asian Democracy* (Oxford: Oxford University Press).

Brundtland, G. (ed.) (1987) *Our Common Future: The World Commission on Environment and Development* (Oxford: Oxford University Press) (the Brundtland Report).

Burnell, P. (2009) 'The Coherence of Democratic Peacebuilding', in T. Addison and T. Bruck (eds) *Making Peace Work: The Challenges of Social and Economic Reconstruction* (Basingstoke, Palgrave Macmillan), 51–74.

Burnell, P. and Calvert, P. (eds) (1999) *The Resilience of Democracy. Persistent Practice, Durable Idea* (London: Frank Cass).

Burra, A. (2010) 'The Indian Civil Service and the Nationalist Movement: Neutrality, Politics and Continuity', *Journal of Commonwealth and Comparative Politics*, 48(4): 404–32

Buzan, B. (1991) *People, States and Fear: An Agenda for International Security Studies in the Post-Cold War Era* (Boulder, CO: Lynne Rienner).

Buzan, B., Waever, O., and de Wilde, J. (1998) *Security: A New Framework for Analysis* (Boulder, CO: Lynne Reinner).

Calhoun, C. (1993) 'What's New about New Social Movements? The Early 19th Century Reconsidered', *Social Science History*, 17(3): 385–427.

Calvert, P. and Calvert, S. (2001) *Politics and Society in the Third World*, 2nd edn (Harlow: Pearson Education).

Cammack, P., Pool, D., and Tordoff, W. (1993) *Third World Politics: A Comparative Introduction* (Basingstoke: Macmillan).

Campbell, H. (2008) 'China in Africa: Challenging US Global Hegemony, *Third World Quarterly*, 29(1): 89–105.

Carey, J. M. and Siavelis, P. (2006) 'Electoral Insurance and Coalition Survival: Formal and Informal Institutions in Chile', in G. Helmke and S. Levitsky (eds) *Informal Institutions and Democracy: Lessons from Latin America* (Baltimore, MD: The Johns Hopkins University Press), 160–77.

Carillo, S. (2007) *Assessing Governance and Strengthening Capacity in Haiti*, World Bank Capacity Development Brief, available online at http://documents.worldbank.org/curated/en/2007/12/8991142/assessing-governance-strengthening-capacity-haiti

Carranza, M. (2004) 'Mercosur and the End Game of the FTAA Negotiations: Challenges and Prospects after the Argentine Crisis', *Third World Quarterly*, 25(2): 319–37.

Casanova, J. (1994) *Public Religions in the Modern World* (Chicago, IL/London: University of Chicago Press).

Castells, M. (2012) *Networks of Outrage and Hope: Social Movements in the Internet Age* (Cambridge: Polity Press).

Cederman, L.-E., Wimmer, A., and Min, B. (2010) 'Why Do Ethnic Groups Rebel: New Data and Analysis', *World Politics*, 62(1): 87–119.

Central Intelligence Agency (2013) *World Fact Book: Iraq Military*, available online at https://www.cia.gov/library/publications/the-world-factbook/geos/iz.html

Chabal, P. (2009) *Africa: The Politics of Suffering and Smiling* (London: Zed Books).

Chabal, P. and Daloz, J. P. (1999) *Africa Works: Disorder as Political Instrument* (London: James Currey).

Chakrabarty, D. (2003) 'Postcoloniality and the Artifice of History: Who Speaks for "Indian" Pasts?', in J. D. LeSueur (eds) *The Decolonization Reader* (London: Routledge), 428–48.

Chandra, B., Mukherjee, M., and Mukherjee, A. (1999) *India after Independence* (New Delhi: Viking Penguin India).

Chandra, K. and S. Wilkinson (2008) 'Measuring the Effect of "Ethnicity"', *Comparative Political Studies*, 41(4/5): 515–63.

Chaney, E. M. and Castro, M. G. (eds) (1989) *Muchachas No More: Household Workers in Latin America and the Caribbean* (Philadelphia, PA: Temple University Press).

Chang, H. (2002) *Kicking Away the Ladder* (London: Anthem Press).

Chapman, A. R. and Ball, P. (2001) 'The Truth of Truth Commissions: Comparative Lessons from Haiti, South Africa, and Guatemala', *Human Rights Quarterly*, 23(1): 1–43.

Charron, N. and Lapuente, V. (2010) 'Does Democracy Produce Quality of Government?', *European Journal of Political Research*, 49(4): 443–70.

Chatterjee, P. (1986) *Nationalist Thought and the Colonial World: A Derivative Discourse?* (London: Zed Books).

Chauvel, R. (2003) 'Papua and Indonesia: Where Contending Nationalisms Meet', in D. Kingsbury and H. Aveling (eds) *Autonomy and Disintegration in Indonesia* (London: RoutledgeCurzon), 115–27.

Chen, S., and Martin R. (2012) *More Relatively Poor People in a Less Absolutely Poor World*. World Bank Policy Research Working Paper 6114, available online at http://elibrary.worldbank.org/content/workingpaper/10.1596/1813-9450-6114

Chenery, H., Ahluwalia, M., Bell, C., Duloy, J., and Jolly, R. (1974) *Redistribution with Growth* (New York: Oxford University Press).

Chibber, V. (2005) 'The Good Empire: Should We Pick up Where the British Left off?', *Boston Review*, 30(1), available online at http://www.bostonreview.net/chibber-good-empire

Choi, S. (ed.) (1997) *Democracy in Korea: Its Ideals and Realities* (Seoul: Korean Political Science Association).

Clapham, C. (2000) 'Failed States and Non-States in the Modern International Order', Paper presented at 'Failed States III: Globalization and the Failed State', Florence, Italy, 7–10 April, available online at http://www.comm.ucsb.edu/faculty/mstohl/failed_states/2000/papers/clapham.html

Clapham, C. (2002) 'The Challenge to the State in a Globalized World', *Development and Change*, 33(5): 775–95.

Cohn, B. S. (1996) *Colonialism and Its Forms of Knowledge: The British in India* (Princeton, NJ: Princeton University Press).

Collier, D. and Levitsky, S. (1997) 'Democracy with Adjectives', *World Politics*, 49: 430–51.

Collier, P., Elliott, V. L., Hegre, H., Joeffler, A., Reynal-Querol, M., and Sambanis, N. (2003) *Breaking the Conflict Trap* (Washington DC: The World Bank).

Connor, W. (1994) *Ethnonationalism: The Quest for Understanding* (Princeton, NJ: Princeton University Press).

Cooper, F. (2002) *Africa since 1940: The Past of the Present* (Cambridge: Cambridge University Press)

Cooper, F. (2003) 'Conflict and Connection: Rethinking Colonial African History', in J. D. Le Sueur (ed.) *The Decolonization Reader* (London: Routledge), 23–44.

Cooper, F. (2005) *Colonialism in Question. Theory, Knowledge, History* (Berkeley, CA: University of California Press).

Cooper, R. (2004) *The Breaking of Nations: Order and Chaos in the Twenty-First Century* (London: Atlantic).

Cornia, G. A. and Court, J. (2001) *Inequality, Growth and Poverty in the Era of Liberalization and Globalization*, UNU Policy Brief No. 4, available online at http://www.wider.unu.edu/publications/policy-briefs/en_GB/pb4/_files/78807311723331954/default/pb4.pdf

Coulon, C. (1983) *Les Musulmans et le Pouvoir en Afrique Noire* (Paris: Karthala).

Craig, A. L. and Cornelius, W. A. (1995) 'Mexico', in A. Mainwaring and T. R. Scully (eds) *Building Democratic Institutions* (Stanford, CA: University of California Press), 249–297.

Cremer, G. (2008) *Corruption and Development Aid: Confronting the Challenge* (Boulder, CO: Lynne Rienner Publishers).

Crook, R. C. (2005) *The Role of Traditional Institutions in Political Change and Underdevelopment*, Center for Democratic Development/Overseas Development Institute Policy Brief No. 4 (Accra: Ghana Center for Democratic Development).

Croucher, S. L. (2003) 'Perpetual Imagining: Nationhood in a Global Era', *International Studies Review*, 5: 1–24.

Dahl, R. (1971) *Polyarchy: Participation and Opposition* (New Haven, CT/London: Yale University Press).

Dauvergne, P. (1997) *Shadows in the Forest: Japan and the Politics of Timber in South East Asia* (Cambridge, MA: MIT Press).

Davidson, B. (1992) *The Black Man's Burden: Africa and the Curse of the Nation-State* (New York: Times Books).

Davis, M. (2001) *Late Victorian Holocausts: El Nino Famines and the Making of the Third World* (London: Verso).

De Tocqueville, A. (2000; 1835, 1840) *Democracy in America* (Chicago, IL/London: University of Chicago Press).

della Faille, D. (2011) 'Discourse Analysis in International Development Studies: Mapping Some Contemporary Contributions', *Journal of Multicultural Discourses*, 6(3): 215–35.

Deshpande, A. and Nurse, K. (2012) 'Introduction', in A. Deshpande and K. Nurse (eds) *The Global Economic Crisis and the Developing World* (London: Routledge), 1–18.

Devarajan, S., Azam, J. P., and O'Connell, S. A. (1999) *Aid Dependence Reconsidered*, World Bank Policy Research Working Paper Series 2144, available online at http://elibrary.worldbank.org/content/workingpaper/10.1596/1813-9450-2144

Diamond, L. (1996) 'Is the Third Wave Over?', *Journal of Democracy*, 7(3): 20–37.

Diamond, L. (2002) 'Thinking about Hybrid Regimes', *Journal of Democracy*, 13(2): 21–35.

Diamond, L. (2004) 'What Went Wrong in Iraq', *Foreign Affairs*, 83(5): 34–56.

Diamond, L. (2012) 'The Coming Wave', *Journal of Democracy*, 23(1): 5–13.

Dicken, P. (2003) *Global Shift: Reshaping the Global Economic Map in the 21st Century* (London: Sage).

Dickson, A. K. (1997) *Development and International Relations: A Critical Introduction* (Cambridge: Polity).

Dirks, N. (2001) *Castes of Mind: Colonialism and the Making of Modern India* (Princeton, NJ: Princeton University Press).

Dirks, N. (2004) *Colonial and Postcolonial Histories: Comparative Reflections on the Legacies of Empire*, UNDP Human Development Report Office Occasional Paper 2004/4, available online at http://hdr.undp.org/en/reports/global/hdr2004/papers/HDR2004_Nicholas_Dirks.pdf

Dodge, T. (2003) *Inventing Iraq* (London: Hurst).

Dodge, T. (2005) *Iraq's Future: The Aftermath of Regime Change*, Adelphi Paper No. 372, available online at http://eprints.lse.ac.uk/38660/

Dodge, T. (2012) 'Iraq's Road Back to Dictatorship', *Survival: Global Politics and Strategy*, 54(3): 147–168.

Doig, A., Watt, D., and Williams, R. (2007) 'Why Do Developing Country Anti-Corruption Commissions Fail to Deal with Corruption? Understanding the Three Dilemmas of Organisational Development, Performance Expectation, and Donor and Government Cycles', *Public Administration and Development*, 27(3): 251–9.

Doorenspleet, R. (2009) 'Public Support versus Dissatisfaction in New Democracies?', in P. Burnell and R. Youngs (eds) *New Challenges to Democratization* (London and New York: Routledge), 95–117.

Downs, E. (2007) 'The Fact and Fiction of Sino-African Energy Relations', *China Security*, 3(3): 42–68.

Doyle, M. W. and Sambanis, N. (2006) *Making War and Building Peace: United Nations Peace Operations* (Princeton, NJ: Princeton University Press).

Drake, C. (1989) *National Integration in Indonesia: Patterns and Policies* (Honolulu, HI: University of Hawaii Press).

Drone Wars UK (2012) 'Mapping Drone Proliferation: UAVs in 76 Countries', *Global Research*, 18 September, available online at http://www.globalresearch.ca/mapping-drone-proliferation-uavs-in-76-countries/5305191

Duffield, M. (2001) *Global Governance and the New Wars: The Merging of Development and Security* (London: Zed Press).

Duffield, M. (2006) 'Racism, Migration and Development: The Foundations of Planetary Order', *Progress in Development Studies*, 6(1): 68–79.

Dunn, R. M. and Mutti, J. H. (2004) *International Economics*, 6th edn (London: Routledge).

Dupuy, A. (2007) *The Prophet and Power: Jean-Bertrand Aristide, the International Commmunity, and Haiti* (Lanham, MD: Rowman & Littlefield).

Eckl, J. and Weber, R. (2007) 'North-South? Pitfalls of Dividing the World by Words', *Third World Quarterly*, 28(1): 3–23.

The Economist (2012) *Pocket World in Figures*, 2013 Edition (London: The Economist).

Ehrlich, P. (1972) *The Population Bomb* (London: Pan/Ballantine).

Elkins, Z., Ginsburg, T., and Melton, J. (2008) 'Baghdad, Tokyo, Kabul . . .: Constitution-Making in Occupied States', *William and Mary Law Review*, 49(4): 1139–78.

Elkins, Z., Ginsburg, T., and Melton, J. (2009) *The Endurance of National Constitutions* (New York: Cambridge University Press).

Elson, D. and Pearson, R. (1981) 'Nimble Fingers Make Cheap Workers: An Analysis of Women's Employment in Third World Export Manufacturing', *Feminist Review*, 7: 87–107.

Elster, J. (1997) 'Ways of Constitution-Making', in A. Hadenius (ed.) *Democracy's Victory and Crisis* (Cambridge: Cambridge University Press), 123–42.

Escobar, A. (1995) *Encountering Development: The Making and Unmaking of the Third World* (Princeton, NJ: Princeton University Press).

Fahim, K. (2013) 'Ruling Islamists, under Attack, Reject Blame for Tunisia's Woes', *The New York Times*, 13 February, available online at http://www.nytimes.com/2013/02/12/world/africa/memo-from-tunis-ennahda-party-rejects-blame-for-tunisias-troubles.html?_r=0

Fanon, F. (1967) *The Wretched of the Earth* (Harmondsworth: Penguin).

Fawcett, L. and Sayigh, Y. (eds) (1999) *The Third World beyond the Cold War: Continuity and Change* (Oxford: Oxford University Press).

Ferdinand, P. (2012) *Governance in Pacific Asia* (New York: Continuum).

Ferdinand, P. (2013) 'Foreign Policy Convergence in Pacific Asia: The Evidence from Voting in the UN General Assembly', *British Journal of Politics and International Relations*, available online at http://onlinelibrary.wiley.com/doi/10.1111/1467-856X.12019/abstract

Ferguson, J. (1997) *The Anti-Politics Machine* (Minneapolis, MN: University of Minnesota Press).

Ferguson, N. (2004) *Colossus: The Rise and Fall of the American Empire* (London: Allen Lane).

Feuerwerker, A. (1983) 'The Foreign Presence in China', in J. K. Fairbank and D. C. Twitchett (eds) *The Cambridge History of China: Vol. 12, Republican China 1912–1949 Part 1* (Cambridge: Cambridge University Press), 128–207.

Fjeldstad, O.-H. and Moore, M. (2008) 'Tax Reform and State-Building in a Globalised World', in D. Bräutigam, O.-H. Fjeldstad, and M. Moore (2008)

Taxation and State-Building in Developing Countries: Capacity and Consent (Cambridge: Cambridge University Press), 235–61.

Fleischer, D. (2010) 'Brazil to Comply with UN sanctions against Iran', *Brazil Focus*, 7 August.

Food and Agriculture Organization (2012) *The State of Food Insecurity in the World 2012* (Rome: FAO).

Frank, A. G. (1969) *Capitalism and Underdevelopment in Latin America: Historical Studies of Chile and Brazil* (New York: Monthly Review Press).

Frank, A. G. (1971) *The Sociology of Development and the Underdevelopment of Sociology* (London: Pluto Press).

Frank, A. G. (1998) *Reorient: Global Economy in the Asian Age* (Berkeley, CA: University of California Press).

Freedom House (2012) *Countries at the Crossroads 2011: An Analysis of Democratic Governance, Volume 11* (Lanham, MD: Rowman & Littlefield).

Friedman, T. L. (2006) 'The First Law of Petropolitics', *Foreign Policy*, 154: 28–36.

Friman, M. (2006) 'Historical Responsibility: The Concept's History in Climate Change Negotiations and its Problem-Solving Potential', MA Thesis in Environmental History, Linköping University, Faculty of Arts and Sciences, Sweden.

Fuest, V. (2009) 'Liberia's Women Acting for Peace: Collective Action in a War-Affected Country', in S. Ellis and I. van Kessel (eds) *Movers and Shakers: Social Movements in Africa* (Leiden: Brill), 114–38.

Fukuyama, F. (1989) 'The End of History', *The National Interest*, 16: 3–18.

Fukuyama, F. (1992) *The End of History and the Last Man* (Harmondsworth: Penguin).

Fukuyama, F. (2013) 'What is Governance?', *Governance*, 26(3): 347–68.

Gallagher, K. P., Irwin A., and Koleski, K. (2012) *The New Banks in Town: Chinese Finance in Latin America*, Inter-American Dialogue Report, February, available online at http://ase.tufts.edu/gdae/Pubs/rp/GallagherChineseFinanceLatinAmerica Brief.pdf

Gamble, A. and Payne, A. (eds) (1996) *Regionalism and World Order* (London: Palgrave).

Gamson, W. A. (1975) *The Strategy of Social Protest* (Belmont, CA: Wadsworth Publishing).

Ganguly, S. (2012) 'An Enduring Threat', *Journal of Democracy*, 23(1): 138–48.

Garcia-Johnson, R. (2000) *Exporting Environmentalism: US Chemical Corporations in Brazil and Mexico* (Cambridge, MA: MIT Press).

Gbowee, L. and Mithers, C. (2011) *Mighty Be Our Powers: How Sisterhood, Prayer, and Sex Changed a Nation at War* (New York: Beast Books).

Ghani, A. and Lockhart, C. (2008) *Fixing Failed States: A Framework for Rebuilding a Fractured World* (Oxford and New York: Oxford University Press).

Ghosh, A. (2002) *The Imam and the Indian* (New Delhi: Ravi Dayal & Permanent Black).

Gill, B. and Reilly, J. (2007) 'The Tenuous Hold of China, Inc. in Africa', *The Washington Quarterly*, 30(3): 37–52.

Gilmartin, D. (2003) 'Democracy, Nationalism and the Public: A Speculation on Colonial Muslim Politics', in J. D. Le Sueur (ed.) *The Decolonization Reader* (London: Routledge), 191–203.

Ginsburg, T., Elkins, Z., and Blount, J. (2009) 'Does the Process of Constitution-Making Matter?', *Annual Review of Law and Social Science*, 5: 201–23.

Giugni, M. (2004) *Social Protest and Policy Change: Ecology, Antinuclear, and Peace Movements in Comparative Perspective* (Lanham, MD: Rowman & Littlefield).

Gloppen, S. and Roseman, M. J. (2011) 'Litigating the Right to Health: Are Transnational Actors Backseat Driving?', in S.Gloppen and A. E Yamin (eds) *Litigating Health Rights: Can Courts Bring More Justice to Health* (Cambridge: Harvard University Press), 246–272.

Glosny, M. (2010) 'China and the BRICs', *Polity*, 42(1): 100–29.

Go, J. (2003) 'Global Perspectives on the US Colonial State in the Philippines', in J. Go and A. L. Foster (eds) *The American Colonial State in the Philippines: Global Perspectives* (Durham, NC: Duke University Press), 1–42.

Goldstone, J. (2003) *States, Parties and Social Movements* (Cambridge: Cambridge University Press).

Goodwin, J. and Jasper, J. M. (2003) *The Social Movements Reader: Cases and Concepts* (Malden: Blackwell Publishing).

Gopin, M. (2000) *Between Eden and Armageddon: The Future of World Religions, Violence and Peacemaking* (New York/London: Oxford University Press).

Gopin, M. (2005) 'World Religions, Violence, and Myths of Peace in International Relations', in G. Ter Haar and J. Busutill (eds) *Bridge or Barrier? Religion, Violence and Visions for Peace* (Leiden: Brill), 35–56.

Gramsci, A. (1992; 1929–35) *Prison Notebooks* (New York: Columbia University Press).

Gray, C. W. and Kaufmann, D. (1998) 'Corruption and Development', *Finance and Development*, 35(1): 7–10.

Gray, J. (2003) *Al Qaeda and What it Means to be Modern* (London: Faber & Faber).

Green, E. D. (2010) 'Ethnicity and Nationhood in Pre-Colonial Africa: The Case of Buganda', *Nationalism and Ethnic Politics*, 16(1): 1–21.

Grimmett, R. F. and Kerr, P. K. (2012) *Conventional Arms Transfers to Developing World 2004–2011*, Congressional Research Services Report, available online at http://www.fas.org/sgp/crs/weapons/R42678.pdf

Grindle, M. S. (2010) *Good Governance: The Inflation of an Idea*, CID Working Paper No. 202, available online at http://www.hks.harvard.edu/var/ezp_site/storage/fckeditor/file/pdfs/centers-programs/centers/cid/publications/faculty/wp/202.pdf

Grugel, J. (2002) 'Conservative Elites and State Incapacities', *New Political Economy*, 7(2): 277–9.

Grugel, J. and Rigirozzi, P. (2012) 'Post-Neoliberalism in Latin America: Rebuilding and Reclaiming the State after Crisis', *Development and Change*, 43(1): 1–21.

Grupos de Poder en Petén: Territorio, política y negocios, (July 2011) <http://www.plazapublica.com.gt/content/insightcrimeorg-peten-de-politica-mafias-y-empresas>

Guha, R. (1989) 'Dominance without Hegemony and its Historiography', in R. Guha (ed.) *Subaltern Studies VI: Writings on South Asian History and Society* (New Delhi: Oxford University Press), 210–309.

Gulbrandsen, Ø. (2012) *The State and the Social: State Formation in Botswana and its Precolonial and Colonial Genealogies* (New York: Berghahn Books).

Hakim, P. (2003) 'Latin America's Lost Illusions. Dispirited Politics', *Journal of Democracy*, 14(2): 108–22.

Halliday, F. (1989) *Cold War, Third World: An Essay on Soviet-US Relations* (London: Hutchinson).

Halliday, F. (1993) 'Orientalism and its Critics', *British Journal of Middle Eastern Studies*, 20(2): 145–63.

Halliday, F. (2002) *Two Hours that Shook the World: September 11, 2001, Causes and Consequences* (London: Saqi).

Halliday, F. (2005) *The Middle East in International Relations: Power, Politics and Ideology* (Cambridge: Cambridge University Press).

Hanna, W. M. (2012) 'Clouded U. S. Policy on Egypt', *Arab Uprisings. The US Policy Challenge*, Project on Middle East Political Science, 4 March, 17–19.

Harff, B. (2003) 'No Lessons Learned from the Holocaust? Assessing Risks of Genocide and Political Mass Murder since 1955', *American Political Science Review*, 97(1): 57–73.

Harrison, G. (2004) 'Sub-Saharan Africa', in A. Payne (ed.) *The New Regional Politics* (Basingstoke: Palgrave), 218–47.

Harvey, F. (2010) 'The Long Road to Rainforest Conservation', *Financial Times*, 28 June.

Haynes, J. (1996) *Religion and Politics in Africa* (London: Zed Books).

Haynes, J. (2007) *Introduction to Religion and International Relations* (Harlow: Pearson Education).

Heathershaw, J. (2011) *Post-Conflict Tajikistan: The Politics of Peacebuilding and the Emergence of Legitimate Order* (New York: Routledge).

Hegel, G. W. F. (1942; 1821) *Philosophy of Right*, trans. with notes by T. M. Knox (Oxford: Clarendon Press).

Hegre, H., Ellingsen, T., Gates, S., and Gleditsch, N. P. (2001) 'Democracy, Political Change and Civil War', *American Political Science Review*, 95(1): 16–33.

Hellman, J. S., Jones, G., and Kaufmann, D. (2000) *'Seize the State, Seize the Day', State Capture, Corruption and Influence in Transition*, World Bank Policy Research Working Paper 2444, available online at http://econ.worldbank.org/external/default/main?pagePK=64165259&theSitePK=469382&piPK=64165421&menuPK=64166093&entityID=000094946_00091405494828

Herbst, J. (2000) *States and Power in Africa* (Princeton, NJ: Princeton University Press).

Heritage Foundation (2013) 'Index of Economic Freedom', available online at http://www.heritage.org/index/ranking

Herring, R. J. (1979) 'Zulfikar Ali Bhutto and the "Eradication of Feudalism" in Pakistan', *Comparative Studies in Society and History*, 21(4): 519–57.

Hirst, P., Thompson, G., and Brompley, S. (2009) *Globalization in Question*, 3rd edn (Cambridge: Polity).

Hobson, J. A. (2004) *The Eastern Origins of Western Civilization* (Cambridge: Polity).

Hoogvelt, A. (1997) *Globalization and the Postcolonial World* (Baltimore, MD: Johns Hopkins University Press).

Horowitz, D. (1985) *Ethnic Groups in Conflict* (Berkeley, CA: University of California Press).

Howard, M. M. and Roessler, P. G. (2006) 'Liberalizing Electoral Outcomes in Competitive Authoritarian Regimes', *American Journal of Political Science*, 50(2): 365–81.

Howard, P. N. and Hussain, M. M. (2013) *Democracy's Fourth Wave? Digital Media and the Arab Spring* (New York: Oxford University Press).

Hudson, V. and den Boer, A. M. (2005) *Bare Branches: The Security Implications of Asia's Surplus Male Population* (Cambridge, MA/London: MIT Press).

Human Rights Watch (2013) *Mexico's Disappeared: The Enduring Cost of a Crisis Ignored* (New York: HRW).

Human Security Report Project (2005) *Human Security Report 2005: War and Peace in the 21st Century* (New York/Oxford: Oxford University Press).

Human Security Report Project (2012) *Human Security Report 2012: Sexual Violence, Education, and War—Beyond the Mainstream Narrative* (Vancouver, BC: Human Security Press).

Huneeus, C., Berrios, F., and Rodrigo C. (2006) 'Legislatures in Presidential Systems: The Latin American Experience', *The Journal of Legislative Studies*, 12(3–4): 404–25.

Huntington, S. P. (1968) *Political Order in Changing Societies* (New Haven, CT: Yale University Press).

Huntington, S. P. (1971) 'The Change to Change', *Comparative Politics*, 3(3): 283–332.

Huntington, S. P. (1991) *The Third Wave: Democratization in the Late Twentieth Century* (Norman, OK/London: University of Oklahoma Press).

Huntington, S. P. (1993) 'The Clash of Civilizations?', *Foreign Affairs*, 72(3): 22–49.

Huntington, S. P. (1996a) *The Clash of Civilizations and the Remaking of World Order* (New York: Simon and Schuster).

Huntington, S. P. (1996b) 'Democracy for the Long Haul', *Journal of Democracy*, 7(2): 3–14.

Hurrell, A. and Narliker, A. (2006) 'A New Politics of Confrontation? Brazil and India in Multilateral Trade Negotiations', *Global Society*, 20(4): 415–33.

Index Mundi (2013) *Iraq Government Profile 2013*, available online at http://www.indexmundi.com/iraq/government_profile.html

Inglehart, R., Basáñez, M., Díez-Medrano, J., Halman, L., and Luijkx, J. (2004) *Human Beliefs and Values: A Cross-Cultural Sourcebook Based on the 1999–2002 Values Surveys* (Mexico: Siglo XXI Editores).

Institute for Applied Economic Research (IPEA) (2013) 'IPEA Data: Brasília', available online at http://www.ipeadata.gov.br

Institute of Development Studies (2010) *An Upside Down View of Governance* (Brighton: University of Sussex).

Inter-Agency Information and Analysis Unit (2012) *Sustainable Development, Green Economy and Oil and Gas in Iraq*, Inter-Agency Fact Sheet, available online at http://iq.one.un.org/documents/469/Sustaible-ble%20Development%20-%20English.pdf

International Crisis Group (2004) *Iraq's Transition on a Knife Edge* (Baghdad/Brussels: ICG)

International Crisis Group (2005) *Unmaking Iraq: A Constitutional Process Gone Awry* (Amman/Brussels: ICG)

International Crisis Group (2006) *In Their Own Words: Reading the Iraqi Insurgency* (Amman/Brussels: ICG).

International Crisis Group (2008) *Iraq after the Surge II: The Need for a New Political Strategy* (Baghdad/Istanbul/Damascus/Brussels: ICG).

International Crisis Group (2011) *Failing Oversight: Iraq's Unchecked Government* (Brussels: ICG).

International Crisis Group (2012) *Déjà Vu All Over Again: Iraq's Escalating Political Crisis* (Brussels: ICG).

International Energy Agency (2008) *Key World Energy Statistics 2008*, available online at http://iklim.cob.gov.tr/iklim/Files/eKutuphane/Key%20world%20Energy%20Statistics.pdf

International Institute for Strategic Studies (2008) 'Middle East and North Africa', *The Military Balance*, 108(1): 225–72.

International Labour Organization (2009) *Global Employment Trends for Women, March 2009* (Geneva: ILO).

International Labour Organization (2012) *Global Employment Trends 2012* (Geneva: ILO).

International Labour Organization (2013) *Global Wage Report 2012/13* (Geneva: ILO).

International Monetary Fund/World Bank (2009) *Global Monitoring Report 2009: A Development Emergency*, available online at http://www.imf.org/external/pubs/ft/gmr/2009/eng/gmr.pdf

Iraq Body Count (2012) 'Iraq Body Count', available online at http://www.iraqbodycount.org/

Isaak, R. A. (2005) *The Globalization Gap: How the Rich Get Richer and the Poor Get Left Further Behind* (London: FT Prentice Hall).

Jackson, R. H. (1990) *Quasi-States: Sovereignty, International Relations and the Third World* (Cambridge: Cambridge University Press).

Jalal, A. (1995) *Democracy and Authoritarianism in South Asia: A Comparative and Historical Perspective* (Cambridge: Cambridge University Press).

Jamail, D. (2012) 'Iraq Execution Spree under the Spotlight', *AlJazeera English Online*, 11 September.

James, C. L. R. (1977) *Nkrumah and the Ghana Revolution* (London: Allison and Busby).

Jenkins, J. C., Jacobs, D., and Agnone, J. (2003) 'Political Opportunities and African-American Protest, 1948–1997', *American Journal of Sociology*, 109(2): 277–303.

Joffe, G. (2011) 'The Arab Spring in North Africa: Origins and Prospects', *The Journal of North African Studies*, 16(4): 507–32.

Johnson, M. and Blas, J. (2009) 'China Drives Commodity Price Rises', *Financial Times*, 19 June, available online at http://www.ft.com/cms/s/0/e7e10432-5b29-11de-be3f-00144feabdc0.html

Joshi, A. and Ayee, J. (2008) 'Associational Taxation: A Pathway into the Informal Sector?' in D. Bräutigam, O.-H. Fjeldstad, and M. Moore (eds) *Taxation and State-Building in Developing Countries: Capacity and Consent* (Cambridge: Cambridge University Press), 183–212.

Kalyvas, S. (2001) '"New" and "Old" Civil Wars: A Valid Distinction?', *World Politics*, 54: 99–118.

Kalyvas, S. (2006) *The Logic of Violence in Civil War* (New York: Cambridge University Press).

Kang, D. C. (2002) *Crony Capitalism: Corruption and Development in South Korea and the Philippines* (Cambridge: Cambridge University Press).

Kapstein, E. and Converse, N. (2009) 'Why Democracies Fail', *Journal of Democracy*, 19(4): 57–68.

Karl, T. L. (1990) 'Dilemmas of Democratization in Latin America', *Comparative Politics*, 23(1): 1–21.

Kashyap, S. C. (1989) *Our Parliament: An Introduction to the Parliament of India* (New Delhi: National Book Trust).

Kavada, A. (2012) 'Engagement, Bonding, and Identity across Multiple Platforms: Avaaz on Facebook, YouTube, and MySpace', *MedieKultur*, 28(52): 28–48.

Kelsall, T. (2011) 'Rethinking the Relationship between Neo-Patrimonialism and Economic Development in Africa', *IDS Bulletin*, 42(2): 76–87.

Kelsall, T. (2012) 'Neo-Patriomonialism, Rent-Seeking and Development: Going with the Grain?', *New Political Economy*, 17(5): 677–82

Kelsall, T. and Booth, D. (2010) *Developmental Patrimonialism? Questioning the Orthodoxy on Political Governance and Economic Progress in Africa*, APPP Working Paper No. 9, available online at http://r4d.dfid.gov.uk/PDF/Outputs/APPP/20100708-appp-working-paper-9-kelsall-and-booth-developmental-patrimonialism-july-2010.pdf

Khan, M. (2002) 'Fundamental Tensions in the Democratic Compromise', *New Political Economy*, 7(2): 275–7.

Khanna, P. (2009) *The Second World: How Emerging Powers are Redefining Global Competition in the Twenty-First Century* (London: Penguin).

Ki-moon, B. (2009) 'New York, 9 December 2009: Secretary-General's Message on International Anti-Corruption Day', available online at http://www.un.org/sg/statements/?nid=4293

Kipling, R. (1987; 1890) 'Tods' Amendment', in R. Kipling, *Plain Tales from the Hills* (London: Penguin), 179–84.

Kitschelt, H. P. (1986) 'Political Opportunity Structures and Political Protest: Anti-Nuclear Movements in Four Democracies', *British Journal of Political Science*, 16(1): 57–85.

Kjaer, M. (2004) *Governance* (Cambridge: Polity Press).

Kohli, A. (2007) *State-Directed Development: Political Power and Industrialization in the Global Periphery* (Cambridge: Cambridge University Press).

Kohli, A. and Singh, P. (eds) (2013) *Routledge Handbook of Indian Politics* (New York: Routledge).

Kraft, H. J. S. (2006) *China and Democracy in the Asia Pacific*, UNISCI Discussion Paper No. 11, available online at http://revistas.ucm.es/index.php/unis/article/download/unis0606230071a/28109

Krauthammer, C. (1991) 'The Unipolar Moment', *Foreign Affairs*, 70(1): 23–33.

Kriesi, H., Koopmans, R., Duyvendak, J. W., and Giugni M. G. (1995) *New Social Movements in Western Europe: A Comparative Analysis* (Minneapolis, MN: University of Minnesota Press).

Lal, D. (2004) *In Praise of Empires: Globalization and Order* (Basingstoke: Palgrave).

Landman, T. (2003) *Issues and Methods in Comparative Politics*, 2nd edn (London: Routledge).

Lange, M. (2009) *Lineages of Despotism and Development: British Colonialism and State Power* (Chicago, IL: Chicago University Press).

Large, D. (2008) 'All Over in Africa', in C. Alden, D. Large, and R. Soares de Oliviera (eds) *China Returns to Africa: A Rising Power and a Continent Embrace* (London: Hurst and Co.), 371–6.

Latin American Commission on Drugs and Democracy (2009) *Drugs and Democracy: Toward a Paradigm Shift*, available online at http://www.drogasedemocracia.org/Arquivos/livro_ingles_02.pdf

Lauth, H. J. (2000) 'Informal Institutions and Democracy', *Democratization*, 7(4): 21–50.

Lawson, L. (2009) 'The Politics of Anti-Corruption Reform in Africa', *Journal of Modern African Studies*, 47(1): 73–100.

Lee, K.-S. (2011) *The Korean Financial Crisis of 1997: Onset, Turnaround, and Thereafter* (Washington, DC: International Bank for Reconstruction and Development, World Bank, and Korea Development Institute), available online at http://www-wds.worldbank.org/external/default/WDSContentServer/IW3P/IB/2011/04/08/000356161_20110408052735/Rendered/PDF/594620PUB0REPL10Box358282B01PUBLIC1.pdf

Lee, Y. H. (1997) *The State, Society and Big Business in South Korea* (London/New York: Routledge).

Leftwich, A. (1993) 'Governance, Democracy and Development in the Third World', *Third World Quarterly*, 14(3): 603–24.

Leftwich, A. (2002) 'Democracy and Development', *New Political Economy*, 7(2): 269–81.

Levi, M. (1988) *Of Rule and Revenue* (Berkeley, CA: University of California Press).

Levitsky, S. and Way, L. A. (2010) *Competitive Authoritarianism: Hybrid Regimes after the Cold War* (New York: Cambridge University Press).

Lewis, P. (2009) 'Growth without Prosperity in Africa', *Journal of Democracy*, 19(4): 95–109.

Lightfoot, S. (2008) 'Enlargement and the Challenge of EU Development Policy', *Perspectives on European Politics and Society*, 9(2): 128–42.

Lin, J. Y. (2011) *From Flying Geese to Leading Dragons: New Opportunities and Strategies for Structural Transformation in Developing Countries*, World Bank Policy Research Working Paper 5702, available online at http://elibrary.worldbank.org/content/workingpaper/10.1596/1813-9450-5702

Lindberg, S. (2006) *Democracy and Elections in Africa* (Baltimore, MD: Johns Hopkins University Press).

Linz, J. J. (1990) 'The Perils of Presidentialism', *Journal of Democracy*, 1(1): 51–69.

Linz, J. J. and Stepan, A. (1996) *Problems of Democratic Transition and Consolidation: Southern Europe, South America, and Post-Communist Europe* (Baltimore, MD: Johns Hopkins University Press).

Lipset, S. M. (1994) 'The Social Requisites of Democracy Revisited', *American Sociological Review*, 53(1): 1–22.

Lodgaard, S. (2007) 'Iran's Uncertain Nuclear Ambitions', in M. Bremer Maerli and S. Lodgaard (eds) *Nuclear Proliferation and International Security* (London: Routledge), 50–70.

Lucas, R. E., Jr (1988) 'On the Mechanics of Economic Development', *Journal of Monetary Economics*, 22(1): 3–42.

Lugard, Lord (1965; 1922) *The Dual Mandate in British Tropical Africa* (London: Frank Cass).

MacQueen, B. (2013) *An Introduction to Middle East Politics: Continuity, Change, Conflict and Co-operation* (London: SAGE Publications).

McAdam, D. (1982) *Political Process and the Development of Black Insurgency 1930–1970* (Chicago, IL: University of Chicago Press).

McAdam, D. McCarthy, J. D., and Zald, M. N. (1996) *Comparative Perspectives on Social Movements: Political Opportunities, Mobilizing Structures, and Cultural Framings* (Cambridge: Cambridge University Press).

McCarthy, J. D. and Zald, M. N. (1977) 'Resource Mobilization and Social Movements: A Partial Theory', *American Journal of Sociology*, 82(6): 1212–41.

McEwan, C. (2009) *Postcolonialism and Development* (London: Routledge).

McGrew, A. (1992) 'A Global Society?', in S. Hall, D. Held, and A. McGrew (eds) *Modernity and Its Future* (Cambridge: Polity Press), 62–102.

McMichael, P. (2008) *Development and Social Change: A Global Perspective*, 4th edn (Los Angeles, CA: Pine Forge).

McMillan, J. and Zoido, P. (2004) 'How to Subvert Democracy: Montesinos in Peru', *Journal of Economic Perspectives*, 18: 69–92.

Maddison, A. (2007) *Contours of the World Economy, 1–2030 AD* (Oxford: Oxford University Press).

Mahon, J. (2004) 'Causes of Tax Reform in Latin America, 1977–95', *Latin America Research Review*, 39(1): 3–30.

Mainwaring, S. and Scully, T. (1995) *Building Democratic Institutions: Party Systems in Latin America* (Stanford, CA: Stanford University Press).

Mair, P. (1996) 'Comparative Politics: An Overview', in R. E. Goodin and H. Klingemann (eds) *A New Handbook of Political Science* (Oxford: Oxford University Press), 309–35.

Malamud, A. (2011) 'A Leader without Followers? The Growing Divergence between the Regional and Global Performance of Brazilian Foreign Policy', *Latin American Politics and Society*, 53(3): 1–24.

Malek, C. (2004) 'International Conflict: The Conflict Resolution Information Service', available online at http://www.crinfo.org/coreknowledge/international-conflict.com

Mamdani, M. (1996) *Citizen and Subject: Contemporary Africa and the Legacy of Late Colonialism* (London: James Currey).

Mann, M. (1986) *The Sources of Social Power, Vol. I* (Cambridge: Cambridge University Press).

Mao, Z. (1977) *Selected Works of Mao Tse-tung* (Peking: Foreign Language Press).

March, J. and Olsen, J. (1984) 'The New Institutionalism: Organisational Factors in Political Life', *American Political Science Review*, 78(3): 734–49.

March, J. and Olsen, J. (2006) 'Elaborating the "New Institutionalism"', in R. A. W. Rhodes, S. Binder, and B. A. Rockman (eds) *The Oxford Handbook of Political Institutions* (Oxford: Oxford University Press), 000–000.

Marx, K. (1970) *The German Ideology* (London: Lawrence and Wishart).

Mayall, J. and Payne, A. (eds) (1991) *The Fallacies of Hope: The Post-Colonial Record of the Commonwealth Third World* (Manchester: Manchester University Press).

Mazrui, A. (1986) *The Africans: A Triple Heritage* (London: BBC Publications).

Mearsheimer, J. (2010) 'The Gathering Storm: China's Challenge to US Power in Asia', *The Chinese Journal of International Politics*, 3(4): 381–96.

Mehta, L. (2006) 'Do Human Rights Make a Difference to Poor and Vulnerable People? Accountability for the Right to Water in South Africa', in P. Newell and J. Wheeler (eds) *Rights, Resources and the Politics of Accountability* (London: Zed Books), 63–79.

Melia, T. O. and Katulis, B. M. (2003) *Iraqis Discuss their Country's Future: Post-War Perspectives from the Iraqi Street* (Washington, DC: National Democratic Institute).

Menkhaus, K. (2006–07) 'Governance without Government in Somalia: Spoilers, State Building, and the Politics of Coping', *International Security*, 31(3): 74–106.

Merrill, D. (1994) 'The United States and the Rise of the Third World', in G. Martel (eds) *American Foreign Relations Reconsidered 1890–1993* (London: Routledge), 166–86.

Mesbahi, M. (ed.) (1994) *Russia and the Third World in the Post-Soviet Era* (Gainesville, FL: University Press of Florida).

Michels, R. (1962) *Political Parties: A Sociological Study of the Oligarchical Tendencies of Modern Democracies* (New York: Collier).

Migdal, J. S. (1988) *Strong Societies and Weak States: State–Society Relations and State Capabilities in the*

Third World (Princeton, NJ: Princeton University Press).

Mill, J. S. (1888) *A System of Logic* (New York: Harper and Row).

Ministry of Commerce, PRC (2009) *China Commerce Yearbook 2009* (Beijing: China Commerce and Trade Press).

Minorities at Risk Project (MAR) (2009) 'Minorities at Risk Dataset', available online at http://www.cidcm.umd.edu/mar/

Mitlin, D and Mogaldi, J. (2013) 'Social Movements and the Struggle for Shelter: A Case Study of eThekwini (Durban)', *Progress in Planning*, 84: 1–39.

Moloeznik, M. P. (2009) *Militarizing Mexico's Public Security*, Center for Hemispheric Defense Studies Regional Insights No. 11, available online at http://www.seguridadcondemocracia.org/biblioteca/Militarizing%20Mexico%202009.pdf

Moon, C. (1994) 'Changing Patterns of Business-Government Relations in South Korea', in A. MacIntyre (ed.) *Business and Government in Industrializing Asia* (Sydney: Allen and Unwin), 142–66.

Moore, M. (2007) *How Does Taxation Affect the Quality of Government*, IDS Working Paper 280, available online at http://www2.ids.ac.uk/gdr/cfs/pdfs/Wp280.pdf

Moore, M. (2011) 'Globalisation and Power in Weak States', *Third World Quarterly*, 32(10): 1757–76.

Mores, M. (2013) *South Sudan: Overview of Corruption and Anti-Corruption*, U4 Expert Answer 371, available online at http://www.u4.no/publications/south-sudan-overview-of-corruption-and-anti-corruption/downloadasset/3034

Morris, A. (1993) 'Birmingham Confrontation Reconsidered: An Analysis of the Dynamics and Tactics of Mobilization', *American Sociological Review*, 58(5): 621–36.

Morris-Jones, W. H. (1987) *The Government and Politics of India* (Huntingdon: Eothen Press).

Mosley, L. (2005) 'Globalization and the State: Still Room to Move?', *New Political Economy*, 10(3): 355–62.

Mote, O. and Rutherford, D. (2001) 'From Irian Jaya to Papua: The Limits of Primordialism in Indonesia's Troubled East', *Indonesia*, 72: 115–40.

Mozaffar, S. (1995) 'The Institutional Logic of Ethnic Politics: A Prolegomenon', in H. Glickman (ed.) *Ethnic Conflict and Democratization in Africa* (Atlanta, GA: African Studies Association Press), 34–69.

Mozaffar, S., Scarritt, J. R., and Galaich, G. (2003) 'Electoral Institutions, Ethnopolitical Cleavages, and Party Systems in Africa's Emerging Democracies', *American Political Science Review*, 97(3): 379–90.

Mutua, M. (2008) *Kenya's Quest for Democracy: Taming Leviathan* (Boulder, CO: Lynne Rienner).

Myrdal, G. (1968) *Asian Drama: An Enquiry into the Poverty of Nations* (Harmondsworth: Penguin).

Nash, K. (2010) *Contemporary Political Sociology: Globalization, Politics, Power* (Chichester: Wiley-Blackwell).

Natali, D. (2010) *The Kurdish Quasi-State: Development and Dependency in Post-Gulf War Iraq* (New York: Syracuse University Press).

Nehru, J. (1942) *An Autobiography* (London: The Bodley Head).

Nehru, J. (1961) *The Discovery of India* (Bombay: Asia Publishing House).

Neuman S. G. (ed.) (1998) *International Relations Theory and the Third World* (Basingstoke: Macmillan).

Newell, P. (2001) 'Environmental NGOs, TNCs and the Question of Governance', in D. Stevis and V. Assetto (eds) *The International Political Economy of the Environment: Critical Perspectives* (Boulder, CO: Lynne Rienner), 85–107.

Newell, P. and Wheeler, J. (eds) (2006) *Rights, Resources and the Politics of Accountability* (London: Zed Books).

Newman, E., Richmond, O., and Paris, R. (eds) (2009) *New Perspectives on Liberal Peacebuilding* (Tokyo: United Nations University Press).

Ngûgîwa Thiong'o (1986) *Decolonising the Mind: The Politics of Language in African Literature* (London: James Currey).

Nijzink, L., Mozaffar, S., and Azevedo, E. (2006) 'Parliaments and the Enhancement of Democracy on the African Continent: An Analysis of Institutional Capacity And Public Perceptions', *Journal of Legislative Studies*, 12(3): 311–35.

Nkrumah, K. (1965) *Neo-Colonialism: The Last Stage of Imperialism* (London: Panaf Books).

Nolutshungu, S. C. (1991) 'Fragments of a Democracy: Reflections on Class and Politics in Nigeria', in J. Mayall and A. Payne (eds) *The Fallacies of Hope* (Manchester: Manchester University Press), 72–105.

North, D. C. (1990) *Institutions, Institutional Change and Economic Performance* (Cambridge: Cambridge University Press).

Nozick, R. (1974) *Anarchy, State and Utopia* (Oxford: Blackwell).

Nye, J. S. (2005) *Soft Power: The Means to Success in World Politics* (New York: Public Affairs Press).

O'Donnell, G. (1994) 'Delegative Democracy', *Journal of Democracy*, 5(1): 55–69.

O'Rourke, D. (2004) *Community-Based Regulation: Balancing Environment and Development in Vietnam* (Cambridge, MA: MIT Press).

Olken, B. A. (2006) 'Corruption and the Costs of Redistribution: Micro Evidence from Indonesia', *Journal of Public Economics*, 90(4–5): 853–70.

Olson, M. (1965) *The Logic of Collective Action: Public Goods and the Theory of Groups* (Cambridge, MA: Harvard University Press).

Olson, M. (2001) *Power and Prosperity: Outgrowing Communist and Capitalist Dictatorships* (New York: Basic Books).

Organisation for Economic Co-operation and Development (OECD) Development Assistance Committee (DAC) (undated)

Organization of American States Hemispheric Security Observatory (2012) *Report on Citizen Security in the Americas 2012* (Washington, DC: Organization of American States).

Ottaway, M. (2003) *Democracy Challenged: The Rise of Semi-Authoritarianism* (Washington DC: Carnegie Endowment for International Peace).

Ottaway, M. (2009) 'Ideological Challenges to Democratization: Do They Exist?', in P. Burnell and R. Youngs (eds) *New Challenges to Democratization* (London: Routledge), 42–58.

Panner, Morris and Beltrán, Adriana, 'Battling Organized Crime in Guatemala' The Americas Quarterly, (Fall 2010) <http://www.americasquarterly.org/node/1899>

Parente, S. L. and Prescott, E. C. (2000) *Barriers to Riches* (Cambridge, MA: MIT Press).

Parry, J. H. (1966) *The Spanish Seaborne Empire* (London: Hutchinson).

Payne, A. (2004) 'Rethinking Development inside International Political Economy', in A. Payne (eds) *The New Regional Politics of Development* (Basingstoke: Palgrave), 1–28.

Payne, A. (2005) 'The Study of Governance in a Global Political Economy', in N. Phillips (ed.) *Globalizing International Political Economy* (Houndmills: Palgrave Macmillan), 55–81.

Perham, M. (1963) *The Colonial Reckoning: The Reith Lectures 1961* (London: Fontana).

Phillips, N. (ed.) (2005) *Globalizing International Political Economy* (Houndmills: Palgrave Macmillan).

Pichardo, N. A. (1997) 'New Social Movements: A Critical Review', *Annual Review of Sociology*, 23: 411–30.

Pierson, P. (2000) 'The Limits of Design: Explaining Institutional Origins and Change', *Governance*, 13(4): 475–99.

Pierson, P. and Skocpol, T. (2002) 'Historical Institutionalism in Contemporary Political Science', in I. Katznelson and H. V. Miller (eds) *Political Science: State of the Discipline* (New York: Norton), 693–721.

Pieterse, J. N. (2011) 'Global Rebalancing: The Eastern and Southern Turn', *Development and Change*, 42(1): 22–48.

Piven, F. F. and Cloward, R. A. (1977) *Poor People's Movements: Why They Succeed, How They Fail* (New York: Pantheon Books).

Polgreen, L. (2006) 'Truce is Talk, Agony is Real in Darfur War', *New York Times*, 14 May, available online at http://www.nytimes.com/2006/05/14/world/africa/14sudan.html

Porter, B. (1996) *The Lion's Share: A Short History of British Imperialism 1850–1995*, 3rd edn (London: Longman).

Posner, D. (2005) *Institutions and Ethnic Politics in Africa* (Cambridge: Cambridge University Press).

Posner, D. and Young, D. J. (2007) 'The Institutionalization of Political Power in Africa', *Journal of Democracy*, 18(3): 126–40.

Powell, G. B. (2000) *Elections as Instruments of Democracy: Majoritarian and Proportional Visions* (New Haven, CT: Yale University Press).

Prakash, G. (1999) *Another Reason: Science and the Imagination of Modern India* (Princeton, NJ: Princeton University Press).

Przeworski, A., Alvarez, M., Cheibub, J., and Limongi, F. (1996) 'What Makes Democracies Endure?', *Journal of Democracy*, 7(1): 39–55.

Puddington, A. (2013) 'Breakthroughs in the Balance', *Journal of Democracy*, 24(2): 46–61.

Purdey, J. (2006) *Anti-Chinese Violence in Indonesia, 1996–1999* (Singapore: Singapore University Press).

Pye, L. W. (1966) *Aspects of Political Development* (Boston, MA: Little, Brown).

Qi, G. (2007) 'China's Foreign Aid: Policies, Structure, Practice and Trend', Paper delivered to Oxford University Conference on New Directions in Foreign Aid, Oxford, June.

Rai, S. M. (ed.) (2003) *Mainstreaming Gender, Democratizing the State? Institutional Mechanisms for the Advancement of Women* (Manchester/New York: Manchester University Press).

Raja Mohan, C. (2004) *Crossing the Rubicon: The Shaping of India's New Foreign Policy* (Basingstoke: Palgrave Macmillan).

Ramo, J. C. (2004) *The Beijing Consensus* (London: The Foreign Policy Centre).

Randall, V. (2004) 'Using and Abusing the Concept of the Third World: Geopolitics and the Comparative Study of Development and Underdevelopment', *Third World Quarterly*, 25(1): 41–53.

Randall, V. and Svåsand, L. (2002) 'Party Institutionalization in New Democracies', *Party Politics*, 8(1): 6–29.

Ravallion, M. (2009) 'Should the Randomistas Rule?', *Economists' Voice*, 6(2), available online at http://www.degruyter.com/view/j/ev.2009.6.2/ev.2009.6.2.1368/ev.2009.6.2.1368.xml

Reilly, B. and Nordlund, P. (eds) (2008) *Political Parties in Conflict-Prone Societies: Regulation, Engineering and Democratic Development* (Tokyo: United Nations University Press).

Remmer, K. (1997) 'Theoretical Decay and Theoretical Development: The Resurgence of Institutional Analysis', *World Politics*, 50(1): 34–61.

Richards, P. (2004) *No Peace, No War: An Anthropology of Contemporary Armed Conflicts* (Oxford: James Currey).

Richmond, O. (2009) 'Liberal Peace Transitions: A Rethink is Urgent', *OpenDemocracy*, 19 November, available online at http://www.opendemocracy.net/oliver-p-richmond/liberal-peace-transitions-rethink-is-urgent

Robinson, G. (1998) 'Rawan is as Rawan Does: The Origins of Disorder in New Order Aceh', *Indonesia*, 66: 127–56.

Rodríguez-Garavito, C. (2010). 'Beyond the Courtroom: The Impact of Judicial Activism on Socioeconomic Rights in Latin America', *Texas Law Review*. 89: 1669–98.

Roett, R. and Paz, G. (eds) (2008) *China's Expansion into the Western Hemisphere: Implications for Latin America and the United States* (Washington DC: Brookings Institute Press).

Rose-Ackerman, S. (2004) *The Challenge of Poor Governance and Corruption*, Copenhagen Consensus Challenge Paper, available online at http://www.copenhagenconsensus.com/sites/default/files/PP%2B-%2BCorruption1%2BFINISHED.pdf

Rose-Ackerman, S. and Truex, R. (2012) *Corruption and Policy Reform*, Yale Law & Economics Research Paper No. 444, available online at http://papers.ssrn.com/sol3/papers.cfm?abstract_id=2007152

Ross, M. (1999) 'The Political Economy of the Resource Curse', *World Politics*, 51(2): 297–322.

Rotberg, R. I. (ed.) (2004) *When States Fail* (Princeton, NJ: Princeton University Press).

Rothstein, B. (2011) *The Quality of Government. Corruption, Social Trust and Inequality in International Perspective* (Chicago, IL: Chicago University Press).

Rothstein, B. and Teorell, J. (2008) 'What is Quality of Government? A Theory of Impartial Government Institutions', *Governance*, 21(2): 165–90.

Rousseau, J. J. (1755) *Discourse on Equality* (London: Everyman/Dent).

Rowden, R. (2011) *India's Role in the New Farmland Grab* http://www.networkideas.org.featart/aug2011/Rick_Rowden.pdf

Rubin, M. (2004) 'Iraq's Electoral System: A Misguided Strategy', *Arab Reform Bulletin*, 20 September, available online at http://carnegieendowment.org/2008/08/20/iraq-s-electoral-system-misguided-strategy/6f04

Rudolph, L. I. and Rudolph, S. H. (1967) *The Modernity of Tradition: Political Development in India* (Chicago, IL: University of Chicago Press).

Rueschemeyer, D. (2004) 'Addressing Inequality', *Journal of Democracy*, 15(4): 76–90.

Rueschemeyer, D., Stephens, E. H., and Stephens, J. D. (1992) *Capitalist Democracy and Development* (Cambridge: Polity Press).

Sahni, V. (2007) 'India's Foreign Policy: Key Drivers', *South African Journal of International Affairs*, 14(2): 21–35.

Said, E. W. (1993) *Culture and Imperialism* (London: Chatto & Windus).

Said, E. W. (1995; 1978) *Orientalism* (Harmondsworth: Penguin).

Samatar, A. I. (1999) *An African Miracle: State and Class Leadership and Colonial Legacy in Botswana's Development* (Portsmouth, NH: Heinemann).

Sangmpan, S. N. (2007) 'Politics Rules: The False Primacy of Institutions in Developing Countries', *Political Studies*, 55(1): 201–24.

Sartori, G. (1976) *Parties and Party Systems: A Framework for Analysis* (Cambridge: Cambridge University Press).

Scarritt, J. and Mozaffar, S. (1999) 'The Specification of Ethnic Cleavages and Ethnopolitical Groups for the Analysis of Democratic Competition in Contemporary Africa', *Nationalism and Ethnic Politics*, 5(1): 82–117.

Scarritt, J. and Mozaffar, S. (2003) 'Why Do Multi-ethnic Parties Prevail in Africa and Ethnic Parties Do Not?', Unpublished paper.

Schedler, A. (1998) 'What is Democratic Consolidation?', *Journal of Democracy*, 9(2): 91–107.

Schedler, A. (2006) *Electoral Authoritarianism: The Dynamics of Unfree Competition* (Boulder, CO/London: Lynne Rienner).

Schedler, A. (2013) *The Politics of Uncertainty: Sustaining and Subverting Electoral Authoritarianism* (Oxford: Oxford University Press).

Schedler, A., Diamond, L., and Plattner, M. (eds) (1999) *The Self-Restraining State* (Boulder, CO: Lynne Reinner).

Scheper-Hughes, N. (1992) *Death without Weeping: The Violence of Everyday Life in Brazil* (Berkeley, CA: University of California Press).

Schneider, B. R. (1999) 'The *Desarrollista* State in Brazil and Mexico', in M. Woo-Cummings (ed.) *The Developmental State* (Ithaca, NY/London: Cornell University Press), 276–305.

Scholte, J. A. (2011) 'Global Governance, Accountability and Civil Society', in J. A. Scholte (ed.) *Building Global Democracy? Civil Society and Accountable Global Governance* (Cambridge: Cambridge University Press), 8–42.

Scott, J. C. (1998) *Seeing Like a State* (New Haven, CT: Yale University Press).

Secretariat of the Convention on Biological Diversity (2000) *Cartagena Protocol on Biosafety* (Montreal: Secretariat of the Convention on Biological Diversity).

Seider, R. (2011) 'Contested Sovereignties: Indigenous Law, Violence, and State Effects in Postwar Guatemala', *Critique of Anthropology*, 21(3): 161–84.

Selznick, P. (1948) 'Foundations of the Theory of Organization', *American Sociological Review*, 13(1): 25–35.

Sen, A. (1990) 'More than 100 Million Women are Missing', *The New York Review of Books*, 20 December, available online at http://www.nybooks.com/articles/archives/1990/dec/20/more-than-100-million-women-are-missing/

Sen, A. (1999a) *Development as Freedom* (Oxford: Oxford University Press).

Sen, A. (1999b) 'Human Rights and Economic Achievements', in J. R. Bauer and D. A. Bell (eds) *The East Asian Challenge for Human Rights* (Cambridge: Cambridge University Press), 88–99.

Sen, A. (2006) *Identity and Violence: The Illusion of Destiny* (London: Allen Lane).

Sharkey, H. (2003) *Living with Colonialism: Nationalism and Culture in the Anglo-Egyptian Sudan* (Berkeley, CA: University of California Press).

Shorter, E. and Tilly, C. (1974) *Strikes in France 1830–1968* (London: Cambridge University Press).

Shugart, M. S. and Carey, J. M. (1992) *Presidents and Assemblies* (New York: Cambridge University Press).

Siavelis, P. (2006) 'Accommodating Informal Institutions and Chilean Democracy', in G. Helmke and S. Levitsky (eds) *Informal Institutions and Democracy: Lessons from Latin America* (Baltimore, MD: Johns Hopkins University Press), 33–55.

Silverman, S. F. (1977) 'Patronage and Community-Nation Relationships in Central Italy', in S. Schmidt, J. C. Scott, C. Landé, and L. Guasti (eds) *Friends, Followers and Factions: A Reader in Political Clientelism* (Berkeley, CA/London: University of California Press).

Singh, S. K. (2007) *India and West Africa: A Burgeoning Relationship*, Chatham House Africa Programme Briefing Paper, available online at http://www.chathamhouse.org/publications/papers/view/108471

Sisk, T. D. (2013) *Statebuilding* (London: Polity Press).

Six, C. (2009) 'The Rise of Postcolonial States as Donors: A Challenge to the Development Paradigm', *Third World Quarterly*, 30(6): 1103–21.

Sklair, L. (1991) *Sociology of the Global System* (London: Prentice-Hall).

Slater, D. (2004) *Geopolitics and the Postcolonial: Rethinking North–South Relations* (Oxford: Blackwell).

Smith, A. D. (1991) *National Identity* (Harmondsworth: Penguin).

Smith, D. (1990) 'Limits of Religious Resurgence', in E. Sahliyeh (ed.) *Religious Resurgence and Politics in the Contemporary World* (Albany, NY: State University of New York Press), 33–44.

Snow, D. A., Soule, S. A., and Kriesi, H. (2004) *The Blackwell Companion to Social Movements* (Malden: Blackwell).

Snyder, R. and Durán-Martínez, A. (2009) 'Does Illegality Breed Violence? Drug Trafficking and State-Sponsored Protection Rackets', *Crime, Law, and Social Change*, 52(3): 253–73.

Staudt, K. (1997) *Women, International Development and Politics: The Bureaucratic Mire*, 2nd edn (Philadelphia, PA: Temple University Press).

Staudt, K. (1998) *Policy, Politics and Gender: Women Gaining Ground* (West Hartford, CT: Kumarian Press).

Stepan, A. (2000) 'Religion, Democracy, and the "Twin Tolerations"', *Journal of Democracy*, 11(4): 37–57.

Stiglitz, J. (1998) 'More Instruments and Broader Goals: Moving Towards a Post-Washington Consensus', WIDER Annual Lecture, Helsinki, Finland.

Stiglitz, J. (2002) *Globalization and its Discontents* (London: Allen Lane).

Stockemer, D. (2011) 'The Successful Creation of Attac France: The Role of Structure and Agency', *French Politics*, 9(2): 120–38.

Strange, S. (1998) *Mad Money* (Manchester: Manchester University Press).

Suberu, R. J. (2008) 'The Supreme Court and Federalism in Nigeria', *Journal of Modern African Studies*, 46(3): 451–85.

Suh, D. (2011) 'Institutionalizing Social Movements: The Dual Strategy of the Korean Women's Movement', *The Sociological Quarterly*, 52(3): 442–71.

Suhrke, A. (2011) *When More is Less: The International Project in Afghanistan* (London/New York: Hurst & Co/Columbia University Press).

Sumner, A. (2010) *Global Poverty and the New Bottom Billion: Three-Quarters of the World's Poor Live in Middle-Income Countries*, IDS Working Paper 349, available online at http://www.ids.ac.uk/files/dmfile/Wp349.pdf

Sutton, P. (1991) 'Constancy, Change and Accommodation: The Distinct Tradition of the Commonwealth Caribbean', in J. Mayall and A. Payne (eds) *The Fallacies of Hope: The Post-Colonial Record of the Commonwealth Third World* (Manchester: Manchester University Press), 106–17.

Swatuk, L. A. and Shaw, T. M. (1994) *The South at the End of the Twentieth Century* (New York: St Martin's Press).

Tan-Mullins, M., Mohan, G., and Power, M. (2010) 'Redefining "Aid" in the China–Africa Context', *Development and Change*, 41(5): 857–81.

Tarrow, S. (1998) *Power in Movement: Social Movements and Contentious Politics*, 2nd edn (Cambridge: Cambridge University Press).

Taylor, I. (2009) *China's New Role in Africa* (Boulder, CO: Lynne Rienner).

Thelen, K. (2004) *How Institutions Evolve: The Political Economy of Skills in Germany, Britain, the United States and Japan* (New York: Cambridge University Press).

Therkildsen, O. (2004) 'The Autonomy of Revenue Authorities in Sub-Saharan Africa: The Case of Uganda', *Forum for Development Studies*, 31(1): 59–88.

Therkildsen, O. and Bourgouin, F. (2012) *Continuity and Change in Tanzania's Ruling Coalition: Legacies, Crises and Weak Productive Capacity*, DIIS Working Paper 2012:06, available online at http://en.diis.dk/files/publications/WP2012/WP2012-06-Continuity-and-change-Tanzania_web.pdf

Thomas, C. and Wilkin, P. (2004) 'Still Waiting after All These Years: The Third World on the Periphery of International Relations', *British Journal of Politics and International Relations*, 6(2): 241–58.

Tilly, C. (1990) *Coercion, Capital and European States, AD 990–1990* (Oxford: Basil Blackwell).

Timmons, H. and Gottipotti, S. (2012) 'Indian Women March: "That Girl Could Have Been Any One of Us"', *New York Times*, 30 December, available online at http://www.nytimes.com/2012/12/31/world/asia/rape-incites-women-to-fight-culture-in-india.html?pagewanted=all

Tomlinson, B. R. (1993) *The New Cambridge History of India, III.3: The Economy of Modern India, 1860–1970* (Cambridge: Cambridge University Press).

Tordoff, W. (1997) *Government and Politics in Africa* (London: Macmillan).

Transparency International (2005) *Global Corruption Report* (Cambridge: Cambridge University Press).

Transparency International (2011) *The Corruption Barometer 2011*, available online at http://www.transparency.org/research/gcb/

Transparency International (2012) *Corruption Perceptions Index 2012*, available online at http://cpi.transparency.org/cpi2012/results/

Transparency International (2013) *The Corruption Perception Index 2012*, available online at http://cpi.transparency.org/cpi2012/

United Nations (2004) *A More Secure World: Our Shared Responsibility—Report of the Secretary-General's High-Level Panel on Threats, Challenges and Change* (New York: United Nations).

United Nations (2009) *Report of the Secretary-General on Peacebuilding in the Immediate Aftermath of Conflict* (New York: United Nations).

United Nations Assistance Mission for Iraq (2007) *Human Rights Report: 1 January–31 March*, available online at http://www.uniraq.org/FileLib/misc/HR%20Report%20Jan%20Mar%202007%20EN.pdf

United Nations Conference on Trade and Development (2003) *Economic Development in Africa: Trade Performance and Commodity Dependence* (New York/Geneva: United Nations).

United Nations Conference on Trade and Development (2008a) *UNCTAD Handbook of Statistics* (Geneva: United Nations).

United Nations Conference on Trade and Development (2008b) *World Investment Report 2008* (Geneva: United Nations).

United Nations Conference on Trade and Development (2009a) *Economic Development in Africa Report 2009* (Geneva: United Nations).

United Nations Conference on Trade and Development (2009b) *Keeping ODA Afloat: No Stone Unturned* (Geneva: United Nations).

United Nations Conference on Trade and Development (2012a) *Handbook of Statistics 2012* (Geneva: United Nations).

United Nations Conference on Trade and Development (2012b) *Economic Development in Africa Report 2012: Structural Transformation and Sustainable Development in Africa* (Geneva: United Nations).

United Nations Department of Peacekeeping Operations (2013) *Peacekeeping Factsheet*, available online at http://www.un.org/en/peacekeeping/resources/statistics/factsheet.shtml

United Nations Development Programme (Various years) *Human Development Reports* (New York/Oxford: Oxford University Press).

United Nations Office on Drugs and Crime (2012) *World Drug Report 2012* (New York: United Nations).

United Nations Standing Committee on Nutrition (2009) *Global Recession Increases Malnutrition for the Most Vulnerable People in Developing Countries* (Geneva: United Nations).

Vaughan, S. and Gebremichael, M. (2011) *Rethinking Business and Politics in Ethiopia: The Role of EFFORT, the Endowment Fund for the Rehanilitation of Tigray*, APPP Research Report 02, available online at http://www.institutions-africa.org/filestream/20110822-appp-rr02-rethinking-business-politics-in-ethiopia-by-sarah-vaughan-mesfin-gebremichael-august-2011

Viswanathan, G. (1990) *Masks of Conquest: Literary Study and British Rule in India* (London: Faber & Faber).

Vogel, D. (1997) *Trading up: Consumer and Environmental Regulation in the Global Economy*, 2nd edn (Cambridge, MA: Harvard University Press).

von Hippel, K. (2004) 'Post-Conflict Reconstruction in Iraq: Lessons Unlearned', in P. Cornish (ed.) *The Conflict in Iraq 2003* (London: Palgrave MacMillan), 200–13.

Walker, A. (2012) *What is Boko Haram?*, United States Institute of Peace Special Report No. 308, available online at http://www.usip.org/sites/default/files/SR308.pdf

Wallerstein, I. (1979) 'The Rise and Future Demise of the World Capitalist System: Concepts for Comparative Analysis', in I. Wallerstein, *The Capitalist World-Economy* (Cambridge: Cambridge University Press), 1–36.

Wallerstein, I. (2003) *The Decline of American Power* (New York: The New Press).

Walt, S. M. (1991) 'The Renaissance of Security Studies', *International Studies Quarterly*, 35(2): 211–39.

Waltz, K. N. (1979) *Theory of International Relations* (New York: McGraw-Hill).

Watt, C. (2011) 'Introduction: The Relevance and Complexity of Civilizing Missions c. 1800–2010', in C. Watt and M. Mann (eds) *Civilizing Missions in Colonial and Postcolonial South Asia: From Improvement to Development* (London: Anthem Press), 1–34.

Weber, M. (1964) *The Theory of Social and Economic Organization*, ed. T. Parsons (New York: Free Press).

Weber, M. (1970) *From Max Weber: Essays in Sociology*, ed. H. H. Gerth and C. Wright Mills (London: Routledge).

Weigel, G. (2005) *Witness to Hope: The Biography of Pope John Paul II, 1920–2005* (New York: HarperCollins).

Weigel, G. (2007) *Faith, Reason, and the War against Jihadism: A Call to Action* (New York: Doubleday).

Weiss, J. (2002) *Industrialisation and Globalisation: Theory and Evidence from Developing Countries* (London: Routledge).

Weiss, L. (2005) 'The State-Augmenting Effects of Globalization', *New Political Economy*, 10(3): 345–53.

Weiss, L. and Hobson, J. M. (1995) *States and Economic Development* (Cambridge: Polity Press).

Weldon, S. L. (2002) *Protest, Policy, and the Problem of Violence against Women: A Cross-National Comparison* (Pittsburgh, PA: University of Pittsburgh Press).

White House (2002) *The National Security Strategy of the United States of America*, September, available online at http://georgewbush-whitehouse.archives.gov/nsc/nss/2002/

Wickramasinghe, N. (2006) *Sri Lanka in the Modern Age* (London: Hurst).

Wilson, D. and Purushothaman, R. (2003) *Dreaming with BRICS: The Path to 2050*, Goldman Sachs Global Economics Paper No. 99, available online at http://www.goldmansachs.com/our-thinking/archive/archive-pdfs/brics-dream.pdf

Wilson, D. and Stupnytska, A. (2007) *The N-11: More than an Acronym*, Goldman Sachs Global Economics Paper No. 153, available online at http://www.chicagobooth.edu/alumni/clubs/pakistan/docs/next-11dream-march%20'07-goldmansachs.pdf

Winters, J. A. (2011) *Oligarchy* (New York: Cambridge University Press).

Wolf-Phillips, L. (1979) 'Why Third World?', *Third World Quarterly*, 1(1): 105–13.

Woodberry, R. D. (2004) 'The Shadow of Empire: Christian Missions, Colonial Policy, and Democracy in Postcolonial Societies', Unpublished PhD Dissertation, University of North Carolina at Chapel Hill.

World Bank (1994) *Adjustment in Africa: Reforms, Results and the Road Ahead* (Washington, DC: World Bank).

World Bank (1997) *World Development Report 1997: The State in a Changing World* (New York: Oxford University Press).

World Bank (2000) *Greening Industry: New Roles for Communities, Markets and Governments* (Washington DC: World Bank).

World Bank (2001) *World Development Report 2001* (Washington DC: World Bank).

World Bank (2003a) *World Development Indicators 2003* (Washington DC: World Bank).

World Bank (2003b) *Breaking the Conflict Trap: Civil War and Development Policy* (Washington DC/Oxford: World Bank/Oxford University Press).

World Bank (2006) *World Bank Development Report: Equity and Development* (New York: World Bank/Oxford University Press).

World Bank (2011) *World Development Report 2011: Conflict, Security and Development* (Washington DC: World Bank).

World Bank (2012) 'Iraq Country Report', available online at http://data.worldbank.org/country/iraq

World Bank (2013) *World Development Indicators 2013* (Washington DC: World Bank).

World Resources Institute (2008) *Correcting the World's Greatest Market Failure: Climate Change and Multilateral Development Banks* (Washington, DC: WRI).

World Trade Organization (2012) *International Trade Statistics 2012* (Geneva: WTO).

Yadav, Y. (1996) 'Reconfiguration in Indian Politics: State Assembly Elections, 1993–95', *Economic and Political Weekly*, 13–20 January: 95–104.

Yamin, A. E. and Gloppen, S. (2011) *Litigating Health Rights: Can Courts Bring More Justice to Health?*, HLS Human Rights Programme Series (Cambridge, MA: Harvard University Press).

Young, C. (1994) *The African Colonial State in Comparative Perspective* (New Haven, CT: Yale University Press).

Young, C. (1998) 'Country Report: The African Colonial State Revisited', *Governance: An International Journal of Policy and Administration*, 11(1): 101–20.

Young, C. (2001) 'Nationalism and Ethnic Conflict in Africa', in M. Guibernau and J. Hutchinson (eds) *Understanding Nationalism* (Cambridge: Polity Press), 164–81.

Youngs, R. (2009) 'Energy: A Reinforced Obstacle to Democratization?', in P. Burnell and R. Youngs (eds) *New Challenges to Democratization* (London/New York: Routledge), 173–90.

Zakaria, F. (1997) 'The Rise of Illiberal Democracy', *Foreign Affairs*, 76(6): 22–43.

Index